Reforming Central and Eastern European Economies

A World Bank Symposium

Reforming Central and Eastern European Economies: Initial Results and Challenges

edited by
Vittorio Corbo
Fabrizio Coricelli
Jan Bossak

The World Bank
Washington, D.C.

HC
244
R3775
1991

The findings, interpretations, and conclusions expressed in this study are entirely those of the authors and should not be attributed in any manner to the World Bank, to its affiliated organizations, or to members of its Board of Executive Directors or the countries they represent.

Because of the informality of this series and to make the publication available with the least possible delay, the manuscript has not been edited as fully as would be the case with a more formal document, and the World Bank accepts no responsibility for errors.

The material in this publication is copyrighted. Requests for permission to reproduce portions of it should be sent to Director, Publications Department, at the address shown in the copyright notice above. The World Bank encourages dissemination of its work and will normally give permission promptly and, when the reproduction is for noncommercial purposes, without asking a fee. Permission to photocopy portions for classroom use is not required, although notification of such use having been made will be appreciated.

The complete backlist of publications from the World Bank is shown in the annual *Index of Publications,* which contains an alphabetical title list and indexes of subjects, authors, and countries and regions. The latest edition is available free of charge from the Publications Sales Unit at the address in the copyright notice or from Publications, World Bank, 66, avenue d'Iéna, 75116 Paris, France.

Library of Congress Cataloging-in-Publication Data

Reforming Central and Eastern European economies : initial results and challenges / edited by Vittorio Corbo, Fabrizio Coricelli, Jan Bossak.
   p. cm.
   Papers from a conference held in Pultusk, Poland, Oct. 4–5, 1990; organized by the Macroeconomic Adjustment and Growth Division of the World Bank.
   Includes bibliographical references.
   ISBN 0-8213-1893-4
   1. Central Europe–Economic policy–Congresses. 2. Central Europe–Economic conditions–Congresses. 3. Privatization–Central Europe–Congresses. 4. Europe, Eastern–Economic policy–Congresses 5. Europe, Eastern–Economic conditions–1989—Congresses. 6. Privatization–Europe, Eastern–Congresses. I. Corbo, Vittorio. II. Coricelli, Fabrizio. III. Bossak, Jan. IV. International Bank for Reconstruction and Development. Economics Dept. Macroeconomic Adjustment and Growth Division.
   HC244.R3775
   338.947–dc2091-27563   CIP

Contents

PART VIII   SUMMING UP AND OVERVIEW   293

Preface

At the request of the World Economy Research Institute (WERI) of the Warsaw School of Economics, the Macroeconomic Adjustment and Growth Division of the World Bank organized a Conference in Pultusk, Poland on October 4-5, 1990. The aim of the Conference was to draw from reform experiences in developing countries some practical lessons for Central and Eastern European countries. The Conference included papers that evaluated international experiences, proposals for reform and progress reports on the initial response to reforms in some of the Central and Eastern European countries.

Most of the papers published in this volume were presented and discussed at the Conference in Pultusk. The papers by Andrés Solimano, providing an historical background, and by Eduardo Borensztein, comparing the three proposals for privatization contained in the volume, were prepared after the Conference.

In addition to the authors of the papers, the Conference brought together a range of distinguished officials and academics from Bulgaria, Czechoslovakia, Hungary, Poland, Romania and Yugoslavia, as well as academics from western countries and representatives of multilateral institutions. The Conference was organized by Vittorio Corbo and Fabrizio Coricelli, of the Country Economics Department of the World Bank, and Jan Bossak of the WERI. Whitney Watriss has done an excellent job of copy-editing the volume in a very short period of time.

Although there are no precedents for the economic reforms being initiated or about to be initiated in Central and Eastern Europe, a careful evaluation of reforms in specific areas that have been carried out in other countries could provide important lessons for the policymakers who are responsible for the reform programs in Central and Eastern Europe. We hope this volume will contribute to providing some guidelines for the unprecedented reforms which are now underway.

Vittorio Corbo
Fabrizio Coricelli

Acknowledgments

This Conference was made possible thanks to the support of the following departments of the World Bank: Europe, Middle East and North Africa, Division 4 (EM4), Country Economics (CEC), Research Administration (RAD) and Development Economics (VDDEC). The staff of the World Economy Research Institute of the Warsaw School of Economics and Barbara Ossowicka of the World Bank provided much support in the preparation and the implementation of the Conference.

Contributors

Eduardo Borensztein
International Monetary Fund,
  Research Department, Washington, D.C.

Jan W. Bossak
World Economy Research Institute,
  Warsaw School of Economics

Guillermo Calvo
International Monetary Fund,
  Research Department, Washington, D.C.

Vittorio Corbo
World Bank, Macroeconomic Adjustment
  and Growth Division, Washington, D.C.

Fabrizio Coricelli
World Bank, Macroeconomic Adjustment
  and Growth Division, Washington, D.C.

William Easterly
World Bank, Macroeconomic Adjustment
  and Growth Division, Washington, D.C.

Stanley Fischer
World Bank, Office of the Vice President,
  Development Economics and Chief Economist,
  Washington, D.C., and Massachusetts Institute
  of Technology, Economics Department, Cambridge,
  Mass.

Roman Frydman
New York University, Department of Economics

Alan Gelb
World Bank, Socialist Economies Reform Unit,
  Washington, D.C.

Stanislaw Gomulka
London School of Economics

Manuel Hinds
World Bank, Europe, Middle East and North Africa,
  Trade and Finance, Washington, D.C.

Miroslav Hrncir
Institute of Economics, Prague

Erika Jorgensen
World Bank, Socialist Economies Reform Unit,
  Washington, D.C.

Miguel Kiguel
World Bank, Macroeconomic Adjustment
  and Growth Division, Washington, D.C.

Johannes F. Linn
World Bank, Country Economics Department,
  Washington, D.C.

Nissan Liviatan
Hebrew University of Jerusalem and
  World Bank, Macroeconomic Adjustment
  and Growth Division, Washington, D.C.

Gabor Oblath
Institute for Economic and Market Research, Budapest

Andrzej Rapaczynski
Columbia University, Law School, New York

Roberto R. Rocha
World Bank, Macroeconomic Adjustment
  and Growth Division, Washington, D.C.

Jacek Rostowski
Polish Ministry of Finance, Warsaw

Jeffrey Sachs
Harvard University, Department of Economics,
  Cambridge, Mass.

Inderjit Singh
World Bank, Socialist Economies Reform Unit,
  Washington, D.C.

Andrés Solimano
World Bank, Macroeconomic Adjustment
  and Growth Division, Washington, D.C.

Jan Svejnar
University of Pittsburgh, Department of Economics

Vito Tanzi
International Monetary Fund,
  Fiscal Affairs Department, Washington, D.C.

Ulrich R.W. Thumm
World Bank, Europe, Middle East and North Africa,
  Washington, D.C.

Stanislaw Wellisz
Columbia University, New York,
  and Polish Ministry of Finance, Warsaw

John Williamson
Institute for International Economics,
  Washington, D.C.

Introduction

Vittorio Corbo, Fabrizio Coricelli and Jan Bossak

Overview

In the last two years, countries in Central and Eastern Europe have initiated major reform efforts with the final objective of creating a Western European-type market economy. Undoubtedly, implementing the reforms has been very difficult. The difficulties have been of three kinds. First, after 40 or more years of a command economy, institutions and the system of incentives are far removed from those required to establish a Western European-type market economy. Therefore, significant changes in institutions and the system of incentives are required. The significant changes needed in the productive and institutional structure are bound to result in important short-term adjustment costs. Second, important political economy problems will emerge as the unavoidable short-term costs of adjustment will occur at the same time that a fundamental redistribution of the political regime takes place. Third, there are no precedents for such far-reaching reforms from which to derive clear lessons on program design.

The conference that gave origin to this volume focused on the economic reforms required to create a market economy and, specifically, on the main challenges. The Central and Eastern European countries have to create the basic structure and institutions needed for a market economy from the ground up and at the same time implement macroeconomic programs aimed at stabilizing large macroeconomic imbalances. The interrelation between these structural issues, which are generally of a microeconomic and institutional nature, and the macroeconomic issues raises fundamental questions about the design and implementation of reform programs. Fundamental tensions between the micro- and macroeconomic dimensions of the reform can arise.

Answering these many questions that the transformation of the Central and European countries poses is an extraordinary challenge for policy-makers and researchers alike. Clearly, a blueprint for the task is not available, and, given significantly different initial conditions across countries, it may even be misleading to search for one. However, despite the unique character of the reform in each country, experience with reform in other parts of the world can provide some useful guidelines. Analyzing the issues raised by reform in the socialist economies against the background of this experience will not only provide insights and guidance but will also help isolate the unique features of socialist economies.

Over the last 10 years the World Bank has gained wide experience in the design and implementation of reform programs. In particular, two reports (*Report on Adjustment Lending 1* [RAL-1] [World Bank 1988] and *Report on Adjustment Lending 2* [RAL-2] [World Bank 1990]), completed in the past two years, provide comprehensive reviews of its experience with adjustment programs. The original motivation of the Conference on Adjustment Lending: Lessons for Eastern Europe, the proceedings of which are contained in this volume, was to draw from those reports the main lessons for reform in Central and Eastern Europe. As these reports do not focus specifically on Central and Eastern Europe, a decision was made to complement the lessons from the reforms supported by the Bank with a set of papers dealing with particular issues that reforms in the Central and Eastern European economies raised.

The volume covers a wide range of issues, touching on key problems at both the macroeconomic and microeconomic levels. In fact, the interplay between macroeconomic and microeconomic issues is the leit-motif of the volume. The structure of the volume reflects this perspective by including analyses of the problems of macroeconomic stabilization, the development and reform of key markets and, finally, privatization. While containing a host of important suggestions derived from the experience of developing countries, the volume also discusses some of the unique features of reform in Central and Eastern Europe, in particular the fact that reform in these economies requires the *creation* of markets and market institutions, and not just the removal of distortions.

The lack of the basic institutions and structures found in market economies makes the traditional models for studying macro and micro policies in market economies inadequate for analyzing the transition of socialist economies. This volume is a first step in isolating some of the unique issues facing these countries in their transition and suggesting appropriate conceptual frameworks.

Part I. Central and Eastern Europe: An Historical Background

Part I provides historical background, drawing especially on the period before the Second World War, when these Central and Eastern European countries had market economies. The paper also provides an overview of the basic conditions in these countries on the eve of the current reform effort.

Part II. The World Bank Experience with Adjustment Lending

Part II consists of two papers that focus on the main lessons for reforming socialist economies, as drawn from the World Bank's experience with adjustment lending. The main objectives are to highlight aspects of adjustment that have general applicability and, at the same time, to stress some specific features of reforming socialist countries that require deviations from the approaches pursued by other countries, such as in the areas of sequencing, the interrelation of macro and micro aspects, and the pace and intensity of liberalization and reforms.

In "World Bank-Supported Adjustment Programs: Lessons for Central and Eastern Europe," Vittorio Corbo draws from the accumulated experience of the Bank four main lessons for Central and Eastern Europe. First, where high inflation—even if repressed—and severe macroeconomic imbalances are present, the adjustment program has to tackle them at the beginning. Second, to achieve a supply response early on in the reform, trade liberalization has to be accompanied by reforms reducing the restrictions on labor mobility and the entry and exit of firms. In this regard, labor market policies, as well as housing policies, and anti-monopoly legislation have to be addressed at the outset of the reform program. Third, although the creation of a full-fledged financial system should be postponed to the later stages, a minimal financial structure capable of channelling working capital financing on the basis of an appropriate assessment of credit risk has to be established at the beginning to facil-

itate the economic restructuring. Finally, institution-building, including the capacity to formulate and execute macroeconomic policies, reduction in the size of the public sector, including moving out fast on privatization and a regulatory framework for the functioning of markets are fundamental conditions for successful reforms.

In "World Bank Adjustment Lending in Central and Eastern Europe," Ulrich Thumm reconstructs the main features of adjustment cum reform programs supported by Sector Adjustment Lending (SALs) from the World Bank in Hungary, Poland and Yugoslavia. The paper also briefly reviews the incipient adjustment program in Czechoslovakia. In his analysis of the recent economic performance of countries in Central and Eastern Europe—which are characterized by large macroeconomic imbalances, external debt problems and low efficiency—Thumm notices the prima facie similarity of this experience with that of other countries, which is very familiar to the World Bank. Despite this similarity in performance, he describes a set of systemic features of socialist economies that make the design and implementation of adjustment in Central and Eastern Europe unique. The lack of private ownership—which is of critical proportions—has been the main stumbling block to a successful restructuring of these economies. Moving from this premise, Thumm argues that, while the socialist economies have undertaken fundamental macroeconomic measures and important reforms in the areas of price and trade liberalization, the transformation of enterprises with respect to both their restructuring or privatization, has been proceeding slowly. While recognizing that their structural, systemic transformation will necessarily take time, Thumm concludes that important steps to create a critical mass of private ownership that can initiate the move toward a market economy have to be taken at the outset of the program, together with macroeconomic measures.

Part III. Speed of Adjustment and Sequencing of Policy Changes

Part III establishes a precise framework for the sequencing of policy measures and structural reforms underlying the transition to a market economy. In "Issues in the Reform of Socialist Economies," Stanley Fischer and Alan Gelb emphasize that the path of the transition and the sequencing of the measures depend crucially on initial conditions. They classify these initial conditions on the basis of: the degree of internal and external macroeconomic imbalance; and the degree of economic centralization. Given that the reform will deal with both macroeconomic stabilization and economic decision-making, the degree of difficulty of the reform and the sequencing of measures in different countries will be determined by their relative position in terms of those factors. Fischer and Gelb then go in detail into the main areas where reforms will be needed. They identify eight main areas and suggest a phased set of policy measures, with a time horizon for each. The eight areas are macrostabilization, a social safety net, institutional reform, price and market reform, small-scale privatization and development of the private sector, large-scale restructuring and privatization, development of an autonomous banking system, and establishment of other financial markets.

Part IV. Stabilization: Design of Programs, Effects on the Economy

Part IV addresses the design of stabilization programs and the choice of policy mix and policy instruments. The two papers provide an interesting perspective by comparing the experience with stabilization programs in Latin American countries and Israel, on the one hand, and that of two socialist economies, Poland and Yugoslavia, which carried out similar stabilization programs in 1990, on the other.

In "Stopping Inflation: The Experience of Latin America and Israel and the Implications for Central and Eastern Europe," Miguel Kiguel and Nissan Liviatan emphasize the common elements between Latin America and Central and Eastern European countries such as Poland and Yugoslavia in terms of both the sources and persistence of inflation and the design of stabilization programs, including the main problems relating to their sustainability. Kiguel and Liviatan stress the difficulty of stopping inflation in chronic high-inflation countries such as Argentina and Brazil. They divide stabilization programs into two main groups. One, labeled "orthodox," is based on fiscal adjustment and the use of money or the exchange rate as "anchors." The other, "heterodox," can be defined as a fiscal adjustment with the addition of price and/or wage controls to deal with the inertial aspects of inflation. Kiguel and Liviatan classify the Polish and Yugoslav stabilization programs as heterodox. They note, however, that in both countries the initial response of the economy differed from that found with typical heterodox programs. In particular, the recessionary impact was larger, and, in the case of Poland, the improvement in the current account did not match the usual experience.

In "Stabilization Programs in Eastern Europe: A Comparative Analysis of the Yugoslav and Polish Programs of 1990," Fabrizio Coricelli and Roberto Rocha discuss the stabilization programs implemented in Poland and Yugoslavia in 1990 at almost the same time. Interest in a comparative analysis of the design, performance and sustainability of the two apparently similar programs being implemented by two reforming socialist countries has

been substantial. Coricelli and Rocha argue that, notwithstanding the apparent similarities, the initial outcomes of the two programs are significantly different, a result that can be explained by the different initial conditions and the different sequence and scope of some policy measures. Finally, the authors discuss the main issues to be addressed in the second stage of the programs, including the unfreezing of the nominal anchors (wages and exchange rates) and crucial structural issues whose solution will determine the prospects for a sustained supply response. Based on an evaluation of the outcomes of both programs, Coricelli and Rocha state that macroeconomic policies alone cannot generate more efficient allocation of resources and efficient natural selection among enterprises. They conclude that the sequencing model traditionally applied in Latin American countries, in which structural reforms are relegated to the later stages of adjustment, does not seem to be applicable to reforming socialist countries, where stabilization and structural reforms—and thus macroeconomic and microeconomic issues—are more closely intertwined.

Part V. Structural Rigidities, Distortions and Inertia in Behaviors: The Supply Response to New Environments and Constraints in Central and Eastern Europe

Part V provides an initial assessment of firms' responses to the reforms in Poland. Because their response to the new institutions and incentives will determinate the ultimate success or failure of the reforms, it is of central importance to obtain a progress report on how firms are adjusting to the reforms. In particular, it is helpful to know if the response is more of a restructuring type or of a wait-and-see type.

In "The Ownership-Control Structure and the Behavior of Polish Enterprises During the 1990 Reforms: Macroeconomic Measures and Microeconomic Responses," Roman Frydman and Stanislaw Wellisz, on the basis of very rich empirical evidence, argue that the stabilization and reform program launched in Poland in 1990 forced firms to adjust and in particular to adopt pricing that largely eliminated shortages in the economy. They also argue, however, that although enterprise behavior is rational in the present framework of institutions and incentives, it is not conducive to greater efficiency because of the structure of rewards and ownership. In particular, they note the persistence of labor hoarding and the recent resurgence of wage pressures, validated by an expansion in credit. Frydman and Wellisz conclude that in the absence of deep changes in the structure of ownership and control of enterprises, a restrictive aggregated demand policy cannot be effective in achieving rationalization and growth. However, an expansionary demand policy will also be ineffective and will result in inflationary pressures. Indeed, they claim that state-owned firms that are managed de facto by workers, will respond to increased demand by raising wages and prices rather than output. Therefore, to restore economic growth, the most needed reform is the development of a well-defined system of ownership and control of enterprises.

In "Life after the 'Big-Bang': Representative Episodes," Erika Jorgensen, Alan Gelb and Inderjit Singh analyze the preliminary results of the Polish reform based on a study using a small sample of enterprises. From this sample they observe that after initial chaos in the first months of 1990, firms began to get a sense of their markets for both inputs and output. The nine case studies of Polish firms indicate that, despite the large, negative shocks, the firms have reacted strongly and positively to the Big Bang. The authors identify positive responses in the areas of marketing-distribution, cost-cutting and finance. They also note that the firms with previous exposure to Western markets were in the best position to undertake the needed adjustments in their operations. However, the authors conclude—in agreement with Frydman and Wellisz—that if the issue of ownership and control of enterpises is not resolved, the adjustment may stall, despite the willingness of firms to modify their behavior.

In "Distortionary Policies and Growth in Socialist Economies," William Easterly draws on the insights of the new growth theory to analyze the interplay between distortions and growth in Central and Eastern Europe. Using this framework, he presents a model that analyzes how distortionary policies can affect growth, and not just the level of output. He shows that the relation between distortions and growth is very non-linear, the implication being that in highly distorted situations—such as those in most socialist economies—small reductions in distortions can have negative effects on growth. An important insight of this work is that, to be effective, reforms must reduce distortions below a critical level. Thus, major reductions in large distortions can have important positive effects on growth. Easterly presents an extension of the model that illustrates the effects that the misallocation of capital has had on growth in the Soviet economy. This extension is used to show that a partial privatization can be harmful for growth, whereas a close to complete or complete privatization of the economy can benefit growth.

Part VI. Adjustment and Reforms: Financial Market, Foreign Trade, Fiscal Sector

Part VI includes three papers that address issues relating to reform of financial markets, foreign trade and fiscal areas. They look at the role of markets and of their cre-

ation and development in the overall reform in socialist economies. Part VI effectively illustrates the size of the problems that Central and Eastern European countries face in trying to move toward market economies given their lack of financial markets, the particular structure of their foreign trade and the inadequacy of the fiscal sector.

In "Financial Aspects of Socialist Economies: From Inflation to Reform," Guillermo Calvo focuses on some financial issues connected with the transformation from planned to market economies. The central theme is that credit in socialist economies has generally taken the form of "bad" credit, i.e., credit that finances ultimately unproductive activities, such as, for instance, the accumulation of excessive inventories. The reason for this problem is a soft budget constraint. In moving to a market-oriented economy, the authorities face the very complicated problem of stopping bad credit and simultaneously making sure that potentially profitable activities have access to financing (to "good" credit). Calvo argues that the lack of information and institutions precludes the expansion of good credit in reforming socialist economies. Simple tight monetary policies, while helping cut bad credit, cannot solve the problem of the "efficiency" of credit. Calvo concludes that the development of a banking system should have priority in the reform. He suggests that if monetary/credit policy relies too heavily on a credit crunch, inflation may be slowed at the cost of equally, if not more disturbing economic problems, such as deep and protracted recession.

In "Adjustment, Trade Reform and Competitiveness: The Polish Experience," Jan Bossak reviews some of the trade policy issues in the reform. He argues that liberalization per se may not be sufficient to dismantle the highly monopolistic structure of industries in socialist economies. He also suggests that the technological and quality gap between East and West is so large that some form of stimulus for specific activities should be introduced.

In "Fiscal Issues in Economies in Transition," Vito Tanzi gives an overview of the main aspects of fiscal policy associated with adjustment programs supported by the International Monetary Fund (IMF). In connection with Central and Eastern Europe, Tanzi emphasizes the problem of institution-building. He stresses that fiscal reform will be a lengthy and effort-intensive undertaking, as the basic fiscal institutions (such as tax and budgetary systems) are either non-existent or very primitive.

Part VII. Panel on Privatization

Privatization has become the Achilles' heel of most of the reform efforts in Central and Eastern Europe. Part VII contains four papers, three of which include proposals for privatization in Central and Eastern Europe, while the fourth provides a comparative assessment of the three proposals. Although they focus specifically on the Polish case, the papers offer a general framework for privatization in reforming socialist countries. All three papers argue for rapid and large-scale privatization. They also share the idea that, because of a lack of financial markets, and the low level of savings, and for political reasons, shares in firms should be distributed freely. Finally, they call in common for the creation of financial intermediaries as an intermediate layer between shareholders and management. These intermediaries would facilitate the control and effective management of the enterprises.

Notwithstanding these common elements, the three papers differ in important aspects. The main difference relates to the role to be played by the state during the transition period.

In "Privatization in Eastern Europe: The Case of Poland," David Lipton and Jeffrey Sachs present a detailed privatization plan, including a timetable. Based on a review of the international experience with privatization, the authors argue that a firm-by-firm approach would fail well before a substantial number of firms could be privatized. They offer a plan for rapid and massive privatization, although they caution that it will not produce rapid efficiency, productivity and managerial gains. Their plan has three stages. First, firms will "corporatize," i.e., be transformed into treasury-owned joint stock companies. Subsequently the treasury will distribute a large component of the shares to workers, the population at large and financial intermediaries such as mutual funds, pension funds and commercial banks, while remaining temporarily the single largest shareholder. Finally, the treasury will sell its shares to "core investors." This plan combines features of the free distribution of shares with the sale of shares contemplated in case-by-case schemes, and it addresses simultaneously the issue of the distribution of wealth and the control of enterprises.

In "Markets and Institutions in Large-Scale Privatization: An Approach to Economic and Social Transformation in Eastern Europe," Roman Frydman and Andrzej Rapaczynski present a view different from that of Lipton and Sachs mainly with respect to the role to be played by the state. Frydman and Rapaczynski call for a drastic reduction in the role of the state, with the mutual funds fully controlled by private investors. This approach relies more on privatization which would take place simultaneously with the creation of a private sector. It stresses the creation of the markets and institutions that are necessary for movement toward a market economy dominated by the private sector. The authors do not believe the state can play an active role in this process.

In "A Note on the Privatization of Socialized Enterpris-es in Poland," Manuel Hinds shares the philosophy of the other two papers, stressing the importance of a free distribution of shares for both equity and macroeconomic considerations (the lack of domestic savings) and the importance of rapid privatization. Some of his recommendations, however, differ from those put forward in the other two papers. In particular, he strongly opposes different voting rights on shares (which Lipton and Sachs propose for the shares held by the treasury) and the holding of shares by commercial banks. Hinds also suggests a clear separation between firms and banks and the creation of capital markets to channel funds to the enterprises. In contrast, the other two papers envisage the development of a financial sector in parallel with privatization and having the financial intermediaries, including the banks, gain control of the enterprises.

In his comments on the above three papers, Borensztein highlights their main points of agreement. He also highlights the points of disagreement, which mainly concern the role of the state and the issue of alternative models of corporate governance.

Part VIII. Summing up and Overview

This section presents the comments of three panelists whose role was to summarize the main findings of the conference and suggest some directions for further research.

From the conference discussions, Stanislaw Gomulka derives four phases for a typical transition. Phase one centers on macrostabilization, phase two on structural adjustment, phase three on the recovery of growth and phase four on sustaining growth and macroeconomic balance. Much of the conference discussions centered around phases one and two. In this regard, Gomulka emphasizes that the paths to transition are distinguished by two main elements: the speed of price liberalization, including current account convertibility; and the speed and scope of privatization. Based on the Polish experience, he argues that both price liberalization and privatization should proceed very fast and notes that while rapid price liberalization is likely to increase the short-term costs of transition, fast privatization could bring about positive effects in the short run.

Johannes Linn tries to identify some of the answers that emerged in the conference to the main questions regarding the timing and sequencing of reforms. He also emphasizes that in recent months there has been an important clarification of the ultimate goals of the reforms, especially as regards private ownership. Linn argues that some ambiguity is still present on the type of labor market these countries are aiming for. Another point relates to measuring and monitoring the impact and progress of reforms using statististical information. As the reforms most likely push activity out of the measured, mainly socialized, sectors, the official statistics tend to overstate their costs.

Jan Svejnar urges that the link between microecomic adjustment and macroeconomic stabilization, addressed in some of the presentations, be stressed more forcefully. He emphasizes three main areas as deserving special attention: capital market imperfections; inter-enterprise credit; and labor market institutions and distortions. Svejnar argues that in designing macroeconomic policies, attention should be paid to those three areas. He notes that bottlenecks in the banking system are indeed a major constraint on growth and the development of a private sector. As to inter-enterprise credit, it tends to weaken considerably the effectiveness of monetary policy and to increase the risks of large-scale insolvency. Finally, on labor market policies, Svejnar emphasizes that considerations of efficiency should lead to a predominance of wage incentives over wage controls. He concludes that the labor market is often treated mechanically at the macro level; however, its functioning, including its institutions, could make or break the whole process of economic transformation in Central and Eastern Europe.

The type of economic transformation being attempted by the reforming socialist countries does not have precedents in recent economic history. Therefore, the road to reform is unknown. The reforms that have been attempted in developing countries have been on a much reduced scale. Nonetheless, there are important lessons to be learned from the experience of these countries. Careful analysis of these experiences could provide important insights, as well as guidelines, for the authorities who are directing the reform effort in the socialist countries of Central and Eastern Europe.

References

World Bank. 1988. *Adjustment Lending: An Evaluation of Ten Years of Experience*. Policy and Research Series No. 1. Washington, D.C.: World Bank.

————. 1990. *Adjustment Lending Policies for Sustainable Growth*, Policy and Research Series No. 14. Washington, D.C.: World Bank.

Part I

Central and Eastern Europe: An Historical Background

2

The Economies of Central and Eastern Europe: An Historical and International Perspective

Andrés Solimano [1]

Current events in Central and Eastern Europe are so far-reaching that a look at the economic (and political) history of the region is critical to understanding the changes fully. Extreme macroeconomic instability, economic reconstruction and structural transformation, integration into a global monetary system, the domestic consequences of changes in international conditions—all are phenomena that Central and Eastern Europe had experienced before socialism was established after the Second World War. Thus, a study of pre-socialist Central and Eastern Europe may provide valuable clues to the current problems of the transition to a market (or capitalist) system. This transition constitutes, in a sense, a *rendez-vous* of the region with its own history (including the problems).

This paper is organized as follows. The next section focuses on the 1920s and 1930s, documenting the formation of the nations in what is today (subject to some territorial changes after the Second World War) Central and Eastern Europe. The problems of macroeconomic stabilization and the issues of economic recovery, integration into the gold exchange standard and the tendency toward protectionism that developed in the second half of the 1920s are reviewed, as are the impact of the Great Depression, the collapse of the gold exchange standard and the policy response of most Central and Eastern European economies to those events of the thirties. The effect of German re-armament on the economies of Central and Eastern Europe in the second half of the 1930s is also addressed. Finally, the section describes the levels of per capita income and the main features of the economic structure in the region in the late 1930s.

The third section begins with a look at the late 1940s. It analyzes the establishment of socialism in the second half of the 1940s in the region, including the policies of nationalization and central planning that were the basis for a socialist (Soviet-style) economy. From a macroeconomic perspective, the implementation of monetary re-

forms in the 1940s and the origin and stabilization of Hungary's hyper-inflation of 1945-46 are discussed. The section then jumps to the late 1980s and early 1990s, when socialism throughout the region collapsed. Some of the initial conditions with which the Central and Eastern European countries began their transition to a market economy are noted, along with some historical and international comparisons of per capita income in the region. The last section offers concluding observations.

Central and Eastern Europe Before Socialism: The Inter-war Period

The end of World War I led to the collapse of the four main monarchies—German, Habsburg, Ottoman and Czarist—that dominated Central and Eastern Europe. In the case of the former Austro-Hungarian Empire, it gave birth to three independent states: Austria, Czechoslovakia and Hungary. The former Hungarian kingdom, however, lost nearly two-thirds of its territory (table 2-1). Yugoslavia acquired the kingdoms of Serbia and Croatia.

Table 2-1. *Central and Eastern Europe Before and After World War I*

	Area (in square kms)		Population (millions)	
	1914	1921	1914	1921
Austro-Hungarian Monarchy	676,433		51,390	
Austria		85,533		6,536
Hungary		92,607		7,600
Czechoslovakia		140,394		13,613
Bulgaria	111,800	103,146	4,753	4,910
Rumania	137,903	304,244	7,516	17,594
Serbia	87,300		4,548	
Yugoslavia		248,987		12,017
Poland		388,279		27,184

Source: Berend and Ranki (1974).

A reborn Poland (the new Polish kingdom) received territories from the Austro-Hungarian monarchy, Germany and Russia. Bulgaria underwent some minor territorial changes, and the kingdom of Romania annexed territories from Hungary and Russia.[2]

All the above countries suffered significant destruction of their physical capital and infrastructure and sizable losses in human capital during the war of 1914-18. Thus, economic reconstruction became the first priority. Poland was the most badly affected by the war, while Czechoslovakia was the least affected by the destruction.

The 1920s

An important economic consequence of the war was the total disorganization of public finances and financial systems in most of the region. That state of chaos rapidly led to extreme macroeconomic instability and hyper-inflation, notably in Austria, Poland and Hungary. The emergence of macroeconomic imbalances and high inflation in the early 1920s was connected to the financing of the war and its aftermath. Besides taxation and the issuance of debt, to a great extent World War I was financed by printing money. The impact of the money creation on prices was restrained temporarily by the extensive price controls and rationing of consumption goods (the military had priority in the allocation of resources). Thus, by the end of the war the population had accumulated large involuntary savings in the form of liquid assets, and this monetary overhang certainly contributed to the outbreak of inflation. Moreover, public finances were strained by the economic reconstruction, which required increased government spending at a time when fiscal revenues were scarce, particularly in those countries that had lost assets at the outset of the conflict.

Socio-political turbulence compounded the macroeconomic instability. A succession of short-lived, ideologically diverse governments ruled during 1918-19 in

the countries of the region. An example was the establishment of a soviet republic in Hungary in March 1919 led by Bela Kun, which was followed by a right-wing government. Conflicts arose over the distribution of income as workers sought to raise the level of real wages, which had been very depressed during the war. However, external conditions left little room to accommodate these demands for higher real wages at home: the reparations payments and ensuing external transfers required an undervalued real exchange rate.

The war reparations sanctioned in the Treaties of Versailles, St. Germain and Trianon adversely affected the countries born of the Austro-Hungarian monarchy, as well as Bulgaria. They put a severe burden on public finances and the balance of payments. The results of the payments of the war reparations and large fiscal deficits financed by printing money (table 2-2) were extreme inflation (table 2-3) and a massive depreciation of the exchange rate in Austria, Hungary and Poland.[3]

Table 2-2. *Fiscal Budgets and Their Financing after World War I*

	Percentage of government expenditures covered by issues of paper money
Hungary	
1920-21	47.9
1921-22	24.1
1922-23	21.0
1923-24	34.4
Austria	
January 1,-June 30, 1919	67.0
July 1, 1919-June 30, 1920	63.0
July 1, 1920-June 30, 1921	58.0
January 1-December 31, 1922	40.0

Source: Sargent (1982).

Table 2-3. *Inflation in Central and Eastern Europe, 1921-24*

	Austria (price index, January 1921=100)	Hungary (price index, July 1921=100)	Poland (price index, January 1921=100)	Czechoslovakia (price index January 1922 =100)
1921				
December	942	196.4	226.9	
1922				
December	17,409	795.2	1,377.7	59.6
1923				
December	21,849	17,000.0	566,055.5	58.8
1924				
March	23,336	49,445.24	975,686.8	60.9
April	23,361	50,823.81	963,927.7	60.2
June	24,267	52,566.6		
September		53,252.3		

Source: Prepared on the basis of Sargent (1982).

The hyper-inflation in Austria, Hungary and Poland in the early 1920s shared some common features: complete demonetization and shifts of the portfolios of domestic residents toward foreign currency and gold; dramatic increases in the fiscal deficits (partly endogenously generated by the reduction in real tax collections induced by the inflation); very rapid depreciation of the exchange rate; and the complete destruction of the contract-structure for goods, labor and financial transactions (see Dornbusch and Fischer 1986; Solimano 1990a; and Wicker 1986).

The stabilization of those hyper-inflationary episodes illustrates, vividly, the interplay between foreign assistance and domestic fiscal and monetary reform in stopping extreme inflation. In Austria and Hungary, the stabilization was framed within a League of Nations reconstruction plan (also signed by Czechoslovakia) that included two protocols: the first established the political and territorial sovereignty of these countries; and the second set out a plan for economic stabilization that tied the granting of an international loan to the adoption of fundamental reforms in the fiscal and monetary areas. Two key conditions were incorporated that the countries complied with. First, they were to institute independent central banks (these banks were to replace the former Austro-Hungarian Bank with its two sections, the Austrian and the Hungarian). The main proviso in the charters of the newly created central banks was a prohibition on the discounting of treasury bills, a practice used so extensively that it had led to the hyper-inflation. Second, the budget was to be balanced through a combination of reduced expenditures and increased taxation.

The League of Nations plan also lowered and clarified the amount and timing of the reparations payments owed to the Reparations Commission. In addition, it lifted the lien on state assets imposed by the original treaty. Those measures were undoubtedly a stabilizing factor, as they reduced current and expected fiscal obligations abroad.[4] The result in Austria and Hungary of the plan was an end to inflation and the stabilization of their currencies in 1924. Poland managed to eliminate the hyper-inflation and stabilize its currency through policies similar to those followed by Austria and Hungary, namely, stabilization of the exchange rate, creation of an independent central bank and balancing of the budget. However, unlike in Austria and Hungary, it achieved the stabilization without a League of Nations loan. Later on, in 1927, when instability in the foreign exchange market started to develop, Poland arranged for a large foreign loan with the help of the League.

Czechoslovakia, formed in 1918, was the only country in Central and Eastern Europe that managed to avoid a period of extreme inflation in the aftermath of the First World War. As shown in table 2-3, it experienced *deflation* in 1922-23 (matching that of dollar prices) following the implementation of conservative fiscal and monetary policies. Czechoslovakia's economic reconstruction went ahead without the detour of its first having to stabilize as its neighbors did.

The second half of the 1920s brought relative prosperity to Central and Eastern Europe. With the consolidation of stabilization, output started to grow, a trend that lasted until 1929 with the onset of the world Depression. Data on the national product for that period show Czechoslovakia's economy starting to grow in the early 1920s, avoiding the slump experienced by the countries affected by hyper-inflation in that period (table 2.4).

Two external factors fueled the recovery of growth in the second half of the 1920s—favorable agricultural

Table 2-4. *Economic Growth in Central and Eastern Europe in the Inter-war Period, as Measured by National Product*[a]
(annual growth rate in percent)

	Czechoslovakia	Hungary	Yugoslavia	Bulgaria
1920-24	4.7	-	3.4	-
1925-29	3.7	5.4	3.7	2.3
1930-33	-2.9	-2.4	-2.1	0.0
1934-39	4.5[b]	2.5	4.0	7.5

a. For Czechoslovakia and Yugoslavia, gross domestic product; for Hungary and Bulgaria, net national product.
b. 1934-37.
Source: Elaborated on the basis of Mitchell (1975).

prices and foreign capital inflows. The favorable agricultural prices benefitted not only the agrarian countries of the Balkans, but also Hungary and Poland. The major inflow of capital, including direct investment, came from the West, with England and the United States the most important sources.

Although the economies of Central and Eastern Europe maintained their trade with the rest of Europe and overseas, a general tendency toward protectionism developed in the region in the mid-1920s. In Hungary, average tariffs were raised from 20 percent, the average level prevailing under the monarchy, to 30 percent by 1925. Romania raised its import duties from 30 percent before the war to almost 40 percent by 1924. Bulgaria hiked its tariff levels to prohibitive levels: for some activities, they reached a level 100-300 percent higher than that before the war (Berend and Ranki 1974, chapter 9).

Most countries in Central and Eastern Europe based their exchange rate system on the gold exchange standard, as proposed in the Genoa conference of 1922 (Nurske 1944 and Kindleberger 1984). This system allowed the central banks (reformed with the assistance of the League of Nations, as noted) to hold their reserves partly in the form of foreign exchange—instead of gold—against notes in circulation and sight deposits. The US dollar and the pound sterling served as reserve currencies. The system worked relatively well for a while, preventing the deflationary tendencies that a "full" gold standard could have generated given the relative scarcity of gold at the time. Nevertheless, toward the late 1920s, following the events in France in 1928, the system came under pressure.[5] (Table 2-5 provides details on exchange rates and prices.)

The response to the loss in confidence in the gold exchange standard in countries such as Poland, Czechoslovakia and Bulgaria was the transfer of their reserve balances from London to Paris when a run against the pound developed. After April 1933, the other reserve currency—the US dollar—also ceased to be eligible for reserve purposes.

The 1930s and After

The economies of Central and Eastern Europe were not immune to the world Depression triggered in 1929. These countries suffered a fall in world demand for their exports, a deterioration in their terms of trade and a cutoff of foreign lending. Agriculture-exporting countries such as Bulgaria, Rumania and Yugoslavia were badly hurt by the drop in agricultural world prices, particularly for wheat and corn (table 2-6), a shock that had both adverse income and balance-of-payments effects. The semi-agrarian countries of Hungary and Poland also suffered directly from the drop in world agricultural prices, as well as indirectly from the squeeze on industrial de-

Table 2-5. *Exchange Rates and Prices in the Inter-war Period*
(dollar and cents per unit of local currency)

	Czechoslovakia		Hungary		Poland		Yugoslavia		Romania		Bulgaria	
	Exchange rate (Crown)	Price level (1929=100)	Exchange rate (Pengo)	Price level (1929=100)	Exchange rate (Zloty)	Price level (1929=100)	Exchange rate (Dinar)	Price level (1929=100)	Exchange rate (Leu)	Price level (1929=100)	Exchange rate (Lev)	Price level (1929=100)
1925	2.97	109	0.0017[a]	116	17.74	n.a.	1.70	n.a.	0.48	n.a.	0.73	95
1926	2.96	103	17.56	102	11.18	91	1.76	101	0.46	n.a.	0.72	87
1927	2.96	106	17.47	109	11.29	103	1.76	104	0.60	n.a.	0.72	88
1928	2.96	106	17.44	112	11.21	104	1.76	107	0.60	n.a.	0.72	94
1929	2.96	100	17.44	100	11.19	100	1.76	100	0.60	100	0.72	100
1930	2.96	89	17.49	87	11.21	89	1.76	86	0.60	78	0.72	82
1931	2.96	81	17.45	82	11.20	78	1.76	73	0.60	60	0.72	67
1932	2.96	74	17.45	82	11.18	68	1.64	65	0.60	54	0.72	59
1933	3.82	72	22.36	71	14.41	61	1.76	64	0.78	52	1.00	53
1934	4.24	74	29.57	71	18.85	58	2.27	63	1.00	52	1.29	54
1935	4.16	77	29.6	78	18.88	55	2.28	66	0.93	60	1.30	55
1936	4.01	77	19.78	80	18.87	56	2.29	68	0.74	69	1.30	56
1937	3.49	82	19.78	86	18.92	62	2.30	74	0.73	78	1.29	63
1938	3.47	81	19.73	87	18.86	58	2.31	78	0.73	78	1.24	65
1939	3.42	93	19.24	86	18.84	57	n.a.	79	0.71	88	1.21	66

n.a. Not available.

a. The Pengo was introduced in 1925 (1 Pengo=12,500 Crowns).

Source: Svennilson (1954).

Table 2-6. *Price Index of Grains, Central and Eastern Europe, 1930-33*
(1929=100)

	Bulgaria		Hungary		Yugoslavia		Romania	
	Wheat	Corn	Wheat	Corn	Wheat	Corn	Wheat	Corn
1930	87	59	55	31	63	46	47	51
1931	72	63	57	29	39	34	45	46
1932	77	59	67	29	54	30	34	37
1933	62	32	44	26	63	26	34	25

Source: Berend and Ranki (1974).

mand associated with the decline in real incomes in the agricultural sector. The more industrialized Czechoslovakia (and Austria) experienced a cut in production in industry, in particular in the capital goods-producing sectors during the great Depression.

National product and the level of prices fell in the early 1930s (tables 2-4 and 2-5), particularly in the period 1930 through 1933. The bankruptcies of German and Austrian banks in 1931 compounded the financial repercussions of the crisis in real economic activity. The attempts to continue servicing the short-term credits from abroad caused large losses in their holdings of international reserves and gold. Hungary had to rescue major banks from bankruptcy; in Yugoslavia, total deposits shrunk by half between 1930 and 1934, a problem that caused several financial institutions to go bankrupt. In Bulgaria the crisis in the banking system showed up in the failure of the important Banque de Sofia and the merger of several other banks.

In contrast with the other countries of the region, Czechoslovakia came through the financial crisis of the early thirties in much better shape than its neighbors did. To a large extent, the reason was that at the time of the adverse shocks in the early 1930s it had a relatively low level of external debt. As table 2-7 shows, in the 1930s Czechoslovakia's external debt (as a share of national income) was roughly a *third* that of the other countries in Central and Eastern Europe. As such, Czechoslovakia was less vulnerable to the increases in foreign interest rates and/or the cut-off in foreign lending.

The policy response to the Depression of the 1930s in the countries being studied here included the imposition of foreign exchange controls and limited currency convertibility. In addition, a system of administrative controls and approvals was initiated for foreign trade. That system dramatically changed the relative freedom of trade that had prevailed in the 1920s (although, as noted, tariffs were not low in that period) and reduced the degree of capital mobility the economies of Central

and Eastern Europe had enjoyed under the system based on the gold exchange standard.

Following the example of Germany, the economies of Central and Eastern Europe initially abstained from a devaluation when facing the adverse external shocks of the early 1930s. To counteract a loss in external competitiveness in most of these countries, the governments instituted a "bonus system." The bonus combined a subsidy for exporters with a tax on imports, which was aimed at increasing the relative prices of traded goods (with respect to home goods) without resorting to a nominal devaluation.[6]

Moreover, in 1933, Czechoslovakia, Hungary and Poland all raised their import duties. Those countries maintained the tariff barriers throughout the thirties and then intensified them in the Second World War with the imposition of additional import controls.

Hungary suspended the payment of its external debt, both amortization and interest, between 1931 and 1933. Romania, Yugoslavia and Bulgaria partially suspended foreign debt service even after the worst of the world Depression had passed. In contrast, Czechoslovakia did not need to suspend its foreign debt obligations. Poland is a special case. Its government did not adopt restrictive policies during the years of the Depression; it tried to maintain the gold standard parity of the zloty and paid the amortization when due. However, this policy proved unsustainable, and in 1936 the government had to reschedule its payments obligations abroad, and it imposed controls over foreign exchange.

An important external factor that shaped developments in Central and Eastern Europe in the second half of the thirties was the establishment in 1933, a period of peace, of a "war economy" in Nazi Germany. The aim was to accelerate growth and secure agricultural products and raw materials to support the re-armament. The countries of Central Europe and the Balkans initially welcomed the measures, for they were suffering from depressed world demand for their products. Moreover, German trade policies after 1933 were conducted on a

Table 2-7. *Indicators of Foreign Debt in Central and Eastern Europe, 1930*

	Hungary	Czechoslovakia	Yugoslavia	Romania
Foreign debt per capita (US dollars)	65.0	34.0	66.0	75.0
National income per capita (US dollars)	116.0	171.0	93.0	107.0
Foreign debt as a share of national income (percent)	56.0	19.9	70.1	70.1

Source: Berend and Ranki (1974).

bilateral basis, with the direct exchange of goods—barter trade—rather than the use of international means of payments, which were scarce in Germany and in the other countries of the region. Several countries of Central and Eastern Europe increased their trade with Germany substantially toward the second half of the 1930s. That trend was particularly noteworthy in Hungary, Yugoslavia and Bulgaria (table 2-8).

In terms of the level of national per capita income, the structure of economic activity, and foreign trade in the region toward the late 1930s, table 2-9 shows the relative backwardness of the countries of Central and Eastern Europe with respect to Western Europe. Austria and Czechoslovakia had the highest per capita income in Central Europe, but their average was still only around 40 percent that of Great Britain, the most developed nation in Western Europe at the time. In turn, Great Britain's national per capita income was nearly *six* times that

Table 2-8. *Composition of the Trade of Central and Eastern European Countries with Germany, 1929 and 1937*

	Exports to Germany percentage of total		Imports from Germany percentage of total	
	1929	1937	1929	1937
Hungary	11.7	24.1	20.0	26.2
Yugoslavia	8.5	21.7	15.6	32.4
Romania	27.6	19.2	24.1	28.9
Bulgaria	29.9	43.1	22.2	54.8

Source: Berend and Ranki (1974).

Table 2-9. *Per Capita National Income in Europe, 1937*
(US dollars)

Western Europe		
	Great Britain	440
	Sweden	400
	Germany	340
	Belgium	330
	Holland	306
	France	265
Central and Eastern Europe		
	Austria	190
	Czechoslovakia	170
	Hungary	120
	Poland	100
	Romania	81
	Yugoslavia	80
	Bulgaria	75

Source: United Nations (1949).

of Bulgaria, the poorest country in Central and Eastern Europe. Moreover, average per capita income in Central and Eastern Europe was around *one-third* the level in Western Europe.

With the exception of Czechoslovakia and Austria, most of the countries of Central and Eastern Europe had a predominantly agrarian economic structure by the late 1930s (table 2-10). The Balkan countries (on average) generated nearly 55 percent of their national income from agriculture (63.3 percent in Bulgaria), Hungary and Poland around 37 percent on average in 1938. Agriculture in those countries was relatively backward, with low growth in productivity, a structure of land tenure in which tiny plots owned by peasants coexisted alongside large unexploited farms owned by relatively wealthy landlords. Surplus labor was another indicator of the low level of agricultural development.

The share of manufacturing in income was just over 53 percent in Czechoslovakia, close to 34 percent in Hungary and Poland and around 23 percent in Yugoslavia, Romania and Bulgaria. In Czechoslovakia, the capital goods-producing sector, chemicals and other heavy branches dominated industry. In contrast, in the less industrialized countries of the region, the manufacturing sector centered around food processing, textiles and other light activities.

The structure of foreign trade in these countries was a reflection of their patterns of development and specialization (table 2.11). In most, the bulk of exports consisted of raw materials and food, whereas their imports entailed mainly manufactured goods and intermediate inputs. Czechoslovakia, however, was a net exporter of manufacturing goods and a net importer of raw materials and food.

As noted, Germany's drive toward war directly affected the economies (and politics) of Central and Eastern Europe. Here a distinction should be made among: the group of countries that was (at least) partly annexed in 1938-39, namely, Czechoslovakia and Austria, or the so-called "Czech-Moravian Protectorate" ; the "satellite" countries—Hungary, Rumania and Bulgaria; and the group of countries that Germany occupied and physically devastated—Poland and Yugoslavia. The members of the Czech-Moravian Protectorate, given its relatively advanced stage of industrialization and financial development, were integrated into the German economy under a system of centralized state control typical of a war economy. Moreover, German intervention in the "protectorate" entailed some confiscation of property, including industry and bank assets.

The war economy did not involve open occupation of Hungary, Romania and Bulgaria, although German control was effective. These countries supplied food, agricul-

Table 2-10. *Structure of National Income by Economic Sectors of Selected Central and Eastern European Countries, 1938*
(percentages)

	Agriculture	Industry	Construction and services	Total
Czechoslovakia	23.2	53.2	23.6	100.0
Hungary	36.5	35.7	27.8	100.0
Poland	39.0	32.2	28.8	100.0
Romania	53.2	28.4	18.4	100.0
Yugoslavia	53.6	22.1	24.3	100.0
Bulgaria	63.3	18.3	18.4	100.0

Source: Berend and Ranki (1974).

tural products in general and raw materials such as iron, bauxite and timber. German involvement in these countries also had some important macroeconomic consequences. As Germany accumulated debts with these countries for unpaid supplies, their national governments printed bank notes to compensate domestic producers for the unpaid orders. Thus, with the German deliveries unpaid, a monetary overhang developed. The governments repressed the inflationary impact of the resulting excessive liquidity by rationing goods. On the supply side, they enacted a system of compulsory deliveries to the state of agricultural goods and raw materials based on fixed quotas that they strictly enforced.

The third group, comprised of Poland and Yugoslavia, was the hardest hit during the war. Both lost their independence, as Germany, Italy and the Soviet Union occupied and split up their territories. In addition, parts of Yugoslavia were annexed to Hungary and Bulgaria. The initial strategy of the Axis countries with respect to Poland and Yugoslavia was outright annihilation through the destruction of their communications systems, physical infrastructure and industrial capacity. However, later that policy changed, as Germany made deliveries of food and raw materials the priority.

By the end of World War II most of the countries of Central and Eastern Europe had suffered enormous losses. Poland and Yugoslavia lost an important part of their population, and their railway systems were severely damaged, as were the roads, infrastructure and communications in general. The capital stock of industry and agriculture was partly destroyed, with an obvious adverse effect on productive capacity.[7]

Table 2-11. *Structure of Foreign Trade in Central and Eastern Europe, 1938*
(percentages of countries' total trade)

	Czechoslovakia	Hungary	Poland	Yugoslavia	Romania	Bulgaria
Exports						
Manufactured goods	71.8	13.0	6.4	0.8	1.9	2.0
Raw materials and intermediate goods	19.8	31.7	65.1	49.5	64.3	66.6
Foodstuffs	8.4	55.3	28.5	49.7	33.8	31.4
	100.0	100.0	100.0	100.0	100.0	100.0
Imports						
Manufactured goods	29.6	30.2	28.4	44.8	68.3	68.0
Raw materials and intermediate goods	57.5	61.5	54.1	50.1	27.3	31.5
Foodstuffs	12.9	8.3	17.5	5.1	4.5	0.5
	100.0	100.0	100.0	100.0	100.0	100.0

Source: Spulber (1957).

The Establishment of Socialism in the Second Half of the 1940s

The end of the Second World War brought far-reaching political and economic changes to Central and Eastern Europe. Territories in Poland, Czechoslovakia, Rumania and Bulgaria were redistributed.[8]

The Soviet Union gained territories at the expense of these countries, while Poland got territories from Germany as retribution. As could be expected, all these changes altered the distribution of agricultural land, natural resources and industrial capital stock in the region. Poland and Czechoslovakia underwent profound changes, as the alteration of their national boundaries was of a sweeping nature. In addition, the Soviet Union specified in the peace treaties how German assets in the former satellite countries of Germany (Hungary, Romania and Bulgaria) were to be disposed of. At the political level, the governments emerging after the Second World War were formed by broad political coalitions ranging from liberal to Communist. The dynamics of the political situation were such that the Communist parties managed to acquire, in various cases through coups d'etat, dominant positions in the governments after 1948.

In keeping with the new political circumstances, the economies of Central and Eastern Europe were reorganized along the lines of the Soviet economic system. The first and most important move was the nationalization of industry, the financial system, and the trade and service sectors, along with agrarian reform, the latter being an old aspiration of the political left and the peasantry. In Czechoslovakia, before the Communist coup d'etat of February 1948, the nationalization laws had brought nearly 57 percent of the total industrial labor force into the state sector. After 1948 that process was accelerated, and by 1949 the private sector accounted for just 3 percent of total employment in manufacturing. In Poland, in 1946 the state sector accounted for nearly 85 percent of total employment in the manufacturing sector for units with over five workers. Industry was almost fully nationalized by the early 1950s. In Hungary, where nationalization had been relatively moderate early on, after 1948 the process was intensified, encompassing medium- and large-scale firms in manufacturing. With some specific differences, the same process occurred in Romania and Bulgaria.

By 1949 the share of the socialized sector in gross manufacturing output ranged from 85 percent in Romania to 92 percent in Hungary, 93 percent in Bulgaria, 94 percent in Czechoslovakia and 100 percent in Yugoslavia (Spulber 1957, p. 83). Thus, the private sector practically disappeared from the productive sphere in a period of around five years.

The nationalization laws contemplated compensation of the former owners of the enterprises through treasury bills, payments of money or paper issued by newly created funds.[9]

The amount of actual compensation is hard to determine, but the widespread presumption is that it amounted to very little. The nationalizations spurred the merging and consolidation of nationalized enterprises, a process that created monopolistic market structures. A few units ended up producing the total supply of given goods. The nationalizations also encouraged vertical integration and required centralized decision-making. Therefore central planning and full state ownership became closely intertwined.

The nationalization of the banking and financial systems was facilitated in Czechoslovakia, Poland and Yugoslavia by the fact that the major financial institutions had no private property after the war. In general, merging and centralization of the banking system into state national banks took place in Poland, Hungary, Romania, Yugoslavia and Bulgaria in the late 1940s. These banks performed several roles: they had a monopoly over the issuance of money and therefore acted as central banks; they regulated the financial system; and they provided short-term credit to enterprises in the context of the planning system. Savings and investment banks (very often just branches of the state national bank) accepted savings from the population and channeled them as financing for investment.

The monetary history of the region after World War II resembled in several ways that of the post-World War I period. Because World War II had been financed by the printing of money (along with rationing), there was a monetary overhang when it ended. Moreover, the reconstruction and the need to recapitalize and expand the nationalized sector after 1945 led to a rapid expansion of the money supply in several Central and Eastern European economies (see table 2-12).

From another angle, the accumulation of excessive liquidity originated in an increase in the wage bill that was overly high relative to the output of consumer goods at fixed prices (the phenomenon of too high wages chasing too few goods) (table 2-13). The resulting shortages in

Table 2-12. *Currency in Circulation in Czechoslovakia, Poland and Yugoslavia, 1938, 1945 and 1948*
(1938=100)

	Czechoslovakia	Poland	Yugoslavia
1938	100	100	100
1945	254	1,878	231
1948	908	12,400	509

Source: Spulber (1957).

consumption goods led to an accumulation of involuntary savings in the form of liquid assets.

As the excessive liquidity threatened to become an inflationary factor, governments implemented monetary reforms to soak up the large monetary balances. The monetary reforms involved at least one of three measures: (1) reduction of the supply of liquid assets through the compulsory exchange of "old" money for "new" money at a given rate of conversion; (2) immobilization of a share of the supply of liquid assets by blocking access to some deposits in the banking system, with the blocked funds going into special accounts (the depositors still owned the full deposits); and (3) the conversion of wages into a new unit at a given rate of exchange.

In several countries of the region, the monetary reforms involved differentiated rates of conversion for bank notes vis-a-vis bank deposits, with a more favorable rate of conversion for deposits (intended to tax speculators who often operated with currency). In addition, a distinction was made based on the amount of liquid assets held by individuals and enterprises, with small holders favored over large ones or private enterprises.[10]

The actual rates of conversion of money varied from country to country. Under the Hungarian monetary reform of December 1945, the rate was 4 to 1 old for new currency bank notes. In Bulgaria, it was 100 to 1 in the reform of March 1947. In Rumania, the rates varied from 100 to 1 to 400 to 1 under the monetary reform of January 1952. Poland blocked bank deposits beginning in December 1944, Czechoslovakia in October 1945 and Bulgaria in March 1947.[11]

The extent to which the monetary reforms were successful in reducing the excess liquidity and inflationary pressures in Central and Eastern Europe is debatable, as, in general, the rate of conversion for wages was more favorable than that for money (Ames 1954). Moreover, reducing the excess liquidity was not easy, and several countries of the region had to implement more than one monetary reform in the period 1945-53.

Hungary suffered a (classic) case of hyper-inflation during its transition to socialism. Moreover, its bout of hyper-inflation was the second one it had faced after the hyper-inflation of the early 1920s. The hyper-inflation of 1945-46 was more intense than the former episode and was more extreme than even the German one of 1923. As in other historical episodes of extreme inflation, Hungary's was associated with the severe increase of the fiscal deficit. As table 2-14 shows, during most of the hyper-inflation, tax revenues financed less than 10 percent of fiscal expenditures. An important element in the deterioration of fiscal finances was the burden imposed by the reparations payments Hungary agreed to in the armistice of January 1945. It owed those reparations mainly to the Soviet Union, but also to Czechoslovakia and Yugoslavia.[12]

The costs of the reparations and occupation accounted for between 23-50 percent of public spending.[13] The fiscal deficit was financed through treasury bills issued by the Hungarian government and discounted by the central bank. In addition, indexation of the money supply is considered to have been a critical contributor to the very high rates of inflation (table 2-15).

The Hungarian stabilization plan of August 1, 1946—designed by the Marxist economist Eugene Varga and backed by the Communist party—consisted of the following measures. In the area of monetary reform, the

Table 2-13. *Consumption Spending and Wages, 1948-51*

(1948=100)

	1948	1949	1950	1951
Czechoslovakia				
Consumption	100	108	118	131
Wage bill	100	112	142	159
Hungary				
Consumption	100	122	134	152
Wage bill	100	131	169	206
Poland				
Consumption	100	101	118	126
Wage bill	100	143	180	256
Romania				
Consumption	100	90	109	111
Wage bill	100	154	210	n.a.

n.a. Not available.
Source: Ames (1954).

Table 2-14. *Public Finances in Hungary, 1945-46*

	Percentage of fiscal expenditures financed by fiscal revenues	Occupation and reparation costs as percentage of fiscal expenditure
1945		
July	6.8	23.0
August	5.3	34.0
September	7.3	23.0
October	5.7	24.0
November	6.6	31.0
December	7.1	40.0
1946		
January	14.2	26.0
February	14.4	32.0
March	13.0	39.0
April	9.8	50.0
May	7.3	38.0

Source: Bomberger and Makinen (1983).

Table 2-15. *Inflation in Hungary, 1945-June 1946*
(price level, January 1945=100)

1945	I	104
	II	124
	III	290
	IV	1,826
1946	I	4,442
	IV	185×10^6

Note: I-IV refer to quarters of the year.
Source: Spulber (1957).

government introduced a new unit, the forint, and initially it imposed a 100 percent reserve requirement on commercial banks. The central bank was forbidden by law from making direct or indirect loans to the government. Discounting of treasury bills was abolished, and the only operation allowed between the treasury and the central bank was lending to finance the acquisition of gold or foreign currencies. In the area of fiscal reform, the tax system was completely revamped, with the tax rates on labor income and property going up, as did the sales tax. The government introduced a turnover tax on enterprises and reduced fiscal expenditures by cutting the number of civil servants and shrinking the size of the army and police. With respect to external financing, the plan entailed external support in the form of tied US loans, increased food supplies granted by the United Nations and an extended payment period for the debt owed to the Soviet Union.

The plan succeeded. Hyper-inflation stopped rapidly: from August 1 to December 1946, inflation rose by only 6 percent, and the rate of inflation in 1947 was approximately 19 percent. Stabilization followed the rapid monetization (the increase in money demand after the stabilization was accommodated), and the stock of money increased by 221 percent between August 31 and December 31, 1946. During 1947, the nominal money stock grew by 132 percent (Bomberger and Makinen 1983). The effects of the stabilization on output and employment are hard to determine given the sketchy data. However, a reduction in employment along with an increase in national product seem to have taken place during 1946 and 1947. Politics took center stage after the achievement of stabilization: in June 1947 a Communist coup d'etat forced the resignation of Prime Minister Nagy. The Communist party took over practically all the ministries, and the state was reorganized in a way that furthered the establishment of socialism. In the economic sphere, nationalization and the imposition of central planning were accelerated.

The Collapse of Socialism in Central and Eastern Europe: The Late 1980s

The seemingly irreversible socialist experiment in Central and Eastern Europe came to sudden, and largely unexpected, end in the late 1980s. The collapse of Soviet-style socialism has both economic and political roots. Central planning led to endemic shortages, slow technical change, low quality goods and over-expanded public sectors. In practice, full employment and social protection had been bought at the price of economic backwardness and a lack of political freedom. Attempts at partial reform in the 1980s often worsened the macroeconomic conditions, as credit and wage policies were relaxed and fiscal budgets turned into deficits. In addition, several Central and Eastern European economies borrowed heavily abroad, accumulating a large external debt that further complicated domestic economic management.

At the political level, more than four decades of one-party rule and authoritarianism generated a (non-official) domestic consensus on the need for a political opening-up and democracy. In 1989, emerging political parties and social movements with an agenda of political transition to a Western-style democracy and the creation of a market economy toppled the authoritarian regimes dominated by the Communist party (or its equivalent).

Table 2-16 gives a broad picture of both the final state of the socialist experiment and initial results of the transition toward a market economy. The image is that of deteriorated economic conditions, as reflected (among other indicators) in the lower growth and higher inflation in the second half of the 1980s. The macro instability was more acute in Yugoslavia and Poland, where near hyper-inflation developed in 1989. To eradicate the inflation and create a more favorable macro environment for a market-oriented economy, both countries adopted sharp anti-inflationary policies in early 1990. Their plans included a large real depreciation of the exchange rate, the deregulation of most controlled prices, tight monetary and credit policies, the correction of fiscal deficits and a drastic lowering of import tariffs.[14]

In addition, both countries are trying to privatize state-owned enterprises, albeit still with only limited success.

Hungary and Czechoslovakia are in better shape, although inflation in the former is considered relatively high. Czechoslovakia, following a long history of macro stability and prudence (that goes back to its pre-socialist period), had not experienced any upsurge in open inflation through the end of 1990, although acceleration in inflation cannot be discarded for the future.[15]

Table 2-16. *Inflation and GDP Growth in Selected Central and Eastern European Countries, 1986-90*
(percentages)

| | Poland | | Yugoslavia | | Hungary | | Czechoslovakia | | Bulgaria | |
	GDP growth	Infl. rate[a]	GDP growth	Infl. rate[a]	GDP growth	Infl. rate[a]	NMP[b] growth	Infl. rate[a]	GDP growth	Infl. rate[a]
1986	1.5	18.0	3.4	89.9	1.5	5.3	2.6	0.50	4.2	1.3
1987	3.4	25.2	-0.5	120.8	3.4	8.6	2.1	0.09	6.1	0.07
1988	0.1	60.0	-1.0	194.1	0.1	15.7	2.3	0.09	2.6	2.3
1989	-1.0	700.0	-2.0	2,700.0	0.5	19.6	1.9	1.44	-1.9	4.4
1990	-12.0	249.0	-3.2	118.6	-6.5	30.0	-3.5	13.9	-12.0	100.0

Source: World Bank.
a. Based on the Consumer Price Index.
b. Net material product.

The economic outlook for Central and Eastern Europe is bleak. The results of 1990 reveal large-scale contraction in economic activity, particularly in Poland, Bulgaria and Yugoslavia, along with stubborn inflation. These trends are worrisome as they may undermine public support for the reform process.

The situation does not leave much room for optimism given the monumental task of transforming a very obsolete economic system into a dynamic one. Currently, the problems of structural transformation are compounded by the disintegration of Comecon (it will entail a big terms of trade deterioration for Central and Eastern Europe vis-a-vis the Soviet Union) and the reluctance of the international capital markets to commit ample credit to the region until the reform is more consolidated.

In looking at the structure of production in Central and Eastern Europe in the late 1980s, the reduced share of agriculture and the relatively high share of industry in output (between 37-60 percent) are evident (table 2-17).[16]

Socialist industrialization significantly altered the production structure of the 1930s (table 2-10). At that time, Bulgaria, Yugoslavia and Romania were predominantly agrarian economies, with the share of agriculture in national income at over 53 percent in 1938. In the late 1980s that share was down to less than 15 percent. However, as will be seen below, socialist industrialization did not bring much prosperity.

The case of Spain provides a useful contrast. A backward Western European country in the thirties, Spain industrialized in the 1950s and 1960s around (protected) market lines and ended up in 1988 with a level of per capita GDP around three times higher than the average for Central and Eastern Europe (table 2-18). In Central and Eastern Europe, socialist industrialization began with an "easy phase," as idle resources could be pulled from the agricultural sector. However, the industrialization turned very capital-intensive, with a heavy focus on

development of the capital goods sector, to the clear detriment of the production of manufactured consumer goods, whose quality was poor.[17]

Table 2-17. *Structure of GDP in Selected Eastern and Central European Countries, 1988[a]*
(percentages)

	Agriculture	Industry	Construction and services	Total
Czechoslovakia	6.4	49.6	34.0	100.0
Hungary	14.0	37.0	49.0	100.0
Poland	10.6	40.4	49.0	100.0
Yugoslavia	14.0	49.0	37.0	100.0
Bulgaria[b]	12.6	58.5	28.9	100.0

a. The shares for Czechoslovakia and Bulgaria correspond to net material product.
b. The shares correspond to 1989.

Table 2-18. *Per Capita GDP in Selected Eastern and Central European Economies, Compared to Western Europe and Selected Latin American Countries, 1988*
(in 1988 US dollars)

Poland	1,860
Hungary	2.460
Yugoslavia	2,520
Czechoslovakia	3,300
Mexico	1,760
Brazil	2,160
Argentina	2,520
Spain	7,740
United Kingdom	12,810
Italy	13,330
Austria	15,470
France	16,090
Germany, F.R.	18,480
United States	19,840

Source: World Bank (1990).

In practice, the industrialization of Central and Eastern Europe was based on a wall of tariffs and prohibitions on imports from the West. The Soviet Union dictated the pattern of specialization, and production was not located on the basis of comparative advantage.

The end of the centrally planned economy in Central and Eastern Europe leaves as a legacy the almost complete dominance of the public sector in the generation of output (table 2-19). After 18 months of transition from socialism, it is clear that privatization is crucial to creating a market economy, although the process faces multiple obstacles of both an operational and political nature.

Finally, a look at recent levels of per capita GDP in several countries of Central and Eastern Europe is revealing. The historical differences between Eastern and Western Europe in the late thirties (table 2-9) were not any narrower after 40 years of socialism (table 2.19).[18]

Quite the opposite, the data suggest (with the usual caveats pertinent to comparisons of real income over time and across countries) that the gap in per capita income has widened spectacularly. For example, while in 1937 Czechoslovakia had a national per capita income just 10 percent below that of Austria, in 1988 per capita GDP in Czechoslovakia was nearly *one-fifth* that of Austria (US$3,300 for Czechoslovakia versus US$15,470 for Austria). In 1988 the per capita GDP of the most developed countries in Western Europe (for example, the Federal Republic of Germany) was 5.6 times larger than that of Czechoslovakia, the most developed country of Central and Eastern Europe. In contrast, in 1937 the national per capita income of Great Britain was just 2.6 times that of Czechoslovakia.[19]

Currently, the average per capita GDP (World Bank data) in Central and Eastern European countries is closer to the levels in Latin American countries such as Mexico, Brazil and Argentina.

Table 2-19. *Size of the State Sector in Central and Eastern Europe*

(percentage of output and employment of the public sector in total output and employment)

	Output	*Employment*
Czechoslovakia (1986)	97.0	
Dem. Rep. Germany (1982)	96.5	94.2
Poland (1985)	81.7	71.5
Hungary (1984)	65.2	69.9

Source: Lipton and Sachs, *Brookings Papers on Economic Activities* (1990), 2:293-341.

Concluding Remarks and Summary

This paper reviewed first the main features of the economic history of Central and Eastern Europe in the inter-war period and the establishment of socialism in the forties. It then looked at the initial results of the transition to a market economy after the collapse of socialism in the late 1980s. A summary of the main findings follows:

• The economic history of Central and Eastern Europe shows episodes of extreme inflation and extreme macroeconomic instability following World War I and in the early 1920s. An example of the economic situation was the hyper-inflation of Poland, Hungary and Austria. Its stabilization in Poland, Hungary and other Eastern and Central European economies required stabilization of the exchange rate, fiscal reform, the establishment of independent central banks and (conditional) foreign financing provided by the League of Nations. Of the countries in the region, Czechoslovakia, which was formed out of territories left over from the Austro-Hungarian Empire, is unique for having carried out its reconstruction after World War I without inflation and with macroeconomic stability.

• The second half of the 1920s in Central and Eastern Europe was a period of relatively high growth, low inflation, moderate protectionism and increasing financial integration in the context of the gold exchange standard system. London and New York were the main financial centers at the time, and the British pound and US dollar were the reserve currencies, in addition to gold.

• The great Depression of 1929-33 hit Bulgaria, Rumania and Yugoslavia particularly hard. The drop in the international prices of agricultural products was an adverse external shock for these agrarian economies. Moreover, the disruption in the flows of foreign financing also hurt the Balkan states, Hungary Poland and even Czechoslovakia, the most industrialized country. The response of the countries of the region to the adverse external shocks and the collapse of the gold exchange standard in the early 1930s included the imposition of foreign exchange controls, the rise in import duties and the suspension of debt payments abroad.

• The initial recovery of most economies in Central and Eastern Europe in the second half of the 1930s was basically driven by Germany. Its war preparations required an abundant supply of agricultural products and raw materials that the Balkan countries, Hungary and Poland could provide. Czechoslovakia's large industrial base was also instrumental to German re-armament. To enhance its control, before the war Germany annexed

Czechoslovakia and Austria (the "Czech-Moravian Protectorate").

- Poland and Yugoslavia suffered the greatest destruction of productive capacity, infrastructure and housing and the most extensive human losses as a result of the occupation and war. Czechoslovakia suffered comparatively less after the conflict.

- After 1945 the nationalization of industrial firms and financial systems and the launching of agrarian reform were the main features of the economic policies implemented by the coalition governments that emerged in Central and Eastern Europe. The drive toward full nationalization and the creation of a system of central planning were fully consolidated after a series of coups d'etat led by the Communist parties in 1948.

- The second half of the 1940s provides an interesting laboratory of monetary reform aimed at reducing excess liquidity. In Hungary, Rumania, Poland and Bulgaria the reforms involved a reduction of the money supply through (differential) rates of exchange between "old" and "new" money. Poland, Czechoslovakia and Bulgaria instituted the blocking of deposits in the banking system between 1945 and 1955. Western European countries such as France, Austria and Belgium implemented some of the same reforms over the same period.

- Hungary in 1945-46 provides a good example of hyper-inflation during the transition to socialism. It later achieved economic stabilization by bringing public finances into balance, stabilizing the currency and arranging for a package of foreign financing, debt and relief from war reparations.

- The collapse of socialism in Central and Eastern Europe in the late 1980s made evident the structural weakness of central planning in improving the standards of living of the population. The economic hardship and closed political systems could not last forever. In several cases, systemic reform has been implemented alongside the macroeconomic stabilization. The initial results have been a massive collapse in economic activity and stubborn inflation. Economic transformation looms as a long and complicated process given the difficult initial conditions for the transition to a market economy. The economies of Central and Eastern Europe are characterized by obsolete and uncompetitive productive capacities, macroeconomic imbalances, lack of modern infrastructure and factor markets, and weak institutions, as well as other problems. In addition, the external environment in the East is not very supportive: the disintegration of Comecon will entail large terms-of-trade losses for Central and Eastern Europe vis-a-vis the Soviet Union, and a massive influx of Western capital is unlikely to happen in the short to medium run. On the political side, the initial euphoria associated with the end of the old regimes is being replaced by a less enthusiastic public attitude toward the hardships of transition. Fragile and changing political coalitions and the temptation of populism clearly reflect these tendencies.

- Finally, an important finding of the paper is that the differences in per capita income between Eastern and Western Europe *widened* under the socialist regimes. In 1937, before the Second World War and socialism, the per capita income of Great Britain, which was the highest in Western Europe at the time, was 2.6 times greater than that of Czechoslovakia, which had the highest per capita income in Central and Eastern Europe. In 1988, the per capita income of the Federal Republic of Germany (which is now greater than that of Great Britain) was 5.6 times greater than the per capita GDP of Czechoslovakia. The average per capita income of Central and Eastern Europe is now closer to the levels in Latin American countries such as Mexico, Brazil and Argentina.

Notes

1. The comments by Bela Balassa, Rudi Dornbusch, Raimundo Soto and Steven Webb on a previous draft are appreciated.

2. See Berend and Ranki (1974) for a full analysis of the economic history of Central and Eastern Europe before and after World War I.

3. Germany's hyper-inflation is not discussed in this paper. For references in the literature see Graham (1930), Bresciani-Turroni (1937), Dornbusch (1987), Sargent (1982), Solimano (1990a), and Webb (1989).

4. The League of Nations loans were not only necessary for the reconstruction of the economies of the recipient countries but also enhanced the functioning of the system of international payments that emerged after the First World War. In fact, the United States required that the Allies—England, France and Italy—honor their war debts with the United States. However, to honor those debts, the Allies required that the losers of the war—Germany, the countries formed from the collapse of the Austro-Hungarian Empire and Bulgaria—transfer to them resources in the form of war reparations. After a few years it became evident that without external support the loser countries would be unable to meet their obligations. Thus, the League of Nations loans involved a recycling of the war reparations payments.

5. Nurske (1944) describes the situation: The fate of the gold exchange standard was sealed when France decided in 1928 to take nothing but gold in settlement of the enormous surplus accruing to her from the repatriation of capital and the current balance of payments. The French gold imports certainly aggravated the pressure of deflation in the rest of the world and specially in London. In London the pressure became unbearable in the end, and the gold parity of the Pound was abandoned.

6. The bonus system was administratively cumbersome, as the size of the subsidy tax varied by currency and trading partner.

7. The estimates of the destruction are rather imprecise. Among the numbers are: Yugoslavia lost 10 percent of its population and half its industrial engines and around 40-50 percent of its agricultural machinery and equipment. In Poland, 40 percent of the railways were destroyed, 85 percent of the housing in Warsaw was devastated, and there was massive destruction of industry and agriculture. See Berend and

Ranki (1974, chapter 13).

8. Hungary was the only country that returned to its pre-war territorial status (see Spulber 1954).

9. The exception was property confiscated from collaborators with the Germans. The compensation of foreigners, when it occurred, in general took an ad hoc form and was tied to trade negotiations and other deals.

10. See Gurley (1953) for an interesting discussion and documentation of the monetary reforms in Western and Eastern Europe. A more recent analysis of the topic is found in Dornbusch and Wolf (1990).

11. The blocking of bank deposits was also part of the monetary reforms in Western Europe after World War II. Examples are Belgium in October 1944, France in June 1945 and January 1948, and Austria, Denmark, Norway and the Netherlands in 1945 (see Gurley 1953).

12. The reparations due were calculated to be US$300 million, payable within a period of six years. The national income of Hungary in 1945-46 is estimated to have been around US$1 billion (see Bomberger and Makinen 1983).

13. The worsening of the fiscal situation in Hungary is also attributable to lower tax revenues, the result of administrative mismanagement after the war, the destruction of records on income and assets during the war, the fall in the level of economic activity and the acceleration in inflation (see Bomberger and Makinen 1983).

14. For a description of the stabilization policies in Poland, see Lipton and Sachs (1990a). A comparative analysis of the Polish and Yugoslav stabilization plans is found in chapter 9, "Stabilization Programs In Eastern Europe: A Comparative Analysis of the Polish and Yugoslav Programs of 1990" by Fabrizio Coricelli and Roberto de Rezende Rocha in this volume. For an analysis of privatization in Eastern Europe, see Lipton and Sachs (1990b).

15. See Solimano (1990c) for an analysis of the Bulgarian case.

16. This number tends to be a bit overstated in Czechoslovakia, where the ratio involves net material product, which excludes several services such as education, health and other "non-productive" activities.

17. See Solimano (1990b) for a discussion of the patterns of productivity growth in socialist economies.

18. The comparison is based on World Bank estimates of per capita GDP in dollars for 1988. Other sources, such as the C.I.A. and Plan Econ, yield higher estimates of per capita income for Central and Eastern Europe.

19. Great Britain had the highest per capita income in Europe in the 1930s.

References

Ames, E. 1954 "Soviet Block Currency Conversions." *The American Economic Review* XIV (June).

Berend, I., and G. Ranki. 1974. *Economic Development in Central and Eastern Europe in the 19th and 20th Centuries*. New York and London: Columbia University Press.

Bomberger, B., and G. Makinen. 1983. "The Hungarian Hyperinflation and Stabilization of 1945-1946." *Journal of Political Economy* 91 (5)(October).

Bresciani-Turroni, C. 1937. *The Economics of Inflation*. London: Allen & Unwin.

Dornbusch, R. 1987. "Lessons from the German Inflation Experience of the 1920s," In R. Dornbusch, S. Fischer and J. Bossons, eds., *Macroeconomics and Finance: Essays in Honor of Franco Modigliani*. Cambridge, Mass.: MIT Press.

Dornbusch, R., and H. Wolf. 1990. "Monetary Overhangs and Reforms in the 1940s." Mimeo. Massachusetts Institute of Technology, Cambridge, Mass.

Dornbusch, R., and S. Fischer. 1986. "Stopping Hyperinflation: Past and Present." *Weltwirtschaffliches Archiv* [Review of World Economics] (Kiel Institute).

Graham, F. 1930. *Exchange Rates, Prices and Production in Hyperinflation: Germany 1920-1923*. Princeton, N.J.: Princeton University Press.

Gurley, J. 1953. "Excess Liquidity and European Monetary Reforms, 1944-1952." *American Economic Review* XLIII (March).

Kindleberger, C. 1984. *A Financial History of Western Europe*. London: George Allen & Unwin.

Lipton, M., and J. Sachs. 1990a. "The Creation of a Market Economy in Eastern Europe: The Case of Poland." *Brookings Papers on Economic Activity* 1:75-147.

————. 1990b. "Privatization in Eastern Europe: The Case of Poland." *Brookings Papers on Economic Activity* 2:293-341.

Mitchell, B.R. 1975. *European Historical Statistics, 1750-1970*. New York: Columbia University Press.

Nurske, R. 1944. "The Gold Exchange Standard." In B. Eichengreen, ed., *The Gold Standard in Theory and History*. New York: Methuen, 1985.

Sargent, T. 1982. "The Ends of Four Big Inflations." In R. Hall, ed., *Inflation Causes and Effects*. Chicago: University of Chicago Press.

Solimano, A. 1990a. "Inflation and the Costs of Stabilization: Historical and Recent Experiences and Policy Lessons." *The World Bank Observer* 5 (2)(July).

————. 1990b. "Macroeconomic Adjustment, Stabilization and Growth in Reforming Socialist Economies. Analytical and Policy Issues." Policy Research and External Affairs (PRE) Working Paper Series #399. World Bank. Washington, D.C.

————. (1990c) "Inflation and Growth in the Transition from Socialism: The Case of Bulgaria." Policy, Research and External Affairs (PRE) Working Paper Series #659. World Bank. Washington, D.C.

Spulber, N. 1957. *The Economics of Eastern Europe*. Cambridge, Mass.: MIT Press and New York: J. Wiley & Sons, Inc.

Svennilson, I. 1954. *Growth and Stagnation in the European Economy*. Geneva: United Nations Economic Commission for Europe.

United Nations. 1949. *Economic Survey of Europe, 1948*. Geneva: United Nations.

Webb, S.B. 1989. *Hyperinflation and Stabilization in Weimar Germany*. New York: Oxford University Press.

Wicker, E. 1986. "Terminating Hyperinflation in the Dismembered Hapsburg Monarchy." *American Economic Review* 76 (3)(June).

World Bank. 1990. *World Development Report 1990*. Baltimore: Johns Hopkins University Press.

Part II

The World Bank Experience with Adjustment Lending

3

World Bank -Supported Adjustment Programs: Lessons for Central and Eastern Europe[1]

Vittorio Corbo

The World Bank introduced adjustment lending in 1979. It grew rapidly in the first half of the 1980s and then leveled off in 1986-88, when it averaged 24 percent of Bank Group lending commitments. In 1989 it reached 27 percent of total lending commitments.

The main differences between adjustment and traditional project lending are that adjustment lending is quick-disbursing and is made conditional on policy reforms. The two principal instruments of this program are structural adjustment loans (SALs), which support economy-wide reforms and institution-building, and sectoral adjustment loans (SECALs), which have more of a sector focus.[2] Another distinction—that between structural adjustment programs and adjustment lending—is also worth noting. Countries have on their own been implementing structural adjustment programs for a long time, and the Bank has been supporting the preparation and implementation of adjustment programs since at least the late 1950s. The quick-disbursing balance-of-payments support for adjustment programs provided under adjustment lending was, however, a new initiative.

The Bank established adjustment lending in response to the difficulty a large number of countries were having by the late 1970s in financing their balance-of-payments deficits. They were also experiencing very weak growth. When the second oil shock hit in 1979, they found themselves ill-prepared to absorb the increasingly higher prices without radical changes in their economic policies and institutions. The common causes of these problems were many years of distortionary trade, regulatory and exchange rate policies and an expansion of the state's role in the allocation of resources. Ultimately, these factors resulted in the inefficient use of resources, discouraged exports and created an internationally uncompetitive structure of production. Countries facing these types of problems were spread throughout the different geographical regions.

As some countries were adjusting to the second oil shock and others were planning the transition from the initial stage of financing the deterioration in their balance of payments to a second stage of adjustment, they also had to contend with the effects of major policy changes in the industrial countries. Following the frontal attack on inflation that most industrial countries initiated in late 1979 and the early 1980s, nominal and real interest rates reached their highest level in 50 years. The industrial countries entered into a major recession, and the prices for primary commodities collapsed. To make matters worse, following Mexico's difficulty servicing its foreign debt in late 1982, commercial lending to developing countries all but disappeared. Current account deficits that were financed without much trouble in 1981 suddenly could not be financed at all.

For most of these countries, adjustment became ever more urgent. In those where large distortions and institutional weakness were preventing the economy from producing as much as it might, removal of the distortions was seen as a less costly option than reducing the current account deficit by lowering expenditures. It was recognized that many developing countries would benefit tremendously from reducing the inefficiency with which they used resources, in particular, by eliminating the excessive regulation and moderating the anti-export bias of their policies. Stabilization programs accompanied by reforms toward market-based allocation were seen as ways to lessen the cost of the oil shock. Not unexpectedly, countries had to initiate adjustment programs, including Chile, Thailand, Uruguay, Ghana and Mexico. Given these developments in the international economy, it is not surprising that adjustment lending grew rapidly in the first half of the 1980s.

The main purpose of adjustment lending is to help member countries restructure their economies to create the conditions for equitable growth while maintaining a sustainable balance of payments. Structural adjustment programs include measures to achieve or consolidate macroeconomic stabilization and the structural transformation of the economy. Adjustment lending facilitates the phased reduction of the current account deficit while a country is introducing reforms, and thereby reduces the short-run costs of adjustment on output, employment and consumption.

The risk of this type of lending is that, while it provides financing to help sustain expenditure levels, it can result in the postponement of necessary reforms. Therefore the Bank attaches conditionalities to ensure that disbursement of the loan is linked to implementation of an agreed-upon program.

Periodically the Bank evaluates the design and implementation of the adjustment programs it has supported. For example, it recently carried out two comprehensive analyses, presented in the Report on Adjustment Lending-1 (RAL-1) and Report on Adjustment Lending-2 (RAL-2) (World Bank 1988a and 1990b, respectively). The Bank also carries out a research program on development policies that has a heavy focus on the current and prospective problems of developing countries. The findings of this research and of research carried out elsewhere provide important underpinnings for the Bank's advice on the design of adjustment lending programs and operations.

The rest of this paper is divided into five sections. The next section looks at the emerging consensus on the optimal design of adjustment programs. The following section presents the main findings of RAL-2 on the effectiveness of adjustment programs and on the experience with implementation. The findings of RAL-2 on policies for the recovery of growth are reviewed in the subsequent section. The next to last section offers some lessons for the design of adjustment programs in Central and Eastern Europe. Some overall conclusions are presented in the final section.

The Emerging Consensus on Program Design

Some important lessons have emerged from analyses of the economic reforms, both successful and unsuccessful, in developing countries. These lessons, which are summarized below, are the basis of an emerging professional consensus on the design of adjustment programs, although the design of an individual country's program needs to take into account its specific economic and political conditions.

For reforms to be successful, they should have a good chance of resulting in major progress toward removing the obstacles to maximum output from existing resources. In countries with significant impediments to resource reallocation in the form of high and variable inflation, restrictions on factor mobility, ill-defined property rights and a large public sector sheltered from efficiency considerations, a reform effort that does not address these barriers has a low chance of success. Furthermore, if these barriers are not removed, the reforms will have low credibility and could unleash responses that cause a deterioration in the economic situation instead of an improvement (Calvo 1989).

In countries that are experiencing acute macroeconomic imbalances manifested in high open or repressed inflation, large fiscal deficits and major balance-of-payments crises, the structural reforms should start by attacking the fundamental causes of the macroeconomic crisis (Fischer 1986; Corbo and de Melo 1987; Sachs 1987; Corbo and Fischer 1990; and Rodrik 1990). Given that the success rate of stabilization programs in countries that have experienced a prolonged period of inflation is very poor, it is dangerous to proceed simultaneously with reforms whose ultimate success depends on the control of inflation (i.e., major trade and financial liberalization). Successful stabilization attempts have involved major fiscal adjustment through cuts in government spending, reductions in large subsidies, lessening of the losses of public enterprises and a drastic reduction in the losses of the central bank (Dornbusch 1989; and Kiguel and Liviatan 1988). In the period immediately after the Second World War, countries that had accumulated a large money overhang during the war years used monetary reform to avoid an explosion in inflation (Dornbusch and Wolf 1990). Reforms to restore macroeconomic stability could require major structural reforms in the operation of public enterprises, the tax system and the financial system (in the latter to establish at least the capacity to evaluate loans on a commercial basis). In countries with a large public sector that contains public enterprises experiencing major losses and where government subsidies are widespread, stabilization could require a major overhaul of the public sector (as in Chile in 1973-76, Mexico in 1982-89 and Argentina starting in 1989). Significant increases in the mobility of labor and flexibility in hiring and firing should be introduced early on to facilitate stabilization. Parallel programs that provide a safety net for the temporarily unemployed can increase the political acceptance of these programs and make them more equitable.

Once enough progress has been achieved in reducing inflation and the balance-of-payments deficit—in a credible way—other structural reforms aimed at improving the allocation of resources and achieving sustainable and equitable growth should be attempted. These reforms would address such areas as the public sector, trade, the financial sector, the regulatory framework and the labor market.

The Main Findings of RAL-2: The Effectiveness of Adjustment Programs and Their Implementation[3]

For countries experiencing acute macroeconomic imbalances and suffering from deep-rooted structural problems that impede a better use of resources and that limit growth, the benefits of a structural reform program will take time to develop. Therefore, to evaluate the effectiveness of adjustment programs adequately, the assessment cannot be started until enough time has elapsed since initiation of the program. Intermediate evaluations, however, can be conducted using indicators of progress with the adjustment. The analyses underlying RAL-1 and RAL-2 followed that route, considering both macroeconomic and social welfare indicators of performance.

Effectiveness of Adjustment Programs— Macroeconomic Indicators

To assess the contribution of adjustment lending to sustainable growth, RAL-2 examined performance in terms of several intermediate indicators of structural transformation—saving, investment and export ratios and the rate of growth of output. Countries were grouped into three categories for the analysis: early intensive-adjustment-lending (EIAL); other adjustment lending (OAL); and non-adjustment-lending (NAL) (table 3-1).[4]

The observed performance of an adjusting country results from (1) the policies that would have been in place in the absence of adjustment lending from the Bank, (2) world economic conditions, (3) the effects of a Bank-supported program and (4) other shocks to the economy (droughts, earthquakes, etc.). To isolate the net contri-

Table 3-1. *Country Classification*

I. EIAL (Early Intensive-Adjustment-Lending Countries) (25)

Bolivia *	Cote d'Ivoire	Madagascar *	Morocco	Tanzania *
Brazil	Ghana *	Malawi *	Nigeria *	Thailand
Chile	Jamaica	Mauritania *	Pakistan *	Togo *
Colombia	Kenya *	Mauritius	Philippines	Turkey
Costa Rica	Korea, Rep. of	Mexico	Senegal *	Zambia *

II. OAL (Other Adjustment-Lending Countries) (25)

Argentina	Guinea-Bissau *	Sierra Leone *
Bangladesh *	Guyana *	Somalia *
Burkina Faso *	Honduras	Sudan *
Burundi *	Hungary	Tunisia
Central African Rep. *	Indonesia	Uruguay
China *	Mali *	Yugoslavia
Congo, People's Rep. of	Niger *	Zaire *
Ecuador	Panama	Zimbabwe
Guinea *		

III. NAL (Non-Adjustment-Lending Countries)(28)

Algeria (NA)	Haiti * (NA)	Paraguay (NA)
Benin * (NA)	India * (NN)	Peru (NA)
Botswana (NN)	Jordan (NA)	Portugal (NN)
Cameroon (NA)	Liberia * (NA)	Rwanda * (NA)
Dominican Republic (NA)	Malaysia (NN)	Sri Lanka * (NA)
Egypt, Arab Rep. of (NA)	Myanmar * (NA)	Syrian Arab Republic (NN)
El Salvador (NN)	Nicaragua (NA)	Trinidad and Tobago (NA)
Ethiopia * (NA)	Oman (NN)	Venezuela (NA)
Greece (NN)	Papua New Guinea (NA)	Yemen Arab Republic * (NN)
Guatemala (NN)		

Notes: EIAL = countries that have received two SALs or three or more adjustment operations, with the first adjustment operation in 1985 or before; OAL = other countries receiving adjustment lending; NAL = countries that did not receive adjustment lending in the period 1980 to 1988; NA = countries that did not adjust although it was necessary for them to do so; NN = other NAL countries.

* IDA low-income countries. Middle income countries are non-IDA countries.

Source: World Bank (1990b), annex table 5.5, pp. 72-78.

bution of the Bank-supported program, a counterfactual scenario was created by estimating the effects on performance of:

- External shocks (in terms of interest rates, terms of trade and non- official lending)
- The economic policies in the pre-program period (indicated by the real exchange rate, ratio of the fiscal deficit to GDP and the annual rate of inflation)
- The initial values of the four selected indicators of macroeconomic adjustment—real GDP growth and the ratios of investment, saving and exports to GDP.

Performance in 1985-88, the period after adjustment was initiated, as measured by the four indicators, was compared with that in 1970-80 and 1981-84. Because some countries started to receive adjustment lending in the early 1980s, the base period 1970-80 corresponds more closely to the period before adjustment lending.[5]

Before-and-after comparisons of the performance indicators were also made, as they provided useful background for the counterfactual analysis (whose results are presented later). Although a program's effectiveness cannot be judged on the basis of before and after comparisons, they are likely to be important to the political viability of adjustment programs. (Before and after results can be obtained directly from table 3.2).

It is possible that exogenous influences that had nothing to do with the Bank-supported adjustment programs could have led to the observed improvement in GDP growth, saving rate and export rate of the EIAL countries in 1985-88, after the Bank-supported adjustment programs started. These influences include higher export prices, lower import prices, lower interest rates on external debt and higher external financing. Therefore, to assess the contribution of an adjustment program to these intermediate objectives, it is necessary to control for these non-program factors. In the report, the contribution of an adjustment program to macroeconomic performance is assessed by comparing the actual performance of a country in the period after adjustment was initiated (1985-88) with an estimated counterfactual scenario of what would have happened in that period in the absence of the program but with the same exogenous influences. These results are shown in table 3-3 (table 3-4 gives the leading and lagging performers for each indicator, after adjusting for other factors).

After explicitly adjusting for the external shocks, initial conditions, levels of external financing and policies followed in the pre-program period, the change in the annual average rate of *GDP growth* in the EIAL countries was higher, although it was not statistically different, from that of all the other countries when measuring changes between 1970-80 and 1985-88. Between 1981-84 and 1985-88, however, the adjustment programs are estimated to have boosted the rate of GDP growth by close to 2 percentage points. (These results have been adjusted for the effects of International Monetary Fund [IMF] programs.) Typically, the successful adjustment programs improved the growth rate as a result of greater exports, which more than offset the short-term contractionary effects of the reform policies. In contrast, the less successful programs did not shift resources rapidly enough from non-tradable to tradable activities so as to increase growth, probably because of market distortions and institutional weaknesses. In some countries with se-

Table 3-2. *Country Performance*

Country groups[a]	Real GDP growth (% per year)			Investment to GDP (% of GDP)			Domestic saving to GDP (% of GDP)			Exports to GDP (% of GDP)		
	1970-80	1981-84	1985-88	1970-80	1981-84	1985-88	1970-80	1981-84	1985-88	1970-80	1981-84	1985-88
EIAL	4.6 (2)	1.3 (3)	4.2 (1)	22.5 (2)	19.9 (3)	18.6 (3)	17.4 (1)	14.8 (1)	17.2 (1)	24.2 (2)	25.1 (2)	28.1 (1)
LIC	4.0	0.1	3.9	22.8	18.4	16.6	16.9	11.8	13.2	29.1	27.3	29.6
MIC	5.5	2.8	4.7	22.1	21.9	21.2	17.9	18.6	22.4	17.9	22.4	26.1
OAL	3.9 (3)	2.3 (2)	3.0 (2)	21.3 (3)	22.0 (2)	20.1 (1)	14.0 (3)	12.7 (3)	13.3 (3)	22.2 (3)	24.4 (3)	23.6 (3)
LIC	3.2	2.1	4.1	18.3	19.3	19.3	8.1	3.3	6.8	18.0	19.4	19.1
MIC	4.8	2.5	1.7	25.0	25.2	21.1	21.4	23.8	21.6	27.5	30.2	29.3
NAL	5.5 (1)	3.1 (1)	2.7 (3)	23.4 (1)	24.1 (1)	20.0 (2)	16.7 (2)	14.0 (2)	14.4 (2)	26.3 (1)	26.1 (1)	24.6 (2)
LIC	4.1	3.1	2.7	17.5	19.1	15.5	9.7	6.0	7.7	19.0	18.1	15.5
MIC	6.2	3.1	2.7	26.2	26.4	22.1	20.1	17.7	17.6	29.7	29.9	28.9
NA	4.7	2.2	1.7	22.2	23.5	19.6	15.7	13.1	13.3	25.7	25.2	22.5
NN	7.0	4.7	4.5	25.6	25.1	20.7	18.6	15.4	16.4	27.3	27.8	28.5

a. LIC = Low-income countries, MIC = Medium-income countries. For the other categories see table 3.1.

b. The rate of growth is calculated from constant price local currency data. The ratios are calculated from current price local currency data. The figures in parentheses indicate the ranking for the variable, with (1) indicating the best performance.

Source: World Bank data.

Table 3-3. *The Effect of Being an EIAL Country*

Period/ dependent variable	Change in rate of growth of GDP[a] (%)	Change in investment/GDP (%)	Change in domestic saving/ GDP (%)	Change in export/GDP (%)
Current prices				
1985-88 with 1970-80	1.3	-4.1**	4.0*	6.4**
1985-88 with 1981-84	2.0*	0.5	4.2**	5.0*
Constant prices				
1985-88 with 1970-80	1.0	-5.6**	2.0	1.2
1985-88 with 1981-84	1.9*	-0.1	5.8**	2.3

a. The rate of growth of GDP is measured at constant prices in both cases, but the estimation procedure requires the use of lagged values of all the performance indicators, the reason for the slightly different estimation of the effect of programs on the rate of growth of GDP in the top and bottom of the table.
* Statistically significant at the 10 percent level.
** Statistically significant at the 5 percent level.
Source: Author's calculations.

vere macroeconomic instability, the programs supported by the initial adjustment loans broke down, a situation that depressed growth in 1985-88.

In the case of *investment*, after adjusting for other factors, the adjustment programs appear to have led to a drop in investment's share in GDP (in current prices) of 4.1 percentage points between 1970-80 and 1985-88. The changes between 1981-84 and 1985-88 were small and not statistically significant. Further, because most EIAL countries carried out a real depreciation in 1985-88, the relative price of investment goods rose. As a result, the effect of the programs was an even larger average reduction—5.6 percentage points of GDP—in the constant price ratio of investment to GDP between 1970-80 and 1985-88. This decline resulted not only from lower public investment, but also from lower private investment, probably caused in part by the greater economic uncertainty at the start of the adjustment program. It should also be mentioned that where an integral aim of the adjustment program was to curtail public (and private) investment programs whose efficiency was low, a decrease in the rate of investment was part of the adjustment.

The reduction in the rate of private investment may have been unavoidable in the initial phase of the adjustment programs (see the next section). Under pressure to reduce public sector deficits, many governments substantially reduced their investment programs (and current expenditures for the maintenance of infrastructure) because of their inability to reduce other expenditures.

However, such reductions in public investment in infrastructure and human capital seriously jeopardized the resumption of private investment and the ultimate success of the adjustment programs. At the same time, however, expansion of efficient public investment enhances the supply response to the reformed incentive structure by increasing the credibility of the adjustment programs and thus contributing to the expansion of private investment.

The decline in investment is a matter for concern, since in most countries sustainable higher growth is likely, later on in the adjustment effort, to require an increase in investment above the average levels of the 1980s. The hoped-for recovery of investment to sustain future growth did not occur in most EIAL countries, although their experience varies (table 3-4). At the same time, the impact of the programs on investment should be viewed with caution. Since adjustment is not estimated to have reduced growth, it must have increased the average efficiency of capital. Indeed, the most efficient way of getting higher growth is just from policy reforms that raise growth without the cost of increased investment.

With respect to the *domestic saving* rate in current prices, after adjusting for the effects of other factors, it increased more in the EIAL countries than it did in other countries (table 3-3). (The domestic saving rate is more appropriate than the national saving rate for measuring the impact of adjustment on resource mobilization, because net factor payments abroad are not deducted and

Table 3-4. *Country Differences in Performance, 1985-88 Compared with 1970-80*

Leading performers[a]	Lagging underperformers[a]
Change in annual average rate of GDP growth	
Korea	Nigeria
Mauritius	Philippines
Morocco	Malawi
Ghana	Cote d'Ivoire
Thailand	Mexico
Saving rate in current prices	
Korea	Nigeria
Chile	Zambia
amaica	Philippines
Mauritius	Senegal
Investment rate in current prices	
Costa Rica	Cote d'Ivoire
Korea	Malawi
Jamaica	Nigeria
Chile	Zambia
Kenya	Philippines
Investment rate in constant prices	
Korea	Malawi
Mauritania	Zambia
Mauritius	Nigeria
Togo	Cote d'Ivoire
Madagascar	Philippines
Export-to-GDP ratio in current prices	
Jamaica	Kenya
Mauritius	Senegal
Chile	Malawi
Korea	Zambia
Mauritania	Brazil
Export-to-GDP ratio in constant prices	
Jamaica	Kenya
Mauritania	Zambia
Korea	Nigeria
Togo	Madagascar
Mauritius	Malawi

a. The designation of leading and lagging performers is based on the performance ranking of each country after adjusting for the effects of initial conditions and the external environment.

Source: Author's calculations.

net foreign transfers are not included.)[6] As a share of GDP, the domestic saving rate rose about 4 percentage points more in the EIAL countries than it did in the other countries, whether using 1970-80 or 1981-84 as the base period.

With respect to the *ratio of exports to GDP* in current prices, after adjusting for other factors the Bank-supported programs had a positive effect, boosting the ratio about 6.4 percentage points of GDP between 1970-80 and 1985-88 and 5.0 percentage points between 1985-88, although with large differences across countries. The strong positive effect of the programs on the ratio of exports to GDP in current prices could in part be the result of the accounting effect of the real devaluations by the EIAL countries in the third period. As to the ratio of exports to GDP in constant prices after controlling for other factors, the adjustment programs on average had a positive, although not statistically significant, effect (table 3-3).

The low and statistically insignificant effect on the ratio of exports to GDP in constant prices raises concern about the speed of the supply response of exports to the changed incentives brought about by a real devaluation. The small and slow average response may have been caused by the absence of the investment needed to increase supplies and by uncertainties about the stability of the improved incentives for exports. For countries with a long history of macroeconomic instability, discrimination against exports and unstable real exchange rates, the export response would be low.[7]

In terms of the *ratio of imports to GDP* in current prices, the structural adjustment programs in the EIAL countries had a small negative effect of 1.7 percentage points from 1970-80 to 1985-88 and a small positive effect of 1.3 percentage points from 1981-84 to 1985-88.[8] Given that in some countries output has been constrained by a lack of imports, the improved access to imported inputs may in part have led to the increase in the efficiency of investment between 1981-84 and 1985-88 by permitting fuller use of productive capacity.

The macroeconomic performance of intensive-adjustment-lending countries has thus been at least adequate along the dimensions of GDP growth, saving, exports and imports, with the very strong performance of some countries more than making up for the declines experienced by others. In the area of investment, however, aggregate performance has been poor, although with important differences across countries.

The Effectiveness of Adjustment Programs—Social Welfare Indicators

Aggregate economic performance does not tell the whole story of the effect of structural adjustment. It is important also to consider what happened to the indicators of consumption, especially by the poorest levels of society, and what happened in the education and health sectors.

In countries with an unsustainable current account deficit, the macroeconomic component of the adjustment program encourages a reduction in aggregate demand, generally through monetary and fiscal restraint.

It also encourages a switch in production from the non-tradable to the tradable sectors, generally through a real devaluation. The reductions in aggregate demand are likely to have negative short-run effects on the growth of output and employment. On the other hand, the structural reforms (economy-wide and sector-specific) improve the efficiency of the economy, have a longer term positive impact on the growth of output and are likely to reduce poverty in the medium to longer run. That is, while the reduction in aggregate demand and the structural reforms are bound to have distributional consequences, the potential adverse short-run effects must be weighed against the longer run benefits.

In countries with high inflation, policies that permanently reduce the fiscal deficit make a major contribution to the reduction of inflation. Lower inflation should help the poor, who are less able to protect the real value of their assets and incomes from inflation. Lowering the fiscal deficit requires a combination of revenue increases and expenditure cuts. On the revenue side, higher income taxes generally do not affect the poor, and the goods they consume can be exempted from excise taxes. As to expenditures, whether the decreases will affect the poor depends on the incidence of the cuts. For example, reductions in health spending could have a negative impact. If, however, the composition of health expenditures were to switch toward preventive medicine and away from curative medicine, which goes mainly to the middle class, the impact on the poor could be softened.

As to structural reforms, changes in relative prices that remove the biases against labor should help reduce poverty in the long run. Devaluation of the exchange rate will help the poor if they produce tradable goods and will hurt them if they consume tradable goods, such as imported necessities. Removal of the ceilings on agricultural prices will benefit the rural poor, who are net producers of food, but hurt the urban poor, who are net consumers of food.

It is difficult to assess the effects of adjustment programs on the poor for three reasons. First, it is inherently difficult to establish causality—to isolate the effects of adjustment programs from other factors—and particularly to determine whether alternative policies would have done better or worse. Second, socioeconomic data on the living conditions of the poor are scarce and often of dubious quality. Although many of the poor work in the informal sector, data on the output of that sector and on other variables are usually not included in official statistics. Third, the adjustment programs are relatively new, and their long-run positive effects probably take longer than the experience with adjustment so far.

While complete analysis of the adjustment programs must await the conclusion of the entire adjustment period, as noted, interim evaluations such as those here are still necessary.[9] In general, the limited cross-sectional data on changes in poverty do not suggest that adjustment lending has on average increased it. Other aggregate data support similar conclusions:

• On average, the rate of growth of private consumption in the EIAL countries recovered in the late 1980s to the rate achieved in the 1970s—and the rate in the late 1980s was higher in total and on a per capita basis in comparison with other groups of countries.

• The socioeconomic indicators of the status of the poor in developing countries or in the EIAL group of countries did not deteriorate in the 1980s on average. The indicators of nutrition improved, and average protein intake continued to rise from 1983-84 to 1986 in all categories of countries, with and without adjustment lending. Infant and child mortality, both indicators of the longer run health status of the poor, continued to improve on average for country categories with and without adjustment lending.

• The shares of central government expenditures for health and education declined on average in the EIAL countries having data. Some of the decline may have occurred because better targeting of public expenditures left middle- and upper-income groups paying for more of the provision of these services or because other levels of government took responsibility for some of these expenditures. In education, there were declining rates of primary school enrollment for the EIAL countries. This trend is inconsistent with restoring sustainable long-term growth, which requires strengthening the human capital base, an important input into growth. In health, the coverage of immunization generally increased in all country groups, a trend that probably accounts for much of the continuing decline in the rates of infant and child mortality.

Program Implementation

Progress with implementation is measured by the share of conditions in the loan agreements that the countries have implemented by the time the final tranche is released. The data on conditionality and implementation (note that relative to RAL-1, RAL-2 used a much expanded sample of loans approved in FY79-88) show most of the same patterns found in the first Report as well as some new ones (Webb and Shariff 1990). Countries began implementing their structural adjustment programs before the adjustment loans became effective and frequently continued implementation after the disbursements ended. Of the conditions in the loan agreements in the sample, 84 percent had been implemented at least substantially—a higher rate than that found with RAL-1—and 66 percent had been implemented fully or more than fully by the time the final tranche was released.

The rate of implementation of loan conditions increased during the 1980s, both for countries that had received adjustment loans since the early 1980s and for countries that started more recently. For the loans in the sample whose final tranche was released in FY89, i.e., since the first Report, 99 percent of the conditions were implemented at least substantially and 80 percent of the conditions as originally written were implemented fully or more. In the rare cases where a condition as originally written came to be seen as unnecessary, the Bank waived the condition, with approval from the Board. If the one loan in the sample for which this eventuality occurred in FY89 is excluded, the rate of full implementation of conditions rises from 80 percent to 88 percent. In short, the final tranches were released only when all the conditions in the loans were at least substantially fulfilled. An important finding is that the implementation rates in countries with higher rates of inflation were lower. This finding once again illustrates the importance of macroeconomic stability.

Governments were more frequently able to develop and maintain political support for the structural adjustment when they designed the program with this condition in mind and were active in explaining the source of the problems addressed by the program, how they planned to tackle them, why that approach was the best option and how people would benefit from the new policy environment. Typically this openness mobilized beneficiaries to become political supporters. While technical considerations sometimes caused unavoidable delays in program implementation, more prompt implementation almost always increased the chances of political support. Awareness of the economic problems that motivated the initial decision for reform was greatest at the beginning, giving the authorities maximum latitude for reform. Support to sustain the new status quo then developed as the structural reform paid off in growth and higher living standards.

Although adjustment programs often call for a reduction in the resources going to the public sector, it is equally important to strengthen public institutions in terms of improved policies, organization and management. Institutional development is essential for both the implementation and ultimate success of many of the reforms the Bank supports. Not surprisingly, actions to improve the efficiency of the public sector, including the design and implementation of public policies, are integral parts of most adjustment operations.

Main Results of RAL-2: Policies That Promote Growth

RAL-2 not only evaluated the effectiveness of adjustment lending but also provided a summary of the research on what policies promote sustainable growth. The lessons from this research are relevant for the design of growth- oriented adjustment programs. In theory, adjustment measures to achieve an adequate supply response should boost investment, particularly in the tradable goods sector. An increase in investment will provide a connection between adjustment, growth and external balance that will ensure the sustainability of the adjustment effort. The reason is that structural adjustment programs change an economy's incentives to increase efficiency and encourage growth. Given the pivotal role of increased investment in the recovery of sustained growth, adjusting countries will need to institute further policy reforms in the later phases of adjustment to remove the impediments to the increase in investment.

This section looks at why adjustment programs have constrained investment and then suggests further policy reforms adjusting countries will need to make to achieve sustainable growth. Specifically, they must address the uncertainty and lack of credibility that often accompany adjustment programs and deter investors, they must foster higher rates of saving by both the public and private sectors, and they must increase the efficiency of investment by removing distortions.

Increasing Investment

To understand what policies are needed to increase investment, it is useful to understand why it declined so frequently during adjustment. One reason for the slow investment response to structural adjustment programs was investor uncertainty about the governments' commitment to carry out the programs. That is, the adjustment programs lacked credibility. Private agents may also have been receiving mixed incentive signals—some associated with the previous policy rules, some with the stabilization package and some with the structural reforms aimed at restoring medium-term growth. This uncertainty about the future economic environment, particularly the incentive structure, left investors reluctant to make fixed investments, as for the most part those investments are irreversible: capital, once installed, can seldom be put to productive use in a different activity, at least not without incurring a substantial cost. Thus, a trade reform that is suspected of being only temporary can reduce investment, as the economic agents postpone their investment decisions while waiting to see whether the reform lasts (Serven and Solimano 1990).

The opposite is also true, however: a stable and predictable incentive structure and macroeconomic policies can further investment, even more so than tax incentives or subsidized interest rates might. Under conditions of great economic and political uncertainty, it is usually prohibitively expensive to make tax and related incentives high enough to have any significant impact on investment (Pindyck 1989). In Argentina, Honduras, Morocco and even Turkey, the investment incentives substantially enlarged government deficits without appreciably increasing investment.

Based on a first look, investment declined because of the reduced availability of financing. Lower external financing forced an important decline in the deficit in the resource balance—defined as the difference between domestic investment and domestic saving—following the debt crisis in 1982 (table 3-5). Because this decline was not matched by a sufficient increase in domestic saving, the deficit was almost entirely reflected in reduced investment. The factors accounting for the drop in investment should be looked at more carefully.

The demand for investment fell for several reasons. For one, public investment contracted because in some cases it was unsustainably high and of dubious productivity. Other reasons were the deterioration in fiscal conditions as a result of the cut in foreign lending and the lack of adjustment in other fiscal expenditures, the rise in international and domestic interest rates, and the sharp acceleration of inflation, which eroded real tax receipts. In the case of private investment, slower or even negative growth discouraged it in several countries, as did the adverse external shocks, the high real interest rates, the uncertainty about the new configuration of relative prices and incentives, and the inability of governments to stabilize their economies. In addition, the debt overhang may have discouraged investment not only through the uncertainty it created but also through its implicit "tax" on future output and the resultant credit rationing in the international capital markets.

Uncertainty and lack of credibility often undermine the effectiveness of macroeconomic policy. There are two aspects to credibility: the internal consistency of the adjustment program; and the government's commitment to carry it out despite possible short-run costs. When credibility is low and the investment response is therefore insufficient to restore growth, a structural adjustment program may entail larger than anticipated social and economic costs.[10] A persistent slump may

Table 3-5. *Gross Domestic and National Saving Ratios in 83 Developing Countries*

Indicator	Group	1970-80	1981-82	1983-84	1985-88
Gross domestic investment (percentage of GDP at current prices)	All	22.4	24.0	20.2	19.6
	Highly indebted	22.8	23.0	18.0	18.4
	Middle income	25.5	28.6	24.4	21.9
	Low income	19.7	20.3	17.0	17.4
Gross domestic saving (percentage of GDP at current prices)	All	16.1	13.7	13.9	14.9
	Highly indebted	20.3	20.1	19.8	20.2
	Middle income	18.3	17.5	17.7	17.8
	Low income	12.5	7.6	8.0	9.9
Resource balance deficit (percentage of GDP at constant prices)	All	6.4	10.3	6.2	4.6
	Highly indebted	2.5	2.9	-1.7	-1.8
	Middle income	7.2	11.1	6.7	4.0
	Low income	7.2	12.7	8.9	7.5
Gross domestic investment (percentage of GDP at constant prices)	All	23.4	24.1	20.6	19.6
	Highly indebted	23.1	22.3	17.1	16.8
	Middle income	25.7	28.6	24.9	22.1
	Low income	21.5	20.7	17.8	18.0
Rate of growth of real GDP (percentage per year)	All	4.7	2.7	1.8	3.3
	Highly indebted	5.0	-0.3	-0.4	2.7
	Middle income	6.1	4.5	3.9	3.2
	Low income	3.5	2.5	0.5	3.5

Source: World Bank Economic and Social Database (BESD).

develop before investors become confident that the adjustment measures will be maintained.

Resolving the problem of a low investment response may be particularly critical for economies with a history of frequent policy swings or failed stabilization attempts. As the recent experience of Bolivia and Mexico shows, while establishing the right economic incentives is a precondition for investment and growth, it cannot guarantee them (Dornbusch 1989).

An assessment of credibility and uncertainty should influence the choice between gradual and abrupt adjustment. Under gradual adjustment, the initial objectives are modest ones that can be achieved with near certainty, so that the government can build its reputation. Abrupt adjustment starts with an over-adjustment—say, an over-depreciation of the exchange rate through large cuts in tariffs—the aim being to frontload the incentives for resource reallocation. However, this approach also concentrates the costs of the adjustment.[11] The choice appears to depend largely on the specifics of each country, with the social distribution of the adjustment costs and policy experience likely to be important factors.

Sufficient external support for the adjustment effort of a committed government can raise the confidence of investors in the sustainability of the adjustment and thus enhance the take-off of investment. Implementation of well-targeted public investment projects that attract private investment may be another important element in getting growth under way. The removal of impediments to resource allocation, the development of financial markets, and a more transparent legal and regulatory framework could also enhance the investment response.

Increasing Saving

To sustain investment for a desirable rate of growth, the adjusting countries have to increase their rate of saving. This need is greatest in the highly indebted countries, mostly in Latin America and Sub-Saharan Africa, whose saving rates fell significantly in the 1980s (table 3.5).

Although public policies can affect public saving directly, there are limits on their effect on private saving. Public saving and the way it is financed affect the economic environment—GDP growth and inflation—and this environment in turn affects decisions on private saving. That is, public and private saving, although analyzed separately here, are closely linked.

To measure *public saving* properly requires defining the public sector comprehensively as encompassing the central and local governments, financial and non-financial public enterprises and the quasi-fiscal operations of the central bank. In many countries, the losses of public enterprises have contributed to the high public deficits. In Bolivia, for example, public enterprise deficits reached 5 percent of GDP before the 1987 stabilization. In Argentina, they have fluctuated between 2 percent and 7 percent since the early 1980s. In Zimbabwe, they were reduced from 9 percent of GDP in 1982 to 4 percent in 1988. In some countries, the losses of the central bank arising from fiscal operations have been even more important than the deficit of the general government or the public enterprises. Often these losses have resulted from operations such as emergency loans at subsidized rates to failing domestic financial systems and from foreign exchange subsidies to domestic holders of foreign debt. In Argentina the central bank's losses have fluctuated between 2 percent and 6 percent of GDP since 1982, while in Chile they were 7 percent of GDP in 1985 and in Venezuela 6 percent of GDP in 1987 (Corbo and Schmidt-Hebbel forthcoming).

Changes in the public sector deficit and in public saving result not only from the direct effects of tax and expenditure policies but also from the interaction of fiscal policy with other policies and with foreign economic shocks.[12] For example, depreciation of the exchange rate affects all budget items that are fixed in foreign currencies or indexed to world prices. A real depreciation increases the budget deficit (relative to GDP) when the public sector has more expenses than revenues denominated in foreign currencies—as in countries where the foreign debt service is a large part of public spending (e.g., Brazil, the Philippines and Turkey). In countries where the public sector obtains much revenue from import taxes or commodity exports—oil in Mexico, phosphates in Morocco and copper in Zambia—a real depreciation tends to decrease the budget deficit.

In most countries the bulk of saving is accounted for by the *private sector*. While government policy can readily alter the disposable income of the private sector, in a market economy it has only limited influence on the share of disposable income that the private sector saves. Key policies that affect private saving are the rate of return on saving, the level and form of taxation, the rate of inflation, the real exchange rate, the flight of capital, the business cycle, the inflows of foreign capital and the rate of growth (table 3-6).

Credit rationing and controls on interest rates discourage saving in many countries. The low or negative real interest rates on deposits and targeted credits reduce the supply of loanable funds and hence effectively ration investment.[13] Financial reforms that raise real interest rates to market clearing levels are justified because they improve the efficiency of resource use, which boosts long-run growth.[14] The effect of higher real interest rates on the level of private saving is ambiguous, however. The reason is that an increase in the real return on saving has two offsetting effects. First, a higher real interest rate decreases the present cost of future consumption, so that it is attractive to consume less now and more in the future and thus to save more today. Second, it is no longer necessary to save as much to achieve a target level of future consumption. A higher real interest rate therefore allows greater consumption both today and tomorrow and reduces the need to save today.

Given this theoretical ambiguity, the effect of the real interest rate on saving becomes an empirical issue. A large body of evidence for both industrial and developing countries shows that, on average, real interest rates or after-tax real rates of return do not have a significant effect on the share of private income that is saved.[15] However, financial liberalization that allows real interest rates to rebound from very negative to near-zero levels often has a positive impact on measured private saving in financially unstable, high-inflation countries. This effect is attributable to reduced flight into consumer durables and foreign capital after the interest rate has risen.

Public policies to raise public saving and hence national saving have a key role in structural adjustment. The evidence shows that the private sector does not reduce its saving one-for-one with tax increases or public spending cuts; it follows that reductions in budget deficits increase national saving. This fact has profound implications for Bank-supported adjustment lending. It was concluded earlier that after controlling for the effect of other factors, the domestic saving rate rose 4 percentage points more in EIAL countries than in any other

Table 3-6. *Public Policy and Private Saving: Effects of Intervening Variables*

	Inflation and relative price instability	After-tax real rate of return on saving	Per capita disposable income			Foreign resource constraint	Foreign income concentrat.	Capital flight	Total effect on saving
			Growth	Trend	Deviation from trend				
Effect of an increase in intervening variable on private saving	-	+	+	+	+	-	+	-	
Policy									
Financial liberalization		?		+ (L.run)			+		+? (L.run)
Fiscal/monetary stabilization	+	?	+ (L.run)	+ L.run)	- (S.run)				+ (L.run)
Selective tax incentives on particular financial assets		+?							+
Shift of taxation from corporations to households							+		+
Shift of taxation from higher to lower income households							+		+
Shift from income to consumption tax		?					+		+
Real exchange rate depreciation			+ (L.run)		- (S.run)			+	+ (L.run)
Foreign capital inflows			+ (L.run)		-				

Notes: L.run = long run; S.run = short run. The signs in the first line indicate the effect of the intervening variable on private saving, while the signs in the remainder of the table denote the fiscal effect of each policy through the corresponding intervening variable.
Source: World Bank (1990b), table 7.2, p. 95.

group of countries. Thus, adjustment programs supported by the Bank have played a significant role in raising aggregate domestic saving and changing its composition in favor of public saving.

Increasing Investment Efficiency

Because resources for investment are scarce, they are costly, and it is therefore vital that the efficiency of investment be increased. Further, because more efficient investment has a higher rate of return, increasing the efficiency of investment encourages savings to stay in the developing economy and not to go into capital flight.

Investment is more efficient with relatively non-distortionary policies, and therefore policy changes that reduce the distortions in resource allocation not only raise the baseline level of efficiency but also tend to raise growth in the long term. The size of the initial distortions and the magnitude of the reduction affect how much growth will respond. Growth-enhancing policies include lowering tariffs, relaxing import quotas, raising or decontrolling domestic interest rates, reducing reserve requirements or mandatory government bond-holdings, reducing government subsidies for the consumption or production of particular goods, and reforming taxes to reduce or eliminate differential treatment of sectors or inputs.

Reforms to improve incentives can proceed in several steps. For example, tariffs can initially be substituted for quotas, both to increase the transparency of incentives and to raise public revenue. Later, tariffs can be reduced as other revenue sources are expanded. Institutional development may be necessary to strengthen the private responses to such changes in incentives. In low-income countries, the lack of well-developed public and private institutions may be an important hindrance to growth even if trade and financial incentives are not distorted. A stable system of civil liberties, well-defined property and contractual rights, and predictable and equitable regulation are widely believed to be particularly important in harnessing the energies of entrepreneurs in Africa (World Bank 1989b). A comparison of the long-run growth experience among many developing countries concluded that the administrative competence of governments was the single most important factor explaining the differences in growth (Reynolds 1985). Political stability and the safeguarding of civil liberties have also been found to increase growth (Kormendi and Mcguire 1985; Scully 1988).

An important finding of the research is that the largest pay-off comes from changing high distortions into low ones. Neither a small reduction in high distortions nor the complete removal of small distortions does

much to foster higher growth in the long run, a conclusion that is based on an examination of country experience and a simulation of a structural model of growth. Since policy-makers have only a limited amount of political capital for correcting distortions, they should concentrate their efforts on the changes that have the largest pay-off in terms of increased growth rates. If more than one major distortion exists, all should be reduced together.

Lessons for Central and Eastern Europe

This section presents some lessons for the design of programs in Central and Eastern Europe from the experience, successful and unsuccessful, with adjustment programs elsewhere.

Although initial conditions are not the same in all Central and Eastern European countries, some common elements exist. At the cost of simplification, the general characteristics are the following. There is large excess demand at existing prices. This situation holds particularly in Bulgaria, Romania and, until recently, Poland. Excess demand is less severe in Czechoslovakia, Hungary and Yugoslavia. When the external debt is large and the balance of payments unsustainable—conditions found in all Central and Eastern European countries except Romania and Czechoslovakia—a large part of foreign trade takes place on non-market terms. At the structural level, there are several problems. The structure of industry in most Central and Eastern European countries is dominated by large state enterprises that are uncompetitive at international prices. There is a lack of labor, land, financial markets and the whole set of institutions and arrangements needed to support a market economy (especially appropriate accounting procedures, property rights, bankruptcy laws and commercial law). At the same time, Central and Eastern European countries have some big advantages—they have very good human capital bases, are next to Western Europe, one of the most dynamic international markets, and have a privileged political relation with the Western European governments.[16]

For Central and Eastern European countries that start with acute macroeconomic imbalances in the form of high open or repressed inflation and/or unsustainable current account deficits, the adjustment program needs to start with stabilization and give priority to reforms that aim to restore macroeconomic balances. Otherwise the success of other reforms will be put in jeopardy. For countries with a history of increasingly binding price controls, stabilization must embody two components: first, elimination of the monetary overhang (a stock problem); and, second, elimination of the public sector deficit (a flow problem). Elimination of the monetary overhang can be achieved through a once-and-for-all increase in the price level or through monetary reform. Coming out of World War II, most European countries used monetary reform (Dornbusch and Wolf 1990). In contrast, in the post-1950s most countries have sought to eliminate the monetary overhang by increasing the level of prices.

Countries with a large monetary overhang that follow the increase in the price level route run the risk that the initial increase in the price level could result in a protracted period of high inflation. Even after taking care of the fiscal adjustment, some countries have found it very difficult to contain the inflation dynamic that usually develops following the initial increase in prices. For example, when Chile liberalized prices in 1973, even though it reached a public sector surplus by 1975, it experienced three-digit inflation until 1977 (Corbo and Solimano 1990). Most of the reduction in expenditures has to be done through fiscal policy, as monetary policy does not have much of a role to play in countries without capital markets and where the main borrowers are public enterprises without a hard budget constraint (the case in Chile in 1973, Mexico in 1983 and Egypt in 1990).

In countries where there is limited flexibility in the labor market, to break the inflation inertia that can follow the liberalization of prices, the drastic reduction in the public sector deficit needs to be followed by some kind of income policy.[17] Israel followed this route in 1985, Mexico in 1987 and Poland in 1990. To avoid a prolonged period of inflation, a permanent reduction in the public sector deficit should be achieved early on in the reform. A permanent reduction in the public sector deficit requires the imposition of a hard budget constraint on public enterprises, a drastic reduction in public sector subsidies and the creation of an efficient tax system. Another lesson is to avoid the temptation to use *only* the nominal exchange rate to bring stubborn inflation under control. The real appreciation that could develop could put the full reform effort in jeopardy (as in Chile in 1978-82, Mexico in 1988-89, Israel in 1986-88, Argentina in 1978-80 and Uruguay in 1980-82).

Socialist countries in transition to a market economy and heavy regulated economies in Africa also face, as countries such as Turkey did in 1980, Chile in 1973 and Mexico in 1982, the problem of how to reduce both the large distortions in relative prices and the distortions resulting from heavily regulated or almost non-existent labor and financial markets. On top of these distortions, there is the additional burden of a large public enterprise sector with low responsiveness to price incentives and the lack of institutions to manage macroeconomic policies and establish a minimum set of rules for the normal functioning of a market economy (i.e., property rights, bankruptcy laws, appropriate accounting procedures, etc.). Therefore, early on the authorities need to face the issue of clarifying property rights and establishing the basic conditions for the functioning of the labor market.

For a country that is about to initiate a major reform effort, the question it has to face from the beginning is the sequence and speed of other reforms. For one, any reform that calls for a major reallocation of resources will need to deal with appropriate and credible relative prices early on. For another, trade reforms have a very high priority in countries that have much to gain from integration into the world economy, such as was the case in Mexico in 1982 and Chile in 1973 and is the case in the Central and Eastern European countries today. The initial stages of a trade reform, such as the replacement of managed trade by open trade, the replacement of quantitative restrictions for tariffs and the reduction of extreme tariffs, should be attempted early on. However, major trade liberalization should be attempted only when clear and credible progress has been achieved in reducing inflation or when there is a clear perceived commitment from the authorities that the anti-inflationary program is a very high priority. In countries with a very uncompetitive domestic economy, trade liberalization may help the stabilization effort, as may have been the case in Mexico in 1988. In countries with a long period of a very isolated domestic economy, trade liberalization could also help in providing a market-based structure for the relative prices of tradable goods, as was the case in Poland in 1990. However, a major fiscal adjustment is necessary to generate a suitable reduction in spending and to avoid a balance-of-payments crisis.

Trade reforms aim to shift investment and labor from non-tradable and highly protected import-competing activities toward export-oriented and efficient import-competing activities. However, unpredictable relative prices (as is usually the case in high inflation economies), the lack of labor mobility, the absence of financial markets, and impediments to the creation of enterprises are major roadblocks to successful trade reform. Therefore, in many of the Central and Eastern European countries privatization and the development of the labor and financial markets could be an important component of the economic restructuring program.

A major study of trade liberalization (Papageorgiou, Choksi and Michaely 1990) found that countries that carried out sustained trade reforms usually had lower fiscal deficits and inflation than did countries where liberalization failed. In some cases, successful trade liberalization was carried out while stabilization was still under way—as in Chile in 1974-79 and Turkey in 1980-84. In more typical cases, either severe macroeconomic instability contributed to the failure of stabilization (Argentina, Brazil and Sri Lanka in the 1960s and Peru, the Philippines, Portugal, Turkey and Uruguay in the 1970s), or stability contributed to successful liberalization (Greece, Korea and Spain and all of Western Europe).

Internal reforms have also been important determinants of the success or failure of trade liberalization. The lack of labor mobility (including restrictions on labor movement within a firm and the requirements for high severance payments), restrictions on the entry and expansion of firms, and restrictions on the exit of firms (including distress financing for firms that will never be profitable at the new undistorted relative prices) can severely reduce the benefits of trade liberalization and jeopardize the whole reform effort. A lack of incentives and regulations that slow or make it costly for firms to restructure or close have been important factors in the failed or costly liberalization attempts in Poland, Hungary, Turkey (in the 1970s) and Yugoslavia. In contrast, deregulation of the labor market played an important role in the success of the trade reforms in Chile (World Bank 1990a). Domestic regulatory policies in Mexico and Morocco that restricted factor and output mobility, including restrictions on the entry and exit of firms, raised the adjustment costs of the trade reforms. In this area, Central and Eastern European countries need to make major efforts.

Conclusions

Based on growing evidence from failed and successful reforms, it can be concluded that:

(1) High open or repressed inflation and other manifestations of severe macroeconomic imbalances, such as unsustainable current account deficits or very large positive real interest rates, need to be tackled at the beginning of an adjustment program.

(2) Restrictions on labor mobility and on the exit and entry of firms should be removed at roughly the same pace as trade is being liberalized so that the reforms can produce an increase in output early on rather than cause unemployment.

(3) The creation of a full-fledged financial system should wait until the stabilization is well-consolidated; however, markets for working capital financing with appropriate mechanisms to assess credit risks should be created early on to facilitate the economic restructuring.

(4) Institution-building, including a capacity to formulate and execute macroeconomic policies and the regulatory framework that support the function of markets, are important complements to successful reforms.

The road to reforms is difficult, but the alternative of perpetual stagnation and deteriorating living standards is even worse. The road is made even more difficult by the lack of much precedent in recent economic history for reforms such as those being initiated today in Central and Eastern Europe. Nevertheless, the evidence reviewed here suggests that output levels will most likely suffer in the early years of a massive economic restructuring. It is very important that governments be aware of these adjustment costs as they are the equivalent of an investment in a better economic system that will emerge as the reforms are implemented. To make this investment highly profitable, governments will need to stick to their policies. As the credibility of the reforms grows, the investment and output responses will materialize.

The road to reform in Latin America is littered with failures that arose from governments' incapacity to achieve and maintain macroeconomic balances and/or their abandonment of well-intended reform efforts in the face of short-term, unavoidable costs. It was a long time before the reforms in Chile in the 1970s and in Mexico in the 1980s produced sustainable growth paths. The record of these two countries could have been improved by addressing some of the issues raised in this paper. Reform-oriented governments should be prepared to sell to the public and to maintain programs that will take two or three years before output levels begin to rise. In the short run, access to external financing to support the adjustment effort can help achieve higher consumption levels and finance part of the investment in activities targeted for expansion as a consequence of the reforms.

Notes

1. The views expressed in this paper are the author's and do not necessarily reflect the views of the World Bank or its affiliated organizations.

2. Both types of loans generally disburse against general imports, with a small list of excluded items.

3. This and the next section draw heavily on World Bank (1990b).

4. The groups of countries and periods used here differ from those in RAL-1. Here the EIAL countries include all the intensive-adjustment-lending countries of RAL-1 plus 13 more. Because another year of performance could be looked at, the RAL-2 intensive adjusters include additional countries whose second or third adjustment loans came after 1985. Within each group, a breakdown has been made between low- and middle-income countries. Low-income countries are defined as all IDA countries (including those receiving a blend of IDA and IBRD loans) and middle-income countries as all the rest.

RAL-1 concluded that by the end of 1987 the 30 countries receiving SALs before '985 performed better on average than did the developing countries not receiving such loans. This conclusion was based on two comparisons: the performance of countries before and after receiving adjustment loans; and the average performance of countries receiving adjustment loans before 1985 and of countries not receiving such loans. The 30 countries receiving loans had modest improvements in performance as compared with the other group of countries, despite a more unfavorable external environment. The 12 countries that received three or more adjustment loans before 1987 had more pronounced improvements.

5. The base period 1970-80 was chosen because it preceded the major shocks of the early 1980s and was not dominated by conditions in a particular year or two. Performance in 1985-88 is also compared with that in 1981-84.

6. The effect of the programs on the national saving rate is also positive but is statistically significant at the 5 percent level only when comparing performance in 1981-84 with 1985-88.

7. On the effect of incentives and uncertainty on exports, see Caballero and Corbo (1989).

8. This result comes from the identity that investment minus saving equals imports minus exports.

9. The central topic of the World Bank's *World Development Report 1990* (World Bank 1990c) is poverty. This report includes additional analyses of the impact of adjustment programs on poverty.

10. Credibility introduces an externality that creates a wedge between the social and private returns on investment. In fact, higher aggregate investment helps sustain the adjustment and therefore results in higher returns on investment. However, the individual investor will ignore this mechanism.

11. On these topics, see Kiguel and Liviatan (1988) and Solimano (1990).

12. Public saving and the deficit are directly linked: the public deficit is defined as public investment minus public saving.

13. For a recent review of financial systems and financial liberalization in developing countries, see World Bank (1989b).

14. This policy prescription is taken from McKinnon (1973) and Shaw (1973).

15. Among the studies presenting growing evidence of the insensitivity of saving in developing countries to interest rates, see, for instance, Giovannini (l985). For an alternative view, see Fry (1988) and the survey by Balassa (1989).

16. For a good description of initial conditions in the Central and Eastern European countries, including the social and political factors, see Lipton and Sachs (1990).

17. Inertia can also result from a lack of credibility or from lagged indexation schemes. The latter form of inertia played a central role in the slow deceleration of inflation in Chile in the period 1978-82 (Corbo 1985).

References

Balassa, B. 1989. "The Effects of Interest Rates on Saving in Developing Countries." World Bank. Washington, D.C.

Caballero, R., and V. Corbo. 1989. "The Effect of Real Exchange Rate Uncertainty on Exports: Empirical Evidence." *World Bank Economic Review* 3(2):263-78.

Calvo, G. 1989. "Incredible Reforms." In G. Calvo, et al., eds., *Debt, Stabilization and Development.* Oxford and Cambridge, Mass.: Basil Blackwell.

Corbo, V. 1985. "Reforms and Macroeconomic Adjustment in Chile: 1974-82." *World Development* (August).

Corbo, V., and J. de Melo. 1987. "Lessons from the Southern Cone Policy Reforms." *World Bank Research Observer* 1(2):111-42.

Corbo, V., and S. Fischer. 1990. "Adjustment Programs and Bank Support: Rationale and Main Results." World Bank. Washington, D.C.

Corbo, V., and K. Schmidt-Hebbel. Forthcoming. "Public Policies and Saving in Developing Countries." *Journal of Development Economics.*

Corbo, V., and A. Solimano. 1990. "Chile's Experiences with Stabilization Revisited." In M. Bruno, et al., eds., *Experiences with Stabilization.* Cambridge, Mass.: MIT Press.

Dornbusch, R. 1989. "Credibility and Stabilization." Massachusetts Institute of Technology. Cambridge, Mass.

Dornbusch, R., and H. Wolf. 1990. "Monetary Overhang and Reforms in the 1940s." Massachusetts Institute of Technology. Cambridge, Mass.

Fischer, S. 1986. "Issues in Medium-Term Macroeconomic Adjustment." *World Bank Research Observer* 1(2):163-82.

Fry, M.J. 1988. *Money, Interest and Banking in Economic Development.* Baltimore, Md.: Johns Hopkins University Press.

Giovannini, A. 1985. "Saving and the Real Interest Rate in LDCs." *Journal of Development Economics* 18.

Kiguel, M., and N. Liviatan. 1988. "Inflationary Rigidities and Orthodox Stabilization Policies: Lessons from Latin America." *World Bank Economic Review* 2:273-98.

Kormendi, R.C., and P.G. Mcguire. 1985. "Macroeconomic Determinants of Growth: Cross-Country Evidence." *Journal of Monetary Economics* 16:141-63.

Lipton, D., and J. Sachs. l990. "Creating a Market Economy in Eastern Europe: The Case of Poland." *Brookings Papers on Economic Activity* 1:75-147.

McKinnon, R. 1973. *Money and Capital in Economic Development.* Washington, D.C.: Brookings Institution.

Meier, G.M., and W.F. Steel, eds. 1989. *Industrial Adjustment in Sub-Saharan Africa.* : Oxford University Press.

Papageorgiou, D., A.M. Choksi and M. Michaely. 1990. *Liberalizing Foreign Trade in Developing Countries.* Washington, D.C.: World Bank.

Pindyck, R. 1989. "Irreversibility, Uncertainty and Investment." World Bank, Policy, Planning and Research Department (PPR) Working Paper No. 183. Washington, D.C.

Reynolds, Lloyd G. 1985. *Economic Growth in the Third World, 1880-1980.* New Haven, Conn.: Yale University Press.

Rodrik, D. 1990. "How Should Structural Adjustment Programs Be Designed?" *World Development* 18(7):933-48.

Sachs, J. 1987. "Trade and Exchange Rate Policies in Growth-Oriented Adjustment Programs." In V. Corbo, et al., eds., *Growth-Oriented Adjustment Programs.* Washington, D.C.: International Monetary Fund-World Bank.

Scully, G. 1988. "The Institutional Framework and Economic Development." *Journal of Political Economy* 96(3).

Serven, L., and A. Solimano. 1990. "Private Investment and Macroeconomic Adjustment in LDCs: Theory, Country Experiences and Policy Implications." World Bank. Washington, D.C.

Shaw, E.S. 1973. *Financial Deepening in Economic Development*. New York and London: Oxford University Press.

Solimano, A. 1990. "Inflation and the Costs of Stabilization: Historical and Recent Experiences and Policy Lessons." *World Bank Research Observer* 5(2):167-85.

Webb, S., and K. Shariff. 1990. "Designing and Implementing Adjustment Programs." World Bank. Washington, D.C.

World Bank. 1988. *Adjustment Lending: An Evaluation of Ten Years of Experience*. Policy and Research Series #1. Washington, D.C.: World Bank.

_____. 1989a. *Sub-Saharan Africa: From Crisis to Sustainable Growth*. Washington, D.C.: World Bank.

_____. 1989b. *World Development Report 1989*. Washington, D.C.: World Bank.

_____. 199ʋa. *Lessons in Trade Policy Reform*. Policy and Research Series #10. Washington, D.C.: World Bank.

_____. 1990b. *Adjustment Lending: Policies for Sustainable Growth*. Policy and Research Series #14. Washington, D.C.: World Bank.

_____. 1990c. *World Development Report 1990*. New York: Oxford University Press for the World Bank.

4

World Bank Adjustment Lending in Central and Eastern Europe

Ulrich R.W. Thumm

The World Bank has been active in adjustment lending in a large number of countries for about 10 years. However, Central and Eastern European countries are relative newcomers to the World Bank, and their participation has been largely limited to project lending.

In dealing with adjustment lending in Eastern Europe, an obvious question is whether there is anything special about adjustment lending in this region as compared with that in other regions and countries, whose experience is summarized in the next section. The third and fourth sections address the above question following an overview of the typical macroeconomic and structural issues facing the Central and Eastern European economies. Based on that information, a set of key elements that ideally should be included in meaningful adjustment programs is postulated.

The fifth section reviews the recent adjustment programs in Yugoslavia, Hungary and Poland, which the World Bank has been supporting with structural adjustment loans (SALs). In addition, the results of prior adjustment lending in Yugoslavia and Hungary are discussed briefly, particularly because their experience is of great importance in the design and implementation of current programs at what is a historically crucial juncture. A few words on the incipient adjustment program in Czechoslovakia are also provided. The key findings are summarized in the concluding section.

A Brief Summary of the Lessons from World Bank Adjustment Lending

The focus of this paper is on Central and Eastern Europe and the World Bank's support through adjustment lending for country-specific reform or transformation programs. Thus, discussion of the Bank's general experience with adjustment lending and related lessons is kept to a minimum (comprehensive coverage is provided elsewhere—see World Bank 1990a; Corbo and Fischer 1990; and chapter 3, "World Bank-Supported Adjustment Programs: Lessons For Central and Eastern Europe," by Vittorio Corbo, in this volume).

The most important lesson from the World Bank's experience is that the largest problems impeding the efficient allocation of resources and limiting growth should be addressed first. In many if not most cases, the largest problems result from acute macroeconomic imbalances that translate into high inflation and unsustainable balance-of-payments deficits. In other cases, the most severe distortions may stem from a interventionist trade regime, pervasive price controls or inefficient financial intermediation. If the largest distortions are not addressed first, the effectiveness of other policy reforms will be greatly hampered if not nullified. In a second-best situation, it is even conceivable that a partial reform program might make the overall situation worse rather than better.

In most cases, effective stabilization and assurance of a minimum level of functioning of the goods and factor markets have to precede structural adjustment. Changing relative prices and allowing resource allocation to proceed in line with such changes are the keys to structural adjustment and greater efficiency of resource use. In the presence of major macroeconomic imbalances such as high inflation, price relations tend to be highly volatile and greatly distorted. This environment precludes a clear perspective on profitability and undermines investor confidence, and thereby impairs greater factor mobility and structural adjustment.

While the need for macroeconomic stability as a precondition for successful structural adjustment can hardly be overemphasized, this emphasis should not distract from other grave distortions and priority areas for corrective action. In Central and Eastern Europe, the establishment of functioning goods and factor markets is a high priority. It will require the liberalization of trade and prices, the promotion of competition and the dismantling of monopolies, development of a financial system with independent financial intermediaries, flexibility in the labor market, and, last but not least, clarification of ownership rights and a critical minimum participation by the private sector in production and distribution to make the decentralized, market-based approach to economic management credible.

Institutional reforms, particularly in the public sector, have also proven to be extremely important. Normally these reforms include a thorough overhaul of the tax system (aimed at non-distortionary taxes that yield sufficient revenues and that are relatively easy to collect at a reasonably low administrative cost) and public enterprise reform (aimed at improving efficiency and ultimately at privatization). In Central and Eastern Europe, in the broadest context of a thorough overhaul of the role of the state in the economy, government expenditures should be curtailed and rationalized, with the ultimate goal of lowering excessive tax burdens.

Another area of great importance for the lasting success of adjustment is the recovery of investment and a concomitant increase in domestic savings to keep the balance of payments sustainable over the longer run. The recovery of investment, particularly private investment, depends most critically on a stable macroeconomic environment as well as on the functioning of markets. Those conditions in turn require removal of the impediments to domestic factor mobility and international trade. Without functioning markets, any recovery of investment after stabilization will result in a continued misallocation of resources, with negative implications for longer term growth and the sustainability of the balance of payments.

In many countries, stabilization and structural adjustment have proven to be controversial because of their perceived social cost. The friction tends to be the greatest the lower the degree of flexibility in the factor markets is. Any adjustment program should explicitly consider the social and distributional implications and, at a minimum, include compensatory measures for the poorest people who might be the worst affected by the structural changes. Ideally, the social mitigation component should be part of a more comprehensive and long-term effort to establish a social safety net that provides minimum support in cases of unexpected social hardship, that maintains the incentives to work and that is fiscally affordable. In the reforming economies of Central and Eastern Europe, where the distribution of income is relatively even, the greatest emphasis needs to be placed on the creation of employment in the private sector, since it is perhaps the most effective means to mitigate the costs of transition.

Finally, it should also be highlighted that "government ownership" of the adjustment program and thus the government's full commitment are critical to the successful implementation of a program. While the conditionality the World Bank attaches to its financing may help spur full implementation, it is not a substitute for government commitment. In the World Bank's experience, many programs have failed for lack of government ownership and commitment. A case in point is the Yugoslavia program of the early 1980s.

Crucial Economic Problems in Central and Eastern Europe

As a result of the dramatic political developments in 1989, economic reform reached a critical, historically unprecedented stage in all Central and Eastern European countries during the course of 1989-90. These countries had earlier attempted different reforms of varying scope at different times; by no means could Central and Eastern Europe be considered a monolithic bloc with regard to their mode of economic organization. Hungary and Poland experimented the most (particularly Hungary, with its adoption of the New Economic Mechanism in 1968) but failed to address until recently the root causes of their well-known and acknowledged economic problems. For most of the post-World War II period Yugoslavia followed its own economic model, although not with any greater success than in other reforming countries. Other countries made other attempts at reform.

As they entered the critical reform stage in 1989/90, each of these countries faced its own specific economic problems. The degree of macroeconomic imbalance varied significantly from one to another. So did, among other factors, the rate of inflation, the acuteness of the shortages, external indebtedness, domestic price distortions, the rate of economic growth and the degree of centralization of economic decision-making.

Despite these differences, there is sufficient common ground to warrant a stylized description of the typical economic problems in the region that need to be addressed through reforms to achieve the common overall objective of a transition to a market economy in order to restore growth and achieve greater social and economic welfare with freedom of consumer choice. To varying degrees, in 1989 all countries in the region faced major internal and external imbalances: excess demand resulted from unsustainable fiscal and/or social enterprise deficits, which spilled over into sizable balance-of-payments deficits and high external indebtedness. (Table 4-1 presents a number of macroeconomic indicators.) In a few countries, most notably Poland and Yugoslavia, the imbalances led to high inflation or, most recently, to hyper-

Table 4-1. *Economic Performance in Selected Central and Eastern European Countries*

Indicator[a]	Years	Hungary	Poland	Yugoslavia	Czech.
Inflation	1980	9.1	9.4	30.9	3.7
	1985	7.0	15.1	72.3	2.3
	1989	17.0	244.5	1,239.9	1.4
	1980-89	8.1	53.1	74.9	1.6
	1984-89	8.9	62.9	106.3	0.9
GDP growth	1980	0.2	-10.0	2.3	2.4
	1985	0.3	3.6	0.5	2.9
	1989	-1.5	0.5	0.8	1.3
	1980-89	2.1	1.4	0.5	2.0
	1984-89	2.5	4.0	0.3	2.5
Export growth	1980	19.7	21.2	18.6	23.7
	1985	-14.8	-2.3	-1.1	-4.0
	1989	15.0	4.5	9.8	8.5
	1980-89	2.9	-0.6	7.3	6.3
	1984-89	5.2	6.7	10.0	2.5
Export/GDP	1980	21.7	14.0	9.1	10.6
	1985	20.3	7.5	15.6	9.8
	1989	22.6	11.4	15.3	11.2
Current account/GDP	1980	-1.7	-1.4	-3.0	-3.5
	1985	-4.1	-0.9	0.7	2.3
	1989	-5.2	-2.8	3.0	0.8
Currency debt	1980	9,090	25,500	18,486	6,850
(mil. US$)	1985	13,955	33,100	18,407	4,608
	1989	20,605	40,578	17,320	7,915
DOD/GDP[b]	1980	40.6	44.9	24.5	16.6
	1985	67.6	46.6	42.1	11.7
	1989	73.8	61.2	28.3	16.3
Debt/XGNFS[c]	1980	151.0	286.5	158.2	85.0
	1985	228.4	508.4	177.9	87.0
	1989	246.1	465.1	105.8	104.0
Debt service/XGNFS[c]	1980	13.5	95.9	32.9	17.2
	1985	60.4	86.0	28.9	17.4
	1989	40.8	75.3	29.4	19.4

a. The current account, export and debt data are in convertible currencies. The aggregate economic activity index is gross social product for Yugoslavia and net material product for Czechoslovakia. The ratios are in percentages of GDP for Yugoslavia.

b. DOD=debt outstanding and disbursed.

c. XGNFS=exports of goods and non-factor services.

Source: Country data, World Bank (1990c); Yugoslavia (various issues).

inflation, mainly as a result of the monetization of enterprise deficits. In other countries, most notably perhaps Bulgaria, the former German Democratic Republic (GDR) and the USSR, the governments repressed inflation with price controls, and the underlying macroeconomic imbalances translated into shortages and consequently into forced savings and an ever-increasing monetary overhang. Multiple and generally overvalued exchange rates aggravated the external imbalances. The preferred tool to keep the imbalances within manageable proportions was the centrally controlled allocation of foreign exchange.

The pervasive state intervention carried down to the microeconomic level. Direct price controls, subsidies and taxes produced grave price distortions, while highly differentiated foreign exchange and trade regimes led to a large number of effective exchange rates. Directed credit allocations at highly negative real interest rates and direct control of investment caused further distortions, and the de facto guarantee of full employment resulted in overstaffing.

The results of this approach to economic management are well-known. The level of efficiency was low, examples being an energy intensity 2 to 3 times higher than in the Organisation for Economic Co-operation and Development (OECD) countries; labor productivity that was 2 to 5 times lower; transport intensity that was 4 to 10 times higher; excessive inventories, perhaps 10 to 20 times higher in relation to GDP than in the OECD countries; low capital productivity as reflected in high incremental capital/output ratios (ICORs); severe environmental problems; a growing technology gap; a lack of competitiveness in the open international markets despite technology imports from OECD countries; and lagging growth and standards of living. (Table 4-2 presents a number of structural and efficiency indicators.) While the standard of living in a country such as Czechoslovakia was about at par with the West European countries before World War II, it is now only one-third to one-half that of Western Europe. Over the years Czechoslovakia lost market shares in the OECD countries and moved toward a "regressive specialization" that replaced its former technology-intensive exports such as machinery with material- and energy-intensive goods such as steel, organic chemicals, fertilizers and textiles.

Although these stylized results may appear dramatic, the underlying causes as summarized in the preceding paragraphs read like familiar stories from other World Bank client countries. An important question to be asked, then, is whether there are any other critical factors that set Central and Eastern Europe apart from the World Bank's typical developing country clients and that constitute some sort of quantum leap in underlying structural problems (and not just the same problems to a greater degree).

A large number of such factors have been at work in Central and Eastern Europe simultaneously for prolonged periods of time: the preponderant importance of political decisions; central planning (albeit to varying degrees across the countries); the total lack of a financial system; the absence of functioning factor markets; the almost complete state ownership of enterprises (or other forms of ownership and management with confused ownership rights that have had severe implications for the functioning of the factor markets); overemphasis on an even distribution of income and thus a lack of performance-related compensation systems; and the overwhelming role of barter trade arrangements within the Council for Mutual Economic Assistance (CMEA) (Hinds

1990; Kornai 1990). This set of structural or systemic features makes the design and implementation of adjustment programs in Central and Eastern Europe unique. The standard tools of stabilization and adjustment with which the international financial institutions have gained ample experience over a long period, most notably during the 1980s, are not quite sufficient for the task in Central and Eastern Europe. The task goes well beyond mere reform and adjustment. Rather, it requires a systemic transformation. While state-owned enterprises are important in many Latin American countries, and their poor performance has unleashed severe crises for entire economies, at the same time these enterprises have been operating in some sort of market environment. Such systems lend themselves to reform. In contrast, in Central and Eastern Europe many of the fundamental rules of a market-based economy have to be designed and established from scratch, a process for which there is little historical guidance.

Based on theoretical considerations of the efficiency of different modes of organizing production and the concrete experience with reform in a large number of countries, it can be concluded that, ultimately, excessive direct state intervention and the critical degree to which private ownership is lacking largely explain the dismal performance of the Central and Eastern European economies (Hinds 1990; Milanovic 1989). The numerous attempts in these economies to decentralize and introduce competition or quasi-competition have not included measures to deal with the crucial issue of ownership and concomitant management of the means of production. It was once thought that market socialism, i.e., decentralization of decision-making along the lines postulated by neoclassical economic theory while maintaining state ownership of enterprises, was a workable system, embodying, as it did, a compromise aimed at retaining the efficiency of a market economy without incurring the undesirable aspects of a capitalist system such as unemployment and social inequality. To date, all attempts have failed.

Pure neoclassical economic theory pays little attention to the importance of ownership in achieving maximum efficiency. However, the growing literature on ownership rights focuses on their critical implications for management and decision-making and thus for the functioning of markets. The implication is that a divorce of the ownership of capital and decision-making over its use will result in inefficiencies (Milanovic 1989). The problem is even more acute if the relations of ownership and management are confused, as is the case in many Central and Eastern European countries that have worker self-managed firms with social ownership or state-

46

Table 4-2. *Structural Indicators*

A. Energy
i. Annual Average Percentage Changes

Years	Countries	GDP	Energy use	Oil consumption	Energy elasticity
1976-79	OECD	3.9	3.0	2.7	0.8
1976-79	Hungary	4.1	3.9	2.14	1.0
1975-79	Poland	3.8	3.7	4.1	1.0
1975-79	Yugoslavia	6.6	2.6	5.6	0.4
1980-82	OECD	0.9	-2.9	-6.6	n.a.
1980-82	Hungary	2.9	0.2	-5.7	0.1
1980-82	Poland	-3.2	-1.4	-5.0	n.a.
1980-82	Yugoslavia	-0.6	3.6	-2.5	n.a.
1983-85	OECD	3.2	1.2	-0.4	0.4
1983-87	Hungary	0.5	0.7	-0.3	1.4
19683-87	Poland	4.6	1.9	1.6	0.4
1983-87	Yugoslavia	-2.0	1.2	-0.1	n.a.

n.a. Not available.
Source: Country data,World Bank; and World Bank (1990b).

ii. Intensity of Use
([TOE] of primary energy per US$1 million of GDP [1975 US$]; purchasing power parity [PPP]-based)

Country group in	1965	1975	1982
OECD-15	682.1	631.7	487.3
CMEA-7	1,312.3	1,145.5	1,138.9
CMEA-3[a]	1,169.6	1,974.1	1,132.5

a. CMEA-3 consists of Hungary, Poland and Yugoslavia.
Source: Gomulka and Rostowski (1988).

B. Transport: Surface Transport in East Europe and OECD[a]
(ton-km per US$1 of GNP)

Countries	Ton-km per 1 $ of GNP
Czechoslovakia	1.6
Hungary	1.8
Poland	2.3
Yugoslavia	0.24

a. The data generally relate to 1988 and do not precede 1984.
Source: EMENA, Technical Department for the infrastructure, World Bank, from International Road Federation, *World Road Statistics 1984-88*.

C. Inventories: Changes in Stock as a Percentage of GDP
(current prices)

	Hungary	Poland	Yugoslavia[a]	Czech.	OECD[b]
1980	1.9	1.6	9.6	6.1	0.28
1981	3.2	-0.2	11.6	2.2	0.45
1982	3.3	7.8	9.3	2.4	-0.41
1983	1.9	4.9	12.6	2.4	-0.15
1984	2.7	5.6	16.3	1.9	1.22
1985	2.5	6.5	18.8	2.1	0.31
1986	2.9	7.0	7.7	2.6	0.36
1987	2.8	6.3	7.0	3.3	0.58
1988	3.9	10.0	5.0	1.4	0.57
1989	5.2	10.0	5.0	2.1	0.53

a. Because of inflationary distortions, the change in stock in Yugoslavia is not reliable.
b. The unweighted average includes France, Germany, Japan and the United States.
Source: IMF, *International Financial Statistics*; World Bank (1990c); Yugoslavia (various issues).

D. ICOR

	Hungary	Poland	Yugoslavia
1980-85	16.5	23.1	37.4
1985-89	27.7	22.2	n.a.

n.a. Not available.
Source: Country data, World Bank.

E. Staffing
(percent)

	Disguised unemployment	Unemployment (1990)
Hungary	10-30	2
Poland	8-10 in manufacturing	7
	20-30 in service	
Yugoslavia	20	11
Czechoslovakia	n.a.	3

n.a. Not available.
Source: Adam (1984); Mencinger (1989); and World Bank.

F. Tax Revenue as a % of GDP, 1985

Countries	%		%
Czechoslovakia	50.7	OECD total	37.2
Hungary	49.9	OECD Europe	38.9
Poland	37.0	EEC	39.5
Yugoslavia[a]	33.7		
Romania	11.5		
Average	35.9		

a. Implies gross social product and a broad case.
Source: Coricelli and Rocha (1990).

G. Money Stock as a Percentage of GDP

	Hungary		Poland		Yugoslavia	
	M1/GDP	M2/GDP	M1/GDP	M2/GDP[a]	M1/GSP[b]	M2/GSP
1982	23.2	47.8	22.7	57.4	20.0	32.6
1983	22.7	47.0	22.6	52.1	17.6	30.0
1984	21.8	45.4	20.6	47.3	14.2	26.3
1985	23.5	47.2	20.0	44.8	10.5	22.6
1986	26.6	51.0	18.5	46.2	9.8	20.4
1987	25.1	48.8	14.9	51.4	9.1	17.4
1988	21.9	43.0	15.7	56.4	7.4	14.3
1989	n.a.	38.3	n.a.	36.8	n.a.	n.a.

n.a. Not available

a. Implies gross social product.

b. The M2/GDP for Poland includes foreign currency deposits valued at black market rates. The ratio for 1989 is at December 31, 1989 exchange rate.

Source: Country sources, World Bank.

H. Importance of Public Enterprises[a] in Selected Countries
(percent of output)

OECD	
France (1982)	16.5 (1973: 11.7;1979: 13.0)
Austria (1978-79)	14.5
Italy (1982)	14.0
Germany, F.R. (1982)	10.7 (1977: 10.3)
United Kingdom (1978	11.1 (1972: 10.2))
United States (1983)	1.3
Developing countries	
Sudan (1980s)	40.0
Guyana (1978-80)	37.2
Venezuela (1978-80)	27.5
Chile (1981)	24.0
India	10.3
Socialist countries[b]	
Czechoslovakia(1986)	97.0
German Dem. Rep. (1982)	96.5
USSR (1985)	96.0
Poland (1985)	81.7 (1980: 83.4; 1970: 82.2)
China (1984)	73.6 (1982: 77.8; 1980: 78.7)
Hungary (1984)	65.2 (1980: 69.8; 1975: 73.3)

a. Government/state-owned corporations.

b. Including government.

Source: Milanovic (1989).

owned firms in which workers' councils ultimately decide on the use of resources.

Some of the weaknesses of market socialism, most importantly the lack of financial discipline at the enterprise level, may even have been exacerbated (Kornai 1990; Brus and Laski 1989; Aslund 1990). Financial discipline and competition, including competition from international trade, can only be exercised in a credible manner when there is a sufficiently high degree of decentralization, autonomy of enterprises and, ultimately, private ownership. Private ownership would make it highly unlikely and extremely difficult to resort to large-scale government support in the case of financial difficulty. Moreover, a predominantly private system has room for other forms of ownership and management, including worker self-management, as financial discipline and even application of the rules of the game to all players are guaranteed or at least have a high degree of credibility.

The great emphasis in Central and Eastern European countries on ownership and the effective exercise of ownership rights, and the implications for enterprise management, is a key aspect of the quantum leap in underlying structural problems referred to earlier. While in an economy with mostly private ownership the exposure of state-owned enterprises to effective competition through trade liberalization and domestic deregulation may be more important in achieving greater efficiency in these enterprises than privatization is (Douglas 1990), in the Central and Eastern European economies with their overwhelming state ownership this pattern does not seem to hold, as evidenced by the failure of previous reform attempts.

Key Elements of an Economic Transformation Program for Central and Eastern European Economies

Given the list of typical policy issues to be addressed in the Central and East European economies and the main lessons from the World Bank's experience with adjustment lending, what should be the key elements of an economic transformation program that can reasonably be expected to succeed?

Most economies with unsustainable balance-of-payments positions requiring adjustment typically face both major macroeconomic and microeconomic distortions that need to be attacked simultaneously. While the programs would obviously vary from country to country, they would follow a by now traditional pattern that entails varying doses of stabilization cum adjustment, typically supported by a series of International Monetary

Fund (IMF) financial programs (e.g., standby arrangements) and World Bank adjustment operations (e.g., structural or sector adjustment loans).

Perhaps the most comprehensive and successful economic adjustment programs in any World Bank client countries to date are Chile and Mexico's, which have been implemented since the mid-1970s and mid-1980s, respectively. Although the Chilean and Mexican programs may be the most comprehensive ones to date, for the most part they lack the systemic dimension clearly needed in Central and Eastern Europe. State ownership of firms was extensive in Chile and Mexico and required far-reaching privatization programs. At the same time, however, the economies had market elements, albeit with gross distortions whose correction constituted the core elements of the programs. In other words, market behavior and private ownership of firms did not have to be "invented" in those countries.

The typical adjustment or transformation program in Central and Eastern Europe has to be broader in scope, with macroeconomic, microeconomic and systemic elements. To have a minimum chance of success, beyond addressing the gravest distortions first, the transformation program has simultaneously to:

- create a stable macroeconomic environment;
- create a market-driven incentives system, together with greater flexibility in the factor markets; and
- create a critical degree of decentralization and competition, with private ownership of firms.

These key elements are crucial, and there is not much room for different sequencing. Most elements have to be present from the outset, and the government's commitment to the comprehensive transformation has to be credible. At the same time, implementation of the different elements will follow different time paths; in particular, privatization and institutional development to support a market economy, especially the development of financial markets, greater flexibility in the labor market and upgrading of the legal system, will take longer than some other elements. It is, therefore, all the more important to pursue all elements simultaneously from the outset. This approach appears to be crucial to bringing about the necessary behavioral changes, particularly in enterprises (International Institute of Finance 1990; Kornai 1990).

A stabilization program may be required at the beginning of the transformation because of high or hyper-inflation, as in the cases of Poland and Yugoslavia and to a lesser degree Hungary and the USSR. Even where inflation is not a major problem at the beginning of the transformation, a stabilization program involving tight fiscal and monetary policies and perhaps a more radical monetary reform to control or eliminate the monetary overhang is still needed. Significant price corrections, including in most cases a depreciation of the exchange rate and an upward adjustment of interest rates, are required, to be effected through the elimination of subsidies and the liberalization of trade so as to align domestic with international prices. These measures could easily trigger high inflation if not controlled through rigorous fiscal and monetary management.

A major realignment of relative prices through the elimination of subsidies, tax reform and liberalization of domestic and international trade, and the imposition of financial discipline on firms through a reformed financial system, would have to be the core elements of any program of transformation aimed at establishing a market-based system. However, only if there is greater factor mobility will the aforementioned measures lead to a reallocation of resources and greater efficiency. Functioning labor and capital markets are indispensable. Persistent rigidity in the factor markets could cause the macroeconomic stabilization to translate into unduly high losses in output and loss in employment.

As experience in Hungary, Yugoslavia and—to a lesser extent—Poland suggests, these core microeconomic reforms by themselves have little chance of producing the expected increase in efficiency unless complemented by a massive transformation of ownership and management that makes financial discipline credible. As to privatization, it is a long-term proposition in light of the sheer proportions of state ownership in Central and Eastern Europe. Nevertheless, a critical mass of private firms has to be achieved in a relatively short period.

Based on World Bank experience in other countries, these changes can be greatly facilitated by mitigating any resulting social hardship through specific support measures for the most adversely affected. That is, adequate provision for a social safety net, in particular unemployment benefits complemented by employment services and training programs, should be made from the outset.

This section has focused on the requirements of domestic policy reform. However, the external dimension is equally important. To succeed, adjustment programs need to be adequately financed. As domestic savings will tend to fall short of investment requirements, external financing on adequate terms will be needed. In the cases of Poland and Bulgaria, adequate external financial support also has to include a lasting solution to the debt overhang.

World Bank-Supported Programs in Central and Eastern Europe

World Bank adjustment lending in the region began with the first SAL to Yugoslavia in 1983. The operation was not successful, and much time elapsed before the second SAL was approved in April 1990, after a preparation period of more than three years. In Hungary, adjustment lending was initiated in 1988 with the Industrial Sector Adjustment Loan (a sector adjustment loan, or SECAL), followed by a SAL, approved in June 1990. (Quasi-adjustment lending in support of industrial restructuring had actually started in 1986 with a series of sector operations—Industrial Restructuring I, II and III—with the latest approved in 1989.) In Poland, World Bank lending was initiated in February 1990 with two project loans. An additional three project loans followed before the first SAL was approved in July 1990.

This section highlights the main features of all adjustment lending operations in the region and provides brief assessments, mainly of program design, in the context of the normative framework specified in the preceding section.[1] A few words are also added on the World Bank's recent recommendations for reform in Czechoslovakia. A summary assessment is provided in the concluding section.

Yugoslavia

The first SAL to Yugoslavia was made in June 1983 in support of the government's adjustment program. The program, entitled Long-Term Program of Economic Stabilization, was based on the recommendations of a high-level Commission on Stabilization. Its focus was the strengthening of market forces in the economy, and its main components were:

• more liberalized external trade policies and allocation of foreign exchange;
• improved pricing policies and enterprise decision-making, with particular emphasis on the agriculture and energy sectors; and
• adjustment of interest rates and improvement of investment planning and allocation.

The program also included a traditional stabilization effort that was supported by an IMF Standby Arrangement.

The reforms faltered, particularly as the stabilization effort could not be sustained for a sufficient period and inflation accelerated. During 1985-86, there was considerable policy backsliding, and by mid-1987 Yugoslavia had essentially fallen back to the situation in 1982-83, when the stabilization and policy reforms were initiated.

In addition to the failure to maintain an adequate macroeconomic environment, which in itself hampered the effectiveness of the structural reforms, the program supported by SAL I tried to address too many issues and was not well-focused on the most crucial ones, such as reform of enterprise management, enforcement of financial discipline, improvement of the financial system, development of a new approach to the employment of labor, and, ultimately, changes in enterprise ownership and the approach to enterprise management. These shortcomings were not the result of absent or misguided analysis. Thorough analysis by the high-level commission and by Bank staff had preceded adoption of the reform program. The lack of success was ultimately also the result of the political situation in Yugoslavia, which led to both lagging implementation and eventually to abandonment of the program. At that time Yugoslavia was not really committed to the transition to a market-based system, and—within the existing legal framework—the federal government was severely limited in bringing about the interregional consensus required for effective implementation of major reforms.

SAL I had been conceived as the first in a series of such loans. It took, however, about seven years to agree on a follow-on operation, which for all practical purposes could be considered as a new operation. This long hiatus reflects the difficulty of designing and agreeing on a program that would address the key issues in a meaningful way and provide for a reasonably stable macroeconomic environment after the inflation degenerated into hyper-inflation in 1989. That time was not entirely lost, however. In the interval the government made substantial progress in amending the constitution and strengthening the institutional setting for enterprise management and the financial sector. It adopted key pieces of legislation such as a new enterprise law (enacted in 1988) and a new banking law (enacted in 1989), along with several other important laws affecting investment.

Yugoslavia's current adjustment program, which is being supported by SAL II, was initiated along with a radical and far-reaching heterodox stabilization program, with support from the IMF. Contrary to previous stabilization attempts, the current program also addresses structural issues such as adjustment of the enterprise and banking sectors, which were seen as two of the root causes of the financial instability and poor economic performance in Yugoslavia.

Other key structural elements incorporated into this new program are:

• further liberalization of the foreign exchange and trade regimes and concomitant domestic price liberalization.

• enforcement of financial discipline by enterprises through restructuring and tighter bankruptcy procedures, together with an adequate interest rate policy. In the short run, the enterprise adjustment will be backed by non-inflationary fiscal support to the enterprises—a sharp departure from the past when enterprises were automatically financed through the banking system and ultimately the central bank.

• broader-based fiscal financing of the social safety net to protect displaced workers without placing a further burden on productive enterprises. This measure will be complemented by specific programs to promote small private sector enterprises.

The program addresses the most crucial issues contributing to the poor performance of the Yugoslav economy and closely follows the normative framework set out in the previous section. Moreover, the program is being strengthened by expanding its coverage to enterprise reform, attention to the financial sector issues and preparation of the ground for bank restructuring, as well as further rationalization of unemployment benefits and improvement of the functioning of the labor market, with additional support from the World Bank.

Key questions remain, however. Given the historically rooted political difficulties, will program implementation be effective? Can the ultimate and systemic root cause of Yugoslavia's economic calamity—the lack of clear enterprise ownership and concomitant management—be addressed effectively, given the possibility of having to liquidate and restructure enterprises and dismiss workers. While the federal government is pursuing such policies, it has yet to demonstrate that the new rules spelled out in recent legislation will be applied and further strengthened. Liquidations and bankruptcies, although obviously not the objectives of the program, are the only credible threats to enterprises to enforce financial discipline and thus improve market behavior, which are key factors in securing macroeconomic stability and efficient resource use. The credible imposition of financial discipline has major implications for the management of enterprises and will necessarily require a significant "cultural" change, particularly in the labor market: through competitive pressure in the goods markets, firms will be forced to cut costs, an eventuality that will no longer permit maximization of the wage fund and other distributable surpluses but rather will lead to the dismissal of excess labor.

Hungary

World Bank adjustment lending in Hungary started with the approval of an industrial sector adjustment loan (ISAL) in 1988 to support the industrial policy reforms the government planned for the period 1985-90. The ISAL was actually preceded by two sector operations, the Industrial Restructuring Loans I and II, approved in 1986 and 1987, respectively, and was followed by the Industrial Restructuring Loan III in 1989. All three restructuring loans obviously also support the program to reform industrial policy through specific restructuring programs at the enterprise level. The first two operations were hybrid, including quick-disbursing components for balance-of-payments support against a set of policy measures that had been designed to improve macroeconomic and sector performance.

The industrial policy reform program has been part of a larger reform effort aimed at macroeconomic stabilization and greater overall efficiency, centering around three key elements:

- increasing domestic and external competition;
- tightening financial discipline in the enterprise sector; and
- facilitating the mobility of capital and labor to enable the restructuring of the industrial sector.

The program design, as modified to deal with the shortcomings observed in 1985-87, stressed the links to macroeconomic performance by: concentrating on the most inefficient subsectors and enterprises receiving the highest budgetary support; cutting producer and consumer subsidies; strengthening tax reform; and providing incentives for convertible currency exports. However, program implementation through the end of 1989 was not very successful. Macroeconomic management continued to falter, and excessive current account deficits in the balance of payments and increasing external financing difficulties emerged. Lax macroeconomic management in the face of interest rates that had not reached adequate levels also had direct negative implications for enterprise behavior. Moreover, enforcement of financial discipline by enterprises lagged, as the liquidation and restructuring plans for important enterprises were delayed. The lagging structural reform in turn fed back into the poor macroeconomic performance, which further weakened the reform.

An additional factor explaining the lagging restructuring has been the CMEA trade arrangements, which provided an easy—and from an enterprise's point of view, profitable—way out. Enterprises participating in the restructuring program actually increased their exports to CMEA markets rather than to convertible currency areas.

Around the end of 1989 the interim government strengthened the impetus for reform, as did the government that took power in 1990. Most importantly, a more rigorous approach to macroeconomic management was put in place based on stricter fiscal and monetary policies, including adjustments of interest rate and foreign exchange policies. At the same time, the structural elements aimed at more disciplined enterprise behavior were strengthened. The revised and strengthened program is being supported by an IMF Standby Arrangement and a World Bank SAL, approved in June 1990. The World Bank is also providing complementary support through previously approved industrial restructuring loans and a recently approved loan for the modernization of the financial system.

The revised program's main structural features are the following:

- ownership reform and privatization based on the Law of Transformation enacted in June 1989 (and other laws) aimed at effective enterprise management by vigorous exercise of ownership rights;
- promotion of competition through further, progressive trade liberalization, domestic deregulation and price reform, greater participation of foreign investment, and tightened financial discipline, to be enforced through stricter application of the bankruptcy legislation and with the help of a financial sector now being strengthened for more effective intermediation;
- eduction of the state's role in the economy, most notably through a sharp reduction in subsidies and the limitation of public investment to core areas of the physical and social infrastructure, in addition to privatization; and
- major reform of social policies, including housing, health, social security and unemployment compensation.

Besides vigorous macroeconomic management aimed at lower inflation and a sustainable balance of payments, the core of the program deals with the reform of enterprise behavior. The design of the program seems to be broadly in line with the norms postulated in the previous section. The proof will be mainly in the implementation. The program addresses the root causes of inefficiency in Hungary, except perhaps for import liberalization, which, after many previous attempts, is still relatively modest in scope and phased over a number of years. Current macroeconomic management has been quite successful in improving the balance of payments (which has gone from a large and increasing deficit to a slight surplus in the current account in the first half of 1990) but less successful in controlling inflation, which has actually accelerated. With regard to enterprise behavior, the acid test will be that liquidations, bankruptcies and privatization actually take place, supported by intensified domestic and foreign competition. The main battle is still ahead, and, judging by the authorities' relatively modest assumptions about future unemployment, it would seem the task of restructuring has been either substantially underestimated or political compromises may be likely regarding the pace of the adjustment.

There is, as noted, no substitute for government ownership, i.e., the government is ultimately responsible for the design and implementation of its reform efforts. However, to the extent that program design and implementation can be strengthened through loan conditionality, the SAL builds on prior experience in Hungary and general lessons learned from World Bank adjustment lending. The government took important actions prior to loan approval, and more specific actions of a crucial nature are required for the release of the loan's second tranche. The authorities designed the macroeconomic framework for the overall program in close consultation with the IMF and the Bank. Monitoring of performance will be based on specific indicators, and there has to be agreement on the future policy course, including the 1991 budget (with special emphasis on the reduction of producer and consumer subsidies) prior to release of the second tranche. Similarly, strong and credible action on privatization, enterprise liquidation and trade liberalization is required for release of the second tranche.

Poland

To some extent, Poland is unique: in addition to the macroeconomic, sector and systemic problems it shares with its neighbors in the region, its creditworthiness is seriously impaired. It has not been able to service its debt with Paris Club creditors since 1982 and has undergone five reschedulings, the latest one in February 1990. While Hungary also is highly indebted (on a per capita basis even more so than Poland), it has managed to stay current with its debt-service obligations. Poland has also had to reschedule its commercial debt on seven occasions; until about a year ago, it managed to pay the interest on all commercial debt but since then has suspended payments on medium- and long-term debt, which accounts for about 90 percent of total commercial debt. Thus, in addition to the "standard" issues of economic

transformation, Poland has to find a longer term solution to its severe debt problem.

Poland joined the World Bank in 1986. Because of its macroeconomic and debt problems, initially it was not considered creditworthy for any lending from the Bank, and a credible stabilization and adjustment program was a prerequisite for initiation of any lending. The Solidarity-led government of Prime Minister Mazowiecki prepared the ground to receive Bank financing when it adopted the Economic Transformation Program on January 1, 1990. That program, which is comprised of a strong heterodox stabilization component and far-reaching structural adjustment measures, is being supported by a standby arrangement from the IMF and a SAL from the World Bank, approved in July 1990, following initiation of project lending in February. Complementary lending operations to support, inter alia, industrial restructuring, financial sector development, agricultural development, and strengthening of the labor market and employment promotion are also under preparation.

The Economic Transformation Program is Poland's most comprehensive and radical attempt to date to stabilize and set the stage for transformation into a market economy. In its combination of macroeconomic and structural or systemic elements, it is certainly the strongest program among the three described in this paper. The stabilization component, which is similar to Yugoslavia's, aims to eradicate inflation, after prior price liberalization, through the pursuit of tight fiscal and monetary policies, with a drastic cut in subsidies and a major adjustment of interest rates, as well as through the use of a fixed exchange rate and partially indexed wages as nominal anchors. The structural or systemic component goes beyond Yugoslavia's or Hungary's, however, in terms of the liberalization of imports and prices and the enforcement of financial discipline of enterprises. Finally, contrary to the other programs, Poland's program aims at comprehensive debt relief from all creditors, a move that appears indispensable to its viability and to laying the groundwork for the restoration of growth and creditworthiness.

More specifically, the stabilization component of the Economic Transformation Program comprises: a virtually balanced budget, to be achieved mainly through a drastic reduction of subsidies; strict control of credit; positive real interest rates; an almost complete liberalization of prices (including major adjustments of still administered prices, particularly in energy); radically changed foreign exchange and trade regimes, with complete import liberalization and a fixed exchange rate after significant devaluation; and a substantial reduction in real wages.

The structural adjustment or systemic component of the Economic Transformation Program comprises three main features:

- enterprise restructuring, privatization and development of the private sector, with appropriate legislation to impose financial discipline, establishment of an adequate institutional framework for enterprise restructuring (including stricter environmental standards) and preparation of the ground for privatization;
- financial sector reform, with emphasis on improved banking regulation and supervision, introduction of adequate accounting and auditing standards (also for non-financial enterprises), and strengthening and phased restructuring of the banking system; and
- establishment of a social safety net, with emphasis on adequate unemployment benefits, employment services, training, a program of minimum social assistance and improved health policy.

Enterprise restructuring and privatization are the Economic Transformation Program's most crucial element. These measures presuppose a reasonable degree of competition, to be achieved through the complete liberalization of imports and demonopolization of (or enhancement of competition in) the domestic economy, as well as a functioning financial system. The demonopolization and financial sector development need to be accelerated to make enterprise restructuring and privatization effective tools in increasing overall efficiency.

The poor performance of enterprises in Poland, as in other socialist economies, was the result of lax financial discipline (or the soft budget constraint, in Kornai's words), i.e., easy access to bank credit at subsidized interest rates, with the funds ultimately originating from the central bank's printing press. The Economic Transformation Program seeks to address financial indiscipline in the short run in two ways: by limiting the overall availability of credit and raising interest rates significantly; and by enforcing the payment of a mandatory dividend on that portion of a firm's revalued capital that was originally provided by the founding organization. The dividend provision, which is stronger than in the past, is a significant financial requirement, particularly as the availability and cost of credit are additional constraints. Failure to pay the dividend to the government would trigger a number of possible actions, including restructuring or liquidation. A possible avenue to restructuring could also be privatization.

The institutional framework to establish financial discipline is relatively strong. However, actual performance (as in the other countries) largely depends on enforcement of the rules and, thus, on determined initiation of liquidation and bankruptcy procedures. While there have been a number of liquidations, generally speaking enforcement has lagged.

Credit ceilings and mandatory dividend payments are essentially short-term devices to enforce financial discipline. In the longer run, a well-functioning and independent financial system as well as increased private ownership of enterprises are more effective guarantees. Both elements are included in the Economic Transformation Program, although both are longer term propositions.

Implementation of the program's structural component lacks vigor, a situation that may also explain the stubbornness of inflation, which, after having dropped sharply from 78 percent in January, hovered around 3-5 percent per month during May-September. The economy is highly concentrated, and monopolistic structures dominate large segments, including the distribution system. Moreover, the persistence of energy subsidies and a somewhat undervalued exchange rate (in spite of the real appreciation since the beginning of 1990) may have provided some sectors with a relatively comfortable initial cushion that diminished the effectiveness of import competition.

Again, as in the other cases, SAL conditionality was designed to strengthen the government's hand in implementing the Economic Transformation Program—to the extent strengthening can be achieved through outside support or requirements. The Bank will closely monitor macroeconomic performance based on a set of key indicators, which also stress the medium-term dimension through an emphasis on savings and investment. Importantly, the macroeconomic conditions for release of the second tranche include agreement on the 1991 draft budget, with particular emphasis on a further reduction in the energy, housing and transportation subsidies, as well as on adequate investment. An effective external financing strategy—which in the case of Poland essentially means debt and debt-service reduction—is another important aspect of the macroeconomic framework. Key structural actions to support the drive toward a market-based system and greater efficiency include: vigorous action on demonopolization in key sectors, such as agricultural marketing, distribution of inputs, transportation and trade; a review of import tariffs and the remaining export restrictions; accelerated enterprise restructuring and privatization based on sound policies and operating principles for the respective institutions; and prudential bank supervision based on new accounting and auditing standards. Ultimately, however, it is obviously the government's commitment to the program and political support that will determine the relative success of its implementation.

Czechoslovakia

Czechoslovakia became a member of the IMF and the Bank only in September 1990. While the previous regime over the years had undertaken some economic reforms, Czechoslovakia was much closer to a centrally planned system than were the other countries. The new government has initiated a few reforms, such as the establishment of a two-tier banking system and limited price liberalization. However, the big push for reform is yet to come, most likely at the beginning of 1991.

As compared with other Central and Eastern European countries, Czechoslovakia has managed its economy more prudently, avoiding high inflation, severe shortages, balance-of-payments problems and excessive indebtedness. However, grave price distortions, low efficiency and heavy dependence on the defense industries and arms exports, as well as on CMEA trade, make a comprehensive approach to economic reform equally urgent. Similarly, given the need for major price corrections, stringent macroeconomic management is indispensable to ensure that the one-time price adjustments do not trigger an inflationary spiral.

The World Bank recently completed an Economic Memorandum on Czechoslovakia. In line with the general lessons from adjustment lending and the specific issues in Eastern Europe as postulated in the previous section, the Bank has recommended a program of simultaneous policy actions in a number of key areas within the context of a prudent and consistent set of macroeconomic policies aimed at creating a stable financial environment:

- far-reaching liberalization of domestic prices;
- liberalization of current account transactions ("internal convertibility");
- changes in the rights and responsibilities of the managers of state-owned enterprises, as well as initiation of privatization and private sector development;
- encouragement of private direct foreign investment; and
- provision of an adequate social safety net.

There has been considerable debate in Czechoslovakia among various factions over the scope and pace of reform. The scope and pace seem to be critical issues in Czechoslovakia, as the population does not appear to be prepared for major sacrifices given the relatively smooth if not impressive functioning of the economy in the past.

However, based on the experience of other countries, ultimately success in transforming the economy will depend on the decisive implementation of a critical mass of simultaneous measures from the outset.

Conclusions

Given the similarity of the macroeconomic, sector and systemic problems in various Central and Eastern European countries, it is not surprising that the approaches to reform and the focus of IMF and World Bank support are quite similar across countries. Obviously the magnitude of the macroeconomic adjustment and the kind of approach (with or without the use of nominal anchors) varies from country to country, as does the relative emphasis on different structural components such as trade liberalization, enterprise restructuring, financial sector reform and privatization.

Experience with previous reform attempts suggests that a critical mass of simultaneous efforts is required for ultimate success. This prescription applies in particular to the stabilization efforts currently being pursued, which need to be complemented by structural adjustment. Short-term macroeconomic stabilization turns out to be relatively easy: Hungary, Poland and Yugoslavia have achieved encouraging results in terms of their balance-of-payments performance, although somewhat less so in terms of controlling inflation. By far the more difficult task, however, is to maintain financial stability in the medium and longer term and to achieve greater efficiency through structural transformation and change in enterprise behavior. It is the behavioral change of enterprises that in the end will determine the supply response.

In the light of experience, the enforcement of financial discipline in the enterprise sector can be considered the acid test of all transformation programs in terms of securing both macroeconomic stability (because of the monetary implications of the soft budget constraint) and greater efficiency of resource use. This summary assessment of the programs therefore focused on the relative strength of that particular aspect of the individual programs.

Enforcement of financial discipline is used here as a broad concept comprising a number of different features, such as competition, a far-reaching change in ownership rights and the concomitant accountability of enterprise management, a credible threat of bankruptcy and liquidation, and ultimately large-scale privatization to bring about a qualitative change in enterprise behavior. These features are prominent in all programs and are supported by World Bank SAL conditionality. However, program implementation, while still at an early stage in all countries, has not been as vigorous as might have been hoped considering the dimension and urgency of the task. The relative inexperience of the administrations and the political controversy are obvious explanations for the tardiness in implementing the reforms.

Regarding competition, the Polish program has gone the farthest in terms of import liberalization and the exposure of domestic industry to international competition. Yugoslavia and particularly Hungary still have a long way to go. However, even in Poland, the remaining subsidies, particularly the energy price subsidies, and possibly a somewhat undervalued effective exchange rate (taking tariffs into account as well) provide many enterprises with a still relatively comfortable cushion. Combined with high concentration and a correspondingly high degree of monopolization that affects domestic distribution systems, a non-tradable activity, these factors have slowed adjustment. However, there are now the first encouraging signs of some enterprise adaptation to the new market environment.

The governments in all the countries have been relatively slow to enforce bankruptcy and liquidation procedures, with Yugoslavia having gone the farthest. To some extent, enterprises have been operating on the back of increasing inter-enterprise credit; in addition, banks have had little choice but to extend more credit to enterprises in financially precarious conditions, even if they do not have a clear perspective on their own restructuring and recapitalization. In all the countries, changes in the nature of ownership rights, restructuring and privatization have also been proceeding slowly, mainly because of political controversy over workers' acquired management rights and expectations of partial or total ownership, adequate valuation of enterprises, lack of domestic capital and the role of foreign investment. A critical mass of private ownership of enterprises with effective management in a competitive market environment seems to be the most effective guarantee for greater efficiency and financial discipline. While all the countries now have enabling legislation in place, actual privatization, except of very small enterprises, is lagging. The task is, however, daunting, given the large number of enterprises and the lack of domestic savings and effective capital markets. Rapid sale of retail outlets and other small units that could be spun off from large conglomerates and a few large-scale privatizations involving foreign capital as well as free distribution of shares to the population at large, combined with effective enterprise control mechanisms through private mutual funds or similar arrangements, are feasible short-run measures that could make an important qualitative difference in the transformation. Acceptance of foreign participation also seems to be crucial, not least for the required inflow of managerial talent.

A critical complement enterprise reform is the development of an effective and independent financial system, with severance of the intimate relationship between banks and non-financial enterprises, a link that is particularly strong in Yugoslavia and—to a lesser extent—in Hungary. While this proposition is long-term, important regulatory measures can be implemented in the short run to strengthen the system and make the banks more autonomous. Ultimately, however, privatization of the banking system is also required.

The experience of the former German Democratic Republic, which is undergoing the most radical and fastest transformation, warrants careful study. However, its conditions are hardly replicable, as other countries lack external support, including direct investment and technical assistance, of comparable magnitude.

Rapid adjustment and transformation have become even more urgent with the impending change in the CMEA trade arrangements toward convertible currency and international prices and the most recent oil price shock. Both events represent a shock on the order of 5 percent of GDP for the Central and Eastern European countries (excluding the USSR). While some additional external financing may become available, additional domestic adjustment is also required.

In summary, all the countries should accelerate their structural transformation to take advantage of the uniquely favorable environment at this historical moment. The World Bank's support through SALs is built on strong conditionality to steer the process in the desirable direction at the appropriate pace. It cannot, however, substitute for the governments' commitment and implementation capacity. In addition, an adequate attack on the root causes of the financial indiscipline and inefficiency is critical: failure to launch one has been a main reason for the failure of past reform efforts. The relative newcomers to economic reform such as Czechoslovakia, Bulgaria, Romania and the USSR should carefully study failed attempts at reform in other countries and apply those lessons in designing and launching their own transformation programs in the most comprehensive way and at the fastest possible pace.

Notes

1. The discussion is based on information available through the middle of 1990. Thus, it is too early in all cases to judge program implementation and actual performance, although some weaknesses in program design and implementation have already surfaced and are mentioned.

References

Adam, J. 1984. *Employment and Wage Policies in Poland, Czechoslovakia and Hungary Since 1950*. New York: St. Martin's Press.

Aslund, Anders. 1990. "Systemic Change in Eastern Europe and East-West Trade." European Free Trade Association (EFTA) Occasional Paper No. 31. Geneva. June.

Brus, Wlodzimierz, and Kazimierz Laski. 1989. *From Marx to the Market. Socialism in Search of an Economic System*. Oxford: Clarendon Press.

Corbo, Vittorio, and Stanley Fischer. 1990. "Adjustment Programs and Bank Support, Rationale and Main Results." Mimeo. World Bank. Washington, D.C. August.

Coricelli, F., and R. Rocha. 1990. "Tax Reform in Socialist Countries: A note on the main issues." Country Economic Department, Macroeconomic and Growth Division (CECMG). World Bank. Washington, D.C.

Douglas, Roger. 1990. "A Brief Account of New Zealand's Evolving Economy." *The United States-New Zealand Council Quarterly Report* (Washington, D.C.) (Summer).

Gomulka, S., and J. Rostowski. 1988. "An International Comparison of Material Intensity." *Journal of Comparative Economics* 12.

Hinds, Manuel. 1990 . "Issues in the Introduction of Market Forces in Eastern European Socialist Economies." World Bank, Europe, Middle East and North Africa Region (EMENA) Discussion Papers. Washington, D.C.

Institute of International Finance. 1990. "Building Free Market Economies in Central and Eastern Europe. Challenges and Realities." Washington, D.C. April.

Kornai, Janos. 1990. *The Road to a Free Economy. Shifting from a Socialist System. The Example of Hungary*. New York and London: Norton.

Mencinger, J. 1989. "Economic Reform and Unemployment." *Privrendna kretanja Jugoslavije* 19 (March).

Milanovic, Branko. 1989. *Liberalization and Entrepreneurship. Dynamics of Reform in Socialism and Capitalism*. Armonk and London: Sharpe.

World Bank. 1990a. *Adjustment Lending: Policies for Sustainable Growth*. Policy and Research Series #14. Washington, D.C.: World Bank.

_____. 1990b. *World Development Report* 1990. Baltimore, Md.: Johns Hopkins University Press.

_____.1990c. *World Tables, 1988-89*. Washington, D.C.: World Bank.

Yugoslavia. Various issues. *Yugoslavia Statistical Survey*. Belgrade: Research Department, National Bank of Yugoslavia.

5

Comments on "World Bank Adjustment Lending in Central and Eastern Europe," by Ulrich R.W. Thumm

Miroslav Hrncir

Just one decade has passed since the World Bank introduced its program of structural adjustment lending. Ten years ago the growing pressures of external indebtedness that resulted from the profoundly changing conditions in the world economy and the failure of development policies in a number of developing countries prompted the World Bank to initiate this program as a more policy-oriented and comprehensive approach to addressing the evolving challenges, in addition to its traditional project-type programs. Ten years later, toward the end of the 1980s, dramatic socio-political changes are taking place in the countries of Central and Eastern Europe, as they endeavor to transform their economies into market-type ones.

What role should the World Bank play in that transformation? Are the experiences with and lessons from adjustment lending in other parts of the world relevant and applicable? What are the common grounds and what are the basic differences in both given conditions and the aims being followed?

The paper presented by Ulrich R.W. Thumm provides a comprehensive analysis of the relevant issues. From the perspective of an observer living in Central Europe, the paper succeeds in identifying and evaluating the conditions and factors calling for structural adjustment lending.

The comments made here focus on three issues specifically. The first concerns the *substance of the transition* being undertaken by the previously centrally planned economies. The paper makes the valid point that its dimensions and goals are far more complex and, consequently, more demanding than has been the case in other parts of the world. Their transition is unique in the sense that it requires a *total change in their economic and social regimes*. The aim in the transition of the economies of Central and Eastern Europe is not only to stabilize, deregulate and liberalize, as was the case in countries where government intervention had been ex-

tensive, such as Spain or Chile several years ago. It also requires simultaneous *basic institutional and systemic changes*. Market agents proper and the entire framework of market institutions need to be created in the course of mass privatization. The result will be a corresponding change in behavior patterns and social values. The relevant issue is thus a *substitution of the existing system*, and not its reform. The concept of reform that involves changing only some of the elements of the given system does not, therefore, seem relevant any more.

Experience with and evaluation of this type of transition have been limited. Not surprisingly, there is no established theory. Considerable knowledge has, however, gradually been accumulated that perhaps represents a rudimentary stage of theory. The analysis presented in the paper suggests a number of relevant conclusions in that respect:

- all the transition programs surveyed in the paper (those of Yugoslavia, Hungary and Poland) aim at implementing comprehensive sets of measures that should guarantee achievement of the desired *qualitative change*. The scope of these sets of measures suggests that the governments are trying to avoid the shortcomings and constraints of the partial approaches to reform pursued in the past.

- macroeconomic stabilization is treated as a *necessary precondition* for the implementation of institutional and systemic changes and the development and efficient functioning of markets.

All the programs are trying to combine the traditional stabilization policies of demand management (through restrictive fiscal, monetary and credit policies) with less orthodox policies on the regulation of wages and personal income, as well as deliberate policies of restructuring and promotion of a supply-side response. This heterodox approach is expected to be more productive, particularly given the conditions with which the countries are starting their reform (monopolistic structure, rigidities and low transparency within the domestic economy, clear property rights, which mostly are still lacking, lax financial discipline and low responsiveness of enterprises to indirect policy measures). Under the circumstances, traditional demand management is likely to be only partly relevant and/or rather costly in terms of the level of economic activity, employment and real wages.

The income and employment levels at which the trade-offs among the various policy objectives will be achieved are thus conditioned on the outcome of both the restrictive measures on the demand side and the policies on the supply side and on the restructuring. Achieving a proper balance between them in the reform packages is likely to be key to the success of the stabilization efforts in the medium and longer terms. At the same time, the transition to a market-type economy requires a multi-dimensional approach, with stabilization policies being just one element. The other interrelated components of a transition package are institutional and systemic changes and policies for restructuring and social adjustment, including the creation of social safety nets and changes in the social values pursued.

The paper shows that, despite the different initial conditions in both the economic and socio-political spheres, the adjustment programs of Yugoslavia, Hungary and Poland are more or less the same. More precisely, they *share the same aims and components*, even if the relative weights attached to them vary.

The multi-dimensional character of the transition implies that *proper timing and sequencing of the various policy steps* as well as *differential time horizons* are issues. The paper does not elaborate on this point. It is therefore important to distinguish here between stabilization measures that can be introduced in one stroke (and shock therapy is an option for the three countries) and those that involve institutional and systemic changes that could become effective only over a certain time horizon. The same applies to changes in social attitudes and values.

The second point refers to the *relation between common principles in the transition processes and country-specific conditions and factors*. In emphasizing the common features of the transitions in the previously centrally planned economies, it is important not to generalize too much. The unique conditions of each country must always be borne in mind. These conditions must be identified and accounted for if the economic and social policies for the transition are to be as feasible and efficient as possible.

The paper discusses the Yugoslav, Hungarian and Polish cases extensively. Czechoslovakia, because it re-

gained its membership in the International Monetary Fund (IMF) and World Bank only in September 1990, is not addressed in detail. The initial macroeconomic conditions in Czechoslovakia appear to be more favorable than those of the other countries examined, particularly with respect to two points: so far, Czechoslovakia has maintained a considerable degree of domestic macroeconomic stability; and it has a relatively low level of foreign debt. These factors are often claimed as Czechoslovakia's comparative advantages. As a result, its stabilization policies do not have to cope with galloping inflation, as was the case in Yugoslavia and Poland. Rather, the task is to avoid such inflation during the transition.

On the other hand, Czechoslovakia's rate of growth has been declining over a longer period than in the other countries—signs of stagflation emerged in the 1980s (when hidden and repressed inflation is accounted for), as did a fall-off in its share of exports to the world markets. Thus, it was maintaining macroeconomic stability at the cost of the future. The high "internal" debt it incurred is manifest in the obsolete capital stock, neglected infrastructure and environmental needs. A disproportionate emphasis on heavy industry and a one-sided orientation toward trade within the Council on Mutual Economic Assistance (CMEA) region contributed to structural rigidities and a low capacity to adjust to the changing pattern of demand. As is rightly stated in the paper, Czechoslovakia is an example of "regressive specialization" : over time it replaced higher value-added exports with lower ones, such as raw materials and intermediate products.

Another point is that the institutional and socio-political framework of Czechoslovakia has corresponded more closely to the traditional type of centrally planned economy than was true in the reforming economies of Hungary and Poland, even toward the end of the 1980s.

Another problem specific to Czechoslovakia is that the external shocks such as the considerable increase in oil prices and the collapse of the CMEA institutions and regional trade coincided with the introduction of a set of measures aimed at deregulating and liberalizing the pricing and foreign exchange regimes, reforms that should represent a turning point on the road to a market economy (including the "internal" convertibility of currency, i.e., current account transactions of residents).

These factors and conditions should be reflected in both the plan Czechoslovakia adopts for its transition and the timing and sequencing of its implementation.

The third comment refers to the *role of the World Bank in the transition* of Central and Eastern Europe. The efficiency of any national economy has two key dimensions: efficiency in the allocation of resources in both static and dynamic terms; and the efficiency of resource use, or technical efficiency. The two dimensions are interrelated. However, it seems that what is most critical to the future development of the previously centrally planned economies are *the extent and pace of restructuring, product innovation and technological change*. Here is where the command-type economy proved most detrimental.

However important stabilization policies are to a successful transition, the main task—an even more demanding and prolonged one—is a successful structural adjustment. It requires a *change in the entire regime affecting the behavior of economic agents, including the driving forces and incentives that underlie workable competition and entrepreneurship*. So far the other countries in Central and Eastern Europe have achieved only modest progress with structural adjustment; none is an obvious success story yet. Structural adjustment is, however, a necessary precondition for sustained growth and development.

The structural adjustment lending of the World Bank should help the countries of Central and Eastern Europe cope with the problems of transition from the very beginning of their efforts. Given the rather distorted data base and low level of transparency of the economies, one issue for the Bank is what criteria it should use to assess the success of its activities in this area. The relevant criterion should be the real contribution of structural ad-

justment lending to the achievement of the goals and priorities being pursued, that is, the extent to which it contributes to the pace of the reforms and to the adoption of measures that would not otherwise be implemented. Such a hypothetical evaluation is, however, very ambitious and perhaps not even viable, especially in connection with the evaluation of policy and institutional changes linked to structural adjustment lending.

A possible option is to look at the degree to which countries have implemented the structural adjustment measures agreed to, including the time horizon of implementation. An alternative criterion is to assess the extent to which the Bank has proceeded efficiently, given its mandate, that is, the amount of resources it has disbursed in light of conditions in a particular country.

At the same time, there is merit to the view expressed in the paper that structural adjustment lending should be accompanied by, or even better preceded by, elimination of the major distortionary factors, particularly through the liberalization of prices and foreign exchange and through tax reform. The World Bank should support those measures. However, ultimately their implementation and the credibility of the effort are the responsibility of the governments of Central and Eastern Europe.

6

Comments on "World Bank–Supported Adjustment Programs: Lessons for Central and Eastern Europe," by Vittorio Corbo and "World Bank Support for Adjustment Lending in Central and Eastern Europe" by Ulrich R.W. Thumm

Stanislaw Gomulka

The paper by Vittorio Corbo discusses the World Bank's vast non-European experience with adjustment lending in terms of policy objectives and actual economic impact. The paper by Ulrich Thumm concentrates on the Bank's policies for Eastern and Central Europe, taking into account the specific systemic features of the post-Communist economies. Both papers provide excellent analyses of significant value to policy-makers. The comments made here are limited to selected economic points and a few policy implications.

The economic competition between the capitalist and socialist systems has centered around the importance of private ownership. In the absence of a convincing economic theory, the competition had to be settled by a practical test, whose outcome is now clear. However, understanding of the precise reasons for the failure of economies based on non-private ownership to perform well is incomplete. Thumm stresses the inability of central authorities to impose financial discipline on enterprises as the key intermediate reason.[1]

He attributes this poor discipline to lax bankruptcy procedures and subsidized interest rates, both of which are real and distinct features of these economies. However, Thumm himself notes the much improved enforcement of financial discipline in state-owned enterprises under the Polish economic transformation program. The government has achieved this discipline through the withdrawal of tax concessions, a policy of non-negative real interest rates, a drastic reduction in other enterprise subsidies and a clear signal to enterprises that the central bank was withdrawing from its role as lender of last resort.

It can be argued that the credibility of the new policy of a hard budget constraint cannot be sustained for long if public ownership continues. There is, however, little evidence of a markedly improved performance by these enterprises. Nor is there any need to put the policy to a serious test. The original fears that under the new circumstances many enterprises, which together constitute a sizable part of the economy, would face bankruptcy have proved unfounded. Their profit margins, which were already high before 1989, increased considerably in the autumn of 1989 and the spring of 1990. The financial data for the largest 500 Polish enterprises, which together accounted for about 65 percent of industrial output in the years 1983-87, also suggest that most state-owned enterprises are both inefficient and profitable. The loss-making enterprises in those years were concentrated largely in the food processing industry because low (fixed) prices were set for products for social and political reasons.

It is true that financial discipline has been more lax under socialism than under capitalism, a systemic feature that must have resulted in efficiency losses. In an exchange with Janos Kornai, the present discussant argued that these losses, and not shortages, have been the major effect of the soft budget constraint (Gomulka 1986, chapter 5). However, this source of inefficiency, given the evidence of good profitability, must have been weaker than the other ownership-related sources of inefficiency. Thumm himself notes the presence of ineffective enterprise management and insufficiently rigorous exercise of ownership rights by the state. This point can be taken further, with emphasis on the lack of sufficient motivation for bright innovators and entrepreneurial managers to perform exceptionally well as a key factor; their efforts would be wasted or socialized. In the absence of such efforts, the competitive pressures and associated threats to income are low even if the number of enterprises were large, which it has not been. It therefore seems that the primary reason the socialist economies have been and are inefficient is precisely this lack of strong positive and negative incentives to do well.[2]

Corbo notes that the origin of the World Bank's increased effort to promote structural adjustment dates back to the oil price shocks of 1973 and 1979. These were externally imposed shocks with negative balance-of-payments implications. The main purpose of the World Bank's involvement has been to help eliminate the balance-of-payments problems through structural adjustment. The economic circumstances of Eastern and Central Europe are, however, quite difficult. In both Poland and Yugoslavia the shocks were internally and deliberately imposed. The World Bank's structural adjustment loans (SALs) came after the introduction of the programs sponsored by the International Monetary Fund (IMF), which were intended rapidly to create a stable macroeconomic environment and a properly functioning price system. These programs produced recessions and therefore balance-of-trade surpluses. Moreover, the World Bank's SAL negotiators typically suggest that governments undertake further rapid price liberalization and complete elimination of subsidies.

The countries of Central and Eastern Europe would like to proceed with these measures, and to do so with considerable speed. However, it should be recognized that price adjustments will have an additional recessionary and inflationary impact. The upshot is that because in Central and Eastern Europe the SAL comes during a deep recession and improved external position, it is difficult to justify on its own terms as a balance-of-payments support program.

Put simply, the structural adjustment problem in Central and Eastern Europe is much different in origin and larger in size than the problems the founders of the World Bank's lending policy had in mind. These differences in circumstances call for a change in the standard objectives and performance criteria, and perhaps also for a lengthening of the period within which these objectives are to be implemented.

Notes

1. Essentially Thumm says the poor performance of enterprises in Poland, as well as in other socialist economies is the result of lax financial discipline, that is, easy access to subsidized bank credit that originated at the printing presses of the central bank. Budget deficits and massive printing of money have only recently become major features of socialist economies.

2. For a detailed discussion of the poor environment for innovation under socialism see, among others, Balcerowicz (1990), Hanson and Pavitt (1987) and Gomulka (1990, chapter 7).

References

Balcerowicz, L. 1990. "The Soviet Type Economic System, Reformed Systems and Innovativeness." *Communist Economies* 2 (1).

Gomulka, S. 1986. *Innovation, Growth and Reform in Eastern Europe*. Madison, Wisc.: Wisconsin University Press.

————. 1990. *The Theory of Technological Change and Economic Growth*. London and New York: Routledge.

Hanson, P., and K. Pavitt. 1987. *The Comparative Economics of Research Development and Innovation in East and West: A Survey*. Cambridge, Mass.: Harvard Academic Publishers.

Part III

Speed of Adjustment and Sequencing of Policy Changes

7

Issues in the Reform of Socialist Economies

Stanley Fischer and Alan Gelb[1]

The formidable challenges facing the reforming European socialist economies are frequently said to be unique. In fact, most of the individual requirements for their reform have been faced before in China and in Latin American and African countries where the combination of a weak private sector, political monopoly, extensive policy-induced distortions and macroeconomic imbalance is not uncommon. There are also lessons to be drawn from the earlier reform experiences of Yugoslavia and Hungary. Nonetheless, the challenge *is* unique in its system-wide scope, its political and historical context and required speed of the reform.

Few socialist countries remain as unreformed planned economies. In the last decade several—for example, China—have instituted some economic reforms while still trying to preserve the state's monopolies over political power, the savings-investment process and social ownership. However, countries such as Hungary, Poland, Czechoslovakia and Bulgaria—and increasingly the Soviet Union—are seeking to institute fundamental changes that will lead to a pluralist political system, well-defined—and substantially private-property rights and the market-based allocation of resources. By most criteria Yugoslavia should be included here. However, in light of its long history of reform and political independence, and non-membership in the Council for Mutual Economic Assistance (CMEA), it regards itself as—and is—*sui generis*. This paper looks at the reform process in countries that have decided to move from a more or a less planned socialist system to a private market economy, in which private ownership predominates and most resources are allocated through the markets. Such reform demands the creation of management skills and legal, regulatory and infrastructural conditions whose development has been set back by decades of socialist development. It also requires fundamental changes in the role and capabilities of the state.

This paper does not address at any length the close interrelationship between economic and political reform.[2]

However, it is noted that the important strategic choices in the reform arise out of the interplay of economics and politics: technocratic solutions alone will not be sufficient in deciding on the path and speed of reform.

Because the reform is both intertwined with political factors and economically complicated, and because there are substantial differences among the reforming countries, no single detailed road map can guide the way to the new systems. Therefore the paper presents general considerations that provide a framework for reform and discusses the choices that have to be made in light of some initial conditions in the reforming countries. In the metaphor of Vaclav Klaus (1990), the finance minister of Czechoslovakia, undertaking reform is like playing chess: while one needs to know the rules and have a sense of strategy, it is not possible to plan each specific move at the beginning.

Although the interdependence among the reforming socialist countries is also very important, the problems posed by the January 1991 reform of the trade and payments institutions of the CMEA are also not addressed at length.[3]

Initial Conditions

Recent data on the economies of the European socialist economies and the USSR are presented in table 7.1. The estimates of gross national product (GNP), aggregate or per capita, vary widely, depending on the source and the conversion method, and none can be regarded as accurate.[4] The 1988 estimates of the US Central Intelligence Agency (CIA) are well above the rates calculated through the exchange rate, which are more relevant to the borrowing status of actual and potential members of the World Bank.[5]

In any case, income levels in the European socialist economies appear to be above the average in Latin America but well below that in Western Europe. Until recent-

Table 7-1. *Basic Data on East European Economies*

	Albania	Bulgaria	Czech.	Ger. Dem. Rep.	Hungary	Poland	Romania	USSR	Yugoslavia	US	Germany, F.R.
Population, 1987 (millions)	3	9	16	17	11	38	23	283	23	244	61
Area (1,000 sq km)	29	111	128	108	93	313	238	22,402	256	9,373	249
GNP (CIA), 1988 (US$ bil.)	n.a.	68	158	207	92	276	126	2,535	154	4,881	1,206
(% of US per capita)	n.a.	38	51	63	44	37	2,852	33	n.a.	n.a.	n.a.
GNP (exchange rate estimates), 1988 (% of US per capita)	n.a.	13	18	45	13	9	16	19	11	100	n.a.
GDP physical indicators, 1980 (% of US per capita)	n.a.	30	42	45	32	27	21	n.a.	22	100	n.a.
Bal. of payments, 1989 (US$ bil.)	n.a.	-1.1	-0.1	0.7	-0.7	-1.3	2.1	0.1	1.5	-115	60
Hard currency debt, 1989 (US$ bil.)	n.a.	5.5	4.0	10.0	15.4	35.6	0.8	30.5	17.7	n.a.	n.a.
Life expectancy at birth, late 1980s (years)	72	72	71	73	70	71	70	69	71	75	75
Infant mortality rate, late 1980s (per thousand)	39	15	13	9	21	24	n.a.	25	24	14	15

n.a. Not available.

Source: GNP (US$ bil.)—United States, Central Intelligence Agency (1989); exchange rate estimates—tentative estimates based in IMF, *International Financial Statistics* data where available and staff estimates in other cases; GDP physical indicators—Erlich (1987, p. 15); and World Bank, *World Development Indicators* and *World Tables* (various issues); Wharton Economic Forecasting (1989); Fink and Havelik (1989).

ly, the former German Democratic Republic (East Germany) was thought to be the most advanced of the European socialist economies, with the CIA (United States, Central Intelligence Agency, 1989) suggesting that per capita income was over 60 percent of the United States' level. A closer look at East Germany has persuaded many that Czechoslovakia has the highest per capita income, followed by Hungary, but this view could change on closer examination of the other countries. Poland and Hungary are heavily indebted in convertible currencies, and Yugoslavia has borrowed intensively.

As measured by their reported Gini coefficients of around 24 (the same as Norway's and a little higher than Sweden's), income is relatively equally distributed in the European socialist economies, whereas the Gini coefficients for the industrial market economies commonly fall in the range 30-35.[6] By international standards, social indicators such as longevity and literacy are high for the income levels of these economies, although there was a relative decline in their social indicators during the past decade and some evidence of recent retrogression.

The European socialist economies experienced similar growth patterns after the immediate post-World War II period. Growth at the extensive margin, based largely on the accumulation of capital through very high investment rates and increasing participation in the labor force, was quite rapid until the seventies, although there was probably less technical progress than in Western Europe. In the late seventies growth gave way to stagnation, worsening shortages and, in some countries, worsening macro-imbalances. By contrast with Western Europe, there was no recovery in the first half of the 1980s.[7] Despite the broad similarities in the structures of the European socialist economies, important differences in their initial conditions will shape their reforms, including:

• the *extent of their macroeconomic imbalances*, both internal and external;

• the degree of the *decentralization of their economic management and extent of the product markets* prevailing before reform of the system begins; and

• the *extent of private sector activity* prior to the reform.

Figure 7.1 depicts the first two initial conditions—macro-imbalances and management decentralization—in seven countries.[8]

Macro-imbalances

Domestic macro-imbalance in a socialist economy can take various forms, from open inflation to the involuntary accumulation of financial claims because of the rationing of acceptable goods and/or the absence of alternative assets (the monetary overhang). Poland probably embarked on reform from the worst macro position, with an overwhelming debt problem and high inflation. Yugoslavia was in better shape on the external side but also suffered from very high inflation and enormous domestic losses in the banking system that threatened macroeconomic stability. The USSR and Bulgaria face major macro-imbalances. Internal disequilibrium appears to be relatively larger in the former, but the burden of foreign debt is much lower,[9] especially if account is taken of its substantial gold reserves. Hungary has the largest external debt per capita and persistent inflation of about 20 percent but a relatively small budget deficit. With low foreign debt and probably only moderate domestic imbalances, Czechoslovakia appears to be in the best macro position. The former East Germany is a special case because it has been reformed out of existence, with the Federal Republic of Germany underwriting its foreign debts and any monetary overhang.

Figure 7-1. *Initial Conditions for Socialist Reform: Degree of Economic Centralization*

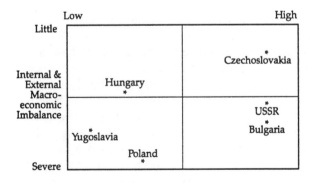

Source: The authors.

The extent and type of macro-imbalances prevailing before the structural reform have an important bearing on the potential speed and design of the reform programs. Although it can be one of the mechanisms for eliminating a monetary overhang, the inflation that accompanies liberalization that is starting from a condition of repressed excess demand is likely to cause serious economic and political difficulties for the reform. Although elimination of the monetary overhang should in principle be possible with a one-time change in the level of prices, rising prices may accentuate the flow disequilibrium by worsening the fiscal balance[10]—thus potentially turning what should be a one-time change in the price level into a more persistent increase in the rate of inflation. High open inflation has to be eliminated for the structural reforms to be effective. Eliminating excess demand is also important for microeconomic reasons: studies of firms in socialist countries suggest that a shift from sellers' markets to buyers' markets is essential to modifying the efficiency and customer orientation of firms.

Countries close to macroeconomic equilibrium have greater latitude to implement those institutional reforms most needed to support the operation of markets before switching over to market mechanisms.[11] Those countries needing urgent stabilization face difficult decisions relative to the sequencing of the stabilization measures (which in the past have typically involved a tightening of controls) and structural reforms leading to a market system.

Markets and Decentralization

Turning to the other axis in figure 7.1, at the start of 1990 Czechoslovakia, East Germany, the Soviet Union and Bulgaria had relatively centralized economies, with a planned system for the supply of materials playing a major role and with enterprise management subject to constant intervention by the ministries.[12] In contrast, Yugoslavia has long been the most decentralized of the socialist countries, with Hungary (since 1968) and Poland progressively moving the distribution of products toward a market basis—although with distorted prices—and according greater autonomy to firms.[13]

With only limited private ownership permitted, decentralization has resulted in self-management of the social or state capital within firms. In addition to the dominant role of the self-managed sector in Yugoslavia, some 70 percent of Hungarian and Polish firms are self-managed.

"Socialism without planning" has distinctive characteristics that have been extensively analyzed. These include a lack of effective balance-sheet constraints on firms because of the "absence" of effective owners and the extensive fiscal redistribution among enterprises, largely motivated by a commitment to full employment effected through the preservation of jobs. This lack of constraints adversely affects incentives and has resulted in chronic scarcities, impelled by a combination of expansionist management unconstrained by considerations of profitability and workers seeking higher pay without fear of layoffs and unemployment.[14] Subsidies divorce incomes from productivity.[15] Relative prices are also divorced from world patterns, with energy, transportation and state rents normally far below world levels, credit cheap and staple foods subsidized. Taxes and subsidies insulate the domestic prices of traded commodities from their world levels.

One symptom of the distorted initial positions from which the European socialist economies are embarking on market reforms is that the market socialist banking system, although superficially transformed from the mono-bank of the centralized system, has no basis for allocating credit according to market criteria and for identifying and pricing risk. In this situation, the allocation of credit is indeterminate, being set neither by plan nor by market. Avoiding severe macroeconomic imbalances in such a system is extremely difficult, essentially because the economic agents have autonomy without responsibility.

Decentralization may reflect a deliberate policy decision to relax central planning in an attempt to gain advantages from market organization without confronting the ideologically difficult issue of ownership and the technically difficult issues involved in transformation into a private market economy. Alternatively, it may result from a power vacuum following a decline in the legitimacy of the government or from a change in government.[16] In many respects, a decentralized socialist economy starts the transition to a private market economy with advantages over its more planned counterpart. Agents are more familiar with the markets, and their response to market incentives is therefore likely to be faster. In addition, as indicated in table 7.1, a larger share of the exports of the less centralized countries goes to countries outside the CMEA area and is thus subject to global competition. Firms in these countries are more likely to have had commercial dealings with foreign firms than are firms in centrally planned systems and are more likely to have had some exposure to the real needs of clients. Especially in light of the depressed condition of CMEA members, the ability to increase exports rapidly to Western markets will be an important determinant of the speed with which the reform can produce results.

On the negative side, reformers of a decentralized economy must address the problem of rendering power-

ful and previously relatively independent firms accountable, whether to the market (by reducing the cross-subsidies and/or offering firms the opportunity to privatize themselves) or directly (by asserting the state's ownership rights and recentralizing decision-making). Removing acquired rights is not easy, especially since the shift toward representative democracy requires maintaining a reasonable degree of consensus.

Together with measures to limit serious abuses from spontaneous privatizations,[17] a blend of carrot and stick is in practice evolving in the reforming countries to deal with decentralized firms that are not yet privatized. The carrots, such as exemption from the wage curbs applied to socially-owned firms and cheap shares for employees, appeal to those in potentially profitable firms. Sticks, such as bankruptcy and dissolution of the worker council if debts, dividends or the annual fee for the state's capital are not paid, threaten the loss-making ones.[18]

Assuming that opposition from its ministries has been overcome, a reforming centralized economy can consider and implement a wider range of options for addressing the ownership and management issues.[19] Despite this advantage, it is unlikely that such economies face an easier transition. On the contrary, their greater distance from a market configuration probably implies more difficulty in reshaping institutions and acquiring the necessary skills.

One important question for a still centralized economy is whether to pass through the stage of market socialism prior to reforming to a private market economy. As this approach would involve first giving ownership rights to the workers and then reclaiming those rights, it is a most undesirable path for reform. Accordingly, an economy starting out from a centralized system should make great efforts to prevent firms' managers and workers from assuming the ownership rights in an early phase of the reform. The government can do so by defining the ownership rights clearly and assigning them as rapidly as possible to agents or institutions outside the enterprises.[20]

The Pre-Reform Scope of the Private Sector

Most of the European socialist economies have for some time codified certain private property rights. However, their private sectors are relatively small (almost zero in Czechoslovakia) and comprise largely crafts and distributive trades.[21] In some cases agriculture is substantially private (75 percent in Poland, whereas agricultural production in Bulgaria is dominated by a few public conglomerates).[22] In certain other socialist countries the private sector is far larger than in the European socialist economies: for example, it accounts for about one-half of the economic activity in Vietnam. Because it is easier to relax restrictions on an existing private sector than to attempt to create a new one from scratch, countries with substantial private sector activity and a private asset base enter into the reform with a notable advantage. The strategy of first empowering the private sector and then progressively reforming the public sector and relying on the private sector to absorb laid-off employees is more viable the larger the initial private sector is.

Elements of Reform

The move to a full market economy requires political changes that recognize the value of diversity and individual initiative and that require a substantial social and political consensus. This consensus seems to exist in Poland, Hungary and Czechoslovakia but is not present in Romania or probably in the Soviet Union. Reform of the economic system also requires fundamental changes in the role and organization of government. It means countless changes in economic structure and behavior. The nature of those changes can be understood by comparing the working of the European socialist economies with those of the more advanced market countries. Table

7.2, which classifies the needed changes, summarizes the discussion of these changes, which follows. The issue of sequencing is discussed in the following section.

Macroeconomic Stabilization and Control

Some analysts, notably Hinds (1990), have raised the question of whether macroeconomic stabilization is possible in a socialist system, or whether it requires a reform of property rights with a clear definition of ownership. Following the recent experiences of Poland and Yugoslavia (as well as considering the measures used to stabilize market countries with large public sectors), it is reasonable to assert that a tightening of the fiscal and credit policies reduces inflation and the current account deficit in socialist as well as in market economies.

However, there are some differences, which are a reflection of the different microeconomic incentive structures in the two systems. As socialist firms know no bottom line, stabilization policies cannot rely on the same responses as those in a market economy. For example, rising interest rates may encourage households to accumulate financial assets, but firms may simply refi-

Table 7-2. *Economic Elements of System Reform*

1.	*Macroeconomic stabilization and control*
	Implementation of stabilization programs
	Creation of tools and institutions for indirect macroeconomic control, monetary and fiscal
	Measures to harden the budget constraints
	Dealing with existing problems (monetary overhang, financial system, bankruptcies)
1a.	*Social safety nets* (at first on an emergency basis)
2.	*Institutional reforms: Human capital and administrative capacity*
	Legal and regulatory institutions
	Business management, including financial sector
	Government decision-makers and administrators
	Information systems (accounting and auditing)
3.	*Price and market reform*
	Domestic price reform
	International trade liberalization
	Distribution systems for products
	Creation of market for housing
	Wages
	Interest rates
4.	*Small- and large-scale enterprise restructuring and privatization*
	Management systems
	Allocation of property rights
	Agricultural land
	Industrial capital
	Housing stock
	Social protection and insurance rights for individuals
5.	*Development of financial markets and institutions*
	Banking systems
	Other financial markets

Source: The authors.

nance the growing interest charges in a giant Ponzi scheme that initially delays reform and then renders it extremely costly. A range of direct controls will therefore be needed to reinforce the indirect measures. These can include: the elimination of ex post subsidies for individual firms and the setting of strict cash limits on them; direct central bank control over the quantity of credit; and controls over public sector wages. Until bankruptcy becomes a credible threat, the proliferation of arrears on inter-firm payments could undermine the control of credit, especially because socialist firms tend to be closely linked in oligopolistic interdependencies.[23] In the face of an inefficient banking system, inter-enterprise credit can play a useful role in facilitating adjustment to rapidly changing circumstances, but the volume and distribution must be monitored, just as with bank credit.[24]

The longer run success of macroeconomic tightening depends on the political resolve and economic skill of the government, which is bound to come under severe pressure when firms run into financial trouble. A skilled government will already be working out criteria and methods for the restructuring of enterprises. It will also have to institute measures—the *social safety net*—to protect the living standards of those adversely affected by the economic reforms. In particular, because job losses are likely to prove the most traumatic consequence of reorganization in economies that have not previously known open unemployment, it is essential that a social safety net for the unemployed be included in the planning of any stabilization cum reform program. In the beginning, measures will have to be instituted on an emergency basis because the European socialist economies have no administrative structures for dealing with open unemployment. Over the longer run, a more complete social safety net will have to be developed.[25]

In addition to measures to discipline firms and address unemployment, *fiscal reforms* must have a high priority. With tax revenues highly dependent on remittances of profits from enterprises, measures to increase their financial autonomy and at the same time absorb the losses that result from restructuring are likely to have a serious impact on the budget. Revenues from privatization are likely to become significant only in the medium term, even if privatization itself is accelerated; increased revenues from privatization and greater efficiency are likely to lead to a lag in the increased costs associated with the restructuring. Because of the uncertain size of any particular tax base in the turbulent reform environment, there are arguments for raising revenues as broadly as possible, subject to the problems posed by inadequate accounting, auditing and enforcement.

Since governments will in the longer term have to maintain macroeconomic control through the indirect levers employed in modern market economies, reform of the fiscal and financial sectors, with a broader perspective than the immediate macroeconomic balance, has to be initiated. This reform is essential to increase the efficiency of the economy and to complement the enterprise restructuring that will result in firms responding to market and interest rate signals. Such responses will not be efficient unless prices are themselves rational—and as discussed below, it may not be possible or desirable to impose tight budget constraints on firms without rational prices. This point illustrates the complementarity among the elements of policy and structural changes and the need (see below) to undertake certain reforms simultaneously.

Estimates of the extent of the monetary overhang vary; it is difficult to evaluate in the absence of most other stores of value. It seems to be significant in the USSR (estimates place it at about one-half of the financial assets held by households) and may exist in some of the smaller countries.

There are several broad options for eliminating the overhang without drawing on foreign exchange reserves or foreign borrowing: a currency reform that freezes or eliminates financial balances above certain levels;[26] reliance on inflation, with incomplete compensation by interest rates; an increase in interest rates on existing assets or introduction of new, higher return assets; and the sale of state assets to the public.

A confiscatory fiscal reform is problematic, especially in the context of a reform aiming to secure private property rights, but can possibly be justified politically as the result of the mistakes of the previous governments and the dubious nature of the activities that allowed individuals to accumulate private wealth. Poland and Yugoslavia in effect took the inflationary route at the end of 1989. However, it is inadvisable that it be taken after the adjustment has started, as it imposes high costs of its own. Raising interest rates on existing assets, such as saving accounts, will help reduce the inflationary pressure from the current overhang (in the case of the USSR, most estimates suggest that raising interest rates to normal levels would not be sufficient to eliminate the overhang).

There are strong arguments for the sale of public assets, especially since this approach can be made consistent with the goal of strengthening the small-scale private sector. The sale of small enterprises and premises for businesses and retail shops is one example. Sale of the housing stock is another, although this action would need accompanying measures to raise the cost and reduce the security of renting, and these, in turn, would require the adjustment of pay levels to reflect the higher rents. Because rents are usually far below maintenance costs, even giving housing away would improve the budget on a flow basis. At the same time, it has to be recognized that privatization is likely to be slow. One possible strategy—it has not yet been used in the European socialist economies—is to combine currency reform with the sale of assets. Asset holdings above a certain level can be frozen and their subsequent use permitted to purchase assets that are being privatized.

Consider now the external balance. Especially once measures are taken to harden the budget constraints and restrain domestic demand, changes in the exchange rate should be effective in switching expenditures and output in the socialist economies, provided that a price reform creates a link between the world and domestic prices for tradables. However, again the distinctive institutional arrangements of the European socialist economies constrain the likely response. Over half the exports of the European socialist economies go to countries in the CMEA system. Many of these products are not of adequate quality and appeal to be acceptable in the world markets. Within the unreformed CMEA system, trade flows were arranged through inter-government protocols rather than being responsive to relative prices.

Except for the USSR (which exports hard currency commodities), the imminent comprehensive reform of the CMEA system toward multilateral, market-based trading (which is a logical complement to the internal reforms) raises the problem that each reforming country's exports must compete in previously sheltered markets with superior products from the West. Reforms in one socialist country as well as in the trading system can render more difficult the short-run task of maintaining an external balance in the other reforming countries. Indeed, exports from certain small European socialist economies to the West could actually *fall* because of the need to divert world-quality products to the USSR to pay for essential imports of fuels and raw materials. In the longer run, however, reform of the CMEA system will have a positive effect on the economies of its members—and certain countries, notably Hungary, have already demonstrated their ability to increase exports to the West quite rapidly.

In sum, stabilization measures involving a combination of controls on aggregates and specific interventions can be effective. However, given their economic rigidities, narrow markets and small convertible currency trade ratios, the response of socialist systems to reductions in expenditures and switching measures is likely to be less rapid and more costly in terms of output than is typical in market economies. Further, the cost of reform is likely to be raised by the simultaneous reforms in the other European socialist economies as a result of the disruption and loss of protected markets.

Institutional and Complementary Reforms

Institutions and professions that are taken for granted in market economies have to be re-created in the reforming socialist economies. Legal, regulatory and information systems need to be reformed to support the markets.[27]

A secure legal environment has to be created for the protection of property rights and the regulation of commercial relations. Accounting and audit systems are needed to organize and monitor information. Needed to complement those reforms are investments in human capital in areas such as accounting, credit and market analysis, and bank inspection. Management skills have to be upgraded and modernized, especially in finance and marketing. In some areas such as financial markets, reform may require a greater role for the state than before.

When assessing the efforts underway to change the legal and regulatory institutions in reforming socialist countries rapidly, it must be remembered that those in market economies have evolved over centuries. Such reforms and the creation of the human capital appropriate to a new system are lengthy processes that constrain the efficiency and speed of reform.[28] They also constitute an area in which foreign assistance may be especially useful in the transition.

Price and Market Reform

Given the mutual interdependence of prices and their sheer number (some 25 million in the planned Soviet economy), the process of moving to a more rational set of prices could be highly complex and extended. Fortunately, the rational price system needed for increased enterprise autonomy to make sense is known: it is world prices. The best way to introduce rational prices is to open the economy to foreign trade. An open trade (and current payments) policy also exposes domestic producers to foreign competition and offers the prospect of more rapid increases in the quality of products through a range of licensing, processing, marketing and other joint-venture arrangements with foreign firms. This route is certainly available to the European socialist economies, which will become more open as they reform and which can expect considerable growth in trade (especially intra-industry trade) with the market economies.[29]

The Polish government's move to current account convertibility (at a heavily depreciated exchange rate) should thus be seen not only as a way to improve the current account, but more importantly as an essential and immediate move to a rational price system that helps force competition. In practice, some price-distorting tariffs will remain—uniform tariffs can be justified as a source of fiscal revenue—and realistically the governments of the reforming European socialist economies are no more likely to move immediately to undistorted trade than are other governments. Nonetheless, world relative prices are the right reference point.

Trade and domestic reforms are mutually dependent. Domestic deregulation of agriculture, industry and services and reform of enterprises have to take place if firms are to respond appropriately to price signals. Some analysts (Nuti 1990) seem to argue for liberalizing the internal markets and reforming administered prices before liberalizing international trade. Such reforms are more likely to succeed if an appropriate price system is already in place, and liberalized trade can be an important element in producing such a price system.

Price liberalization is also necessary for the credible long-term hardening of the budget constraints. Until prices are rational, profits and losses are not necessarily good indicators of efficiency and are therefore not good guides for decisions on which firms should be closed and which should obtain financing for increased investment. Closing a firm whose output price is being held below its social value is not necessarily the optimal response to its financial losses. Firms cannot easily be held accountable for their profitability if the government sets their prices.

Because of past patterns of industrial organization, additional measures may be required to develop competitive markets. These are likely to include active and early demonopolization of the transport, distribution and trade systems. They may involve the break-up of large conglomerates that evolved not in response to market imperatives, but to reduce the problems of control and to secure inputs often in shortage under the socialist system. Although demonopolization is needed, it should be approached from an international perspective, especially in a small country. As a method of enhancing competition, the opening up of trade is likely to be preferable to fragmenting firms to achieve competition in the domestic market.

So far, this paper has considered only product prices and markets. However, the creation of factor markets and the liberalization of factor prices are also important, and they are discussed later.

Enterprise Reform

Enterprise reform—in all sectors, not just industry—is the heart of the transformation. As in all areas, this process requires interrelated changes: the imposition of bottom line discipline; definition and change of ownership; and reform of management arrangements.

The ownership issue is a political minefield: workers in worker-managed firms believe they have substantial claims on the firms; while insider sales of firms by and to former managers and bureaucrats (spontaneous privatizations) create inequities. How to respond to such sales, which are likely to be the first response to liberalized regulations, is an important policy question for governments. Political opposition to the initial bursts of spontaneous privatization in Hungary and Poland resulted in their suspension and a lull in privatization activity in those countries. Sales of firms before their value can be determined through a realistic price system are likely to be inequitable ex post, and nationalist sentiment in all countries will put some limits on the role of foreign ownership.[30] The ownership of agricultural land poses another set of politically charged issues.

Corporatization, which involves a change in the status of a firm into a joint-stock or other corporate form, is normally the first stage of enterprise reform. However, restructuring and privatization are the two real phases. Opinions on which should come first differ. Proponents of *slow privatization* argue that firms should be sold off gradually after restructuring, when there is a more rational price system, the new rules of economic behavior have begun to emerge and a real business class has had time to develop to exercise the ownership function. The prices of firms will be more realistic and the sales process more equitable, both because the new owners will pay the right prices and because the government will obtain more revenue. The privatization in Great Britain is cited as evidence supporting this approach. Proponents also point to the need for "real owners"—private agents with a long-term view and sufficient equity in a given firm to encourage them to play an active role and to give them a strong measure of control. They also suggest that *premature privatization* may unnecessarily create interest groups of shareholders who object to the removal of distortions, such as subsidies, which has an adverse impact on the value of their assets.

Supporters of *fast privatization* argue that more comprehensive and rapid ownership reform is necessary to increase efficiency.[31] A further argument is political. Without the power of a substantial capitalist class behind it—and it is agreed that such a class will not emerge rapidly—the reform will surely be subverted and prematurely terminated by the interest groups representing adversely affected segments of society, such as potentially laid-off workers and redundant bureaucrats. Reform must be radical and fast-moving to deny such groups the opportunity to coalesce. It is widely accepted that more rapid privatization reduces the expected total sales revenue to the state; fast privatizers argue, however, that the benefits of a rapid and irreversible shift to private production outweigh the costs of reduced state revenue and that the higher tax revenues from a more efficient economy will offset the loss in revenue from rapid privatization.

A number of schemes have been proposed to achieve the goal of rapid privatization in an equitable and politically acceptable fashion, and in doing so to overcome the problem posed by the uncertainty of asset valuation. The schemes typically involve creating shares in the companies and distributing them broadly within the country. Since most proposals recognize that very dispersed ownership does not provide a basis for effective control, they also include a mechanism to create a dominant shareholder or group of shareholders to monitor the management of the individual companies. Some offer employees preferential access to a block of shares as an efficiency incentive and to render the process acceptable to them.

Two approaches can be considered:

(1) create holding companies or unit trusts to be the dominant shareholders, sufficient in number to ensure competition among them. The state can retain a block of shares for later sale or distribution to citizens, a measure that would ensure that the public participates in the benefits of privatization. The government can also offer citizens shares in the holding companies, so that they have an opportunity for diversified portfolios. The difficulty is to ensure that the dominant shareholders operate like private owners, which they are not (unless they consist of foreign owners who have sufficient wealth to buy the shares). There is also a risk that privatization may stall at some intermediate stage.

(2) distribute the shares in each enterprise equally across the population and initiate trading arrangements to enable dominant ownership groups to emerge. Whether an effective ownership group would actually result and whether the large ex post inequities that are likely to arise are acceptable because of ex ante fairness are important questions.[32]

No country has yet implemented schemes of these types, but they are being actively discussed, and implementing legislation has been passed in Czechoslovakia and Poland.[33]

The reforming European socialist economies are likely to adopt a variety of approaches in practice. Consider first firms in potentially competitive sectors, and suppose that price reform and macrostabilization have progressed sufficiently so that reasonable judgments about viability are possible.[34] Small weak firms should be closed and their assets and premises sold off; small stronger firms could be privatized rapidly, possibly being sold to all or some of their employees, with the state of-

fering some seller financing. The state would have to handle the large weak firms, with extensive restructuring needed to move them into the private sector if they are not closed.[35]

The larger firms with potential are the crux of the privatization problem. Many could be privatized relatively rapidly, at least in part. Foreign investors are already active in each country. In some cases they could either take on the role of dominant shareholder (possibly on a temporary basis) or could manage the firm under contract to a domestic holding company. Shares in such firms could be distributed under the schemes discussed above.

Whatever the precise rapid method used, it is likely that state holding companies will play an important ownership role in the transition. Given the scarcity of domestic owners and the undesirability of a fire sale to foreigners, there seems to be no alternative. Some form of holding company structure would likely also be needed under the slow privatization option, as a vehicle through which the state could assert its ownership during the restructuring. In the longer run, the holding companies could be privatized; alternatively they could be converted into pension funds by transferring to them the appropriate liabilities. Foreign management may be a useful intermediate stage; so might foreign ownership, although there are political limits to this option, and it is inappropriate to sell national assets off too cheaply on the basis of very short-term considerations.

In line with European tradition, and considering the regulatory difficulties, natural monopolies should probably not be privatized early on, unless perhaps this action is particularly needed to attract large foreign investments to facilitate restructuring and modernization.

Financial Markets and Institutions

Development of financial markets and private sector financial institutions, including banks, is an essential step in the transition to a market economy and in moving investment decisions away from government control. Many reforming socialist countries have already taken steps in this direction, including moving from a mono-bank to a two-tier banking system. Several of the European socialist economies are also discussing the rapid creation of a stock market. However, there are important differences between enterprise reform and the reform of financial institutions that suggest a need to treat these latter reforms differently.

More so than with other sectors, financial markets depend on underlying legal and informational systems and skills that barely exist in the European socialist economies. Further, the problems with existing loan portfolios, which are very substantial, have to be addressed before a sound banking system can emerge. The loan losses, which originated when the central bank's portfolio was allocated to the commercial banks, will have to be moved off the balance sheets and allocated either to depositors or other lenders or be absorbed by the budget. In addition, the large loan losses that will appear when relative prices and demand patterns shift as a result of the domestic and trade reform will need to be handled similarly. The banks should be recapitalized and expected to function as market institutions only after the economy has settled down sufficiently to enable loan portfolios to be kept reasonably clean. Before then, the proliferation of banking institutions should be constrained and the emphasis on competition in financial markets moderated, although some entry of foreign banks, as participants or managers of domestic institutions, can play an important role.

The differences between banking reform and enterprise reform exist because the condition of the firms determines the state of the banks' portfolios, their earning potential and their equity (assets corrected for expected loan losses less liabilities). If their equity is zero or negative, as is the case in several and possibly all European socialist economies, banks face perverse incentives in mobilizing and allocating credit that lead to viable borrowers being crowded out. If the banks' budget constraint is hardened without restructuring their portfolios, they will attempt to compensate for the high share of non-performing loans by raising charges to paying clients.[36] The latter will face extremely high costs of credit because of large banking spreads. Under such conditions it is likely that mainly firms in potential financial trouble will borrow from the banks.

A truly competitive banking system cannot be expected to emerge before the enterprise restructuring and price reform are substantially under way. This conclusion raises several sequencing issues that are addressed below, including the question of how new firms are to be financed early on in the transition. Other important questions to be considered are the ownership of the banks (they should not be owned by client firms) and whether the banks should have an ownership role as in Germany and Japan. That last point is less important at the start of reform, because the banks have no obvious capability to exert a positive ownership role.

The Sequencing of Reforms

Administrative feasibility alone ensures that not all reforms can be instituted simultaneously. The more fundamental reason for sequencing the reforms is that some changes are preconditions for others: for instance, macroeconomic stabilization is needed if price reform is to be successful. The systems and skills that have to be in place for the markets to work need to be developed. To give an important example, financial liberalization is extremely risky unless a sound system of accounting, auditing, prudential regulation and supervision is in place and unless the macroeconomy is reasonably stable.

The sequencing problem has been extensively studied in the analysis of the structural adjustment of developing economies. While some rules of thumb have emerged,[37] the more important conclusion is that a linear sequence of individual policy changes is not the right approach. The problem is better thought of as one of how to *package* the reforms: the need is to introduce groups of complementary policy reforms sequentially.

The details of the reform path any country will follow depend on the state of the economy, on the tolerance of the population for the disruptions that are sure to accompany the reform and on the political situation. Nonetheless, figure 7.2 presents an outline of a prototype reform for a representative European socialist economy with initial conditions somewhere between those of Poland and Czechoslovakia.

For countries with high inflation and non-sustainable balance-of-payments deficits, macroeconomic stabilization has to be the initial priority. The severity of the program and the range of the accompanying structural reform measures will reflect the extent of the initial imbalances and political judgments about what the population will accept. A new government, or a government with support for radical change, has far more leeway, which it should use, as it is harder to impose tough measures later.

In the extreme case of Poland, the government pursued a stabilization program consistent with a move toward a market system. The program included sharp cuts in firm-specific subsidies and tight credit limits, as well as trade liberalization on a major scale and at a heavily depreciated exchange rate. In high inflation countries, it may be necessary in the initial phase of stabilization to fix the nominal exchange rate to provide a nominal anchor for the price level. It is also necessary to create an emergency safety net that shifts social protection off the shoulders of firms so as to facilitate the allocation of resources, which allocation means, in the case of labor, unemployment.

While initial success in reducing inflation from very high levels can be achieved within a few months, stabilization can be assured only by following consistent policies over periods of years. During that time, measures to allow indirect macroeconomic control should be put in place. It may take years for the expectation of macroeco-

Figure 7-2. *Sequencing of the Reform*

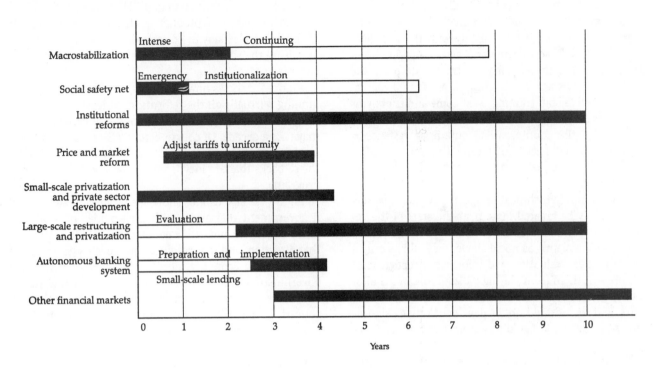

Source: The authors.

nomic stability to become sufficiently ingrained to affect long-term economic decision-making. A particularly difficult stage for reforming governments comes a few months after success with the initial phase, when unemployment is rising, firms are beginning to experience financial difficulties and closings are in sight. Because inflation is lower, the demand for reflation—meaning an easing of credit constraints and reinstatement of some subsidies—mounts. For this reason alone, governments have to move quickly after stabilization to formulate measures for the emergency restructuring of firms. Price reform for goods is shown taking place early as a prerequisite for decentralization and tightening of the budget constraints, with trade reform an important element. Progressive reductions in state interventions continue the process.

Wage determination presents a major challenge. In socially-owned firms (the great majority), wage-setting cannot be left to the market early in the process because the firms are not operating under correct price and management signals. At the same time, wages must respond to inflation and changing relative prices, including those (such as the introduction of more realistic rents) needed to place the housing sector on a sound basis. Wage guidelines or formulae have to be used initially in non-privately owned firms;[38] wage determination can in-

creasingly be left to the market as firms are restructured and privatized.

Realistic interest rates are needed to attract depositors into the banking system and to provide a reasonable measure of the cost of financial resources to firms. However, it will not be possible to leave the determination of interest rates to the market until far into the reform because appropriate incentive structures for firms and banks will not be in place. Premature reliance on the financial market as an instrument of indirect economic management is likely to raise real interest rates to the point where they create financial difficulty even for firms that would be sound in normal times, as well as to provoke costly financial crises.

Measures to eliminate discriminatory regulation against the private sector can be taken at the start of the process.[39] Privatization of small firms can also start immediately, with small-scale commercial bank lending needed in support. Whether or not some holding company mechanism is used as an intermediate stage or some shares are distributed across the population, preparation for the restructuring and "real" privatization of most larger firms is likely to take several years and execution to take much longer. Nonetheless, preparation, including corporatization, has to begin as soon as possible. Clarification of ownership rights and the transfer of responsibility for the direction of firms to boards of directors should be implemented as rapidly as possible.

Reform of the banking system involves several stages. Preparation can begin immediately with the establishment of suitable accounting and asset valuation standards, reform of the banking, contract, enterprise and bankruptcy laws and the drafting of prudential regulations, as well as staff training. Next come audits of firms and banks and asset valuations, followed by portfolio restructuring (the counterpart to enterprise restructuring), allocation of losses and recapitalization. Only after this process is complete can a market-based banking system emerge.[40]

From a purely technical perspective, equity markets can probably be created quite near the start of the reform. However, apart from their possible initial role in consolidating claims as noted above, they will be only a facade because valuation and information deficiencies will prevent them from playing a useful role in the allocation of resources.[41] Evolving such a role will take years, and they should not be developed on any significant scale until the banking system has been restructured.

It is important that the reform of the financial sector not outrun the reform of enterprises. This caveat raises the important question of how the emerging private sector is to obtain financial services in the interim. One possibility is to establish specialized financial institutions for the private sector. However, a better solution, given the need for the banks to acquire the capabilities needed to serve private clients, is to implement a *two-track strategy* for the banking system, with service departments for the private sector in all major banks, albeit on a small scale initially, and the separation of assets in private and publicly owned entities.

No separate line is shown in figure 7.2 for *international trade*. The reason is that reform of trade in goods is treated as an element of price reform. Current account convertibility, which means essentially unrestricted access to foreign exchange for current account transactions, is desirable early on in the reform program.[42]

It is particularly important to make provisions early in the process for the treatment of foreign investors. Capital account convertibility should come later, when expectations of stability have been established.

This simple treatment of the trade and payments issues ignores the need for reserves to be adequate prior to liberalizing the current account. Poland's reserves had been augmented by standby agreements, and Poland enjoyed a de facto moratorium on its debt service; Yugoslavia had accumulated reserves prior to initiating its major reforms. Countries in the position of Bulgaria, with essentially no reserves, face greater risks in opening their current accounts. Also ignored are the complications that will arise from the changing CMEA regime. In addition to the issue of product quality discussed above, CMEA reform is likely to exacerbate the reserve problem by raising the share of trade for which a normal reserve cover is needed.

Figure 7.2 shows how much has to be done at the beginning. Virtually all the reforms, or at least their planning, have to start quickly, even though implementation may take a decade. Of course, figure 7.2 exaggerates the precision of the process, and it certainly does not show the setbacks that are inevitable in any economic reform program.

Figure 7.2 also cannot show one other vital element. A government that starts with a clear idea of what it wants to achieve and with a popular mandate to move in that direction, and that resolutely pursues its goals, will transform the economy more successfully than will a government and society that is not sure what it wants. For this reason, reform is more likely to succeed in those countries where there is a consensus on the necessity of moving to a normal private market economy.

The Role of Foreigners

The success of economic reform in European socialist economies depends heavily on the extent to which the reforming governments open their economies to foreign trade, capital and expertise and on the response of Western economies and governments. Opening up to foreign trade immediately puts in place the right price signals and allows countries to benefit from larger markets and from foreign technologies. The proximity of Western Europe makes these benefits obvious to the reforming governments and to those contemplating reforms.

The reforming governments have welcomed foreign direct investment, although it is not yet taking place on a large scale except in the former East Germany. It will be necessary for the governments of the European socialist economies to develop a systematic approach to foreign investment and foreign ownership, recognizing that the right approach is not to create special incentives for foreign investors but rather to create conditions favorable to both domestic and foreign private investment.

Official foreign finance is also needed to ensure reserves, cushion the short-run impact of stabilization and help develop the infrastructure. Bilateral support except in the case of the former East Germany has been limited so far. However, the multilaterals have started lending on a large scale. The potential role of the new European Bank for Reconstruction and Dvelopment (EBRD) as a lender to the private sector is important, especially given the reluctance of commercial banks to become involved, but it will take some time to work out how public money should be channelled to the private sector.

Foreign expertise from both the private and official sectors is avidly solicited by European socialist economies. It is essential to expand the use of management contracts and other methods of using experts with the practical knowledge of how to run businesses and the other institutions that support a market economy.

What should Western governments do to help the reform? They cannot intervene directly in the intense political ferment that in the end will determine many aspects of the reform. However, they can make four important contributions:

- *Market access*. With generally restrictive domestic spending policies and the need to upgrade to Western standards, access to the markets of industrial countries is vital for a rapid return to growth. It is extremely important that the industrialized countries open their markets to exports from the European socialist economies.
- *Technical assistance*. The needs of the reforming countries are enormous. Because of their relatively high levels of literacy and numeracy, the pay-off from a period of intensive and well-coordinated technical assistance will be high. Direct firm-level assistance can be especially useful.
- *Financial assistance*. Some countries, especially Poland, are embarking on reform with crushing debt burdens. Relief is an essential ingredient of reform, as is continued access to capital to finance the restructuring and provide a cushion during the transformation. Assistance aimed directly at cushioning the impact of restructuring can also play an important role.
- *Coordination*. Present aid efforts are so ill-coordinated that they stretch the already overstretched implementation capacities of the reforming governments. Coordination has to be improved.

Conclusion

This paper presented a definition of the main components of programs to reform the socialist economic systems with the aim of transforming socialist economies into private market economies. Initial conditions that shape reform were discussed, together with the complementarities between the major elements of reform and the need for certain reforms to precede others if the program is to be consistent. The paper then sketched out an illustrative schedule for such a program for a representative country.

In practice, any given country will face many choices concerning its reform path. Some choices involve the *target of the reform*, that is, the ultimate form of the private market economy. The organization of such economies is quite well-defined in general terms, but there are important differences across industrial countries, for example, in terms of the role of the state, the coverage of social insurance and the methods of collective bargaining. Economic theory offers relatively little guidance for making decisions on the distribution of wealth across the population. There are also important choices to be made concerning the role of foreign ownership and control. Such differences obviously will affect the design of specific programs.

Even with consensus on the elements of reform, *implementation* can generate substantial debate. For example, the approach to regulating natural monopolies differs between the United States and Europe; similarly, the tax codes and banking regulation and supervision are not uniform. In some of these areas, flaws are apparent in certain potential models that have evolved over time.[43] More often, the most important consideration in shaping reform may be to ensure consistency with potential trading partners and sources of capital, so that differential regulation does not impede economic integration.

The important strategic choices arise, however, out of the inter-play between economics and politics. System reform is an intensely political process, and the imperatives of political sustainability may dominate analysis of the reform: indeed, the major differences between the alternative proposals for reform reflect, to a large extent, different strategic views of what will be sustainable. The time needed to reform institutions, create skills—including the re-instatement of a business class—and establish valuations argues for a measured pace of reform. However, a slow pace has costs, including prolonged uncertainty and perhaps an extended period of poor management of assets. It runs the risk that opposition to the changes will coalesce to terminate the process. This risk argues in favor of a rapid approach, but in that case the markets are apt to be liberalized prior to adequate preparatory steps. Owners will be created early, either in the form of various holding arrangements or spontaneously by trading claims, distributed in some across-the-board manner. This rapid approach to reform has definite merits, especially if reserves have been built up to tide the country over the period of economic disruption that is likely to follow. However, it, too, runs high risks because of the potential for chaos.

Especially in this situation, technocratic solutions are not sufficient. In addition to trying to define optimal, or even feasible, transition strategies, economists must have an eye for the major inconsistencies, risks and dead-ends likely to result from strategies driven by political processes. They must seek ways to defuse such problems, if possible before they become serious enough to undermine the reform. At the same time, politicians have to recognize that the neglect of economic factors has caused the present crises and that political considerations alone cannot drive the reform.

Notes

1. Work on this paper was begun when Fischer was chief economist at the World Bank. The opinions expressed are those of the authors and are not the official views of the World Bank. The authors are indebted to Bela Balassa, Olivier Blanchard, Rudiger Dornbusch and Imre Tarafas for their helpful comments.

2. Political reform may be needed prior to economic reform to prevent the latter from being stalled by an entrenched bureaucracy. However, as a reflection of the complex political-economic interactions, successful, partial economic reform can provide space for political reform. Providing alternative private career paths for the *nomenklatura*, or bureaucracy (a contentious issue in several countries) could also ease certain aspects of the political reform.

3. The CMEA is an essentially bilateral system of trade relations, with the Soviet Union the dominant trading partner with each of the smaller Central and Eastern European countries. Yugoslavia is not a member of the CMEA. Payments among CMEA countries are expected to be made in hard currencies, at world prices, beginning in 1991.

4. The estimates shown in the row "GDP physical indicators" are close to the estimates of the purchasing power of real incomes. See Fink and Havelik (1989) for a discussion of alternative income estimates.

5. The exchange rate-based estimates—which use actual exchange rates for countries such as Poland and Yugoslavia that have reformed their exchange arrangements and staff estimates for the other countries—imply that all European socialist economies would be eligible for World Bank borrowing based on the income criterion.

6. Inter-regional income differences account for much of the observed inequality in socialist countries, essentially because of limited equilibrating resource flows in the factor markets. For this reason Yugoslavia's Gini coefficient is relatively high. For a discussion of this effect in rural China, see Byrd and Gelb (1990).

7. As with the estimates of real income, the growth rates of the socialist economies are subject to debate. In some cases, including East Germany, the high reported growth rates are known to have been the result of statistical manipulation. Nevertheless, the general picture in the European socialist countries is one of quite high growth rates that declined sharply from the latter half of the seventies, followed by stagnation during a period of attempts at reform. This situation is very different from China's, whose economy stagnated prior to the reforms initiated in the 1970s and then grew rapidly thereafter.

8. The relative positions of the countries in figure 7.1 necessarily reflect a degree of judgment. Some countries included in table 7.1 are omitted from figure 7-1 for lack of information.

9. In March 1990 the USSR published a list of its debtors and identified overall international assets of US$145 billion, of which $74 billion were owed by CMEA members and $71 billion by developing countries (*Oxford Analytica* 1990). It is not clear to what extent these debts are collectible, but at least on paper the USSR has developed a substantial net international credit position that could give it some leeway in adjusting its external accounts. Bulgaria has also extended credit to developing countries, notably in the Middle East. Reform of the CMEA system will probably be to the advantage of the USSR but adverse for Bulgaria.

10. This situation could arise as a result not only of the Tanzi effect, in which real tax revenues decline as inflation rises, but also because partial price decontrol may require increasing government subsidies to maintain the prices of necessities constant.

11. For examples of authors who advocate such a pattern, where the institutions needed to support the markets are put in place prior to each stage of liberalization, see Svejnar (1990) and the so-called sequential approach outlined in Rosefielde (1990).

12. For descriptions of the Soviet and Chinese patterns of management, see Hewitt (1988) and Tidrick and Chen (1989).

13. China is a distinctive case. It adopted a two-tier approach to decentralization and markets, with state firms and a material supply system coexisting with a growing non-state sector (largely in agriculture and rural industry) and with trading increasingly occurring on a market basis but with different prices for similar commodities. In its reform, China has also experimented with regional differentiation, with some provinces and special zones moving far more rapidly toward markets and pluralistic forms of ownership. (See Byrd and Lin 1990.) Regional decentralization has progressed a long way. (Many of the prerogatives that firms have gained in the European socialist economies have been captured by the lower levels of government in China.)

14. Authors differ in the emphasis they place on the relative importance of the absence of a well-defined bottom line for management and the responsibility of management to workers in accounting for the performance of decentralized firms in European socialist economies. (For examples, see Kornai 1990 and Hinds 1990).

15. China's rural economy can be said to consist of product markets without factor markets, as individuals cannot move easily and interregional resource flows are constrained. However, communities face quite hard budget constraints, and fiscal mechanisms to equalize incomes across them are limited, so that, on a group basis at least, incomes reflect the availability and productivity of local factors.

16. Czechoslovakia made moves in this direction, with workers in some firms effectively dismissing their managers through votes of no confidence, but it has also taken steps to reassert centralized control as a prelminary step in the move to a private market economy.

17. In spontaneous privatization, which is initiated by management, the firm is sold or its assets are leased to a private corporation in which the managers and possibly workers have an interest. Spontaneous privatization emerged in Hungary and Poland, and somewhat later in Yugoslavia; it is also taking place in the Soviet Union.

18. Poland and Yugoslavia have adopted variants of the carrot and stick approach. In the former, failure to pay a dividend to the government triggers intervention; in the latter, late payment on debts is the trigger.

19. Czechoslovakia is a case in point, with the famous voucher scheme being only one of many proposals under consideration (see Klaus 1990).

20. This point does not argue against some employee shareholding or representation on boards, as in co-determination. However, there should be an independent locus of control on the board.

21. For example, limited forms of private property were legally protected beginning in 1955 in Hungary, and their scope has been progressively enlarged, notably in 1968 and 1982. Private property in China and the USSR, on the other hand, has lacked a formal legal underpinning.

22. For reviews of the private sector in four European socialist economies, see Webster (1990, Annex IA-ID).

23. Central planning is facilitated by minimizing the number of firms to reduce the complexity of control. Spontaneous entry and exit processes are virtually absent under socialism.

24. Yugoslavia has instituted a centralized reporting system covering both bank and inter-enterprise credit. Late payments on either can trigger intervention and bankruptcy.

Both the phenomena discussed in this paragraph have their counterparts in market economies: firms facing a high risk of bankruptcy may attempt to borrow at very high interest rates—a tendency that leads lenders to ration credit at market interest rates; and inter-firm credit, sometimes called the gray market, tends to expand when bank credit is constrained.

25. The far lower levels of productivity in the European socialist economies should be borne in mind when assessing the applicability of Western European social insurance systems, with their relatively high levels of benefits. Because of the initially quite equal income distribution in the European socialist economies, it may be difficult for them to formulate comprehensive social insurance schemes and at the same time widen the differentials to create adequate incentives.

26. See Dornbusch and Wolf (1990) on the effectiveness of currency reforms in dealing with the post-World War II monetary overhang in several countries.

27. One suggestion is that a reforming economy take over and adapt a complete legal and regulatory system from a market economy with which it has historic and cultural ties. For example, Hungary and Czechoslovakia might adopt and adapt the Austrian framework. The former East Germany has essentially adopted the institutions of the Federal Republic.

28. Consider, for example, that in the United States it takes a minimum of five years to train an examiner to deal with the smallest and simplest bank.

29. While open foreign trade provides a rational price system for traded goods, it does not do so for non-traded goods. Moreover, until the capital account of the balance of payments is opened, interest rates and the prices of assets can also diverge from world levels. In a large, closed economy such as the USSR, it is less clear that a rapid move to world prices is the most appropriate strategy. However, even in the case of the Soviet Union, rapid liberalization of trade, combined with a gradual reduction in tariffs, would provide potential markets for exporters and an important element of potential import competition for domestic monopolists, conditions that would help create an appropriate relative price structure.

30. hina's rural reform, in which communes were in effect privatized to their members, is the most impressive example of the reform of property rights among the socialist countries. Lin (1989) has shown that the introduction of the household responsibility system was responsible for most of the increase in agricultural output associated with the Chinese reforms. Such reforms are probably far more difficult in an industrial setting and in a less authoritarian system.

31. Discussion of the Hungarian reform provides examples of the distinction between the schools of slow and fast privatization, with Kornai (1990) as a slow privatizer and the Blue Ribbon Commission (1990) arguing for fast privatization. The periods that have been suggested in various studies as appropriate for privatization of a major part of industry range from less than 3 years to around 30 years.

32. Without an adequate information base, a stock market established at an early stage of reform would not be able to offer a useful basis for valuation or any indication of desirable investment patterns. The initial purpose of the exchange is, however, quite different.

33. See Lipton and Sachs (1990) for presentation of a rapid privatization scheme for Poland involving the distribution of shares.

34. In the early stages of reform, many potentially viable firms are likely to experience severe liquidity, and possibly solvency, difficulties because of their exceptionally depressed markets, disruption of CMEA trade and exceptional interest charges. These short-run difficulties greatly complicate the task of deciding whether to close or support a given firm.

35. It seems doubtful that the private sector could handle the restructuring of very large, weak industries because of the potential political reaction.

36. This process is apparently taking place in Yugoslavia.

37. For example, when inflation is rapid, macroeconomic stabilization is needed before reforms to change relative prices, such as trade reforms, are undertaken; the goods markets should not be liberalized later than the factor markets; and the capital account should generally be opened after the trade account.

38. In the case of Poland, wages were *partially* indexed.

39. Hungary, Poland, Czechoslovakia and Yugoslavia have all taken steps to place private firms onto the same legal and regulatory footing as public firms.

40. This is not to say the banks cannot be active participants in the restructurings—centers of expertise can be usefully developed in the banks. At the same time, responsibility for the process and its financing must lie outside the banking system.

41. In China, for example, equity issues can be found despite the absence of laws defining private property rights. Liabilities combining features of debt and preferred shares are also issued, but without clear definition of the holders' rights and the basis for their returns.

42. Some countries may elect to use dual exchange rates and import licensing for some transitional period. In these cases, it would be important for firms to have access to foreign exchange and automatic import licenses in the free foreign exchange market.

43. For example, few would now recommend adopting the organization of the US banking industry or the institutional fragmentation of its regulators.

References

Blue Ribbon Commission: Project Hungary. 1990. *Hungary in Transformation to Freedom and Prosperity*. Indianapolis, Ind.: Hudson Institute, April.

Byrd, William, and Alan Gelb. 1990. "Why Industrialize? The Incentives for Local Community Governments."In William Byrd and Lin Qingsong, eds., *China's Rural Industry*. New York: Oxford University Press.

Byrd, William, and Lin Qingsong, eds. 1990. *China's Rural Industry*. New York: Oxford University Press.

Dornsbusch, Rudiger, and Holger Wolf. 1990. "Monetary Overhang and Reforms in the 1940s." Mimeo. Massachusetts Institute of Technology. Cambridge, Mass.

Erlich, Eva. 1987. "Absolute and Relative Economic Development Levels and Their Structure 1937-1980." Mimeo. Budapest.

Feige, Edgar L. 1990. "Perestroika and Socialist Privatization: What Is to Be Done and How?" Working Paper 1. International Center for Economic Growth. March.

Fink, G., and P. Havelik. 1989. "Alternative Measures of Growth and Development Levels: Comparisons and Assessments." In Joint Economic Committee, *Pressures for Reform in the East European Economies*. Washington, D.C.: US Government Printing Office, October.

Hewitt, Ed A. 1988. *Reforming the Soviet Economy: Equality Versus Efficiency*. Washington, D.C.: The Brookings Institution.

Hinds, Manuel. 1990. "Issues in the Introduction of Market Forces in Eastern European Economies." World Bank. Washington, D.C. January.

Klaus, Vaclav. 1990. Address to the Conference on Development Economics, World Bank. Washington, D.C., May 1990.

Kornai, Janos. 1990. "The Road to a Free Economy: Shifting from a Socialist System: The Case of Hungary." January.

Lin, Justin Y. 1989. "The Household Responsibility System in China's Agricultural Reform: A Theoretical and Empirical Study." A paper prepared for the 20th Anniversary Conference of the Graduate Program in Economic Development, Vanderbilt University, Nashville, Tenn., October 15-17, 1989.

Lipton, David, and Jeffrey Sachs. 1990. "Creating a Market Economy in Eastern Europe: The Case of Poland." A paper presented to the Brookings Institution. Washington, D.C. April.

Milanovic, Branko. 1990. "Income Distribution in the USSR." Mimeo. Socialist Economic Reform Unit, World Bank. Washington, D.C., January.

Nordhaus, William. 1990. "The Longest Road: From Hegel to Haggle." Yale University. New Haven, Conn.

Nuti, Domenico Mario. 1990. "Stabilization and Reform Sequencing in the Reform of Socialist Economies." A paper presented to the Economic Development Institute (EDI) Seminar, World Bank, Washington, D.C., March 1990.

Oxford Analytica. 1990. July 26.

Rosefielde, Steven. 1990. "Market Communism at the Brink." *Global Affairs*.

Svejnar, Jan. 1990. "A Framework for the Economic Transformation of Czechoslovakia." University of Pittsburgh. Pittsburgh, Pa. January.

Tidrick, Gene, and Chen Jiyuan. 1989. *China's Industrial Reforms*. New York: Oxford University Press.

United States. Central Intelligence Agency. 1989. *Handbook of Economic Statistics*. Washington, D.C.: CIA.

Webster, Leila. 1990. "Private Sector Development in Eastern Europe." Draft. Industry Division, Industry and Energy Department (IEN-IN), World Bank. Washington, D.C. July.

Wharton Economic Forecasting. 1989. *World Economic Outlook* (October).

World Bank. Various issues. *World Development Indicators*. Washington, D.C.: World Bank.

————. Various issues. *World Tables*. Washington, D.C.: World Bank.

Yasin, E. 1989. "Modern Market Institutions and Problems of Economic Reforms in the USSR." A paper presented at the Conference on Economic Reform and Integration, Luxembourg, March 1989.

Part IV

Stabilization: Design of Programs, Effects on the Economy

8

Stopping Inflation: The Experience
of Latin America and Israel and the Implications
for Central and Eastern Europe

Miguel A. Kiguel and Nissan Liviatan

This paper examines the inflation-stabilization experience of the chronic high-inflation countries of Latin America and Israel and relates it to recent events in Poland and Yugoslavia. The hope is that, despite the structural and institutional differences between market and centrally planned economies, the experience of Latin America and Israel can shed some light on the nature of inflation and on some of the difficulties that the Central and Eastern European countries are likely to face during stabilization.

Latin America and Israel offer one of the richest laboratories for studying inflation and stabilization. Table 8-1 shows annual rates of inflation for a selected group of countries (Israel is not included in the table), which can be grouped into three categories based on their inflationary history. First, there are the low-inflation countries such as Colombia and Costa Rica, where inflation has remained relatively stable and low by Latin American standards. Some of these countries have experienced temporary bursts of inflation for one or two years (e.g., Costa Rica in 1982-83), but these episodes have usually been reversed quickly, with inflation returning to low levels thereafter. Second are the chronic high-inflation countries (in the terminology of Pazos 1972), whose high rates of inflation have persisted for long periods. Argentina, Brazil, Chile, Israel, Mexico, Peru and Uruguay are in this group. The third category includes a number of countries that have experienced hyper-inflation. Within this group are countries that prior to hyper-inflation had had a tradition of low inflation (such as Bolivia and Nicaragua) and others that had experienced chronic high inflation (such as Argentina, Brazil and Peru).

A central reason for differentiating among the countries' experiences with inflation is that the effectiveness of alternative stabilization strategies largely depends on a country's inflationary history. As will be discussed, the speed and ease with which inflation can be brought down

and price stability can be sustained are heavily influenced by whether the country has mechanisms that allow it to live with high levels of inflation. For example, the orthodox approach has been very effective in stopping hyper-inflation in traditionally low-inflation countries, as evidenced from the experience of Bolivia in the mid-eighties and Europe in the 1920s and after World War II (see, for example, Dornbusch and Fischer 1986, Sargent 1982 and Sachs 1986). In addition, this approach has been effective in stopping inflationary outbursts in traditionally low-inflation countries.[1] On the other hand, the orthodox approach has by and large not been very successful in achieving rapid and drastic reductions in inflation in chronic high-inflation countries.[2]

This paper looks at those aspects of inflation in Latin America and Israel that are potentially relevant to understanding current developments in Central and Eastern Europe, especially Poland and Yugoslavia. The focus is mainly on the following issues:

(1)   what are the similarities and differences in the underlying causes of inflation, and where in the inflation process were these countries prior to stabilization? It is argued that Latin America and Central and Eastern Europe have many common elements with respect to inflation. For example, there are many similarities in the reasons for the permanent increase in inflation during the debt crisis in Yugoslavia on the one hand and in Brazil and Mexico on the other and in the characteristics of the inflation that emerged thereafter. Likewise, Poland and Yugoslavia experienced some of the same mechanisms that fueled inflation in Argentina and Brazil, especially the difficulty of enforcing hard budget constraints on public sector enterprises and of limiting the amount of credit granted by the banking system.

(2)   the outcomes of the programs in those two socialist countries are compared with similar programs

Table 8.1. *Inflation (As Measured by the Consumer Price Index) in Latin American and Eastern European Countries*
(percent in annual terms)

Year	Argentina	Bolivia	Brazil	Chile	Colombia	Costa Rica	Mexico	Peru	Uruguay	Czech.	Poland	Hungary	Romania	Yugoslavia
1960	27.30	11.53	29.53	n.a.	3.87	0.79	4.93	8.66	38.50	n.a.	n.a.	n.a.	n.a.	9.30
1961	13.39	7.58	33.42	n.a.	8.67	2.43	1.61	5.92	22.75	n.a.	n.a.	n.a.	n.a.	8.72
1962	28.32	5.88	51.84	n.a.	2.49	2.68	1.20	6.64	10.91	n.a.	n.a.	n.a.	n.a.	10.14
1963	23.90	-0.71	70.08	n.a.	31.98	2.93	0.59	6.07	21.25	n.a.	n.a.	n.a.	n.a.	5.88
1964	22.20	10.18	91.88	45.98	17.64	3.32	2.34	9.79	42.37	n.a.	n.a.	n.a.	n.a.	11.35
1965	28.63	2.86	65.69	28.84	3.51	-0.66	3.57	16.39	56.56	n.a.	n.a.	n.a.	n.a.	33.26
1966	31.91	6.95	41.30	23.08	19.85	0.18	4.22	8.84	73.46	n.a.	n.a.	n.a.	n.a.	25.52
1967	29.20	11.20	30.46	18.75	8.15	1.21	3.02	9.78	89.28	n.a.	n.a.	n.a.	n.a.	6.63
1968	16.21	5.49	22.01	26.32	5.84	4.09	2.33	19.09	125.34	n.a.	n.a.	n.a.	n.a.	5.13
1969	7.57	2.22	22.66	30.44	10.13	2.63	3.37	6.24	20.97	n.a.	n.a.	n.a.	n.a.	9.13
1970	13.59	3.84	22.36	32.48	6.85	4.65	5.21	5.03	16.31	n.a.	n.a.	n.a.	n.a.	9.53
1971	34.73	3.69	20.14	20.03	9.05	3.08	5.26	6.79	23.95	n.a.	1.10	n.a.	0.60	15.70
1972	58.45	6.51	16.56	74.84	13.45	4.60	5.00	7.22	76.48	n.a.	-0.10	n.a.	0.00	15.93
1973	61.25	31.49	12.68	361.53	20.76	15.21	12.04	9.49	97.00	n.a.	2.48	3.39	0.70	19.48
1974	23.47	62.83	27.60	504.73	24.28	30.07	23.75	16.89	77.21	n.a.	7.05	1.80	1.09	21.98
1975	182.93	7.98	28.97	374.73	22.93	17.37	15.15	23.62	81.41	n.a.	2.26	3.84	0.20	23.49
1976	443.97	4.50	42.04	211.81	20.23	3.49	15.79	33.48	50.62	n.a.	4.41	5.23	0.50	11.15
1977	176.00	8.10	43.68	91.94	33.05	4.17	29.00	38.05	58.20	n.a.	4.90	3.91	0.60	14.66
1978	175.52	10.36	38.70	40.12	17.79	6.01	17.46	57.85	44.55	n.a.	8.10	4.69	1.98	14.09
1979	159.51	19.73	52.70	33.36	24.70	9.18	18.17	66.69	66.84	n.a.	7.03	8.98	1.84	20.68
1980	100.76	47.23	82.79	35.14	26.54	18.13	26.36	59.15	63.48	n.a.	9.41	9.29	1.52	30.88
1981	104.48	28.57	105.57	19.69	27.48	37.06	27.93	75.43	34.05	0.82	21.20	4.51	2.20	39.83
1982	164.78	133.33	97.78	9.94	24.55	90.12	58.92	64.45	18.99	5.07	100.82	7.02	16.93	31.51
1983	343.82	269.05	142.14	27.26	19.76	32.62	101.76	111.15	49.20	0.95	22.10	6.40	5.19	40.23
1984	626.72	1,281.40	196.98	19.86	16.14	11.95	65.54	110.21	55.30	0.95	15.01	8.65	1.11	54.71
1985	672.15	11,749.60	226.86	30.70	24.04	15.05	57.75	163.40	72.22	2.28	15.10	7.01	-0.39	72.27
1986	90.10	276.34	145.24	19.48	18.88	11.84	86.23	77.92	76.38	0.50	17.69	5.27	-0.08	89.77
1987	131.33	14.58	229.66	19.87	23.30	16.85	131.83	85.85	63.57	0.08	25.21	8.73	n.a.	120.80
1988	342.96	15.99	682.30	14.69	28.11	20.83	114.16	667.03	62.19	0.16	60.00	15.80	n.a.	194.09
1989	3,079.35	15.01	1,286.98	17.03	25.84	16.51	20.01	3,398.59	80.45	1.40	244.55	n.a.	n.a.	1,239.87

n.a. Not available
Source: International Monetary Fund (various issues).

in Latin America and Israel. The working assumption is that Poland and Yugoslavia used the exchange rate as the nominal anchor for their programs, and in this sense they pursued exchange rate-based stabilization. In addition, the paper evaluates the positive initial results of Poland and Yugoslavia's programs in reducing inflation and whether the impact the programs have had on output and the balance of payments is comparable to that under similar programs in Latin America and Israel.

(3)   what difficulties have Latin American countries had in sustaining low rates of inflation, maintaining an external balance and coping with unemployment under their alternative strategies, and what lessons can be drawn for countries in Central and Eastern Europe?

(4)   in what ways can the specific institutional characteristics of Central and Eastern European countries, especially regarding ownership, affect the evolution of macroeconomic variables during stabilization? It is argued that a delay in establishing rules for privatization is likely to raise savings (and hence improve the current account), as agents increase their holdings of liquid assets to take advantage of the unique opportunities that privatization of public sector enterprises will create.

The paper is organized as follows. The next section describes the main features of chronic high-inflation countries and discusses some of the reasons that make disinflation difficult in these types of countries. Also discussed are the reasons why stabilization in chronic high-inflation countries is different from that in hyper-inflationary ones. It is postulated that Yugoslavia has the basic features of a chronic high-inflation country, while the evidence on Poland is mixed, although in many respects Poland resembles a chronic high-inflation country. The third section presents a discussion of the experience with alternative stabilization strategies in chronic high-inflation countries. In particular, it examines the experience with orthodox and heterodox stabilization programs. While both types of programs use fiscal adjustment as a central component of stabilization, the heterodox programs also use price and wage controls (usually in the form of a freeze) and a fixed exchange rate. Among the orthodox programs, some use a fixed or pre-announced exchange rate as a way to "anchor" the price level (exchange rate-based stabilization), while others use money (or domestic credit) as the nominal anchor (money-based stabilization). The current stabilization efforts in both Poland and Yugoslavia incorporate elements of the two types of stabilization programs and hence are difficult to characterize in an unambiguous

way. Nevertheless, the nature of these programs is explored and related to the results of similar ones in Latin America. (The analysis in the second and third sections draws heavily on the authors' previous work on this topic, in particular, on Kiguel and Liviatan 1988, 1989 and 1990a).[3] The paper wraps up with a discussion of policy issues. Special attention is paid to the issue of sequencing. It is argued that stabilization is difficult and costly to maintain unless the privatization issue is addressed from the start.

Inflation and Stabilization

Chronic High-Inflation Countries

A number of features characterize chronic high-inflation countries. First, inflation in these countries has typically gone up over the years. In Brazil and Israel, for example, inflation was around 20 percent in the early seventies, 40 percent in the mid-seventies, 100 percent in the early eighties and 200 percent toward the mid-eighties. Although there were more fluctuations in Argentina's inflation, the average rate increased from the sixties to the seventies and from the seventies to the eighties.

A second characteristic is that temporary shocks tend to have a permanent effect on inflation. In Brazil and Israel the oil shocks caused the increases in inflation during the seventies. Likewise, the *permanent* increase in inflation in Brazil and Mexico during 1982-83 was associated with the maxi-devaluations carried out in response to the beginning of the debt crisis. In contrast, in low-inflation countries (e.g., Costa Rica and most countries in the Organisation for Economic Cooperation and Development [OECD]), adverse external shocks have only *temporary* effects.

A third characteristic is the asymmetry observed in inflation: it ratchets up in response to adverse shocks but does not fall in the same manner when the economy experiences a favorable shock. This pattern is clear in Brazil and Israel, where inflation did not drop in the periods when the terms of trade improved. In practice, inflation tends to display downward rigidity in these economies. Finally, chronic high-inflation countries tend to institute mechanisms (such as indexation of wages and tax revenues) that allow them to live with inflation. These mechanisms help avert the redistribution of income and wealth that is usually associated with inflation in low-inflation countries, while at the same time reducing the disruption in production that would occur as a result of nominal shocks. In Brazil, for example, it has been argued many times that, because of the indexation of wages, prices and the exchange rate, relative prices have remained stable, and inflation has not adversely affected production and exports.[4]

Paradoxically, this ability to cope with inflation is why stabilization tends to be difficult and lengthy in these countries. Because indexation lessens many of the costs of inflation, the pressures for stabilization are weaker than in low-inflation countries, and hence stabilization can be postponed. A lack of credibility about the success of a stabilization program is usually a more formidable obstacle in chronic high-inflation countries because there is no compelling reason in the short run (especially from a political-economic perspective) to undertake a costly process of disinflation when the economy can continue to grow and trade can expand in an inflationary environment.[5] Unfortunately, if a program is not credible, inflation is likely to display downward rigidity (sometimes referred to as inertia) as firms and workers continue to set prices and wages on the expectation that the program will fail. This situation creates an inflationary bias in the economy that not only slows the speed with which inflation comes down but also leads to an overvaluation of the currency, a deterioration in the current account and an increase in real wages. In the end, all these factors might lead to the abandonment of the stabilization effort.

A second reason that makes disinflation difficult in chronic high-inflation countries is that the causes of inflation are not always clear. In fact, the changes in the government's budget deficit do not usually explain the changes in inflation (contrary to what is widely believed). The links between the budget deficit, seigniorage (or revenue from money creation) and inflation are typically very weak in these countries. For example, inflation in Brazil and Israel has risen in steps over the years despite relatively stable budget deficits and levels of seigniorage. Liviatan and Piterman (1986) discussed the Israeli case, but Brazil is its mirror image. The pattern of their inflation is peculiar (as illustrated in figures 8-1-A and 1-B): inflation stays relatively stable at a plateau for a number of years, it is then destabilized, usually by a balance-of-payments crisis, and it subsequently rises to a new, higher plateau. Interestingly, the upward movement to the new plateau in these episodes is not linked to increases in the budget deficit as predicted by the fiscal view, but instead to maxi-devaluations in response to external shocks. On the other hand, in Argentina there has been a close relationship between budget deficits (and seigniorage) and inflation (as shown in figure 8-1-C). The overall evidence shows that the causes of inflation are indeed diverse in chronic high-inflation countries. There is no single explanation that holds for all places at all times. Instead, judgment coupled with good economic analysis are essential to understanding the various episodes.

Figure 8-1: *Inflation (As measured by the Consumer Price Index) and Devaluation, Brazil and Israel, and Fiscal Deficit and Inflation, Argentina*

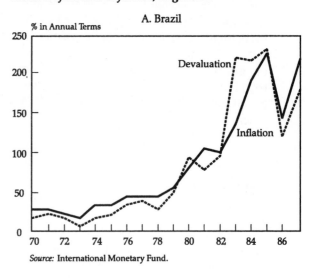

A. Brazil

Source: International Monetary Fund.

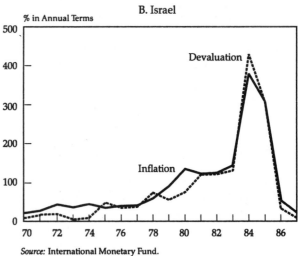

B. Israel

Source: International Monetary Fund.

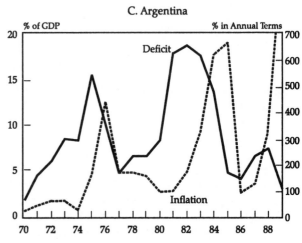

C. Argentina

Source: De Pablo and *International Financial Statistics.*
Note: Inflation rate in 1989 is 3,080 percent.

88

Hyper-inflation

Stopping hyper-inflation in countries that otherwise have no tradition of inflation is in many ways easier than stopping chronic-high inflation. This is confirmed by the recent stabilization program in Bolivia (basic data on Bolivia are included in table 8-2).[6] The characteristics of its stabilization resembled the pattern discussed in Yeager (1981), Sargent (1982) and Dornbusch and Fischer (1986): the government stopped the inflation abruptly with an orthodox program that included elimination of the budget deficit, monetary discipline and a fixed exchange rate.

There are at least three reasons why stabilization is easier in hyper-inflationary as compared with chronic high-inflation countries. First, with hyper-inflation the causes of the inflation are clear: large budget deficits financed by money creation. In Bolivia, for instance, the level of seigniorage rose significantly (exceeding 12 percent of gross domestic product [GDP]) during the hyper-inflation, compared with an average of 2 percent of GDP in the late seventies and early eighties. These levels of seigniorage are extraordinarily high by international standards and cannot be sustained for prolonged periods at a stable rate of inflation.[7] Second, hyper-inflation is extremely costly and hence is not sustainable. In Bolivia, growth collapsed and tensions mounted during the hyper-inflation, conditions that generated support for a serious stabilization program. Hyper-inflation eliminates many of the credibility problems typical of chronic high-inflation countries.

A third, and important, reason for the sudden fall in inflation in Bolivia and in other well-known cases is that by and large the countries traditionally had low rates of inflation for prolonged periods. Their hyper-inflation was an isolated episode. In Bolivia, the rate of inflation in the sixties and seventies was not much different from that in many industrialized countries.

This third point is particularly important because it suggests that once hyper-inflation is stopped, inflation returns to its previous level (which in Bolivia was low). It also suggests that restoring price stability after hyper-inflation in a chronic high-inflation country could be very different from stopping it in a low-inflation economy. To the extent that hyper-inflation does not remove the perception that the economy can function in a high-inflation environment, then firms and workers might expect that once the hyper-inflation is eliminated, inflation would go back to previous levels. In addition, the government might be willing to tolerate a high, but stable, rate of inflation, which after all is much lower and less disruptive than hyper-inflation. Thus, restoring price stability after hyper-inflation in a chronic high-inflation country is likely to be much more difficult and costly than the evidence indicates.

There have not yet been any cases where hyper-inflation has been stopped in chronic high-inflation countries. However, there are a few instances in Latin America of chronic high-inflation countries experiencing hyper-inflation for the first time (namely, Argentina, Brazil and Peru). The failure of recent attempts to stop hyper-inflation in Argentina and Brazil suggest that the challenge could be more formidable than the findings of Sargent (1982) suggest.

A quick review of these episodes is potentially relevant for current developments in Poland and Yugoslavia. The recent history of inflation in Argentina and Brazil is summarized in figure 8-2.[8] For the first time (in 1989) these two high-inflation countries experienced hyper-inflation. In Argentina the acceleration in inflation that

Table 8.2. *Bolivia: Annual Indicators*

	Budget deficit (% of GDP) (1)	Seigniorage (% of GDP) (2)	Inflation average (3)	GDP growth (4)	Unemployment (5)	Terms of trade (6)
1980	9.0	3.2	47.2	1.2	5.8	100.0
1981	7.8	1.6	28.6	−0.4	9.7	99.7
1982	14.7	12.2	133.3	−5.6	10.9	98.1
1983	19.1	10.0	269.0	−7.2	13.0	99.3
1984	27.4	15.9	1,281.4	−4.0	15.5	104.1
1985	11.7	8.8	11,749.6	−4.0	18.0	104.3
1986	1.3	2.3	276.3	−2.9	20.0	81.9
1987	4.1	1.6	14.6	2.2	21.5	n.a.
1988	3.1	1.6	16.0	2.8	18.0	n.a.

n.a. Not available.

Source: Column (1), 1980–84 from Morales (1988) and 1985–88 from International Monetary Fund (1989), other columns from Morales (1988), columns (2) and (3) from World Bank (various issues).

Figure 8-2. *Inflation (As measured by the Consumer Price Index), Argentina and Brazil*

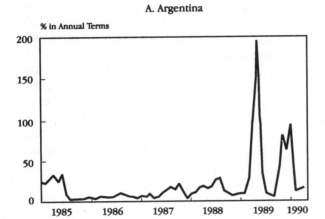

A. Argentina

% in Annual Terms

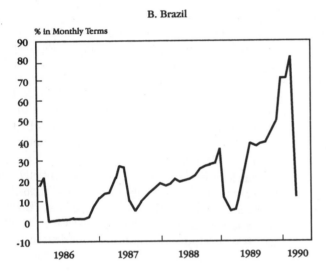

B. Brazil

% in Monthly Terms

eventually led to the hyper-inflation started around February 1989, coinciding with the collapse of the Plan Primavera (or Spring Plan); it continued for around a year (with a temporary period of price stability in the second half of 1989). In Brazil, the hyper-inflation was shorter, lasting around three months, and the inflation rates were much lower than in Argentina.

The interesting feature is that, although both Argentina and Brazil adopted very similar, orthodox stabilization programs in March 1990 to deal with the hyper-inflation, neither was successful in achieving price stability (of the type achieved in Bolivia).[9] The stabilization programs in Argentina and Brazil had many features in common with the Bolivian program: a balanced budget on a cash basis (or even a surplus in some months); very tight money; and a stable exchange rate.

In spite of the similarities in their approaches to stabilization, neither Argentina nor Brazil eradicated their inflation. Instead, it remained around 10 percent a month for a few months and then crept up above 20 percent a month some months later. While it could be argued that the inflation has not receded because the governments could not fully commit to future deficits and hence the fiscal adjustment was not credible in the longer term, this problem is in fact common to hyper-inflation elsewhere. Sachs (1986), for example, forcefully argues that the Bolivian program was not fully credible either, and yet low inflation was sustained.

The view here is that the difficulty of stopping inflation in chronic high-inflation countries is not fully related to the inability of governments to deal with the fiscal deficit. Perhaps as important a reason is the generalized perception among agents that these economies can function with high inflation and that the government will not fight inflation if it stabilizes at the old rates.

In summary, hyper-inflation cannot be stopped always and everywhere in the same way. The inflationary history of the country matters. Stopping hyper-inflation in chronic high-inflation countries is different from stopping it in low-inflation ones. The rate of inflation that prevails once hyper-inflation is stopped most likely will relate to the rate of inflation in place prior to the hyper-inflation.

Inflation in Central and Eastern Europe

Inflationary History

While the inflationary history of Central and Eastern European countries is certainly different from that in Latin American and in Israel, there are many parallels worth pointing out. The comparison is more applicable to the high-inflation countries (namely, Poland and Yugoslavia). The inflation in Yugoslavia has many features in common with the chronic high-inflation countries in Latin America. The rate has continuously exceeded 30 percent a year since 1981, with a tendency to accelerate over time. In addition, many of the institutional arrangements characteristic of chronic high-inflation countries, such as wage indexation and foreign exchange deposits, are also prevalent there.

Poland is difficult to classify precisely. Inflation remained in the 20 percent range between 1980 and 1987 (with the exception of 1982), but in 1988-89 it increased sharply. It could be argued that Poland is essentially a low-inflation country that underwent a *temporary* increase in inflation in 1988-89. Alternatively, it could be argued that the recent inflationary experience in Poland already shows some of the signs observed in chronic high-inflation countries.

The latter view seems more correct for two reasons. First, although Poland had low rates of inflation for a number of years, it promulgated wage indexation and other institutions characteristic of chronic high-inflation countries. In fact, the rapid acceleration in inflation that took place in 1988-89 can in part be explained by the fact that the inflationary bias observed in many chronic high-inflation countries was also present in Poland. Second, the pattern of inflation after the January 1990 stabilization program resembled the recent experiences of Argentina and Brazil as opposed to that of Bolivia, in the sense that inflation remained at levels that are high by international standards, and certainly above what can be acceptable on a long-term basis.

The Causes for Inflation

A separate issue is understanding in what respects the causes of inflation in Poland and Yugoslavia are similar to those of Latin America (table 8-3 gives basic macroeconomic indicators for the two countries). In Yugoslavia, as was the case in Brazil and Israel, the increase in inflation in the early eighties was associated with the maxi-devaluations undertaken to improve the external sector and reduce the real wage.[10] Because formal and informal indexation mechanisms were in place, the period of devaluations led to an increase in inflation. This interpretation of events is consistent with Rocha (1990), who argues that the accelerations in inflation in 1983-85 and 1987-89 were largely driven by exchange rate shocks. As in Brazil, the devaluations that triggered the increase in inflation were used to reduce the real wage in order to restore external balance.

While there was an increase in seigniorage in recent years coinciding with the large acceleration in inflation (see table 8-3), the causality between seigniorage and inflation is difficult to establish unambiguously in Yugoslavia. It is conceivable that, unlike the case of Bolivia, seigniorage increased as a result of a policy of aggressive devaluations, whose main objective was to improve export performance. In the end, however, they led to an increase in inflation. The data presented in Rocha (1990) broadly support this view. The argument could be as follows: because the devaluations increased the costs of servicing the foreign-denominated debt and raised the cost of imported inputs, they led to larger deficits of public sector enterprises. Ultimately the National Bank of Yugoslavia, as lender of last resort, financed these losses, printing money to keep the enterprises functioning, a measure that was reflected in a higher level of seigniorage.

It is worth pointing out that during this period the policy-makers did not use any instrument to anchor the price level. The supply of money was endogenously determined by the need to finance public sector enterprises; the exchange rate was continuously devalued to maintain an undervalued exchange rate, while wages were indexed. Without a nominal anchor in place, inflation could be easily destabilized even in the absence of any fiscal imbalance. This type of problem was also observed in the chronic high-inflation countries in Latin America (for example, in Brazil in the late seventies and early eighties).[11]

The causes of the recent inflation in Poland are somewhat different. The 1980 blip in inflation has many similarities with the experience of other low-inflation countries attempting to improve the external sector. A policy of devaluations succeeded in reducing the real wage and improving the current account. The high level of inflation only lasted a short while, mainly because at that time Poland was a low-inflation country and many of the mechanisms that tend to perpetuate inflation in chronic high-inflation countries were absent. On the other hand, the more recent inflationary episode was different. According to Lipton and Sachs (1990), an austerity program in early 1988 based on cuts in subsidies and sharp increases in consumer prices caused the acceleration in inflation. They also argue that because the program lacked popular support, it rapidly confronted a tide of wage demands. By early 1989 the price spiral accelerated further as a result of the adoption of wage indexation and the introduction of foreign exchange-denominated deposits, a situation that was compounded later that year by the liberalization of food and agricultural prices.[12]

These developments indicate that, as in Yugoslavia, there was no nominal anchor for the price level. Wages were indexed, the exchange rate followed a crawling peg and the money supply was accommodating. One difference, however, is that in contrast to other stabilization programs discussed in this paper, the Polish program did not attempt to improve the current account (since it had already done so in the early eighties). A second related, and perhaps more important, difference is that real wages increased during this period, as opposed to the fall observed in programs aimed at improving the current account. The implication is that increases in the nominal wages were the main force behind the inflation. As in Yugoslavia, seigniorage also increased significantly in 1989, coinciding with the time when inflation reached hyper-inflationary levels, although the causality between seigniorage and inflation remains unclear, as in many other instances.

Table 8-3.A. Macroeconomic Indicators, Yugoslavia, 1980–89

Indicators	1980	1981	1982	1983	1984	1985	1986	1987	1988	1989
Inflation (%)	30.9	39.8	31.5	40.2	54.7	72.3	89.8	120.8	194.1	1,240.2
Devaluation (%)	29.9	41.9	43.8	84.7	64.6	76.8	40.4	94.4	242.2	1,041.3
Real wage (index)	119.6	117.6	113.7	103.7	97.3	100.0	108.1	100.3	92.5	n.a.
Real exchange rate (index)	n.a.	98.2	85.8	80.2	97.0	99.9	100.7	82.1	91.2	108.6
GMP[a] growth (%)	2.3	1.4	0.5	-1.0	2.0	0.5	3.6	-1.0	-2.0	n.a.
Industrial production (index)	87.7	91.9	90.6	91.7	96.9	100.0	103.7	103.1	103.5	105.0
Industrial employment (index)	85.5	88.7	91.5	93.7	96.7	100.0	103.8	107.0	107.4	107.4
Consumption as percent of GMP[a]	52.7	51.8	51.5	51.1	48.2	47.4	44.7	65.0[c]	67.3[c]	69.4[c]
Investment as percent of GMP[a]	35.1	31.0	29.6	25.2	21.9	21.8	20.1	22.6[c]	20.9[c]	19.9[c]
Balance of payments (millions of US dollars)										
Exports	8,978.0	10,929.0	10,241.0	9,914.0	10,254.0	10,622.0	11,084.0	11,803.0	12,779.0	13,560.0
Imports	15,064.0	15,757.0	13,334.0	12,154.0	11,996.0	12,223.0	13,096.0	13,010.0	13,329.0	15,002.0
Trade balance	-6,086.0	-4,828.0	-3,093.0	-2,240.0	-1,742.0	-1,601.0	-2,012.0	-1,207.0	-550.0	-1,442.0
Current account	-2,291.0	-635.0	-464.0	274.0	559.0	833.0	1,100.0	1,219.0	2,487.0	2,427.0
Public sector (1% of GSP)[b]										
Revenues (broad def.)	n.a.	38.7	37.2	36.7	34.8	33.7	38.2	34.5	33.5	34.7
Expenditures (narrow def.)	n.a.	31.9	30.2	29.4	27.2	26.1	30.3	29.4	25.8	26.3
Deficit										
Enterprise losses	1.6	1.3	2.2	2.9	2.1	2.8	3.0	6.6	5.7	15.0
Seigniorage										
Currency	n.a.	n.a.	1.6	1.3	1.2	2.0	2.8	2.0	2.5	5.9
M1	n.a.	n.a.	4.1	3.9	4.0	3.4	5.7	5.2	5.7	5.7
Reserve money	n.a.	n.a.	8.0	12.6	12.0	11.6	13.9	25.8	33.5	78.1

n.a. Not available.
a. GMP. Gross material product.
b. GSP. Gross social product.
c. Based on changes in % of GSP.
Source: World Bank and International Monetary Fund data.

Table 8-3.B. *Macroeconomic Indicators, Poland, 1980–89*

	1980	1981	1982	1983	1984	1985	1986	1987	1988	1989
Inflation (%)	9.4	21.2	100.8	22.1	15.0	15.1	17.7	25.2	60.0	244.5
Devaluation (%)	10.1	15.7	65.8	7.9	23.7	29.9	19.1	51.2	62.4	234.3
Real wage (index)	118.8	124.8	94.0	95.8	96.9	100.0	102.3	99.0	112.6	126.0
Real exchange rate (index)	70.9	78.5	97.9	118.9	116.3	100.0	78.2	56.5	51.6	57.2
GDP[a] growth (index)	n.a.	–9.98	–4.8	5.6	5.6	3.6	4.2	2.0	4.5	109.6
Industrial production (index)	101.11	87.4	85.8	91.4	96.4	100.0	104.3	107.5	112.7	96.9
Industrial employment (index)	108.2	107.7	102.2	101.2	100.5	100.0	100.2	99.7	98.1	94.8
Consumption as percent of GDP[a]	66.9	74.1	62.7	64.8	63.3	61.7	61.1	60.0	57.1	76.7
Investment as percent of GDP[a]	24.7	18.7	20.1	20.1	20.8	21.3	21.9	22.6	22.5	21.5
Exports as % of GDP[a]	28.1	23.2	19.4	17.2	17.7	18.3	18.2	22.6	22.8	18.3
Imports as % of GDP[a]	31.1	25.3	17.3	15.5	15.7	16.9	16.8	19.0	20.0	16.6
Trade balance as % of GDP[a]	–2.9	–2.1	2.1	1.8	2.0	1.4	1.4	3.6	2.7	1.7
Current account as % of GDP[a]	–5.8	–8.2	–4.0	–2.3	–1.7	–1.3	–0.9	–0.4	–1.0	–2.7
Revenues as % of GDP[a]	48.3	41.7	43.3	39.1	39.7	40.8	39.9	34.2	35.6	30.8
Expenditures as % of GDP[a]	49.5	53.2	46.3	41.2	41.9	41.9	41.0	37.7	37.0	37.0
Deficit as % of GDP[a]	1.2	11.4	2.9	2.1	2.2	1.2	1.1	3.5	1.4	–6.2

n.a. Not available.

a. GDP: Gross domestic product.

Source: World Bank and International Monetary Fund data.

93

Soft Budget Constraints

A common problem in these two countries was the difficulty in imposing hard budget constraints on public sector enterprises. A firm that has a soft budget constraint has an incentive to run deficits, which in the end are financed by credit from the banking system. In effect, this system amounts to granting firms the "privilege" of indirectly printing money (or getting seigniorage), which is a source of inflation. There could be an additional inflationary bias if, as shown in Aizenman (1989), each firm chooses its deficit optimally, taking the total level of seigniorage in the economy as given (i.e., each firm decides its "seigniorage" while keeping constant the amount of seigniorage that other firms receive). However, if all firms behave in this manner, two things happen: the rate of inflation increases; and each firm gets a smaller amount of seigniorage than expected because the demand for money falls as a result of the rise in inflation. Paradoxically, total seigniorage could decline if the economy is already on the wrong side of the Laffer curve.[13]

Soft budget constraints are not exclusive to socialist economies. In Brazil, for example, it is well-known that the central bank has had difficulty controlling the money supply, as it has ended up monetizing the losses of public sector enterprises and government agencies and providing easy credit to the provincial banks. Likewise, in Argentina much of the monetization in the eighties was caused by the losses of public sector enterprises and the financial sector and by the deficits of the provinces. Those two Latin American countries have had the same difficulty imposing hard budget constraints as the transforming economies in Central and Eastern Europe are confronting now.

What the hard budget constraints entail is a centralization of control over overall macro-management, with especial emphasis on monetary policy.[14] In Central and Eastern Europe the governments are imposing hard budget constraints on the enterprises at the same time they are following policies aimed at decontrolling prices and decentralizing production decisions. These two objectives are compatible, and in effect they represent the reversal of the previous system in which the decentralization of macro-decisions created an inflationary bias in the economies, while centralization of production decisions resulted in widespread inefficiencies.

Stabilization Strategies

Broadly speaking, two alternative stabilization strategies can be distinguished. The orthodox approach is based on elimination of the budget deficit and the use of money or the exchange rate to anchor the price level. Within this approach there is money- and exchange rate-based stabilization, depending on which of these variables is used as the nominal anchor. The heterodox approach, which in effect is a version of the orthodox exchange rate-based stabilization, initially supports the fiscal adjustment with price and wage controls to deal with the inertial aspects of inflation.

There is extensive literature analyzing orthodox and heterodox programs in Latin America and Israel (for example Bruno, et al. 1988, Kiguel and Liviatan 1988 and 1989, and Ramos 1986, among others). This paper summarizes the main findings with the objective of drawing lessons for Central and Eastern Europe.

The Orthodox Approach

The orthodox approach has been effective in stopping hyper-inflation episodes in low-inflation countries. It has been less effective in the chronic high-inflation ones, especially in the short run.

Money-based programs. There are few examples of money-based stabilization programs in chronic high-inflation countries. The Chilean stabilization program of 1974-75 is one of the few. It was a comprehensive effort that combined a major fiscal adjustment with a monetary crunch aimed at stopping inflation.[15] The effect on inflation was disappointing. Despite a major anti-inflation effort, the rate fell only marginally between 1973 and 1975. This disappointing outcome was accompanied by a dramatic rise in unemployment (from 4.6 percent in 1973 to 16.8 percent in 1975), a large fall in GDP (exceeding 14 percent in 1975) and an improvement in the current account. In early 1990 Argentina and Brazil were pursuing monetarist programs to stop their hyper-inflation (see the previous section). In these two cases inflation fell initially—monthly inflation dropped at the beginning to one-digit levels—but the success lasted for only several months: inflation later bounced back to rates above 20 percent a month in both countries. As in Chile, both programs were recessionary and led to an improvement in the current account.

The sluggishness with which money-based programs reduce inflation and their high costs in terms of output and unemployment explain why this approach is seldom used in the chronic high-inflation countries. In most cases where money-based programs have been adopted, the monetarist phase has been short, with the authorities eventually shifting to a strategy that uses the exchange rate as the nominal anchor.[16]

Exchange rate-based stabilization. Exchange rate-based stabilization is a program designed to reduce inflation that combines a package of fiscal adjustment with the exchange rate as the nominal anchor. The exchange rate rule can take the form of a fixed exchange rate (as in Chile in 1980) or a pre-announced rate of devaluation (as in the *tablitas* in the late seventies in Argentina, Chile and Uruguay).[17]

Exchange rate-based stabilization is usually more effective than money-based stabilization in bringing down inflation. In Chile, for example, the combination of a tight fiscal stance and the announcement of a schedule of future daily values of the exchange rate embodying decreasing rates of devaluation was more effective in reducing inflation than was the monetarist phase. Nevertheless, the inflation was very persistent, remaining above the pre-announced rate of devaluation for a prolonged period. As a result, the real exchange rate appreciated, and in the end the economy was stuck with an overvalued currency, difficulties in the external sector and the threat of a balance-of-payments crisis.

The experience with the pre-announced exchange rate in Argentina and Uruguay, as well as in other countries that adopted exchange rate-based stabilization programs, indicates that overvaluation is unavoidable in programs of this type and needs to be viewed as a necessary cost for stopping inflation. Because of this problem, however, countries need to devise a strategy for solving the overvaluation issue. Typically the solution is to change the nominal anchor as devaluation of the exchange rate is used to change the real exchange rate. At least transitorily, money should replace the exchange rate as the nominal anchor (the strategy adopted in Chile in 1982-83 to overcome the real appreciation).

The Heterodox Approach

Heterodox stabilization programs are those that supplement orthodox measures—namely, tight fiscal and audit policies and a fixed exchange rate—with income policies. They are usually the first stage in a long-term stabilization effort. The distinctive feature of these programs is the initial and temporary use of price and wage controls and a fixed exchange rate to achieve a rapid reduction in inflation. Once the controls are removed, the program essentially becomes an orthodox exchange rate-based stabilization program. Most orthodox programs start with a period of tight money before they switch to the exchange rate as the nominal anchor—one difference between orthodox and heterodox programs.

Few programs satisfy the definition of heterodox presented here. There were just two examples in the eighties: the Israeli program of 1985 and the Mexican program of 1987-88.[18] Both programs initially used income policies to achieve a rapid reduction in inflation;

in both cases the exchange rate was the main nominal anchor and was fixed at the beginning; and both maintained the fiscal adjustment throughout.[19] There were differences in the degree to which the two countries applied controls. In Israel, the controls were economy-wide, while in Mexico the government opted to allow a large number of prices to be determined freely. However, these differences were ones of degree and not substance. Basically, the philosophy behind the two programs was the same.[20]

One feature of heterodox programs is the ease with which they bring inflation down during the early phase of the program. This initial fall in inflation, however, is not an indication of success because this outcome is common to both successful and unsuccessful programs (the latter include those that imposed price-wage controls but did not persist on the fiscal side). A second feature is that the initial costs of bringing inflation down are not very large (as opposed to under money-based orthodox programs). In Israel, unemployment went up marginally for just two quarters, while in Mexico there were no indications of costs in terms of unemployment and output growth as a result of the stabilization efforts.

The first stage is, however, the easy part of a heterodox stabilization program. Typically, the difficulties appear later. By using the heterodox approach, policymakers tend to postpone many of the problems that appear early on in money-based orthodox programs. The use of controls does not remove the credibility problem that orthodox programs face in chronic high-inflation countries, and this difficulty has to be confronted later when prices and wages are liberalized (the stage in which flexibility is created). This stage is the more difficult one in a heterodox program, since only then do policy-makers have to rely on traditional nominal anchors (either money or the exchange rate) to bring inflation down. The typical problems in the flexibility stage are a resurgence of inflation, an increase in real wages, high interest rates, an appreciation of the real exchange rate and a deterioration in the current account.

Outcomes under Exchange Rate- and Money-based Stabilization

The outcomes of money- and exchange rate-based stabilization not only differed in terms of inflation but also the evolution of output, the current account, the real exchange rate and other key macroeconomic variables.[21]

Exchange rate-based stabilization. Most of the exchange rate-based stabilization programs are characterized by a sequence of expansion and recession in GDP growth and by a deterioration in the current account.[22] This pattern is robust in the sense that it is observed in programs that started as heterodox as well as those that started as orthodox and is common to those that did and did not undertake a robust fiscal adjustment. For example, a large number of programs in Argentina and Uruguay began with a reduction of the fiscal deficit, which, however, was maintained only for a limited time (from one to three years).[23] These stabilizations were characterized by initial booms in output, increases in real wages, real appreciations and subsequent recessions. In some cases the collapse of the exchange rate regime was associated with a severe crisis (such as in 1980–81 in Argentina and the 1972 collapse in Uruguay).

Similar developments were also observed in exchange rate-based stabilization programs that continued to be supported by a fiscal adjustment. This pattern prevailed in the Chilean and Uruguayan *tablita*-type stabilizations around the end of the 1970s and in the Israeli stabilization of 1985. In the case of Chile, the fiscal accounts were in surplus throughout the last three years of the program, while Israel ran a surplus in the first two years. Yet in all these cases output cycles were observed, ending in severe recessions in the Southern Cone countries and a prolonged recession in Israel (Kiguel and Liviatan 1990a). Real appreciation of the domestic currencies and the emergence of current account problems were also observed (except in the case of Israel). Thus the phenomenon of temporary growth cannot be explained solely by a lack of fiscal balance.

What is the explanation for the difficulty of maintaining a stable exchange rate when the government's budget is balanced? One possible explanation is that the nominal anchor lacks credibility. Suppose that agents expect that the government will not sustain the program over the longer run and that it may end up in a balance-of-payments crisis, as has been true in the past. In this case agents will expect tight credit conditions in the future or the introduction of trade restrictions, expectations that will induce them to shift expenditures to the present period. In an exchange rate-based stabilization these expectations tend to become self-fulfilling, since the central bank supplies the foreign exchange reserves to finance the expenditure boom and/or capital flight. This situation may explain the actual consumption booms often observed in these programs.

This expansionary tendency may also explain part of the rise in real wages and the real appreciation.[24] In addition, a lack of credibility in the persistence of the official exchange rate policy will give rise to expectations of devaluations in excess of the actual ones, a situation that will tend to raise real wages (or prevent them from fall-

ing) even when the expenditure boom subsides. This factor exacerbates the recession.

Money-based stabilization. In view of the difficulties found with exchange rate-based stabilization, is it not preferable to use the money supply as the nominal anchor? A basic feature of money-based stabilization is that the recessionary costs appear up front, in contrast to exchange rate-based programs, where the costs appear at a later stage as a result of the real appreciation and the deterioration of the current account. The immediate recessionary effect of money-based programs is mainly attributable to the short-term downward rigidity in prices and wages and the lack of credibility, which in part may be related to skepticism about whether the government will stick with tight money.

Another difference between the two strategies is that, with money-based programs, it is unusual that targets be set for expansion of the money supply, while under exchange rate-based programs it is very common to announce targets for the exchange rate (including a full peg or a pre-announced rate in the *tablita* fashion). A number of reasons can explain this difference. First, there is a stronger incentive to set targets for the exchange rate because its definition is clear and it is easy to measure and control. With the money supply, on the other hand, there are different monetary aggregates that could be subject to targets, and information on these aggregates is not readily available. Second, the difficulty of predicting the demand for money during disinflation makes it very hard to establish targets for the money supply (especially in the case of the narrow aggregates). Increases in the money supply are not inflationary if accompanied by an increase in money demand. Under an exchange rate rule, on the other hand, this problem does not arise because money is endogenously determined through the balance of payments. Third, the costs associated with a lack of credibility (and the persistence of inflation) are easier to absorb in the short run under an exchange rate rule than under a monetary rule. In the former case, they usually lead to a real appreciation and a deterioration in the current account; however, because real interest rates are relatively low, an exchange rate rule does not usually have strong recessionary effects. Under a monetary rule, on the other hand, persistence in inflation leads to even tighter money, high interest rates and a more pronounced recession.

In comparing the two strategies, it is observed that exchange rate-based stabilization has the advantage of avoiding large initial recessionary costs.[25] However, it should not be thought that the recessionary costs of bringing inflation down can be avoided altogether. There is usually a period of real appreciation even with exchange rate-based programs, as inflation persists while the government adheres to the exchange rate rule. A maxi-devaluation is not usually the solution to this recessionary period because it amounts to abandonment of the rule. In addition, the country needs to reduce domestic expenditures in the future in order to service the external debt that accumulated during the period of current account deficits.

The Stabilization Programs in Yugoslavia and Poland

An Impressionistic Look at the Outcomes

The stabilization programs in Yugoslavia and Poland combined elements of both heterodox and orthodox strategies. The heterodox component was the use of wage controls (either directly or through tax-induced incentives), which in Yugoslavia were supplemented by price controls for a small number of goods (around 20 percent of the consumer basket). Prices were by and large more flexible than in most heterodox programs in Latin America.[26] The orthodox part was the fiscal adjustment, of which a central part in both countries was the imposition of hard budget constraints on public sector enterprises. This measure was crucial because to a large extent the deficits of these enterprises rather than that of the central governments were the source of the money creation (in this respect the nature of the deficits were similar to Argentina and Brazil's). Both programs fixed the exchange rate (which in effect became the main nominal anchor) and tightened domestic credit to the enterprises.

While there are similarities regarding the behavior of inflation and output, developments were not exactly the same. Inflation fell drastically in the two countries: in Yugoslavia it was stopped in its tracks (as in past hyper-inflations), while in Poland inflation remained at a low level (around 4-5 percent a month). The disinflation led to large output costs in both countries, which were especially large in Poland.

How do these outcomes compare with the experience of other countries? First, it seems that the costs of reducing inflation were larger than was true under the exchange rate-based stabilization programs in Latin America and Israel, and certainly larger than those incurred in stopping hyper-inflation. In fact, the reduction in output and the improvement in the current account were more common under money-based stabilization programs (e.g., Chile 1973-75). At the same time, the rapid initial fall in inflation is characteristic of programs that rely (even if partially) on some type of wage controls (the heterodox component), an element that was present in both countries.

There are at least two reasons why these exchange rate-based programs were more recessionary that similar programs in Latin America. First, as argued by Calvo and Coricelli (1990), in part the recession was driven by a tightening of domestic credit that worked through the supply side. In addition, as happens in most monetarist programs, the current account improved. In this respect, the programs had a stronger monetarist flavor than did many exchange rate-based programs in Latin America.

A second, important factor for the recession cum improvement in the current account is related to the delay in defining a policy for the privatization of public sector enterprises. It is now certain that most public sector enterprises will be privatized in the near future and that this move will create great opportunities for those individuals who are liquid. It will also create an incentive to increase private saving, so that domestic absorption will decline and the current account improve. The improvement in the current account should not, however, be taken as evidence that the programs are credible, in part because it is not yet clear whether they will succeed and what will happen to the exchange rate in the case of failure. Instead, the improvement in the current account indicates that the potential gains from purchases of public enterprises (the saving motive) outweigh the increase in demand resulting from the temporary nature of the stabilization effort. More importantly, it also suggests that resolving the privatization issue will add to the recovery of economic activity.

Finally, it seems that both countries are still in the early stages of their stabilization process. While they succeeded in bringing inflation down before experiencing full-blown hyper-inflation, none has achieved sustainable price stability. Experience shows that the most difficult task is sustaining a low rate of inflation. Many programs in chronic high-inflation countries have maintained low levels of inflation for prolonged periods, but eventually their initial success was reversed because it could only be maintained at the cost of an overvalued exchange rate, very high real interest rates, low real wages, or unrealistic expectations about the sustainability of the cuts in government expenditures or the increases in tax revenues.

Policy Issues Based on the Latin American Experience

There are three additional lessons from Latin America that could be relevant for Central and Eastern Europe. First, none of the successful stabilization programs (including Israel, Mexico and Bolivia's) has been able to bring annual inflation down below 20 percent. This situation is a puzzle, because the same outcomes are observed in Bolivia, which stopped a hyper-inflation, and in the chronic high-inflation countries (e.g., Chile, Mexico and Israel). In addition, the phenomenon does not seem to be related to the specific form of the exchange rate rule—Mexico adopted a crawling peg, while Israel used discrete devaluations—and cannot be explained by fiscal considerations, since deficits do not appear to have been a major factor in affecting inflation in any of these countries.

Second, stabilization has proved to be a long-term endeavor in the chronic high-inflation countries in Latin America where markets already existed. It is likely to take even longer in Central and Eastern European countries where a large number of structural reforms need to be undertaken simultaneously.

Third, and a related factor, the costs of failure should not be underestimated. Each new stabilization attempt that fails to bring inflation down makes stabilization more difficult the next time around. The repeated failure of stabilization attempts in Argentina and Brazil since the Austral and Cruzado plans are good examples of what happens. Both countries experienced a period of inflation-stabilization cycles in which the inflationary outbursts became more pronounced after each failed attempt at stabilization (see figure 8-2), eventually reaching hyper-inflationary levels, while the difficulty in keeping inflation low, even for short periods, became larger over time. These arguments can be used to make a case for maintaining and deepening the stabilization effort.

Finally, it is important to examine briefly in what ways stabilization in centrally planned economies could be different from that in market economies as a result of the differences in institutional arrangements and the system of incentives. Specifically, it is argued here that the imposition of hard budget constraints on firms when the issue of ownership is not settled, as is now the case in both Poland and Yugoslavia, changes the nature of the relation between firms and workers and could lead to an undesirable response by managers. Prior to the imposition of a hard budget constraint, there is an implicit long-term relationship between a firm and its workers because the firm is likely to continue functioning in the future and hence workers have implicit tenure. Although the state is the formal owner of the firm, workers still identify with the interests of the firm.

Once the hard budget constraint is imposed, the nature of this relationship changes. Workers in effect lose their tenure, since they are not sure whether the firm will survive under the new rules and whether they will retain their jobs. This situation causes a shift in the objective function of the workers (and hence managers), who place more emphasis on maximizing short-term revenue, even at the cost of depleting the capital stock and inventories, and less concern about the long-term viability of the firm.

The above discussion indicates that imposing a hard budget constraint on firms while the issue of ownership is not settled could have detrimental effects on the capital stock and on the long-term viability of firms and hence growth. It argues in favor of settling the ownership issue before imposing the hard budget constraint on firms.

Notes

1. As discussed in Lizano and Charpentier (1990) with respect to Costa Rica.

2. For a discussion of this topic see Kiguel and Liviatan (1988).

3. These were prepared as part of the World Bank research project, "Stopping High Inflation," RPO 674-24.

4. While indexation usually lowers the costs of nominal shocks, at the same time, by reducing the variability in relative prices, it also makes the adjustment to real shocks more difficult and costly.

5. The costs of inflation appear much later, usually as inflation reaches hyper-inflationary levels. Experience indicates that there is no such thing as a high stable rate of inflation. Once inflation is high, if it is not brought down through a drastic and persistent stabilization program, it will eventually run out of control.

6. The Bolivian hyper-inflation and subsequent stabilization are analyzed in Sachs (1986) and Morales (1988), among others.

7. For a thorough discussion of this topic see Kiguel and Liviatan (1988).

8. See Kiguel and Liviatan (1990b) for a comparison of the recent inflation-stabilization experience in Argentina and Brazil.

9. Bolivia did not fully eliminate the inflation: it has held at an annual rate of around 20 percent since stabilization.

10. Rocha (1990) provides an extensive analysis of inflation in Yugoslavia in the eighties.

11. There are many examples of inflationary episodes caused by a policy of aggressive devaluations aimed at achieving a real depreciation (e.g., Mexico in 1987 and Israel in 1984). The perception that the real exchange rate (a relative price) can be affected by manipulating the exchange rate is misleading, because it ignores that domestic prices adjust to bring the real exchange rate to a level that is consistent with the underlying policies and overall macroeconomic conditions.

12. There are also cases in Latin America of increases in inflation that were driven by wage push pressures of the type just described. In Argentina, for example, in 1983-84, first the military government and then the Alfonsín administration attempted to increase real wages by raising nominal wages. The policy backfired in the end, as is now happening in Poland, because inflation increased the rise in nominal wages and thereby reduced the real wage.

13. Some of these issues are analyzed in Aizenman (1989).

14. In Argentina, for example, the finance minister recently requested personal control over the budgets of public sector enterprises, a measure that increased centralization of decision-making. This arrangement was devised as a way to impose hard budget constraints on the enterprises.

15. For a thorough analysis of this program see, for example, Ramos (1986), Corbo (1986), Edwards and Edwards (1987), and Corbo and Solimano (1990).

16. This sequence was observed in the Chilean program just discussed, as well as in the 1959 and 1976 stabilization programs in Argentina.

17. These programs are described and analyzed in Corbo and de Melo (1985) and Ramos (1986), among others.

18. The Mexican program cannot be fully evaluated yet, since two and a half years is not a long enough period according to the authors' criteria. Progress has been good, however, and the prospects are promising.

19. The Israeli program is analyzed in detail in Bruno and Piterman (1988), Bruno and Meridor (1990) and Liviatan (1988 and 1990), among others, and the Mexican program in Ortiz (1990). See also Kiguel and Liviatan (1989).

20. There also were a number of heterodox programs in the sixties in Latin America. The Brazilian stabilization program of 1964–67 (analyzed in Simonsen 1974 and Cardoso and Fishlow 1990, among others) is an example of a successful one. The Austral plan in Argentina in 1985 (analyzed in Heymann 1987 and Kiguel 1989, among others) started as a heterodox program, but the government later relaxed the fiscal adjustment and abandoned the program.

21. Heterodox programs are considered here as exchange rate-based stabilization. Although initially the exchange rate is part of a broader set of anchors, it usually becomes the main nominal anchor in the second stage once the controls are removed.

22. This finding is documented in Kiguel and Liviatan (1990a), where a large number of money- and exchange rate-based stabilization programs in Latin America and Israel are examined in detail.

23. Kiguel and Liviatan (1990a) discussed these episodes.

24. Calvo (1986) and Calvo and Vegh (1990) explain how a cash-in-advance model can generate these transitory aspects. For alternative explanations, see Kiguel and Liviatan (1990a).

25. Typically, heterodox exchange rate-based stabilization programs exhibit some initial recession. However, it was usually small relative to the ones observed under money-based stabilization in the sample of countries studied by the authors and in industrial countries.

26. The Mexican program is undoubtedly the most similar because most prices continued to be freely determined. In practice, however, there were informal pressures on firms to limit their price increases.

References

Aizenman, Joshua. 1989. "Competitive Externalities and the Optimal Seigniorage." Mimeo. University of Chicago. Chicago.

Bruno, Michael, and L. Meridor. 1990. "The Costly Transition from Stabilization to Sustainable Growth: Israel in Its Third Phase." Mimeo.

Bruno, M., and S. Piterman. 1988. "Israel's Stabilization: A Two Year Review," pp. 1-47. In M. Bruno, et al., eds., *Inflation Stabilization*. Cambridge, Mass.: MIT Press.

Bruno, M., G. Di Tella, R. Dornbusch and S. Fischer, eds. 1988. *Inflation Stabilization*. Cambridge, Mass.: MIT Press.

Calvo, Guillermo A. 1986. "Temporary Stabilization: Predetermined Exchange Rates." *Journal of Political Economy* 94:1319-29.

Calvo, Guillermo, and Fabrizio Coricelli. 1990. "Stagflationary Effects of Stabilization Programs in Reforming Socialist Countries: Supply Side Vs. Demand Side Factors." Mimeo. World Bank. Washington, D.C.

Calvo, Guillermo, and Carlos Vegh. 1990. "Credibility and the Dynamics of Stabilization Programs: An Analytical Framework." Mimeo. International Monetary Fund. Washington, D.C.

Cardoso, Eliana, and Albert Fishlow. 1990. "The Macroeconomics of Brazilian External Debt," pp. 269-391. In Jeffrey Sachs, ed., *Developing Country Debt and Economic Performance*. Chicago, Ill.: University of Chicago Press.

Corbo, Vittorio. 1986. "The Use of the Exchange Rate for Stabilization Purposes: The Case of Chile." In M. Connally and C. Gonzalez, eds., *Economic Reforms and Stabilization in Latin America*. New York: Praeger.

Corbo, Vittorio, and Jaime de Melo. 1985. "Liberalization with Stabilization in the Southern Cone of Latin America." *World Development*, special issue (August).

Corbo, Vittorio, and Andrés Solimano. 1990. "Chile's Experience with Stabilization Revisited." Mimeo. World Bank. Washington, D.C.

Dornbusch, Rudiger, and Stanley Fischer. 1986. "Stopping Hyperinflation Past and Present." *Weltwirtschaftliches Archiv* (April).

Edwards, Sebastian, and Alejandra Cox Edwards. 1987. *Monetarism and Liberalization: The Chilean Experience*. Cambridge, Mass.: Ballinger Publishing Co.

Heymann, Daniel. 1987. "The Austral Plan." *American Economic Review* 77 (2):284-87.

International Monetary Fund. Various issues. *International Financial Statistics*. Washington, D.C.: World Bank.

Kiguel, Miguel A. 1989. "Inflation in Argentina: Stop and Go Since the Austral Plan." World Bank, Policy, Planning and Research (PPR) Working Paper. Washington, D.C.

Kiguel, Miguel A., and Nissan Liviatan. 1988. "Inflationary Rigidities and Orthodox Stabilization Policies: Lessons from Latin America." *The World Bank Economic Review* 2 (3)(September):273-98.

———. 1989. "The Old and the New in Heterodox Stabilization Programs: Lessons from the 1960s and the 1980s." World Bank, Policy, Planning and Research (PPR) Working Paper No. 323. Washington, D.C.

———. 1990a. "The Business Cycle Associated with Exchange Rate Stabilizations." Mimeo. World Bank. Washington, D.C.

———. 1990b. "The Inflation Stabilization Cycle in Argentina and Brazil." Mimeo. World Bank. Washington, D.C.

Liviatan, Nissan. 1988. "Israel's Stabilization Program: A Three Year Perspective." World Bank, Policy, Planning and Research (PPR) Working Paper No. 91. Washington, D.C. September.

———. 1990. "The Process of Restoring Macroeconomic Balance in Israel." Mimeo. World Bank. Washington, D.C.

Liviatan, N., and S. Piterman. 1986. "Accelerating Inflation and Balance of Payments Crises: Israel 1973-1984," pp. 320-46. In Yoram Ben-Porah, ed., *The Israeli Economy*. Cambridge, Mass.: Harvard University Press.

Lipton, David, and Jeffrey Sachs. 1990. "Creating a Market Economy in Eastern Europe: The Case of Poland." *Brookings Papers on Economic Activity* 1:75-147.

Lizano, Eduardo, and Silvia Charpentier. 1990. "External Debt and Economic Policy: The Case of Costa Rica." Mimeo. World Bank. Washington, D.C.

Morales, Juan-Antonio. 1988. "Inflation Stabilization in Bolivia," pp. 307–46. In Michael Bruno, G. Di Tella, R. Dornbusch and S. Fischer, eds., *Inflation Stabilization*. Cambridge, Mass.: MIT Press.

Ortiz, Guillermo. 1990. "Mexico Beyond the Debt Crisis, Towards Stabilization and Growth with Price Stability." Mimeo. January.

Pazos, F. 1972. *Chronic Inflation in Latin America*. New York: Praeger.

Ramos, Joseph. 1986. *Neoconservative Economics in the Southern Cone of Latin America, 1973-83*. Baltimore, Md.: The John Hopkins University Press.

Rocha, Roberto. 1990. "Inflation and Stabilization in Socialist Countries: Some Lessons from the Yugoslav Experience." Mimeo. World Bank. Washington, D.C.

Sachs, J. 1986. "The Bolivian Hyperinflation and Stabilization." NBER Discussion Paper No. 2073. National Bureau of Economic Research. New York.

Sargent, Thomas J. 1982. "The End of Four Big Inflations." In R.E. Hall, ed., *Inflation: Causes and Effects*. Chicago, Ill.: University of Chicago Press.

Simonsen, Mario Henrique. 1974. "The Anti-Inflation Policy." In Mario Henrique Simonsen and Roberto de Oliveira Campos, eds., *The New Brazilian Economy*. Rio de Janeiro: Crown Editores Internacionais.

Yeager, Leland B. 1981. *Experiences with Stopping Inflation*. Washington, D.C.: American Enterprise Institute.

9

Stabilization Programs in Eastern Europe: A Comparative Analysis of the Polish and Yugoslav Programs of 1990

Fabrizio Coricelli and Roberto de Rezende Rocha[1]

Dissatisfaction with their performance and concern over the acceleration of inflation led the governments of Poland and Yugoslavia to implement stabilization cum restructuring programs at the end of 1989. Their programs, which they launched at approximately the same time (December 18, 1989 in Yugoslavia and January 1, 1990 in Poland), comprise measures designed not only to stabilize inflation at low levels but also to change the structure of their economic systems.

The stabilization components of both programs would ordinarily be classified as heterodox, since they include incomes policy measures in addition to a significant fiscal adjustment, the imposition of credit controls and the relaxation of exchange rate and trade controls. The restructuring components of the two programs also share some similarities. Both attempt to force inefficient enterprises into bankruptcy, albeit through different methods. However, in neither case is there a clearly defined strategy to deal with bankrupt enterprises, including what the precise role of privatization in the overall reform strategy will be. In fact, both countries are still elaborating several aspects of their restructuring components.

Both programs brought about a substantial reduction in inflation in the first semester of 1990 without recourse to widespread price controls. In the case of Poland, inflation was reduced from a peak of 78 percent in January to 3.5 percent in June. In the case of Yugoslavia, inflation went from a peak of 60 percent in December 1989 to almost 0 percent in May and June 1990. The performance of the two programs in the second semester of 1990 was less satisfactory, with monthly inflation rates of around 5 percent in Poland and ranging between 3 percent and 8 percent in Yugoslavia.

Both countries experienced a sharp contraction in economic activity following the implementation of their programs. During 1990, real GDP fell by 12.5 percent and 7.5 percent in Poland and Yugoslavia, respectively.

The contraction of activity was particularly strong in the industrial sector, as indicated by negative growth rates of 20 percent and 10 percent, respectively. Although the contraction in output was concentrated in the first semester of 1990, the prospects for a sustained resumption of growth are still uncertain in both countries.

The implementation of two apparently similar programs by two reforming socialist countries at almost the same time has produced great interest in a comparative analysis of their design, performance and sustainability. Such is the objective of this paper. To this end, the paper investigates the possible differences that underlie the similarities of the two programs and that may account for the better initial performance of Yugoslavia's program (a sharper reduction of inflation with smaller losses in output). The paper identifies significant differences in the initial conditions in the two countries, as well as in the sequence and degree of some policy measures. These differences may explain the disparities in the early results. Finally, the paper identifies the most important issues that the two countries will have to address in the second stage of their programs. These include the unfreezing of nominal variables and resolution of the critical structural problems affecting both economies.

The next section provides some background information on inflation in the two countries during the 1980s. The following section examines the conditions in the two economies before stabilization. A comparison of the components of the two programs is presented in the subsequent section, followed by a section that analyzes the initial results of the programs and points to the possible causes of the more severe recession in Poland. It also identifies the likely causes of the revival of inflation in Yugoslavia during the second semester of 1990. The final section assesses the main issues facing the second stage of the reform in the two countries. Much more detailed analyses of the two programs appear in the two appendices (appendix 1 deals with Poland, appendix 2 with Yugoslavia).

Background

The histories of inflation in Poland and Yugoslavia during the last decade are quite different. As shown in figure 9-1, inflation in Poland was more erratic than that in Yugoslavia. The dominant feature in the first half of the decade in Poland was a jump in 1981-82, while in the second half inflation showed an upward trend until 1988, followed by another jump in 1989 when it reached 640 percent. In Yugoslavia inflation was more or less stable until 1983. After that year it accelerated almost continuously, reaching 2,700 percent in 1989. In general, the rates of inflation in Yugoslavia were much higher than in Poland (except in 1982) and than the OECD average for the decade.

These differences in the path of inflation reflect in part differences in the structure of the two economies. Until the early 1980s Poland had a centrally planned economy, when it initiated a gradual decentralization. Yugoslavia had already replaced its central planning with a system of self-management in the early 1960s. As a result, there was much less interference in the price system in Yugoslavia. Unlike in Poland, price controls in Yugoslavia were rarely strong enough to repress inflation. In fact, they bore a greater resemblance to the controls prevailing in other high inflation countries such as Brazil (which has always had controls of some sort).

The phenomenon of high inflation in Yugoslavia was closely associated with the turnaround in the current account during the 1980s—typically inflation accelerates as the current account shifts from a deficit to an increasing surplus. Two major factors underlay the close association between inflation and the current account in Yugoslavia. First, the need to reduce the real wage to levels consistent with a given depreciated real exchange rate required an increase in the rate of inflation—the Pazos-Simonsen mechanism (see Dornbusch 1987, Pazos 1978 and Simonsen 1989). This factor became more important at the end of the decade, with the increase in real wage rigidity occurring after the formal introduction of wage indexation in 1987.

Second, the conditions that prevailed after the reversal of the flows in external financing considerably wors-

Figure 9-1: *Inflation in Poland and Yugoslavia, 1980-90* (percentage change per annum)

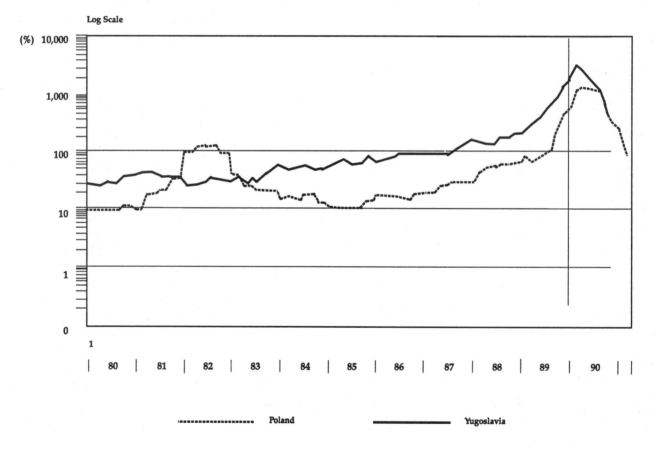

ened the financial situation of Yugoslav enterprises, where the fundamental imbalances of the Yugoslav economy were located (the non-financial public sector ran surpluses throughout the 1980s). Large losses in foreign exchange as a result of interest and principal payments, combined with stagnant output and increasing overstaffing, resulted in greater enterprise losses in the 1980s. The enterprise imbalances spilled over to the central bank, since the latter had to absorb large amounts of foreign liabilities in an effort to protect the enterprises and commercial banks from even greater financial difficulty. As a result, the central bank ran a quasi-fiscal deficit that became an independent source of monetary expansion. The various attempts at stabilization failed to address the hidden losses in the system and were abandoned soon after implementation.

Unlike in Yugoslavia, the non-financial public sector in Poland ran deficits during the 1980s, while enterprise accounts showed small surpluses. The fiscal deficits were, however, kept at moderate levels (1-2 percent of gross national product [GNP]) during most of this period, the exceptions being 1981 and 1989, when the deficit was much larger (10 percent and 8 percent of GNP, re-

spectively). In addition, the negative transfer of resources from abroad, as measured by the non-interest current account surplus, was much smaller in Poland (2-3 percent of GNP) than it was in Yugoslavia (5-7 percent of GNP).[2]

These numbers indicate that the underlying rate of inflation consistent with "fundamentals" was lower in the case of Poland. At the same time, the much stricter price controls in Poland make it more difficult to associate the movement of inflation with the fundamentals.[3]

In addition, there is some association between price controls and budgetary performance via the subsidies. For instance, the outburst of inflation in 1982 coincided with a sharp reduction in the deficit from 1981 to 1982, a phenomenon that occurred again from the first to the second half of 1989.

Conditions Preceding Stabilization

Conditions in the Polish and Yugoslav economies preceding the two stabilization programs are summarized in table 9-1. In Poland, the sharp increase in inflation during 1989 was the result of not only the increased fis-

Table 9-1. *Initial Conditions in Poland and Yugoslavia*

Variable	Poland	Yugoslavia
Background		
Inflation	640% in 1989	2,700% in 1989
Output growth	1.4% in the 1980s, 0% in 1989	0.7% in the 1980s, 0.8% in 1989
Rate of unemployment	0% in the 1980s, 0% in 1989	13% in the 1980s, 14% in 1989
Other Conditions in 1989		
GNP	US$66.2 billion	US$67.0 billion
Current account	US$1.8 billion deficit	US$24.billion surplus
Gross debt	US$40.6 billion	US$17.3 billion
Reserves	US$2.5 billion	US$6.1 billion
Black market premium	400% average in 1989 40% before the plan	10% average in 1989, 30% before the plan
Fiscal/enterprise balance	Fiscal deficit of 7.2% of GNP	Fiscal surplus of 0.7% of GNP Enterprise losses of 15% of GNP Central Bank losses of 4-5% of GNP Large volume of non-performing loans
Seigniorage	13.5% of GNP	12% of GNP
Ratio of M3 to GNP	47.8%	33.1%
Share of foreign exchange deposits in M3	69.3%	69.5%

Source: Various national sources.

cal deficit (7.2 percent of GNP, the bulk of which was incurred in the first semester) but also the successive price shocks related to the liberalization of food prices (August), the first round of adjustment of energy prices (October) and repeated devaluations accompanied by the introduction of formal wage indexation.

In Yugoslavia, various factors contributed to the open inflation of 2,700 percent in 1989. First, a large real devaluation in mid-1988 in the context of formal wage indexation caused wages and prices to escalate. Second, although the government abandoned its target for the real exchange rate in mid-1989, an explosion in real wages in the second semester sustained the inflationary pressure. Finally, the hidden losses in the system, which had not been corrected, constituted a permanent source of monetary expansion and inflation. Pressure on the money supply was further increased by the large buildup in foreign exchange reserves over the year. In 1989, seignorage revenues on base money reached 13.5 percent and 12 percent of GNP in Poland and Yugoslavia, respectively.

The fiscal deterioration in Poland during 1989 was partly attributable to the fall in real tax revenues, which in turn resulted in part from lags in the collection of taxes—the Olivera-Tanzi effect (see Olivera 1967 and Tanzi 1977). As shown in table 9.2, the revenue loss amounted to 7 percent of GNP.

In Yugoslavia, on the other hand, the erosion of fiscal revenues in the 1980s tended to be offset by adjustments in the tax rates and contributions, as well as by the partial indexation of some taxes. In the years when these measures proved insufficient to stabilize real tax revenues, the government adjusted expenditures so as to prevent a deficit. These factors make estimation of the Olivera-Tanzi effect more difficult in the case of Yugoslavia.

Yugoslavia enjoyed a more comfortable external position before 1990 than did Poland. The large current account surplus of 1989—US$2.4 billion—and the successful debt rescheduling of 1988 allowed foreign reserves to rise to US$6.1 billion at the end of 1989. Poland, in contrast, ran a current account deficit of US$1.8 billion in 1989 and ended the year with much lower reserves—US$2.5 billion (much of which was not useable

as pledged against obligations). In addition, in Yugoslavia the excess demand for foreign exchange at the official rate was mild, as suggested by a barely positive black market premium (figure 9.2). In Poland, the black market premium was still very large in 1989, despite the real devaluations after 1987. The size of the premium there reflected the magnitude of the exchange rate misalignment and possibly some residual monetary overhang.

It is important to bear such differences in mind when examining the rationale for some of the preparatory measures taken in 1989, especially in view of the goal in the two programs of substantially reducing the exchange rate and trade controls. As shown in figure 9.3, both countries devalued their currencies in real terms in November and December 1989. However, in the case of Poland, the more adverse external conditions and the large exchange rate misalignment dictated the need for much sharper real devaluations. The same factors seem to explain why Poland restricted the introduction of convertibility to current account transactions, while in Yugoslavia convertibility was also extended to the capital account.

Figure 9-2: *Black Market Currency Premia in Poland and Yugoslavia, 1980-90*

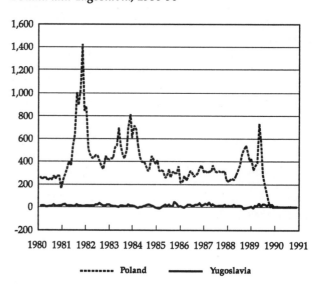

Table 9-2. *Total Fiscal Revenues in Poland and Yugoslavia, 1985-89*[a]

(percent of GDP)

	1985	1986	1987	1988	1989
Poland	n.a.	49.4	46.9	48.0	40.8
Yugoslavia	33.7	38.2	34.5	33.5	34.7

n.a. Not available.

a. Using a broad definition of the public sector in both countries.

Source: World Bank.

Figure 9-3. *Real Effective Exchange Rate Indices, Poland and Yugoslavia*
(1988=100)

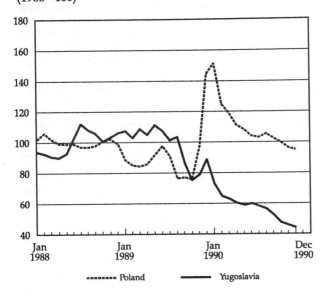

------- Poland   —— Yugoslavia

Both countries adjusted public sector prices at the end of 1989. However, in Poland some of the administered prices were so low that even after the very sharp corrections made in that period (100 percent increase in energy prices in October), the prices remained substantially below international levels and had to be further corrected at the start of the program.

The two countries shared a severe problem of excess personnel in the enterprise sector. In the case of Poland, the extent of the problem is indicated by a rate of unemployment barely above 0 percent throughout the 1980s. In Yugoslavia the rate of unemployment was around 14 percent in 1989, a slight increase over the 13 percent average for the whole decade. Although this higher rate of unemployment (concentrated on new entrants) in Yugoslavia seems to rule out the existence of overstaffing, a major cause of enterprise losses was indeed excess personnel, estimated to have reached 20 percent of the labor force in 1988 (Mencinger 1989).

The two countries also shared a problem of flight from domestic assets and increasing velocity. While hardly a novelty in high inflation countries, in both countries the payment of negative real interest rates on domestic deposits—a policy designed to provide subsidized credits to enterprises—accelerated the flight from domestic assets. In addition, the foreign exchange deposits in the financial systems of both countries are also likely to have facilitated the shift out of domestic money. Between 1980 and 1989 the share of foreign exchange deposits in M3 increased from 20 percent to 69 percent in Poland and from 30 percent to 65 percent in Yugoslavia. In 1989 the ratio

of M3 to GNP in Poland and Yugoslavia had declined to 47 percent and 33 percent, respectively.

A Comparison of the Two Stabilization Programs

A summary comparative description of the Polish and Yugoslav stabilization programs is provided in table 9.3. On first examination, the two programs look strikingly similar. The income policy components are basically the same, including: (1) a temporary freeze on the exchange rate that both countries extended to one year; (2) wage controls (with a complete freeze in Yugoslavia and partial indexation with very low coefficients in Poland); and (3) a temporary freeze on public sector prices.[4]

However, note that Yugoslavia made all its price corrections before the start of its program, whereas Poland made large corrections to its energy prices (400 percent) on January 1, 1990.

Both programs included a significant fiscal adjustment—7 percent and 5 percent of GNP in Poland and Yugoslavia, respectively. In the case of Poland, the adjustment was designed to close the fiscal deficit, whereas in Yugoslavia it was essentially designed to cover new, non-traditional expenditures. These included the quasi-fiscal operations of the central bank (servicing of foreign liabilities and subsidies to favored sectors), transfers to the bank restructuring program and the social program, and coverage of some enterprise arrears.

Both programs set targets for the growth of net domestic assets. In the case of Poland, the net domestic assets of the banking system were to grow at 20 percent in the first quarter and 8 percent in the second, whereas in Yugoslavia these assets were to expand at slightly negative rates in the two first quarters. Both programs allowed for the monetization of foreign exchange inflows.

A first reaction to these figures might be that the monetary program in Yugoslavia was much tighter. However, two critical factors necessitate modifying this conclusion. First, the Polish program allowed for an increase in domestic credit in anticipation of the price jump that would result from the large correction in energy prices in January 1990, a jump that later proved to have been severely underestimated. Second, the Yugoslav program was preceded by a substantial real monetary and credit expansion in December 1989. As shown in the next section, these and other factors resulted in a much tighter monetary stance in Poland.

Both programs called for a substantial relaxation of the exchange rate and trade controls, although Yugoslavia maintained some quota restrictions (amounting to 12 percent of total imports). Yugoslavia also introduced

Table 9-3. *Summary Description of the Polish and Yugoslav Programs*

Components	Poland	Yugoslavia
Incomes policy	3-month freeze on the exchange rate (dollar) after large adjustment in December 1989, later extended to 1 year	6-month freeze on the exchange rate (deutschemark) after some adjustment in December, later extended to 1 year
	Partial and lagged wage indexation, with very small coefficients	6-month freeze on nominal wages
	6-month freeze on energy prices, after large corrections in January 1990	6-month freeze on energy and other public sector prices (20% of the Consumer Price Index), after corrections in December 1989
Fiscal policy	Expected fiscal adjustment of 7% of GNP	Expected fiscal adjustment of 5% of GNP
Monetary policy	Controls over net domestic assets of the banking system	Controls over the net domestic assets of the Central Bank
	Setting of the discount rate at 36% per month in January 1990, up from 7% in December 1989	Setting of the discount rate at 23% per annum; full liberalization of other interest rates
Exchange and trade policies	Partial convertibility (current account only)	"Full" convertibility (some capital restrictions have remained)
	Elimination of quotas and relaxation of licenses	Reduction of quotas and relaxation of licenses
Enterprise/bank reform	Enforcement of bankruptcies through the "dividend tax"	Enforcement of bankruptcies through 60-day tolerance limit for arrears
	Evolving plans for enterprise restructuring and privatization	Bank restructuring program; evolving plans for enterprise restructuring and privatization

Source: The authors.

full currency convertibility, while Poland restricted convertibility to current account transactions.

Interruption of the explicit or implicit subsidization of inefficient enterprises and free operation of the Darwinian-Schumpeterian law of natural selection were implicit in both programs. Thus, the programs contained measures to preclude enterprise recourse to inter-enterprise credits and arrears,[5] so that inefficient enterprises would be forced into bankruptcy. In the case of Yugoslavia, a limit of 60 days of arrears was established as the trigger for bankruptcy procedures. The government was able to enforce this rule by means of a centralized system of payments among enterprises and banks. In Poland, enterprises were ordered to pay dividends to the government based on the book value of their funding capital.

The two governments announced plans to restructure and privatize enterprises and banks. Yugoslavia issued a bank restructuring program, to be managed by a bank rehabilitation agency and supported by budgetary resources. Although the agency was created in mid-1990, enterprise restructuring moved slowly, pending the establishment of specialized regional institutions. In addition, the strategy for linking restructuring and privatization was still being debated during the course of 1990, partly as a result of different positions among the various republics.

In Poland, the government made a commitment to a large-scale privatization plan at the start of the program, and the legal framework for the plan was spelled out in a privatization law passed in July 1990. However, the legislation was "enabling" rather than "programmatic." Thus, no significant cases of bankruptcy (40 to 50 minor cases of bankruptcies occurred), restructuring or privatization were observed in the first nine months following initiation of the program. The recognition that further delays in privatization could ultimately jeopardize the success of the program led to the introduction of a much more ambitious plan in December 1990. The objective of the plan is to privatize 50 percent of industry in three years. To this end, the plan relies on a free distribution of vouchers to the public and the creation of financial intermediaries to control the enterprises (see chapter 21, "Markets and Institutions in Large-Scale Privatization: An Approach to Economic and Social Transformation in Eastern Europe" by Roman Frydman and Andrzej Rapaczynski in this volume).

Before moving on to an examination of the initial results, some comments about the implementation of the heterodox programs in the two socialist countries are in order. Incomes policy support to stabilization is commonly justified on the grounds that it reduces the unnecessary losses in output that are usually associated with purely orthodox programs. The possible reasons for these losses have been investigated extensively, including imperfect information (Lucas 1973), long-term or staggered wage contracts (Fischer 1977 and Taylor 1979), backward wage indexation, coordination problems (Dornbusch and Simonsen 1988) or monopolistic price setting (e.g., Rotemberg 1987 and Blanchard and Fischer 1989).

Although the microfoundations of socialist and market economies are clearly different, the case for including an incomes policy in the stabilization programs of the former may be even stronger. In addition to the importance of this policy in breaking the inflationary inertia in the Yugoslav and Polish economies (both countries formalized backward indexation rules in the late 1980s), it has a role to play given the absence of markets for both labor and capital, and it can counterbalance the influence of the workers' councils in wage determination. Under these conditions, the link between aggregate demand policies and the short-run behavior of wages and prices is likely to be weaker than in market economies,[6] making the case for nominal anchors stronger.

Examination of the Initial Results

Analysis of the initial results of the two programs reveals two well-defined periods. During the first semester both programs achieved a substantial reduction in the rate of inflation, as shown in figure 9.4. In the case of Yugoslavia, the monthly inflation rates were reduced to zero at the end of the semester, while in Poland they were around 3-5 percent (see also table 9.4 and the two appendices).[7]

The performance of both programs was more mixed after June. In the case of Poland, monthly inflation remained at around 5 percent, proving more persistent than anticipated. In Yugoslavia, there was a revival of inflationary pressures, as indicated by monthly inflation rates ranging between 3 percent and 8 percent in the

Figure 9-4. *Monthly Price Changes in Poland and Yugoslavia*
(percent change over the previous month)

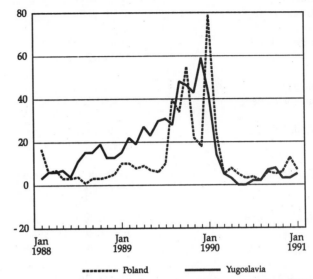

- - - - - - - Poland   ——— Yugoslavia

second semester. Therefore it is useful to examine first the results for the first semester and then to identify the main problems that emerged during the second semester.

A sharp contraction in economic activity followed implementation of the two programs in both countries, as shown by the deseasonalized indices of industrial production in figure 9.5. The decline in industrial production during 1990 was much more pronounced in Poland (-20 percent, with a decline in socialized sector production of about 28 percent and an increase in private sector

Figure 9-5. *Industrial Production Indices in Poland and Yugoslavia*
(1985=100)

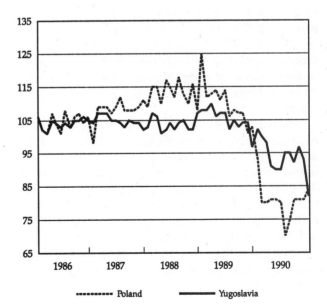

- - - - - - - Poland   ——— Yugoslavia

Table 9-4. *Results of the Polish and Yugoslav Programs During 1990*

Variable	Poland	Yugoslavia
Inflation (Dec.-Dec.)	1989: 640% 1990: 250%	1989: 2,700% 1990: 120%
Output growth	Industry: -20.0% GDP: -12.5%	Industry: -10.5% GDP: -7.5%
Rate of **unemployment**	1989: 0% 1990 (Dec.): 6.1%	1989: 14.2% 1990 (mid-year) 14.9%
Trade balance	1989: US$0.2 billion surplus 1990: US$2.2 billion surplus	1989: US$1.5 billion deficit 1990: US$4.7 billion deficit
Current balance	1989: US$1.8 billion deficit 1990: US$0.7 billion surplus	1989: US$2.0 billion surplus 1990: US$2.7 billion deficit
Reserve position	Dec. 1989: US$2.5 billion June 1990: US$3.9 billion Dec. 1990: US$6.8 billion	Dec. 1989: US$6.1 billion June 1990: US$8.6 billion Dec. 1990: US$6.7 billion
Black market premium	Reduced to zero	Reduced to zero in December; increased to 20% during the year

Monetary aggregates	Cumulative real changes:
	
	        M1 M3
	Dec.-June: -15% -42%
	Dec.-Dec.: 58% -42%
		Cumulative real changes:
		
		        M1 M3
		Dec.-June: 49% -5%
		Dec.-Dec.: 40% -20%

Share of foreign exchange **deposits** in M3	Dec. 1989: 69% June 1990: 42% Dec. 1990: 31%	Dec. 1989: 65% June 1990: 51% Dec. 1990: 46%

Source: Various national sources.

production of about 24 percent) than in Yugoslavia (-10 percent). Although the post-stabilization recession was severe in both countries, it should also be noted that the decline in economic activity cannot be blamed entirely on the stabilization, since it started in the second semester of 1989, after a "peak" of activity in the first half of that year.[8]

The more severe recession in Poland was also reflected in the relative behavior of imports and the trade balance in the two countries, although in this case a number of other factors were also at work, most notably the sharper pre-plan real devaluation in Poland (figure 9.3). The immediate import contraction was more severe in the Polish case, as shown in figure 9.6. In addition, it was not followed by a recovery, unlike the case of Yugoslavia. Whereas the Polish trade balance shifted into a surplus, in Yugoslavia the trade deficit increased.[9]

The first reason for this difference in output performance was the much stronger direct supply shock arising from the increase in input prices in Poland. A second likely reason is the tighter monetary stance in the Polish program in the first semester, even though a first inspection of the two monetary programs suggests otherwise. Figure 9.7 illustrates the differences in the quarterly evolution of the real stock of money (M1 and M3) in the two countries. Between December 1989 and June 1990, real M1 grew by 50 percent in Yugoslavia and 15 percent in Poland, as measured by calendar price indices. In the case of M3, the difference is also large. There was a decline of only 5 percent in Yugoslavia versus 40 percent in Poland.[10]

In the second semester the situation is somewhat different. The process of remonetization continues in Poland and is reversed in Yugoslavia. As discussed in more

Figure 9-6. *Convertible Currency Area Trade Balance, Poland and Yugoslavia 1988-90*

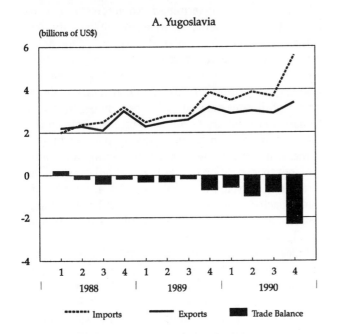

A. Yugoslavia

(billions of US$)

····· Imports   —— Exports   ■ Trade Balance

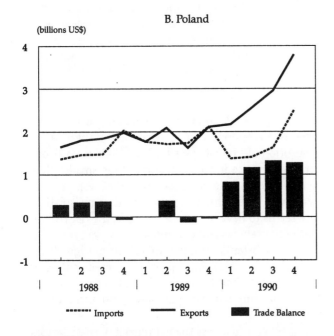

B. Poland

(billions US$)

····· Imports   —— Exports   ■ Trade Balance

Figure 9-7. *Monetary Indices, Poland and Yugoslavia* (fourth quarter, 1988=100)

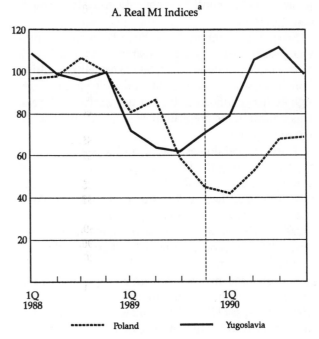

A. Real M1 Indices[a]

····· Poland   —— Yugoslavia

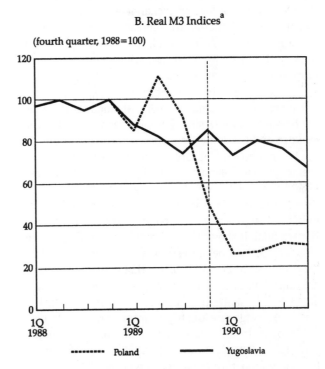

B. Real M3 Indices[a]

(fourth quarter, 1988=100)

····· Poland   —— Yugoslavia

a. The number following the year refers to the quarter for that year.

detail below, in Yugoslavia that pattern essentially reflects excessive credit expansion in Yugoslavia in the second semester, resulting in a revival of inflation and a loss of foreign reserves.

The comparative evaluation of the two monetary programs in the first semester centers on four major points. First, in Yugoslavia, all exchange rate and price corrections were carried out before the plan and were smaller in magnitude than those in Poland. Therefore, the sub-

sequent impact on prices was also smaller. In Poland, the various prior price and exchange rate adjustments combined with the large increase in energy prices in January

1990 (400 percent) resulted in a price increase in January whose magnitude (100 percent from the beginning to the end of the month) was not anticipated by the monetary program.

Second, as mentioned, the Yugoslav monetary program was preceded by a large real increase in the stock of base money in December 1989 (25 percent), resulting from increased domestic credits and some increased foreign exchange inflows in the last two weeks of the year. This growth in the pre-plan stock of money was not observed in Poland.

Third, the net domestic assets of the central bank of Yugoslavia during the first semester behaved according to the program—basically flat in nominal terms. In the case of Poland, the net domestic assets of the banking system did not rise to the targeted level, essentially because of the better than expected budgetary performance. There was no attempt to divert credit within the ceilings to the enterprises.

Fourth, large inflows of foreign exchange resulted in a substantial increase in net foreign assets in both countries. In the case of Poland, the inflows were generated in the trade account, while in the case of Yugoslavia they were generated by increased workers' remittances and the repatriation of foreign exchange assets held abroad by enterprises. Although the increase in net foreign assets was even greater in Poland, the other factors, most notably the price jump in January, produced a much more severe monetary crunch.

The conclusion that monetary policy was tighter in Poland based on a comparison of real money stocks may not be valid, however, since it implicitly assumes that the real demand for domestic money was equally strong in the two countries. The large price shocks at the start of the program in Poland may initially have created adverse expectations that lowered the demand for money. In any case, the above comparison reveals interesting differences in the design of monetary policy in the two programs. In particular, it shows the desirability of carrying out all price corrections before establishing the monetary targets. Another interesting point is that in neither country did households convert their stocks of foreign exchange deposits into domestic currency deposits, despite the frozen exchange rate and higher interest rate on domestic deposits. In the Israeli stabilization program such a conversion constituted an important source of non-inflationary monetary expansion (Liviatan 1988). The absence of conversion in Poland and Yugoslavia could signal an initial lack of credibility of the program, particularly of the exchange rate policy.[11]

It is natural to look at nominal interest rates as an indicator of liquidity conditions that result from an immediate contraction in the supply of money and the reshuffling of the portfolios of asset holders. However, in both countries the exogenously determined discount rates influenced the determination of interest rates considerably, making them poor indicators of liquidity conditions. In Yugoslavia, interest rates on short-term deposits were relatively stable during the year (10-15 percent per year), in spite of the large fluctuations in monetary conditions in this period. In Poland, short-term deposit rates moved from 15 percent per month in January and February to 5-6 percent per month in the following months, becoming slightly positive in real terms. Lending rates were much higher in both countries, but that situation to a large extent reflects the non-performing loans in the banks' portfolios, and not just liquidity factors. Finally, the real devaluation in Poland may also account for the stronger initial contraction of activity relative to Yugoslavia.[12]

Indeed, the first indications are that the unambiguously adverse supply-side effects of a real devaluation were not offset by the expansionary effects on the demand side. In the traded goods sector, it is unclear whether the increase in foreign demand offset the contractionary supply-side effects. In the case of non-traded goods, it is most likely that the demand-side effects were also contractionary. The wealth effect was largely negative, as indicated by the 40 percent real decrease in M3, while some redistribution of real income from wages to profits is also likely to have depressed demand.[13]

A complete comparative evaluation of the initial results of the stabilization programs requires a more detailed analysis of the impact of policies on real incomes in the two economies. In both countries, there was a substitution of explicit taxes for the inflation tax. However, the increase in explicit taxation was smaller than the volume of inflationary taxation in 1989, especially in Yugoslavia. When this factor is looked at in isolation, there seems to have been an increase in the net real income of households and enterprises. However, real wages also fell substantially in the two countries (figure 9.8). In part the reason was the removal of the credit subsidies for enterprises. Thus the decline in real wages indirectly reflects the elimination of inflationary financing of enterprise losses.

It is difficult to assess the net impact of these factors on real incomes. In addition, the situation is likely to be highly differentiated across households and enterprises. While the real wage adjustment may have allowed several enterprises to operate without a loss (without meaning that they became efficient), in other cases there would still have been a loss even with a further substantial reduction in the real wage. In fact, during the first semester the wage ceilings became non-binding for several enterprises in both countries. The tightening of

Figure 9-8. *Real Wage Indices, Poland and Yugoslavia*
(1985=100)

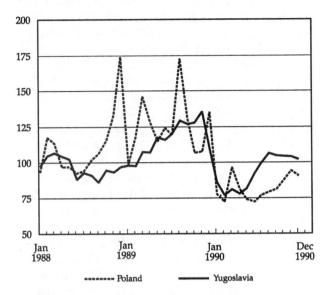

-------- Poland   ——— Yugoslavia

Figure 9-9. *Dinar Bank Credits and M1*
(billions of dinars)

A. Nominal

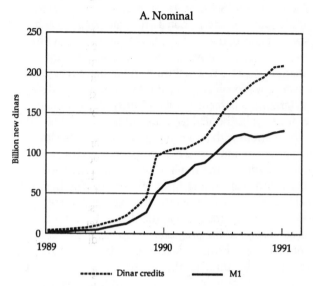

-------- Dinar credits   ——— M1

B. Real
(base=1985)

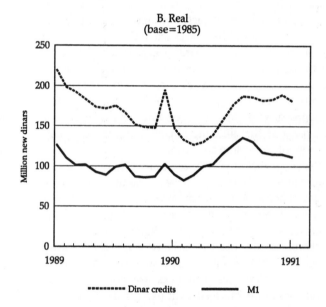

-------- Dinar credits   ——— M1

credit during the first semester had a strong impact on the enterprise sector. In Yugoslavia, 7,000 enterprises had difficulty making payments to banks and other enterprises, 3,000 had accumulated arrears for 30 days and 350 were declared bankrupt. A large number of enterprises was reported to have interrupted their wage payments (especially in May) to postpone bankruptcy. At the end of the first semester the situation was, however, highly differentiated, with a group of enterprises increasing wages above the ceilings and another group unable to make wage payments within the ceilings.

Pressure to relax the monetary policy mounted in the first semester and led to a relaxation after June. The shift to a relaxed monetary stance was achieved mostly through the implementation of measures to increase the multiplier. These measures produced a rapid increase in the stock of bank credits after June (figure 9.9). The easing of monetary policy led to further increases in wages and contributed to a revival of inflation in the second semester. It also aborted the expected shake-out of the industrial sector by keeping loss-making enterprises afloat and allowing them to resume wage payments.

Concern over the revival of inflation led the central bank to return to a tight monetary stance in early October. However, pressed by enterprises to continue lending, commercial banks reduced their reserves below the required levels, a move that weakened the central bank's control over monetary policy.[14]

Further evidence of the difficulties faced by the central bank in conducting monetary policy was the unusual episode of December 1990, whereby one regional branch of the central bank expanded credits by US$1.8

billion equivalent in Dinars to finance the payment of wages and pensions (*The Economist* 1991) in the region, without notifying the board of governors. The monetary impact of the domestic credit expansion was largely offset by a substantial loss in foreign reserves during the same period. However, these events raised obvious doubts about the sustainability of the stabilization program.

In Poland, despite the sharp contraction in industrial output, no bankruptcies occurred. Nor did the expected shake-out of the industrial sector, with inefficient enterprises sinking under the pressure of the elimination of subsidies, take place.[15]

The Darwinian-Schumpeterian process of natural selection did not operate. As noted, the main trigger mechanism for bankruptcy procedures is a failure to pay the dividend tax. The appropriateness of this mechanism as the main trigger for restructuring and/or bankruptcy is, however, questionable. First, the tax was not burdensome (around 6 percent of total profits). Second, many enterprises paid the dividend tax while also failing to meet obligations with other enterprises and banks. However, neither creditor firms nor the banks initiated bankruptcy procedures, the implication being some sort of collusive behavior among firms and banks. The inefficiencies arising from these inter-linkages among enterprises is one of the main issues that has to be tackled in the second stage of the program.

Both fiscal and credit policies were relaxed after July, in an attempt to stimulate the economy. The relaxation of credit policies opened the way to a significant increase in real wages and contributed to a certain revival of inflation. In an attempt to reduce these inflationary pressures, credit policy was tightened in the fourth quarter, with the imposition on each commercial bank of strict ceilings on credit to the socialized sector. However, the overall credit expansion largely exceeded the targets, mainly because of sharp growth in credit to the non-socialized sector, which was exempted from the ceilings. Despite the tightening of credit to the socialized sector, wage pressures in this sector remained unabated, a point that revealed the difficulty of containing wages under the present ownership structure.

Developments in 1990 raise a more general issue: under the present structure of these economies, macroeconomic policies alone cannot generate efficient natural selection. Inter-enterprise credits link "good" and "bad" enterprises, opening the way for chains of bankruptcies involving "good" enterprises. Moreover, if the banking system is inefficient and, in the case of Yugoslavia, controlled by enterprises, resources are not necessarily channelled to the more efficient uses. Under these conditions, the attempt to enforce hard budget constraints may result in a generalized credit crunch—as seems to have happened in the first semester of 1990 in Poland—with unclear effects on efficiency.

Assessment of the Main Issues

The issues that policy-makers in Poland and Yugoslavia will have to address include some that belong to the stabilization component per se and others that are of a structural nature. In the first group, the most important issues are the unfreezing of the exchange rate, the intro-

duction of a new wage policy and the adequacy of the fiscal support for the restructuring component of the two programs. This group of issues also includes the need to reduce the servicing of external debt in order to avoid a drain of scarce resources that ideally should be channelled toward restructuring the economy. The second group comprises the restructuring and privatization of enterprises and banks and the development of the labor and financial markets.

Recognition that the real exchange rate in Yugoslavia had severely appreciated led to a 30 percent corrective devaluation in January 1, 1991. In the case of Poland, the real appreciation is probably not so severe as in the case of Yugoslavia, given the large real devaluation at the start of the program. Obviously, if inflation does not quickly subside, the extent of the real appreciation is likely to become unsustainable during 1991.

Although the exchange rate correction in Yugoslavia seemed unavoidable, given the rapid loss of foreign reserves at the end of 1990, it did result in increasing rates of inflation at the start of 1991 (5 percent and 10 percent in January and February, respectively). This increase in inflation happened despite the introduction of a new package of measures designed to contain the impact of the devaluation, which included a freeze on nominal wages paid by loss-making enterprises and new regulations designed to prevent other episodes of monetary decontrol. Success at preventing the re-emergence of an exchange rate-wage-price spiral will obviously depend on more effective implementation of wage and monetary policies, a task that will require a high degree of consensus among the various republics.

Despite the present uncertainty regarding the continuing implementation of these measures, they do reflect a recognition that some form of wage policy is needed, especially while the labor markets are not sufficiently developed and the problem of ownership rights is not adequately solved. The design of a wage policy for the transition is indeed a difficult task. On the one hand it has to counteract the excessive influence of the workers' councils. On the other hand, it should minimize the inefficiencies arising from strict and generalized wage controls, which can hinder the recovery of economic activity.

This point is also relevant in the case of Poland, where a wage policy was maintained in the first half of 1991. However, the government introduced several changes. First, it shifted the control of wages from the wage bill to the wage per worker to eliminate the constraints on expanding firms. Second, wage increases became conditional on profitability performance. Finally, private firms were excluded from the wage ceilings, and corporatized firms were partially exempted from the tax penalties on wage increases above the ceilings. However, the government retained the monthly indexation of wages, with adverse effects on inflationary inertia.

Fiscal support for restructuring is another critical issue in the two countries. While the fiscal adjustment has proven sufficient to close the deficit in Poland and to absorb the central bank's deficit in Yugoslavia, it does not seem to be consistent with the intention of implementing a serious restructuring program in both countries. For instance, it has become clear that the fiscal commitments to the social program in Yugoslavia would have been inadequate had the loss-making enterprises really been forced into bankruptcy. The initial fiscal commitments to the financial restructuring also proved largely insufficient at the end of the year.

In the area of restructuring, a wide range of issues needs to be considered. At the level of each enterprise, restructuring entails laying off excess personnel, writing off debts in justified cases, making selective investments capable of improving the efficiency of existing capital, changing management and so on. It also entails closing enterprises that cannot become profitable even with the above measures. At the level of each bank, restructuring involves a detailed evaluation of its portfolio, the removal of bad loans from the portfolios, a severing of the links between banks and enterprises, and the introduction and enforcement of prudential financial regulation and supervision. A crucial question related to the restructuring of enterprises and banks is who will be in charge of this formidable task and under what system of incentives. An approach to restructuring that is excessively centralized and excludes privatization may not only prove too slow to implement, given the institutional deficiencies, but may also produce an undesirable selection of enterprises and sectors for restructuring. A more rapid move toward large-scale privatization seems to be required to minimize the risks of wasting resources during the restructuring and to enhance the prospects of a sustained supply response. (For a detailed discussion of this issue, see Hinds 1990 and Lipton and Sachs (1990), as well as chapter 21, "Markets and Institutions in Large-Scale Privatization: An Approach to Economic and Social Transformation in Eastern Europe" by Roman Frydman and Andrzej Rapaczynski in this volume).

While forcing inefficient enterprises into bankruptcy is an important step in the right direction, in the absence of well-functioning labor and capital markets that permit an efficient reallocation of resources across firms and sectors, a large pool of unemployed could be generated for a protracted period. The impossibility of developing a true labor market without developing in parallel a market for capital again raises the issue of privatization (see Hinds 1990). In addition, the development of a labor

market will require that policy-makers address the issues of housing ownership and financing, two notorious obstacles to labor mobility in socialist countries.

While Poland and Yugoslavia acknowledge the importance of these issues, they have been addresssing them too slowly. Failure to provide prompt solutions to these problems could lead to a protracted stagnation of output and a return to high inflation. In this regard, the model of sequencing traditionally applied to Latin American countries, in which structural issues are relegated to later stages of the adjustment programs, does not seem to be applicable to reforming socialist countries, in which stabilization and structural reforms are much more closely intertwined.

Appendix 1. Stabilization in Poland

Background

The Polish stabilization program of January 1990 is undoubtedly one of the most radical attempts to transform a socialist economy into a market economy quickly. In addition to the severity of Poland's macroeconomic situation, the government chose to pursue a "cold turkey" approach to stabilization (whence the label "Big Bang"), because of the disillusionment with the *gradualist* reform strategy followed in the 1980s. That strategy, which relied on increased enterprise decentralization but within a context of continuing state interference in the allocation of inputs, licensing of imports and exports, and determination of prices, had not provided visible improvements in efficiency. In fact, the partial decentralization of enterprise decision-making—reminiscent of the idea of "market socialism" —in a context of absent factor markets and persistent soft budget constraints actually contributed to a widening of the macroeconomic imbalances in the 1980s. Several rescheduling agreements of the external debt partly masked the severity of the external position and allowed Poland to grow at relatively high rates in the period 1983-88 and to maintain relatively high rates of investment growth (figure 9-1-1).

On the other hand, the rate of inflation averaged above 50 percent in the 1980s, a condition that prima facie put Poland in with the "chronic inflation" countries (figure 9-1-1).[16]

However, the persistent inflation during the 1980s reduced significantly the stock monetary overhang, a point on which Poland's experience differed from the typical experience of the centrally planned economies with rigid price controls, such as Bulgaria and the Soviet Union. Accordingly, the underlying inflationary pressures in the 1980s came, overall, more from flow than from stock fac-

Figure 9-1-1: *Selected Macroeconomic Variables, Poland, 1980-90*

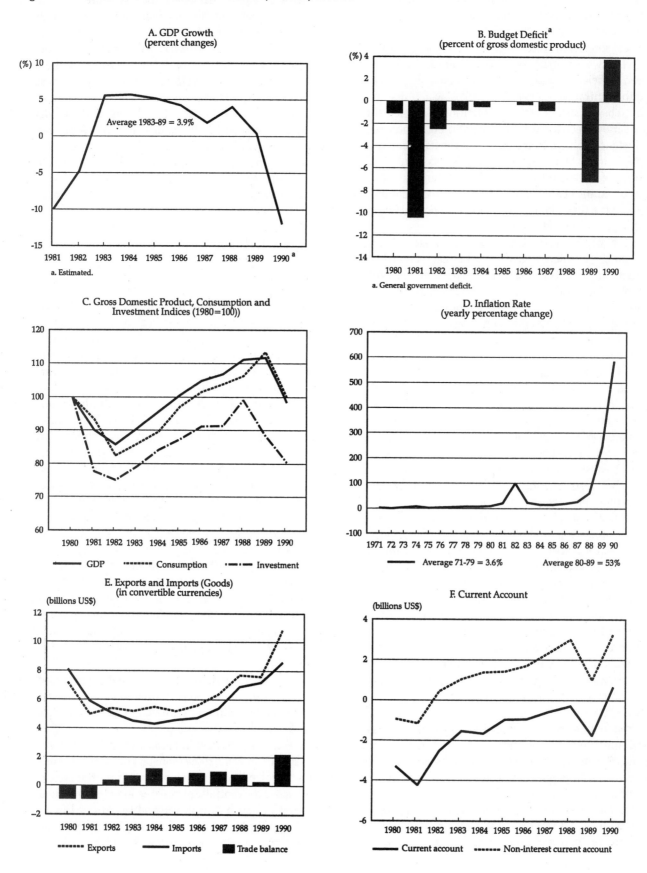

A. GDP Growth
(percent changes)

Average 1983-89 = 3.9%

a. Estimated.

B. Budget Deficit[a]
(percent of gross domestic product)

a. General government deficit.

C. Gross Domestic Product, Consumption and
Investment Indices (1980=100))

——— GDP   ·········· Consumption   ·—·— Investment

D. Inflation Rate
(yearly percentage change)

Average 71-79 = 3.6%   Average 80-89 = 53%

E. Exports and Imports (Goods)
(in convertible currencies)

(billions US$)

········ Exports   ——— Imports   ■ Trade balance

F. Current Account

(billions US$)

——— Current account   ········ Non-interest current account

114

tors (Lipton and Sachs 1990). In this regard, cost-push factors, such as the cost of labor and the prices of imports, played a fundamental role in the context of a price-setting system dominated by "cost-plus" behavior. However, the widespread price controls that prevailed until the end of 1989 and that affected about 50 percent of total retail sales complicate the analysis of inflation. Although repressed inflation does not seem to have been a "chronic" phenomenon in Poland in the 1980s, the mixed system of controlled and free prices tended to adjust slowly to excess demand and to generate large gaps between the controlled and free prices, with adverse effects on the budget. Thus, an inflation that behaved erratically, "stop-and-go" phenomena and the inertia elements in the catch-up between controlled and free prices were not only important features of Polish inflation in the 1980s but were particularly important in the acceleration of inflation in 1989.[17]

Large disequilibria did indeed precede the "corrective" jumps in the price level, mainly in 1982 and 1988-89, with relatively stable rates of inflation of 20 percent per annum inside the peaks, a rate that was high by European standards.

Preliminary econometric results confirm this pattern (table 9-1-1). The regression, which tries to separate

presence of inertia elements in the inflation. These can be traced mainly to the de facto full indexation of wages to prices throughout the period 1983-89 and, after 1985, to an exchange rate policy aimed at stimulating exports through continued "competitive" devaluations.

Discrete shocks to the *price level*, usually through a change in administered prices, tended to be translated into a persistent higher level of *inflation*. Thus, the system, with its generally accommodating monetary policy, lacked a nominal "anchor." In the mixed system of free and controlled prices, price controls proved to be a pure substitute for the missing anchor. Indeed, price controls had an adverse effect on the fiscal budget—as they implied subsidies—and with passive money this channel fueled inflation.[18]

The price controls gave rise to various types of subsidies to cover the difference between the price and production costs; the subsidies were channelled to both households and enterprises. Moreover, when the input subsidies were reduced through increases in the administered prices, especially those of energy—as, for instance, in 1988—sizable subsidies on interest rates cushioned the enterprises from these adverse supply shocks. Only in 1990 did this compensation disappear,

Table 9-1-1. *Poland: Inflation in the 1980s*
(quarterly regression 1983-89)[a]

DLCPI = 0.72*DLCPI(-1) + 0.42*DLWAGES + 0.1*DLOER + 0.23*DLM3/RS - 0.63*ECM

$$\text{DLCPI} = 0.72*\text{DLCPI}(-1) + 0.42*\text{DLWAGES} + 0.1*\text{DLOER} + 0.23*\text{DLM3/RS} - 0.63*\text{ECM}$$

(7.1)   (7.1)   (7.1)   (2.8)   (-3.5)

$R^2 = 0.97$; DW = 1.33; e = 0.0042

Note: DLCPI = the rate of inflation; DLWAGES = the rate of change in wages; DLOER = the rate of change in the official exchange rate; DLM3/RS = the change in the ratio of household broad money to retail sales; and ECM = the error correction term, defined as the difference between prices and costs (wages plus the exchange rate). The t-statistics in parentheses

a. The equation in the main text is part of a system estimation, in which prices and wages are estimated simultaneously.
Source: Commander and Coricelli (1990b).

cost-push factors from monetary disequilibria—as measured by the change in the ratio of household money to retail sales—indicates that, overall, cost-push factors were the main determinants of price inflation in the period 1983-89.

However, if the coefficients in the above equation are used, in the period of accelerating inflation in 1988 up to the third quarter of 1989, monetary imbalances exerted important pressure on inflation. Indeed, 20 percent of the increase in prices in that period is explained by the monetary disequilibrium, while cost-push factors accounted for the remaining 80 percent, with 65 percent attributable to wages and 15 percent to the exchange rate.

The fact that inflation remained relatively high following the jump in the price level in 1982 suggests the

with the simultaneous elimination of both types of subsidies.

In general, the system allowed the enterprise sector to register net profits in the aggregate without, as before 1989, large deficits for the consolidated government sector (including transfers for the service of the foreign debt). Therefore, a "pure" fiscal explanation of underlying inflation does not seem to be relevant to the Polish experience in the 1980s. Nevertheless, as noted, sizable hidden subsidies, mainly in the form of implicit subsidies for interest rates, were channelled to the enterprises, accounting for a significant portion of the seigniorage from money creation. According to some estimates, the interest rate subsidies amounted to an average of 6 percent of GDP in the period 1984-88.[19]

The subsidies on interest rates thus allowed firms to operate with positive profits, compensating them for the high costs of the inefficiency in production, such as overstaffing and the generally high intensity of inputs in production, common symptoms of soft budget constraints. The largely negative real interest rates on lending were accompanied by even more negative real rates on deposits. As a result, households increasingly shifted out of zloty-denominated assets and into foreign currency deposits (table 9-1-2). The base for the inflation tax

reduction in the fiscal and monetary disequilibria, paving the way for the stabilization program of January 1, 1990.

The first phase. The wage push initiated in the second half of 1988 gained strength at the beginning of 1989, the result being sizable increases in real wages and a real appreciation. In addition, the budget deficit deteriorated sharply during the first half of 1989 because of a substan-

Table 9-1-2. *Poland: Monetary Indicators*

	1985	1986	1987	1988	1989
	(percent of GDP)[a]				
M1	20.1	19.5	18.5	14.6	10.1
Broad money	44.3	46.2	51.5	56.5	47.5
	(percent of broad money)				
M1	44.3	40.3	32.0	20.8	21.9
Currency	19.6	16.8	12.0	9.9	11.5
Quasi money	55.7	59.7	68.0	79.2	78.1
Zloty	75.1	68.8	53.7	35.1	30.7
Foreign currency	24.9	31.2	46.3	64.9	69.3
Socialized sector	26.9	24.9	26.6	19.4	25.1
Non-soc. sector	73.1	75.1	73.4	80.6	74.9

a. Average stock, geometric mean.
Source: National Bank of Poland; International Monetary Fund, *International Financial Statistics*.

was progressively reduced in the 1980s as the currency substitution advanced, a pattern that increased velocity in terms of M1 and reinforced the inflationary pressures—open or repressed—arising from the need to finance both the budget deficit and the hidden subsidies to the socialized sector.

During 1987-88, and then again in 1989, the authorities attempted to impose more stringent financial discipline on the enterprises by tightening bank credit. However, given the predominantly soft budget constraints, the attempts to enforce financial discipline through credit ceilings were largely ineffective, with enterprises bypassing the ceilings by extending credit to each other. The ratio of inter-firm credit to bank credit to the socialized sector went from about 50 percent at the end of 1987 to 70 percent at the end of 1988 and 155 percent at the end of 1989.

Preparation for the Stabilization Program and Other Developments in 1989

Two clearly distinct phases, separated by the change in government, characterized 1989. In the first, which corresponds to the first three quarters, there was a sharp deterioration in the macroeconomic situation. In the second, corresponding to the last quarter of 1989, when the new government was in power, there was a marked

tial decline in revenues and, to a lesser extent, increased expenditures.[20]

The consolidated budget of the general government moved from an initial balance in 1988 to a deficit of 7.2 percent of GDP in 1989. It should be noted that 80 percent of the state's budget deficit (excluding extra-budgetary funds) in 1989 was accumulated in the first half of the year. The deficit was financed mainly through central bank credits and money creation.

Interestingly, the worsening of the "fundamentals" in the first half of 1989 did not immediately result in hyperinflation. In the first half of 1989 the monthly rate of inflation averaged 7 percent and did not accelerate during the period. The cumulative increase in prices was about 60 percent with respect to December 1989. This lack of synchronization between the acceleration of inflation and worsening fundamentals is consistent with the stop-and-go nature of the system, with its widespread price controls, in which a widening of monetary imbalances generally precedes corrective price increases. That growing monetary imbalances were created in the first half of 1989 can be inferred from the rapidly depreciating exchange rate in the parallel market, a signal of a loss in confidence in the domestic currency. The share of foreign currency deposits increased from 65 percent at the end of 1988 to 71 percent at the end of June 1989.

The outburst in the rate of inflation occurred in August, when retail prices jumped to 39.5 percent from 9.5 percent in July. The liberalization of food prices in August at a time of significant excess demand caused a jump in those prices. Wage earners tried to catch up to the increased food prices by demanding higher wages, in effect indexing wages de facto to food prices, which were rising more than the average price level. This phenomenon may have contributed to further inflationary pressures in the non-food sector as well. Formal institution of a wage indexation rule in April and the policy of adjusting the official exchange rate to catch up with the black market exchange rate further increased the inflationary inertia. The official exchange rate, which had depreciated roughly in line with inflation in the first seven months (about 65 percent), was depreciated by 680 percent in the remaining months of the year, when the cumulative increase in inflation was 320 percent.

The second phase. The new government, which took office in September, tried promptly to halt the deterioration in the macroeconomic situation, instituting several measures to tighten credit policy, reduce the budget deficit, curb the wage increases and correct the prices of energy and other highly subsidized goods. The adjustments in the prices of energy produced an initial acceleration in inflation in October. A reduction of the periodicity of wage adjustments from quarterly to monthly and the frequent exchange rate devaluations also fueled inflation.[21]

In December real wages were 27 percent above their level in October, while the official exchange rate depreciated by 260 percent in the period October-December.

After October, however, the improvement in the fundamentals did exert downward pressure on inflation, which decelerated sharply from 54.8 percent to 17.7 percent in December. At the same time, the premium of the parallel market over the official exchange rate was substantially reduced by the end of 1989, an indication of a significant improvement in the monetary disequilibria. Three main factors explain this reduction of the premium: the devaluation of the official exchange rate; the slowdown in the rate of growth of the money supply, linked to the improvement in the budget deficit; and the reduction in the monetary overhang as a result of the large cumulative increase in prices during 1989.

As to currency substitution, the shift from domestic to foreign currency deposits was halted in the second half of the year, and the share of foreign currency deposits in broad money declined from 71 percent in June to 69 percent at the end of December.

The tightening of bank credit to enterprises was partially compensated for by the flourishing of a thick inter-firm credit market, which partly cushioned the enterprise sector from the squeeze in official credit. Inter-firm credit declined by only 9 percent in real terms during 1989, compared with a decline of 65 percent in real terms in bank credit to the non-government sector. The result was a dramatic increase in the size of inter-firm credit relative to official credit, from 63 percent at the end of 1988 to 145 percent at the end of 1989.

To sum up, the deterioration in the macroeconomic situation was most severe in the first half of 1989. The rapid increase in the rate of inflation to almost hyper-inflationary levels in the second half of 1989 was the result of a combination of factors, the foremost being: the liberalization of food prices; large adjustments in administered prices, particularly energy; continuous devaluations of the exchange rate; and the formalization of a backward wage indexation scheme with progressively shorter periodicity for adjustments. Accordingly, wage indexation and the exchange rate policy turned the "corrective" increases in the price level associated with the reduction in the subsidies for food and energy prices (August and October) into sustained higher inflation. Moreover, anticipation of the January 1990 program is likely to have affected developments at the end of 1989 and to have exerted further pressure on inflation. Significant purchases and hoarding by households were detected, along with the accumulation of inventories by enterprises. Finally, the wage spike in December 1989 reflects the anticipation of the price corrections carried out in January 1990, since, through a complicated indexation rule, the December increase was linked to both price changes in November and expected changes in January.

The Stabilization Program of January 1990

The stabilization program, launched on January 1, can be defined as *heterodox*, with two nominal anchors, the nominal wage and the exchange rate, and fiscal and monetary tightening. The wage policy consisted of a lagged indexation of the *wage bill* with low coefficients.[22]

The wage ceilings were to be enforced through a steeply progressive tax penalty. The exchange rate was frozen at 9,500 zlotys per US dollar, after the unification of the parallel and official markets, and the decreed "internal" convertibility of the zloty (for current account operations but not for capital account operations). The freeze of the exchange rate was preceded by a sharp depreciation of 46 percent, and the measure resulted in a significant overshooting of the parallel market rate prevailing on average in December (about 30 percent).[23]

It was expected that the exchange rate would be defended by a special fund (of US$1 billion) to be made available by foreign banks, as well as by the interest rate policy.

The fiscal components relied on a balanced budget, to be achieved in 1990. An increase in revenues of about 4 percent of GDP and a small reduction in expenditures of around 1 percent of GDP were to produce an adjustment in the budget. The government undertook discretionary measures—which were to have supplemented the automatic rise in real revenues from the expected reversed Olivera-Tanzi effect—to increase revenues: it raised the basic rate of the turnover tax from 15 percent to 20 percent; it revalued tenfold the fixed assets of the socialized enterprises, the basis for the dividend tax; and it drastically curtailed tax exemptions and relief. On the expenditure side, the main gains were expected to come from a reduction in the subsidies on the order of 8 percent of GDP.

The monetary components relied on tight credit conditions in the first quarter of 1990 that were partially loosened in the following three quarters of the year. Net domestic assets were expected to grow by about 20 percent in nominal terms in the first quarter, a level that implies a real decline of 30 percent, and to grow at an average quarterly rate of 7-8 percent in the rest of the year, a level that is above the expected rate of inflation. This policy would have guaranteed a small real increase in net domestic assets by the end of the year. The credit ceilings were complemented by an interest rate policy geared to maintain positive real rates throughout the year. Given expected inflation of about 30-35 percent, the government set the refinancing rate of the National Bank of Poland, which was to serve as a sort of leading rate, at 36 percent in January.

Amendments to the banking law strengthened the independence of the central bank. This measure likely signalled to actors in the economy that the central bank was abandoning its role as lender of last resort.

Fundamental liberalization measures accompanied the above macroeconomic policies. The *price system* was liberalized almost entirely—only 5 percent of goods sold at the retail level remain subject to price controls—and simultaneously the administered prices of energy products were raised more than 400 percent so as to reduce the subsidies. The *trade system* was liberalized by abolishing the quantity controls on imports and replacing them with tariffs and by reducing the quotas for exports of basic commodities.

Finally, the government announced a program of privatization and restructuring of the industrial sector, including new rules establishing triggers for the initiation of bankruptcy and restructuring of enterprises. In this regard, failure to pay the dividend tax (a tax on the value of the funding capital of a firm) was established as the main instrument for triggering these procedures.

To summarize, the design of the program was based on the assumption that the nominal anchors would help reduce inflation very fast, and, accordingly, monetary balances and credit, after an initial tight condition meant to defend the nominal anchors, were expected to grow considerably in real terms starting in the second quarter of 1990. The planned decline in real terms in the first quarter was based on the assumption that the growth of nominal credit and monetary aggregates would lag behind the rate of inflation, pushed up temporarily by the increase in energy prices. However, it was thought that the decline in real wages would give room to enterprises to absorb the price shock (see also Lipton and Sachs 1990). That the program was not intended to squeeze aggregate demand can be inferred from the expectation of a current account deficit of more than 7 percent of GDP in 1990 (compared with a deficit of 2.6 percent of GDP in 1989).

Initial Results

The initial results of the stabilization program can be characterized as *stagflationary*, at least in the first two months following the start of the stabilization measures. A sharp drop in output was accompanied by an acceleration in the rate of inflation, which remained persistent and relatively high given the depressed economy. Using a terminology suggested by Polish economists (Kolodko and McMahon 1987), the economy experienced a shift from a condition of *shortage-flation*—caused by the combination of high inflation and large shortages of goods—to one of stagflation.

The rate of inflation, after jumping to 78.6 percent in January 1990, declined to 23.9 percent in February and to an average monthly rate of 5 percent in March-June. After falling to 1.8 percent in August, it bounced back to 4.7 percent in September and 5.7 percent in October, 4.9 in November and 5.9 in December, pushed by the large increases in the prices of oil products and administered prices. Notwithstanding the external negative shock and successive increases in administered prices, the persistently high rate of inflation, which oscillated around 4 percent per month for more than 10 months, was unexpected. Given the larger than anticipated fiscal adjustment and drop in output, this persistence was puzzling, although it is similar in some ways to Brazil and Argentina's experience with stabilization programs. When fiscal and monetary explanations for this phenomenon are ruled out, the main factors can be identified as: (1) the slow movement toward a higher equilibrium price level for both tradable and non-tradable goods; and (2) the de facto high degree of indexation of wages to prices since March 1990.

The profile of the decline in output shows that the drop was concentrated at the beginning of the program and that thereafter output remained practically flat, with some signs of a possible recovery surfacing in August-September. Along with the decline in output sold, initially enterprises drew down significant quantities of inventories of both inputs and finished products. Employment in the socialized sector responded with a lag to the drop in output, and in the year as a whole employment was about 10 percent below its level in the same period in 1989. Unemployment, practically non-existent before 1990, increased after February 1990 at an average of 100,000 people per month, reaching about 1.15 million people in December (more than 6 percent of the labor force). "Statistical" real wages declined sharply in the first six months of 1990, while they increased significantly in the third quarter (about 20 percent over the second quarter) and fourth quarter. Despite this increase, for the year as a whole they declined by about 30 percent.

Marked improvements took place in both the fiscal and the external accounts. The fiscal accounts moved into a sizable surplus in the first half of 1990 (about 3 percent of GDP was expected for the whole year), despite the acceleration in inflation in the first quarter and the decline in output. The improvement continued in the third quarter, although a deficit was experienced in the last quarter of 1990. The main factor behind this unexpected surplus was a surge in tax revenues, mainly on enterprise profits, which at the end of 1989 (which is the tax base for 1990 payments) were much larger than anticipated as a result of large capital gains on enterprise dollar deposits. The trade balance displayed a remarkable improvement, with a surplus of US$2.7 billion (for convertible currency trade) for the year as a whole, with exports in convertible currencies increasing by more than 40 percent and imports by 10 percent. The change in

gross reserves fully reflected the improvement in the current account.

On the monetary side, net domestic assets grew well below the ceilings of the program in the first half of the year, while the growth of the stock of money was in line with nominal targets because of the monetization of foreign reserves (table 9-1-3).

This trend was reversed in the second half of the year, however, and the net domestic assets of the banking sector (NDA) overshot the credit ceilings of the program. While the contemporaneous increase in real wages and real credit raises concerns about possible excess liquidity in the system, the evidence for the third quarter, particularly the continued increase in foreign reserves, points to a "remonetization" of the economy.[24]

It is worth noting that part of the increase in bank credit appears to have resulted from the substitution of inter-firm credit with bank credit, a positive phenomenon. Developments in the fourth quarter were more worrisome, however, as the financing needs of the government sector increased with the shift to a budget deficit.

The real decline in the stocks of money and credit has been substantial. In the first quarter, net domestic assets and broad money declined by 54 percent and 44 percent in real terms, respectively. In the second quarter net domestic assets continued to decline in real terms, while broad money increased in real terms because of the large inflows of international reserves.

The National Bank refinancing rate was set according to expected inflation, the aim being to produce slightly positive real rates. In January, the refinancing rate was 36 percent, in February 20 percent, in March 10 percent, in April 8 percent, in May 5.5 percent and in June 4 percent. After declining to 2.5 percent in July-September, it was raised to 3.5 percent in October and again to 4.5 percent in November, following the increase in the rate of inflation. Ex post, the rates were negative in real terms in January-February and roughly in line with inflation in the following months.

Table 9-1-3. *Poland: Monetary Survey, December 1989-September 1990*

	1989.IV	1990.I	1990.II	1990.III	1990.IV
Gross reserves	24.1	26.8	36.7	50.4	46.8
Domestic credit	40.0	50.8	63.4	81.8	110.4
Credit to government (net)	6.5	2.7	-11.1	-18.1	-8.2
Credit to non-gov't.	33.5	48.1	74.5	99.9	118.6
Other	31.8	35.3	36.5	35.0	34.8
Broad money	96.0	112.9	136.6	169.2	192.0
Inter-firm credit	47.3	75.1	82.6	77.3	82.6[a]

Note: The roman numerals following the years refer to the quarters of the year.
a. November.
Source: National Bank of Poland.

The magnitude of the initial results was largely unexpected; the discrepancy is so large that the normal bias, which often seems to characterize predictions about stabilization programs, whereby inflation tends to be underestimated and growth overestimated, cannot explain it.[25]

Before turning to possible interpretations of the initial results, it is important to emphasize that there were no slippages in the implementation of the program during the first semester. More controversial is the issue of slippages in the second half in the areas of both credit and wage policies. However, given that in both areas developments in the first semester were well below the targets of the program, it is not too surprising that some overshooting took place in the second semester.

Obviously, the real issue is whether these trends are sustainable in future months and consistent with a decline in inflation. In the first semester the two nominal anchors of the program, the exchange rate and the nominal wage, were maintained without trouble and actually appeared to be non-binding as the increase in wages stood below the ceilings and the exchange rate stabilization fund made available by western countries was not used, with a build-up of international reserves. As to the monetary program, the ceilings (on both net credit to the government and net domestic assets) were respected with ample margins, and interest rates were set as programmed. Although some overshooting of the targets took place in the third quarter, even then no pressure was exerted on the exchange rate, and the wage increases were consistent with the original indexation scheme, given that the increases derived from use of the "reserve" accumulated in the first quarter, when wages rose well below the norm.

Assessment of the most recent trends and the policy prescriptions for the next months depend crucially on the analysis of the results of the program so far, in particular of the unexpected outcomes, such as the sharp recession, the fiscal improvement and the sizable current account surplus. One possible, and actually widespread, reading of the initial results of the program interprets the recession as a standard Keynesian phenomenon of demand contraction. For Poland, the appearance of *demand barriers* would certainly represent a fundamental break with the past, when the economy was traditionally *supply constrained*. The large drop in real wages would thus be the main source of the contraction in output, and the larger than expected decline in output would seem consistent with the larger than expected fall in real wages.

Without denying the possibility that this drop in demand could have been the source of the drop in output, several doubts can be raised. First, it is widely recognized that in 1989, at least in the first three quarters, the economy experienced excess demand, with worsening shortages. Therefore, when real wages are measured using official price indices, they reflect—in the terminology of Polish economists—"statistical" rather than actual real wages (see also Lipton and Sachs 1990). These "statistical" real wages largely overestimate real purchasing power in 1989 and thus overestimate the drop in real purchasing power in 1990, as measured by the decline in the "statistical" real wages.

Second, measured retail prices likely overestimate the actual rates of inflation, as a significant proportion of retail trade in 1990 took place outside the state distribution channels, at prices estimated to be 20-30 percent below officially recorded prices.

Third, the downturn in production actually began in 1989, specifically, in the second half, when "statistical" real wages were still well above their 1988 levels.

Fourth, although a decline in domestic demand was clearly envisioned in the program, an increase in foreign demand should have sustained output.

Finally, the behavior of the financial savings of households appears at odds with the view of a household sector experiencing severely constrained liquidity forced to adjust its demand for goods downward. In particular, the availability of a large stock of foreign currency deposits made by the household sector—which is an abstraction from distributional issues, which may be important—means that households were not constrained in borrowing at the outset of the program for the most part. Given the temporary character of the income policy scheme, it remains to be explained why households did not deplete their stock of foreign currency deposits to protect their levels of consumption. Indeed, in US dollar terms, household deposits in foreign currency increased in the first six months following the start of the program (table 9-1-4).

More generally, a main limitation of the above view is that it takes as exogenous elements that are actually endogenous, particularly the decline in real wages, which is assumed to be the ultimate source of the decline in output.[26]

An alternative explanation that is favored here emphasizes that the focus of the stagflationary effects of the program should be on the enterprise sector and its reaction to the large supply shock arising from the elimination of the subsidies for both input prices and interest rates. According to this view, the credit crunch associated with both the policy-determined tightening of official credit and the sudden increase in credit risk played the main role in transmitting the effects of the initial supply shock.

Table 9-1-4. *Poland's Foreign Currency Deposits*
(billions of US$)

	1988	1989				1990		
	IV	I	II	III	IV	I	II	III
Total	5.4	5.8	6.8	7.2	7.2	6.0	5.9	6.2
Households	4.3	4.5	4.5	4.8	4.9	5.0	5.2	5.6
Enterprises	1.1	1.3	2.3	2.4	2.3	1.0	0.7	0.6

Source: National Bank of Poland.

While it has generally been observed that the jump in the rate of inflation can reflect the effects of the price liberalization in the context of the liquidity overhang, the larger than expected increase in the rate of inflation in January can be mainly ascribed to cost-push factors linked to the devaluation of the exchange rate and the lifting of the subsidies decreed at the outset of the program as a main element in the rationalization of the price system. While the importance of these targets to achieving greater efficiency in the economy and to reducing pressures on the budget is not questioned here, it is important to stress that the recessionary impact of a tightening of credit when there is a large increase in the prices of inputs has been overlooked. In Calvo and Coricelli (1990), it is estimated, although by an admittedly rough calculation, that the credit crunch, measured as the gap between actual and required liquidity, necessary to permit enterprises to maintain the same level of production of 1989 was on the order of 60 percent at the beginning of 1990. To appreciate the magnitude of the crunch, note that in January 1990 working capital credit from the banking system to the socialized sector declined in *nominal* terms—in a context of increased prices for domestic inputs of 400 percent, large increases in the prices of foreign inputs as a result of the devaluation at the outset of the program, and of a jump in interest rate costs.

Although the squeeze somehow loosened in the following months, by the end of June 1990 the stock of credit to the non-government sector was 20 percent below its level in real terms at the end of 1989. This partial loosening of the credit squeeze seems consistent with the fact that, after dropping sharply in January, industrial output remained flat in the following months. A similar argument applies to the third quarter, which shows some recovery in economic activity. At the end of the third quarter, real credit to the non-government sector had essentially recovered its level of December 1989. In the fourth quarter credit to the socialized sector declined in real terms while production remained flat.

In a static framework, the sharp reduction in subsidies for enterprises represents a supply shock that even in a competitive industry would cause a reduction in output and an increase in prices. This simple story seems to accord with several phenomena characterizing the first results of the stabilization program. However, it would imply a simple shift from a distorted equilibrium to an undistorted and efficient equilibrium. At the micro level, this explanation suggests that firms operating only thanks to subsidies should have gone bankrupt after the elimination of these subsidies, while efficient firms should have survived after the Big Bang. However, the first months following the stabilization display a different picture that indicates a widespread recession without significant bankruptcies. This phenomenon casts doubt on the working of a Schumpeterian, efficient natural selection.

The explanation postulated here, without denying the relevance of the above static factors, relies on a different mechanism. Specifically, it emphasizes the role of the credit markets in transmitting the effects of the supply shock. The sharp reduction in the stock of real credit from both the banking system and within the enterprise sector itself accounts for the observed recession.[27]

By increasing the price of inputs, the stock of liquidity necessary at the beginning of the period to operate at the old level of production increased sharply. The lack of a sufficient stock of liquidity likely induced firms to reduce their purchases of inputs, with a consequent fall in output. This phenomenon, which is related to the adequacy of the initial stock of liquidity, occurs independently of the behavior of the price of outputs. The increase in prices, accompanied by the compression in real wages, helped firms reconstitute their liquidity. Accordingly, both the fall in real wages and the good profit performance of Polish industry during the first months of the deep recession can be explained. The good profit performance of enterprises in particular is puzzling for those who share the view that a recession is induced by "demand barriers."

The actual working of the credit crunch and the relative role of the quantity of credit versus its cost (interest rate) are still uncertain, given the presence of direct controls over bank credit.

In this connection, the behavior of the inter-firm credit market may provide important clues. As noted, in 1989 the stock of inter-firm credit, despite a slight decline in real terms, grew much faster than official bank credit did. According to data up to March 1990, although smaller than the decline in official credit, the stock of inter-firm credit declined by about 33 percent in real terms in the first quarter of 1990 (compared with a decline in bank credit of 46 percent in real terms in the same period). It continued to decline in real terms in the second quarter and also in relation to bank credit. Starting in July it even declined in nominal terms. In the remaining months of 1990, the inter-firm market did not provide a relevant cushion to the squeeze of official credit. Moreover, it is conjectured here that a large component of inter-firm credit in 1990 represents an accumulation of arrears rather than a "voluntary" extension of new credit. This phenomenon is consistent with the view of a sudden increase in *credit risk*, likely associated with the signaled withdrawal of the central bank from its role as lender of last resort.[28]

The extremely simplified mechanism just described has to be amended to accommodate the impressive improvement in the trade balance observed after January 1990. Indeed, in general recessions led by temporary supply shocks should result in a worsening of the trade balance (consumption tends to decline less than output).[29]

However, if the behavior of inventories held by enterprises is considered as well, the "model" used here can account for a temporary improvement in the trade balance. The liquidity crunch will induce enterprises to deplete their stock of inventories to reconstitute their liquid balances—in other words, there will be a shift in the "portfolio" of enterprises from inventories to money. As a result, total absorption in the economy by households and enterprises can decline more than output—although the decline in consumption falls short of the decline in output—and thereby yields an improvement in the trade balance. The data on inventories are, however, ambiguous, as inventory accounting is unclear. According to the authors' calculations, the stock of inventories declined sharply at the beginning of 1990 and was, at the end of September, still well below its level in 1989.

Demand-side factors certainly played a role. Household savings increased during the year so that no consumption "smoothing" took place. This increase occurred as households likely tried to reconstitute their real stock of financial wealth, eroded by high inflation (see chapter 11, "The Ownership-Control Structure and the Behavior of Polish Enterprises During the 1990 Reforms: Macroeconomic Measures and Microeconomic Responses" by Roman Frydman and Stanislaw Wellisz in this volume). In addition, the increase in unemployment could have induced an increase in precautionary savings. Finally, a further element (mentioned in the main text)

might have been the shift in the distribution of income in favor of profits.

Appendix 2. Stabilization in Yugoslavia

Background

The reversal of external financing flows during the 1980s forced Yugoslavia to undertake drastic measures to balance its external accounts. The external adjustment consisted primarily of large real exchange rate devaluations and, initially, quantitative restrictions on imports. Although these measures were able to generate increasing current account surpluses, economic activity stagnated, and inflation accelerated almost continuously (figure 9-2-1). Moreover, the absence of fiscal imbalances in the economy might suggest that the nature of inflation in Yugoslavia is entirely non-fiscal.

While it is true that many hyper-inflationary episodes are triggered by balance-of-payments difficulties and large exchange rate devaluations, the complete absence of fiscal imbalances from the overall picture in the case of Yugoslavia is intriguing. Indeed, even the "balance-of-payments view of inflation" recognizes the role of fiscal deficits in the determination of inflation, although that role is assumed to be less central than under the "fiscal view of inflation." In the former view, the exchange rate has the central role, while fiscal deficits contribute to inflation mostly through endogenous interactions with the exchange rate and the inflation rate itself (see for instance, Dornbusch 1987, Dornbusch and Fischer 1986, Liviatan and Piterman 1986, and Montiel 1989).

This appendix will show that, while non-fiscal factors played a role in the acceleration of inflation during the 1980s, especially at the end of the decade, the existence of fundamental domestic imbalances also contributed decisively to the inflationary process. These fundamental imbalances were originally located in large segments of the enterprise sector, but gradually spilled over to the financial system, resulting, among other things, in a quasi-fiscal deficit in the central bank.[30]

A major non-fiscal factor that contributed to higher inflation was the need to reduce real wages and ensure a given real devaluation of the exchange rate—the Pazos-Simonsen mechanism (see Dornbusch 1987; Dornbusch and Simonsen 1988; Pazos 1978; and Simonsen 1989). This mechanism became more important after the introduction of wage indexation in 1987. In particular, the large real devaluation of mid-1988 (figure 9-2-2) in the context of wage indexation and monetary accommodation, triggered a significant increase in the rate of inflation (figure 9-2-3). During the last three quarters of 1989, the relation between real wages and inflation

Figure 9-2-1. *Selected Macroeconomic Variables for Yugoslavia, 1977-89*

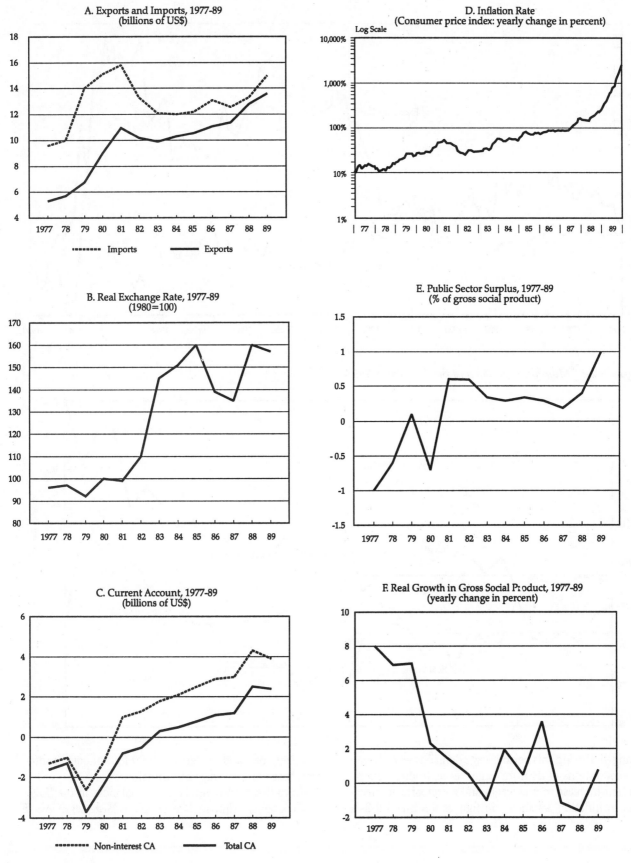

A. Exports and Imports, 1977-89
(billions of US$)

········ Imports   —— Exports

D. Inflation Rate
(Consumer price index: yearly change in percent)

B. Real Exchange Rate, 1977-89
(1980=100)

E. Public Sector Surplus, 1977-89
(% of gross social product)

C. Current Account, 1977-89
(billions of US$)

········ Non-interest CA   —— Total CA

F. Real Growth in Gross Social Product, 1977-89
(yearly change in percent)

Figure 9-2-2. *Real Exchange Rate and Real Wages*
(1980=100)

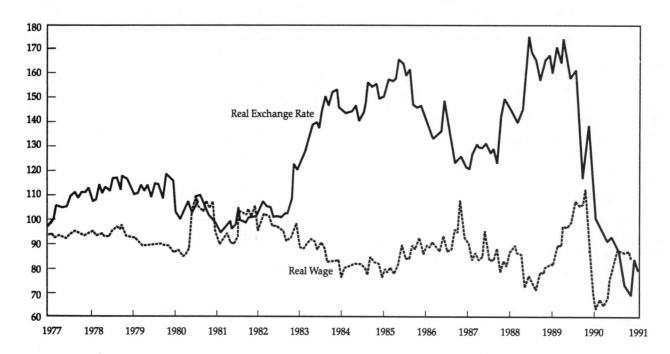

Figure 9-2-3. *Monthly Inflation and the Real Wage, 1987-89*

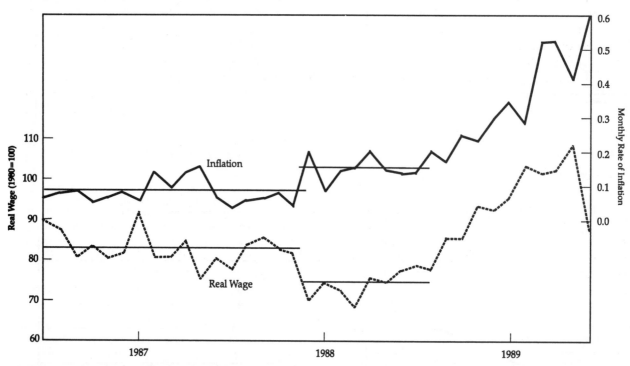

changed. During this period, wage demands were driven by expectations of a future wage freeze, leading to a 40 percent increase in real wages and a dramatic acceleration in inflation, as shown in figures 9-2-2 and 9-2-3.

(see Helpman and Leiderman 1990 for a model of inflation based on real wage increases).

As to the fundamentals, the imbalances in the Yugoslav economy originated, as noted, in large segments of the enterprise sector. Already in the late 1970s a significant number of enterprises were recording losses. During the 1980s the amount of the losses increased significantly (table 9-2-1). Although these numbers are

the system. This redistribution gained momentum in the 1980s as a result of the reversal of financing flows and the successive exchange rate shocks in the economy. The phenomenon of accelerating inflation in Yugoslavia

Table 9-2-1. *Enterprise Losses*
(% of GSP)

	1980	1981	1982	1983	1984	1985	1986	1987	1988	1989
Enterprise losses	1.6	1.3	2.2	2.9	2.1	2.8	3.0	6.6	5.7	15.0
Seigniorage on base money	1.8	2.7	2.7	1.6	3.9	3.6	4.2	4.9	5.7	12.0

Source: SDK, National Bank of Yugoslavia, Knight (1984) and Rocha (1991).

affected by many accounting problems, they indicate a deteriorating trend that is highly probable. One likely cause for this increase in losses was the sharp real devaluations undertaken in the mid-1980s (enterprises initially held 80 percent of Yugoslavia's external debt). Another likely cause was the growing numbers of redundant workers in the enterprises, estimated to have reached 20 percent of the labor force in 1988.[31]

An obvious question is how the enterprise losses were financed. During the 1980s there were two basic sources of financing. The first comprised various forms of inter-enterprise financing, including voluntary transfers from profit-makers to loss-makers inside the same industrial holding, as well as inter-enterprise credits and arrears. The second consisted of bank credits on subsidized terms. The banks, which were controlled by the enterprises, were able to continue this policy of credit subsidies until almost the end of the decade only by paying even more negative real interest rates on domestic deposits.

During the 1980s enterprises' financial imbalances spilled over into the central bank. Several enterprises revealed themselves unable to service their foreign liabilities. The central bank absorbed the foreign liabilities of enterprises located in less developed regions, thus adding to its own foreign liabilities. The central bank also absorbed the stock of foreign exchange deposits in the commercial banks, a measure designed to protect the banks from foreign exchange losses.[32]

The reluctance of the central bank to charge positive real interest rates on its credits, while facing mounting payments on its foreign liabilities, resulted in a quasi-fiscal deficit that constituted an independent source of monetary expansion.

Ultimately, inflation in Yugoslavia engineered a complex redistribution of real resources from holders of domestic assets toward the financing of hidden losses in

can also be interpreted as resulting from an external-internal transfer problem, as in other debtor countries (Cohen 1988). The ultimate beneficiaries of the internal redistribution were the enterprises, which were the major recipients of Dinar credits at subsidized terms, and the holders of foreign exchange deposits.

The precise magnitude of the inflationary financing of hidden losses is difficult to assess. On the one hand, not all the seignorage revenues on base money (changes in base money as shares of gross social product [GSP]) shown in table 9-2-1 were channeled toward the financing of hidden losses. For instance, in 1988 and 1989 roughly half the seignorage revenues on base money were absorbed by the large build-up of foreign reserves that preceded the stabilization program. On the other hand, the base of inflationary taxation was broader than base money, since it included the whole Dinar deposit base. The introduction of indexation on time deposits above three months in mid-1988 reduced the base of inflationary taxation. However, the implicit taxation of shorter term deposits remained substantial.[33]

The combination of accelerating inflation and negative real interest rates on deposits resulted in a drastic portfolio shift out of domestic assets, as illustrated in figure 9-2-4. The share of foreign exchange deposits in broad money increased from less than 30 percent at the start of the decade to more than 65 percent in 1989. It is quite possible that the existence of foreign exchange deposits facilitated the shift out of domestic money and thereby also contributed to inflation by accelerating the increase in velocity.

The failure to correct the internal imbalances was a major cause of the failure of the several stabilization attempts of the mid-1980s, which relied mostly on wage-price controls. Particularly noteworthy was the stabilization program of mid-1988, which attempted to curb inflation essentially through the establishment of

Figure 9-2-4. *Real M2, Foreign Exchange Deposits and M3*
(base=1985)

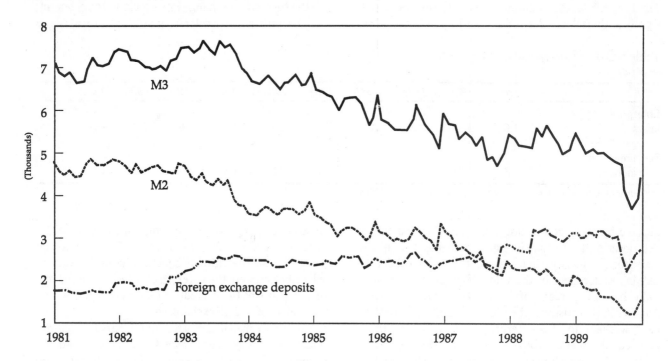

progressively declining targets on the growth of money and wages and through the indexation of time deposits. This measure was introduced as an attempt to reduce the subsidization of credits and to impose financial discipline on enterprises. No fiscal policy support to stabilization was envisaged in the 1988 program.

The inconsistencies of the mid-1988 program were aggravated by a real devaluation whose rationale was unclear, since the country was already running a large current account surplus and was also engaged in debt rescheduling negotiations with private foreign banks. In fact, the real devaluation defeated one of the main purposes of the external debt rescheduling, which was to relieve the pressure of external debt payments on the domestic economy.

The attempt to maintain the real exchange rate depreciated in the context of formal wage indexation resulted in a strong acceleration of wages and prices, as noted above. The real devaluation also increased the burden of foreign interest payments, thus offsetting in part the benefits of the rescheduling of commercial debt. The pressure to finance hidden losses, particularly the central bank's own deficit, led policy-makers to abandon the monetary targets soon after their implementation. Faced with higher real interest rates on bank credits, several enterprises simply stopped paying, a step that considerably worsened the already severe problem of non-performing loans in the commercial banks.

Developments in 1989 and Preparations for the 1990 Program

The failure of the 1988 stabilization program showed the futility of implementing another program without addressing the fundamental domestic imbalances. Thus, during 1989, consensus was reached about the need to generate a surplus in the non-financial public sector in order to cover losses elsewhere in the economy, even though there was less certainty about the required magnitude of the fiscal adjustment, as well as the best strategy for dealing with the loss-makers.

In the case of the central bank's own deficit, the solution was clear, consisting basically of the transfer of the servicing of its foreign exchange liabilities and agriculture subsidies to the federal budget. In the case of enterprises and commercial banks, the situation was less clear. Although enterprise losses were regularly calculated, frequent changes in accounting rules and a lack of harmonization in accounting procedures decreased the reliance on available figures. The situation of the commercial banks was not fully transparent either. While the share of non-performing loans was known to be large, the estimates were tentative.

More important, the design of a well-defined strategy to deal with the loss-makers had not been completed. For instance, there were still doubts over whether to provide a fiscal subsidy to loss-makers while submitting them to restructuring programs (involving lay-offs, debt write-offs, selective improving investments, changes in management, etc.), or whether to let the Darwinian-Schumpeterian law of natural selection operate freely. In this case, the number of bankruptcies was expected to increase much more rapidly, and the fiscal resources would be directed toward social programs, as opposed to the loss-making enterprises themselves. Finally, although privatization was already accepted as an essential component of the overall strategy, the mechanisms and timing of its introduction, as well as its interactions with the restructuring program, had not been fully worked out.

During 1989, progress in the establishment of the preconditions for a stabilization program was more advanced in the macroeconomic area. First, the debt rescheduling agreements of mid-1988 and the large current account surplus achieved in 1989 (US$2.4 billion) resulted in an increase in international reserves from US$3.3 to US$6.1 billion. An adequate level of reserves was deemed essential to ensure the initial credibility in the program, which was to include the introduction of currency convertibility[34] and a substantial degree of import liberalization. In the fiscal area, all the changes in legislation required for the transfer of the fiscal operations of the central bank to the federal budget and the introduction of a new sales tax were completed.

The dramatic acceleration in inflation in 1989 (figure 9-2-3) affected the elaboration of a stabilization program that same year. As noted, several causes contributed to the acceleration. First, the attempt to maintain the real exchange rate depreciated in the presence of wage indexation required an acceleration of inflation to achieve a reduction of the real wage. Second, in the last three quarters of 1989 the real exchange rate target was partly abandoned, but the very strong increase in real wages kept the pressures on inflation. Finally, the hidden losses in the economy had not been eliminated and still constituted a permanent source of monetary expansion and inflation. In addition, during 1989 the pressures on money supply were compounded by the large build-up of foreign reserves by the central bank. The perception that inflation was running completely out of control motivated the launching of the plan at mid-December, despite the awareness of some loose ends.

The Stabilization Program of 1990

The stabilization program of 1990, as it was called, contained a variety of measures in the areas of income, fiscal, monetary and trade policy. The program also included a currency reform that eliminated four zeros off the old Yugoslav Dinar. The program can be classified as heterodox, even though it did not include the imposition of widespread price controls for goods and services as happened under other heterodox programs of the mid-eighties. In addition to elements commonly found in other heterodox programs, the Yugoslav one included a financial and industrial restructuring cum privatization component that was supposed to affect most of the Yugoslav economic system, although this component had not been fully worked out at the start of the program.

The incomes policy consisted of a six-month freeze on the exchange rate, on nominal wages and on the prices of a set of goods (mostly in the areas of energy and transportation) that accounted for 20 percent of the consumer price index. The prices of the other goods and services remained completely free. The exchange rate was frozen at 7 new Dinars per deutschemark right after a devaluation of 20 percent on December 18. The devaluations preceding the program were supposed to have corrected the overvaluation that had occurred in the second half of 1989, but they were rapidly eroded by the price increases that followed (figure 9-2-2).[35]

Moreover, there was no attempt to use a larger real devaluation to neutralize the impact of the introduction of currency convertibility and the reduction in import restrictions.

The government froze nominal wages in December at the November levels adjusted for a 20 percent increase. Although it was known that the freeze could cause a substantial erosion in real wages, they actually reached their highest level of the decade in the second half of 1989 (figure 9-2-2). Thus, it was felt that a larger initial correction of nominal wages was not needed before the freeze. The prices of energy, transportation and some other goods were frozen on December 18 after a series of adjustments in November and the first half of December. As with the exchange rate, the level of the price adjustments seems to have been based on an expectation of rapidly declining rates of inflation after the program.

The fiscal policy component of the program consisted basically of the assumption of several non-traditional expenditures by the budgets of the federation and the republics and the maintenance of a small budgetary surplus. The non-traditional expenditures included the servicing of foreign liabilities of the National Bank of Yugoslavia, interest subsidies for agriculture, transfers to the bank restructuring program, transfers to the social safety net, and coverage of some enterprise arrears.

The overall expansion of fiscal expenditures and maintenance of the budgetary surplus required an increase in tax revenues of approximately 5 percent of GSP. The increase in revenues was expected to come partly from exogenous increases in tax revenues (3.5 percent of GSP) as a result of the introduction of a new federal sales tax, higher customs duties and unspecified increases in the republics' tax rates, and partly from endogenous increases in real tax revenues resulting from the stabilization itself (1.5 percent of GSP)—the inverse Olivera-Tanzi effect (Olivera 1967 and Tanzi 1977). Estimation of the Olivera-Tanzi effect was complicated by the constant changes in the tax rates in the 1980s, designed mostly to offset the inflationary erosion of real tax revenues. In addition, in 1989 a partial indexation mechanism was applied to the collection of the basic sales tax.[36]

Monetary policy consisted essentially of a freeze on the nominal stock of the central bank's net domestic assets, while also allowing the central bank to monetize the foreign exchange inflows resulting from the program. However, it should also be noted that there was a substantial real increase in the central bank's domestic credits and base money during December 1989 (figure 9-2-5). Thus, monetary policy was less restrictive at the very start of the program than might have seemed at a first examination.

Finally, the restructuring cum privatization component included various measures that were still being developed or were running into problems with implementation. For instance, although the program called for the financial restructuring of the commercial banks and the commitment of fiscal resources for this purpose, the agency that presumably was to lead the bank restructuring program was created only in mid-1990.

On the side of enterprise reform, it was finally decided that the program would not provide financing for lossmakers out of budgetary resources. It was expected that the program would therefore result in a large number of bankruptcies. To prevent enterprises from circumventing the lack of financing by lending to each other, on January 1, 1990 the government introduced strict enforcement of the payments rules. The rules stated that enterprises which had not met their obligations within 60 days would be declared bankrupt and closed. Enforcement of this rule was possible because of a clearing system that centralized the payments among enterprises and banks.

Although the decision to force inefficient enterprises into bankruptcy was in principle worthy of praise, the strategy for dealing with bankrupt enterprises and the accompanying institutional and legal framework were still incomplete. Regional institutions that would presumably be placed in charge of restructuring and privatization had not yet been created. In addition, although the program included the commitment of fiscal support to a social safety net, the amount of resources required seems to have been underestimated.

Figure 9-2-5. *Exchange Rate and Prices, Wages and Prices, and Base Money and Prices, 1988-91*

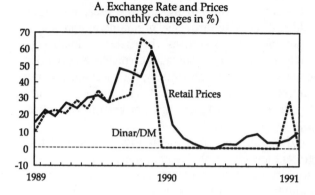

A. Exchange Rate and Prices
(monthly changes in %)

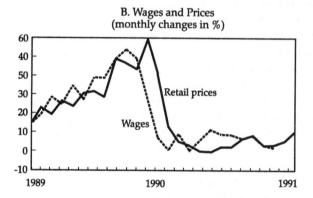

B. Wages and Prices
(monthly changes in %)

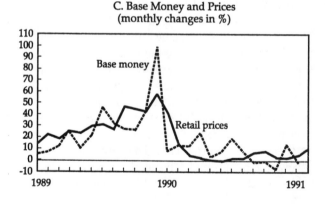

C. Base Money and Prices
(monthly changes in %)

First Results of the 1990 Program

Although it is too early to make a final judgment on the 1990 program, it is possible to assess the initial results and to identify the problems. As shown in table 9-2-2 and figure 9-2-5, the first point to be made is the program's success in halting inflation during the first semester without recourse to widespread price controls. The index measuring variations in the retail prices by calen-

Table 9-2-2. *Monthly Variations of Retail Prices, December 1989-February 1991*
(percent)

| | 1989 | 1990 | | | | | | | | | | | | 1991 | |
	Dec	Jan	Feb	Mar	Apr	May	Jun	Jul	Aug	Sep	Oct	Nov	Dec	Jan	Feb
(A)	59	42	13	5	3	0	0	2	3	7	8	3	3	5	10
(B)	64	17	8	3	0	0	0	5	2	1	10	n.a.	n.a.	n.a.	n.a.

n.a. Not available.

Notes: (A) Classical Index, computed from mid-month to mid-month.

(B) Supplementary Index, computed from beginning to end of month.

Source: Federal Institute of Statistics.

dar month (computed since December 1989) shows that the decline in inflation at the start of the program was actually more pronounced than the classical index suggests. However, table 9-2-2 also indicates a revival of inflationary pressures after July.

Industrial production fell by 10 percent in 1990, while GDP fell by 7.5 percent. However, these figures might overstate the recessionary impact of the program. As shown in figure 9-2-6, economic activity in the socialized sector, which was unusually strong in the first half of 1989, had already weakened considerably in the second half of that year. In addition, the stability of electricity production and the creation of large numbers of small private sector enterprises during 1990 may indicate that production in the private sector (not fully captured in the statistics) was not affected to the same degree.

In spite of the decline in output, the increase in the real tax revenues of the federation was impressive (figure 9-2-6). As mentioned, the increase reflects both endogenous and exogenous factors. Total revenues rose less in real terms, however, a reflection in part of the difficulty of collecting taxes from an economy in recession and the absence of significant exogenous tax adjustments at the local level. Although the public sector overall generated a small surplus in the first nine months of 1990, a development that caused concern was the rapid growth in traditional expenditures by the federation, including the wages of federal employees, as they absorbed resources that should ideally have been channelled to the restructuring programs.

The accumulation of reserves was indeed substantial—US\$4 billion between December 1989 and September 1990—and the stock of reserves rose to more than US\$10 billion, or 60 percent of the gross external debt. On the side of the current account, the freezing of the exchange rate and the introduction of convertibility led to a rapid recovery in the level of workers' remittances starting in the last days of December. On the side of the capital account, the same factors, combined with the imposition of tight controls on domestic credit, led enterprises to repatriate foreign exchange assets previously held abroad.

Figure 9-2-6. *Output, Real Tax Revenues and the Trade Balance*

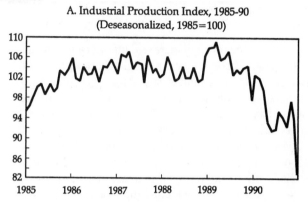

A. Industrial Production Index, 1985-90
(Deseasonalized, 1985=100)

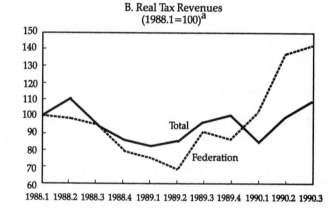

B. Real Tax Revenues
(1988.1=100)[a]

a. The figure following the year (.1-.4) refers to the quarter of the year.

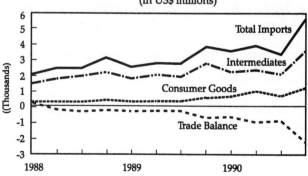

C. Imports and the Trade Balance, 1988-90
(in US\$ millions)

These foreign exchange inflows were the fundamental source of the expansion in base money during the first months of the program (table 9-2-3). After the December

There are no clear indications that monetary policy was unduly restrictive at the start of the program. Interest rates on time deposits were around 12-15 percent per

Table 9-2-3. *Balance Sheet of National Bank of Yugoslavia, December 1989-December 1990*
(billions of dinars)

	Dec.	Mar.	Jun.	Sept.	Dec.
Net foreign assets	26	44	58	66	39
Net domestic assets	135	131	131	141	165
Base money	26	40	53	71	69
Foreign exchange liabilities to banks	135	135	136	136	135

Source: National Bank of Yugoslavia.

"blip" (partly the result of increased inflows) and the January "crunch," base money expanded in keeping with the increase in National Bank of Yugoslavia's net foreign assets. The result was a real increase of 70 percent in the stock of base money between December 1989 and September 1990 (measured by calendar inflation).

The reshuffling of the portfolios of asset-holders at the start of the program is shown clearly in table 9-2-4. During the first three quarters, the increase in net foreign assets was accompanied by a rapid increase in M1 (driven especially by currency). The growth of Dinar time deposits was much slower, actually remaining below the rate of inflation. Finally, the stock of foreign exchange deposits was essentially stable. The fact that households did not convert their foreign exchange deposits into Dinar deposits could reflect an initial lack of confidence in the program. In the Israeli stabilization program, the conversion of dollar-linked deposits into domestic deposits constituted a basic source of non-inflationary monetary creation (Liviatan 1988).

Of course, the evaluation of portfolio shifts resulting from the program also has to consider the repatriation of foreign exchange assets previously held abroad by enterprises and the conversion of deutschemarks and dollars held "under the mattress." The first was shown to be substantial (around US$2 billion), while there is less information about the second.

year, an indication that liquidity conditions were not very tight.[37]

The level of the lending rates was much higher— around 30-35 percent per annum. These high intermediation spreads reflect to a large extent the severe problem of non-performing loans in banks' portfolios, rather than tight liquidity. In any case, the high lending rates tended to aggravate the financial conditions of the enterprises and increase their financial distress, creating obvious complications for the program.

Even though monetary policy did not seem unduly restrictive, the implementation of the program, combined with strict enforcement of the new payment rules, had a strong impact on enterprises. During the first semester of 1990, 7,000 of them fell into some kind of arrears, 3,000 were unable to make their payments within 30 days, and 350 were declared bankrupt. A large number of enterprises attempted to postpone bankruptcy by not paying wages. At the end of the first semester the situation was, however, very differentiated, with several enterprises increasing wages above the ceiling and several others unable to make wage payments within the ceiling. It was reported that a large number of enterprises did not make any wage payments in May to avoid the 60-day trigger mechanism for bankruptcy.

Pressure to relax the monetary policy mounted during the first semester of 1990 and produced a relaxation

Table 9-2-4. *Monetary Survey, December 1989-December 1990*
(billions of dinars)

	Dec.	Mar.	Jun.	Sept.	Dec.
Net foreign assets	-61	-39	-29	-16	-46
Net domestic assets	306	314	333	355	388
M1	51	75	100	125	127
Dinar time deposits	42	43	50	57	59
Foreign exchange deposits	152	157	154	157	156
M3	245	275	304	339	342

Source: National Bank of Yugoslavia.

starting in June. The relaxation was accomplished mostly by implementing measures to increase the multiplier, although central bank credits also increased somewhat. The result was a rapid increase in the stock of commercial bank credits after that month (figure 9-2-7). This increase led to a further rise in wages and a revival of inflationary pressure in the second semester. The relaxation of monetary policy also aborted the expected shake-out of the industrial sector by keeping loss-makers afloat while allowing them to resume wage payments.

Figure 9-2-7. *Dinar Credits and M1, 1989-90*

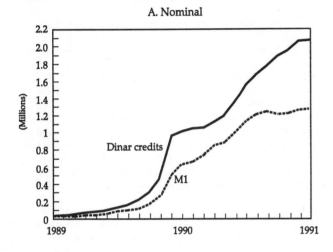

A. Nominal

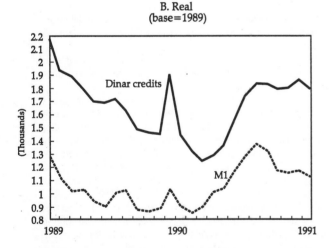

B. Real
(base=1989)

Concern over the revival of inflation led the central bank to shift back to a restrictive monetary policy in early October. However, there are indications that the banks avoided a contraction in credit by not complying with the reserve requirements. A further indication of the difficulty the central bank was having conducting monetary policy was the unusal episode of December 1990, whereby one of the regional branches of the central bank report-

edly increased credits by US$1.8 billion equivalent of Dinars in order to finance pensions and enterprise wages ("No Such Thing as a Free Dinar" 1990), a step it took without prior notification to the board of governors. The increase in domestic credits did not translate into monetary expansion in the fourth quarter because of the US$3 billion loss of foreign reserves that happened during the same period. As shown in tables 9-2-3 and 9-2-4 and figure 9-2-7, the increase in domestic credits was almost fully matched by a decrease in net foreign assets. The result was roughly constant stocks of base money, M1 and M3. Thus, although there was no further escalation in inflation late in the year, the rapid loss in reserves created obvious doubts about the sustainability of the stabilization program. The recognition that the real exchange rate had become severely overvalued led to a corrective 30 percent devaluation in January 1, 1991. In addition, the convertibility of the Dinar was abandoned in December, as the government interrupted sales of foreign exchange to households to prevent a further loss of reserves.

The devaluation of January 1, 1991 resulted in increasing rates of inflation in January and February (5 percent and 10 percent, respectively), despite the reimposition of controls on the wages of loss-making enterprises and the efforts to reestablish control over monetary policy. Furthermore, the exchange rate again became severely overvalued as a result of the accumulated increase in prices.

An Assessment of the Main Issues

The Yugoslav program of 1990 is an additional example of an exchange rate-based program lacking adequate correction of domestic imbalances. The program was very successful in the first semester but started to falter in the second half of the year. Enterprises continued to run losses, wages increased beyond the ceilings, fiscal resources were diverted toward wage payments of public sector employees, and, finally, monetary policy became largely accommodating. Although the maintenance of the exchange rate freeze and the open trade account prevented a further escalation of inflation late in the year, the drastic overvaluation of the exchange rate and the rapid loss of reserves ultimately forced the government to make a corrective devaluation and to suspend the convertibility of the Dinar.

The challenge faced by policy-makers in 1991 is to avoid the reemergence of an exchange rate-wages-prices spiral. The only solution to this problem is a return to the discipline of the first semester of 1990, including the reinstitution of some kind of enforceable wage policy. Although the measures taken in early 1991 are a step in the right direction, the prospects for their sustained implementation are still unclear, as it depends on a high degree of consensus among the various republics.

Fiscal policy also needs to be strengthened to support the restructuring program, since the initial fiscal commitments to the reforms were clearly insufficient. For instance, the resources allocated to the social program would clearly have been inadequate had loss-makers really been forced into bankruptcy. Final estimates of the quality of the portfolios of the commercial banks also indicated the need for more fiscal support for the financial restructuring program. The fact that the public sector ran a small surplus is almost completely irrelevant, as the imbalances in the Yugoslav economy were never located in the non-financial public sector but rather in other sectors of the economy.

Events in the second semester of 1990 also indicate that, for the stabilization to be successful, there must be much faster progress in the area of enterprise and bank restructuring and privatization. To some extent, the slow progress reflects institutional and human resource constraints on implementation of the restructuring effort. It also reflects the absence of adequate fiscal commitment to the reforms. Finally, it reflects insufficient political resolve to deal effectively with the loss-makers and the associated increase in unemployment. Until these problems are effectively tackled, however, the prospects for stabilization and growth will be highly uncertain.

Notes

1. The authors are grateful to Guillermo Calvo, Vittorio Corbo, Alex Cuckierman, Miguel Kiguel, Nissan Liviatan, Branko Milanovic and Jeffrey Sachs for their helpful comments on an earlier version of the paper. The authors are also grateful to Rodney Chun for his very competent research assistance. The views expressed in the paper are the authors' and do not necessarily reflect the views of the World Bank or its affiliated organizations.

2. In fact, Poland managed to run current account deficits throughout the 1980s, while Yugoslavia ran increasing current account surpluses after 1983.

3. Even in countries with open inflation, it may be difficult to establish a continuously close relationship between budgetary developments, money creation and inflation. See Sargent and Wallace (1981), Bruno and Fischer (1987) and Drazen and Helpman (1888) for theoretical demonstrations of the possibility of weak links in the short run and Kiguel and Liviatan (1990) for a recent examination of the Argentine and Brazilian cases.

4. In July both countries made some adjustments to the administered prices.

5. A common phenomenon in socialist countries that is known to weaken the power of monetary policy considerably.

6. This point is acknowledged by Kornai (1990), who also stresses the importance of wage controls in the initial phase of reform programs. See also Rocha (1991) for evidence on the absence of the Okun relationship in Yugoslavia.

7. Newly computed calendar indices for both countries, which are provided in table 9.4 and in the two appendices, show that inflation ac-

tually declined faster than indicated by the regular indices.

8. It appears that private sector activity is more reflected in the Polish figure than in the Yugoslav figure. If this is true, the difference in output performance may be larger than indicated.

9. The large current account surplus in Yugoslavia is generated from workers' remittances and tourism.

10. The real decrease in the Yugoslav M3 is a somewhat stronger 12 percent when the foreign exchange assets held abroad by Yugoslav enterprises are included. However, it is still a much smaller decrease than in Poland.

11. In both countries, the decline in the share of foreign exchange deposits in broad money was almost entirely attributable to the real increase in the stock of domestic money.

12. In the case of Yugoslavia, the real exchange rate in the first quarter of 1990 had already appreciated relative to the level in December.

13. The evaluation of the net impact of a real devaluation on output is complicated by the notorious multiplicity of channels (see Lizondo and Montiel 1989 for a recent survey). When the devaluation is carried out in the context of a stabilization program, it is further complicated by the simultaneous implementation of other policies.

14. This problem arose as a result of the control exercised on the banks by the enterprises.

15. An interesting simulation by de la Calle (1990), based on data on domestic resource costs computed by Konovalov (1989a), estimated that the stabilization program would have led to a contraction of about 20 percent in industrial output, a contraction led by the bankruptcy of enterprises, particularly in inefficient sectors. His predictions on the sectoral fall in output display a recession much more uneven than the one that actually took place.

16. The Polish rate of inflation in the 1980s was extremely high by European standards, even excluding 1989. The average for the period 1981-88 was 35 percent, compared with 5 percent for industrial countries, 38 percent for developing countries, 8 percent for Hungary and 1.3 percent for other Central and Eastern European countries, excluding Yugoslavia.

17. A macroeconomic analysis of the dynamics of inflation in a mixed system of free and controlled prices can be found in Commander and Coricelli (1990a).

18. Commander and Coricelli (1990a) show several cases in which this mixed system of free and controlled prices, with "passive" money, can generate explosive rates of inflation.

19. Saldanha (1989). The interest rate subsidies were measured by the difference between the nominal rates for credit and the rate of inflation. However, when the inflation tax on the monetary holdings (currency plus demand deposits) of enterprises is netted out, the net subsidies in the period 1984-88 fall to about 2-3 percent of GDP.

20. Note that wage push and budget deficits are directly linked through the wages of the public sector, which are tied institutionally to wages set in the socialized sector (see Gomulka 1990).

21. The government did not anticipate this effect, and it tried to reduce the wage-price spiral by lowering the coefficient of indexation and forbidding wage increases in excess of the indexation rules. With accelerating inflation, however, the shortened interval of adjustment had a negative impact that dominated the moderating effects of the reduced coefficients of indexation.

22. The wage bill was indexed to the changes in prices in the preceding month according to the following coefficients: 0.3 in January, 0.2 in February-April (a coefficient that was ultimately maintained through June), 1 in July and 0.6 thereafter. This decision was taken to compensate for the effects on real wages of the administered increase of energy prices in July. The rationale is not fully clear, however, because by July enterprises had accumulated significant room to increase their wage ceilings, as in the first six months they had stayed well be-

low the ceilings imposed.

23. The parallel market was very volatile in December: while the reduction in the overhang and the previous real exchange rate depreciations pushed the parallel rate down to the level of the official rate in mid-December, in the last days of the month the rate approached 9,500 zlotys in anticipation of the decision actually made on January 1, 1990.

24. Moreover, almost half the increase in credit to non-government was channelled to the non-socialized sector: households, farmers and private firms.

25. van Wijnbergen (1982) has emphasized the presence of a consistent bias of this type in IMF-supported stabilization programs.

26. The policy implications of this demand-led view of the recession are straightforward: they imply some form of demand stimulus. However, the stimulus can be achieved with different policies and different degrees of policy activism. A "non-activist" possibility would be not to change the policies and to let the decline in inflation, induced by the contraction in demand, reconstitute real monetary balances, and hence demand and output. A more activist approach would favor either increasing demand through a looser wage policy or more expansionary fiscal policy or turning monetary policy around with a much more accommodative credit policy (similarly to the recent experience in China in 1990).

27. Calvo and Coricelli (1990) provide a simple analytical model that illustrates this phenomenon.

28. In addition, the central bank strengthened its supervision of the criteria that commercial banks are to follow in extending credit. It appears that an assessment of creditworthiness is a condition for the extension of credit.

29. The fall in supply reduces the permanent income of workers/households, which accordingly reduces their consumption. Therefore, the fall in real wages and in consumption is a response to the credit crunch and the attendant fall in supplies, and is not an exogenous source of the recession.

30. More detailed analysis of inflation in Yugoslavia is provided in Rocha (1991), Bole and Gaspari (1990), Gaspari (1988), Mates (1987) and Mencinger (1987).

31. See Mencinger (1989). That should be compared with an open unemployment figure of 14 percent.[

32. The stock of foreign exchange deposits (mostly held by residents) is not part of Yugoslavia's external debt. In the early 1980s, the stocks of external debt and foreign exchange deposits amounted to US$20 billion and $11 billion, respectively.

33. Therefore, the impressive correlation between enterprise losses and seignorage in table 9-2-1 is somewhat misleading, since the central bank did not finance enterprises directly. The inflationary financing of all hidden losses is more complex, involving the financing of central bank losses from base money creation and the financing of enterprise losses through subsidized bank credits. See Rocha (1991).

34. The dollar value of the stock of domestic currency and sight deposits was $3.7 billion in December 1989. Thus, the level of reserves would be sufficient to cover a large portfolio shift out of domestic assets.

35. However, the real effective exchange rate relative to December 1989 in figure 3 understates the real devaluation that occurred right before the freeze, since it is measured by the *average* exchange rates in December adjusted by the Consumer Price Indexes in Yugoslavia and abroad.

36. These measures succeeded in maintaining the ratio of fiscal revenues to GSP at around 35 percent during the second half of the 1980s.

37. However, the constancy of nominal rates raises doubts about its value as an indicator of liquidity. It is possible that the constancy of the free deposit rates reflects the maintenance of the discount rate at 23 percent per year during the first semester.

References

Blanchard, O., and S. Fischer. 1989. *Lectures on Macroeconomics*. Cambridge, Mass: MIT Press.

Bole, V., and M. Gaspari. 1990. "The Yugoslav 'Way' to Hyperinflation." Processed. Belgrade.

Bruno, M., and S. Fischer. 1987. "Seignorage, Operating Rules and the High Inflation Trap." NBER Working Paper No. 2413. National Bureau of Economic Research, New York. October.

Calvo, G., and F. Coricelli. 1990. "Stagflationary Effects of Stabilization Programs in Reforming Socialist Countries: Supply Side vs. Demand Side Factors." International Monetary Fund and World Bank. Washington, D.C. August.

Cohen, D. 1988. "The Management of Developing Countries' Debt: Guidelines and Applications to Brazil." *The World Bank Economic Review* 2 (1) (January): 1-48.

Commander, S., and F. Coricelli. 1991a. "The Macroeconomics of Price Reform in Socialist Countries: A Dynamic Framework." World Bank, Policy, Research and Affairs (PRE) Working Paper no. 555. Washington, D.C.

—————. 1991b. *Price Wage Dynamics and the Transmission of Inflation in Socialist Economies: Empirical Models for Hungary and Poland*. Policy, Research and External Affairs (PRE) Working Paper Series. Washington, D.C.: World Bank, March.

de la Calle, L. 1990. "Macro and Microeconomic Linkages of the Polish Reforms." World Bank, Washington, D.C.

Dornbusch, R. 1987. "Lessons from the German Inflation Experience of the 1920s." In R. Dornbusch and S. Fischer, eds., *Essays in Honor of Franco Modigliani*. Cambridge, Mass.: MIT Press.

Dornbusch, R. and Fischer, S. 1986. "Stopping Hyperinflation: Past and Present." *Weltwirtschaftliches Archiv* 122 (1)(April):1-47.

Dornbusch, R., and M. Simonsen. 1988. "Inflation Stabilization: The Role of Incomes Policy and of Monetization." In R. Dornbusch, etc., *Exchange Rates and Inflation*. Cambridge, Mass.: MIT Press.

Drazen, A., and E. Helpman. 1988. "Inflationary Consequences of Anticipated Macroeconomic Policies." *Quarterly Journal of Economics*.

Fischer, S. 1977. "Long-Term Contracts, Rational Expectations and the Optimal Money Supply Rule." *Journal of Political Economy* 85 (February).

Gaspari, M. 1988. "Financial Crisis in Yugoslavia Since the Early 1980s: Causes and Consequences." A paper presented at the Conference on Financial Reform in Socialist Countries, Florence, Italy, October 1987.

Gomulka, S. 1990. "Reform and Budgetary Policies in Poland, 1989-90." In "Economic Transformation in Hungary and Poland." *European Economy* (43).

Helpman, E., and L. Leiderman, 1990. "Real Wages, Monetary Accommodation and Inflation." *European Economic Review* 34:897-911.

Hinds, M. 1990. "Issues in the Introduction of Market Forces in Socialist Economies." World Bank. Washington D.C. January.

Kiguel, M., and N. Liviatan. 1990. "The Inflation Stabilization Cycles in Argentina and Brazil." World Bank, Policy, Research and External Affairs (PRE) Working Paper Series No. 443. Washington, D.C. August.

Knight, P. 1984. "Financial Discipline and Structural Adjustment in Yugoslavia." World Bank Staff Working Paper No. 705. Washington, D.C. November.

Kolodko, G., and W. McMahon. 1987. "Stagflation and Shortageflation: A Comparative Approach," *Kyklos* 40:176-96.

Konovalov, V. 1989a. "Poland: Competitiveness of Industrial Activities: 1961-86." World Bank. Washington, D.C.

——————. 1989b. "Yugoslav Industry: Structure, Performance and Conduct." Mimeo. World Bank. Washington, D.C. November.

Kornai, J. 1990. *The Road to a Free Economy. Shifting from a Socialist System: The Case of Hungary*. New York: Norton.

Lipton, D., and J. Sachs. 1990. "Creating a Market Economy in Eastern Europe: The Case of Poland." *Brookings Papers on Economic Activity* 1:75-147.

Liviatan, N., 1988. "Israel's Stabilization Program." World Bank, Policy, Planning and Research Department (PPR) Working Paper Series No. 91. Washington, D.C. September.

Liviatan, N., and S. Piterman. 1986. "Accelerating Inflation and Balance of Payments Crises, 1973-84." In Yoram Ben-Porath, ed., *The Israeli Economy*. Cambridge, Mass.: Harvard University Press.

Lizondo, J., and P. Montiel. 1989. "Contractionary Devaluation in Developing Countries: An Analytical Overview." *IMF Staff Papers* 36 (1)(March).

Lucas, R. 1973. "Some International Evidence on Output-Inflation Trade-Offs." *American Economic Review* 63 (June).

Mates, N. 1987. "Some Specific Features of Inflation in a Heavily-Indebted Socialist Country." *Economic Analysis and Workers' Management* 21 (4):419-32.

Mencinger, J. 1987. "Acceleration of Inflation into Hyperinflation: The Yugoslav Experience in the 1980s." *Economic Analysis and Workers' Management*, 21 (4):399-418.

——————. 1989. "Privredna Reforma i Nezaposlenost" [Economic Reform and Unemployment]. *Privredna Kretanya Jugoslaviye* (March).

Montiel, P. 1989. "Empirical Analysis of High-Inflation Episodes in Argentina, Brazil and Israel." *IMF Staff Papers* 36 (September).

"No Such Thing as a Free Dinar." *The Economist*. 1991. January 12, p. 44.

Olivera, J. 1967. "Money, Prices and Fiscal Lags: A Note on the Dynamics of Inflation." *Quarterly Review* (Banca Nazionale del Lavoro) 20 (September).

Pazos, F. 1978. *Chronic Inflation in Latin America*. New York: Praeger.

Rocha, R. 1991. "Inflation and Stabilization in Yugoslavia." Processed. World Bank. Washington D.C.

Rocha, R., and F. Saldanha. 1991. "Fiscal and Quasi-Fiscal Deficits, Nominal and Real: Some Conceptual and Measurement Issues." Processed. Washington D.C. World Bank.

Rotemberg, J. 1987. "The New Keynesian Microeconomic Foundations." *NBER Macroeconomics Annual*.

Saldanha, F. 1989. Processed. "Self-Management: Theory and Yugoslav Practice." World Bank. Washington D.C.

Sargent, T., and N. Wallace. 1981. "Some Unpleasant Monetarist Arithmetic." *Quarterly Review* (Federal Reserve Bank of Minneapolis) (Fall).

Simonsen, M. 1989. "Inercia Inflacionária e Inflaçao Inercial" [Inflationary Inertia and Inertial Inflation]. In F. Barbosa and M. Simonsen eds., *Plano Cruzado: Inrcia x Inpcia*. Rio de Janeiro: Editora Globo.

Tanzi, V. 1977. "Inflation, Lags in Tax Collection, and the Real Value of Tax Revenue." *IMF Staff Papers* 24 (March).

Taylor, J. 1979. "Staggered Price-Setting in a Macro Model." *American Economic Review* 69 (May).

van Wijnbergen, S. 1982. "Stagflationary Effects of Monetary Stabilization Policies, a Quantitative Analysis of South Korea." *Journal of Development Economics* 10:133-69.

10

Comments on "Stopping Inflation: The Experience of Latin America and Israel and the Implications for Central and Eastern Europe" by Miguel A. Kiguel and Nissan Liviatan

John Williamson

It is a tribute to the authors of this paper that "Kiguel-Liviatan" is rapidly becoming a compound noun akin to "Friedman-Schwartz." Their paper provides an admirable framework within which to organize an assessment of the policy problems facing the countries of Eastern and Central Europe, which are trying not to succumb to chronic inflation. However, precisely because their conclusions, which are based on a careful and broad-ranging analysis of the comparative experience of different countries, are becoming so influential, it is the duty of a discussant to be particularly conscientious in examining whether the policy conclusions may depend on questionable analysis.

The intellectual framework of Miguel Kiguel and Nissan Liviatan is summarized in the 2x4 classification displayed in table 10.1 of this paper.[1] They argue that fiscal consolidation is a necessary but not sufficient condition for stabilization, which they also see as requiring a nominal anchor that the authorities are prepared to make credible even at the cost of a recession. The authors observe that a recession typically comes sooner with a money-based nominal anchor than with an exchange rate-based one. They draw the important distinction between chronic high-inflation countries and what by analogy can be called low-inflation countries. They claim that the latter seem to have far less difficulty stabilizing inflation after some shock pushes the rate far above its previous level. They also make the interesting

and important point that in both groups of countries stabilization seems *at best* to take inflation back down to where it was before the inflationary acceleration began.

Kiguel and Liviatan argue that inflationary pressures may persist for a time after stabilization if the public doubts the government's determination to stick with its proclaimed nominal anchor (the phenomenon of inflationary inertia). If the government stands by the anchor, the result will be short-run deflation; to the extent that wages are sticky downwards, the recession may persist into the medium term. Because prolonged inflation is politically painful and (at least superficially) economically wasteful, the government will be tempted to seek some way of accommodating what it hopes will be a once-over price rise. Unfortunately, this accommodation is difficult to carry out without undermining the credibility of its commitment to stand by its nominal anchor. As a result, what the government initially intends as a once-and-for-all accommodation often becomes a resumption of inflation.

On examination, this account of inflationary inertia embodies two distinct hypotheses. Hypothesis one is that agents (unions in particular, although not necessarily exclusively) can and do choose to enforce a set of real income claims that are higher than what would be consistent with a full employment equilibrium on the basis of announced macro policies. Hypothesis two is that what causes agents to act in this way is their lack of

Table 10.1 Kiguel-Liviatan Framework

Fiscal consolidation	Nominal anchor			
	None	Money supply	Exchange rate	Wage rate
Yes				
No				

Source: The author.

confidence in the credibility of the government's announced policy intentions.

The principal criticism of Kiguel and Liviatan's paper is that it goes along with practically all the literature of the last 15 years in assuming that hypothesis two is the only possible explanation for why agents choose to behave according to hypothesis one. However, another strand of the literature (it largely died out in the English language after Hirsch and Goldthorpe [1978] but has survived in the Portuguese language in Brazil) argues that agents make real income claims above the level consistent with equilibrium because they have become accustomed to thinking that such a level is their just entitlement. For example, claims that are now collectively inconsistent may have been established at some time in the past, before the economy confronted an oil price increase or a debt crisis and when its ability to pay was greater. Alternatively, and of particular interest for present purposes, the inconsistent real income claims may have been nurtured by past inflation itself.

Consider figure 10-1, "Simonsen's saw-tooth diagram," which is familiar in the Brazilian literature. It shows the movement of the (representative) real wage over time under conditions of steady-state inflation. After the wage settlement at time t_1, the real wage rises to its peak level w^*. It then is gradually eroded by inflation until the next wage increase at time t_2. The hypothesis is that labor tends to think of its just wage as w^* rather than the mean w'. If after stabilization—after the government has cut back its own demands on the economy—labor attempts to establish the real wage at w^* rather than at w', the authorities will again have to choose between recession and the resumption of inflation. A refusal to accommodate inflation will create a recession of whatever severity is needed to batter the real income claims down until they are consistent with reality (i.e., to w').

Liviatan, in replying to these sorts of comments at the conference in Pultusk, made the point that, if labor really believed it was entitled to w^* rather than w', then rational expectations would lead it to claim a still higher real wage than w^* in order to raise the average real wage from w' to w^*. The implication is that a steady-state inflation such as is shown in figure 10-1 is not a feasible equilibrium. To the contrary, rather than implying that inconsistent real income claims cannot explain inflationary inertia, Liviatan's observation may explain the stylized fact that it is more difficult to prevent a 20 percent inflation from accelerating than to prevent a 2 percent inflation from doing so, and likewise that a 200 percent inflation is far more prone to explode than a 20 percent one.

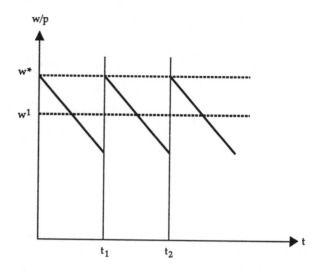

Figure 10-1. *Simonsen's "saw-tooth diagram"*

Note also that inconsistent real income claims seem to provide a readier explanation than the credibility argument does for Kiguel and Liviatan's stylized fact that after a successful stabilization the rate of inflation tends to return to its pre-disturbance level rather than to zero. It is really rather difficult to see why a lack of credibility should so regularly prevent even a new government from being believed when it proclaims its determination to eliminate inflation, to the point where the government feels compelled to accommodate more or less the rate of inflation prevailing before destabilization started. In contrast, if agents are content to acquiesce in the reestablishment of their former real incomes but unwilling to abandon their former claims, then inflation will settle down again at its former rate under passive money (i.e., in the absence of a nominal anchor).

The credibility explanation of inflationary inertia views government as engaged in a game with labor in which its optional strategy is to pre-commit. The alternative view suggests that pre-commitment may not have much effect because people do not pay much attention to whether their micro claims are consistent with the government's macro plans. They revise their claims only when they perceive the government's plans to be in conflict with their micro realities. The government may be better advised to devote energy to educating the public about the implications of its macro plans for the agents' micro alternatives. Presumably Helmut Schmidt was doing so during his chancellorship, when he is reputed to have spent some 20 percent of his time talking to trade union leaders.

The alternative view casts doubt on the wisdom of a government making a strong commitment to a fixed exchange rate as the nominal anchor. It suggests that the reason this strategy has so often collapsed is that agents tend to pursue their inherited real income claims regardless of whether they would be serving their own best interests if the government indeed stuck to its plans. As the currency becomes progressively more overvalued because of the persistence of inflationary inertia, then people may start to notice, but by then the betting has started on how soon the government will renege on its pledges and devalue, an expectation that is only reinforced by the government's increasingly more desperate proclamations of its determination to defend the parity. The process ends when a devaluation occurs and leaves the government's credibility in tatters.

Must Poland repeat this sad story? The remarkable social solidarity witnessed in 1990 and people's willingness to accept real wage cuts give rise to more optimism that it can be avoided than Kiguel and Liviatan express. However, this optimism is not based on Poland's continuing to defend a fixed nominal exchange rate. To the contrary, it appears that the exchange rate is too brittle to serve as a satisfactory nominal anchor for more than the first few months, or at most for the first year or two, after a stabilization program is implemented. (The European Monetary System [EMS] is moving toward the point where fixed exchange rates may make sense, but to imagine that Eastern Europe can leapfrog the 25 years of history that have gotten Western Europe to where it is today is fanciful.) Relying on the money supply is little better, since it too produces strong distortions (high real interest rates, an overvalued currency, recession and balance-of-payments deficits) that are prone to undermine confidence that the government will maintain its policies. The wage rate is worse, for it generates a disequilibrium in relative wages whose effects become progressively more severe.

The most promising candidate for nominal anchor in the longer run is a target for the growth of nominal income (Gordon 1990; and Williamson and Miller 1987[2]). It is true that a nominal income target is effectively the same thing as a price target under conditions of high inflation, and as such it is not a candidate for the role of nominal anchor in the initial months after the introduction of a stabilization program. However, once inflation has been brought down to single digits, it has all the advantages of a money anchor (in particular, it is about as easy to track and control), plus the enormously important attraction of being consistent with a real exchange rate peg (i.e., a crawling peg that moves to offset differential inflation so as to maintain constant competitive-

ness, a condition that assures prospective investors in export industries that their returns will not be held hostage to the need to reduce inflation). It is the most neutral nominal anchor available. It can be adapted to combat the inevitable setbacks rather than confronting the government with a stark choice of surrendering or fighting to the finish whenever events turn out less favorably than anticipated.

Economists have embraced the doctrine that policy should always be consistent with the public's forming its expectations rationally. Few economists would abandon that position because of evidence, of which there is now plenty, that expectations are often *not* formed rationally. The conclusion that surely *should* be drawn from the evidence that expectations are often not formed rationally is that policy should be robust against the mechanism by which expectations are formed. A pegged exchange rate as nominal anchor fails that test: it performs satisfactorily *only* if a lack of credibility is the sole source of inflation inertia.

It is to be hoped that in future work Kiguel and Liviatan analyze the merits of a nominal income target—and that this analysis be made available in time to prevent Eastern and Central Europe from relying on the ability of fixed exchange rates to conquer inflation.

Notes

1. It would have been helpful for Kiguel and Liviatan to have used this taxonomy to organize their discussion and to have abandoned the use of emotionally charged words such as "orthodox" and "heterodox." In normal English those two words are antonyms, and it is disconcerting to find the latter defined as a version of the former. Moreover, their definition of heterodoxy has the paradoxical effect of excluding the Austral and Cruzado Plans from the category, despite the fact that the term was initially coined to describe them.

2. Williamson and Miller actually suggested a target for the growth rate of nominal domestic demand rather than nominal income so as to build in pressures to correct balance-of-payments disequilibria. The difference is not, however, central to the present discussion.

References

Gordon, Robert. 1990. "The Phillips Curve Then and Now." In P. Diamond, ed., *Growth, Productivity, Unemployment: Essays in Honor of Bob Solow's 65th Birthday*. Cambridge, Mass.: MIT Press.

Hirsch, Fred, and John Goldthorpe. 1978. *The Political Economy of Inflation*. London: Martin Robertson.

Williamson, John, and Marcus H. Miller. 1987. *Targets and Indicators: A Blueprint for the International Coordination of Economic Policy*. Washington, D.C.: Institute for International Economics.

Part V

Structural Rigidities, Distortions and Inertia in Behaviors: The Supply Response to New Environments and Constraints in Central and Eastern Europe

11

The Ownership-Control Structure and the Behavior of Polish Enterprises During the 1990 Reforms: Macroeconomic Measures and Microeconomic Responses

Roman Frydman and Stanislaw Wellisz[1]

This paper analyzes the behavior of the socialized sector in Poland during the first seven months of the reform program launched by the government in January 1990. The principal purpose of the January 1 reforms was to fight hyper-inflation. Optimists also hoped that financial discipline and demand constraints would induce enterprises to rationalize pricing, production and employment. They further hoped that market pressures would drive the least efficient enterprises into bankruptcy. The pessimists, on the other hand, feared that managers, following the cost-plus principle, would raise prices in response to costs and, if demand proved insufficient, simply slash production. There was also much skepticism about bankruptcy: given the tightly knit network of exclusive suppliers and subcontractors and exclusive customers, the financially strong firms would, it was argued, prop up the financially weak ones lest bankruptcies produce a chain reaction.

In retrospect it is clear that pressures on the product market induced by the reforms have forced firms to adopt pricing that has largely eliminated shortages. However, the reform-related loosening of bureaucratic controls and political change have made managers more than ever beholden to labor. As a consequence, cuts in production have thus far not been matched by corresponding cuts in the labor force. There has been some cost rationalization, but here, too, managerial incentives are weak.[2]

It is shown here that in the absence of external accountability, a characteristic of the post-command phase in the Central and Eastern European economies, the only external instrument of control over enterprises has been the government's credit policy. That credit policy, coupled with the internal structure of incentives of the socialized enterprises, can explain the wage dynamics during the first eight months of the reforms. The evidence seems to suggest that, given the rewards and constraints, managers strive to behave rationally. In turn, those rewards and constraints are deeply rooted in the ownership and control structure of the Polish economy.[3]

The Economic Reforms

Under the "classical" Soviet-type system that prevailed, with some modifications, from the late 1940s to the end of the 1970s, the economy was organized along hierarchic-bureaucratic lines. Enterprises were looked upon as administrative units, with no associated ownership rights, and their behavior was subject to the dictates of the plan. Industry was heavily concentrated for ease of control. The reward system was based on fulfillment of plan targets, and management was accountable to the higher levels of the command structure. Market considerations played a subordinate role.

During the 1980s the government progressively relaxed the bureaucratic controls. The reforms embraced an ever-widening number of industries, and by the end of the decade only some of the key sectors (mining, transport and communications, and basic industries) remained under centralized control. In other sectors, enterprises were permitted to choose their sources of supply, market their products, change the assortment of products, and decide, within limits, on the volume and direction of investments made out of retained profits. The government also gradually phased out the allocation of foreign currency at official, artificially low rates. It permitted enterprises to retain an increasing share of their foreign exchange earnings and to use them to import approved products, mainly producer goods, or to sell the retained foreign exchange at auction.[4]

Despite the loosening of controls, much of the bureaucratic-administrative structure held firm. For example, until the end of 1988 major enterprises continued to have only one marketing agent and a single source for principal inputs. For other firms the heavy concentration of industry and trade barriers limited the range of choice. Most important of all, ownership and control rights remained unclear. Enterprise managers continued to face the possibility of arbitrary bureaucratic interference. An enterprise that set its prices at a level that government bureaucrats deemed excessive could be accused of gouging and be ordered to make a roll-back. On the other hand, if an enterprise made losses, it could receive a subsidy. The subsidies, which were subject to administrative discretion, were granted easily to strategically important enterprises, for example, coal mines or steel producers.

The profit bonus payable to management and employees was an insufficient incentive to pursue profit-maximizing policies. For purposes of calculating the bonus, the subsidy was counted as part of the profit. Moreover, the profit incentive was blunted by taxes designed to discourage "excessive" wage raises. In contrast, there were significant incentives to create shortages by setting prices below the market-clearing level. In a shortage situation the entire output could readily be sold regardless of quality. Letting preferred customers jump the queue and reserving high quality products for them gave power to the individuals who could dispose of the product. They in turn could exact favors that enhanced their real income.

The environment within which the socialized sector enterprises were operating changed abruptly with the reforms introduced on January 1, 1990. Most of the subsidies were eliminated: before the reforms, administered prices applied to an estimated 50 percent of the nominal value of legal transactions, a proportion that fell to 10 percent. The subsidies for coal, energy and transport were drastically reduced. To compensate for the subsidy reductions, the price of coal was increased on average by 500 percent, electricity 200 percent and transport 200 percent.[5] The zloty was devalued by 58 percent and made convertible for transactions on the current account.

The government also took measures to tighten demand. Real interest rates that had been negative prior to the reforms were henceforth to be positive. The rationing of credit at preferential rates was discontinued. To stop the price-wage spiral, tight limits were imposed on wage increases. From April until December 1989, wages were indexed at 80 percent of the cost of living index, and workers could obtain even higher wages through bargaining. Beginning in January the permissible increases were tied not to the wage level but to the wage bill, and the degree of indexation was reduced to 30 percent; in February and March it was further reduced to 20 percent; thereafter it was subject to monthly revision. Enterprises that exceeded the permissible increase were subject to heavy penalty taxes.

The Socialized Sector

In 1989 the socialized sector in Poland, which generated an estimated 75 percent of the gross national product, consisted of over 21,000 enterprises. Of these, 9,000 were funded by central or local authorities, and 12,000 were cooperatives. In December of that year the public sector employed 8.6 million workers, of whom just over some 4 million were in industry, the sector that is the focus here (table 11.1). There were a total of 5,486 industrial enterprises, including 2,463 cooperatives, most of them small units. Large- and medium-scale units were, with few exceptions, centrally funded.

Who owns Polish public enterprises? Is there a residual claimant who has the right to dispose of the property? How does that owner exercise control? There are no clear answers to these questions, although they are critical to understanding the pattern of behavior of the economy. The initial capital of the enterprises has come from a budgetary allocation administered through a "funding body," i.e., a ministry or local authority.[6] Enterprises have no legal standing. Therefore a going concern cannot be sold, although the funding body may dispose of the assets of a bankrupt enterprise. Management has the right to sell selected assets, subject to the approval of the Workers' Council.[7] The Council's approval is also needed to change the enterprise into a genuine joint-stock company or to privatize it.

In large enterprises the funding body chooses the managing director, also subject to the approval of the Workers' Councils. In smaller enterprises the Workers' Councils nominate this person and the funding body approves. The Workers' Councils are empowered to remove the managing director or to suspend him or her.

The banks that grant operating credit to the enterprises exercise financial control. The funding body does not exercise control except over enterprises that go into bankruptcy. Net income is divided between the state budget and the enterprise. The former collects the "dividend," a lump sum based on the value of the funding capital, and a tax on an enterprise's profits over and above the dividend.[8] The profit accruing to the enterprise is allocated to the "development fund," i.e., to investment, and to the "personnel fund," i.e., to wage and salary premia and social amenities. The allocation of the funds is at the discretion of the Workers' Councils, with the credit-granting banks influencing the choice. The Workers' Councils also decide how to split the bonus between labor and management. Under the rules now in force, bonuses in excess of the amount permitted by indexation are subject to heavy penalty taxes.

Labor organizations are also important players. The original, submissive, government-sponsored unions col-

Table 11-1. *Employment and Value Added in Socialized Industry*

	Employment on December 31, 1989		Value added on June 30, 1990
	in '000	*in %*	*(billions of zlotys)*
Industry of which:	4,016.3	100.0	109,641
Coal	482.5	12.0	1,576
Fuel	53.5	1.3	8,564
Energy	119.1	3.0	4,480
Steel production	142.1	3.5	10,388
Non-ferrous metals	60.2	1.5	6,017
Metal working	241.4	6.0	5,152
Machine-tools	407.4	10.1	9,895
Precision-tools	68.3	1.7	1,495
Transport equipment	311.3	7.8	7,870
Electronics equipment	247.7	6.2	6,029
Chemical	278.4	6.9	10,160
Construction materials	131.2	3.3	2,842
Glass	47.9	1.2	1,015
Ceramics	24.9	0.6	451
Wood products	157.9	3.9	2,508
Paper	45.5	1.1	1,560
Textiles	320.2	8.0	5,681
Clothing	175.6	4.4	1,756
Leather	132.4	3.3	1,789
Food	408.6	10.2	18,391
Animal feed	6.1	0.2	181
Printing	44.4	1.1	745
Other	109.7	2.7	1,096

Source: Central Statistical Office (Warsaw) data.

lapsed with the formation of Solidarity. When Solidarity was outlawed, the government created a new union organization, the OPZZ. To gain legitimacy among the workers, the OPZZ assumed a belligerent stance and survived even Solidarity's regaining its official right to exist in 1989. It is something of a paradox that under the new regime Solidarity is closely associated with the government, while OPZZ aggressively represents workers' particularist interests.

As elsewhere in Europe, Polish legislation protects workers from sudden mass dismissal. Management must notify the union prior to a planned group lay-off, that is, a lay-off of 10 or more percent of workers in enterprises with 1,000 or fewer workers or 100 or more workers in enterprises above that size. The union has the right to obtain financial information concerning the enterprise and to present a counter-proposal. This step is followed by negotiations, although, in the case of a disagreement, the manager has the last word. It must be borne in mind, however, that the Workers' Council may dismiss the manager. Therefore, when managers need to reduce the labor force, they generally opt for gradual attrition.

Effects of the Reforms on Enterprise Behavior

The analysis of enterprise behavior presented here is based on aggregate data for the socialized sector. Also presented are conclusions drawn from a preliminary analysis of a survey of 315 enterprises conducted by the advisory group to the economic committee of the council of ministers.

Price and Output Behavior

In January 1990 the retail price index rose by almost 80 percent (table 11.2). In the aggregate, this increase reflects the effects of the cost-push from the supply shock. In December 1989 there had been a sharp rise in producer prices: those realized by the metal-working industry rose 61 percent, machine tools by 56 percent, the chemical industry by 60 percent and construction materials by 52 percent.[9] The December price increases affected the January production costs. In addition, as mentioned, the prices of coal, fuel, energy and transport were raised drastically as of January 1, 1990.

Table 11-2. *Retail Prices January1989-August1990*

Year	Month	December 1988=100	Previous month=100
1989	January	111.0	111.0
	February	119.8	107.9
	March	129.5	108.1
	April	142.2	109.8
	May	152.4	107.2
	June	161.7	106.1
	July	177.1	109.5
	August	247.1	139.5
	September	331.9	134.4
	October	513.6	154.8
	November	628.5	122.4
	December	739.8	117.7
1990	January	1,328.6	179.6
	February	1,644.8	123.8
	March	1,715.6	104.3
	April	1,844.2	107.5
	May	1,929.1	104.6
	June	1,994.7	103.4
	July	2,066.5	103.6
	August	2,103.7	101.8

Source: Central Statistical Office (Warsaw) data.

An upper-bound measure of the supply shock effect can be obtained by substituting the exogenous price changes in an input-output table.[10] This calculation, based on a 39x39 input-output table, yields a 77 percent price increase in the retail price index, a rate that closely matches the actual increase (table 11.3).

As the input-output table indicates, the supply shock affected the capital goods sector more strongly than it did the more labor-intensive consumer goods sector (middle column of table 11.3).[11] In the producer goods industries, actual price increases (right-hand column of table 11.3) exceeded the price increases based on the input-output prediction. The machine tool, precision tool and transport equipment industries are the three notable exceptions. In the case of the first two, exports play an important role; hence, a significant component of the aggregate realized price is determined in the world market. Much of the transport equipment was sold under long-term contracts. More importantly, as will be discussed below, domestic sales of the three sectors declined more drastically than they did for the rest of industry. In the construction, leather, textile and clothing sectors, the price increases were substantially lower than indicated by the input-output table. All three sectors experienced a greater decline in output than did industry as a whole.

In January 1990, the output sold by socialized industry was 10 percent lower than in December 1989 (21 percent lower than in January 1989). The output sold by the mining sector declined by 1 percent (7 percent), while the output sold by manufacturing declined by 11 percent (22 percent). Most of the branches of heavy industry experienced little decline in sales; in some, such as metallurgy, the January 1990 sales were higher than those in December 1989. However, sales of machine tools declined by 25 percent (12 percent), of precision tools 34 percent (13 percent) and of transport equipment 34 percent (25 percent). The decline in light industry, 11 percent (18 percent), was slightly more severe than in manufacturing as a whole, and the consumer durable branches were hard hit. Clothing sales dropped by 11 percent (77 percent), leather goods by 14 percent (23 percent).

When a recession occurs in Western market economies, a decline in production in heavy industry often precedes and is more severe than the decline in the consumer goods' sector. In the Polish case, exactly the opposite has been true. The decline started and was very deep in the consumer goods sectors, and enterprises in those sectors lowered their price mark-ups significantly. Output sold by the producer goods sector declined initially by a lesser percentage, while the mark-ups increased.

It is hypothesized that different explanations stemming from the structure of the Polish economy are needed to understand the behavior of the two sectors. It is the view here that the fall in output and reduction in mark-ups in the relatively competitive consumer goods sector were caused by the decline in consumer demand. The strongly monopolized producer goods industries, insulated to a larger extent from market shocks, switched, under the impact of the stabilization measures, from a policy of below-market clearing to monopolistic pricing.

Household Behavior and the Consumer Goods Sector

The stabilization measures caused an immediate and profound decline in constant-price household incomes.[12] The index of the money income of the Polish population declined from 100 in July 1989 to 68.5 in January 1990 at constant prices. During the same period the constant price index of household expenditures declined from 100 to 63.5. In February there was a further drop in incomes and an even deeper drop in expenditures. These figures suggest that the propensity to consume decreased in a period of declining real incomes. This phenomenon can be explained by the "Pigou effect." The hyper-inflation drastically reduced the value of zloty holdings. Following stabilization, the real value of the US dollar on the Polish market dropped steadily. The rise in the propensity to save is the consequence of the effort by households to rebuild their assets.

Table 11-3. *Results According to the Input-Output Table, January 1990*
(percent)

	Hypothetical increase of prices based on increases in costs	Actual increase in prices in January
	(December 1989=100)	*(December 1989=100)*
Industry		
Coal	285.0	404.0
Fuel	205.2	294.0
Energy	218.0	300.3
Steel production	218.9	235.0
Non-ferrous metals	174.7	285.0
Metal-working	194.4	197.0
Machine-tools	184.6	175.4
Precision-tools	174.3	167.2
Transport equipment	188.9	162.5
Electric machinery	180.1	186.3
Chemical	186.9	207.2
Construction materials	202.9	224.0
Glass	179.3	203.6
Ceramics	181.3	187.7
Wood products	182.5	170.4
Paper	192.1	182.4
Textiles	173.3	159.3
Clothing	164.5	135.0
Leather	170.7	152.8
Meat	175.8	190.0
Other food products	178.1	150.0
Animal feed	182.0	290.0
Printing	175.6	180.0
Other	181.1	183.0
Construction		
General	186.1	149.0
Production & services	184.4	148.0
Specialized	186.4	146.0
Other	173.0	145.0
Agriculture		
Vegetable products	199.5	220.0
Animal products	188.5	162.2
Agriculture services	182.8	220.0
Forestry	188.8	170.0
Transport	241.0	280.0
Telecommunication	182.0	180.0
Trade	183.8	160.0
Other branches of production	166.0	185.0
Public services	204.7	240.0
Average price realized by producer	193.7	196.8
Retail price	177.0	179.6

a. The profit rates in each industry are assumed to be equal to the average of historical rates.
Source: Andrew Berg, Dariusz Jasczynski and Jan Rajski.

A comparison of the average propensity to consume during the first six months of 1990 with the corresponding figure for 1989 supports this conjecture (figure 11.1). Within that period, real household incomes dropped by 36 percent, household expenditures by 41 percent. As a consequence, the average propensity to consume declined from 0.84 to 0.78. Other evidence comes from changes in household assets: between January and June 1990 real household incomes dropped 8 percent, but dollar-denominated household holdings (the main store of non-agricultural wealth) rose from US$4.9 billion to US$5.2 billion (table 11.4).

Other, less readily quantifiable considerations also support the demand constraint hypothesis. Hoarding of

Figure 11-1. *Average Propensity to Save Out of Money Incomes and Real Household Income*

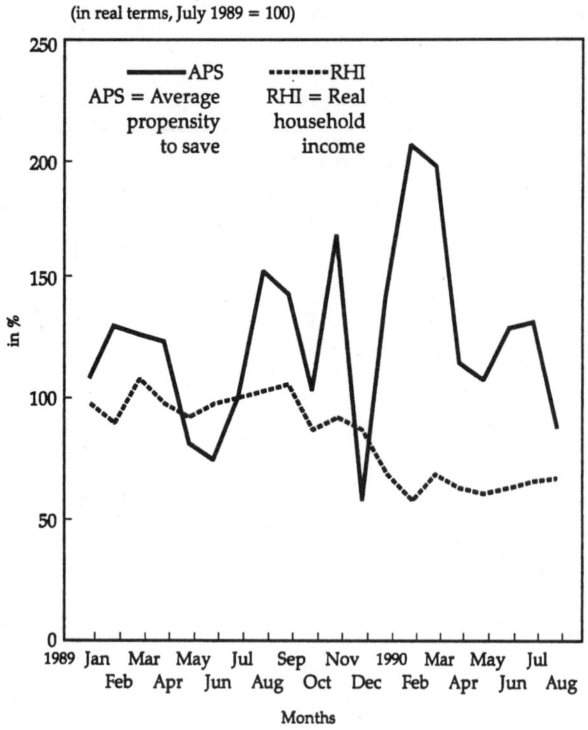

(in real terms, July 1989 = 100)

Legend:
— APS
APS = Average propensity to save
······ RHI
RHI = Real household income

Source: Central Statistical Office (Warsaw) data.

durables, which occurred during the hyper-inflationary period, subsided, and households rebuilt their cash balances (figure 11.2). Foreign consumer goods became somewhat more readily available. It is also possible that the private sector produced more goods.[13] In the pre-reform period, the public sector was able to sell all its production, regardless of quality. Since the reforms, defective goods remain unsold.

The Producer Goods Sector

The producer goods industry consists of large enterprises, interlinked by a traditional administrative structure. Under the old regime these enterprises produced mostly for each other, and a complex system of subsidies and protection from outside competition shielded them from market pressures and from the necessity of paying much attention to the future use of their products by the consumer goods industry.

As discussed, prior to the reforms below-equilibrium pricing was prevalent throughout the economy. The hard line taken on new subsidies and the reduction of existing ones induced enterprises to cover their costs. Under the new rules enterprises were free to raise prices. Clearly, the shortage-creating pricing strategy was no longer possible, and enterprises now sought to set prices at profit-maximizing levels.

Table 11-4. *Household Dollar Deposits, January 1989–August 1990*

Year	Month	Household dollar deposits (millions US$)	Index (January 1989 =100)
1989	January	4,139	100.0
	February	4,402	106.4
	March	4,464	107.9
	April	4,516	109.1
	May	4,561	110.2
	June	4,458	107.7
	July	4,550	109.9
	August	4,618	111.6
	September	4,762	115.1
	October	4,864	117.5
	November	4,863	117.5
	December	4,925	119.0
1990	January	4,911	118.7
	February	4,969	120.1
	March	5,040	121.8
	April	5,123	123.8
	May	5,214	126.0
	June	5,252	126.9
	July	5,409	130.7
	August	5,599	135.3

Source: Central Statistical Office (Warsaw) data.

Figure 11-2. *Real Wages and Stock of Money in Households*
(in constant July 1989 prices)

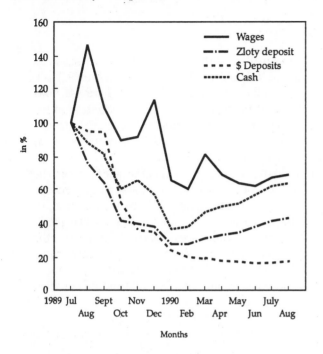

Source: Central Statistical Office (Warsaw) data.

Although both the consumer and producer goods sectors attempted to raise prices to profit-maximizing levels,[14] as has been stressed, the initial outcomes in terms of prices and output were quite different in the two sectors. An explanation of this disparity lies not in the differences in motivation of the enterprises but in the difference in constraints. The consumer goods sector experienced a severe shift in its demand curve, while industries in the producer goods sectors traded with each other and so at first were less affected by the demand or credit constraints.

Price and Output Behavior in Later Months

The initial price adjustments took place under highly uncertain cost and demand conditions, and profits plummeted (table 11.5). There is evidence that as the economic environment became more stable, enterprises engaged in search behavior that led to improved profits.[15] The survey (referred to above) shows that enterprises that initially raised their prices by a wide margin tended to lower their prices later on, whereas those that raised them relatively little, or in some cases not at all, later made upward adjustments. In January 1990, 92 percent of the surveyed enterprises raised their prices; of these, 60 percent lowered them in February, 54 percent in March and 49 percent in April. Of the firms that raised

Table 11-5. *Sales and Net Profits of the Socialized Sector, January 1989–July 1990*
(billions of zlotys, constant December 1988 prices)

Year	Month	Sales	Net profits	Net profit/ sale ratio (%)
1989	January	4,498	504	11.1
	February	4,108	551	13.4
	March	5,379	550	10.2
	April	3,764	430	11.4
	May	4,328	632	14.6
	June	6,000	896	14.9
	July	2,841	320	11.3
	August	4,028	439	10.9
	September	5,493	746	13.6
	October	3,517	711	20.2
	November	4,221	794	18.8
	December	5,013	1,904	38.0
1990	January	3,315	425	12.8
	February	3,050	467	15.3
	March	3,414	535	15.7
	April	3,039	353	11.6
	May	3,399	434	12.8
	June	3,265	436	13.4
	July	3,001	304	10.1

Source: Calculated on the basis of Central Statistical Office (Warsaw) data.

their prices in January, 21 percent increased them in February, 10 percent in March and 15 percent in April. However, these price increases were much lower than those in January. This picture is representative of the economy as a whole: even as hyper-inflation subsided, prices continued to rise (table 11.2).

After the initial fall, aggregate output continued to decline, albeit at a lower pace; by July it stabilized, and in August it increased, following a real rise in wages in July. As time has progressed, the demand constraint has apparently reached heavy industry: by June 1990 most branches experienced a decline in output of 25-30 percent relative to June 1989. Interestingly, this drop is about the same percentage as was experienced by light industry in January.

Foreign Trade

Changes in the patterns of exports and imports demonstrate that the Polish socialized sector is flexible. The domestic recession and the devaluation of the zloty increased the profitability of sales to hard currency countries. During the first six months of 1990, such exports, reckoned in constant dollars, were 20 percent higher than during the same period a year earlier. Imports from the convertible currency and ruble areas declined. It is interesting to note, however, that imports of machines from the convertible currency areas rose, while purchas-

es from domestic producers as well as from the ruble area countries went down—a clear indication that Polish industry was seeking to modernize.

Employment

Employment in the socialized sector declined throughout the 1980s. In 1989 alone it fell from 9.2 million to 8.6 million, or close to 7 percent. There was, however, no overt unemployment, for the expansion of the private sector created a sufficient number of jobs to employ the workers shed by the socialized sector as well as new entrants into the labor force.

In 1990 the rate of reduction of the labor force in the socialized sector quickened, but, unlike in production, there was no dramatic break with past trends. In January, in the face of a drop in output of close to 30 percent, employment fell by just over 1 percent. In the months that followed, the rate of labor-shedding accelerated somewhat, although it never surpassed 2 percent a month. In total, during the first eight months of 1990 employment in the socialized sector declined by 870,000, or about 10 percent (table 11.6).

During the first three months of the year, output per employed worker was about 26 percent lower than during the first three months of the previous year (table 11.7). Group lay-offs were insignificant (table 11.8), the reason being that according to the rules such lay-offs require a 60 to 90 day notice. Moreover, the unions as well

Table 11-6. *Employment in the Socialized Sector, January 1989-August 1990*

Year	Month	Employment ('000)	Change over the previous month ('000)	(%)
1989	January	9,189	—	—
	February	9,184	-5	-0.05
	March	9,092	-92	-1.01
	April	9,009	-83	-0.92
	May	8,954	-55	-0.61
	June	8,874	-80	-0.90
	July	8,864	-10	-0.11
	August	8,771	-93	-1.06
	September	8,721	-50	-0.57
	October	8,715	-6	-0.07
	November	8,690	-25	-0.29
	December	8,600	-90	-1.05
1990	January	8,508	-92	-1.08
	February	8,414	-94	-1.12
	March	8,305	-109	-1.31
	April	8,199	-106	-1.29
	May	8,040	-159	-1.98
	June	7,950	-90	-1.13
	July	7,844	-106	-1.35
	August	7,734	-110	-1.42

— Not applicable.
Source: Central Statistical Office (Warsaw) data.

Table 11-7. *Production Sold per Worker in Socialized Industry, January 1989-August 1990*

Year	Month	Zlotys ('000)	Corresponding month of previous year=100 (%)	January 1989=100 (%)
1989	January	246.2	117.9	100.0
	February	217.2	100.3	88.2
	March	243.6	101.8	98.9
	April	224.8	107.5	91.3
	May	227.4	99.4	92.4
	June	241.8	103.3	98.2
	July	189.4	98.0	76.9
	August	205.1	94.9	83.3
	September	221.9	98.8	90.1
	October	214.7	102.9	92.5
	November	214.7	91.0	87.2
	December	227.2	102.1	92.3
1990	January	185.3	75.3	75.3
	February	160.6	73.9	65.2
	March	179.3	73.6	72.8
	April	165.7	73.7	67.3
	May	175.6	77.2	71.3
	June	176.5	73.0	71.7
	July	169.9	89.7	69.0
	August	183.3	89.4	74.5

Source: Central Statistical Office (Warsaw) data.

Table 11-8. *Unemployment, 1990*
(last day of the month)

	Jan.	Feb.	Mar.	Apr.	May	June	July	Aug.
Rate of unemployment (%)	0.4	1.1	2.0	2.6	3.3	4.2	5.2	6.1
Unemployment ('000)	56	152	267	351	443	568	699	820
of which (%):								
Group lay-offs	4.3	4.5	5.7	7.8	9.5	10.2	11.3	12.2
Other separations	n.a.	n.a.	64.3	7.8	9.5	10.2	11.3	12.2
Unemployed for more than 3 months before registration	n.a.	n.a.	30.0	43.8	44.8	42.0	39.2	37.0

n.a. Not available.
Source: Central Statistical Office (Warsaw) data.

as the Workers' Councils pressured management not to discharge workers. The hope that the anti-inflationary squeeze would lead to a rapid improvement in the allocation of labor proved unjustified. Nevertheless, over the next four months productivity improved, and by August it recovered to within 13 percent of that of the previous year. The index does not, of course, take into account the noticeable improvement in the quality of products.

Wages

During the first half of 1990 money wages consistently rose less than permitted by indexation (table 11.9). Month by month there was an accumulation of arrears—sums that could be paid to workers without incurring tax penalties. However, the rate of accumulation declined uniformly. In July and August the wage increases

Table 11-9. *Wage Indicators and the Evolution of Average Wages in Five Main Sectors of the Socialized Economy, January-August 1990*

		Jan.	Feb.	Mar.	Apr.	May	June	July	Aug.
		(percent)							
1.	Indexation coefficient	0.3	0.2	0.2	0.2	0.6	0.6	1.0	0.6
2.	Increase in retail prices (%)								
	Forecast	45.0	23.0	6.0	6.0	2.5	3.0	5.5	3.0
	Actual	78.6	23.9	4.7	8.1	5.0	3.4	3.6	1.8
3.	Actual wage increase (%) (without bonuses from profits)	5.2	5.4	10.5	2.5	8.7	5.6	14.4	5.2
4.	Maximum allowable rate of growth of wage fund (increase relative to the previous month)								
	According to the price forecast	13.5	4.6	1.2	1.2	1.5	1.8	5.5	1.8
	According to actual prices	23.6	4.8	0.9	1.6	3.0	2.0	3.6	1.1
		('000 zlotys per employee)[a]							
5.	Actual wage without bonuses from profits	618.3	651.9	720.1	738.2	802.2	846.8	969.2	1,019.9
6.	Maximum wage (the wage norm)	734.3	778.1	795.8	819.1	860.3	887.6	934.8	958.3
7.	Monthly employment relative to the previous month	98.9	98.9	98.7	98.7	98.1	98.9	98.4	98.6
8.	Forecast norm	674.4	776.8	797.9	815.8	847.8	885.8	952.0	965.2
9.	Unused norm based on the forecast	56.1	124.9	77.7	77.5	45.6	39.0	-17.2	-54.8
10.	Unused norm based on the forecast as % of the previous month's wage	9.6	20.2	11.9	10.8	6.2	4.9	-2.0	-5.7
11.	Unused cumulative norm	116.0	242.3	318.0	398.9	457.1	498.1	463.8	402.2

a. Indexation base in '000 zlotys = 587.9.

Source: Calculated on the basis of Central Statistical Office (Warsaw) data.

exceeded the amount permitted by indexation, and the cumulative arrears started to decline.

The question is why this pattern of wage behavior occurred, and more particularly, the extent to which the indexation rule actually constrained the wage increases.[16] In examining this question, it is necessary to start by explaining the indexation system introduced in January. It is easiest to do so using actual data, as displayed in table 11.9. The indexation specifies the maximum total wage payments (the maximum wage fund) for every enterprise and every month. The maximum wage or wage norm (line 6) is obtained by dividing the maximum wage fund by the employment. A fall in employment automatically increases the wage norm per worker. Table 11.9 presents a computation of the wage norms for the aggregate economy.

The January 1990 wage norm is obtained by multiplying the December 1989 indexation base of 587,900 zlotys by the maximum allowable rate of growth of wages. Since the actual rate of inflation in January was 78.6 percent and the indexation coefficient was .3, the maximum allowable rate of growth of the wage fund was 23.6 percent (line 4). When this figure is adjusted for the change in aggregate employment (line 7), the result is the norm for January, 734,300 zlotys. An enterprise that exceeded the norm was subject to a 200 percent tax on the excess payments below 3 percent of the norm and a 500 percent tax on payments higher than 3 percent.[17]

Wages are set monthly. Since the norm is set on the basis of the ex-post inflation rate, enterprises have to predict the inflation rate to predict the norm for the coming month. The only widely publicized forecast in Poland is published by the Ministry of Finance. Hence table 11.9 supposes that this forecast is used to predict the norm. Since a 45 percent rate of inflation was forecast for January, the forecast increase in the wage norm was assumed to amount to 13.5 percent (line 4) and the corresponding forecast of the norm to equal 674,400 zlotys (line 8). As it turned out, on average the enterprises actually paid a wage of 618,300 zlotys (line 5). Thus, the ex-post unused norm was 116,000 zlotys (line 11), and the unused norm based on the forecast was 56,100 zlotys (line 9). The ex-post January norm in turn serves as the basis for February's calculations.

To return to the question of whether the indexation system constrained the wage increases actually paid by the enterprises, it is also possible that the low wage increase granted in January reflects management's caution given the uncertainty. While wages rose in February, on average the increase was only 33,600 zlotys (line 5). Although this increase is a 5.4 percent rise over the actual January wage (line 3), the gap between the wage norm (whether computed ex post or ex ante) and wages more than doubled (lines 5 and 6). The unused reserve grew in February from 116,000 zlotys to 242,300 zlotys per worker. The unused reserve grew further over the next four months, although at a diminishing rate, and by June it amounted to close to 500,000 zlotys, compared with a monthly wage of almost 850,000 zlotys.

It is therefore difficult to claim that, during this period, the indexation rule significantly restrained wages. It should not be concluded, however, that it had no effect. Although average wages were below the norm, some enterprises paid the maximum permitted under the norm or even surpassed it. In January the treasury received 1.75 billion zlotys in penalty taxes, and these payments increased every month, reaching 267.8 billion in June. For the first six months of the year the penalty taxes amounted to 608 billion zlotys, or about 2 percent of the wage fund.

The indexation rule also cannot explain the rapid increase in wages that occurred in July and August. In July the government adopted full indexation to gain public acceptance of the administered price increases (notably for coal),[18] but the rate of inflation was not expected to surpass 4 percent. The actual wage increases exceeded 14 percent. The raises were not confined to enterprises with unused reserves, witness the fact that the penalty tax payments amounted to 640 billion zlotys—that is, more than the total for the previous six months. The

wage increases granted in August further reduced the aggregate unused reserve.

To conclude, although it cannot be denied that the indexation cum penalty tax system had a restraining effect on wages in the case of some enterprises, the view here is that this mechanism was not a major determinant of the evolution of the average wage since January 1990. It is necessary to look for additional explanations of the wage dynamics in response to the credit and interest rate policy.

Interest Rate and Credit

In December 1989, the last month prior to the introduction of the stabilization program, retail prices were rising at 17 percent a month. The discount rate of the National Bank of Poland was set at 13 percent. Since the stabilization program was widely publicized, expectations were that prices would rise sharply in January and that credit would be tightened. In anticipation of these developments, enterprises attempted to build up inventories of raw materials, a decision that led them into heavy debt. The proportion of inventories financed by enterprises from retained earnings fell from 48 percent at the end of June 1989 to 38 percent at the end of December, while accounts payable rose from 30 percent to 34 percent.

December also brought windfall profits. The US$2.4 billion in the enterprise accounts were revalued from 3,800 zlotys per dollar to 6,500 zlotys to reflect the official devaluation of the zloty; the revaluation yielded close to 6.5 billion zlotys. Thus, at the beginning of the program, the enterprises were in a relatively strong financial position.

On January 1, 1990 the National Bank of Poland raised the discount rate to 36 percent a month. It expected that this rate would exceed the average rate of inflation for January–February. However, prices rose faster than foreseen, and the ex-post January real rate of interest was strongly negative (table 11.10). The new rates applied, however, to old as well as new debt. The rate increase imposed a burden on the heavily indebted sectors of the economy, especially agriculture and construction, which were granted special relief for interest payments.[19]

Inflation subsided in February, and although the nominal discount rate was reduced to 20 percent, the ex-post real rate was positive. In the following months, in anticipation of a further decline in the rate of inflation, the discount rate was gradually reduced.

The monetary authorities were subject to strong, contradictory pressures. On the one hand, high rates of interest were considered important to holding the price line. On the other hand, the continuing recession and deepening unemployment were used as arguments to ease credit. Under the policy that was adopted, the ex-ante real discount rate declined month by month. Credit was eased. For the first six months of the year, the real ex-post discount rate was positive. In July, however, it once again became negative.

During the first months of the stabilization program, credit to the socialized sector did not change in nominal terms, so that it registered a decline of about 50 percent in real terms.[20]

The implication is that the enterprises perceived the increase in the nominal rate as an increase in real costs. There may have been other reasons, as well, why enterprises reduced their indebtedness. In view of the accumulation that took place toward the end of 1989 and the decline in demand, the enterprises appropriately reduced their inventories and thereby decreased the need for inventory financing. Given the high nominal rates on loans and the uncertainty concerning real rates, the enterprises also found it preferable to increase the degree of self-financing. On the whole, thanks to the amassed inventories of raw materials and their highly liquid positions, the enterprises did not seem to have been severely constrained by inputs of raw materials. In February and March the growth of nominal credit exceeded the rate of inflation. At the end of the first quarter, credit in real terms was 37 percent lower than at the end of December 1990. With the decline of nominal and real interest rates, credit was gradually rebuilt.

It is striking that the time path of the enterprises' wage policy parallels that of credit policy. The tight credit period of February through April occurred at a time when wage payments lagged behind the norm. As credit eased, the percentage gap between the wages paid by enterprises declined. When, in July, the ex-ante real interest rate turned negative, nominal wages increased by 14.4 percent, and for the first time in 1990 they exceeded the norm[21] (table 11.9). This also occurred in August, the last month for which data were available.

It is hypothesized here that this parallelism of the time paths of interest rates and wages indicates the di-

Table 11-10. *Monthly Interest Rates, January-July 1990*
(percent)

	Jan.	Feb.	Mar.	Apr.	May	June	July
				(nominal)			
National Bank of Poland							
discount rate	36.0	20.0	10.0	8.0	5.5	4.0	2.5
6-month time deposits	17.0	13.0	6.5	5.0	3.4	3.5	2.0
1-year credit: Minimum	36.0	20.0	9.0	7.5	5.0	4.0	2.5
Maximum	62.0	23.0	12.0	9.5	8.0	5.5	2.6
				(real based on the actual point-to-point inflation rates)			
National Bank of Poland							
discount rate	-33.9	14.0	3.7	1.6	0.7	0.4	-1.2
6-month time deposits	-43.1	7.3	0.4	-1.2	-1.3	-0.0	-1.7
1-year credit: Minimum	-33.9	14.0	2.7	1.1	0.2	0.4	-1.2
Maximum	-21.3	16.8	5.6	3.0	3.1	1.9	-1.1
				(based on the forecast inflation rates)			
National Bank of Poland							
discount rate	-6.2	-2.4	3.8	1.9	2.9	1.0	-2.9
6-month time deposits	-19.3	-8.1	0.5	-0.9	0.9	0.5	-3.3
1-year credit: Minimum	-6.2	-2.4	2.3	1.4	2.4	1.0	-2.9
Maximum	11.7	0.0	5.7	3.3	5.4	2.4	-2.8
Memo items:							
Rate of retail price							
inflation (point to point)	106	5.3	6.1	6.3	4.8	3.6	3.8
Retail price inflation rate (forecast)[a]	45.0	23.0	6.0	6.0	2.5	3.0	5.5

a. Forecasts of inflation rates are available only for average rates. Also note that since the point-to-point inflation rate in February was much lower than the average rate, the ex-ante real rate in February was actually higher than the rate reported in the table (and was probably positive).

Source: Calculated on the basis of Central Statistical Office (Warsaw) and National Bank of Poland data.

rection of causation from the government's credit policy to the wage policy of enterprises. The missing link in this chain of causation is provided by the demand constraint coupled with the incentive structure in Polish enterprises.

Incentives and Responses

Price and Output Response

In a situation of declining demand for labor such as the one that has prevailed since January 1990, the unions and the Workers' Councils have strongly opposed group lay-offs. A manager is unlikely to gain approval for a group lay-off unless this measure is required to save the enterprise from bankruptcy.[22] As a consequence, as shown by the unemployment statistics, the decline in employment in the socialized sector is almost entirely the result of individual dismissals for cause and of people quitting (table 11.8).

In enterprises that are not threatened by bankruptcy, the number of workers remains constant as long as output does not exceed "capacity," defined here as the output that the normal labor contingent could produce working the usual weekly hours. When output is below capacity, there is labor-sharing. The drop in measured output per worker that occurred in 1990 strongly suggests that labor-sharing took place.[23]

The above observations suggest that as long as an enterprise is not threatened by bankruptcy, the manager takes the size of his labor contingent as fixed. It can be argued that, under these circumstances, the manager will strive to maximize value added. As long as payments are below the norm, workers can pressure for higher wages. Moreover, both management and labor derive benefits from enterprise profits in the form of bonuses and social amenities. Workers also benefit from investments that lighten the work burden or improve the working environment.

Insofar as a part of all current non-labor inputs are bought on credit, a rise in interest rates boosts production costs ceteribus paribus.[24] Costs obviously also rise with increases in the prices of material inputs. In January 1990, costs increased sharply for both reasons. In the absence of knowledge of demand conditions, and given the widely publicized forecast of a drop in demand, managerial prudence called for a low wage policy. In the ex-ante sense, low wages were also in the interest of labor. The reasons for, and the probable effects of, the anti-inflationary policy received wide publicity, and workers were well aware that enterprises might go bankrupt. Under these circumstances job security was more important than wages.[25]

Credit was very tight in February, but easier credit over the ensuing months lowered the cost of inputs. With product prices and output unchanged, enterprises were able to raise wages. This highly simplified model is consistent with the parallel movement of wages and interest rates.

The argument thus far is that the lowering of interest rates reduces the costs of production and, with a given demand, raises value added, so that there is a possibility of raising wages as long as the norm is not binding. However, for marginal enterprises, that is, for those threatened with bankruptcy, employment is a control variable. A Workers' Council is likely to agree to a group lay-off if the alternative is bankruptcy or a reduction of all wages below an acceptable minimum. Unemployment compensation is indexed to the overall wage level; hence, ceteris paribus, this minimum is an increasing function of the wage norm.

As a first approximation, it can therefore be assumed that in enterprises on the verge of bankruptcy there is no labor-sharing and that workers' pay, which is determined by the minimum acceptable wage, is equal to their marginal product. Thus, in the case of marginal enterprises, wage increases constitute a cost push.

Wages also influence prices via agriculture. An average Polish family spends 50 percent of its income on food. The limits imposed on exports maintain the Polish prices of most major foods at a lower than world price level, and, in the short run, supply in most cases is very inelastic. Agricultural products have a 50 percent weight in the retail price index. In the short run, a rise in wages induces a rise in agricultural prices and in the retail price index.

This model, as they all do, simplifies reality. Nevertheless, it throws light not only on overall price and wage movements, but also on specific, seemingly anomalous, instances. Thus, although in July and August credit was eased and wages rose above the norm, inflation in August was the lowest since the stabilization began.[26] However, in August the prices of the products of the light consumer industries rose, although, as noted, this sector is the least profitable. Its wages also lag the most relative to the norm. Hence it may be inferred that bankruptcy looms as a possibility in this sector.[27]

The Rationalization of Production

Consider now the problem of the rationalization of production. Rationalization measures that increase value added without causing labor redundancy are clearly beneficial to workers. The efficiency incentive is, of course, blunted by the norm and by the limitations imposed on bonus payments. It is clear, nevertheless, that the imposition of a hard budget constraint and elimination of the subsidies spurred enterprises to seek more profitable markets, cheaper sources of supply and improved production methods. Two-thirds of the enterprises covered by the survey reported that in 1990 they introduced changes in the organization of production. About the same proportion reported changes in the assortment of products. Fewer than 50 percent reported changes in production technology.

At one time the belief that the withdrawal of subsidies would cause widespread bankruptcies that would weed out production and increase overall efficiency was fairly common. In free market economies an enterprise goes bankrupt if it fails to meet its fixed obligations. In the absence of long-term debt, the payment of the dividend was adopted as the solvency test. The dividend, however, is a misnomer: it is in fact a capital tax that at present is set at 32 percent of the funding capital, that is, at the (inflation-adjusted) depreciated value of the capital provided by the funding authority. The impact of the dividend is unequal. New enterprises are subject to a higher one than are old ones, which have depreciated their original capital and made new investments out of retained profits. Overall, it is estimated that the dividend is equal to 8 percent of the book value of fixed capital. Since the annual rate of inflation surpasses 8 percent of a wide margin, the overall impact of the dividend is very small.

So far, except for a few enterprises in the food processing sector—the hardest hit by current recession—there have been no bankruptcies. There are two main reasons, in addition to the insignificant level of the dividend. An enterprise may delay bankruptcy through decapitalization—it may either fail to keep up the stock of its fixed capital, or it may sell some of its operations (usually the profitable ones) to the private sector. By such means it might be able to meet its current obligations and keep on paying its workers. There is no reason to believe, however, that decapitalization is, in all cases, the rational course from the point of view of the management of capital. Second, given the tightly knit network of suppliers, subcontractors and customers, the bankruptcy of a weak unit may deprive a strong one of an important source of supplies or an important outlet. Therefore, financially strong enterprises have an interest in supporting financially weak ones through the extension of inter-firm credit. This credit puts off the day of reckoning but increases the danger of a chain reaction in which sound creditors will go bankrupt because of the insolvency of the debtors.

The structure of control also discourages modernization of the labor-saving type. It has been argued here that redundancy is not a proximate reason for group dismissals. However, since the Luddite movement if not before, workers have been well aware that they can be replaced by machines, and at a time of growing unemployment they are not likely to favor labor-saving improvements as long as they have a voice in management and as long as there is unemployment. Thus, the incentives for achieving efficient production in the long run are weak. Indeed, they may be even weaker now than they were under the planning system, for at that time workers had no fear of unemployment.

Is There a Role for an Expansionary Aggregate Demand Policy?

Poland has overcome its 1989 hyper-inflation, but the economy is now in a state of stagflation. Orthodoxy calls for the continued application of anti-inflationary measures until such time as price stability is firmly restored. Yet political pressures are mounting to relax the controls and apply standard Keynesian measures to cure the recession.

On the demand management side the authors tend to agree with the opponents of expansionary policy. As long as the control structure of enterprises is not modified, this policy is likely to result in higher wages and lead to renewed inflationary pressures. The cost of the short-run gains in output may therefore be too high.

In conclusion, the authors do not think that, in the absence of deep changes in the structure of ownership and control of enterprises, restrictive aggregate demand policy is an effective way to achieve rationalization and growth. The crux of the matter lies in the definition of ownership and control: there is no well-defined owner who seeks to maximize the present value of the returns on capital and who is able to determine the use of resources. Under the orthodox planning system, faulty and highly irrational as it was, the government exercised control. In the present transitional state, there is none. Emergence of a new private structure of control requires widespread privatization.[28]

Notes

1. The authors benefitted from discussions with Guillermo Calvo and Fabrizio Coricelli. They also thank Dariusz Jaszczynski for excellent research assistance and informative discussions and Jan Rajski for help with the data. Roman Frydman gratefully acknowledges a grant for this project from the C.V. Starr Center for Applied Economics at New York University.

2. For an analysis of the relationship between the disciplinary effect of the pressures on the product market and the problem of control over enterprise management in the 1990 reforms, see Chapter 21, "Markets and Institutions in Large-scale Privatization: An Approach to Economic and Social Transformation in Eastern Europe," by Roman Frydman and Andrzej Rapaczynski, in this volume.

3. For earlier related analyses, see Calvo and Coricelli (1990), Frydman, Wellisz and Kolodko (forthcoming), Lipton and Sachs (forthcoming) and Phelps' (forthcoming).

4. For earlier related analyses, see Calvo and Coricelli (1990), Frydman, Wellisz and Kolodko (forthcoming), Lipton and Sachs (forthcoming) and Phelps' (forthcoming).

5. From July 1990 on, the price of coal was no longer administered. Instead, it was "negotiated," i.e., set by mutual agreement between the sellers and the principal buyers. The remaining subsidy for coal was discontinued.

6. As the government's structure has evolved, the number and designation of the funding bodies have changed. At present, industry is under the tutelage of a single Ministry of Industry. Other funding bodies include the Ministry of Transport and the Ministry of Telecommunications.

7. The Workers' Councils originated as part of the effort by anti-Communist forces to loosen the Party's grip on the economy. The law creating them was passed in September 1981, at a time when Solidarity exercised considerable influence. However, most were set up during the ensuing period of martial law, when Solidarity was suspended and eventually outlawed. The Councils are elected by secret ballot for a three-year period. In some enterprises, notably in several steel mills, they have been captured by Solidarity; in others, the elections have caused little excitement, and in practice the Councils have come close to being tools of management. However, Council membership confers power, and the Councils now constitute a lobby of some importance.

8. The dividend is a 32 percent tax on the funding capital. It does not apply to capital generated through the reinvestment of profits. On average, the tax amounts to 8 percent of estimated total capital, although the percentage varies greatly from firm to firm.

9. Realized prices are the weighted average of the prices obtained by enterprises for domestic sales and for exports to the ruble bloc and to convertible exchange countries.

10. This statement applies, sensu stricto, to a perfectly competitive economy. In the Polish case the calculation assumed that profit margins remained constant.

11. Because of the high degree of aggregation, the changes in sectoral prices differ, in some cases very markedly, from those of the sectors' major products. For instance, the sectoral price rise indicated for the coal mining sector is much lower than the exogenous price rise of coal because the sector embraces, in addition to coal production, various ancillary activities and services, such as canteens, miners' housing and rest homes.

12. A distinction is drawn here between the statistical concept of changes in real income and the welfare concept. The latter assumes that the quality and assortment of goods remain constant, as does search time. The former, which for the sake of clarity is called here changes in money income at constant prices, makes no such assumptions. Stabilization and liberalization improved the availability of goods and their quality; hence, the real drop in income in the welfare sense was less severe than the statistical decline.

13. During the first six months of 1990, employment in private non-agricultural activities increased 2 percent. There is no sectoral breakdown, and no data on output.

14. As will be discussed, the enterprises are modeled as striving to maximize the value added at the firm level, subject to various constraints.

15. By March 1990, profits in constant prices rose to 97 percent of the 1989 level, although output was 27 percent lower.

16. The following analysis, based on new data, substantially extends and revises the authors' earlier discussion in Frydman, Wellisz and Kolodko (forthcoming).

17. The tax rates were changed on July 28, retroactive to January 1. Under the new rules a 100 percent tax is payable on the excess of wages over the norm if the excess does not surpass 3 percent of the norm, 200 percent on a 3-5 percent excess and 500 percent on an excess over 5 percent.

18. Administrative fixing of the price of coal was abolished in July, but the administration retained the right to delay price increases by three months. In July, the mining industry was permitted to raise prices by 15 percent; prices will be raised again in October.

19. All debtors were permitted to capitalize 60 percent of the interest payments on old debt, with interest paid only on the remaining 40 percent. However, agriculture was granted a 50 percent subsidy for its debt payments; in the case of credit for construction, the subsidy was to be 32 percent of the interest on the total debt, so that debtors had to pay interest on only 8 percent of the debt.

20. According to the IMF, total credit to non-financial public enterprises amounted to 30.6 trillion zlotys at the end of December 1989 and 31.8 trillion zlotys at the end of January 1990. The index of prices realized by industry, as defined earlier, rose 110 percent.

21. Wages above the norm could be paid without incurring penalties because of the accumulated reserves resulting from the shortfalls in wage payments during the previous months.

22. As discussed in the second section, the manager needs the approval of the Workers' Council to effect a group lay-off. He or she may, however, dismiss individual workers for cause.

23. An alternate hypothesis is that this measure of output per worker is faulty, since it does not take into account the quality improvements that took place since the introduction of the anti-inflationary program. Doubtless there is some truth to that contention, but it fails to explain (1) the increased frequency with which paid and unpaid leaves have been granted to workers and (2) the acceleration in the reduction of employment in the socialized sector.

24. Calvo and Coricelli (1990) have proposed a connection between the costs of inputs and credit and restrictions on output on the supply side. They also provide some empirical evidence that the credit crunch has caused the initial drop in the output of the socialized sector. More empirical research is needed to disentangle the demand and supply explanations of output dynamics during the 1990 reform.

25. From the partial equilibrium point of view of the average enterprise, the low wage decision was correct. By raising wages to the level permitted by the norm, such an enterprise would have incurred losses.

26. As discussed, the 15 percent increase in the price of coal accounts, in part, for the price increase in July.

27. A stronger test of the model would require examining the relation between prices, wages and group lay-offs. At present, the relevant data are not available.

28. For an analysis of these issues see chapter 21, "Markets and Institutions in Large-scale Privatization: An Approach to Economic and Social Transformation in Eastern Europe," by Roman Frydman and Andrezj Rapaczynski, in this volume.

References

Calvo, Guillermo, and Fabrizio Coricelli. 1990. "Stagflationary Effects of Stabilization Programs in Reforming Socialist Countries: Supply-Side vs. Demand-Side Factors." Mimeo. World Bank and International Monetary Fund. Washington, D.C. September.

Frydman, Roman, Stanislaw Wellisz and Grzegorz Kolodko. Forthcoming. "Stabilization in Poland: A Progress Report." In Emil-Maria Claassen, ed., *Exchange Rate Policies of Less Developed Market and Socialist Economies.*

Lipton, David, and Jeffrey Sachs. 1990. "Privatization in Eastern Europe: The Case of Poland." *Brookings Papers on Economic Activity*, 2:293-341.

Phelps, Edmund S. Forthcoming. "Sub-normal Unemployment in Socialist Economies." In Emil-Maria Claassen, ed., *Exchange Rate Policies of Less Developed Market and Socialist Economies.*

12

Life after the Polish "Big Bang":
Representative Episodes of Enterprise Behavior

Erika A. Jorgensen, Alan Gelb and Inderjit Singh

Polish firms recently experienced a series of economic shocks that occurred in three overlapping waves. First there was the severe macroeconomic instability (from August 1989 to February 1990). Then in January 1990 the government implemented a package of economic policy measures that has come to be called the "Big Bang". It consisted of strong stabilization measures, liberalization of the trade regime and creation of a convertible currency. The government also took important steps toward reforming the industrial system by freeing most prices and eliminating most subsidies. Last, there was the exogenous shock of the disintegration of the regime of international trade of the Council of Mutual Economic Assistance (CMEA), a process that is ongoing. By coincidence, the five-year cycle of planned CMEA trade ended in 1990. Through the spring of 1990 the enormous political and economic upheavals occurring all over Central and Eastern Europe and in the Soviet Union made it increasingly clear that standard negotiation of the next five years of CMEA trade was unlikely. Even the remaining contracts for 1990 came into question as doubts about delivery and payment grew and as governments backed away from the subsidies promised to exporters as part of the original bilateral agreements.[1] At the time, Poland was selling 45 percent of its exports under the CMEA system, equal to 9 percent of GNP. Of these non-convertible currency exports, 54 percent consisted of machinery and transport equipment. Thus, when the CMEA arrangements broke down, a key market for Polish exports dried up completely.

The first wave of economic shocks gained strength through 1989 with a sharp rise in inflation and tightening of credit. The January 1990 reforms (preceded by some preliminary policy changes in September 1989) then fundamentally transformed the environment in which firms were operating, with promises of still more change. Growing doubts about the future of the CMEA trading system became a serious worry by March 1990.

The result was that for the first few months of 1990 uncertainty and chaos reigned in the industrial sector. Firms struggled to gain a sense of the nature of their markets for inputs and outputs. Domestic demand continued to fall, credit remained tight, and expectations about the important CMEA market became ever more pessimistic.

What Poland now needs to pull itself out of this economic quagmire is a strong supply response to the reforms in the form of an expansion of industrial production, which will come about as the aggregate effect of the behavior of individual industrial firms. The question is if and when that supply response will occur. Given the string of negative shocks cited above, it would not have been surprising had firms become paralyzed by the uncertainty and unable to react.

Contrary to that expectation, it seems, based on an analysis of a sample of nine Polish industrial firms, that they reacted strongly and often positively. This paper explores the response of those firms to the January 1990 economic reforms in Poland and the contemporaneous shock of the breakdown in CMEA trade.

The Methodology and the Sample

The Methodology

This paper describes some of the microeconomic responses of a small sample of nine industrial firms to the Big Bang during the first six months of the economic reform (January to June 1990). The information about the firms in the sample was obtained during visits by a World Bank team to each firm during June and July 1990, at which time managers were interviewed and basic data on financial and real variables were collected.

This direct approach was used for a number of reasons. First, aggregate data often obscure important behavior at the sectoral or subsectoral levels and suffer from lags in availability. In the case of this study, timeliness was very important. Second, it is more difficult to assess the condition of firms on the basis of centrally collected data in a reforming socialist economy than it is in a capitalist economy, where changes in the recorded rates of bankruptcy, profitability and investment provide important information for tracking the impact of policy changes. Third, the macroeconomic data in socialist economies may be of especially poor quality because of non-standard collection practices and inadequate conceptual definitions. This situation is exacerbated in Poland by the distortions in the economic environment, such as the high rate of inflation in 1989. Fourth, when change is both drastic and ongoing, recorded data become more difficult to interpret, and the lags before which patterns become apparent may be overly long. Finally, it is difficult to analyze the impact of macroeconomic policies in socialist economies. As such, micro analysis becomes all the more important.

Given the above problems, a decision was made to talk directly with the managers of industrial firms to gain insights into their responses to the economic reforms and to use the results as context when examining the statistical data from the firms. This approach yields first-hand evidence of the perceptions of the managers as to their firms' changing budget constraints, evolving objectives and shifting scope of possible actions. The combination of data from the statistical agency and interviews with management at individual firms can provide clear and timely insights into recent economic behavior, as well as guidance on key areas for government action. This direct examination can also assist in forecasting the likely direction of the supply response.

There are a number of other advantages to using firm-level data and interviews to analyze the reaction to the Big Bang. First, the microeconomic impact of macroeconomic policies is immediately evident from firm-level data. Retrieving the data directly from the enterprise avoids the inevitable delays in the collection of macroeconomic data. Interviews with managers give insight into how these economic agents perceive current reform policies and can disclose divergences between the objectives of the managers and the government. Second and more important, the behavioral responses to macroeconomic policy changes may well be different in a reforming socialist economy than in a market economy, especially in the case of state-owned industrial firms. Problems of ownership and control may dominate their reactions, leading to objectives that are quite different from those of privately owned firms. Third, important obstacles to adjustment by firms may have caused them to react in ways different than expected to the changes in the macroeconomic environment, and those factors may

have been overlooked. For example, firms may be so influenced by the uncertainty over ownership and control by the policy-makers or so paralyzed by the general uncertainty of the economy that they react to new economic policies in seemingly perverse ways. Last, there has been much variation in the performance of firms, with some doing well and others badly even within the same subsectors. Interviews with firm managers can provide some sense of whether particular characteristics render firms flexible in the face of change and whether successful adjustment is mostly a matter of luck and historical accident.

The Sample

State-owned industrial firms were the focus of the field trip. They have accounted for almost 90 percent of the net material product (NMP) in industry in recent years in Poland and almost 90 percent of industrial employment. The private firms are too small in the aggregate to absorb much labor in the short run or to affect total production. As a result, it is the aggregate response of the state-owned firms in industry that is crucial for a macroeconomic supply response led by the industrial sector.

Since timeliness was a primary goal, only nine firms were visited: seven state-owned enterprises, one cooperative and one private joint venture (for purposes of comparison). The firms covered a wide range of industrial subsectors, including engineering, transport equipment, chemicals, electronics, light industry, food industry, and wood and paper. They also covered the range of product markets, including domestic, CMEA export and hard currency export.

Without examining the entire universe of firms in Poland, it is impossible to know whether the few firms in the sample are representative of Polish industry as a whole in terms of initial conditions or responses to the Big Bang, as similar information on the entire industrial sector is not readily available. A few preliminary comparisons can be made, however. Table 12-1 displays some of the basic characteristics of the firms in the sample, of the average firm in the Lista 500 (the top 500 state-owned firms when ranked by sales), and of the average firm in Polish state-owned industry overall. The average firm in the sample had sales close in volume to the Lista 500 average in 1989 but greater employment. The sample firms also had significantly higher shares of exports in total sales.

This range of firms provided a broad picture of industrial behavior but ruled out any formal comparative analysis, since sectoral differences could not be captured within the small sample.

Although a sample of only nine firms offers sparse information, their behavior does provide insight into the issue of when and if a supply response will emerge to revive the Polish economy from the deep recession induced by the profound economic reforms. This first cut at understanding firm-level responses needs to be followed by more detailed and quantitative analysis of a larger sample of firms to test the generalizability of the findings. Nevertheless, the information presented here offers much-needed anecdotal evidence of the microeconomic responses and focuses further debate and analysis.

The 1990 Policy Package

Beginning in 1981, Poland undertook a partial economic reform that significantly diminished the role of central planning in the economy. Enterprises gained some autonomy, although with much variation across sectors. For example, firms that produced consumer goods were allowed to make decisions about most aspects of current operations. Another measure established some self-management of firms through the introduction of the Workers' Councils, with limited rights in enterprise decision-making. However, the government maintained its control through informal bargaining between its financial authorities and enterprises that determined the levels of prices, interest rates and tax rates for the enterprises. Unfortunately, this system of compromised central control discouraged financial discipline by the firms and eventually created serious macroeconomic imbalances in the Polish economy.

The further reforms introduced from 1987 to 1989 failed to improve the macroeconomic conditions, although they did help set the stage for the drastic reforms of the new Solidarity government. For example, the system of centralized allocation of inputs was pared back to just five commodity groups, and firms were given greater freedom to set the prices of their outputs. In August 1989, the government freed the prices of agricultural inputs and products. These goods accounted for approximately 20 percent of GDP, so that the share of goods with decontrolled prices reached 50 percent of gross domestic product (GDP).

Despite these measures, by mid-1989 it became clear the macroeconomic situation was unsustainable. Inflation was already 100 percent at the start of 1989, and in the last semester of that year it hit 2,000 percent.

When the new Polish government took power in September 1989, it responded immediately with a policy of steady devaluation of the zloty. In January 1990, it implemented extensive stabilization and liberalization measures to reverse Poland's soaring inflation and push the economy much of the way toward a free market orientation.

The stabilization component of the program was heterodox in nature, using both the wage and exchange rate as nominal anchors for price stability. The predicted budget deficit for 1990 was reduced to 1 percent of GDP by cutting the subsidies for consumption and production. The government tightened credit by increasing interest rates sharply and reducing the quantity of credit. To create a nominal anchor, it instituted an incomes policy that involved levying a heavy tax on firms that exceeded the government-mandated wage increases, a measure designed to repress the nominal wage. Another nominal anchor was the pegging of the zloty to the dollar at a fixed rate, resulting in a large devaluation of almost 60 percent. This devaluation allowed the simultaneous introduction of many policies directed at the liberalization of trade. The government unified the foreign exchange market, eliminated the restrictions on access to foreign exchange and replaced the quantitative restrictions on imports with a unified customs tariff.

The Big Bang package also included important steps toward the creation of a market economy. The government lifted almost all the remaining controls over wholesale and retail prices except for energy. In addition, it instituted unemployment insurance and other social assistance programs that formed the beginnings of a safety net to ease and encourage adjustment by labor. The unemployment insurance legislation passed in January 1990 also allowed employers to fire employees on one month's notice. The combination of openness to the world markets and liberalization of domestic prices was intended to shift relative prices to reflect scarcity, an important step in encouraging the reallocation of resources toward more productive uses.

Firms had to cope not only with these macroeconomic policy shocks but also with other policy changes that had a primarily microeconomic focus. The monopoly position of the central distribution system was eliminated by law, and anti-monopoly legislation was prepared to counteract the high concentration of Polish industry. The government instituted a number of policies to harden the budget constraint[2] of state-owned firms. For example, the levy on the fixed assets of state-owned enterprises was modified as of January 1990.[3] The assets of the enterprise that formed the base for the tax were adjusted for inflation, and the link between the tax and current profits was eliminated. Non-payment of the tax now triggers rehabilitation (similar to bankruptcy proceedings except that the government as owner initiates the rehabilitation). The slashing of the subsidies, contraction of bank credit and strengthening of the threat of bankruptcy proceedings together hardened the budget constraint for state-owned enterprises and forced an improvement in resource reallocation.

The impact of the Big Bang at the aggregate level was generally in the direction intended by policy-makers, although the disintegration of the CMEA trading system intensified the negative shocks on demand. Inflation (as measured by the Consumer Price Index [CPI]) fell to a monthly rate of 5 percent by March 1990 and stayed there until September. Industrial production dropped more sharply than expected, contracting by 30 percent in the first five months of the year (compared with the same period in 1989). The industrial subsectors that experienced the largest contraction were light industry, mining, food processing and minerals. At the same time, registered unemployment rose sharply to 107,000 people by the end of February and 500,000 by the end of May. Real incomes fell by 35 percent from January through May. On the other hand, the trade account improved greatly, despite the problems with CMEA partners. Total exports increased by 8 percent in real terms in the first five months of 1990 as compared with the same period in 1989. The increase was driven by exports to hard currency countries, which rose by 15 percent, whereas exports to the CMEA remained unchanged. Over the same period, imports fell by 29 percent in volume, split between a 32 percent contraction in imports from CMEA countries and 27 percent from convertible currency areas (World Bank sources).

The harshness of this contraction of the economy succeeded in squeezing inflation from the system. The important question is when a supply response will occur. This issue of the resumption of growth has crucial political dimensions, since a lengthening and deepening recession eventually wears down the patience of any electorate. Over time the political costs of worsening economic conditions are high, especially in a country such as Poland, where employment has always been secure and where many social benefits remain tied to employment.

The Effect of the Big Bang Policy Package at the Firm Level

Despite the great uncertainty, the firms actively adjusted to the triple shock of the liberalization of the product market, depressed domestic demand and collapse of CMEA demand for Polish exports. Since they entered 1990 with relatively large financial cushions and since wages were not the dominant portion of their production costs, they had made only modest cuts in their work forces. Moreover, they took assertive action in two areas: they energetically and creatively pursued new export markets in response to the decline in domestic demand and uncertain CMEA trade; and they established a system of inter-firm notes in response to the severe credit squeeze, as reflected in a sharp rise in receivables and payables.

It also seems that firms were suffering from a vacuum of ownership. However, the partial self-management did not appear to be a source of perverse behavior, perhaps because the repression of the nominal wage as part of the government's stabilization package significantly constrained the power of the Workers' Councils, the representative bodies elected by the workers in a state-owned firm,[4] and the trade unions.

The numerous and dramatic changes in policy outlined above drastically altered the environment in which Polish enterprises were operating. For one, the budget constraints they faced were significantly hardened by the removal of most subsidies and the tightening of credit, as well as by the increased threat of enforcement of the bankruptcy procedures. The harder budget constraints tended to encourage a reallocation of resources from unprofitable to profitable firms. In other words, as of 1990, the profitability of enterprises mattered. For another, the liberalization of trade and devaluation of the exchange rate altered the relative profitability of the sectors and together shifted relative prices in favor of tradables. The removal of the subsidies and the general freeing of prices also changed relative profitability across firms and sectors. The generally worsening demand conditions had a differing effects, since the CMEA market, formerly the most secure of selling places, almost closed and the domestic market, especially for investment goods, collapsed. By process of elimination, the hard currency export market became the strongest and steadiest source of demand for Polish goods.

This shift in relative profitability (driven by changes in the structure of prices and in demand) should have encouraged the reallocation of resources toward newly profitable sectors. More specifically, it would have been expected that firms would lay off labor to cut costs and therefore that labor and other resources would be freed to be reallocated across sectors to match the new relative prices. Some firms would go bankrupt, a move that would free capital assets for reallocation, while others would sell off some plants and equipment, a step that would also encourage the reallocation of capital. Since the real devaluation of the zloty was large, in general there should be a shift of labor and capital toward tradable activities. Profit margins would fall since the import competition and perhaps new domestic competition (especially at the level of distributors and retailers) would severely curtail the ability to pass prices on to consumers. As described below, an examination of the behavior

160

of industrial firms in the small sample corroborates these expectations.

The Responses of Industrial Firms to the Big Bang: Some Findings from a Field Trip

The average firm in the sample is significantly larger on both counts than the average firm in all of industry. The sample firms on average also had significantly higher overall exports as a share of sales and somewhat higher profits in 1988 and 1989. Thus, the sample does not consist of extraordinary firms (by these sample measures).

An Overview of Shocks and Responses at the Level of the Firm

The behavior of firms and their responses to the combination of changed government policies and other economic shocks are discussed in general and with respect to the following areas: marketing and distribution; exporting; cost-cutting measures; and credit and financing.

The Response in General

The responses of firms in the sample reflected what is known of the industrial response overall. Output and employment decreased, with the drop in output greater than that in employment, as would be expected in firms long used to hoarding labor in a socialist setting and reluctant to or unable to fire workers. More interesting are the differences in the condition of the firms, in their assessments of the shocks that were most important to them, and their choice of response, especially to the continuing uncertainty.

Managers were asked which were the most important external shocks to industrial firms since the "Big Bang" reforms from a list of issues that included price liberalization, greater import competition, the breakdown in CMEA trading arrangements, the lack of a formal distribution system, the depressed domestic demand, the tight bank credit, the irregular inputs, the uncertain property and ownership rights, and the general uncertainty about economic conditions in the near future. In the case of firms that were ailing, the managers identified demand conditions as the overriding problem with which they had to cope. Managers of firms oriented toward the domestic market saw the depressed domestic demand as crucial. In contrast, the electronics firm, because of its heavy orientation to the CMEA, said it was suffering mainly from the evaporation of CMEA orders. The other issues were often seen as irritants and difficulties and not as fundamental to the survival of the firms.

With this obvious emphasis on market conditions, the firms that were performing best were, as expected, oriented toward the hard currency export markets.

The sample of nine firms entered 1990 in quite a strong position, as many Polish firms did, having earned high profits relative to sales in 1989—the average was 42 percent for the nine firms in the sample (figure 12-1). By comparison, the Lista 500 firms displayed profits of 34 percent of sales and industry as a whole, 31 percent (Table 12-1). Oligopolistic market power may explain part of that pattern, but far more important was the near-hyperinflation of the last quarter of 1989, which drove their profits up. Profit as a share of sales doubled between 1988 and 1989 for all three groups of firms. The firms had little net debt (because of gifts of capital, the erosion of their bank debt by inflation, and transferring to the government foreign exchange losses on foreign debt). (Table 12-2 shows an average ratio of total liabilities to equity of well under two for 1989.) The amount of the government-mandated dividend tax (a levy on the original capital of the firm) was modest relative to profits, averaging 2 percent of sales in 1989. The reasons for the low level of payments were past retention of earnings and the fact that the Basic Assets Funds (the original capital of the firm) had not been revalued in line with inflation. Further, the Enterprise Funds (investments made from retained earnings) were large relative to the Basic Assets Funds. The share of wages in costs was low—13 percent of sales. As such, while firms reported experiencing a serious liquidity squeeze starting near the end of 1989, most had a deep cushion against bankruptcy as a result of retained profits in the past.

During the interviews, the firms indicated that their output for the first six months of 1990 was running 20-30 percent below that of 1989 on average, although there was considerable variation: some firms were working at no more than 50 percent of capacity while others, notably in garments and food processing, were running near

Figure 12-1. *Net Profit Before Tax* (average for sample firms)

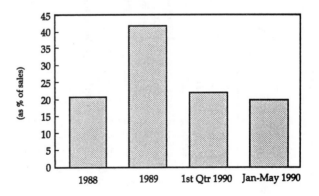

Table 12.1: Characteristics of the Sample of Polish Industrial Firms

Firm	Main product	Sector	Sales (millions US$)[a] 1989	Employment (thousands) 1989	Total exports (% of sales) 1988	1989	Exports to Zone II[b] (% of sales) 1988	1989	Net profit before tax[c] (% of sales) 1988	1989
State-owned firms										
1	Machine tools	Engineering	4	0.5	n.a.	69	n.a.	64	38	132
2	Computer printers	Electronics	27	3.1	67	80	0.1	0.2	31	41
3	Electric generators	Engineering	13	3.3	10	15	0.5	3	26	33
4	Basic chemicals	Chemicals	77	6.2	27	26	22	23	17	36
5	Textiles	Light industry	18	3.8	7	11	4	7	10	32
6	Garments	Light industry	8	2.4	n.a.	19	n.a.	12	23	36
7	Trucks	Transport equipment	76	13.8	4	4	0.8	0.4	12	16
State-owned cooperatives										
8	Food processing	Food industry	63	8.7	81	83	62	73	14	19
Private joint ventures										
9	Wood furniture	Wood and paper	44	5.5	31	21	31	21	16	32
Averages for firms in sample			37	5.2	32	36	17	23	21	42
Average for Lista 500 firms[d]			31	3.2	21	21	n.a.	n.a.	16	34
Average for all industrial firms[e]			4	0.6	18	18	11	12	15	31

n.a. Not available.
a. Polish zloty have been translated to US$ at average exchange rate for 1989 of 3502 ZL/US$.
b. Exports to Zone II are exports to hard currency areas. For ALL INDUSTRIAL FIRMS, reported government number may be too high due to conversion problems.
c. Net profit before tax is before company profits tax, excess wages tax and dividend tax. It includes non-sales income and extraordinary profits and losses.
d. Lista 500 firms are Poland's largest 500 state-owned firms ranked by sales, excluding mining.
e. All industrial firms are state-owned firms and include fuel and power as well as industry.
Sources: Interviews with firms; and data from Central Statistical Office of Poland, Central Planning Office of Poland and others.

Table 12.2. *Overall performance and the structure of costs for the sample of Polish industrial firms*

Firm	Main product	Sales growth[a] (in %)			Net profit before tax[b] (% of sales)				Change in employment[c] (in %)			Total costs[d] (% of sales)		
		1989	1990	1990 1st qtr Jan-May	1989	1989	1990	1990 1st qtr Jan-May	1989	1990	1990 1st qtr Jan-May	1989	1990	1990 1st qtr Jan-May
State-owned firms														
1	Machine tools	41	9	25	38	132	42	37	-8.0	-4.0	-4.0	41.7	60.4	73.5
2	Computer printers	18	-1	16	31	41	36	35	-21.8	-3.7	-6.3	55.4	62.9	74.1
3	Electric generators	15	19	68	26	33	16	21	-6.3	-6.2	-9.6	80.3	71.3	65.6
4	Basic chemicals	22	18	55	17	36	27	23	-2.7	-1.5	-5.3	77.5	83.0	79.4
5	Textiles	21	-6	11	10	32	15	4	-10.8	-9.2	-17.8	76.2	112.5	128.8
6	Garments	30	n.a.	8	23	36	n.a.	22	-1.6	n.a.	-0.4	53.4	n.a.	99.5
7	Trucks	20	-17	-11	12	16	11	7	-4.5	-4.0	-18.3	63.6	84.6	102.4
State-owned cooperatives														
8	Food processing	33	3	34	14	19	7	7	-1.1	-1.2	-1.2	139.8	87.1	77.9
Private joint ventures														
9	Wood furniture	61	n.a.	n.a.	16	32	n.a.	n.a.	n.a.	18.2	18.2	67.8	n.a.	n.a.
Averages for firms in sample		29	4	26	21	42	22	20	-7.1	-1.5	-5.0	72.8	80.3	87.6
Average for Lista 500 firms[e]		26	n.a.	n.a.	16	34	n.a.	n.a.	-8.4	n.a.	n.a.	64.8	n.a.	n.a.
Average for all industrial firms[f]		26	7	n.a.	15	31	n.a.	n.a.	-3.0	-5.9	n.a.	68.2	n.a.	n.a.

(continued)

163

Table 12.2. Overall performance and the structure of costs for the sample of Polish industrial firms (continued)

Firm	Main product	Wages (% of sales)			Material costs [g] (% of sales)			Taxes [h] (% of sales)			Dividend tax [i] (% of sales)		
		1989	1990 1st qtr	1990 Jan-May	1989	1990 1st qtr	1990 Jan-May	1989	1990 1st qtr	1990 Jan-May	1989	1990 1st qtr	1990 Jan-May
State-owned firms													
1	Machine tools	12.1	18.1	8.4	23.8	38.0	46.2	7.3	2.8	6.2	2.7	4.1	1.3
2	Computer printers	7.9	10.0	7.5	36.7	47.8	52.5	6.6	15.0	14.7	1.3	0.8	0.6
3	Electric generators	19.4	12.7	9.2	38.1	38.3	38.2	13.8	8.5	9.8	5.0	0.7	3.9
4	Basic chemicals	7.2	4.8	3.6	59.2	70.1	66.4	12.0	12.5	11.1	2.3	3.6	2.0
5	Textiles	13.7	12.4	13.7	51.4	86.1	82.2	16.9	20.9	18.1	2.7	5.6	4.0
6	Garments	17.6	n.a.	19.8	23.5	n.a.	60.9	29.6	n.a.	25.4	0.9	n.a.	1.1
7	Trucks	11.4	15.4	19.8	40.8	45.7	56.0	22.9	16.9	23.0	1.0	3.4	2.9
State-owned cooperatives													
8	Food processing [j]	10.3	7.3	7.6	102.0	19.6	20.8	4.2	2.2	2.3	—	—	—
Private joint ventures													
9	Wood furniture [j]	14.2	n.a.	n.a.	31.2	n.a.	n.a.	10.6	n.a.	n.a.	—	—	—
Averages for firms in sample		12.6	11.6	11.2	58.1	43.2	52.9	13.8	11.3	13.8	2.3	3.0	2.3
Average for Lista 500 firms [e]		8.3	n.a.	n.a.	57.7	n.a.	n.a.	26.0	n.a.	n.a.	1.9	n.a.	n.a.
Average for all industrial firms [f]			12.0	8.7	n.a.	43.9	n.a.	n.a.	n.a.	n.a.	n.a.	n.a.	n.a.

n.a. Not available.

a. Sales growth is % change in sales from beginning of year measured in US$, using an average exchange rate of 3502 ZL/US$ for 1989 and 9500 ZL/US$ for 1990.

b. Net profit before tax is before company profits tax, excess wages tax, and dividend tax. It includes non-sales income and extraordinary profits and losses.

c. Change in employment is % change since beginning of year.

d. Total costs are material costs (including cost of raw materials and energy, other material inputs, maintenance and servicing, subcontracting, and depreciation) and non-material costs (including wages, payroll taxes and other overhead on wages, interest paid, property taxes and import duties).

e. Lista 500 firms are Poland's largest 500 state-owned firms ranked by sales, excluding mining.

f. All industrial firms are state-owned firms and include fuel and power as well as industry.

g. Material costs include cost of raw materials and energy, other material inputs, maintenance and servicing, subcontracting and depreciation.

h. Taxes include turnover tax, company profit tax, excess wage tax, payroll taxes, property taxes and import duties.

i. Dividend tax is a levy on the original capital of the firm.

j. These firms pay no dividend tax.

Sources: Interviews with firms; and data from Central Statistical Office of Poland, Central Planning Office of Poland and others.

full capacity. This general contraction does not show up in the simple measures of sales growth for the first quarter and for May of 1990 (table 12.1). One reason is that sales are deflated only by the exchange rate; another is that many firms have strong seasonal patterns for their sales.

In addition, production in many industrial branches (e.g., for the maker of large electrical generators) is forward-looking, based on orders for future delivery; thus, production will fall more quickly than will current sales. The pattern of average inventories as a share of sales provides some insight as well. (See table 12-2). From 21 percent of sales in 1989, average inventories of materials and products soared to almost 60 percent during the first quarter of 1990, in the after-effects of the high inflation of January and February. For the truck manufacturer, inventories of materials soared upwards to 400 percent between 1989 and the first quarter of 1990. At the same time, inventories of finished goods jumped by over 2,500 percent (but constituted less than 5 percent of total inventory). Average inventories for all the sample firms fell after March, to average 46 percent for the first five months of 1990, as firms learned to economize on stocks.

As a consequence of the price liberalization and tight fiscal and monetary policies since January, domestic demand fell sharply, especially for firms producing investment goods. The interviews suggested that the first six months of economic reforms were a period of turmoil. Except in the case of agricultural goods, which had been freely traded since mid-1989, the markets were volatile and highly segmented for the first quarter of the year. Firms found it hard to estimate demand and to price inputs and products, in part because the border prices provided an imperfect guide. In addition, in some cases the supplies of inputs became more uncertain, mainly because of the disruption of the state-controlled distribution channels and the problem of finding a replacement for a troubled or uncooperative monopoly domestic supplier. New private distribution channels and markets were in the nascent stage of development.

Marketing and Distribution

The behavioral response of the firms in the sample to the creation of markets was extensive. The steps they took in the areas of purchasing, marketing and distribution to adjust to the post-reform environment included:

• the creation of sales departments, sometimes with travelling salespeople, and the development of more direct links with clients, especially abroad.

• the setting up of factory shops that sold at very low margins;
• the sponsoring of new distributors, for example, of clothing, to bypass the large state distributors that were forced in 1990 to widen their margins to finance high and slow-moving inventories;
• special auctions and attendance at exhibitions and fairs;
• a searching for foreign firms that could provide marketing expertise through a joint-venture arrangement (as well as the provision of technology and capital);
• an increase in the quality and appeal of products, for example, by importing certain critical components from the West or acquiring licenses for high visibility brand-name products. Some of the firms were planning to install new capacity to meet the perceived changes in demand, although they indicated that it was hard to assess new investments in the rapidly changing situation.

In some cases, these efforts to develop a marketing strategy seem to have been quite effective. For example, the truck manufacturer interviewed had begun to sell 80 percent of its output to individuals or small clients for cash, whereas such clients had previously accounted for no more than 20 percent of sales. The garment-maker estimated that it was introducing some 500 different garment products per year, compared with a few dozen a year ago, including high-value lycra bathing suits made under license. This behavior was a dramatic change from a product line previously dominated by low-value standardized products, for which demand had fallen sharply. However, some firms that made significant efforts in marketing and distribution found they were to no avail. For example, the electronics firm, most of whose market was in the USSR, began contacting past customers to sell directly and was planning a junket across the USSR to demonstrate its product line to enterprises that already had some of its equipment. It was clear this bold move was unlikely to pay off. Similarly, the textile producer was suffering from the strong competition for imports in the depressed domestic market. It tried to coordinate closely with garment-makers to increase specialization and customization, but their costs remained far too high. Again, success seemed linked to previous experience with the hard currency market.

Export Response

A number of factors affected CMEA demand for Polish products. The appreciation of the zloty against the transferable ruble relative to the zloty rate with the US dollar lowered the profitability of the negotiated prices for exports to the CMEA. In some cases, the exclusion of products from the inter-government trade protocols and the elimination of export subsidies also diminished profitability. In other cases, such as the manufacturer of a computer printer, the economic reforms turned exports at previously agreed prices into loss-making sales, while attempts to negotiate price increases under the contracts met with resistance from foreign purchasers. By mid-year, firms with long production cycles, such as the producer of electric generators, faced the immediate effects of the failure to negotiate the next five-year cycle of CMEA agreements to begin in 1991. In addition, the general uncertainty, especially in the German Democratic Republic, led to the suspension of orders for production by Polish firms.

With respect to sales, the firms continued to use the foreign trade enterprises (FTEs), state-owned firms that had monopolies over exporting, despite the strong movement away from domestic state-owned distributors. The FTEs are likely to have a continuing role in exporting to both Zone I (CMEA) and Zone II (hard currency) markets: managers perceived some FTEs to be operating effectively and providing good quality service for the sales margin they demanded. This opinion contrasted strongly with the generally poor perception of the usefulness of the former monopoly domestic distributors. It may be that the FTEs possessed scarce and valuable information and skills that Polish firms typically did not possess. On the other hand, those managers interviewed during the field trip believed that the percentage sales commissions the state intermediaries charged for some foreign and almost all domestic sales were too high, even though the rate was generally around 5 percent of the sales price. These commissions seem modest by market economy standards, a point that suggests that Polish firms were not accustomed to the substantial costs of promotion and sales. At present, Polish firms see such expenditures as unproductive and as possible areas for cost-savings rather than as a priority for increased investment.

In general, the firms interviewed believed that exports to the West were more profitable than those to CMEA partners, that Western markets had superior potential for growth and that such exports would be a central part of their strategy for survival. Virtually all of the firms had had some exposure to Western markets before 1990 (although sometimes indirectly through the FTEs). The interviews strongly indicated that those firms with more prior exposure to Western firms had a definite advantage in formulating a viable strategy for survival. This advantage seemed to come partly from the relative attractiveness of hard currency exports given depressed demand elsewhere, but also from an awareness of capitalist ways of doing business.

Cost-Cutting Measures: Employment, Wages and the Costs of Material Inputs

Because many firms in the sample had cut production significantly and were pessimistic about the outlook for sales, they attempted strong cost-cutting measures. Given the sharp increases in the cost of inputs, notably power and water, and the progressively more competitive product markets, which limited the ability of firms to pass the higher costs on to customers, their margins were squeezed in 1990. As a result, as shown in figure 12-2, their profits before taxes as a percent of sales, which had doubled from 1988 to 1989, fell from an average of 42 percent in 1989 to 22 percent for the first quarter of 1990 to 20 percent for the first five months of 1990. These profits include extraordinary profits and non-sales income, such as sales of assets and of inventory. By using the total costs of production for comparison, it can be calculated that in 1989 the firms reaped profits not directly related to production of 15 percent of sales. This share fell to 8 percent in the first five months of 1990, but the textile firm (with extra profits of 33 percent of sales) and the garment manufacturer (with extra profits of 23 percent of sales) in this period remained dependent on income sources other than sales of goods for their financial health (table 12-3). Also of interest is that the ranking of the firms in the sample by profit rate does not change much from 1988 to 1989 to the two points in 1990, partly because of sectoral differences between the firms but also partly because of the general quality of each firm.

Policy-makers anticipated that a response of firms to the Big Bang would be to fire labor. Although the data on industrial employment are difficult to interpret, aggregate employment (i.e., mainly in state-owned enterprises) declined by around 3 percent in 1989 for the industrial sector as a whole, while Lista 500 firms reduced their labor forces by 8.4 percent.

During the same time, the enterprises in the sample reduced employment 7 percent. With these significant cut-backs in 1989, it is not so surprising that firings in the first semester of 1990 were modest. For the sample firms, employment declined by another 2 percent in the first quarter of 1990 while for all of industry, employment fell by 6 percent. By the end of May 1990, the firms had laid off about 5 percent of the labor force they had at the beginning of the year (table 12-3). Clearly, firms are being forced to lay off workers. Initially, however, they are doing so by laying off casual workers and those close to retirement. In light of the nearly 20-30 percent decline in output, the 7 percent decline in the labor force

Table 12.3. Financing by the sample of Polish firms

Firm	Main product	Total liabilities/equity (ratio at end of period) 1988	1989	Average receivables[a] (in weeks of sales) 1989	1990 1st qtr	1990 Jan-May	Average payables[b] (in weeks of sales) 1989	1990 1st qtr	1990 Jan-May	Receivables/payables (ratio at end of period) 1988	1989	1990 March	1990 May	Average inventories[c] (% of sales) 1989	1990 March	1990 May
State-owned cooperatives																
1	Machine tools	0.53	1.47	20.4	8.7	7.2	8.4	2.1	2.7	1.7	2.4	11.1	3.4	21	39	36
2	Computer printers	0.93	1.12	9.3	4.6	4.6	3.8	2.0	3.3	2.1	2.5	2.1	1.0	25	44	40
3	Electric generators	5.20	1.50	8.0	6.2	6.8	7.1	4.2	5.0	2.3	0.9	1.7	1.4	36	57	40
4	Basic chemicals	1.12	1.43	10.9	5.0	5.3	6.3	1.9	2.6	1.7	1.7	3.5	2.2	8	20	13
5	Textiles	0.93	2.07	11.0	9.9	10.9	7.8	8.2	10.5	1.2	1.4	1.1	0.9	23	70	54
6	Garments	0.27	2.70	7.0	n.a.	7.8	1.9	n.a.	5.9	3.9	3.7	n.a.	1.0	12	n.a.	40
7	Trucks	0.99	2.10	9.0	5.8	8.0	7.7	9.3	16.5	1.3	1.1	0.4	0.3	20	110	100
State-owned cooperatives:																
8	Food processing[d]	—	—	9.3	4.7	4.3	3.4	1.3	1.4	2.5	2.7	4.6	3.3	50	73	38
Private joint ventures:																
9	Wood furniture	4.22	3.13	32.0	n.a.	n.a.	26.4	n.a.	n.a.	1.1	1.2	n.a.	n.a.	15	n.a.	n.a.
	Averages for state-owned firms:[e]	1.42	1.77	10.8	6.7	7.2	6.1	4.6	6.7	2.0	2.0	3.3	1.5	21	57	46

n.a. Not available.
a. Average receivables are the average of beginning of year and current receivables, expressed in weeks of sales during the period.
b. Average payables are the average of beginning of year and current payables, expressed in weeks of sales during the period.
c. Average inventories are the average of beginning of year and current inventory stocks, as a % of sales during the period.
d. No comparable equity measure was available for these firms.
e. Averages for state-owned firms exclude firms 8 and 9.
Sources: Interviews with firms; and data from Central Statistical Office of Poland.

is a clear indication that reducing labor and labor costs is the last resort.

Despite the lay-offs, for a number of reasons there was still overstaffing. In the eyes of managers, employees valued job security very highly. Wages were a secondary, although still important, consideration. Desire for ownership of the firm ran a distant third. Despite this worker concern with job security and the legal constraints on group firing, employment did adjust, with an average decline of 7 percent since the beginning of the year for the firms in the sample. Some firms reduced their labor significantly: since January both the textile firm and the truck manufacturer eliminated 18 percent of their labor force. At some firms negotiations were underway to reduce staffing even further. Workers approaching pensionable age and casual workers appear to have been the first to be laid off. The private wood furniture firm stands out as the only firm taking on new labor in 1989 or 1990.

The cost of labor also fell as a result of lower wages — real wages declined quite substantially. This drop was offset in part by the elimination of the shortages of goods and related queuing. By way of comparison, wages at the firms in the sample remained constant as a share of sales through the first five months of 1990 (figure 12-2 and table 12-3). However, the ratio of wages to profits rose: the first five months showed an average ratio of wages to profits of .56, up from .30 in 1989 for the sample. The most dramatic increases in this ratio occurred with the textile manufacturer and the truck maker, followed by the food processor and the garment maker. The excess wages tax, in existence through the 1980s[5] but greatly

strengthened in January, was a powerful constraint on raising wages and bonuses,[6] partly because of its financial cost to the firm and partly because payment of the tax was one of the indicators prompting government review of the firm's condition. The tax was designed to offer an incentive to reduce the labor force, meaning the Wages Fund would be shared among fewer employees. In the past, however, this has not seemed to be a major incentive to lay off employees, although there are indications that companies are now considering lay-offs to permit higher pay.

A parallel process was occurring on the input side, with firms searching for more diversified suppliers. This search was not easy because of the market dominance of a few producers and the higher costs of many imports. In addition, firms eagerly revised the nature of their contracts with suppliers, since they no longer desired the long-term and inflexible contracts common and attractive in a shortage economy. Potential import competition was a factor in holding down prices, but in many cases domestic goods were still cheaper than close foreign equivalents. This continuing gap offered a breathing space to some firms hard-hit by the abrupt transition from virtually full protection to almost no protection. For example, steel prices were said to have been lower than international prices for comparable qualities, a situation that provided some steel-using firms in the sample, such as the machine tool maker, with a competitive advantage.

Credit and Financing

The credit squeeze that began in the latter part of 1989 affected the balance sheets of even the most profitable firms. Since the firms in the sample were not heavily in debt, however, in most cases the rise in interest rates did not in itself seriously damage profits. An exception was food processing, which faced high costs for credit because of the seasonal production cycle.

In general the firms responded to the tight credit in several ways. For example, the manufacturer of electrical generators, fearing that the high rates of interest in January and February 1990 would continue, secured prepayment from a large client and paid off all its debt. More commonly, however, firms experienced a sharp rise in payables, which was mirrored in rising receivables. For the firms in the sample, this pattern became evident between March and May of 1990 (figure 12-3 and table 12-2). Average payables stood at six weeks of sales for the state-owned firms in the sample in 1989, fell to five weeks during the first quarter, and rebounded to reach seven weeks for the first five months. All of the sample firms experienced a rise in receivables between March

Figure 12-2. *Cost Structure of Production* (average for sample firms)

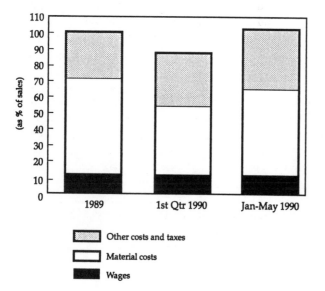

Figure 12-3. *Average Receivables Plus Payables*
(average for sample state-owned firms)

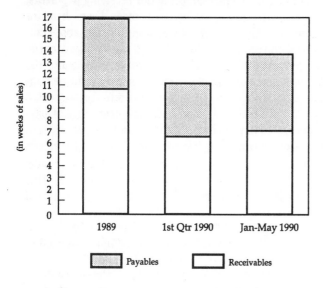

and May of 1990. At the same time, average receivables amounted to 11 weeks of sales in 1989 and then stabilized at around seven weeks during the first five months.

Did the Big Bang Create a New "Sink or Swim" Environment for Firms?

The Old Regime for State-Owned Enterprises

There has been a general withdrawal of government from the active ownership of firms. The decentralization of control in the 1970s had still left the government with financial control over firms. In the 1980s, however, the government paid a large portion of the direct subsidies to the citizenry rather than to the enterprises. For example, in 1988 enterprises received only one-third of the total subsidies, divided into two types: compensation for distortions in the pricing of output, a measure that concentrated on the coal mining sector; and transfers to loss-making firms, a measure that was focused on the food industry and the fuel and power sectors. More important for industrial firms in other sectors was the effect of the indirect subsidies created by a complicated system of subsidized credit and foreign exchange. Schafer (1990) documented the softness of the budget constraints on the Lista 500 firms as a result of government policies, including firm-specific subsidies and tax rebates. The removal of the subsidies in 1990 eliminated the last shred of active government involvement except for the ongoing attempt to harden the budget constraint through bankruptcy proceedings.

The Credit Crunch

Credit from the banking sector was tight and interest rates high, a central feature of the Big Bang's anti-inflationary focus. It was expected that the cut-off of cheap credit would push inefficient firms toward bankruptcy and encourage credit to be directed toward the most creditworthy borrowers. However, firms evaded this constraint through substitution and innovation. Anecdotal evidence supports the claim that banks simply channeled the remaining credit to their biggest borrowers. Other firms were highly credit-constrained, although many did not face an immediate danger of bankruptcy since their profits were so high in 1989. Thus, liquidity rather than solvency was the problem.

The managers agreed in the interviews that the priorities of their firms in making payments were, first, the dividend tax due the government, second, other taxes and wages, and, last, the payables due suppliers, since it was possible to stretch these liabilities out with no real penalty. Thus, suppliers' credits were the buffer in the system, allowing firms a margin of adjustment during the credit crunch. The firms in the sample kept ahead of the inter-firm credit game by delaying their own payables while accelerating their own receivables. This strategy reduced their creditworthiness but generated working capital. The end-of-period ratio of receivables to payables rose from 2.0 at the close of 1989 to 3.3 in March 1990. It then fell dramatically to 1.5 by the end of May (table 12-2). The declining excess of receivables over payables illustrates the credit generated by this behavior.

The use of payables and receivables as a mechanism for financing inter-firm transactions was not new. Socialist firms were notorious for accumulating unpaid inter-firm commitments. Prior to the January reforms, the payables plus receivables for the firms in the sample were around 17 weeks equivalent of sales (figure 12-3). This ratio dropped in the first quarter of 1990, and the ratio of payables to receivables rose. The implication is that once the firms were forced to be responsible for their own cash flows, they probably insisted on some clearing of inter-firm accounts and improvement of their own financial position. By the end of May 1990, volume of suppliers' credits had risen, and the ratio of receivables to payables had fallen sharply, a change that suggested a growing need for credit. Managers reported both that bank credit was generally unavailable and that they expected few or no losses from their own debtors, on the assumption that if the government pushed the debtors into bankruptcy, it would take on responsibility for the bankrupt firm's liabilities.

A more interesting analysis emerges if the sample firms are split into two rough categories: firms deemed likely to fail; and those more likely to survive. The electronics firm, totally dependent on the CMEA market, and specifically the Soviet market, the textile manufacturer with outdated machinery, few exports and buildings protected by historic landmark status, and the truck maker, also with little export experience and growing import competition, and with soaring payables and inventories, were clearly having trouble. The other six firms had comparatively good chances of surviving. These two groups had different patterns of the ratio of receivables to payables. All the firms showed a rise in this ratio for the first five months of 1990 as compared with the first quarter, but only the three failing firms also showed an increase for the first quarter as compared with 1989. That is, the failing firms were using suppliers' credits to generate working capital from the beginning of the year, while the surviving firms delayed until April. A significant development in 1990 was the transformation of suppliers' credits into negotiable inter-firm notes that cost far less than bank credit. The very tight credit squeeze notwithstanding, firms found an innovative way to avoid the disruption of the squeeze.

This inter-firm credit yielded some benefits. In the face of the rigidities of the banking system, it allowed firms to maintain a margin of flexibility for production. This credit was also used to finance new distributors, which in turn made the markets more competitive. However, continued growth without regulation poses an increasing risk of cascading bankruptcy. These worries were not new developments: toward the end of 1989 the government was considering a scheme to net out such debt across all firms.

The Pressure of Import Competition and the Need to Export

The new trade regime had a strong impact on the markets for both inputs and outputs and on relative prices. The fierceness of the import competition across sectors varied, but the low value and continuing depreciation of the zloty moderated competitive pressure overall. However, the exchange rate alone cannot protect domestic producers. For example, the truck manufacturer was charging sales prices far below world prices for a truck of similar size, but since the quality of its trucks was far lower, the firm continued to face strong competition from imported used trucks from Western Europe. International competition came almost entirely from the Western countries. Although Western markets were hard to penetrate, they were what the firms focused on for survival. For Polish firms, the best market in the medium term may well be the CMEA, but in the short

run firms saw the future of the CMEA markets as highly uncertain. Firms had doubts about receiving payments, especially from the USSR, that made them hesitant about fulfilling existing contracts and worried about collecting on receivables. According to the managers of the sample firms, for the CMEA to become a viable alternative market more quickly, trade would have to be conducted at international prices, the rate for the ruble would have to be adjusted and the uncertainty of payment would have to be resolved. Thus, in the short term they concentrated on investing in developing Western markets.

Exit Policy for State-owned Enterprises

Progress was made in defining more clearly the exit policy for firms through the gradual implementation of the January 1990 bankruptcy law and the growing focus on privatization as a way to shift most of the decisions on exit to private agents. Bankruptcy has become more of an institution although the process is not yet completely credible. For example, the firms in the sample still believed there was an implicit government guarantee of inter-firm credit.

The dividend tax—the levy on fixed assets—involved monthly mandated payments that each state-owned firm had to make to the government as the provider of the original capital of the firm. Non-payment of the tax was supposed to trigger recovery or bankruptcy procedures, according to the January 1989 law on the finances of state enterprises. However, not until the government reaffirmed this threat of rehabilitation of non-paying firms in January 1990 did the dividend payment become a top priority of firms.[7] Beginning in January 1990, the dividend became a fixed 32 percent of the capital base, with no link to profits or other performance measures. Because of the high rate in 1989, the government also ordered a revaluation of the Basic Assets Fund of the enterprises in January 1990 by a factor of 14. Despite the tax's name, the fixed nature of the payment made it less like the capitalist dividend that is normally paid to shareholders and more similar to an interest payment on senior debt. Whatever the case, its importance is small for most firms: the dividend tax averaged only 3 percent of sales in the first quarter of 1990 for the firms in the sample, and for no firm did it reach higher than 6 percent of sales.

As mentioned, firms assumed the government would provide a bail-out on inter-firm credit, although they also believed they had to cut costs and increase sales to survive. This sort of confusion will persist until an active, functioning bankruptcy procedure is in place. Firms said they were expecting privatization to occur in the near future (within a year or so) and that the game for them was to survive until then and to place themselves in as favorable position as possible for privatization, including making themselves attractive to foreign partners.

Ownership, Control and Privatization

A central and continuing problem for the long-run adjustment of state-owned firms is clear definition of the rights of ownership and control, a problem intertwined with the move toward privatization. Ownership and control of state-owned enterprises in Poland, as in most socialist economies, are subtle issues because of complications posed by the legal and institutional rules governing operations, the important implications of the current structure of ownership on enterprise behavior, and the influence that de facto ownership and control might have in determining what is a fair settlement of property rights during privatization. At the time of the interviews, the new Privatization Law of July 1990, which circumscribes the possibilities for transforming state-owned property, was not in effect.

The firms were suffering from a vacuum of ownership, with an ill-defined system of control over the enterprise. The managers at a minimum clearly understood that the formal owner of the firm was the treasury. However, the control and supervision the Ministry of Industry once exercised had declined to zero, even in strategic industries. The role of local government had increased, but in very specific areas — zoning approvals, environmental control and social benefits for employees. Those areas did not include direct control over the financial condition of firms. The Workers' Councils exercised some control, but it was limited. In practice, the general managers of the firms had almost all the power over decision-making, except in a few enterprises with strong unions that had created particularly activist Workers' Councils. It should be noted that job security for employees was almost universally quoted as an objective of management, partly because of the influence of the Workers' Councils and partly because some managers were former members of Workers' Councils and/or trade union activists. A further reason was that Solidarity was the ruling party.

All state-owned firms have elected Workers' Councils with formal powers covering all aspects of management. The Workers' Council of a firm must approve the distribution of profits, the sale of fixed assets and the appointment of deputy directors. Most importantly, they must recommend the appointment of the general manager, based on nominations by the Ministry of Industry (with final approval by the Ministry). Management serves at the pleasure of the Workers' Councils. All but two of the sample firms had very recently changed their general manager.

The actual role played by the Workers' Councils, whether active or passive, depends, however, on the individuals elected to them. All the firms visited described relations between management and the Workers' Councils as good, with no serious disputes. They frequently commented that the Workers' Council was helpful, perhaps because it provided a counterweight to the trade unions. It should be noted that by constraining pay, the excess wage tax has defused one of the main potential areas of contention among management, Workers' Councils and trade unions.[8]

Based on the interviews with management, the Workers' Councils did not seem to consider themselves to be owners, although they exercised some rights that were usually reserved for owners. Typically, management doubted that workers wanted to be shareholders in the firm where they worked. Ownership was seen as posing extra risks for Colon workers without corresponding benefits, unless the firms were very secure and profitable. Only in the machine tool firm, which had an excellent capital stock and almost no liabilities, did workers express a desire to buy shares. Without exception, management and workers assumed that the employee shares would have to be purchased (perhaps at some discount) and would not be distributed free of charge.

The possibility of joint ventures with foreign firms has been one source of pressure for speedy resolution of the ownership issue: the managers of Polish firms view this option favorably and are eager to be able to commit to a joint venture. Foreign partners are seen as bringing some particular advantages: market access and marketing expertise; technology and licenses; modern management methods; and new capital.

Some involved breaking up the firm into different entities to facilitate joint ventures. The search for foreign partners, while not the sole element of adjustment strategy, was intense. Partners were perceived to offer advantages of market access and marketing expertise, technology and licenses, modern management methods, and new capital. With ownership status unresolved, however, potential foreign partners were asking for government guarantees on their investments. The terms of the offers were not always favorable to the Polish firm, especially if the firm was doing badly and was in great need of foreign assistance. For example, the electronics firm was negotiating a contract with a Western firm to provide some new technology under license, some joint production and some guarantees of distribution in Western markets. However, the prospective Western partner was not providing any capital and was demanding a very high fee for its services. On the other hand, the electrical generator maker was negotiating a very favorable arrangement that resulted in the acquisition of 75 percent of the firm by a Western firm in the same business in August. Overall, the favorable view of joint ventures among managers of Polish firms, and managers' eagerness to be able to commit to a joint venture, placed pressure on the government to resolve the ownership issue.

With the ownership issue unresolved and privatization not proceeding, state-owned firms nominally belonged to the Treasury while local governments exercised some regulatory powers, and management and the Workers' Councils co-managed most aspects of these firms' operations. Decision-making by the firms under these circumstances was subject to complex considerations and considerable uncertainty.

Conclusions

Management interviews and basic financial data from nine Polish manufacturing firms in June and July of 1990 provide insights into the behavior of state-owned firms in the first six months after Poland's "Big Bang." The observations at the firm level are based on but a partial picture of the response to the Big Bang. Some conclusions, however, do emerge. In particular, the aggregate unemployment rate is not a good measure of the speed of adjustment of the industrial sector because of firms' abilities and incentives to continue to absorb labor costs. In general, the extensive adjustment to the changed conditions and long-term horizon exhibited in the sample of firms reflect flexibility in their behavior, albeit not necessarily with assured successful outcomes in all cases.

As noted, it is unclear if the firms in the sample are representative of the response in the industrial sector. They may well have been above average in their adjustment. However, in the aftermath of the demand and shock of the liberalization of the product market associated with the Big Bang, there is evidence of significant positive adjustment by state-owned firms in some industrial sectors under conditions that were unfamiliar and uncertain. Although some firms were failing, others were actually thriving in 1990. Overall, the best-placed firms appeared to be those with previous exposure to selling in Western markets.

Positive responses occurred in a number of areas. Firms were trimming and rationalizing labor use, although, for the better firms, lay-offs were not necessarily a good indication of the degree of adjustment because wage costs were relatively small and could be absorbed by the generally high profit cushion. The firms were also cutting input costs by searching for new suppliers and

rewriting contracts with existing suppliers. They were actively searching for new markets and new products. In response to the tightening of credit in the first semester of 1990, the firms expanded suppliers' credits and created inter-firm notes.

Some institutional features were influential in the firms' behavior. In those in the sample, the role of the Workers' Councils appeared to be positive; in some cases, the Councils were playing a useful role for management vis-a-vis the trade unions. This relationship could, however, have been a honeymoon caused by the excess wages tax, which was effective in curbing wage increases. The excess wage tax alleviated the wage pressure that would likely otherwise have been induced by the vacuum of ownership created by the decentralized control of firms, especially under continued inflation. However, despite the favorable effect of this tax, the ownership issue was beginning to inhibit the implementation of longer term survival strategies, especially the pursuit of joint ventures with Western firms. Resolution of this issue was growing in importance, because continued delay, despite the willingness and ability of firms to change their behavior, could stall adjustment.

This view of firm behavior was derived at a time when the transition to a market economy was far from complete. Uncertainty was extreme. A new tax structure, including a personal income tax and a VAT, were not yet in place to replace the socialist tax structure that had been heavily dependent on revenues from state-owned firms. The social safety net required further development and refinement. The process by which privatization was to take place had not yet been fully specified. Most important, the medium-term success of individual manufacturing firms, which in aggregate can underlie a positive supply response necessary to revive the economy, evidently required new investment, both foreign and domestic.

There was life after the Big Bang, at least for the sample of firms that were investigated, although the quality of life differed. However, a revival of investment awaits clarification of future uncertainties, in particular regarding privatization, the system of financial intermediation, the role of the excess wage tax, and the future role of the Workers' Councils under a Solidarity government.

Notes

1. See Schrenk (1990a) for a discussion of the workings of the CMEA and the trade patterns that resulted.

2. This phrase comes from Kornai (1979) and is further developed in Kornai (1986).

3. In 1989 the government had introduced a statutory tax on the original assets of state-owned firms that it misleadingly called a "dividend," to be paid to the Treasury as the owner.

4. The Workers' Councils were introduced in 1981 as part of

Poland's first program of reform. They were given limited powers in decisions of firms.

5. During the 1980s, as part of a continued effort to re-establish financial discipline over firms, the government imposed a series of taxes on excess wages that took the general form of progressive taxes on wage increases above a government-mandated maximum. However, frequent exemptions undermined the impact on wage levels.

6. The Big Bang package included a measure to control wages by greatly increasing the excess wage tax. The tax was to be levied on firms that raised wages by more than 30 percent of official inflation in January 1990 and 20 percent in February, March and April. Frydman, Wellisz and Kolodko (1990) argued that the excess wage tax was a binding ceiling on wage payments even though the government usually did not invoke the tax. The penalty arose if wages exceeded the mandated share of actual inflation. However, firms had to set the level of wages one month in advance based only on a forecast. For the first four months of 1990, the wage payments of firms slowly made up for the significant underpayment in January caused by the underprediction of inflation for that month by the Ministry of Finance.

7. The dividend tax was instituted in 1989 to reduce the role of bargaining in the taxation of firms. It required firms to pay a tax on that portion of their capital stock which was funded centrally as opposed to that part of capital funded out of retained earnings. Specifically, the base for this tax is the enterprise's founding fund, or Basic Assets Fund, defined as the total value of its assets in December 1983. The tax rate was linked to the bank rate of interest for re-financing, set by the National Bank of Poland. The setting of an upper bound for the dividend payments—25 percent of profits—and the 75 percent reduction in payments allowed for public utilities and agricultural sector firms compromised the uniform application of this levy.

8. The firms in the sample generally had two main unions, Solidarity and OPZZ (founded by the Communist Party during the period of martial law in response to the rise of Solidarity), with roughly equal membership. Often there is a third small, non-party-affiliated union. The share of non-union workers was sometimes as high as 40 percent. The scope of activity by the trade unions is legally confined to approval of lay-offs and wage agreements.

References

Calvo, Guillermo, and Fabrizio Coricelli. 1990. "Stagflationary Effects of Stabilization Programs in Reforming Socialist Countries: Supply Side vs. Demand Side Factors." Mimeo. Macroeconomics and Growth Division, Country Economics Department, World Bank. Washington, D.C., August

Frydman, Roman, Stanislaw Wellisz and Grzegorz Kolodko. 1990. "Stabilization in Poland: A Progress Report." Mimeo. A revised version of a paper presented at the May 1990 Conference on Exchange Rate Policies of Less Developed Economies and Socialist Economies, Berlin. Department of Economics, New York University, New York, May.

Kornai, Janos. 1979 "Resource-Constrained Versus Demand-Constrained Systems." *Econometrica* 47 (July):802-20.

———. 1986. *Kyklos* 39:3-30.

Lipton, David, and Jeffrey Sachs. 1990. "Creating a Market Economy in Eastern Europe: The Case of Poland." *Brookings Papers on Economic Activity* 1:75-147.

Schaffer, Mark. 1990. "State-Owned Enterprises in Poland: Taxation, Subsidization, and Competition Policies." A paper prepared for the (PHARE) Project, DGII, European Commission. School of European Studies, University of Sussex, Brighton, England, February.

Schrenk, Martin. 1990a. "The CMEA System of Trade and Payments: Today and Tomorrow." Discussion Paper No. 5. Strategic Planning and Review Department, World Bank. Washington, D.C., January.

———. 1990b. "Poland: Reform of the Economic System." Mimeo. Socialist Economies Reform Unit, Country Economics Department, World Bank. Washington, D.C., March.

13

Comments on "Life after the Polish 'Big Bang': Representative Episodes of Enterprise Behavior," by Erika A. Jorgenson, Alan Gelb and Inderjit Singh

Jan Svejnar

This well-motivated paper by Erika A. Jorgenson, Alan Gelb and Inderjit Singh is an impressive analytical report on a visit to nine Polish industrial firms in the summer of 1990. It contains a lucid discussion of the initial conditions of the enterprises as well as their responses to the major policy changes that took place in early 1990.

To summarize, the salient feature of the initial conditions of the firms in the sample is that they entered the Big Bang period in good shape. Unlike their counterparts in some other countries (e.g., Czechoslovakia and Hungary), the Polish firms had relatively high profits and low debt. They were also subject to a low capital tax, and their wage bills on average accounted for only 13 percent of sales. All the enterprises had experience with Western firms and markets. Moreover, managers and workers effectively shared power in the environment of poorly defined ownership and control rights. The main goal of the workers was job security, a goal that the managers shared, as the paper implies. The second goal of workers was the growth of wages, while ownership of enterprise capital came third.

The fundamental change in economic policies that took place at the start of 1990 exerted strong downward pressure on enterprise profits as demand fell and the cost of inputs (especially those of power and water) rose. With the old distribution system gone and a new one not yet in place, supplies of inputs became more uncertain, and export orders from the countries in the Council for Mutual Economic Assistance (CMEA) collapsed. The elimination of the subsidies and imposition of a credit squeeze constrained the cash flow of enterprises significantly. Finally, the government imposed a stiff incremental tax on the wage bill to forestall inflationary increases in wages.

The paper clearly documents the rapid response of the nine Polish firms to this dramatic change in circumstances. Instead of becoming overwhelmed and paralyzed, the enterprises took measures to generate demand

for their products and increase (or limit the decline in) the prices of their products. This effort to adjust led to the creation of marketing departments, the position of traveling salesman, etc.—i.e., to labor-intensive measures that were sensible per se and took into account the primacy of job security as an enterprise goal. The firms decreased their reliance on middlemen for domestic sales (an area where they could rapidly develop their own expertise). They used foreign trade middlemen to stimulate exports to hard currency areas. Although real wages fell, the ratio of the wage bill to total revenue remained roughly constant. Employment declined by about 5 percent in the first six months of 1990 as casual workers were laid off and early retirements took place. The credit squeeze led to an outburst of inter-enterprise credit (in the form of an increase in payables and receivables); enterprises expected this growing system of inter-enterprise financing to be sustainable. Finally, all firms engaged in an intensive search for foreign partners.

The authors argue, and document convincingly, that the response of the Polish firms to the new environment was very substantive. They also make the case that the response was in the "right direction." On the whole, they are right on this point. However, it can also be argued that it is necessary to distinguish between adjustments that are socially desirable and those that benefit only the firm.

The fact that there was a significant response by enterprises to the major change in exogenous factors confirms the findings about enterprise behavior in other countries. Most studies in developing and socialist countries reveal how enterprises exploit government-imposed constraints and regulations to their advantage, in the process frequently generating socially inefficient outcomes. The present study documents responses to government measures that were aimed at relaxing the regulations and constraints. Hence, to a large extent most of the observed enterprise responses (e.g., measures to stimulate demand, find more lucrative markets and use quasi-fixed factors such as labor more intensively) were efficiency-enhancing from the social standpoint. However, where the government imposed constraints, the firms responded by exploiting these to their (i.e., the owner-insiders') advantage. The incremental tax on the wage bill is a good example. It stimulated lay-offs of casual workers and early retirements, as the insiders strove to increase their wages. Whether this outcome was socially efficient or inefficient depends on the marginal product of labor inside and outside these firms (the shadow wage), information that is not readily available. Similarly, there is no information on the other likely impacts of this particular wage regulation — the loss of skilled workers and the negative effect on effort and work quality. Since one of the salient features of socialism was the low level of individual effort, it can be surmised that the negative impact of the wage regulation on productivity could be significant.

It is also worth stressing the potentially very dangerous phenomenon the paper points out — the rapid growth in inter-enterprise credit. Both theory and evidence from other socialist economies (e.g., Yugoslavia) suggest that participation by enterprises in this financial network extends the longevity of failing firms and tends to develop into a game between a large number of colluding enterprises and the government. Insolvency on the part of a few firms then threatens to paralyze the entire enterprise sector, a situation that poses a dilemma for the government. The government's inability to prevent the escalation of inter-enterprise credit may subsequently force even conservative governments to bail out failing firms for fear of the large-scale repercussions of individual bankruptcies.

Overall, the paper offers a very valuable microeconomic diagnosis of the Polish economy in transition. It covers most major areas of the economic activities of enterprises and interprets the main findings in a consistent conceptual framework. The paper leaves a profound impression of the significant changes taking place and of the need to follow future developments closely.

14

Distortionary Policies and Growth in Socialist Economies[1]

William Easterly

This paper discusses several applications of endogenous growth models in socialist countries. The next section reviews the evidence on distortions in resource allocation in socialist countries, particularly the Soviet Union. The following section presents a model of how distortions in resource allocation affect growth, discussing the model under the assumption of a fixed savings rate, and then considering what saving rate a planner might choose if the distortions are taken as given. In the subsequent section, the model is applied to an example of distorted allocation of capital stocks in the Soviet Union. The model is then generalized to consider the effects of partial reform in socialist economies. Some conclusions are presented in the final section.

Introduction

The apparently spectacular failure of the economic system of central planning has led to a reassessment of the system's long-run effects. Although estimates of socialist growth are highly uncertain, it is increasingly clear that it has been comparatively poor when the high rate of investment is considered.

However, according to the standard neoclassical growth model developed by Solow (1956), distortionary policies (and all other economic policies) affect only the level of income and not its rate of growth. Given the existence of non-reproducible factors, constant returns to scale and diminishing returns to each factor, steady-state growth can only take place through exogenous technological change.[2] On these grounds, the alleged long-run growth effects of socialist policy have often been dismissed (e.g., Lucas 1988). A general conclusion is that distortionary policies are not that important in

explaining the large differences in income levels, nor should they be given much weight compared with, for example, stabilization policies (Rodrik 1990).[3]

The literature on endogenous growth, following on the work of Romer (1986, 1987 a and b, and 1988), Lucas (1988) and Barro (1989a and b), presents models in which policies can have significant effects on long-run growth. These models variously relax the assumptions of constant returns to scale (Romer and Lucas), the dependence on non-reproducible factors (Rebelo 1990) and diminishing returns to each factor (Jones and Manuelli 1990). Barro (1989a) and Barro and Sala-i-Martin (1990) have discussed how tax rates can distort savings decisions and lower growth, while the government services financed by those taxes can potentially raise private productivity and increase growth. Rebelo (1990) and King and Rebelo (1990) have similarly shown how differences in tax rates can translate into large differences in growth rates. While much empirical testing of these models remains to be done, the empirical work discussed in this literature has tended to confirm strong effects of policy on growth (Barro 1989b and Romer 1989).

Distortionary Policies in Socialist Countries

Although the endogenous growth models strongly support the emphasis given to policies, so far they have not paid much attention to the special characteristics of policies in socialist countries. The salient fact about these policies is that they cause severe distortions in the allocation of resources. Prior to recent reforms, conditions such as the lack of property rights and production incentives, labor hoarding and labor immobility excessive inventories and unfinished construction, quantitative allocation of inputs by planners and severe misalignment of relative prices severely distorted the resource allocation in these countries.[4] One special feature of the incentive system in socialist economies is the so-called "ratchet effect," whereby improved performance only results in an increase in plan targets for future performance.

Table 14-1 shows the growth performance of selected socialist economies. While their performance does not compare badly with that in the rest of the world, their rates of investment are much higher. Their reasonable growth performance suggests that the effects of even severe distortions can be offset by sufficiently high rates of saving. The informal sector is also thought to play an important role in many of these countries, just as in distorted developing countries, and can help maintain growth. In the Soviet Union, for example, the shadow economy has been estimated at 20 percent of gross domestic product (GDP).[5]

Recent developments in Central and Eastern Europe have led to much questioning of these officially estimated growth rates. For example, the Czech economist Miroslav Hrncir has pointed out the following anomaly. Per capita growth in Czechoslovakia since the war is officially estimated to have been faster than that in Austria. Yet he estimates that the standard of living in Czechoslovakia is now less than half that in Austria, while immediately after the war it was roughly equal. Table 14-2

Table 14-1. *Growth and Investment in Socialist Economies*

	Gross domestic investment (as % of GDP^{a}1988)	*Growth 1960-88 (percent)*
China	38	6.0
Poland	33	4.4^b
Hungary (1971-89)	25	3.1
Algeria	31	3.9
Yugoslavia	39	4.8
Soviet Union	33	2.6-5.6^c
Average low-income (excluding China/India)	18	4.3
Average middle-income (Africa, East Asia, South Asia, EMENA, LAC)^d	25	5.3
Average OECD	22	3.4

a. Gross domestic product.

b. Refers to growth in net material product (NMP), 1960-86.

c. 1965-88.

d. EMENA—Europe, Middle East and North Africa Region, World Bank; and LAC—Latin America and the Caribbean Region, World Bank.

Sources: World Bank data except: Poland, World Bank (1990); Yugoslavia, growth (Yugoslavia, various issues); and Soviet Union (Ofer 1990).

gives different estimates of per capita growth in four socialist countries based on comparisons of these countries with US per capita income growth in 1948 and 1988 (different estimates of Soviet growth will be discussed in the next section).

The literature identifies a number of distortionary practices characteristic of socialist economies. Production is said to be biased toward heavy industry and capital-intensive agriculture, a reflection of the Marxist obsession with large-scale physical capital. The service sector and housing have received far less emphasis. Table 14-3 confirms this pattern: it shows that the share of capital devoted to the production of goods (industry and agriculture) is far higher in the Soviet Union that in Organisation for Economic Co-operation and Development (OECD) economies, while the share of residential dwellings is only half as large. It is highly unlikely that this structure corresponds to the preferences of Soviet consumers. In a word, socialism produced too many steel factories and tractors and too few houses. This overemphasis on heavy industry and capital-intensive agriculture has been blamed for the recent economic stagnation in the Soviet Union, specifically, for the slowing of technological progress and the lack of competitiveness in the world economy (Ofer 1987, and see also Gomulka 1986).

Another characteristic bias of socialist economies is excessive use of inputs. Thumm[6] shows how the energy use per unit of output in Council for Mutual Economic Assistance (CMEA) countries was more than twice as large as that in OECD countries, while the use of transport per unit of output was 4 to 10 times larger. The Soviet Union has a ratio of gross output to net output considerably larger than that in the United States.[7] This use of inputs reflects their subsidization and the soft budget constraint facing producers.

The high cost of transport in socialist economies is indicative of the inefficient spatial distribution of production. Hewett (1988) has shown how the vertical integration of Soviet ministries leads them to ship inputs from one of "their" enterprises to another even if there is a closer plant of another ministry producing the same input. For administrative reasons the ministries have also preferred highly concentrated production, which means that sometimes one plant is supplying the entire vast Soviet territory. This monopolization of production implies that production can easily be disrupted by local incidents. For example, the cigarette shortage in the Soviet Union in 1990 is alleged to have been the result in large part of ethnic strife that disrupted the production of cigarette filters by the sole producer, located in Armenia.

Table 14-2. Measures of Per Capita Income Growth
(percent)

A. Per capita income: Ratio to U.S. per capita income in the same year

	UN 1948	GNP method 1988	Fischer-Gelb physical indicators method 1980	Exchange rate method 1988
Czechoslovakia	28.6	51.0	42.0	18.0
Hungary	14.3	44.0	32.0	13.0
Poland	20.6	37.0	27.0	9.0
Bulgaria	9.7	38.0	30.0	13.0

B. Per capita income: Growth per annum

	GNP method 1948-88	Physical indicators method 1948-80	Exchange rate method 1948-88
Czechoslovakia	3.48	3.23	0.82
Hungary	4.89	4.58	1.74
Poland	3.49	2.85	-0.11
Bulgaria	5.54	5.67	2.75

Note: Per capita growth in the United States, calculated from the International Monetary Fund's *International Financial Statistics* data, is as follows:
1948-1980 1.990 percent
1948-1988 1.989 percent
Sources: United Nations, Economic Commission for Europe (1948, Table E, p. 235); Fischer and Gelb (1990); GNP method—United States, Central Intelligence Agency (1989); physical indicators method—Erlich (1987); exchange rate method—International Monetary Fund, *International Financial Statistics* (various issues) and World Bank staff estimates.

Table 14-3. Percentage Distribution of Capital Stocks, 1987

	Agriculture (A)	Industry (I)	I+A	Dwellings (D)	Other (O)	D+O	I+A+O	(I+A)(D+O)	(I+A)(D)
Soviet Union	14.2	32.2	46.4	18.6	35.0	53.6	81.4	0.87	4.38
Industrial market economies	5.0	23.4	28.4	35.9	35.6	71.6	64.1	0.40	1.78
United States	2.8	22.4	25.2	45.6	29.2	74.8	54.4	0.34	1.19
Australia	3.5	24.4	27.9	27.7	44.4	72.1	72.3	0.39	2.61
Belgium	1.5	20.5	22.0	35.2	42.8	78.0	64.8	0.28	1.84
Finland	7.5	19.9	27.4	33.8	38.8	72.6	66.2	0.38	1.96
Germany, F.R. (1986)	3.6	20.1	23.7	44.2	32.1	76.3	55.8	0.31	1.26
Greece	10.7	21.6	32.3	34.5	33.2	67.7	65.5	0.48	1.90
Norway (1986)	9.7	28.6	38.3	26.4	35.3	61.7	73.6	0.62	2.79
Sweden (1983)	4.1	25.0	29.1	41.0	29.9	70.9	59.0	0.41	1.44
Great Britain	1.8	28.0	29.8	35.1	35.1	70.2	64.9	0.42	1.85

Source: USSR—Soviet data; industrial economies—OECD data.

Of course, the phenomenon of pervasive shortages in socialist economies is caused fundamentally by the absence of flexible pricing that matches supply and demand. This situation and the scarcity of retail services imply queueing costs to consumers. Casual observation suggests these costs are large.

Socialist countries are also characterized by resources wasted on large stocks of inventories and unfinished construction. These conditions reflect the easy credit to enterprises, the soft budget constraint and the efforts of enterprises (and consumers) to hedge against shortages and cutbacks in resources. Thumm[8] shows that the accumulation of inventory was many times higher in Hungary, Poland, Czechoslovakia and Yugoslavia than it was in the OECD economies. As table 14-4 reveals, the accumulation of inventory in the USSR was also excessive by international standards: it averaged 2.7 percent of GDP over 1981-88, compared with 0.4 percent in the OECD countries. Unfinished construction in the USSR amounted to 83 percent of investment in 1988 and as much as 164 percent of investment in the electrical energy sector.

A Model of Endogenous Growth with Distortionary Policies

This section presents an endogenous growth model that attempts to capture some of the special features of the distortionary government policies in socialist countries.[7] Only the permanent, steady-state effects of such policies are considered. It postulates a model of constant returns to scale in reproducible capital, as in Rebelo (1990). Capital is broadly defined to include both physical and human capital. Two types of capital, variously interpreted as formal and informal sector capital, imported and domestic capital, and "heavy" and "light" capital, are defined as producing the single output. Distortion is defined as any government policy that causes the marginal products of the two types of capital to diverge from the optimal resource allocation. The relationship between this rate of distortion and growth is then discussed, with attention paid to both fixed saving rates and optimal sav-

ing. Throughout the paper, it is assumed that the economy is insulated from the international financial markets, although trade in goods is considered. While the model is highly stylized, the results seem to offer insight into some of the characteristics of socialist countries discussed above.

Production

Equation (14-1) shows the production function for the analysis:

$$(14\text{-}1) \qquad Y = (\gamma_1 K_1^\rho + \gamma_2 K_2^\rho)^{\frac{1}{\rho}}.$$

Output Y is a CES function of the two generic types of capital, K_1 and K_2, with the elasticity of substitution $1/(\rho - 1)$. Since no fixed inputs enter the production function, sustained growth is feasible through the accumulation of physical and human capital. For simplicity's sake, population is assumed to be fixed throughout the analysis. This type of production function can be justified as being an asymptotic approximation to one in which fixed inputs become less important at high incomes (Jones and Manuelli 1990; Easterly 1990b). Others have argued that spill-overs from the accumulation of physical and human capital produce a linear relation between output and capital (Romer 1987b). Finally, Rebelo (1990) has shown that sustained growth requires only a core of capital goods that can be produced without fixed inputs, as in equation (14-1).

The distortion is defined as the differential between the marginal products (rates of return) of the two types of capital, as follows:

$$(14\text{-}2) \qquad \frac{\frac{\partial Y}{\partial K_1}}{\frac{\partial Y}{\partial K_2}} = e^\tau$$

where τ is the exponential rate of the sales tax (or tariff) on investment in type 1 capital.[8]

Profit-maximizing producers will rent the two types

Table 14-4. *Inventories—Flows as a Percent of Gross Domestic Product*
(current prices)

	1981	1982	1983	1984	1985	1986	1987	1988	Average 1981-88
OECD	0.1	-0.4	-0.2	1.2	0.3	0.4	0.6	0.6	0.4
USSR	5.8	4.3	4.3	2.9	2.7	0.8	-0.1	1.0	2.7

Sources: OECD—Thumm (1990); and USSR—Soviet data.

of capital such that equation (14-2) is satisfied. The implication is that the following will be the ratio of type 2 to type 1 capital (denoted B), derived from equations (14-1) and (14-2):

$$(14\text{-}3) \qquad B = \frac{K_2}{K_1} = \left[\frac{\gamma_2}{\gamma_1}\right]^{\frac{1}{1-\rho}} \frac{\tau}{e^{1-\rho}}.$$

The distortion τ induces more of type 2 capital to be held than is socially optimal. The elasticity of substitution $[1/(\rho -1)]$ determines how strongly the ratio of capital inputs will respond to increases in the distortion.

The accumulation of the two types of capital is considered next, first under fixed saving rates, then under optimal saving behavior. Two interpretations of this distortion in socialist economies are relevant. The τ could measure the ex-post differential in the rates of return that results from non-market allocation of investment across types of capital, as is the case under central planning. Capital is usually allocated according to other criteria than its rate of return across alternative uses. For example, the aforementioned excessive investment in the production of goods and underinvestment in services implies that the latter offers a higher rate of return. Alternatively, τ could measure the implicit tax on formal income in socialist economies, where individuals retain little of the additional income from improved performance because of the lack of property rights and aforementioned "ratchet effect." Capital in the shadow economy—where a person can keep much of the reward from the productive effort—would be represented by K_2. Because of the risk of penalties under the law, the rate of return on illegal activity will be much higher than that in the formal sector. Thus, this simple set-up captures many of the stylized realities of government distortions in socialist economies.

Other interpretations of the capital types and distortions are also illuminating (although analytically equivalent). According to one, it can be assumed that the economy produces a single domestic good with capital made up of imported goods (K_1) and the domestic good itself (K_2). Both goods are assumed to be traded, and the economy is assumed to be small in international trade. The price ratio of the two goods is thus fixed and can be normalized at unity. The distortion rate τ can then be a misalignment of the exchange rate, a tariff on the imported capital good or an import quota determined by planning (defined as the equivalent tariff rate).

Yet another interpretation is that two types of capital are formed out of the single domestic output in an autarkic economy. The first type, called formal sector capital, is subject to a sales tax at the moment of purchase for investment. The second type, informal sector capital, evades the sales tax. The two types of capital can be formed from domestic output at zero installation cost. However, they differ in other characteristics such as location or institutional form of ownership, and these characteristics cause them to enter into production differently and also determine whether they can be hidden successfully from the authorities.

Although the analysis is presented in the form of a sales or import tax on type 1 capital (the most common types of taxation in socialist countries), the taxes can be shown to be equivalent in steady state to a tax on the income from type 1 capital.[9] Thus, the analysis would be the same for an analysis of a proportional income tax (on both the labor earnings from human capital and the profits from physical capital) that is widely but incompletely evaded. The tax is also equivalent to other government actions that imply either extra unit costs for investment in the formal sector, such as investment licenses or other regulatory requirements, or implicit proportional deductions from income, such as government expropriation of property or a ratcheting upward of plan targets. The analysis is the same if the different types of capital are subject to differential rates of implicit or explicit subsidization/taxation, such as would occur with directed credit schemes or quantitative allocation of foreign exchange.

Capital Accumulation with Fixed Saving Rates

With a lump-sum rebate of tax revenues, the income of the private sector is equal to total output Y. As in the original Solow model, it is assumed that a fixed proportion, s, of this income is saved. Since it is assumed that the economy is closed to inflows of foreign financial capital, saving will equal investment (I_1) in type 1 and type 2 capital goods:

$$(14\text{-}4) \qquad I_1 + I_2 = sY.$$

It is assumed that the rate of depreciation of capital (α) is the same for both types.

The growth rate for the economy in a steady state is then given by the following:

$$(14\text{-}5) \qquad g = s\left[\frac{(\gamma_1 + \gamma_2 B^\rho)^{\frac{1}{\rho}}}{1 + B}\right] - \alpha.$$

It can be shown that growth is unambiguously negatively related to the distortion rate τ. This finding is intuitively clear since it is known that output for a given level of capital is maximized at zero distortion. Equation (14-5) simply represents saving out of output as a ratio to existing capital. This equation is the growth analogue to the standard result in the Solow model that a tax on capital will reduce the steady-state capital/labor ratio and lower output (see, for example, Atkinson and Stiglitz 1980).

It is more illuminating to present a graph of the relationship between the rate of distortion and growth for plausible parameter values (figure 14-1) [10] The relationship approximates a logistic curve, with flat segments at the low and high rates of distortion. In this simulation, growth approaches a minimum as the distortion τ goes to infinity. Increases in the distortion from zero are not very costly at first but show increasing costs in terms of lost growth as the distortion grows. This pattern is the dynamic analogue to the well-known static principle of increasing marginal costs of distortions, which in this case reflects diminishing returns to increased use of type 2 capital. The flattening of the curve as τ increases reflects the gradual disappearance of type 1 capital. As the use of type 1 capital approaches zero, the damage caused by additional increases in the distortion becomes slight.

The finding of a growth rate always above a certain minimum even as distortion approaches infinity is intuitively plausible in light of the socialist experience discussed earlier. The possibility of substituting informal capital for formal capital could explain why output and growth do not fall to catastrophic levels even with almost unlimited distortion in the allocation of resources. This possibility could also explain why high rates of saving could enable socialist economies to grow respectably. With finite losses from an arbitrarily large

distortion, sufficiently high increases in saving could offset the negative growth effects of distortionary policies. For example, in this simulation the loss in growth from an arbitrarily large distortion is 5 percentage points, which could be offset by an increase of 20 percentage points in saving. While such high saving imposes a severe cost on the population, it is within the range of feasibility.

The non-linear shape of the growth-distortion relationship also has implications for policy reforms. Elimination of small distortions is practically pointless according to this model, since it means just a backwards movement along the initial flat part of the curve. Similarly, modest reductions of very large distortions have virtually no impact, since the tax rate of an activity that is at a very low level has little weight. This result implies, for example, that market reform in socialist countries must reach some critical mass to have a growth effect. This model supports the idea of the "Big Bang" as in Poland in 1990, although this conclusion is only from the point of view of a permanent gain rather than any transitional advantage.

The elasticity of substitution plays a critical role in this analysis. The results just presented will only hold when the elasticity of substitution is strictly greater than one, the implication being that neither input is essential for production. (The simulation just presented assumed an elasticity of 2.) Figure 14-2 shows the consequences of distortions on growth under alternative elasticities of substitution. With an elasticity equal to unity, output goes to zero as type 1 capital is more heavily penalized, since this input is essential for production. Growth declines asymptotically to depreciation of the capital stock ($-\alpha$) without replacement. With an elasticity equal to 3, on the other hand, growth stays above a minimum of over 2 percent no matter how large the distortion.

Figure 14-2 shows that the flat part of the curve at low rates of distortion with inelastic production is much larger than the flat portion with highly elastic production. The point made earlier about small distortions not being costly is stronger the more inelastic production is. Similarly, the flat part of the curve at high rates of distortion is longer (and the loss in growth smaller) the more elastic production is. Modest reform of large distortions is more ineffective the greater the elasticity of substitution is. To summarize, a reform strategy based on this model should be affected by the assumption about the substitutability of formal and informal capital. If it is believed that substitutability is high, the emphasis should be on very large reductions in the large distortions, since moderate reductions will have little effect. For example, if it is believed that there is substantial replacement of the formal economy by the underground

Figure 14-1. *Distortion and Growth - Alternative Assumptions*

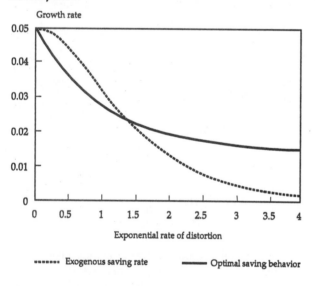

Growth rate

Exponential rate of distortion

- - - - - - - Exogenous saving rate   ——— Optimal saving behavior

Source: Computer simulation by the author.

Figure 14-2. Growth and Distortion - Alternative Elasticities of Substitution (exogenous saving rate)

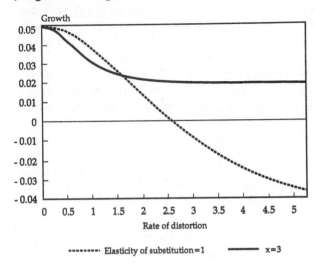

Source: Computer simulation by the author.

economy under socialism, then a drastic market reform is needed to make efficient use of formal capital and thus to raise growth. If it is believed that substitutability is low, it is pointless to bother with small distortions, but even moderate reductions in large distortions will be effective. The growth benefit of reform is greater the more inelastic the production structure is.

Capital Accumulation with Optimal Saving Behavior

This section considers the implications of optimal saving behavior to see how saving responds to distortion. Assume that a beneficent planner seeks to maximize the present discounted value of the utility of future consumption:

$$(14\text{-}6) \quad \int_0^\infty e^{-rt} \frac{c^{1-\sigma}}{1-\sigma} dt.$$

Utility is given as an isoelastic function of total consumption C where the intertemporal elasticity of substitution is $1/\sigma$.

Consumption is given by the excess of income over investment spending. The investment in type 1 capital is taxed (implicitly or explicitly) at an exponential rate, $\exp(\tau)$, as before (in other words, the planner is powerless to alter the distortions induced by the system but can at least alter the rate of saving)[11]:

$$(14\text{-}7) \quad C = Y - e^{\tau}I_1 - I_2 + T,$$

while the equations of the accumulation of capital are simply:

$$(14\text{-}8) \quad \dot{K}_1 = I_1 - \alpha K_1$$

and

$$(14\text{-}9) \quad \dot{K}_1 = I_2 - \alpha K_2.$$

The condition that investment is irreversible was not explicitly imposed.

Showing that the planner solving this maximization problem will allocate investment between the two types such that equation (14-2) continues to hold is a straightforward matter. That is, τ will be equal to the wedge between the marginal products of the two types of capital. In steady state, both types of investment and capital, along with consumption and output, will all grow at the same rate, which will be given by:

$$(14\text{-}10) \quad g = \frac{r_2 - \alpha - r}{\sigma},$$

where r_2 is the marginal product of type 2 capital, given by the following,

$$(14\text{-}11) \quad r_2 = \gamma_2 (\gamma_1 B^{-\rho} + \gamma_2)^{\frac{1}{\rho} - 1},$$

and B is the ratio of K_2 to K_1 given by equation (14-3). Growth is given by the familiar condition that the optimal growth of consumption is equal to the difference between the net marginal product of capital and the rate of time preference times the intertemporal elasticity of substitution. Since the marginal product of type 2 capital goes down when type 1 capital is taxed more heavily, growth is unambiguously a negative function of the distortion rate τ. A plot of the growth-distortion relationship for a simulation with the same parameter values as before is shown in figure 14-1, which also shows the relationship under exogenous saving behavior.[12]

Marginal costs no longer rise with increased distortion under optimal saving behavior. Even small distortions are costly, because they cause both a decrease in saving and a static efficiency loss. However, with endogenous saving, the growth consequences of very large distortions may be less severe than under fixed saving rates. The reason is that the rate of saving actually increases at very high rates of distortion.

The reasons for this result are examined below. It is a straightforward proposition to show that the optimal propensity to consume out of total capital ($K_1 + K_2$) is given by:

$$(14\text{-}12) \quad \frac{c}{K_1 + K_2} = (r_2 - \alpha)(1 - \frac{1}{\sigma}) + \frac{r}{\sigma} + \frac{r_2(e^\tau - 1)}{1 + B}$$

The first two terms in this expression are familiar: the optimal propensity to consume out of wealth (capital) will increase with the net rate of return if the intertemporal elasticity of substitution is less than one, while if it is equal to one, this propensity will be the rate of time preference. The third term gives the amount of the lump-sum transfer of the tax revenues to consumers as a ratio to the capital stock. These revenues are entirely consumed. As the tax rate increases, optimal consumption declines because the rate of return falls, and the income effect is assumed to outweigh the substitution effect. The consumption decline is partially offset by the consumption of lump-sum tax revenues, but these do not affect the growth rate, and the lump-sum transfer disappears as the tax rate increases. The increase in saving as a share of income in response to the high levels of distortion explains why distortion causes less of a fall in growth in the optimal saving case (given the assumption of the simulation of an intertemporal elasticity of less than one, as is supported by most empirical evidence).

This result gives an unusual perspective on the high rate of saving and respectable growth in the socialist economies. The high saving rate imposed by planners could be optimal given the extensive distortions, although of course the distortions themselves are neither necessary nor optimal. If the intertemporal elasticity is less than one, then optimal consumption will fall with increased distortion—the substitution of present for future consumption is outweighed by the income effect of the higher level of distortion. The rise in saving when the level of distortion is greater implies a less severe decline in growth. Thus, the intertemporal elasticity of substitution is as critical in this analysis as the production elasticity of substitution between the two capital types is.

Estimating the Growth Effects of Distortions

A simple model such as the one presented in this paper can be used to estimate the growth effects of severe distortions of resources on actual economies. Although these calculations belong to the "back-of-the-envelope" genre, they can provide a useful first approximation in advance of more detailed, time-consuming studies. Such calculations are useful because they give an idea of what the likely growth benefit of reforms to correct these distortions will be. To illustrate how such calculations can be made, one involving the misallocation of capital stocks in the Soviet Union, as described earlier, is presented here.

Some general remarks about the effects that the distortions induced by central planning have had on output and growth in the Soviet Union are in order. Most analy-

ses of the effect of distortions have been carried out in the context of the traditional Solow model, in which distortions in the allocation of resources only have output effects. Nevertheless, their conclusions can be extended in straightforward manner to the endogenous growth models. The definitive study on the output effect of Soviet central planning is found in Desai (1987). She uses a clever and imaginative method to measure the deviation of Soviet resource allocation from that which would pertain under a market economy. She estimates production functions for a number of sectors for which data on sectoral capital and labor are available. She then calculates the loss of output caused by the failure to equate the marginal rates of substitution of capital and labor across sectors, as would occur under perfect competition. She estimates a loss in output of 4-10 percent across sectors and over time.

One problem with this approach is that it is probably not likely that marginal rates of substitution are equated even in capitalist economies because of departures from perfect competition, government capital and ex-post miscalculations by producers. Thus, the comparison amounts to one between output in the Soviet Union and an unreal situation that may not exist in any other economy. Another approach would be to compare the structure of Soviet resource allocation directly with that in similar market economies, assuming that only the distortions attributable to central planning induce the differences. This assumption, while extreme, still affords a useful first approximation.

A second problem with this analysis is that not all of the misallocation of resources at all levels can be measured. To be precise, it is also necessary that the misallocation of resources between types of capital and types of labor be measured, with each successive level of disaggregation discovering new sources of distortion and output loss. It is like the famous Russian *matryozhka* doll, which successively opens up to yield smaller and smaller facsimiles of the same doll.

This section measures the loss of output and growth attributable solely to the misallocation of capital across alternative types. This distortion may well be relatively minor when compared with the other distortions caused by central planning. Nevertheless, it is analyzed here because the data are readily available.

Addressing the growth effect of distortions in the Soviet Union is complicated by the fact that there are many alternative estimates of Soviet growth. Capital accumulation is also difficult to measure, and again there are several alternative estimates. A crude way to measure the differential growth loss of the Soviet system is to compare the relationship between growth and investment in the Soviet Union with the average for all other economies. It is then possible to calculate how much lower or higher Soviet growth is when compared with the growth that should be expected from Soviet investment rates, if the average pattern for all other economies holds. Table 14-5 shows the difference between Soviet growth and the "expected" growth rate using the alternative estimates. The resulting estimates of the differences in growth range from plus 0.4 percent to minus 2.6 percent. The issue will remain unresolved until a better estimate of Soviet growth is available. The opinion of most experts, however, seems to be swinging toward the lower estimates.

A version of the model that illustrates how the growth effect of the misallocation of capital in the Soviet Union could be calculated indirectly is presented here. It is assumed that the common production function for all countries is given by:

$$(14\text{-}13) \quad Y = A \left(K_1^{\alpha} K_2^{1-\alpha} \right)^{\beta} H^{1-\beta}$$

where H is human capital (i.e., the capital embodied in the labor force) and K_1 and K_2 are two types of physical capital among which there is misallocation. The optimal allocation of capital, assuming that both are formed from a single domestic output and thus have the same user cost, would be given by the following:

$$(14\text{-}14) \quad \frac{K_2}{K_1} = \frac{1-\alpha}{\alpha} \cdot$$

The level of output that results from the optimal allocation of capital would be given by:

$$(14\text{-}15) \quad Y = A \left[\alpha^{\alpha} (1-\alpha)^{1-\alpha} \right]^{\beta} K^{\beta} H^{1-\beta}$$

where K is now all physical capital, or the sum of K_1 and K_2. It is assumed that an optimal allocation of capital

would take place under a market system where private producers are maximizing profits.

However, a suboptimal allocation of capital that deviates by t percent from the optimal allocation is observed:

$$(14\text{-}16) \quad \frac{K_2^s}{K_1^s} = (1+t) \left[\frac{1-\alpha}{\alpha} \right] \cdot$$

It can be calculated that the output (Y_s) given by this suboptimal allocation of capital will be proportional to the optimal level of output as follows:

$$(14\text{-}17) \quad \frac{Y_s}{Y} = \left[\frac{(1+t)^{1-\alpha}}{1+t(1-\alpha)} \right]^{\beta} \cdot$$

Output will always be lower for any deviation t of capital stocks from the optimal allocation.

The growth effect of this deviation from maximum output can be analyzed as follows. In steady state, the growth rate will be given by the common rate of growth of physical and human capital. Thus, the growth rate could be written in terms of the growth of physical capital, where a fixed rate of investment in physical capital, s_k, out of income (presumably determined by the planners) is assumed:

$$(14\text{-}18) \quad g = s_K \frac{Y}{K} - \delta.$$

The decrease in the growth rate associated with the misallocation of capital will be given by:

$$(14\text{-}19) \quad g - g_s = s_k \left[\frac{Y - Y_s}{K} \right] = s_K \left[1 - \frac{Y_s}{Y} \right] \frac{Y}{K}$$

where g_s is the rate of growth with the misallocation of capital. The effect of the misallocation of capital in the form of overinvestment in the production of goods (industry and agriculture) on growth is estimated to be 0.16 percent per year (the effect on output is about 2 percent,

Table 14-5. *Comparison of Actual Soviet Growth with That Expected from Cross-Section Regressions of Gross Domestic Product (GDP) Growth Investment Share of GDP.*
(percent)

	Differential between Soviet growth and expected growth based on investment rate (Ofer) of 29.3 percent	Estimated Soviet GDP growth rate (1960-85) according to source
Official	0.4	5.6
PlanEcon Report	-0.9	4.3
Central Intelligence Agency	-1.8	3.5
Dikhanov[a]	-1.8	3.4
Selyunin and Khanin	-2.6	2.6

a. 1960-89.

Source: Ofer (1987) and (1990), Aslund (1989), Dikhanov (1990) and Vanous (1986).

in line with typical estimates of the deadweight losses attributable to distortions)[13] Lest this level seem small, note that over the six decades of central planning the loss from this distortion alone would amount to 10 percent of output.

A calculation focusing on the misallocation of capital in the form of underinvestment in dwellings (holding other distortions constant) yields a growth effect of 0.29 percent per year, equivalent to a 19 percent loss in output over six decades.[14] These tentative calculations suggest that tracking down the loss in growth attributable to distortionary policies could in the end yield quite a large number.

The Problems of Partial Liberalization

Two applications of the model can give insight into the dangers of a partial correction of the distortions in the highly distorted socialist economies.[15] First, as shown earlier, the relationship between distortions and growth is highly non-linear—at high levels of distortion small reductions in the distortions have almost no effect on growth. A certain minimum level of reform is needed to pass the threshold where there is a significant pay-off to growth. The reason is that it is necessary to breathe life into previously moribund sectors or types of capital before much effect on growth takes place.

A second application of the model is to consider more than one distortion. Here partial liberalization means correcting some types of distortion but not others. It is well-known in the economic literature (under the heading of the analysis of the "second-best") that removing some distortions while allowing others to remain can create a worse situation than leaving all the distortions unchanged.[16] It is not surprising that the model presented in this paper can be extended to show that what is true of one-time effects on income is also true for growth rates.

Here the example of the privatization of a formerly planned socialist economy is used. The model is generalized to have three types of capital, which under central planning were determined by fiat without regard to their relative marginal products. Output is given by:

$$(14\text{-}20) \quad Y = A \; K_1^{1-\alpha_2-\alpha_3} \; K_2^{\alpha_2} \; K_3^{\alpha_3}.$$

It is assumed as before that all types of capital can be formed from a single domestic output. Under a market system, the marginal products of the three types of capital would be equated, since they have the same user cost. The distortions induced by central planning can be defined as the deviations between the marginal products of the capital. There are now two independent deviations to measure, as before, as the exponential wedge between

marginal products:

$$(14\text{-}21) \quad \frac{\partial Y}{\partial K_2} \Big/ \frac{\partial Y}{\partial K_1} = e^{\tau_2}$$

and

$$(14\text{-}22) \quad \frac{\partial Y}{\partial K_3} \Big/ \frac{\partial Y}{\partial K_1} = e^{\tau_3}.$$

The implication is that the ratios of capital stocks with these distortions will be given by:

$$(14\text{-}23) \quad \frac{K_2}{K_1} = \left[\frac{\alpha_2}{1-\alpha_2-\alpha_3} \right] e^{-\tau_2},$$

and

$$(14\text{-}24) \quad \frac{K_3}{K_1} = \left[\frac{\alpha_3}{1-\alpha_2-\alpha_3} \right] e^{-\tau_3}.$$

The total loss of output attributable to the two distortions can be calculated as follows:

$$(14\text{-}25) \quad \tau = 1 - \frac{e^{-\alpha_2\tau_2-\alpha_3\tau_3}}{1-\alpha_2-\alpha_3+\alpha_2 e^{-\tau_2}+\alpha_3 e^{-\tau_3}},$$

and output will be given as a function of total capital K (equal to the sum of the three types) as follows:

$$(14\text{-}26) \quad Y = \Phi (1-\tau) K$$

where Φ is the ratio of output to capital in the absence of any distortion, defined as:

$$(14\text{-}27) \quad \Phi = A (1-\alpha_2-\alpha_3)^{1-\alpha_2-\alpha_3} \alpha_2^{\alpha_2} \alpha_3^{\alpha_3}.$$

The growth rate can be determined by assuming a fixed saving rate out of income s and a fixed depreciation rate k, so that output growth is given by the rate of increase in the capital stocks as follows:

$$(14\text{-}28) \quad g = s\Phi (1-\tau) - \delta.$$

This simple model can be used to simulate the effects of partial liberalization, defined as a reduction of one of the distortion rates with the other left unchanged. A real world example will help to motivate such a partial liberalization. Suppose that the government announces a partial privatization of the economy, such that private firms and households can freely buy and sell capital types 1 and 2 but not type 3, which the state continues to own and determine. The partial privatization is equivalent to eliminating the distortion τ_2 but continuing the distortion τ_3. That is, households will now be able to allocate their resources among the two forms of private capital such that their marginal products are equated in order to use them efficiently. The third type of capital will, however, still be determined by the state, at such a level that τ_3 does not change by assumption.

What will be the effect on growth of such a partial liberalization? It is possible the liberalization will *lower* the rate of growth and *worsen* the distortions.[17] This possibility is greater the higher the share of non-privatized capital is in production and the higher the uncorrected distortion is. To illustrate this point, the derivative of the total distortion τ with respect to the one distortion rate τ_2 can be calculated as follows:

(14-29)

$$\frac{\partial \tau}{\partial \tau_2} = \frac{\alpha_2 (1 - \tau) \left[(1 - \alpha_2)(1 - e^{-\tau_2}) + \alpha_3 (e^{-\tau_3} - 1) \right]}{1 - \alpha_2 - \alpha_3 + \alpha_2 e^{-\tau_2} + \alpha_3 e^{-\tau_3}}$$

This derivative could be negative (the implication being that reducing τ_2 will raise the total distortion τ) if the rate of the other distortion τ_3 is high and if the share of non-privatized capital α_3 is high. An illustration of this possibility is given by a simulation of the model for plausible parameters, shown in figure 14-3.[18] In figure 14-3, the share of non-privatized capital is 45 percent. As can be seen, the relationship between the distortion rate τ_2 and growth, when the other distortion τ_3 is held constant, can be either positive or negative. Beginning at the maximum point A, a reduction of this distortion through partial privatization would worsen the distortions and lower growth by almost 1 percentage point.

The reform does not have to be perfect, however. As long as either the share of non-privatized capital is

small, or the distortion τ_3 is small, the removal of distortion τ_2 will still raise growth. As figure 14-4 shows, if the non-privatized capital is relatively unimportant, with a share of only 5 percent, then the partial liberalization will raise growth.

Another interpretation of equation (14-29) is that it shows the wisdom of reducing the largest distortion where only one can be changed. If an effort is made to reduce the smaller distortion, then the other larger distortion makes a perverse effect more likely. Put another way, the lowest-return activities should not be liberalized while leaving the highest-return activity untouched. This conclusion also has an implication for sequencing. If only one distortion can be corrected at a time, then the larger one should be corrected first. Otherwise there will be a negative supply effect before the second phase of reform.

This model gives quite clear policy counsel—partial liberalization that leaves a large portion of the economy subject to administrative fiat may well worsen growth rather than improve it.[19] However, this possibility is no excuse for not reforming. As noted, perfection is unnecessary: as long as the share of the unliberalized sector or the uncorrected distortion is relatively "small," less than complete liberalization will still lead to increased growth. If a choice must be made between two distortions, the largest one should always be reduced first to avoid perverse effects from the liberalization.

Figure 14-3. *Relation of One Distortion to Growth with Other Distortion Unchanged* (unprivatized sector 45%)

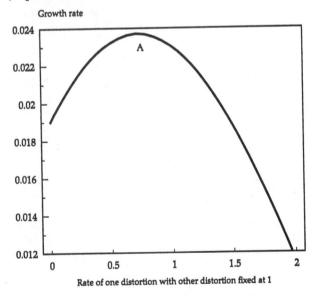

Source: Computer simulation by the author

Figure 14-4. *Relation of One Distortion to Growth with Other Distortion Unchanged* (unprivatized sector 5%)

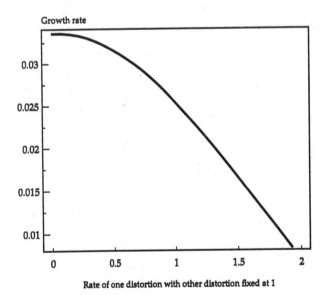

Source: Computer simulation by the author

Conclusions

A stylized model was presented in this paper to show how government-induced distortions can affect the rate of growth in an endogenous growth model, both with and without saving effects. The results suggest that predicting the effect of distortions on growth depends heavily on structural parameters and initial conditions, especially the elasticity of substitution of the different types of capital, the shares of each type of capital being distorted, and the initial distortion. While this model is too simple to give detailed policy advice, it suggests some basic principles. The policy-maker should attempt to identify and move along the steeply-sloped portion of the growth-distortion relationship. In the exogenous saving model, this advice means ignoring the small distortions and making large reductions in the very high levels of initial distortions. If more than one distortion exists and only one can be addressed, the largest distortion should be the one corrected.

While the model is highly stylized, it provides insight into the need for radical reform in socialist economies—for a "Big Bang." Radical reforms will encounter strong political resistance, but so will partial reforms. The question is why carry out a politically costly partial reform that brings little benefit when a radical reform with not much higher political costs can revolutionize the economy?

Notes

1. This paper is a revised version of the one prepared for the Conference on Adjustment and Growth: Lessons for Eastern Europe, held in Pultusk, Poland, October 4-5, 1990. I benefitted substantially from comments by my discussant, J. Rostowski, and the conference participants and from discussions with Robert Barro, Stanley Fischer, Robert King, Ross Levine, Sergio Rebelo and Thomas Wolf on related work. The research assistance of Piyabha Kongsamut and Maria Christina Almero is gratefully acknowledged. The author alone is responsible for any remaining errors. All views expressed are those of the author and not necessarily of the World Bank.

2. More precisely, the standard neoclassical model assumes that the marginal product of each factor goes to zero as that factor increases, with other factors held constant (the Inada condition). Jones and Manuelli (1990) recently explored the implications of relaxing this assumption

3. The growth effects of distortionary policies could be preserved in the Solow model if the focus were on the transition to a steady state. Corden (1971), for example, showed strong growth effects of trade policy in the Solow transition. However, King and Rebelo (1989) have convincingly demonstrated that the Solow transition can explain very little of the long-run growth rate without generating counterfactual implications for the interest rate.

4. An entertaining example of the misallocation of capital under central planning is given by Hewett (1988, p. 175). Because of a shortage of certain critical consumer goods, the Tochmash factory in the USSR in 1987 was ordered to produce flashlights, although it was designed to produce machinery for making socks. This machinery was in short supply at the time, while socks were on the list of critically scarce consumer goods.

5. The Report of the Shatalin Commission appointed by Gorbachev and Yeltsin, as quoted in the *Washington Post*, September 21, 1990.

6. See Chapter 4, Ulrich Thumm, "World Bank Adjustment Lending in Central and Eastern Europe," in this volume.

7. The excessive use of inputs is all the more striking in light of the downward bias attributable to their lower relative prices in socialist economies.

8. Op. cit., Thumm, this volume.

9. This section draws on the model presented in Easterly (1990a).

10. If the income from type 1 capital is what is taxed, then the income tax rate t equivalent to the exponential sales tax τ is $t = 1 - \exp(-\tau)$.

11. This equivalence is noted by Atkinson and Stiglitz (1980, p. 237).

12. The parameter values are $s = .2$, $\alpha = .05$, $\gamma_1 = \gamma_2 = .5$ and $\rho = .5$. Sensitivity testing confirms that the shape of the function is the same for alternative values except for ρ, as noted in the text.

13. The variable T is the lump-sum transfer, ex-post equal to $e^{\tau} I_1$ but treated by the consumer as fixed.

14. The additional parameters for the simulation are sigma = 7 (intertemporal elasticity = .14) and r = .1. The sensitivity of the results to these parameters is discussed below.

15. The calculation is made with data on capital stocks from 1987. It assumes a capital share of 0.4, a capital/output ratio of 4.33 (the OECD average) and a physical investment share of output of 0.33 (the Soviet investment share in 1987 came from Ofer 1990).

16. The cost of this distortion cannot be added to the previous one, as there is some overlap between the two since only pair-wise distortions are being considered.

17. Here partial liberalization means a permanent partial change. In addition, this model does not address the desirable phasing of reforms during the transition.

18. The canonical article is Lipsey and Lancaster (1956).

19. Of course, the privatization will also have favorable effects on the incentives to save and invest, which could well outweigh the possible negative effects of the partial reform.

20. The parameters are $A = 1$, $\alpha_2 = .45$, $\alpha_2 = .45$, $\alpha_3 = .05$ or $.45$, $\tau_2 = 1$ and $s = 0.2$.

21. There is also a political argument against partial reform. It could allow some well-connected private sector operators to capture the rents from the remaining distortions. This enrichment of a few private individuals could provoke a political backlash against privatization in general. This situation may explain the widespread hostility toward the private cooperatives in the Soviet Union.

References

Aslund, Anders. 1989. *Gorbachev's Struggle for Economic Reform.* Ithaca, N.Y.: Cornell University Press.

Atkinson, A. and J. Stiglitz. 1980. *Lectures on Public Economics.* New York: McGraw-Hill.

Barro, Robert J. 1989a. "A Cross-Country Study of Growth, Saving and Government." NBER Working Paper No. 2855. National Bureau of Economic Research. Cambridge, Mass.

————. 1989b. "Economic Growth in a Cross Section of Countries." A paper prepared for the Conference on Human Capital and Growth, State University of New York (SUNY), Buffalo, NY (May 1989).

Barro, Robert J., and Xavier Sala-i-Martin. 1989. "Economic Growth and Convergence Across the United States." National Bureau of Economic Research. Cambridge, Mass.

————. 1990. "Public Finance in Models of Economic Growth." NBER Working Paper No. 3362. National Bureau of Economic Research. Cambridge, Mass.

Corden, M. 1971. "The Effects of Trade on the Rate of Growth." In J. Bhagwati, et al., eds., *Trade, Balance of Payments, and Growth: Papers in Honor of Charles P. Kindleberger.* Amsterdam: North-Holland Publishing Company.

Desai, Padma. 1987. *The Soviet Economy: Problems and Prospects.* Oxford: Basil Blackwell.

Dikhanov, Yuri. 1990. "Real Growth Rates: 1913-1989." *Business in the USSR* (4)(September).

Easterly, William. 1990a. "Endogenous Growth in Developing Countries with Government-Induced Distortions." A paper presentedthe World Bank Conference on Adjustment Lending, September 12-13, 1990.

————. 1990b. "How Does Growth Begin? Models of Endogenous Development." Mimeo. World Bank. Washington, D.C.

Erlich, E. 1987. "Absolute and Relative Economic Development Levels and Their Structure in 1980." Mimeo. Budapest.

Fischer, S., and A. Gelb. 1990. "Issues in Socialist Economy Reform." Mimeo. World Bank. Washington, D.C. September.

Gomulka, Stanislaw. 1986. Growth, *Innovation and Reform in Eastern Europe.* Madison, Wisc.: University of Wisconsin Press.

Hewett, Ed. A. 1988. *Reforming the Soviet Economy.* Washington, D.C.: Brookings Institution.

International Monetary Fund. Various issues. *International Financial Statistics.* Washington, D.C.: IMF.

Jones, Larry, and Rodolfo Manuelli. 1990. "A Convex Model of Equilibrium Growth." *Journal of Political Economy* 98(5):1008-38.

King, Robert, and Sergio Rebelo. 1989. "Transitional Dynamics and Economic Growth in the Neoclassical Model." NBER Working Paper No. 3185. Cambridge, Mass

————. 1990. "Public Policy and Economic Growth: Developing Neoclassical Implications." *Journal of Political Economy* (October).

Lipsey, R.G., and K. Lancaster. 1956. "The General Theory of Second Best." *Review of Economic Studies* 24(1)(October):11-32.

Lucas, R.E. 1988. "On the Mechanics of Economic Development." *Journal of Monetary Economics* 22(1)(July):3-42.

Ofer, Gur. 1987. "Soviet Economic Growth: 1928-1985." *Journal of Economic Literature* XXV (December):1767-1833.

————. 1990. "Macroeconomic Issues of Soviet Reforms." NBER *Macroeconomics Annual* 1990. Cambridge, Mass.

Rebelo, Sergio. 1990. "Long Run Policy Analysis and Long Run Growth." NBER Working Paper 3325. National Bureau of Economic Research . Cambridge, Mass.

Rodri, 1990. "How Should Structural Adjustment Programs Be Designed?: *World Development* 18(7):933-47.

Romer, P.M. 1986. "Increasing Returns and Long-Run Growth." *Journal of Political Economy* 94(5):1002-37.

————. 1987a. "Growth Based on Increasing Returns Due to Specialization." *American Economic Review* 77(2)(May):56-62.

————. 1987b. "Crazy Explanations for the Productivity Slowdown." In S. Fischer, ed., *NBER Macroeconomics Annual.* Cambridge, Mass.: MIT Press.

————. 1988. "Endogenous Technological Change." University of Chicago, Chicago. May.

————. 1989. "What Determines the Rate of Growth and Technological Change?" Policy, Planning and Research (PPR) Working Paper Series, WPS 279 World Bank. Washington, D.C.

Solow, Robert. 1956. "A Contribution to the Theory of Economic Growth." *Quarterly Journal of Economics* 70(February):65-94.

United Nations. Economic Commission for Europe. 1948. *Economic Survey of Europe in 1948.* New York: United Nations.

United States. Central Intelligence Agency. 1989. *Handbook of Economic Statistics.* Central Intelligence Agency. Washington, D.C.:-CIA

Vanous, Jan. 1986. "Developments in Soviet and East European National Income, 1950-85." *Plan Econ Report* II(50-52)(December).

Yugoslavia. Various issues. *Statistical Yearbook of Yugoslavia.*

World Bank. 1990. *World Development Report* 1990. New York: Oxford University Press.

15

Comments on "Distortionary Policies and Growth in Socialist Economies" by William Easterly[1]

Jacek Rostowski

The main comments made here address the applicability of William Easterly's model to centrally administered economies of the Soviet kind in which nearly all allocative decisions related to production and investment are made on the basis of administrative orders. The comments do not apply to economies such as those of Hungary, Poland or Yugoslavia at the present time, in which a very large number of these decisions are made on a market basis and for which Easterly's model is suitable. Moreover, endogenous growth models, which allow distortions in the allocation of resources to affect not only the level of output but also the rate of growth of an economy, are a definite improvement over the traditional Solow-type exogenous growth models, which do not allow for such an outcome.

The weakness of Easterly's model is that it does not allow the growth rate of centrally administered economies to decline over time, as suggested by both theoretical considerations and historical experience. As Ludwig von Mises and Friedrich von Hayek pointed out over 50 years ago, the problem with centrally administered economies is not just that resources are allocated inefficiently, but that the process of allocating them is inefficient. The reason is that in such economies the informational and motivational roles of the price system are not allowed to operate. Because of the all-pervasive principal agent problems, the people directly in charge of productive resources at the level of the factory or shop have little motivation to make the best possible use of them. Since the price system cannot fulfill its informational role, the degree of information managers have about the current and future behavior of suppliers and customers is less than it would be in a market economy. Hayek in particular stresses this aspect of the problem, pointing out that a single price carries in synthetic form an enormous amount of information regarding production possibilities and the preferences and expectations of a vast number of suppliers and consumers of many goods and

services for which supply and demand are interrelated. This information could never be collected, let alone transmitted, to all those concerned directly. Similarily, those making investment decisions (the central planners) are not motivated to allocate resources optimally. Instead, they are likely to be affected by various kinds of ambitions for bureaucratic empire-building. However, even if they were properly motivated, they could not make high quality decisions because they do not have good information on which to base them. Only a price system can provide that information.

Imagine an economy that becomes centrally administered after a peaceful Communist revolution. At time t0 all its resources are optimally allocated (or as optimally allocated as the previous capitalist market economy could have allocated them). From time t1 on, however, two things begin to happen. First, there are changes in the "state of nature" (final consumer demand, the availability of raw materials, technology, international prices, etc.), so that the original allocation of resources becomes less and less optimal. This process is called "optimality drift." Even if planners' responses to this drift result in a better allocation of resources than if there had been no response whatsoever (an assumption that is made for the moment), nevertheless the overall allocation of resources in the economy will be ever more suboptimal on average since, as already said, a centrally administered economy allocates resources in an inferior way to that of a market economy, and a larger and larger proportion of all resources will have been allocated under the centrally administered economy. During this process the degree of distortion in the economy will have grown, i.e., the situation is as if, in Easterly's terms, the number or magnitude of the tax wedges increases. As the degree of distortion grows, the long-run rate of growth of the economy should decline.

The only question is how long the long run is. Clearly, over time so few of the resources in the economy will remain that had been allocated under the market economy that the effect of the optimality drift will have less and less impact on the average optimality of resource allocation in the economy and, therefore, less and less impact on the economy's growth rate, which will settle at some low but positive level. This process may or may not be sufficiently extended over time to account for the observed decline in the growth rates of centrally administered economies over their history. In addition, the high rates of investment that centrally administered economies tend to have may even result in an acceleration of growth in the early years of the system, a situation that further confuses the empirical picture.

It is possible, however, to take a more extreme position than the above one on the efficiency of resource allocation in a centrally administered economy. That more extreme position, which would be consistent with the reasoning of von Mises and Hayek, would claim that a centrally administered economic system *generates no useful information whatsoever regarding* the allocation of resources. That claim does not mean that no useful information exists in the system. Quite a lot of useful information is left over from the previous market system, and this information (although it becomes more and more out of date with the passage of time) can be useful to central planners (the key resource allocators, who are assumed to some extent to be interested in good resource allocation within the economy).

The centrally administered economy, then, has the following history. In the early years central planners have access to a large amount of information inherited from the previous market system, information that is relatively up-to-date. As a result, although the allocation of resources is inferior to that in a market economy, the difference is only one of degree, and if nothing else were happening, the drift scenario described above would take place. However, the critical point (one that is not properly taken into account in the drift scenario) is that under this system the market is not constantly "verifying" the allocation of resources, i.e., the system is not continuously generating new information that allows the optimality of previous allocations of resources to be assessed as a market economy does. As a result, two processes increase the amount of "noise" or "informational entropy" in the system and make it ever harder for planners to make good decisions regarding the allocation of resources. The first is that the information inherited from the market economy becomes ever more out of date with the passage of time. The second is that planners do not know to what extent a new allocation decision is correct, so that as more and more decisions are made under the centrally administered economy, the amount of correct information available to planners declines. Although an omniscient entity could always say at any point just what the degree of distortion in the economy is, and, indeed, identify the ex-post distortions, the planners cannot do so. They do not know to what extent they have misallocated any given resources in the past. Therefore they have to assume that all resources are well-allocated. However, since that assumption is mistaken, it increases the likelihood of present errors. The greater the amount of resources is in the economy that have been allocated under the centrally administered economy, the greater the degree of error involved in this Panglossian assumption. As a result, the quality of resource allocation by planners must decline continuously. To illustrate what is meant, consider the following sketch of a model, assuming an economy subject to exogenous stochastic shocks. Let

$X^t ij$ = actual allocation of resource i to activity j at time t.

$\hat{X}^t ij$ = optimal allocation of resource i to activity j at time t.

$$\bar{X}^t ij = \left| \hat{X}^t ij - X^t ij \right| / X^t ij$$

$$\bar{X}^t ij = at + b \sum_{ij} \bar{X}^{t-1} ij + u^t \text{ where } a>0, b>0 \text{ and } u \text{ is}$$

randomly distributed.

Thus the passage of time (t) causes a deterioration in resource allocation because of the declining relevance of the information inherited from the previous market-based system. The direct impact of this effect is represented by the coefficient b, whereby the aggregate value of past errors in the allocation of resources $\left[\sum_{ij} \bar{X}^{t-1} ij \right]$

increases the error in the allocation of any particular resource in the present, because past errors are noise that reduces the amount of correct information available to planners. Thus, in a centrally administered economy errors accumulate, $\sum_{ij} \bar{X}^t ij$ and grow with time, whereas in a market economy new errors in the allocation of particular resources by particular actors are offset by improvements in the allocation of the same resources by other actors or in the allocation of other resources. Thus, in a market economy

$$\bar{X}^t ij - c \bar{X}^{t-1} ij + u^t \text{ where } c<0$$
or even
$$\bar{X}^t ij = c \left[\bar{X}^{t-1} ij \right]^2 + u^t \text{ where } c<0,$$

where u^t is a randomly distributed variable representing new errors, which takes positive values. The result is that the total expected value of the misallocation of all resources will remain positive but constant, so that:

$$E\left[\sum_{ij}\overline{X}_{ij}^{t}\right] = d \quad \text{where } d>0.$$

What is more, the increase in "informational noise" in the centrally administered economy has no natural upper bound, so that the lower bound for the amount of correct information in the system is zero. This is because not all useful information is lost when particular resources previously allocated under the market system are reallocated under the centrally administered economy. Given that initially they are allocated in a system in which a lot of correct information exists (inherited from the market economy), they are likely to be allocated in such a way that the amount of information embodied in their allocation does not decline to zero immediately. However, each subsequent reallocation of those resources is likely to reduce the amount of useful information embodied in their allocation. Thus the process of "information noise" in the economy can go on forever.

Since the lower bound for the amount of useful information in the system is zero, the implication is that, in the long run, the output of a centrally administered economy is zero (also, resources are totally randomly allocated). This implies that not only would growth rates decline during the life of the centrally administered economy, but that they would ultimately become negative and would remain negative until output reached zero. Historically one is unlikely to observe such a phenomenon, since such a system would become politically unacceptable to both the elites and the population long before zero output was reached. It is worth noting, however, that the history of the USSR since 1975 is not at variance with such a model.

Notes

1. I would like to thank Stanislaw Wellisz for his very useful comments and encouragement.

Part VI

Adjustment and Reforms: Financial Market, Foreign Trade, Fiscal Sector

16

Financial Aspects of Socialist Economies: From Inflation to Reform[1]

Guillermo A. Calvo

This paper focuses on some of the financial issues involved in the market-oriented economic transformations in socialist countries. The central theme is the tension between "bad" credit policy—that which gives rise to inflationary spirals—and "good" credit policy—that which prevents unnecessary credit crunches and contributes to the efficient allocation of resources.

The next section explores the implications of bad credit by means of a simple model in which credit is used to accumulate inventories (which are essentially wasteful). The model is capable of depicting a situation in which inflation and inventories are excessive—a depiction that appears to be in line with the data emerging from several pro-reform socialist countries. This type of inflation is somewhat different from that associated with fiscal deficits. To drive this distinction home, the credit/inventories-driven process is called a "money machine."

The third section studies the implications of trying to deactivate the money machine by (1) increasing the interest rate on bank credit, (2) setting domestic credit targets and (3) removing the subsidies for inventory goods. The first two measures are shown to be potentially successful, while the last one emerges as likely to fail and even to be counterproductive.

The fourth section examines the role of good credit. The main theme is that the market is likely to provide good credit at optimal levels only under rather stringent conditions. For example, it is shown that the market could fail to supply efficient levels of credit if the domestic credit markets are segmented or if there are problems with the credibility of policy.

Financial policy is the subject of the fifth section. The focus is on policies that help the market achieve efficient solutions. One message is that monetary policy should be the main instrument used to accommodate the initial increases in prices after price decontrol. The section discusses why that accommodation should not be thought as a reactivation of the old money machine. The role and nature of monetary and credit policy in the medium term are also discussed briefly. The need for bank supervision and the dangers of playing with short-term interest rates to postpone a crisis are covered.

Some final remarks are presented in the last section.

Bad Credit: A Money Machine

The conventional fiscal deficit as such does not play a central role in inflation in the socialist countries. Instead, credit is the pivotal factor. This section presents an equilibrium model of credit-driven inflation. To simplify, the possibility of transitory disequilibria is omitted (although they may give rise to relevant phenomena in pre-reform socialist countries, such as queues).[2]

Assume that

$$(16\text{-}1) \quad \dot{M} = P_k z,$$

where M, z and P_k denote the money supply, new inventories and nominal price of the stock, k, of inventories, respectively. Equation (16-1) says that the central bank extends credit to firms to purchase (newly produced) inventories[3] and that the supply of money expands only because of that financial operation. For the time being, credit is assumed to be granted at zero interest.[4] Equation (16-1) depicts a typical money machine in pre-reform socialist countries.

There are two types of industries: producers of inventory; and producers for consumption. The outputs of new inventories and of consumption goods, denoted by $\bar{z}$ and $\bar{y}$, respectively, are assumed to be constant over time. The consumption sector is assumed to utilize $\alpha \bar{y}$ units of inventories per unit of time $(\alpha > 0)$.[5] Therefore, at full capacity utilization, the accumulation of inventories, $\dot{k}$, is given by

$$(16\text{-}2) \quad \dot{k} = \bar{z} - a\bar{y} - \delta k ,$$

where δ (> 0) stands for the constant rate of depreciation of the inventories.

At each point in time there is a "collateral" constraint whereby total bank credit cannot exceed the value of the inventories. Formally,

(16-3) $M \le P_k k$,

or, defining p as equal to P_k/P, where P is the price of consumption goods,

(16-4) $m \le pk$,

where m is the real monetary balances in terms of consumption goods. This assumption is not indispensable for a relevant money machine model but is included in the present one to show that collateral constraints are not sufficient to stop a money machine.

It is assumed that consumers are the final holders of money and that their demand for real monetary balances (in terms of consumption) is interest- and income-inelastic, a condition that implies that m is constant over time. In fact, since it is assumed that the central bank has no domestic credit target and, as will be argued, firms have incentives to borrow as much as possible, the collateral constraint will always be binding, i.e., $m = pk$. Therefore, the price of inventories in terms of consumption, p, satisfies $p = m/k$; p is the relative price that will ensure that there is no excess demand for credit (given the collateral constraint). Notice that, under these conditions, p declines as the stock of inventories expands (an anticipated result based on standard demand-supply considerations), while p increases as the demand for money goes up.

From equation (16-1) and the inelasticity assumptions about m,

(16-5) $p\bar{z} = \pi m$,

where π is the rate of inflation for consumption goods. Hence, from equations (16-1) and (16-5), and given that the collateral constraint (equation 16-3) is binding,

(16-6) $\pi = \dot{M}/M = \bar{z}/k$.

Equality between the rate of inflation, π, and the rate of expansion of the money supply, $\dot{M}/M$, is perfectly standard in no-real-growth models such as the present one and needs no further discussion. However, the rightmost equality between the rate of expansion of the money supply, $\dot{M}/M$, and the ratio of the flow of new inventories, $\bar{z}$, to the stock of inventories reflects the workings of the money machine. To verify it, notice that since the collateral constraint (equation 16-3) is binding, then $M = P_k k$ (i.e., the money supply equals the nominal value of the stock of inventories); thus, $\dot{M}/M = \bar{z}/k$, as stated in expression (16-6), can be obtained immediately from the latter equation and the money machine equation (16-1). In other words, the flow of new inventories governs the flow of new money, while the stock of money is directly related to the stock of inventories.[6]

In particular, from equations (16-2) and (16-6), at steady state where $\dot{k} = 0$,

(16-7) $\pi = \delta / (1 - (\alpha\bar{y}) / \bar{z})$.

Consequently, if the production of new inventories is greater than what is necessary to satisfy current production needs (i.e., if $\alpha\bar{y} < \bar{z}$), then the equilibrium rate of inflation, π, is positive. Moreover, given that credit was assumed to be granted at zero interest, it follows that, at steady state, the real interest rate from holding inventories, i.e., $\delta - \pi$, is negative. By continuity, if the system starts near its steady state, the real interest rate from holding inventories will be negative (as asserted before).[7]

It is assumed that a firm will accept credit from the central bank to the extent that the credit operation and associated accumulation of inventories do not decrease the firm's net worth. This practice is a weak form of the profit-maximization assumption. In the present context, it implies that firms will demand bank credit if the real interest rate from holding inventories is not positive. Therefore, from previous remarks, firms would have an incentive to borrow from the central bank, a condition that ensures that the rate of inflation (equation 16-7) is consistent with a situation in which all agents operate according to their postulated behavioral rules.[8]

Notice that this money machine is not captured by conventional budget-deficit accounting. Moreover, no firm receives "excessive" credit, since each firm can fully repay its loans by liquidating its stock of inventories.

Deactivating the Money Machine

Some policies aimed at deactivating the money machine (equation 16-1) are examined next. In particular, the effects of (1) increasing the interest rate on bank credit, (2) setting a domestic credit target and (3) removing the subsidies for inventory goods are studied.

Interest Rate

Let interest on bank credit be denoted by i_m (In the earlier analysis it was assumed that $i_m = 0$.) Suppose that the interest on bank loans cannot be capitalized. Hence, equation (16-1) becomes

(16-8) $\quad \dot{M} = P_k z - i_m M.$

It can easily be shown that equation (16-7) becomes

(16-9) $\quad \pi + i_m = \delta/(1 - \alpha \bar{y}/ \bar{z}).$

Thus, inflation declines, point for point, as i_m is increased. The direction of the effect of i_m on inflation is straightforward. According to the money machine equation (16-8), interest payments, $i_m M$, contribute to monetary absorption. Hence, the larger the interest on bank loans, i_m, is, the lower the expansion of the money supply will be and the lower the rate of inflation will be.

Since this model holds only for situations in which the real interest rate on inventory holdings is not positive—otherwise the demand for bank credit for inventory holding would be nil—the maximum level of i_m compatible with this solution of the model is the one that yields $i_m = \pi - \delta$. Hence, given equation (16-9) and with $\pi - \delta = i_m$, the minimum rate of inflation that can be generated by raising the rate of interest on bank loans (while keeping the real inventory rate of interest negative or zero)—a rate that is denoted by π_{min}—satisfies

(16-10) $\quad \pi_{min} = \delta \dfrac{1 - \alpha \bar{y}/\bar{z}2}{1 - \alpha \bar{y}/\bar{z}} > \delta.$

Domestic Credit Target

Now consider the case in which i_m is set high enough to make the accumulation of inventory unattractive to firms. Since the collateral would be nil, there would be no stock of credit outstanding, and, under the above extreme assumptions, money would disappear from the system. However, it is possible to extend the model to the case in which the money stock has an exogenous, central-bank determined, component. In this case the system would be fully anchored by the monetary target. Notice that *for that kind of regime to hold, it is necessary only to generate slightly positive real interest rates for inventory.* Based on the above reasoning, as the economy enters such a domestic credit-target regime, the rate of inflation is capable of taking a sudden dive toward the level compatible with a (supposedly much lower) nominal target.

It should be noted, however, that success in stopping inflation is accompanied by a sharp fall in the demand for inventories. This situation has several implications. If the inventories are internationally tradable, (1) such a drop in demand will bring about a sharp trade surplus. However, to the extent inventories are not fully tradable,

(2) their price will take a nose-dive, and (3) production for inventory will collapse.

Importantly, the fall in the price of inventories may put consumption firms in a state of virtual bankruptcy. These firms satisfied the collateral constraint under the old set of prices but not under the new one. Note that this type of bankruptcy does not obey any clear efficiency principle, and the bankruptcies are more likely to occur the higher the interest rates on bank loans are.

There is, however, a brighter side to the collapse of production for inventory. The economy had accumulated excessive inventories. Therefore, unless those firms could be fully oriented toward foreign markets, there is no need for their output to be positive in the short run.

On the other hand, when inventories reach their optimal long-run levels, their production will have to resume to maintain optimal levels and take account of growth effects. This point is worth keeping in mind because momentary stoppage of production should not necessarily mean scrapping those industries—a phenomenon that is likely to happen if there is poor access to long-term credit markets or privatization is slow to materialize. This situation suggests that inventory-type industries should perhaps be high on the list of privatizations. Moreover, the possibly sharp contractionary effect of the anti-inflationary policy underscores the relevance of establishing safety nets for those previously employed in inventory-type industries.

In a more realistic model, a large number of firms will produce goods that end up in the inventory of some other firm(s). Therefore, the rise in bank interest rates may lead to a generalized temporary loss in output. This outcome is, in principle, welcome. However, in a realistic set-up, firms need credit for reasons other than just the accumulation of inventory. Thus, the sudden fall in inventory prices may cut their access to the credit market (e.g., because they did not comply with the collateral constraint)—a situation that would give rise to a typical credit crunch.[9]

The Price of Inventories

Recall that the model presented in the second section is not capable of determining nominal prices. Thus, if the authorities set P_k at a higher level, although all nominal magnitudes will take an equiproportional upward jump, the equilibrium rate of inflation (under the assumptions of the second section) will remain the same. Hence, an upward revision of the price of inventories is ineffective as an anti-inflationary device.

Suppose, instead, that the central planner exogenously determines the relative price of inventories in terms of consumption goods. Let this exogenous relative price be denoted by $\bar{p}$, and assume that interest on bank credit is nil (as in the second section). With expression (16-4), it can easily be verified that if $\bar{p}$ is larger than its equilibrium value in the model presented in the second section, then the collateral constraint is never binding, and firms will be credit-rationed (a realistic feature of pre-reform socialist economies). Hence, according to equation (16-5), if the monetary authority is capable of insuring that firms use credit only to buy *new* inventory goods (as specified in equation 16-1), the rate of inflation is given by

(16-11) $\pi = \bar{p}\bar{z}/m.$

Note that the rate of inflation given by equation (16-11) is larger than the value given by the right-hand-side expression in equation (16-7). The reason is that by increasing the price of inventories, the credit needed to finance the production of inventories becomes larger, a phenomenon that results in a larger expansion of the money supply and thus in higher inflation.[10]

This scenario provides an interesting example of misguided policy. In this economy inflation is partly fueled by an over-accumulation of inventories. However, if the authorities attack the problem by increasing the relative price of inventories, more inflation will follow, *even when the monetary authority simultaneously resorts to credit rationing*. The basic reason is, once again, that the higher relative price of inventories gives rise to a higher rate of growth of the money supply.

Good Credit

Bad credit gives rise to inflation. This scenario is, of course, not the only form of, or role for, credit. The monetary authority could, for example, expand the supply of money at an exogenous rate and let the interest rate be determined "by the market." In such a case, bank credit is determined by the money multiplier, and in principle low inflation can coexist with bank credit. A difficulty with this kind of money supply rule policy is that the resulting supply of money could be "too small" relative to prices, and output could suffer. If prices are perfectly flexible, this nuisance may turn out to be minor. However, if wages are downward inflexible, or if the exchange rate is fixed (as in some post-reform socialist countries), then a relatively small real supply of money can give rise to a credit crunch and consequent loss in output.

Too little credit is therefore a possibility. This eventuality is, of course, never true in the stylized model in the second section because credit is assumed to play no productive role. In practice, however, credit appears to be essential for the operation of both capitalist and socialist societies. For example, inter-firm credit has blossomed in countries such as Poland and Hungary, and trade credit appears to be indispensable for modern international trade.

How can bad and good credit be differentiated? This question is perhaps one of the central issues facing the monetary authorities in the newly market-oriented socialist economies. The trade-off is clear. (1) Although tight central bank credit has a good chance of stopping the inflationary spiral, in the process credit could turn out to be too small, and a serious (and inefficient) fall in output could follow. On the other hand, (2) while an accommodative credit policy results in full employment, inflation could be driven to levels that are unacceptably high.

The Best of Both Worlds?

In some scenarios the above-mentioned trade-off is non-existent. Such is the case, for example, in a regime of fixed exchange rates with free trade and perfect international mobility of capital. The latter implies that the domestic interest rate equals that of the international markets. Thus, from the point of view of firms, credit is granted as in the pre-reform regime. There exists a given interest rate at which credit is liberally granted if solvency conditions are satisfied (e.g., the type of collateral condition assumed in the second section). The main difference with the model of that section, however, is that domestic prices are tightly linked to their international counterparts. Therefore, the rate of inflation mimics the international one, the implication being equality between domestic and international real interest rates. Moreover, since the latter are normally not negative, this regime will exhibit efficient stocks of inventories.[11]

This regime requires a relatively efficient financial system. Suppose, for example, that households have perfect access to the international capital markets[12] but firms depend only on domestic financing. If the domestic financial system is efficient, the household sector can easily accommodate the greater demand for credit by firms. This process works as follows. The increased demand for credit tends to raise domestic interest rates above international levels, a situation that makes it attractive for households to exchange foreign for domestic currency and deposit the proceeds in some domestic financial intermediary. The flow of these funds will continue until domestic and international interest rates are equalized. In turn, the funds are funnelled to the firms sector in the form of new credit.[13] However, if the financial system is not well-developed—as seems the case in most socialist economies—international funds may be too slow to come or potential lenders could call for much higher domestic interest rates. Thus, a credit crunch could be hard to avoid.

Imperfect Financial Markets

The above discussion illustrates how easy it could be for an economy to fall into credit crunch difficulties. This subsection discusses other reasons for the failure of the credit market.

Consider the realistic case where, in the pre-reform period, no firm is allowed to go bankrupt. For example, if a firm develops financial troubles, the central bank steps in as the lender of last resort. This situation, it is believed here, is one important reason that inter-firm credit is such a common and relevant feature of the financial regimes of pre-reform socialist economies. The central bank offers full insurance, the implication being that firms can lend to one another with no risk of default.[14] Imagine now that the authorities announce that the central bank will stay away from the credit insurance business and that that policy announcement has some credibility. How will the "market" react?

Operation under a full insurance system implies, most likely, that lenders have had little incentive to collect information about borrowers. Thus, the market starts off with very little information. Consequently, the removal of a lender of last resort has implications that go beyond monetary policy—it has microeconomic informational aspects as well. Thus, in the short run a reduction in official credit to firms is unlikely to be matched by an expansion of *private* credit (including, in particular, inter-firm credit). Eventually, private credit may emerge full bloom, but there is likely to be a period of credit shortage during the transition that is not trivial. The duration of this transition is likely to depend on the pace, breadth and depth of the financial reform.

Another source of imperfection in the credit market is less-than-complete credibility of policy. There are many reasons why a policy announcement is not fully credible (see Calvo 1989), not the least of which is that the politician who makes the policy announcement is likely to have a finite—not to say short—political life, particularly in cases involving radical economic reform. Suppose, for instance, that the policy is expected to be changed if it leads to a credit squeeze (and resulting loss in output) for a period longer than a certain critical one. Assume, in addition, that if there is a change in the policy regime, potential lenders expect that the government will go back to the old ways of paying negative real rates of return on bank savings (through, for example, partial confiscation of deposits). There are at least two possible equilibrium outcomes. In the "good" outcome, lenders are confident of the success of the present policy. In the "bad" one, lenders expect that a credit crunch will develop and that the next government will confiscate part of their bank savings. The good outcome is an equilibrium, because if everybody believes the policy will be continued, funds will flow into the banking system at the slightest sign of a differential between domestic and international interest rates. Hence, a credit squeeze will never happen. On the other hand, the bad outcome is also an equilibrium, because if lenders fear the development of a credit crunch, they will be afraid to put their savings into bank accounts. Therefore, if the stabilization program exhibits credit crunch conditions at the beginning, no funds will be forthcoming, and the credit crunch will actually take place. Notice that the bad outcome is an equilibrium independent of whether or not the lenders are right in expecting that a long enough credit crunch will give rise to a policy change.

Financial Policy

The central message of the previous discussion is that while a passive credit policy may give rise to inflation, the stoppage of official credit flows may be associated with output losses that are not called for by efficiency-type considerations. A credit crunch could develop for reasons ranging from the lack of adequate financial intermediaries to just the expectation on the part of potential lenders that a credit crunch could occur.

Early Stages of Reform

Typically, a market-oriented reform in the socialist economies starts with a radical program of price liberalization. The rationale is that free prices are indispensable for efficient resource allocation.

In this respect, the recent Polish stabilization plan suggests some useful lessons. A salient characteristic of the Polish experiment is that real credit to socialized firms (in terms of the cost of production) appears to have fallen by more than 30 percent. This decline suggests that a credit crunch could partly account for the estimated 20-30 percent drop in the output of the socialized sector. The case of Poland is very illuminating, because households hold a substantial amount of savings in dollar-denominated assets and, as shown by Calvo and Coricelli (1990), few of the assets for which there are official records (i.e., dollar-denominated bank deposits) have been converted into zloty accounts. This case resembles the one discussed in the third section, where a credit crunch develops even when the economy as a whole has access to international funds.

The Polish experiment supports to some degree the view that price reforms in socialist economies may have to be accompanied by an aggressive expansion of credit at the beginning of the program—particularly when the price reform leads to an initial drastic increase in the price of some key factors of production. A contrary view, however, is that such a credit expansion might not deactivate the money machine because that type of credit responds to price rises and thus is like the bad credit that originally set the money machine in motion.

A closer look at this issue reveals that the two points of view are not mutually contradictory. In fact, both offer relevant insights. Care is necessary when distinguishing between stocks and flows. High inflation is fueled by large *flows* of money into the system, not by a possibly large infusion of money at the time the prices of raw materials go up (i.e., by a *stock* change in the money supply at the beginning of the program). The latter avoids the credit crunch and cannot per se generate inflation. Hence, the first view, which says that an initial credit/money expansion may be beneficial, is correct, but at the same time the second view is also right in warning against continuing this money accommodation policy in the future. Indeed, the main message of the second point of view is that the authorities should make absolutely clear that the initial credit accommodation is a one-time event. Firms and individuals should not expect credit/money accommodation to be repeated in the future, unless the system is subject to a new exogenous price-level shock (or any other exogenous shock against which monetary accommodation is ex ante agreed, and clearly announced, to be desirable).

A lesson of the Polish stabilization experiment is that a reform that entails a large increase in the prices of some key raw materials should perhaps be accompanied by a comparable, one-time increase in central bank credit to firms. Furthermore, the central bank could help tidy up the initial conditions by substituting central bank credit for inter-firm credit. Central bank credit may be liberally granted and can even take the form of a transfer to the firms sector. The higher supply of money so generated may not fuel further inflation to the extent that the firms keep a higher stock of monetary balances to carry out their ordinary transactions.

A difficulty with the proposed solution to the initial credit crunch problem is that before the reform takes place there is little or no information about the post-reform demand for credit. Hence, errors are inevitable. What is the best policy response if errors are detected? Following are some tentative thoughts.

First, if the initial expansion of credit proves excessive, prices will overshoot, or greater than programmed reserves will be lost (if the monetary authority intervenes in the foreign exchange market). In this instance, a good case can be made for biting the bullet and letting prices and the exchange rate rise without a substantial loss of reserves. Attempts to prevent the loss in reserves by, for example, increasing the interest rates on bank deposits are likely to backfire (Calvo 1990a).

Consider now the case in which credit is insufficient to sustain full employment. The view postulated here is that belated attempts to provide more central bank credit could be dangerous because they may be taken as a signal that the monetary authorities have resorted to reactivating the old money machine. Thus, prices may start to rise as in the pre-reform regime, a situation that in turn will generate another credit crunch unless the authorities come back later with even greater official credit, and so on. One alternative that deserves attention is to lower the costs of production. This measure could be implemented by reinstating some input subsidies or, in some cases, by appreciating the domestic currency. Since this type of policy goes to the heart of the credit crunch policy, it is likely to boost production. Furthermore, if the country has been facing a sizable loss in output, the stimulus to output could go a long way toward alleviating the government's budget deficit that this policy may entail.

The Medium Term: Sequencing and Interest-rate Policy

The Latin American experience strongly suggests leaving financial liberalization to the later stages of a reform program. In this respect, the central observation is that early financial liberalization may magnify the distortions. These distortions may be the result of: (1) incomplete dismantling of the commodity taxes or subsidies; (2) market imperfections, such as the presence of monopolistic firms—a relevant consideration for reforming socialist economies; or, perhaps more subtle but not less relevant, (3) government policy announcements that lack total credibility with the private sector. The following remarks focus on the credibility-related distortions, since they are likely to be relatively less familiar to the reader.

Credibility distortions were mentioned earlier in connection with the credit crunch difficulties, although in those instances a free financial system may play a welfare-enhancing role. There are, however, cases in which the interaction between the lack of credibility and the free financial markets is counterproductive. Suppose there is incomplete credibility about the success of the anti-inflationary program and that, as a consequence, the rate of devaluation expected by the private sector is larger than the one contemplated in the program. The latter implies that the nominal rates of interest on deposits and loans will tend to be higher than if there were full credibility. At the same time, however, the domestic prices of tradable goods will tend to be governed by the *actual* exchange rate, the implication being that their rate of inflation may follow closely the *actual* rate of devaluation rather than the expected one. Since, as argued above, the nominal interest rate reflects the *expected* rate of devaluation (which, by assumption, is higher than the *actual* rate), it follows that the (ex-post) real interest rate on tradable goods will tend to be higher than if the stabilization program was fully credible. How high the ex-post real interest rate is will depend on the gap between expected and actual devaluation, i.e., the credibility gap. This gap brings about unplanned redistributions of wealth from borrowers to savers. If firms are net borrowers, the credibility gap implies a redistribution from firms to households. As the previous discussion suggests, this redistribution is particularly harmful to firms producing tradable goods, some of which may be driven into bankruptcy that is *unrelated to any efficiency consideration*.[15]

This example shows that financial intermediation could have harmful effects on the economy when the policies do not enjoy full credibility, even though other better known distortions have been eliminated. This situation is very unfortunate because reforming socialists economies—given the novelty and extreme nature of their reforms—are likely to have serious credibility problems, at the same time that, as argued above, they could greatly benefit from access to credit to relieve credit crunches.

Reforming socialist economies are notorious for their lack of financial services. Thus, despite the above-mentioned credibility complications, it is posited here that financial institutions should be developed. However, the credibility issue suggests that the financial policy should be aimed at preventing the magnification of distortions. This objective may be aided by implementing *conservative* banking and financial policies.

In that respect, it seems advisable to provide incentives for longer run financial deposits and loans, since long-term assets may help reduce the probability of financial crises (see Calvo 1990b). To avoid the syndrome of high interest rates, loans and deposits could be indexed to the "market" exchange rate.[16] The indexation could be phased out later as credibility is established. Finally, the financial institutions have to be closely supervised. There is a worldwide tendency for the fisc (including the central bank) to bail financial institutions out when they face so-called systemic problems. This practice tends to remove the incentives for financial institutions to react to perceived global financial problems. In addition, the "free insurance policy" implicitly granted by the fisc may actually embolden financial institutions to take even larger risks when a systemic disarray looms. Therefore, the probability and depth of systemic financial crises may be greatly enhanced unless the financial institutions are well-supervised.

Finally, it is advised that special caution be taken about paying interest on bank reserves. Several Latin American countries have fallen into this trap. Remunerated bank reserves allow banks to pay interest on deposits, even if the deposits are never lent. This practice provides the central bank with a new instrument with which to stave off currency runs or to counteract less dramatic portfolio shifts that would result in higher black market premia. Furthermore, a rise in deposit interest rates induces an increase in the demand for central bank liabilities that, at least for some time, may help reduce the fiscal deficit. Unfortunately, however, the fiscal deficit actually gets worse, or public debt rises further, as the interest on reserves has to be paid. Moreover, quelling a crisis by means of this interest rate instrument is likely to result in even more critical difficulties in the future (see Calvo 1990b).

Final Remarks

Credit is central to the functioning of market economies. It is the vehicle by which the surplus of one agent can be utilized for production or for consumption by other agents in the economy. It is essential to the efficient allocation of resources. However, by their very nature, credit contracts entail one party transferring resources to the other—and receiving in exchange only a promise of future transfers in the opposite direction. Thus, credit markets require trust and, above all, well-defined property rights.

By all accounts, the credit markets in reforming socialist economies are still heavily dependent on the central bank. Even in cases in which inter-firm credit has mushroomed, the central bank has insured much of those loans by operating as a lender of last resort. Thus, in those countries the trustworthiness and validity of property rights necessary for the functioning of credit markets have still to be tested. In the short run, enterprises in reforming socialist countries will find themselves still heavily dependent on central bank credit. In fact, such a dependence could be more pronounced during the early stages of the reform. The reason is that the withdrawal of the central bank as lender of last resort may substantially increase the riskiness of the inter-firm loan market.

Consequently, the first stages of a market-oriented reform program are likely to be characterized by a credit shortage. At first sight, this condition may appear paradoxical because the typical complaint of many of these economies—particularly those that suffer from high inflation—is that credit is excessive. These two opposing roles of credit, and their mutual tension, provided the background to the present paper.

This paper looked at a simple example of what was labeled bad credit. Such credit, which is granted by the central bank, gives rise to both inflation and the misallocation of resources. In the example presented here, the misallocation took the form of an overaccumulation of inventories. However, as pointed out at the outset of this section and as was discussed in the paper, there is also good credit. It may not, however, materialize in the short run to the extent necessary for a successful program of reform.

In particular, the paper emphasized the importance of working capital—the relevance of ensuring that there is enough liquidity in the hands of enterprises to conduct their regular operations. In this regard, it was argued that the removal of input subsidies could generate a serious liquidity crunch that—in view of the characteristic imperfections in the credit market in the first stages of a reform program—could not be offset by the private sector. As a result, the productive sector could be choked off just because there are not enough financial instruments to carry out the productive transfer of resources. In addition, this paper showed that during the first stages of a market-oriented reform, the credit market could be further weakened by the sometimes enormous reallocation of resources required by efficiency. This possibility was illustrated by the sharp fall in demand for inventories during the early stages of the plan when the earlier money machine induced an overaccumulation of inventories.

The major general point of this paper is that financial markets are unlikely to spring to life any time soon after the initiation of market-oriented reform and to contribute to a much better allocation of resources. Further, the paper suggests that if monetary/credit policy relies too heavily on a credit crunch, while inflation may be slowed, it will be at the cost of equally, if not more, disturbing economic problems, such as deep and protracted recession.

Notes

1. I am grateful to Fabrizio Coricelli for his useful comments. The views expressed in the paper do not necessarily represent those of the International Monetary Fund.

2. Although important to a full description of the inflationary process in socialist economies, a focus on rationing equilibria may lead to a failure to see some of the fundamental *monetary* forces behind inflation.

3. In practice, bank credit for purchasing "old" inventories is also a likely possibility. Allowing for that type of credit would give rise to an even more powerful money machine than the one discussed in this section. However, such an extension of the model is not discussed here because it is not pertinent to the central points.

4. Incentives for firms to "demand" this type of credit are dealt with later in this section.

5. To simplify the exposition, the economy is assumed to be closed to international trade. However, in a later discussion this assumption is relaxed.

6. The price of inventories, P_k, is involved in these relationships. However, it washes out completely because it enters multiplicatively in both relationships.

7. Equation (16-7) implies that the rate of inflation *declines* as the flow of inventories, $\hat{z}$, increases. This result is somewhat counterintuitive because the accumulation of inventories is the main factor behind the money machine. However, as the discussion around equation (16-6) shows, although inflation is an increasing function of the *flow* of money, it is also inversely related to the *stock*. For this reason, in the present model, π is equal to $\hat{z}/k$, and not just to z. From equation (16-2), at steady state (i.e., $\dot{k} = 0$), $k/\hat{z} = (1 - \alpha \hat{y}/\hat{z})/\delta$. Hence, at steady state the ratio $\hat{z}/k$ *declines* as the flow of inventories, $\hat{z}$, increases, a phenomenon that explains the above (possibly) counterintuitive result. It will be shown below, however, that the association between inflation and the flow of inventories would be positive if the central planner fixed the relative price of inventories with respect to consumption, p.

8. Notice that absolute prices, P and P_k, are not determined by the model. This situation is a well-known feature of interest rate-based monetary policy (see Sargent and Wallace 1975 and Calvo 1983). In the present context an easy remedy is to assume, realistically, that the central planner chooses, for example, the initial nominal price of consumption (i.e., the nominal price of consumption at some initial time 0, say). Afterwards the price of consumption is determined by the inflation equation (16-7), while that of inventories is given by equation (16-5).

9. This issue will be explored later.

10. Under the present assumption, the conventional result in socialist economies—That inflation is an increasing function of the flow of inventories—is recovered.

11. Furthermore, bankruptcy for not satisfying the credit constraint (equation 16-4) would be avoided if the inventories were internationally tradable.

12. This case is not as extreme as it sounds: in several socialist economies households have a sizable share of their portfolios in the form of foreign exchange. Thus, borrowing from the international markets can be closely emulated by, for instance, households lending to firms, with the latter using the proceeds to buy capital goods abroad. The country as a whole lowers its foreign financial assets, a condition that is equivalent to the country increasing its international financial liabilities (i.e., international borrowing).

13. See Frenkel and Razin (1987) for a fuller exposition of this case.

14. Pre-reform firms have few investment opportunities aside from holding inventories. Hence, risk-free inter-firm loans may be attractive even though the inflation and interest rate controls could result in negative real interest rates.

15. The cases of Argentina and Chile during the late 1970s and early 1980s provide clear-cut illustrations of this type of impasse. See, for example, Calvo (1986) and Edwards (1985).

16. The same applies to government debt obligations (see Calvo 1990a and b).

References

Calvo, Guillermo A. 1983. "Staggered Prices in a Utility-Maximizing Framework." *Journal of Monetary Economics* 12:383-98.

————. 1986. "Fractured Liberalism: Argentina under Mart!nez de Hoz." *Economic Development and Cultural Change* (April):511-33.

————. 1989. "Incredible Reforms." In G. Calvo, R. Findlay, P. Kouri and J. Braga de Macedo, eds., *Debt, Stabilization and Development.* Oxford: Basil Blackwell, Inc.

————. 1990a. "Are High Interest Rates Effective for Stopping High Inflation?" International Monetary Fund. Washington, D.C. February.

————. 1990b. "Credibility Crises and Economic Policy." International Monetary Fund. Washington, D.C. January.

Calvo, Guillermo A., and Fabrizio Coricelli. 1990. "Stagflationary Effects of Stabilization Programs in Reforming Socialist Countries: Supply Side vs Demand Side Factors." International Monetary Fund and World Bank. Washington, D.C. August.

Edwards, Sebastian. 1985. "Stabilization with Liberalization: An Evaluation of Ten Years of Chile's Experiment with Free-Market Policies, 1973-83." *Economic Development and Cultural Change* (January):223-54.

Frenkel, Jacob A., and Assaf Razin. 1987. "The Mundell-Fleming Model a Quarter Century Later: A Unified Exposition." International Monetary Fund, *Staff Papers* 34 (4)(December):567-620.

Sargent, Thomas J., and Neil Wallace. 1975. "Rational Expectations, the Optimal Monetary Instrument, and the Optimal Money Supply Rule." *Journal of Political Economy* 83:241-54.

17

Adjustment, Trade Reform and Competitiveness—The Polish Experience

Jan W. Bossak

The first section of this paper reviews the primary development strategies pursued in recent decades. It makes the point that the inward-looking strategies pursued in Latin America have generally been unsuccessful, while the outward-looking ones found in some East Asian countries have led to significant and stable economic growth. Many economists are urging the Central and Eastern European countries to heed this lesson and to pursue export-led growth. The section concludes by defining what an outward-oriented strategy consists of.

The following section looks at the challenge of adjusting an economy while maintaining growth. It presents some characteristics of successful growth-oriented policy packages, emphasizing both the need for internal commitment by governments to achieving stabilization and adjustment with the least possible disruption to growth and the role that the developed countries must play in furthering the adjustment effort. A key issue is the inability of countries to develop the required investment resources because of their huge debt burdens.

A number of the issues raised by adjustment in two areas—the importance of being clear as to the purpose of adjustment and the appropriate content of an adjustment program and other factors related to successful implementation—are reviewed in the third section. The recent policy reforms are described next, followed by a discussion of the foreign debt problem and the need for assistance by lenders and the developed world.

The main conclusion of the paper, presented in the final section, is that the countries of Central and Eastern Europe need to implement a long-term policy that addresses the structural issues and emphasizes exports, and they have to stand behind the effort. However, it is unlikely that any policy package, no matter what the degree of governmental commitment, can succeed without debt relief and an inflow of external funds.

Outward-Oriented Development: The Emerging Orthodoxy

The Success of Outward-Oriented Development Strategies

In the 1980s, after two to three decades of rapid growth, Latin America, Africa, the Middle East and Central and Eastern Europe registered a decline in economic development. The growth of the previous decades had all too often been founded on development strategies that had failed to emphasize economic efficiency and international competitiveness and that had relied heavily on financing from abroad (World Bank 1989). While in the majority of the countries in Latin America in the 1980s, restrictive, deflationary domestic policies and real devaluations reduced imports and increased exports, a situation that often led to trade surpluses, their macroeconomic efforts to improve the balance of payments resulted in recession and a decline in per capita incomes. After several years of trying to adjust their economies, most of the heavily indebted countries not only failed to resume growth but also to reduce inflation and foreign debt.

In East and Southeast Asia, in contrast, the newly industrialized economies generally pursued sound macroeconomic policies and tried to maintain the competitiveness of their economies, especially in terms of exports. Generally they adapted well to the shocks of the 1970s and early 1980s. To a large extent, their success was a result of their maintaining high levels of savings, investment and export promotion. In the 1980s, when they tried to improve their fiscal balances in combination with a reduction in their investment ratios, they did not experience a substantial decline in the rate of growth of total factor productivity and technological progress. As a result of changes in relative prices, levels of spending and profitability, their international competitive capacity increased, and they experienced substantial export surpluses.

As noted, none of the adjustment efforts undertaken in Latin America produced results comparable to those in the successful East Asian countries. However, recently those Latin American nations that pursued sounder fiscal policies recorded a moderate improvement (Chile, Mexico and Colombia). Some of the countries that strengthened their fiscal balance also started to liberalize their foreign trade and used devaluations in the real exchange rate to improve their export price competitiveness, increase the volume of exports and restrict imports.

The widely acknowledged success of outward-oriented development and adjustment has drawn the attention of many Central and Eastern European countries. According to Sachs, a new orthodoxy is emerging that links recovery in a debtor country to a shift to outward-oriented development strategies designed to produce export-led growth. Followers of this new orthodoxy describe the policy content of these strategies as consisting of:

- liberalization of the trade regime
- real exchange rate devaluations and unification of the exchange rate
- privatization of state enterprises
- maintenance of a small budget
- reduction in government intervention in the economy
- deregulation and
- demonopolization and the fostering of competition.

According to Khan (1990), the International Monetary Fund (IMF) and the World Bank have been attaching ever greater importance to the promotion of exports, mainly by advocating real exchange rate devaluations to raise the profitability of exports and supplies. To support liberalization efforts, the World Bank is gradually increasing the role of structural adjustment loans (SALs) and sectoral adjustment loans (SECALs). Both institutions are cooperating with interested countries in working out medium-term adjustment programs to support outward-oriented structural adjustment.

Some Definitions

The outward-oriented developing economies, especially those of East Asia, have certainly outperformed the economies of Latin America. Therefore, it is plausible to link much of this superior performance to their development strategies and the role of export policy. However, outward-oriented export-led growth, export promotion and liberalization are not synonymous. An outward-oriented strategy implies liberalization of the trade and payment regimes in order to align domestic with international prices and to encourage both exports and imports by setting a realistic exchange rate and removing import restrictions. According to Bhagwati (p. 285), an outward-oriented strategy is mainly a matter of setting price incentives in such a way as to ensure that the home market does not become more lucrative than the foreign market.

An outward-oriented strategy has two basic themes: liberalization; and an export development strategy. Liberalization is in fact a laissez-faire and non-interventionist policy involving the eventual removal of all major economic distortions related to government activity not only in foreign trade and payments but also in the domestic economic system and policies. Liberalization is the opposite of protectionism. In an extreme case, it rejects the idea of active trade and industrial policies and assumes the superiority of exchange rate adjustment and macroeconomic policies.

It is doubtful that there is a universal recipe for solving current and long-term development problems through liberalization. Countries are at different stages of economic development and face different economic conditions. They vary not only in their level of per capita income but also in the level of development of their market institutions and forces. Therefore, many advocates of the liberal approach also see the need for country-specific program designs, within the context of an outward-oriented strategy.

Adjustment programs are also not synonymous with macroeconomic policy, liberalization and a package of government non-interventionism. To the contrary, adjustment programs are part of a conscious state policy in which liberalization of the economic system and policy plays a crucial but not exclusive role in creating a sound basis for future balanced and effective long-term growth.

Advocates of liberalization are cautious about the order of liberalization and the coordination of liberalization and macroeconomic stabilization policies. An important issue is the way in which liberalization is implemented: step-by-step or via radical, comprehensive therapy. The most difficult and controversial question is how quickly to liberalize the capital market. Because premature liberalization is dangerous, it is often argued that liberalization of the capital account should be virtually the last step in a liberalization program.

An export promotion or export development strategy differs from liberalization in that it gives a clear priority to aggressive government promotion of exports while often delaying the liberalization of imports and subsequent adjustment of domestic to international prices and liberalization of capital movements, which are introduced only gradually following a build-up of international reserves. Those countries that intend to pursue an outward-oriented strategy but are burdened by a large foreign debt and are afraid of suddenly exposing their inefficient, inflexible economies to international competition often prefer an export development strategy.

An export development strategy often involves considerable government activity. This intervention can be of a great importance in establishing the credibility and commitment of the government, which are vital in inducing investors to risk investing in the development of export industries. Typically, the strategy calls for state encouragement of savings, investment and technological progress. According to Michel Camdessus, the managing director of the IMF, the countries that are best able to protect growth during the difficult adjustment period are those that maintain a strong export performance, that keep domestic savings and investment from falling sharply and that are able to share the adjustment burden between increased supply and reduced aggregate demand. This package requires not only a set of macroeconomic policies but also structural ones (including elements of liberalization and industrial policy) that enhance international competitive capacity.

Export development strategies should eventually lead a country out of external disequilibrium and import restrictions and on to liberalization. The success stories of Japan, Korea, Taiwan and Malaysia obviously confirm this observation. Moreover, their experience indicates that export development strategies may be efficiently pursued with active government trade and industrial policies and in some cases in the presence of regulated financial and capital markets (Bossak 1990). It also indicates that successful development may be furthered by high quality government, macroeconomic and systemic reforms and structural policies (Bossak 1990).

Adjustment with Sustainable Growth: The Challenge

According to Camdessus, a central mission of the Fund is to support adjustment for durable growth. In countries in which inflation and balance-of-payments crises are major problems, it is extremely difficult to achieve adjustment with growth. Before 1982, about 2 percent of the annual gross national product (GNP) of the highly indebted countries consisted of resources from abroad. Since then, these countries have been transferring roughly 3 percent of their GNP abroad a year (World Bank 1989). Domestic savings would need to rise by 5 percent of GNP to offset this change in net transfers. Despite extraordinary efforts, no country has

succeeded both in restoring adequate net investments and in resuming growth. The Brady plan indicates that at last the US government and creditor banks alike have concluded that debt reduction has to be part of a solution to the debt crisis (Antowska and Malecki). A debt reduction initiative has official support and funding from the IMF and the World Bank, provided the countries involved undertake effective adjustment programs.

A key question, however, is what "effective adjustment programs" means. According to Barber Conable, president of the World Bank, countries must undertake stabilization efforts within the framework of an adjustment program that permits sustainable growth. A successful adjustment program is one that achieves an appropriate macroeconomic balance, that simultaneously raises the level of output obtainable from existing resources, and that discourages excessive spending and inefficient investments that are not growth-enhancing. To be successful, growth-oriented programs have to overcome such problems as distorted factor and commodity prices, inefficient public sector enterprises and protectionism extended to inefficient and uncompetitive industries. In addition to a more efficient allocative mechanism, which is critical to achieving sustainable growth and the development of competitive industries, domestic savings must be raised and additional resources obtained from abroad to diminish the cost of servicing the foreign debt.

The right kind of adjustment will not take place by chance. It requires that a government implement a set of macroeconomic and structural policies that encourage saving, sound investment, cost-saving technology, financial stability and exports. It is also important that creditors assist the countries by providing adequate financing, maintaining open and growing markets and fostering appropriate exchange and interest rates.

The key issue in the pursuit of adjustment and growth is to find a combination of macroeconomic policies that can attain the stabilization objectives while also supporting structural adjustment with the least disruption to growth. A key point is that *stabilization alone does not guarantee growth*. Moreover, the specific policy package designed to induce structural change and growth will vary from country to country.

Greater economic efficiency and improved productivity of investments require the elimination of macroeconomic distortions, as well as measures to improve the efficiency of the public sector. Constantine Michalopulos, senior economic adviser in the World Bank's Policy and Review Department, is of the opinion that two sets of policies are important to stimulate a shift in resources and an increase in the supply of tradables: a macroeconomic policy mix; and other policies aimed at promoting the mobilization of resources, an increase in the efficiency of their use and the restructuring of production in favor of tradables.

Some Issues Raised by Adjustment

The Purpose of Adjustment

A country's adjustment program can also be seen as a response to the ever- changing environment in which a given society seeks ways and means to achieve economic progress. Adjustment may be required in response to external and internal conditions. These conditions may be unexpected, sudden events or the result of long-term processes. They may involve not only new economic phenomena but also fundamental political changes, as in Central Europe. It is of fundamental importance to diagnose accurately why adjustment is necessary as a basis for designing the adjustment program. That is, any adjustment program must be based on the answer to the fundamental question—adjustment for what purpose? The program must then be directed toward that end.

Typically, the objectives of economic adjustment include:

- price stabilization
- reduction or elimination of the current account deficit or achievement of a surplus to service and reduce the foreign debt
- increase in economic efficiency and the level of technology
- greater flexibility and adaptability in order to secure a dynamic comparative advantage and to make the economy less vulnerable to external shocks and
- more savings and investment.

All these objectives are components of a competitive economy capable of achieving sustainable, long-term, balanced and open growth and of securing gains from the international division of labor (see figure 17.1).

The Implementation of Adjustment

The causes for and objectives of adjustment have important implications for what should be done. Only when this information is clearly understood should the policy mix, the role of macroeconomic policy, the scope of the needed reforms of the economic system, and the industrial and trade policies be considered. Further integral parts of these considerations are who will be responsible, how the adjustment program will be implemented, and what the role of the state and market forces will be. With respect to the latter, a key point is how the two can be combined harmoniously to respond in the most rational and efficient way to the changing environment.

If the thesis that reforms must be tailored to individual cases is accepted, it is important to recognize that adjustment of a given system to new developments, or a transformation, is not the same as reform. Reform means modifications of a system without changing its core elements and the logic of its functioning. Transformation means moving from an old system to a new one (Bienkowski and Bossak 1990). In the case of the Central and Eastern European countries, the adjustment is being accompanied not by reform but by a fundamental transformation into a new economic order. Transformation means not only dismantling of the old systems but building new ones in their place.

Because the process takes time and is politically highly sensitive, a serious question arises over what ways and means to use at the time of the systemic transformation to secure efficient structural adjustment. Should real structural adjustment be postponed until the systemic transformation is completed, or should the two be pursued in parallel by temporarily substituting state intervention for the market mechanism?

Another important question is whether the macroeconomic stabilization measures should be followed by a transformation of the economic system (including liberalization of the trade regime) that is comprehensive enough to overcome the following:

- recession, which to a large extent is caused by the macroeconomic stabilization measures
- the structural problems that result in a misallocation of resources
- technological backwardness
- monopolies and limited competition
- underdevelopment of the market infrastructure and
- the debt overhang.

The response of Central and Eastern Europe to absorption and switching measures has been less elastic than that in market economies because of supply rigidities. The institutions, economic agents and professions that are taken for granted in market economies have to be re-established and developed. Human capital and management have to be upgraded. To resolve these problems, governments need to adopt a set of macroeconomic measures and structural policies that address them appropriately using market mechanisms. The set of measures should be aimed at mobilizing resources and savings and channeling them into the most productive uses, support cost-saving technology, increase total factor productivity, ensure factor mobility and high eco-

Figure 17.1. *Basic Components of the Competitive Strength of a National Economy*

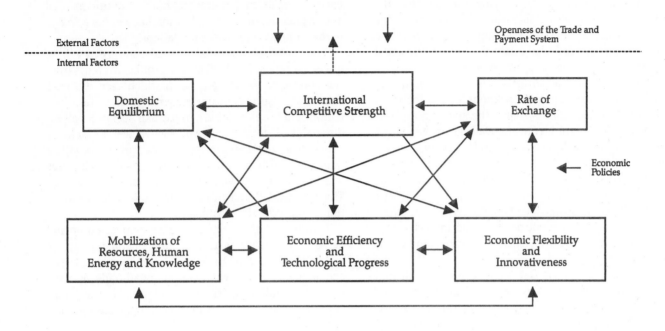

Source: Bossak (1984).

nomic flexibility, encourage the development of highly efficient and competitive export-oriented industries and secure financial stability.

Policy Reforms under the New Polish Regime

In a report prepared by the United Nations Development Programme and the World Bank, the main conclusion was that macroeconomic disequilibrium and systemic problems seriously constrain trade policy. Internal macroimbalances in the form of shortages, excess demand and liquidity were seen as the main factors inhibiting the expansion of exports. This report confirmed the results of earlier studies prepared at the Foreign Trade Research Institute and World Economy Research Institute that the main factors inhibiting trade performance are systemic in character and are associated with macroeconomic disequilibrium; that is, they are outside of trade policy.

The stabilization program and systemic reforms undertaken by the Solidarity-led government beginning in January 1990 have changed the situation radically. The macroeconomic policy contains five main elements:

(1) liberalization of virtually all prices to clear demand and supply in the market and remove the price distortions to the rational allocation of resources.

(2) introduction of the internal convertibility of the zloty and the setting of a unified, undervalued rate of exchange for the zloty, abolition of the preferences favoring exporters and introduction of new customs tariffs.

(3) restrictive income policies, based on a barrier-type tax levied on wages and increases in salaries above the established coefficient.

(4) restrictive monetary policies aimed at reducing the financial liquidity of enterprises and promoting stabilization and growth in zloty saving deposits.

(5) restrictive fiscal policies that limit spending, increase revenues and press for surpluses in para-budgetary funds.

Parallel with efforts to stop inflation and stabilize the economy, the Polish government undertook measures to transform the economic system. First and foremost among them were liberalization of the regime and reform of the financial and budgetary systems. These systemic measures were followed by the introduction of new legislation aimed at clearing the way for the transformation of ownership and development of the wider range of market economy institutions and mechanisms needed to establish the institutional infrastructure for the factor markets.

One aim of the transformation of the economic system was to change the basic relations among the main actors in the economic system: the state, enterprises and labor. The intent was to change labor-management relations at the workplace and to create new types of relations between enterprises. The Solidarity-led government is firmly committed to enterprise restructuring, privatization and private sector development. Without dominant private ownership of the means of production, the factor markets cannot develop, and market forces therefore cannot lead to an efficient allocation and use of resources.

The Memorandum of Development Policy published in September 1990 assumes major changes in the ownership structure of the Polish economy through a program of privatization of state-owned enterprises, promotion of the formation of new private companies and a radical improvement in performance. Legislative initiatives have been undertaken to amend, among others, the Civil Code, the Civil Procedure Law, the Law on Land Management and Real Estate Expropriations, the Housing Law and the Law on Financial Management of State Owned Enterprises. All those amendments aim to reduce the legal and regulatory obstacles to the expansion of private sector activity.

The government regards privatization as a key element in the transition to a market economy and an important stimulus for balanced economic growth. The Law on Privatization of State Owned Enterprises provides a general framework for privatization. The main economic objectives of privatization are to encourage savings and more rational, economic use of resources, to ensure the allocation of resources along the lines of comparative advantage, to stimulate technological, organizational and managerial progress and to raise total factor productivity. Transformation of state-owned enterprises into joint-stock companies owned by the treasury, institutional and private investors will enable the basic factors of a capital market to be introduced. Establishing this market is an important prerequisite for enhancing flexibility and competition and therefore for achieving greater allocative mobility and more efficient use of resources.

Privatization, private sector development and enterprise restructuring will change attitudes and human behavior, especially toward savings, innovation, risk-taking, work discipline, the role of the labor unions, modernization, commitment to the company and job security. In addition, the growing number of unemployed and the development of a labor market will have an important impact on industrial relations.

The privatization of state-owned enterprises will be either voluntary, in which case the initiative comes from the enterprise, or obligatory, in which case it comes from the treasury, typically triggered by the enterprise's continuing losses or failure to pay a dividend. Small industrial and commercial enterprises will be sold or leased. Non-viable enterprises without prospects will be liquidated. Distressed but seemingly viable enterprises will be restructured with the support of a state agency. This process will lead either to their sale or transformation into a joint-stock company.

Parallel with these activities, a demonopolization and deregulation program will be implemented to foster competition. Special attention is to be given both to the demonopolization of wholesale and retail trade, agricultural trade and the distribution sector and to the deregulation of telecommunications, banking, insurance and transport.

Development of the private sector by encouraging new entries and promoting investments, including by foreign capital, will be supported by the removal of the remaining legal barriers, the provision of institutional and infrastructural support and access to credit and technical assistance. Success in this field is closely linked to an improvement in the banking and credit sector and to growth-enhancing tax reforms.

An important element of enterprise restructuring, privatization and private sector development is the founding of a capital market and the development of a modern banking system.

The structural reform and transformation program includes reform of the trade and currency and exchange rate regimes. The managed trade system, which is based on licensing and predominantly centrally allocated foreign exchange, with a complicated system of subsidies, taxes and countervailing duties, has been transformed into a liberal, transparent, market-based system that opens the country to foreign competition and world price signals. The government is committed to maintaining this open trade regime and an appropriate exchange rate to ensure the international price competitiveness of Poland's tradables. The liberal, open trade system is to complement the liberal price-setting system and provide the competitive pressure to combat the monopolistic position of many enterprises. The government assumes that an open trade system will support efficient enterprise restructuring and the allocation of resources according to comparative advantage.

Liberalization of the trade system has opened the way to an almost complete elimination of quantitive restrictions and the administrative allocation of foreign exchange. Moreover, the government has abolished import licensing for practically all traded products. There is some licensing of exports to ensure an adequate domestic supply of products whose prices are still state-controlled and to prevent the re-export of some products imported under special arrangements with the Council on Mutual Economic Assistance (CMEA).

Liberalization of the trade regime has been accompanied by reform of the customs tariff. The average tariff for manufactured goods is around 12 percent, with lower tariffs for imported capital goods. The main objective of the tariff reform has been to stimulate efficiency by lowering the level of effective protection.

The government has also decided to liberalize the transfer of dividends for foreign investors by simplifying the procedures for profit repatriation and making investments more attractive.

The Foreign Debt Problem

The short- and medium-term macroeconomic policy makes price stabilization and achievement of an export surplus priorities at the expense of the rate of growth and employment. The main objective of the so-called structural reform and systemic transformation program is to establish a market economy. It is assumed that price stabilization and market forces in particular will ensure greater efficiency and competitiveness and enhance economic growth. The role of the state will be limited to macroeconomic management and support for the undistorted functioning of market forces.

The question is whether the macroeconomic policies and market forces alone are capable of solving such real structural problems as the significant foreign debt, the inefficiency of mining and heavy industries, and the technological gap. The foreign debt problem in particular has to be taken seriously. There are two options. One is to assume a liberal market economy system and pressure for substantial debt forgiveness. The other is to assume a market economy with active, positive industrial and trade policies aimed at securing the expansion of exports necessary to service and repay the principal of the debt.

The optimists assume that the Western democracies will support the extraordinary effort to introduce a liberal economy by a substantial debt reduction on the part of official and commercial creditors. They also assume that the macroeconomic policy and systemic reforms will create the foundation for a viable economy that will enable a gradual acceleration in productivity, growth and

technological progress. According to Nasilowski, without debt forgiveness Poland will have to achieve a 5 percent rate of growth in national income to service the debt and keep real incomes stable.

To attract foreign capital, Poland needs, beyond the measures already taken, to develop a sound vision for how to solve the debt problem and to foster the development of competitive industries and modern infrastructure. The assumption that the less restrictive macroeconomic policies and systemic reforms alone will lead to growth in excess of 5 percent seems unrealistic. It seems particularly unrealistic given the Persian Gulf and Soviet oil crises, which constitute very serious external challenges to the fragile democracy and pro-market liberal economic transition and stability in Poland (and in Central Europe generally). Both crises create supply bottlenecks and lead to a forced transfer of domestic savings abroad that inflates local prices and crowds out private investment.

The direct losses the Gulf conflict has caused Poland and the other Central and Eastern European economies seem to be overshadowed by the indirect ones. The Central Planning Board of Poland estimates that Poland stands to lose US$2.5 billion from Iraq's invasion of Kuwait, with $1.7 billion of that consisting of broken contracts or the elimination of likely contracts. It also includes $170 million worth of assets that Polish civil engineering contractors and private citizens left behind in Iraq and Kuwait and $500 million in non-payments of Iraq's debt to Poland. On top of these losses comes the new oil price hike: it is estimated that in 1991 alone the additional bill for oil will cost Poland over $2.5 billion. The inflationary effects of this external development will be dramatic, irrespective of whether the prices of crude slide back to their pre-Gulf crisis level.

The switch to dollars and world prices in Poland's trade with the Soviet Union in 1991 will cost an additional US$1.5-2.5 billion, depending on the level of world oil prices. The unification of Germany will result in a contraction in exports of 35-40 percent in terms of Poland's trade with the former German Democratic Republic.

These external shocks will not allow for less restrictive macroeconomic policies. Therefore, it is highly doubtful that the liberal systemic reforms alone, accompanied by restrictive fiscal, monetary and income policies, can overcome the deep structural misallocation of resources and dramatic switch to new, more demanding markets. Despite the exceptional adjustment efforts, without substantial debt relief, some net inflow of foreign capital and an active structural adjustment policy, Poland may enter a long and painful recession, accompanied by political turmoil and stalled negotiations, on the debt problem. Poland's disequilibrium is a deep-seated structural one that requires not only a contraction—and switching across sectors—in demand and systemic reforms, but also positive economic policies that will help overcome the weakness of the supply side, the low productivity, the technological, organizational and managerial backwardness, the misallocation of resources, and the distorted industrial organizational structure (dominated by relatively large state enterprises and underdeveloped medium and small ones that are necessary for a competitive environment and greater economic flexibility).

Conclusion

The conclusion is that Poland will not be able to overcome the economic stagnation and to develop a significant and efficient competitive export base unless it implements a long-term policy that addresses the major structural problems comprehensively, unless the government is actively involved in its implementing that policy and unless it receives simultaneous substantial debt relief accompanied by a net inflow of foreign savings.

The elimination of the hyper-inflation and initiation of the systemic reforms are indisputable achievements of the Balcerowicz adjustment program. However, to be sound, the stabilization needs to achieve greater economic efficiency.[1] The increase in the export surplus as a result of the recession and the switching effect of the devaluation in the real exchange rate of the zloty are transitory. In fact, the decline in output and lack of progress in improving economic efficiency and technology are clear evidence of the weakness and transitory character of the export surplus achieved in 1990. It is true that restrictive income, fiscal and monetary policies, coupled with a real devaluation of the zloty, resulted in a sharp decline in imports and relatively higher profitability of exports. However, gradual progress with the price stabilization will increase aggregate demand and import demand and absorb some exportables. The export surplus will decline and eventually may turn into a deficit. The macroeconomic price stabilization measures and real exchange rate devaluation have increased the competitiveness of exports at the expense of the absorption of a higher share of domestic savings and of a declining national product. Therefore, the export surplus is not only a product of the recession, but it is also undercutting the stabilization efforts.

The development of exports should play a more positive role, especially in the structural adjustment and economic recovery. At a time when the fixed nominal rate of exchange plays the role of nominal anchor, excessively restrictive income, fiscal and monetary policies

may undermine the development of a viable export sector. With the progress on price stabilization and systemic transformations, a structural policy is needed that addresses the real structural problems and that strengthens export capacity and competitiveness based on improved productivity, quality and elasticity of export supply.

In order simultaneously to achieve success in short-term stabilization and lay the basis for long-term economic growth, a set of policies has to be implemented harmoniously. This set needs to involve macroeconomic policies, systemic reforms and active, positive economic policies tuned to the mobilization of savings, release of hidden layers of energy and innovation and the efficient allocation of resources along the lines of dynamic comparative advantage.

The main message of this paper is that *those countries in Central and Eastern Europe that are able to achieve macroeconomic balance, to promote efficiency, to protect the growth of efficient industries during the difficult time of adjustment and to encourage export expansion based on a set of macroeconomic and structural adjustment policies have the highest chance of succeeding, as long as their efforts are seriously assisted by foreign creditors and supported by their own societies.*

Notes

1. A real adjustment policy corrects the disequilibrium, while a quasi-adjustment program only represses it.

References

Antowska, J., and Z. Malecki. "The Brady Plan." Institute of Finance, Warsaw.

Bhagwati, J. "Outward Orientation. Trade Issues." In V. Corbo, M. Goldstein and M. Khan, eds., *Growth-Oriented Adjustment Programs*. Washington, D.C.: International Monetary Fund and World Bank.

Bienkowski, W., and J. Bossak. 1990. "Adjustment and Competitiveness." A paper presented at the IREX-PAN Conference.

Bossak, J. 1984. "Socio-economic Factors Behind Competitive Strength of Japanese Economy." (CSPS), Warsaw.

——————.1990. *Japonia. Strategia rozwoju w punkcie zwrothnym*. Warsaw: PWN.

Khan, M. 1990. "The Macroeconomic Effects of Fund-Supported Adjustment Programs." IMF Staff Papers. International Monetary Fund, Washington, D.C. June.

Nasilowski, M. In *Polityka Finansowa, Nierównowaga i Stabilizacja*. Warsaw: Instytut Finansów.

Sachs, J. "Trade and Exchange Rate Policies in Growth-Oriented Adjustment Programs." In V. Corbo, M. Goldstein and M. Khan, eds., *Growth-Oriented Adjustment Programs*. Washington, D.C.: International Monetary Fund and World Bank.

United Nations Development Programme and World Bank. "Poland, Policies for Trade Promotion."

World Bank. 1989. *World Development Report 1989*. Washington, D.C.: World Bank.

18

Comments on "Adjustment, Trade Reform and Competitiveness—The Polish Experience" by Jan W. Bossak

Gàbor Oblath

Although the notes that follow go beyond Jan W. Bossak's paper, most of the points raised are closely related to the problems he discusses.

The major message of the paper—that to restore viable economies in Central and Eastern Europe, policies designed to achieve stabilization and external adjustment in the very short run are inadequate—is very apropos. The reason is that the systemic transformation taking place in several Central and Eastern European countries, which has few, if any, historical precedents, involves fundamental changes in the basic institutions and workings of both the economy and society. This kind of transformation is different from changing the orientation of a country's trade regime from inward-looking to outward-looking or from protectionist to liberal or from import-substituting to export-promoting. (As noted by Bossak, these terms, although often used interchangeably, may describe different aspects of a foreign trade system.) Instead, the challenge facing the Central and Eastern European countries wishing to replace their inherited socialist systems with market economies entails a far more difficult undertaking than the above-mentioned switches in trade orientation entail.

The above statement does not imply that international experience related to policies aimed at changing the trade orientation of various countries is irrelevant for Central and Eastern Europe. To the contrary. It does imply, however, that due consideration must be given to the underlying differences in basic institutions. The direct applicability to Central and Eastern Europe of Southeast Asia's positive experience with "structural policies" and the kind of government involvement that seems to have worked there give rise to profound skepticism; implementing similar policies in Central and Eastern Europe is not feasible. One of the problems Central and Eastern Europe faces is the governments' deep involvement in the day-to-day life of the economies of the region. Substantial deregulation and liberalization—which require the withdrawal of government from several activities—is necessary to revitalize these economies. What the government should do is assist in the *creation* of the markets and institutions that help markets to function rather than continuing with the same public activities and trying to pick the winners in international competition. The inevitable change in the orientation of trade policy, i.e., the opening up of these economies to the world market, involves larger adjustment costs, in relative terms, than has been the case in less inward-looking countries. Although, because of previous or present price controls, comparisons of this sort (i.e., comparisons related to effective protection) are difficult to make, several signs indicate that the economies of Central and Eastern Europe have been far more closed in their trade policy than most developing countries are or have been.

An important reason for, and an indication of, this stronger inward-orientation relates to the extremely important role of the Soviet (and Council for Mutual Economic Assistance [CMEA]) markets for the manufactures of the smaller Central and Eastern European countries. These markets have been virtually separate from the world market, involving completely different prices and standards than those that apply to world trade. A large part of Central and Eastern Europe's manufacturing industry has been designed for this (presently shrinking) market. The major part of the goods produced by industries oriented toward the CMEA market are "home goods" in the trade policy sense—they cannot be switched to world markets, at least not without a large extra cost (in the form of significantly lower prices).

This orientation of trade toward the CMEA market is the origin of the most serious trade problem the small Central and Eastern European countries face nowadays. Beginning in January 1991, the CMEA will switch over to convertible currency payments among the Soviet Union and other Central and Eastern European partners. It is not at all clear how serious the short-term costs of this change will be. Even before the mid-1990 Gulf crisis and increase in oil prices, it was estimated that the costs in Hungary would be between US$1 and $1.5 billion. Even the approximate magnitude of the short-term costs gives an idea of the extent and implications of the protection offered by the CMEA market.

Evidence of the special but strong inward orientation and protected nature of Central and Eastern Europe's economies is the very large difference between purchasing power parities (PPPs) on the one hand and market or commercial exchange rates on the other. The extent of this difference does not fit into the Balassa explanation based on relative income levels and relative prices of traded goods in terms of non-traded goods. It can, as interpreted here, be explained only by the fact that the quality of tradables (including services related to tradables) in Central and Eastern Europe is much lower than it is in the West. This disparity indicates that tradables were strongly protected. When exporting to the West, it turns out that because of differences in quality, tradables fetch a lower foreign trade price than that implied by PPP comparisons. This fact is reflected in the commercial (official) exchange rate in both Poland and Hungary.

This point leads to the issue of exchange rate policy in adjustment strategy. While strongly opposing the popular ideas often raised by past and present Central and Eastern European policy-makers, according to whom the exchange rate should be *the* instrument of anti-inflationary policy, this discussant has serious doubts about the rationality and efficiency of large devaluations to promote exports in the Central and Eastern European context. Consider Hungary's experience and problems, and not the issue of seeking the "nominal anchor" for stabilization purposes. In Hungary, large devaluations may trigger the acceleration of inflation because of the low efficiency of monetary policy. The problem of arrears (i.e., non-payments or inter-enterprise forced credits) substantially diminishes the efficiency of monetary policy, especially in periods of monetary tightening. A devaluation cannot, however, work without efficient monetary control. Therefore, without establishing a healthy monetary system, large devaluations might, instead of having real effects, contribute to a significant acceleration of inflation.

The other problem is related to supply response proper and the *kind* of supply response required for adjustment. Clearly, the precondition for adjustment is a durable change in the real exchange rate: that change depends on monetary policy, as indicated. However, even if a durable decline in the real exchange rate can be achieved, the question of how swift and what kind of export increase can be expected remains.

At this point the issue raised by Bossak concerning short- and long-term adjustment becomes relevant. With the details passed over here, there is a danger that devaluation *in itself* might reinforce the traditional and inefficient structure of exports. Investment is what is really needed, both domestic and foreign, to improve these countries' non-price competitiveness, not just the selling of low quality products at ever-decreasing prices. If structural policies are understood as measures involving strong incentives for, and promotion of, export-oriented investments, then the application of structural policies is fundamentally appropriate, but only in this sense.

For reasons mentioned above—namely, the inflationary repercussions of large devaluations and doubts about a swift and healthy supply response—the best course would be for Hungary to continue with a gradual, instead of a drastic and quick, trade liberalization policy, accompanied by a transitory increase in the tariff for liberalized products. This tariff increase would be less inflationary than changes in the exchange rate leading to similar effects, and it could be removed gradually.

Bossak's concern over the debt problem of Poland is very real; other countries in transforming Central and Eastern Europe face a similar problem. This concern is closely related to the points discussed at the beginning of these comments—that an exceptionally comprehensive transformation has to take place that alters (and not simply reforms) the economic systems of Central and Eastern Europe. If the West is interested in the success of these changes, it should assist the transformation by lifting the pressure to achieve day-to-day, i.e., very short-term, continuous improvements in the trade balances with the heavily indebted, transforming Central and Eastern European countries. These countries transferred very large sums of net resources in the 1980s, while their debt grew continually. For example, Hungary's external debt increased more than twofold in the 1980s, while a net resource transfer abroad of almost US$3 billion (roughly equal to the net inflow of resources in the 1970s) took place. The conditions imposed by the International Monetary Fund call for significant increases of this transfer in the coming years—the period that seems most critical to the transformation. The basic difficulty is that continuing a short-run trade surplus necessitates heavy restrictions on the domestic economy, which in turn lead to a decline in gross domestic product (GDP). Thus, the burden of the debt service increases. A vicious circle might evolve in which, because of the ever-increasing restrictions, very little adjustment takes place, and the necessary surplus in the trade balance is achieved at continually growing costs in terms of a falling GDP.

These dangers are extremely serious. To be sure, some kind of unconditional debt forgiveness is not recommended. Debt relief, in itself, cannot solve the problems of Central and Eastern Europe. However, if serious, well-designed and promising programs for revitalizing any of the Central and Eastern European economies are designed, and it is clear the debt overhang is constraining their implementation, it would be in the interest of the West as well as a generous act to lighten the burden of the debt service. This point is the other very important message in Bossak's paper. He is completely correct in this conclusion.

19

Fiscal Issues in Economies in Transition

Vito Tanzi [1]

Restructuring and the Institutional Requirements

Recently, the countries of Eastern and Central Europe have abandoned the economic and political ideology that determined their economic policies and institutions over the past four decades (and longer for the Soviet Union). They have started a process of reform and transformation aimed at replacing central planning with a largely market-based economic system similar to that common in the West. The strongest forces pushing for this transformation are the widely recognized failures of the Marxist-Stalinist ideology and the growing awareness of the large differences in the standards of living between centrally planned and market-oriented European countries. These differences cannot be justified on the basis of cultural and historical factors or differences in resource endowment. Half a century ago, for example, the populations of Czechoslovakia and Hungary had incomes similar to or perhaps even higher than those of Austria. Today, the Austrians have much higher standards of living. The Soviet Union has enormous natural resources compared with the West European countries but a much lower per capita income.

The transformation to a market economy will require the dismantling of many institutions and the establishment of new and often very different ones. If the transformation could be instantaneous, it would be easy. Once the new institutions were in place, the countries could channel their energies toward reducing, if not eliminating, the income gap that separates them from the West. Unfortunately, the transformation is likely to be difficult and time-consuming for several reasons. First, while the populations of these countries may favor the idea of a market-oriented economy, abandonment of existing institutions will have, especially during the transition, major impacts on particular groups, who are likely to oppose changes that will affect them negatively. For example, pensioners and many others will oppose the re-moval of food subsidies. Workers and managers will oppose the privatization of their enterprises for fear of losing their jobs or power. Those who have benefited from free, or almost free, housing will oppose privatization of the housing stock. In short, existing institutions have constituencies and lobbies that, although they may welcome the change to a market economy in the abstract in the belief that it will generate Western standards of living, will oppose the immediate negative costs of the changes. During the transition, the costs of restructuring will be current and visible while the benefits will be future and uncertain. Doubts will inevitably arise as to the wisdom and the speed of the change. These doubts will pose additional obstacles to the introduction of the required policies. If the resistance of the opposition is strong—and recent events imply it will be—existing institutions, or at least some of them, may hang on for some time. This situation will increase the cost of the transition, raise uncertainty and delay realization of the full benefits of the economic transformation.

Second, the creation of new institutions requires time, some more than others. At some point, when many of the old institutions have been dismantled or at least rendered ineffective and the new ones have not yet been fully installed, a kind of institutional vacuum will arise. Both economically and politically this period will pose the greatest difficulties.

A third and related point is that the establishment of each institution will have its own dynamics. That is, the time needed to create an institution, say, a new tax system, will depend on technical requirements more than on the need to have that institution in place. The realistic sequencing is likely to be different from the ideal one. The staggered introduction of institutional changes will create uncertainty, since at each step the possibility that the next step may not be taken will influence decisions by individuals and enterprises.

Fourth, and an important point, is the interdependence of institutions and skills. Modern economies are somewhat like ecological systems: their various components—institutions, industries, professional skills, etc.—support and feed each other. Each industry or institution depends on the existence of other industries and institutions. Take, for example, the tax system or the financial system. To function effectively in a modern market economy, they need well-developed legal frameworks as well as particular accounting, legal and managerial skills. They will require that information be processed and presented in certain ways. Economic relations in a market economy are based on legal, accounting and financial frameworks, such as contract law, corporate law, bankruptcy law, financial laws and regulations, and tax laws and regulations, that have developed over many years, in some cases over decades and centuries. Some contracts and obligations are implicit, but they are still generally observed in a modern market economy because society has come to accept them.

Over the years, the advanced Western economies have achieved some sort of "ecological balance" among their institutions and available skills. The demand for certain institutions and skills has led to their development, at times after periods of difficulties and the commission of errors. A balance between required and available skills and institutions is unlikely to exist or to develop quickly in a country that in a short period has transformed itself from a centrally planned to a market economy. For example, accounting skills will be lacking, and it will therefore be difficult to prepare balance sheets and income and loss statements for newly privatized enterprises. This situation in turn will hinder the introduction and enforcement of a modern corporate income tax. Privatization will be hampered by the lack of Western-style managers with business school backgrounds.

The lack of these skills will prevent the smooth and quick establishment and functioning of Western-style institutions. It would be naive to assume that Western institutions can be copied and transplanted as long as the right legal, accounting, financial, managerial and other skills required by Western-style market economies are not available. The implication is that the institutions to be created, especially during the transition, must be simple so as not to make excessive demands for particular skills. Some observers have argued that the high educational levels of the populations of Central and Eastern Europe will facilitate the transition to a market economy. Unfortunately, this assumption is only partly true: a high level of education does not guarantee that the *required* skills are available or can be easily acquired. The skills that are not available and that cannot be acquired within the countries given the absence of teachers are exactly the ones that the newly transformed market economies will need the most.

Restructuring and the Fiscal Institutions

General Background

The Eastern and Central European countries have entered the transition period with levels of government expenditures ranging from around 50 percent to over 70 percent of their gross domestic product (GDP) or in the case of Czechoslovakia, of their net material product (table 19.1). These are extremely high levels, especially in light of the relatively low per capita incomes in these countries. These high expenditures are the result of subsidies for families and enterprises and of government financing of the preponderance of public enterprise investments. The privatization of public enterprises and the removal, or at least the reduction, of subsidies would reduce these public expenditures. However, other factors will push in the opposite direction, especially during the transition.

The transition and restructuring will inevitably increase unemployment significantly, as some public enterprises are closed or are forced to restructure their production toward goods that are sufficiently competitive and of good enough quality to be sold in a market econo-

Table 19.1. *General Government Expenditures of Central and Eastern European Economies*
(percent of GDP)

	1982	1983	1984	1985	1986	1987	1988	1989
Bulgaria	54.7	53.7	51.9	55.2	61.4	64.7	63.7	61.9
Czechoslovakia[a]	67.0	67.4	67.4	69.8	69.8	71.2	74.1	76.6
Hungary	61.2	61.9	59.4	61.1	64.9	61.6	63.0	59.0
Poland	52.2	47.6	48.4	48.2	49.7	47.7	48.0	48.1
Romania	n.a.	n.a.	n.a.	n.a.	n.a.	n.a.	n.a.	n.a.
USSR	49.3	48.6	48.9	49.8	52.2	52.3	53.3	51.4

n.a. Not available
a. Percent of net material product.
Source: Various national sources.

my and in an open environment. If the economies are dynamic and if political or social obstacles do not prevent labor mobility, the period of unemployment may not be too long for many workers. In particular, private sector activities and especially the expansion of the labor-intensive service sector, which is now very undeveloped, could generate substantial demand for labor. Still, the costs of adjustment in terms of unemployment could be large, as the recent experience of Poland, the former German Democratic Republic and other countries shows. Regardless of how dynamic these economies prove to be, unemployment will rise. As a consequence, the government will need to play a role in providing unemployment compensation and retraining those who lose their jobs. Such measures will have an impact on public spending.

Removal of the subsidies for food, lodging, energy, transportation, cultural and recreational activities, public utilities and so forth will reduce public spending. However, it will also sharply reduce the real incomes of vulnerable groups such as pensioners, invalids and children. Thus, there will be a need to adjust pensions and other entitlements. Once again, there are spending implications. Within this same area it is important to mention that the public enterprises have been responsible for important social security and welfare functions. Implicit in the privatization of these enterprises, or even the pressure to make them more competitive, is that the state will need to assume some of these functions.

In part because of the importance of consumer subsidies, money wages have been very low in most of these countries. Removal of the subsidies will create strong pressures to increase money wages. Workers in these countries will make increasing use of a weapon widely used by Western workers—the right to strike. Should government workers get an increase in money wages, public spending will go up.

The need to spend more for some services such as education and health will also create pressure for greater public expenditures. In some of these countries the student/teacher ratio is far higher than in the West, and the quality of health services is very low. In many of these countries, low levels of spending for operations and maintenance have left the social infrastructure in very poor condition. Restoration of this infrastructure to a reasonable state as well as the provision of services (such as telephones) that are not now available will create additional pressure for public spending.

It is unlikely that all enterprises will be privatized. It is improbable that the public enterprises will become efficient enough in a relatively short time to turn a profit, that, given the changing economic situation. Thus, they will continue to need subsidies. Some subsidies may be directed toward enterprises that are restructuring. Finally, substantial sums will have to be spent to create the new institutions needed in a market economy, such as central banks, commercial banks, tax administrations, budget offices, new faculties in the universities and so forth. Some funds may be gained from the dismantling of the planning and other offices (internal security) required by a planned economy but not by a market economy. Nevertheless, at least in the short run the pressure for greater public spending will be substantial.

The bottom line, then, is that for several years the countries of Eastern and Central Europe will continue to require levels of public expenditure far higher than what would be expected from international comparisons, given their per capita incomes. These high levels will make it essential to scrutinize closely the allocation of the expenditures and the efficiency with which they are used. They will also require that government revenue remain high. These requirements have implications for budgeting and for tax policy and administration.

Budgeting

In Western countries the budget office is legally responsible for preparing the budget, for making basic decisions as to the level of total spending and its allocation among the various ministries and functions, and for ensuring that the objectives sought by the budget are being achieved at the lowest cost. In these countries, while the budget office determines total spending on the basis of macroeconomic considerations, its allocation is at least influenced by requests from the spending units.

In centrally planned economies, the budget office has been far less important; its role has been subordinated to that of the planning office. It has had little if any control over productive expenditures, i.e., investment spending, which has been determined by the plan, and it has had little control over important extra-budgetary accounts for military spending, national security and the like. The basic decisions on total spending and to a certain extent on resource allocation have been made by the top levels of the bureaucracy, in long-term plans, with little or no influence by the spending agencies. Thus, the yearly budgets have been little more than instruments to promote and implement the objectives of the plan rather than those of the spending agencies. Another problem with this budgetary system relates to the classifications used. No distinction has been made between ordinary revenues and borrowed funds. Thus, excessive borrowing has showed up as a budgetary surplus. On the other hand, too sharp a distinction has been made between the productive and non-productive sectors (all others). Considering how inefficiently capital has been used, this terminology has made a mockery of the concept of efficiency. In addition, little attention has been paid to cash management; no cost has been imputed for maintaining idle cash. Finally, there often has been no specific budget law, or it has been largely ignored.

The shift toward a market-oriented economic system has made clear that these budgetary procedures and practices must be replaced by a more decentralized, transparent and efficiency-oriented system. Under this new system, the level of spending for the budget year must be more closely related than in the past to projections of the behavior of revenue and the economy in general over the budget year. The allocation of total spending must be based more on the submissions of the spending agencies. Labels such as productive and nonproductive must not determine the priority of spending categories. The budget office must have staff trained to assess the merit of requests by the spending agencies, it must have a greater say in determining the size of total spending, and it must be able to provide more useful classifications of spending categories. On the basis of this information it should be possible to classify spending according to economic or functional category. Cash management must also be improved, with recognition of the opportunity cost of keeping cash idle.

In sum, the budget office must have skills and manpower it does not now have. Only if the budgetary function is greatly improved will the budget office be able to play a role similar to that of the budget offices in industrial countries. At the same time, an effective budget office cannot be developed overnight. Apart from the cost, it requires individuals with skills not now available, as well as well-thought-out legislation. It also requires that political obstacles to the reorganization of that office be removed. This reorganization inevitably implies a loss of political power for many groups that used to have greater discretion over on the use of public resources. These groups will attempt to prevent budgetary reform.

Tax Policy and Administration

The transformation of the economies of Eastern and Central Europe from command to a market orientation has profound implications for their tax systems. Traditionally these countries have collected substantial revenue from taxes, particularly three of them—turnover, profits and payroll. Although the specifics of the application of these taxes differ from country to country, the basic principles are broadly similar. The following discussion focuses on those principles to show the potential effect of the reforms on revenue. The differences among the countries are ignored.[2]

Turnover Taxes. Given the traditional way in which turnover taxes have been applied in the centrally planned economies, they can be thought of either as taxes charged on the sales made by state enterprises to retail shops or simply as the difference between the prices charged to consumers (minus a small profit margin for the retailers) and the prices received by producers. Turnover taxes are not charged on sales between producers. Since both the producer prices and the retail prices are fixed by the department of prices and thus are known, these taxes acquire qualities similar to those of specific taxes.[3] That is, the tax revenue can be calculated once the volume of sales is known. In cases where, for social or planning reasons, the government has wanted to subsidize the consumption of particular products, these taxes have become negative and thus amount to subsidies.

Turnover taxes have at times been applied with hundreds or even thousands of rates. This situation would be a nightmare for Western-style tax administrations, which have difficulty coping with a few rates for value-added taxes (VATs). Nevertheless, governments in Central and Eastern Europe have collected from the turnover taxes revenue far greater than that Western countries have collected with VATs.[4]

The method of collection has been very simple and highly effective. All payments between enterprises and between enterprises and retailers have been made through credit transfers within state banks. Cash payments have not been allowed, and there have been no other forms of payment. Since the prices were administratively fixed and known to the banks, they could calculate the tax liability on the basis of the volume of sales. Thus, the taxes were transfers from the accounts of the retailers to the government's account. In other words, the banks would reduce the balances of the retailers by the required amount and credit part of that amount to the enterprise and part to the state as a tax payment.

This simplified description highlights the great dependence of the turnover tax on two elements—price controls and the method of payment. Moreover, with this system there is no need for a Western-style tax administration. The taxes are simply transfers of a part of the gross revenues of enterprises before they receive those revenues. This system could not survive the liberalization of prices and methods of payment. When prices are no longer fixed and are thus no longer objectively known to the banks, and when payments can be made through different channels and by different means (cash, checks, credit and so forth), it is no longer possible to rely on this system.

Hungary, Czechoslovakia, Poland and Romania need to reform their turnover taxes as a consequence of the price liberalization and financial reforms. Hungary has led the way in freeing most prices and in reforming the tax system. In 1988, it introduced a VAT with two rates—

15 percent and 25 percent—that replaced various turnover taxes. These rates are very high but are necessitated by the decision to exempt large sectors from the tax and by the need to maintain high levels of revenue. Preparation for the introduction of the VAT took more than two years during which time new administrative mechanisms were set up. The change was facilitated by the fact that, as in most centrally planned economies, much of the production takes place in a relatively small number of large enterprises. With liberalization and privatization, and with the growth of small enterprises and services, this situation will undoubtedly change, and Hungary will face greater problems maintaining current rates.

Czechoslovakia is planning to replace its many turnover taxes with just four, which would have rates of 0 percent, 12 percent, 22 percent, and 32 percent, as an intermediate step. The new rates would be levied on the basis of wholesale prices, to take effect January 1, 1991. It eliminated the negative turnover taxes on food in July 1990 by raising retail prices, and it was planning to introduce similar changes for energy prices in December 1990. Special excise taxes will be levied on particular products (alcohol, tobacco, gasoline, coffee and passenger cars) to maintain the level of revenue. These changes will facilitate the liberalization of prices. However, major changes will need to be made to the tax administration since the traditional system for collecting turnover taxes will no longer be feasible. Without these changes, tax revenue could fall substantially.

In January 1990 Poland reduced the rates of its turnover tax to 14 and is contemplating the introduction of a VAT.

Tax on Profits. The taxes levied on profits in centrally planned economies have had little in common with those used in the West. One difficulty is that without proper accounting it is difficult to define profit, especially in the case of socialized enterprises.[5] The definition of profit is distorted by the price controls, the extremely low interest rates paid by the enterprises, the distorted rules of amortization that often assume lives of assets and buildings much longer than is the case in the West (and much longer than the actual economic lives of the assets), the valuation of inventories, and the discretionary nature of what expenses enterprises can claim as costs. In these countries, the taxes on the profits of state enterprises have not been based on an ex ante and objective, even if distorted, concept of profit. Rather, the concept of profit has often been arbitrary, such as a fixed proportion of the producer's turnover, and often the enterprise has negotiated the taxes based on that arbitrary concept so that they amount to ex post taxes.[6]

Price liberalization and privatization will require profound changes in the way profits are taxed. They will also require clearly determined ex ante rules. They will further require that profits be better measured to approximate the economic concept.[7] These skills required to achieve these determinations (accounting and managerial skills) are now lacking and will take some time to develop. Once the switch to a Western-type taxation of profits is made, the role of the tax administration will also change, since it will be responsible for determining the accuracy of the tax declarations and will need to have the ability to challenge taxpayers when their declarations are suspect.

During the transition the revenue from this tax is likely to fall and will remain much lower even after the transition is completed. It should be recalled that the revenue from taxes on profits in the West is only a small proportion of the revenue collected from this tax in the centrally planned economies.

Payroll Taxes. The third major source of revenue—payroll taxes—is similar to that in the West. The taxes are collected directly from the enterprises as a proportion of the payroll. Since the payroll is often met by *cash* transfers from the banks, they can simply withhold the proportion required by the tax. Once again, this system is efficient and simple; it does not require a tax administration to handle the collection, especially where the payroll tax rate is proportional.

Other Taxes. Some of the remaining taxes are largely presumptive ones, as, for example, the taxes on land and on private activities. These taxes are often negotiated ex ante with the taxpayers and, once they are determined, require little if any checking on the part of the tax administration. There has been little or no attempt to base them on objective criteria of income or profits.

Concluding Remarks

A few basic conclusions can be drawn from the brief discussion in the previous sections. First, the centrally planned economies have been very effective in developing revenue systems that, at low administrative (but not efficiency) costs, have succeeded in raising levels of revenue comparable to those in the most advanced industrial countries. They have achieved this success, however, at high efficiency costs, since the taxes probably made a distorted economy even more distorted,[8] and they probably greatly reduced the incentives of the enterprises to become more efficient. This point applies particularly to the taxation of profits. The remarkable feature of this overall system of taxation is that no real tax administration was needed, so that many of these countries have never developed one in the Western sense. By Western standards, and with respect to the needs of market economies, the existing tax administrations appear somewhat primitive.

A second basic conclusion is the great fragility of this revenue system with respect to the changes required to transform these countries into market economies. The transformation will largely destroy the basis for the turnover taxes and, to a lesser extent, the profit taxes. These countries must pay a lot of attention to the creation, almost from scratch, of a new and modern tax system that will almost surely yield less revenue than the one it will replace. The implication is that the level of public spending must be sharply reduced to prevent major macroeconomic problems. Large fiscal deficits have already appeared in some of these countries, especially the Soviet Union, where tax revenue has fallen in part as a consequence of the ongoing reforms. These deficits need to be contained and reduced if they are not to create major economic imbalances and problems (such as high rates of inflation, balance-of-payments difficulties and higher unemployment) that will make the populations question the wisdom of the change toward a market economy. In fact, fiscal deficits are more dangerous in these countries because of the difficulty of covering the shortfalls through sources other than inflationary financing.

A third conclusion is that the existing tax administrations, which are much smaller and less powerful than those in the West, must be substantially expanded and strengthened and must be given greater powers. This change is particularly important if, as argued by Kornai (1990, p. 118), "Nowadays, people in general consider it a laudable act, rather than something to be ashamed of, if someone defrauds the state...." Staff with the skills required to administer the new taxes will need to be trained, perhaps with foreign assistance. New techniques of administration will need to be developed that reflect local conditions.

A fourth conclusion is that the transition from a centrally planned to a Western-style tax system will need to include an "inter-regnum" period in which one tax system will have been abandoned and the new one will not yet have been fully implemented. Thus, temporary sources of revenue will need to be developed to prevent revenue from falling too fast and fiscal deficits from becoming too large.

The experience of several of these countries confirms that tax revenue will fall once they start the transition. For example, in China the ratio of revenue to gross national product fell from 34.4 percent in 1978 to 20.4 percent in 1988. In Hungary the ratio of revenue to GDP fell from almost 60 percent in 1983 to less than 50 percent in 1989, in Poland from 43.4 percent in 1982 to around 30 percent in 1989, and in the Soviet Union from 47 percent in 1985 to 41 percent in 1989.

In this interregnum period, excise taxes can play an important role in generating revenue, and simplified versions of the turnover tax can help until they are replaced by full-fledged VATs. Imports can also contribute to the revenue needs, perhaps through an across-the-board minimum tax imposed at the time the exchange rates are adjusted. Western-style income taxes on individuals must be introduced, although they may not be immediately productive.

Finally, policy-makers in these countries must resist the temptation to see the fiscal instruments in the same light as they saw the plan, that is, as a way to replace the judgment of the market with their own. Although equity has always been an important objective of fiscal policy, this objective must be pursued mainly by using the fiscal instruments to moderate the distribution of income that would result from the free play of the market.[9]

Fiscal policy must not interfere with the choices of the market by promoting certain activities over others. That lesson should have been learned from the experiences of developing and developed countries alike.

226

Appendix 1. Statistical Tables

Table 19-1-1. *General Government Tax Revenue of Central and Eastern European Economies, 1986*
(in percent of GDP)

	Bulgaria	Czecho-slovakia	Hungary	Poland	Romania[a]	Yugos-lavia	USSR	OECD
Profit taxes	18.7 ⎫		11.1	11.0	13.5	6.4	16.0	3.0
	⎬ 25.1							
Income taxes	4.0 ⎭		0.8	3.8	6.0	8.6	3.9	12.1
Turnover taxes	16.5	15.9	16.7	11.6	9.8	6.8	11.5	11.5
Social security contributions	9.7	5.9	16.6	10.3	7.2	8.1	3.3	9.3
Customs duties	0.5	0.7	3.5	2.8	0.9	1.8	7.2	n.a.
Other	0.2	1.0	3.5	4.1	n.a.	5.0	3.8	2.2
Total	49.6	48.6	52.5	43.6	37.4	36.7	45.7	38.1

n.a. Not available.

a. 1988.

Sources: National sources for all countries. For OECD, *Revenue Statistics of OECD Member Countries* (Paris, 1988).

Table 19-1-2. *Bulgaria: Level and Composition of Tax Revenue*
(in percent of GDP)

	1985	1986	1987	1988	1989[a]
Tax revenue	46.1	49.6	46.3	47.4	49.3
Profit tax	19.2	18.7	18.9	21.2	23.3
Income tax	4.0	4.0	4.0	4.0	4.1
Turnover tax	12.6	16.5	13.3	11.6	11.2
Customs duties	0.4	0.5	0.4	0.8	0.8
Social security contributions	9.7	9.7	9.5	9.5	9.6
Other	0.2	0.2	0.2	0.3	0.3

a. Preliminary or estimated.

Sources: National data.

Table 19-1-3. *Czechoslovakia: Level and Composition of Tax Revenue*
(in percent of GDP)

	1985	1986	1987	1988	1989
Tax revenue	50.7	48.6	50.5	50.7	54.9
Profit tax ⎫					
⎬	26.9	25.1	26.2	25.1	21.4
Income tax ⎭					
Turnover tax[a]	16.3	15.9	15.6	15.8	17.6
Customs duties	0.5	0.7	1.4	2.2	1.0
Social security contributions	5.9	5.9	6.3	6.7	15.0
Other	1.0	1.0	1.0	1.0	n.a.

a. Includes internal market differential.

Sources: National data.

Table 19-1-4. *Hungary: Level and Composition of Tax Revenue*
(in percent of GDP)

	1984	1985	1986	1987	1988	1989
Tax revenue	52.6	49.9	52.2	52.4	54.0	49.0
Profit tax	12.6	9.6	11.1	11.9	8.4	7.0
Income tax	0.9	0.9	0.8	0.8	4.7	5.5
Turnover tax	17.9	16.7	16.7	16.9	22.6	17.6
Customs duties	3.4	3.1	3.5	2.8	3.0	4.0
Social security contributions	11.7	15.7	16.6	15.5	14.4	14.3
Other	6.0	3.9	3.5	4.5	0.8	0.5

Sources: National data and staff estimates.

Table 19-1-5. *Poland: Level and Composition of Tax Revenue[a]*
(in percent of GDP)

	1985	1986	1987	1988	1989
Tax revenue	43.4	43.6	40.5	40.2	36.8
Profit tax	10.7	11.0	11.0	12.1	10.2[b]
Income tax	3.7	3.8	3.6	3.5	3.4
Turnover tax	12.3	11.6	10.6	10.8	8.9
Customs duties	2.8	2.8	2.4	2.0	1.1
Social security contributions	10.6	10.3	9.5	7.9	8.7
Other[c]	3.3	4.1	3.4	3.9	4.5

a. State budget and social insurance funds.

b. Includes dividend payments based on enterprise capital.

c. Real estate tax, excess wage tax, and tax payments by the nonsocialized sector and the population, charges on stock revaluation, and temporary levies.

Sources: National data.

Table 19-1-6. *Romania: Level and Composition of Tax Revenue*[a]

	1988	1989
Tax revenue	37.4	42.4
Profit tax	13.5	11.1
Income tax	6.0	6.8
Turnover tax	9.8	14.7
Customs duties	0.9	1.0
Social security contributions	7.2	8.7

a. In Romania there are as yet no official estimates of gross domestic products. Unofficial ones have been used.

Sources: National data.

Table 19-1-7. *USSR: Level and Composition of Tax Revenue*
(in percent of GDP)

	1985	1986	1987	1988	1989[a]
Tax revenue	43.4	42.0	41.5	38.8	38.5
Profit tax	15.2	16.0	15.3	13.5	12.3
Income tax	3.9	3.9	3.9	4.1	4.5
Turnover tax	12.6	11.5	11.4	11.5	11.9
Customs duties	8.4	7.2	7.5	6.3	6.3
Social security contributions	3.3	3.3	3.4	3.4	3.5

a. Preliminary or estimated.
Sources: National data.

Table 19-1-8. *Yugoslavia: Level and Composition of Tax Revenue*
(in percent of GDP)

	1985	1986	1987	1988	1989[a]
Tax revenue	33.1	36.7	34.5	33.2	34.7
Profit tax	5.4	6.4	5.2	4.9	5.7
Income tax	7.6	8.6	8.5	7.1	9.7
Turnover tax	6.6	6.8	6.0	6.9	5.3
Customs duties	2.6	1.8	2.5	3.1	1.8
Social security contributions	6.3	8.1	8.3	7.3	8.9
Other	4.6	5.0	4.0	3.9	3.3

a. Estimates.
Source: *Statistical Yearbook of Yugoslavia*, 1990.

Notes

1. The views expressed in this paper are personal ones and may or may not reflect official positions of the International Monetary Fund. The assistance received from Lazlo Garamfalvi is much appreciated.

2. For a good discussion of the tax systems of these countries, see Gray (1990).

3. However, discretionary price adjustments have been frequent. Thus, effective tax rates can change considerably over time. Still, the new prices are known.

4. In Western countries it has been very difficult to achieve revenues from VATs greater than 10 percent of GDP. The centrally planned economies have reached or exceeded 15 percent with the turnover taxes.

5. A World Bank mission that visited nine enterprises in Poland was given eight different definitions of profit.

6. Furthermore, the formal rates have been very high.

7 Additionally, the tax rates will need to be much lower and to fall into line with those that prevail in the rest of the world.

8. Second-best arguments make this a qualified conclusion.

9. It is very likely that the distribution of income will become less equal during the transition. The governments should do their best to moderate the situation, but only in ways that minimize the damage to efficiency.

References

Gray, Cheryl W. 1990. "Tax Systems in the Reforming Socialist Economies of Europe." World Bank Working Paper, WPS 501. Washington, D.C.

Kornai, Janos. 1990. *The Road to a Free Economy*. New York: W.W. Norton and Company.

Ofer, Gur. 1990. "Macroeconomic Issues of Soviet Reforms." Mimeo. March 9-10.

Part VII

Panel on Privatization

20

Privatization in Eastern Europe: The Case of Poland

David Lipton and Jeffrey Sachs[1]

The transformation of the Eastern European economies into market economies requires comprehensive action on three fronts: macroeconomic stabilization; liberalization of economic activity; and privatization of state-owned enterprises.[2] Each of these is a monumental task. Nonetheless, privatization stands out as the most difficult and novel of the three, both conceptually and politically. There are enormous challenges in transferring state-owned property—which constitutes around 90 percent of the industrial capital in Eastern Europe—to private hands in a manner that is rapid, equitable and fiscally sound and that accomplishes two fundamental goals: the efficient operation of the resulting private enterprises; and the development of efficient capital markets.

The task of privatization in Eastern Europe is not widely understood in the West, partly because misleading analogies have been made to privatization in other parts of the world.[3] In a typical country that has recently "privatized" some state enterprises, only a handful of firms—perhaps up to a few dozen—have been sold by the government to the private sector. These sales may have made an important economic difference in some sectors, but they have not involved a fundamental transformation of the economy. The amount of capital transformed through privatization has generally been a small proportion of total business capital and national income, and the economies typically had large, private industrial and financial sectors before the privatization.

In Eastern Europe, privatization is a very different task, involving nothing less than the complete redefinition of property rights for literally thousands of enterprises. Privatization means the creation anew of the basic institutions of a market financial system, including: corporate governance of managers; equity ownership; stock exchanges; and a variety of financial intermediaries, including pension funds, mutual funds and investment trusts. The importance of such financial intermediaries can be gauged from the fact that institutional investors now hold more than half the value of shares in the United Kingdom, Italy and Japan, as well as more than half the value of the New York Stock Exchange.[4] The economic challenge, then, is to combine the redefinition of property rights with the creation of vital financial market institutions. The political challenge is also awesome: to design a mechanism for creating private property rights that can win broad, lasting social approval (and prevent special interests from paralyzing the process through a fight for the spoils).

Ironically, the rush of investment bankers and Western experts who have been proposing privatization strategies in Eastern Europe has not addressed the real needs of privatization. Not surprisingly, the bankers have focused almost exclusively on a *firm-by-firm* strategy not unlike the programs in which they have participated in other parts of the world. In Eastern Europe, however, the likelihood is that this customized approach would bog down for political, economic and financial reasons well before a significant proportion of state firms are actually privatized.

In this paper, the authors review the enormous scope of the privatization task, and suggest means for a rapid, efficient and equitable transformation of state property into private property. The focus will be Poland, where the authors serve as economic advisors. Some of the problems discussed are more urgent in Poland than elsewhere. Particularly problematic, for Poland, is the fact that the workers' councils are powerfully organized in many enterprises and are fighting for worker self-management and against privatization. Nonetheless, most of the analysis of privatization in Poland applies throughout Eastern Europe.

The authors offer one disclaimer at the outset. Even though rapid privatization is favored, it is doubtful that privatization will produce immediate, large increases in productivity or managerial efficiency. The real gains from private ownership will take years to manifest themselves—the length of time needed for managers to be upgraded, supervisory boards to gain experience, stock markets to improve the quality of valuation of enterprises, and real economic restructuring to take place. Nonetheless, the authors believe that to enjoy those enormous long-term gains, it is necessary to proceed rapidly and comprehensively on creating a privately owned, corporate-based economy in Eastern Europe.

Since privatization is such a vast topic and cannot be treated comprehensively in a single paper, it is important to spell out what is *not* discussed here. The problems of "small-scale" privatization of retail shops and smaller industrial enterprises are not addressed.[5] The socially complex question of *restitution* of the property, or reprivatization as it is called in Eastern Europe, that was nationalized in the 1940s through 1960s is not touched on. The ground-up development of the private sector in Eastern Europe, which is at least as important, and in Kornai's view, even more important, than the privatization of state enterprises is not discussed.[6] Finally, relatively little is said about the crucial question of managerial compensation, which can provide a vital link between the interests of managers and the interests of the owners of the enterprises.

The Debate over the Pace of Privatization

Perhaps the central debate about privatization in Eastern Europe concerns the feasible pace of an effective privatization strategy. Some authors believe that efficiency gains from private ownership and private capital markets are so overwhelming that the process must be speeded up as much as possible. Advocates of rapid privatization are typically confident that even if quick privatization initially leads to an inappropriate distribution of ownership with, for example, too diffuse ownership, or firms in the wrong hands, then the capital markets will encourage a reshuffling of ownership through takeovers, mergers and buy-outs so that there is a proper matching of owners and firms. For these analysts, privatization should be undertaken as rapidly as possible to reap the full benefits of private ownership.

Many authors who take this point of view have recently called for a free distribution of the enterprises into private hands as a way to speed privatization.[7] In Poland, the landmark study calling for a free distribution of shares to speed privatization by Lewandowski and Szomberg (1989). In Czechoslovakia, the Minister of Finance, Vaclav Klaus, and his deputy, Dusan Triska, have been outspoken advocates of rapid privatization through the sale of enterprise shares for vouchers. In Hungary, Liska has been an outspoken advocate of a free distribu-

tion of shares to the population. Other important and influential pieces are those by Hinds (1990) and Frydman and Rapaczynski (1990). Other researchers advocating rapid privatization through a free distribution of shares include Olivier Blanchard and Richard Layard, Fernando Saldanha and Branko Milanovic and Anders Aslund. The president of the Hungarian-American Enterprise Fund, Alexander C. Tomlinson, has also proposed rapid privatization through the free distribution of shares (Tomlinson 1990). *The Economist* (July 21, 1990), too, has advocated rapid privatization in this manner.

For other analysts, privatization should take place at a more measured pace to ensure the development of effective enterprise ownership. In the view of Kornai (1990, p. 82), the apparatus of the state:

is obliged to handle the wealth it was entrusted with carefully until a new owner appears who can guarantee a safer and more efficient guardianship. The point is not to hand out the property, but rather to place it in the hands of a really better owner.

Kornai believes that to bring about effective ownership, the enterprises should be sold carefully and mostly on a one-by-one basis, rather than freely distributed to the public.

The authors are sympathetic to the concerns that Kornai raises. As he stresses, the privatization strategy should focus on establishing effective ownership and corporate governance, rather than on simply transferring nominal ownership to the private sector. The secondary market for corporate control, which might operate, for example, through takeover bids on a stock market, will not be reliable enough to ensure efficient matches between enterprises and owners. Nonetheless, the authors believe that privatization can proceed faster than a one-by-one sale of enterprises would dictate. The process can be accelerated, through the free distribution of shares in a manner consistent with the development of effective ownership.

One reason that rapid privatization is stressed here is that the current pattern of ownership in Eastern Europe is itself prone to massive inefficiencies. The potential costs of overly rapid privatization must be traded off with the high costs of maintaining the present system in which state-owned enterprises lack clear incentives (or actually have perverse incentives) in the face of the market forces now being introduced in Eastern Europe. However, the authors' reasons go further than that, to the politics of privatization. In their opinion, the real risk in Eastern Europe is not that the privatization will be less than optimal, but that it will be paralyzed entirely. Unless hundreds of large firms in each country are quickly brought into the privatization, the political battle over privatization will soon lead to a stalemate in the entire process, with the devastating long-term result that little privatization takes place at all.

Consider the current political situation. While the state enterprises are presumably owned by the state, the various components of ownership—including the rights to use the property, to benefit from financial returns, to benefit from financial returns and to dispose of the property—are in fact jointly in a shifting and imprecise way, among managers, workers and the state. In this situation, workers and managers have incentives to wrest the income and assets of the firm away from the state, often in ways that are highly inefficient and politically explosive.

If property rights are not clearly defined in the near future, enormous energy will likely be wasted in a bruising fight over property rights. As in Argentina, for example, the nation's political and social energy will be spent defining the rules of the game, rather than operating efficiently within stable rules. Groups of workers and managers, both at the enterprise level and at the political level, will surely try to strengthen their claims (both legal and implicit) over the enterprises in ways that will further confuse the ownership structure. Their efforts simply block the state's political and legal capacity to privatize the firms at a later date. Insiders such as influential bureaucrats and state managers might well use their positions to grab an inordinate share of the state property. Such actions could undermine the public consensus to proceed with privatization.

Workers' desires to block privatization might also increase rapidly in the near future if, as expected, unemployment rates rise sharply in Eastern Europe. Workers might assume, with some justification, that their job tenure will be undercut by a privatization of their firm. Even if workers in a particular enterprise do not actually block privatization, they may attempt to bargain with the government, demanding, for example, a cut in the enterprise's debts, or various guarantees on employment levels as their "price" for letting the privatization go forward. If the government becomes enmeshed in case-by-case bargaining, there will be no end in sight, given that hundreds of large enterprises must be privatized.

These fears of paralysis are not hypothetical. In almost all countries where privatizations have been attempted, there have been major political obstacles to the case-by-case approach. These obstacles are likely to develop more rapidly in Eastern Europe given the thinness or, in some cases, non-existence of capital markets, the difficulties of valuation, the likelihood that privatizations will be followed by lay-offs and the sheer number of firms that must be privatized. Already, after just a hand-

ful of privatizations, Hungary has entered into a heated internal debate over political accusations that the privatization process is selling Hungarian assets too cheaply to the rest of the world. The first director of the Hungarian State Property Agency was fired in part because of the controversial flotation of shares in the tourist agency Ibusz on the Austrian stock exchange. In Poland, an increasingly powerful coalition of interests that favor worker management is already organizing itself against widespread privatization.

The authors propose a series of detailed steps to address the various pitfalls of privatization. At the outset, it is recommended that hundreds of the largest enterprises be converted into Treasury-owned joint-stock companies to ensure that the enterprise sector is indeed transformed into corporate form. Right from the start, some firms could be managed on a case-by-case basis (for instance, where a private bidder comes forward). Most firms, however, would follow a special track emphasizing the rapid distribution of shares. A portion of shares would be given at a low price or at no charge to workers, and another portion of shares would be transferred rapidly and free of charge to various financial intermediaries (such as mutual funds, pension funds and commercial banks). Shares in these intermediaries will in turn be distributed or sold to households. Finally, the government would retain a portion of shares of each enterprise and would gradually sell them off as a *block* to "core investors" who are to take a key role in management of the enterprise.[8] In this way, it is hoped that rapid privatization through free distribution can be combined with the advantages of case-by-case sales.

Current Ownership Patterns in Poland

The government of Poland aspires to an ownership structure like that of Western Europe. First, the bulk of the productive sector should be held in private hands. Second, the ownership of large enterprises would be predominantly in corporate form, with shares held by households, financial intermediaries and other non-financial firms. Third, financial markets should be developed to facilitate the trading of shares.

As can be seen in table 20-1, the proportion of enterprise capital in state hands in Poland and the rest of Eastern Europe is vastly above the proportion in Western Europe.[9] Nowhere in Western Europe does the share of state ownership currently exceed 20 percent. Even the Social Democratic regimes in Scandinavia—which serve as a role model for many politicians in Eastern Europe—have very little state capital, and almost none in the industrial sector.[10]

Table 20-1. *Size of the State Sector, Measured by Output and Employment, Selected Countries*

(percent)

Country	Output	Employment
Command economies		
Czechoslovakia (1986)	97.0	...
East Germany (1982)	96.5	94.2
Soviet Union (1985)	96.0	...
Poland (1985)	81.7	71.5
China (1984)	73.6	...
Hungary (1984)	65.2	69.9
Market economies[a]		
France (1982)	16.5	14.6
Austria (1978-79)	14.5	13.0
Italy (1982)	14.0	15.0
Turkey (1985)	11.2	20.0
Sweden	...	10.6
Finland	...	10.0
United Kingdom (1978)	11.1	8.2
Germany, F.R. (1982)	10.7	7.8
Portugal (1976)	9.7	...
Denmark (1974)	6.3	5.0
Greece (1979)	6.1	...
Norway	...	6.0
Spain (1979)	4.1	...
Netherlands (1971-73)	3.6	8.0
United States (1983)	1.3	1.8

a. Excludes government services, but includes state-owned enterprises engaged in commercial activities.

Source: Milanovic (1989), Tables 1.4 and 1.7.

State-owned Industrial Firms in Poland

Poland had 3,177 state enterprises in the industrial sector as of 1988.[11] The country aims to privatize most or all of these firms, so that the ownership structure in industry will approach Western Europe's. As in Western Europe, privatization is likely to come first in industry and small-scale services and then later, and perhaps to a lesser extent, in utilities, communications and railway transport. Privatization is typically more complicated in these latter cases, since the output markets in these sectors tend to be less competitive than in industry. Therefore, in those cases privatization must be accompanied by a regulatory apparatus for controlling the pricing and output decisions of the privatized firms.[12]

While some observers have worried that privatization in Eastern Europe should be delayed until after widespread demonopolization has occurred, the authors do not believe that monopoly power is an urgent problem in the industrial sector. Since most Polish industry is now subjected to strong international competition resulting from a policy of low tariffs and free trade, the problem of industrial monopoly is rather small even in sectors that are dominated by a few firms. Indeed, the Polish Ministry of Finance recently reviewed the competitive environment facing the 500 largest industrial enterprises and concluded that there are few cases, if any, where concerns over monopoly power should stand in the way of rapid privatization.

To some extent, the figure of 3,177 state-owned industrial enterprises exaggerates the task of privatization, since output and employment are concentrated in the top few hundred firms. The size distribution of firms by employment, output and earnings is shown in table 20-2. Note that the top 500 firms, ranked by sales, account for 40 percent of employment, 66 percent of sales and 68 percent of new income in the socialized industrial sector.[13] If most of the top 500 firms can be privatized, then an important part of the industrial sector, as measured by employment, sales and net income, will have been privatized.

It is useful to divide the task of privatization into three categories depending on the size of the firms. *Large*-scale privatization refers to firms that are too large to be sold or distributed to a single Polish buyer. For these firms, privatization will require that ownership be vested in several groups of owners or sold to a large foreign buyer. *Medium*-sized privatization refers to firms in which a majority stake can be sold to a single buyer, either through a management-worker buy-out or in a sale to an outside group. *Small*-scale privatization refers to very small firms, mainly in retail trade but also to some extent in the industrial sector. In these cases privatization will be accomplished mainly by transferring ownership to the firms' workers through a lease or an outright purchase.

As a working assumption, the Polish authorities are presently focusing on the 500 largest industrial firms as the universe for large-scale privatization, although the privatization program will simultaneously go forward on small-, medium- and large-scale enterprises. Since large-scale privatization is the most difficult kind of privatization, and since such privatization will involve the bulk of the industrial sector, the focus in this paper is on these firms.

Legal and Political Aspects of Ownership

Many of the deepest problems of privatization arise from the ill-defined current ownership structure in Poland and in the rest of Eastern Europe.[14] In Western thought, ownership entails several rights over a resource: the right to determine its use; the right to the

Table 20-2. *Poland: Size Distribution of State Enterprises, 1990*

Number of enterprises	Sales[a]		Net Income[a]		Employment[b]	
	Billions of US$	*Percent of total*	*Billions of US$*	*Percent of total*	*Thousands of workers*	*Percent of total*
Top 100	18.1	39	2.9	43	711	18
Top 200	23.1	49	3.6	53	1,036	26
Top 300	26.5	57	4.0	59	1,261	31
Top 400	29.1	62	4.4	65	1,461	36
Top 500[c]	30.9	66	4.6	68	1,612	40
Total of socialized industrial sector	46.8	100	6.8	100	4,051	100

Note: Firms are ranked by sales in the *Lista 500* and *Informacja Statystyczna*.

a. Data are annualized from January-June 1990.

b. Employment refers to 1989 employment levels.

c. Sixteen firms have been dropped from the top 500 firms. The remaining 484 firms are used as a proxy.

Source: *Lista 500* and *Informacja Statystyczna*.

earnings of the resource; and the right to dispose of the resource. In Eastern Europe, however, those rights are now rather vaguely distributed among the workers, managers and state bureaucracies.

Under classical central planning, the state maintained all ownership rights. The enterprise had a "founding organ," usually a branch ministry, which maintained formal oversight of the enterprise. The enterprise's functions, of course, were largely determined by the central plan. It was during the process of reform Communism (in Yugoslavia after 1948, Hungary after 1968, Poland after 1980 and the Soviet Union after 1985) that the situation became highly muddled.

Part of the process of reform Communism in all these countries was the granting of increased operational and financial autonomy to the enterprise.[15] In Poland, these reforms were adopted in September 1981, with the Law on State Enterprises and the Law on Self-Management of the State Enterprises' Employees, just before the imposition of martial law. In theory, the enterprises were to become largely self-managing and self-financing, with less reliance on transfers from the state. Investment spending was to come increasingly from retained earnings rather than from a budgetary allocation. The enterprises were to develop more of their own work plans, with less top-down direction from the bureaucracy. In this way, enterprises were to become increasingly subject to market forces.

It is well-known that these decentralizing reforms in Poland, and elsewhere in Eastern Europe, were at best partial, and failed to create hard budget constraints for the enterprises.[16] Under reform communism enterprises escaped from central planning into an endless series of negotiations with the bureaucracy over taxes, subsidies, prices and output rather than into a true market environment. Nonetheless, the devolution of power upon the

enterprises did blur many of the ownership rights previously exercised by the central bureaucracy.

Workers' Councils

It also raised the question of which group was to assume these rights. In all countries, the formal answer was that *the workers of the enterprise* exercised responsibility for the enterprise, usually through a collective assembly of all the enterprise workers (such as an annual shareholders' meeting) and through a representative workers' council, which was to govern the enterprise between meetings of the general assembly.

A workers' council in Poland is composed of 15 workers who are elected by secret ballot for two-year terms. The councils are charged with "the information of the enterprise's annual plans, investment decisions, changes in the scope of enterprise activities, acceptance and approval of the annual balance and decisions on merger and enterprise dissolution" (see Sajko 1987, p. 1372). In most enterprises, the workers' councils have been given the power to appoint the manager. In enterprises of "primary importance" the workers' councils have been given veto power over the choice made by the government.

Note that the development of the workers' council was not the only logical alternative for Eastern Europe, although it was universally taken to be the one most consistent with Marxist ideology. Another possibility, for example, could have been the classic state-owned enterprise in the British tradition, which is governed by an independent board of directors appointed by the government.[17] The board of directors possesses some operational independence from the government and appoints the management, approves its plans and monitors its performance.

Interestingly, privatization would now be much easier had enterprises taken the form of British state enterprises. In that case, the enterprise would already be in the corporate form, and privatization would merely involve the transfer of control from the board of directors to the new private owners. In the case of worker-managed firms, however, privatization requires a disenfranchisement of the workers' council at the same time that corporate governance is vested in a new board of directors.

In practice, the workers' council played a lesser role, even under the communist system, than set forth in the legislation. While workers' councils were set up in roughly 90 percent of Poland's state enterprises, it is commonly estimated that they have been fully effective in only about 15 percent of the enterprises, al though these have typically been among the larger enterprises (Rudolf 1988, p. 424). In many other firms, where workers' councils were not effectively organized, the state enterprise managers acted with considerable independence not only from the workers but from the state bureaucracy as well.

Consequences of Greater Autonomy for Enterprises

The Communist party, when it was in power, also played a key role in management of the enterprises. Not only was the choice of managers heavily influenced by the *nomenklatura* system," in which the party nominated politically acceptable directors, but also important decisions for the enterprise were referred to the "enterprise collective body," which was composed of the first secretary of the party, together with the managing director of the enterprise, the chairman of the trade union and the chairman of the workers' council (Rudolf 1988, p. 426).

After the collapse of Poland's Communist regime, the independence of the enterprises increased enormously. Of course, the *nomenklatura* system collapsed, as did the direct intervention of the party in enterprise matters. In many enterprises, the workers' councils gained new strength and ousted enterprise managers. In other cases where the workers' council remained weak, the state managers inherited the powers ceded by the bureaucracy and the party. Although in March 1990 the rights of the workers' councils were reaffirmed, emphasizing that "the council must approve the decision by the enterprise to sell assets, to form or to enter into an existing trade company, to buy shares of stock in corporations, or to sell off shares in those corporations," there have been few legal changes in the power of the workers' councils.[18]

As the room for maneuver increased for the enterprises, the problems arising from the muddled ownership structure became acute. Workers and the managers gained control over the firm but lacked clear title to the assets of the firm; they therefore had an overwhelming incentive to try to appropriate the capital income of the firm and to strip the firm of its assets. As Lewandowski and Szomberg (1989, p. 258) put it, "There is still no one to lose anything from the decapitalization of state property." For example, with increased freedom to set wages, the workers' councils pressured managers to raise wages to absorb an increasing amount of the firms' cash flow. Liberalization in 1987-88 therefore ushered in an enormous real wage explosion and a wage-price spiral.[19]

The possibilities for asset stripping became even more dramatic when various property laws were changed during 1988-89, in the final period of Communist rule. First, the private sector was liberalized, and state firms were allowed to do business with the private sector. Second, joint ventures with foreign partners were encouraged. As a result of the changes, managers quickly discovered ways to appropriate state property by making sweetheart deals with an outside partner, in a process that quickly became known as "spontaneous privatization." Lewandowski and Szomber called the process "legal parasitism."

Consider the case of joint ventures. The enterprises were given enormous freedom to enter into joint-venture arrangements with little central control. Many state managers, particularly in firms without strong workers' councils, quickly realized that they could make deals with foreign partners. They would grant the foreign partner a highly favorable stake in the enterprise, and in return the foreign partner would grant the manager an attractive position in the new venture. The manager effectively traded the state property for personal gain.

Even more egregious cases ensued in which the state enterprises entered into contracts with newly established private firms in which the manager had a personal stake. The manager might then lease to the private firm the plant and machinery of the state enterprise at highly favorable terms. The profits of the state enterprise would thereby be transferred to the private firm. These abuses became recognized by the general public in 1989 and led to an enormous storm of protest. The public realized that during the Communist-managed transition to a market economy, the Communist-appointed managers were appropriating the best property for themselves. The public's revulsion against spontaneous privatization was intense and surely helped to speed the demise of the old regime.

Since the start of 1990, Poland's industrial enterprises have had almost complete freedom with regard to pricing, production and international trade decisions. Thus the autonomy of the enterprises has been greatly enhanced. At the same time, administrative means have been introduced to cope, however imperfectly, with the anomalous ownership structure. Wage controls have been put in place to prevent enterprises from appropriating their own profits, and indeed profitability of the industrial sector increased markedly during 1990, despite a domestic recession.

While the government's oversight of joint ventures has been strengthened, there is anecdotal evidence to suggest that at least some joint-venture arrangements still serve the self-interest of managers. In addition, while new conflict of interest laws have been put in place to prohibit spontaneous privatizations through sweetheart deals, the effectiveness of these regulations is not yet clear. The government has also undertaken to review and reverse cases of conflicts of interest that occurred in the past.

In some ways, however, recent reforms have made it harder, not easier, to define real claimants to the assets and residual income of a firm. On the one side, the government has drawn a sharper line between an enterprise's earnings and the state budget. Enterprises now receive fewer transfers from the state budget and are allowed to retain more of their earnings after paying various corporate taxes, but they are not free to distribute those earnings through wage payments without incurring substantial penalties under the excess wage tax law. In addition, because there are clearly no private shareholders to whom the profits can be distributed, the residual income remains with the firm. There, the retained earnings can be used for only two purposes: to amass financial wealth; or to make investment expenditures.

It can be expected that unless the claimants of the residual income are quickly defined through the privatization, management and workers will, through indirect means, find ways to enrich themselves. Some of the profits might be enjoyed through a reduced work effort or through low-return investments, such as in new factory cafeterias, for example, that benefit the incumbents of the firm.

In yet a final facet of the ownership rights debate, most legal analysts in Poland believe that the state remains the holder of enterprise capital, but even this point has become muddled. The book value of the capital of a firm has been divided between the "founder's fund," which represents the initial capitalization of the firm, and the "enterprise fund," which reflects the book value of retained earnings. Some managers and workers' groups have asserted that the enterprise fund should be viewed as already belonging to the enterprise, while most legal scholars in Poland assert that the enterprise fund as well as the state fund belong to the state.

Privatization and Worker Management

The shift to a Western European ownership structure will require that enterprise governance be removed from the workers' councils and managers and placed squarely in a supervisory board (or board of directors) controlled by the owners of the enterprise.[20] In essence, privatization requires first that certain ownership rights now vested in the enterprises, and particularly in the workers' councils, be eliminated so that the property rights can be transferred to the real owners.

The transfer of power to private owners poses a significant political challenge to the governments of Eastern Europe, since support for worker control and worker ownership remains powerful in many enterprises and in some political circles. Not only was the worker management ideology validated in the years of struggle against central planning, but it also enjoys well-organized support in enterprises that have active workers' councils. These councils now aim to strengthen their control and perhaps to win outright ownership of the firms. In enterprises facing cutbacks in employment, many workers view their workers' councils as the best hope for avoiding lay-offs and protecting workers' interests, if not the interests of the capital.

It is clear that for political reasons, and perhaps for ethical reasons as well, that workers will have to be partially compensated for the transfer of control from the workers' councils to private owners. After all, workers stand to lose property rights because of privatization. The standard suggestion is that workers should be allowed to purchase a *limited proportion of shares* (20 percent according to the Polish Privatization Law) in their enterprise at a discounted price when the firm is privatized. The practical question is whether this concession will be politically palatable, at least enough so to permit the privatization to move forward smoothly. It is possible that even with the concession of favorable purchase terms for shares, some workers' groups will fight to slow the privatization to assert their claims for complete worker control.

There are strong reasons, on grounds of equity as well as efficiency, for rejecting the workers' strong demands to deliver greater firm ownership to them. First, workers were never really granted ownership of their enterprises in the Communist reform because doing so would have created vast and unjustifiable inequalities in income and wealth. Only 4 million of Poland's 18 million workers are actually employed in the state-owned industrial sector, so that less than one-fourth of the workers would receive any benefits from the full distribution of ownership to the industrial workers. Moreover, some workers are in highly profitable firms while others are in loss-making firms. Thus, to give the workers ownership of their respective firms would be highly capricious in its distributional consequences.

From an efficiency standpoint, it makes little sense for workers to own their own enterprises (or to lease the capital in their enterprises), except in the case of small, labor-intensive operations. Worker ownership or labor-management tends to cut firms out of the capital markets. Outside investors tend to shun enterprises in which workers have a controlling interest, since 3they can act opportunistically to absorb all of the income of the firm in the form of wage compensation.[21] Moreover, it makes little sense for workers to hold most of their equity wealth in their enterprise, since on diversification grounds they should hold financial capital and human capital in separate investments.

Ironically, many supporters of US employee stock ownership plans (ESOPs) have traveled to Eastern Europe recently to organize support for worker ownership. The effect in many ways has been pernicious. In the United States, the ESOP tends to promote a modest extent of worker ownership, almost always below the 20 percent threshold envisioned by the Polish authorities.[22] As shown in table 20-3, there are less than 50 industrial firms in the United States that employ more than 1,500 workers in which employees own more than 25 percent of the shares. There are still fewer in which the workers own a majority stake in the enterprise. These firms account for a tiny proportion of the industrial labor force. Yet, in Poland, the US ESOPs have been known to support the political case for more complete worker management and ownership.

The Polish Privatization Law

In June 1990, the Polish Parliament overwhelmingly passed the new Act on the Privatization of State-Owned Enterprises, which is designed to be the guiding legislation for privatization. The act does not embrace a single strategy for privatization but rather sets a general framework that could accommodate a variety of strategies.

The history of the legislation is enlightening. In the fall of 1989, just after the Solidarity-led government ascended to power, it tried to introduce a Law on Transformation of State Enterprises, which would have converted state enterprises into joint-stock companies with the treasury as the sole owner (this process is usually termed "corporatization," or sometimes "commercialization"). The Transformation Law stalled in the Parliament and was ultimately withdrawn as a result of

the objections of workers' groups, who rejected the state's claim to sole ownership of the enterprises.

The Mazowiecki government then went ahead with the Act on Privatization, which in many ways reflects the confused state of affairs. The new law allows for the transformation of state enterprises into treasury-owned joint-stock companies under the direction of a new Ministry of Property Transformation, and also provides that the process should be approved by the state enterprise manager, the workers' council and the founding organ. Thus, the enterprises are given a veto. The state, however, retains a trump card, since the Prime Minister, on the motion of the Minister of Ownership Transformation, can order the transformation of an enterprise. In the end, there remains the delicate balancing act between the interests of workers, managers and the state.

The act has several other key provisos but in general provides enough flexibility that the government has a very wide range of options. Most of the legislation seems to envision a standard case-by-case privatization. Several articles in the act detail how shares are to be sold to the public, with the workers getting a discount of half-price on up to 20 percent of the shares.[23] Once again, flexibility is built into the act by allowing the Council of Ministers (the executive body of the government) to permit State Treasury shares to be sold in a different manner to those specified in the act. The act also provides that shares might be distributed for vouchers, or "scrip," issued by the government but does not specify how that is to be done. The Deputy Prime Minister publicly stated during the debate on the law that the free distribution of shares, through one mechanism or another, would play some role in the privatization.

During the period between corporatization of the firm and its sale, the enterprise is to be governed by a supervisory board, of which two-thirds are appointed by the government and one-third elected by the workers. A maximum of two years can pass between the time of corporatization and privatization (defined as the point in which the state's holdings fall to less than half of the shares).

The law also restricts the role of foreign investors, who are allowed, in the aggregate, to purchase up to 10 percent of the shares of an enterprise without restriction but who must obtain government approval for ownership of more than 10 percent. The Mazowiecki government had stressed that it would be liberal in granting access to foreign investors, although it emphasized that the process must be controlled to prevent abuses and to monitor the extent of foreign participation in the economy. Since the law builds in so much flexibility, it is clear that politics, and policy choices, rather than the le-

Table 20-3. *United States: Employee Ownership of Large Industrial Firms*

Company	Business	Persons employed
Ownership greater than 50 percent		
Science Applications	Research and development	10,000
Parsons Corporation	Engineering	10,000
Amsted Industries	Manufacturing	8,300
Weirton Steel	Steel manufacturing	8,100
Avondale Shipyards	Shipbuilding	7,500
W.L. Gore Associates	High-tech manufacturing	5,000
Simmons Company	Furniture manufacturing	4,900
Republic Engineered Steel	Steel manufacturing	4,900
Graybar Electric	Electrical equipment manufacturing	4,700
Treasure Chest Advertising	Printing	4,000
National Steel & Shipbuilding	Shipbuilding	4,000
Stebbins Engineering	Engineering	4,000
CH2M Hill	Engineering	2,300
Northwestern Steel and Wire Steel	Manufacturing	2,300
McLouth Steel	Steel manufacturing	2,000
Cranston Print Works	Textile printing	1,800
Okonite Company	Wire and cable manufacturing	1,700
North American Rayon	Rayon manufacturing	1,500
Total		87,000
Percent of total manufacturing employment[a]		0.4
Ownership between 25 percent and 50 percent		
Phillips Petroleum	Petroleum	28,400
PMC Corporation	Industrial manufacturing	28,000
Tyson Foods	Chicken processing	25,000
Ashland Oil	Oil refining	22,800
USG	Construction material	22,000
Colt Industries	Industrial products	19,700
Olin Corp.	Chemicals/defense	17,000
Hallmark Cards	Greeting cards	15,521
Lowe's Companies, Inc.	Lumber and hardware	14,700
CBI Industries	Energy and manufacturing	11,400
Stone and Webster	Engineering	10,000
Harcourt Brace Jovanovich	Publishing	8,000
Herman Miller Inc.	Furniture manufacturing	5,000
Dentsply International	Dental equipment	3,500
Applied Power, Inc.	Automotive equipment	3,400
Swank, Inc.	Leather goods	3,100
Anderson Corporation	Window manufacturing	2,800
Tyler Corp.	Cast iron pipes	2,700
H.K. Porter	Manufacturing	2,600
Nationwide Automotive	Auto supplies	2,200
U.S. Sugar	Sugar manufacturing	2,100
Granite Construction Co.	Highway and heavy construction	2,000
Anthony Industries	Recreation products	2,000
CF&I Steel	Steel manufacturing	2,000
Quad/Graphics	Printing	2,000
Ormet Inc.	Aluminum manufacturing	1,700
E-Systems	Electronics	1,500
Total		261,121
Percent of total manufacturing employment[a]		1.4

a. Total manufacturing employment in US equals 19,167,000 employees.

Source: National Center for Employee Ownership (1989) and U.S. Labor Department.

gal constraints of the new privatization act, will determine the pace and strategy of privatization.

In August and September of 1990, Deputy Prime Minister Balcerowicz publicly outlined the shape of the privatization program to be developed by the Mazowiecki government. The program would not be based on the case-by-case sale of medium- and large-scale enterprises through initial public offerings. Instead, privatization would be accelerated by means of several techniques, including, among other things, the discount sales of shares to workers and a voucher system to place shares in the hands of the public.

Corporate Governance and Financial Intermediaries

A privatization program in Eastern Europe must do more than simply return enterprise ownership to private hands. The government should also strive to create an ownership structure that will effectively oversee the management of the newly privatized assets. That is, the government should foster an effective structure of corporate governance. Moreover, the government should encourage the development of financial intermediaries that will be important both for monitoring enterprises and for allowing the private sector to diversify the risks of property ownership.

Creation of adequate long-term oversight of management is strongly emphasized for two main reasons. First, there can be little confidence in the current managerial class in Eastern Europe. Many managers owe their positions to their Communist party allegiances rather than to their technical competence. Further, many competent managers won their positions because of their engineering expertise, which was crucial in a planned economy, rather than their ability to navigate the enterprise in the uncharted waters of an open market economy. Thus, an enormous effort will have to be made to evaluate current managers and to train and promote new managers.

Second, Eastern Europe lacks many of the individual and institutional actors that are normally involved in corporate governance in the West. Therefore, special care must be taken to assure that at least some institutions capable of effective corporate governance are created. In particular, unlike in normal market economies, Eastern European countries cannot rely on corporate oversight by: the original families and entrepreneurs that established an enterprise; outside directors that have a long involvement with an enterprise and understand its history and corporate culture; a vast financial press and investment analysis sector that investigates, reports and evaluates management behavior; or regula-

tory institutions such as the Securities and Exchange Commission, which pursue investigations of malfeasance and which require various forms of disclosure that are widely analyzed by the investment community.

The basic proposal described in the next section, is that the ownership of most enterprises should be divided up into *tranches* among various groups and financial institutions that will each have an incentive to monitor the enterprise and promote sound management. In the proposal, a portion of the shares is sold or given to workers; another part is transferred to pension funds and commercial banks; another part is transferred mainly to mutual funds that in turn will be owned by individual households; and another part is sold in a block to a "core investor" group that commits both to hold a substantial proportion of the shares for several years and to manage the firm.

A Strategy for Achieving Effective Corporate Governance

There are two essential tasks in establishing effective governance of the productive capital now in state hands. The first, more urgent, task is to introduce a provisional system of corporate governance that can monitor a firm's management and prevent both managers and workers from squandering its capital income and capital assets before full privatization takes place. The second, longer term task is to foster a structure of ownership in which the new private owners will be in a strong position to manage their newly acquired assets.

A vital first step to privatization is the conversion of state enterprises into corporate form (their corporatization), to concentrate the property rights of the enterprise in a corporate board of directors appointed by the owners. Inevitably, given a realistic timetable for any privatization scheme, the initial boards of almost all enterprises will have to be appointed by the government, with the subsequent boards to be appointed by private owners as they emerge during the privatization. To reduce the enormous administrative burden of creating a large number of corporate boards, the task should initially be focused on the 500 largest firms.

The urgency of corporatization results from the complete inadequacy of the current structure of governance, in which the manager is completely unmonitored in most firms or is monitored by workers' councils in others. It is stressed here that the lack of effective governance has already produced enormous social, political and economic problems that are likely to continue or worsen despite attempts at administrative controls.

Corporatization was one of the first steps in the recent German economic unification. The *Treuhandanstalt*, the state property trust, mandated the conversion of all 8,000 state enterprises into corporate form by administrative decree. So far, the Poles, Hungarians and Yugoslavs have avoided this step for fear of running into political conflict with the powerful workers' councils (known as "enterprise councils" in Hungary). These governments also fear being accused of politicizing the economy by attempting to reconcentrate control in the hands of the state.

The political risks of corporatization pale in comparison with the potential economic gains. If the principle is not accepted early in the privatization, managers and workers' councils together with the state will likely end up bargaining over the terms for privatizing on a firm-by-firm basis, thus paralyzing the process. Moreover, without early corporatization there will be no effective way of replacing the most incompetent managers in enterprises that have weak or non-existent workers' councils. Since the boards of directors will monitor joint-venture arrangements and other major corporate decisions, the ability to forestall "spontaneous privatization" will be greatly enhanced.

At the same time, the risk of politicizing the process through appointing boards of directors can be significantly reduced if, first, the task is largely and visibly subcontracted to professional institutions, such as a consortium of Polish and international management advisory firms, and, second, the initial board of directors is made provisional until the enterprise is at least partially privatized (at which point, the new owners would assume some of the responsibility for forming the board of directors). In fact, Polish company law requires that the first board of directors be constituted for one year, while subsequent boards of directors be constituted for a three-year tenure.

The long-term challenge of the privatization program is to create a structure of ownership in which the owners have effective control over the enterprises. For example, if ownership of the enterprises is too widely dispersed, the individual owners will have very little incentive to monitor the management.[24] Moreover, it will be useful to match firms with appropriate owners in the privatization itself, rather than relying on subsequent trading to establish the "right" owners for the firm. The market for corporate control through takeovers is highly flawed, with significant externalities and asymmetries of information. Therefore, the market cannot be relied upon to do a good job in matching potential owners and firms: many efficient takeovers may never be achieved, and many inefficient takeovers may be consummated.[25]

These concerns lead to three principles for establishing effective long-term control over privatized firms. First, the privatization should avoid creating an atomistic ownership structure for the large enterprises, in which hundreds of thousands or millions of owners each retain a small number of shares. Most ownership of the large enterprises should be held by intermediary firms such as pension funds, mutual funds or commercial banks, or by large owners with concentrated stakes. This principle also conforms to the idea that small investors should hold diversified portfolios, through mutual funds perhaps, rather than shares in a single enterprise.

Second, the privatization should be designed to foster at least one significant non-financial investor in each major industrial enterprise. This investor would hold around 20 percent of the shares and would create a "stable core" of ownership of the firm, to use a concept developed in the French privatization. In the privatizations of the 1980s, the French believed that their capital markets were too thin to rely primarily on public placements as the dominant method of privatization. They also lacked the investment banks that had guided public placements in the United Kingdom. Most importantly, there was concern that no single owner or ownership group would emerge with a significant stake in each enterprise.

Therefore, the French devised a scheme known as the "stable core." This involved soliciting a bid from a single investor, or group of investors working together, to buy 20 percent or more of an enterprise. This group committed a sum of money, prepared a management proposal and submitted its financial bid. It also committed to hold its shares for at least five years. After review of the bids, the French government designated a winner to serve as the stable core. The winning bid was selected not only on the share price offered, but also on the financial strength of the bidder, its reputation and experience, and the quality of its management plan.[26]

In Eastern European privatization plans, as in the French plan, governments would attempt to market a 20 percent block of shares in each enterprise to an investment group that could be domestic, foreign or mixed. This group would be vested with significant representation on the corporate board in return for a requirement that the investor group hold the enterprise for a specified period of time, perhaps three to five years.

Furthermore, the Eastern European countries should create a legal and institutional environment in which financial intermediaries play a more active oversight role than is typical in the United States and United Kingdom. The need for oversight by financial intermediaries results from the lack of other institutions or individuals in Eastern Europe that can be relied upon to help oversee an enterprise's corporate management. Thus, a great effort will be needed to economize on information that will be vital in corporate governance. Since banks, pension funds and mutual funds will have such information, these institutions should also be assigned a major role in the governance.

As a first step toward strengthening the hand of the financial intermediaries, the Eastern European economies should aim to develop universal banking, as in Germany and Japan,[27] where the commercial banks hold stakes in corporate assets and play an active role in the oversight of the enterprises.[28] The new banks should place representatives on the corporate boards of directors and strengthen their capacities to participate in the restructuring of troubled firms. Of course, qualified banks cannot be created at once, but it will be far easier to build up the operational capacity of a dozen large banks (perhaps through management contracts with foreign banks) than to rely on the decentralized oversight of thousands of individual enterprises.[29]

As a second step toward strengthening the oversight by financial intermediaries, newly-created mutual funds and pension funds should be encouraged to appoint representatives to the boards of directors of enterprises in which they hold shares, and to create the institutional capacity to monitor closely a large number of firms. When the mutual funds and pension funds are initially licensed, for example, they could be required to present plans detailing how they will appoint directors to corporate boards and how they will develop the expertise to monitor these companies. One possibility is that they might subcontract the management oversight to an international management consulting firm.

The proposal that mutual funds and pension funds be so actively involved in corporate oversight may seem unusual, but it should be noted that several recent analysts have argued that the same change should apply in the United States.[30] One proposal in the US context is for the institutional investors to appoint a new class of professional, outside directors who would serve full-time on a small number of boards of directors (perhaps six boards per person) for corporations held by the investors.[31] These new directors would constitute a "critical mass" on each board, but would serve together with traditional, outside directors (such as chief executive officers [CEOs] of other companies) and inside directors. The proposal for Poland is more natural in view of the fact that the newly developed financial intermediaries will have a much smaller task with regard to portfolio management than is usual in the United States. The reason is that the market for corporate shares will be considerably smaller and less liquid there than in the United States. Thus, they will have the time to focus somewhat more on corporate governance and rather less on portfolio management.

The Role of the Stock Market in Privatization

It is doubtful that the stock exchange can or should play a major role in the privatization or more generally in the development of financial markets in Eastern Europe in the next few years. While each country will surely develop a stock exchange, the liquidity of the new exchanges will be low, and their capacity to raise corporate capital or serve as a market for corporate control will be highly circumscribed. Moreover, information concerning the fundamental valuation of firms will continue to be limited for many years, since firms will be operating for the first time in a market environment. Thus, it can be expected that the markets will be subject to extreme volatility and will tend toward insider trading, not only because asymmetries of information will be pronounced, but also because the policing of the exchanges will be imperfect in the first few years. Nor are there likely to be many firms with a capital value that is large enough to support many institutional investors and small shareholders.

In general, the continental European economies rely much less heavily on stock markets than do the United Kingdom and the United States for raising and trading corporate wealth and for gaining corporate control.[32] One sign of the smaller role of the stock market in Western Europe is the low number of listed companies in most European countries. Austria, for example, has only 81 listed Austrian firms; Finland, 78; Norway, 122; Sweden, 135; and Switzerland, 177. In addition, hostile takeovers in these countries scarcely occur. There is little evidence to suggest, however, that this relative dearth of stock market activity has hindered effective corporate governance: many observers feel that the opposite is true—that active stock market trading encourages a short-term bias in managerial decisions. Given the difficulties of establishing an active stock exchange for a large number of firms, it seems safe to recommend that Eastern Europe follow the West European lead, at least initially, and downplay the institutional role of the stock exchange.

A Strategy for Privatization

At the outset a basic question was posed: how can a very large number of enterprises be privatized quickly while at the same time establishing an effective structure of corporate governance? It is argued here that a large role must be played by new institutional investors and a relatively small role by the stock market. Following is a description of a strategy for privatization that might be used for transferring ownership and control to private owners.

One key point in this strategy is that much of the privatization should be accomplished through a free distribution of shares to various groups, including workers, pension funds and mutual funds, rather than through the sale of shares in an initial public offering, which was standard practice in the well-known British privatizations. In Eastern Europe, the free distribution of shares helps sidestep the difficult, costly and time-consuming process of enterprise valuation and recognizes the scarcity of financial capital in private hands.

There is good reason to expect that the problem posed by asset valuation will be far more severe in the case of Eastern European enterprises than has been the case in the West. The economic environment is shifting in fundamental ways as the transformation to market economies proceeds. Not only is the domestic environment undergoing a profound change, but in several countries, international trade is being liberalized and currency convertibility introduced. The Comecon system governing trade and payments among the Eastern European countries will be revamped in January 1991. Furthermore, the legal and regulatory environment is also changing. Indeed, the level of interest rates needed to discount future profits for the purpose of valuation could be greatly influenced by the strategy for stabilization itself. As a result of all of these changes, many key relative prices have shifted and will continue to do so. Finally, in many enterprises there will be changes in the structure of management or in management itself that will have profound effects on the value of the enterprise. These factors each pose fundamental conceptual problems for asset valuation and, taken together, cast grave doubts on the viability of privatization schemes that require careful valuation of assets as a prelude to the sale of enterprises.[33]

Another key point in the strategy is that most enterprises should be privatized in a common manner to avoid debates between the government and individual enterprises. To the extent that a common procedure is followed, it will be harder for individual enterprises to attempt to bargain for special advantages in the course of the privatization. At the same time, however, it should be possible for an enterprise to proceed outside of the common procedure (for example, if it receives an attractive bid) and yet remain subject to various due process standards and government oversight.

Before detailing a method of privatization that uses a direct distribution of shares, consider the four fundamental limitations of initial public offerings in the Eastern European context. First, public offerings require a careful valuation of each firm and a great deal of finan-cial preparation. They tend to be time-consuming under normal circumstances and would be far slower in Eastern European, where valuation of firms is nearly impossible and where the financial infrastructure for initial public offerings does not yet exist. Second, the financial capital currently in the hands of the public is a small fraction of the value of the enterprises to be privatized, assuming a reasonable market interest rate (and thus a reasonable price/earnings ratio for the firm). Thus, any attempt to sell a large proportion of the enterprises would create serious financial problems. Third, initial public offerings are typically used, as has been the case in Britain, to secure a widespread ownership of shares by small investors (in order to create "peoples' capitalism"). While this aim is desirable, it does not generally produce an effective structure of corporate governance and, from a logistical point of view, is surely inappropriate for all but the largest enterprises. Fourth, reliance upon initial public offerings would lead to the privatization of only the most profitable enterprises and leave the marginal or unhealthy enterprises—which are viewed as less marketable—in the hands of the government.

Consider each of these four points in more detail. Table 20.4 shows the total worldwide number of privatizations through public offerings between 1980 and 1987, according to a World Bank study. The United Kingdom accomplished 13 initial public offerings during this period, and the country with the largest number, Italy, accomplished 15. Many authors have discussed the laborious preparations involved in each initial public offering. Since there is as yet no stock exchange in Poland, no Polish investment banks and, indeed, no tradition of valuing enterprises for public sale, privatization through initial public offerings would likely be quite slow in Eastern European countries.

The normal problems of initial public offerings are greatly compounded by the shortage of public savings with which to purchase shares. Table 20.5 presents a rough illustration of this problem. Assume that the firms are valued as a multiple of annual earnings, with three alternatives considered: price/earnings ratios of 6, 8 or 10. In each case, the market value of the 500 largest enterprises is compared with the financial savings of private households, which consists of currency and bank deposits. Even for the lowest price/earnings ratio of 6, the value of the largest enterprises is roughly 2.5 times the current stock of savings.

Thus, the shares could not be sold quickly unless one of three things happened. First, the price/earnings ratio could fall sharply, leading to the sale of enterprises for close to nothing to those in the public who hold cash. Second, the government could lend money to the public for share purchase, in the form of grand leveraged buy-

Table 20-4. *Completed Privatizations by Method, Various Countries, 1980-87*

Country	Completed public offerings	Completed private sales	Completed worker/ management buy-out
Africa			
Equatorial Guinea	0	6	0
Gabon	0	1	0
Gambia	2	1	1
Ghana	0	1	0
Guinea	0	25	0
Ivory Coast	1	18	5
Mali	0	2	0
Mauritania	0	1	0
Niger	0	12	0
Senegal	0	4	0
Sierra Leone	1	1	0
Uganda	0	1	0
Zaire	0	0	0
Asia and the Pacific			
Bangladesh	4	1	0
Japan	3	2	0
Korea	2	5	0
Malaysia	2	5	0
Singapore	12	0	0
Sri Lanka	1	4	0
Taiwan	2	3	0
Thailand	1	1	0
Papua New Guinea	1	0	0
New Zealand	1	3	0
Europe			
Austria	2	0	0
Denmark	1	0	0
France	14	10	1
Germany	6	0	0
Italy	15	17	1
Netherlands	1	0	0
Spain	5	25	0
Sweden	1	1	0
Turkey	2	0	0
United Kingdom	13	18	12
North and South America			
United States	1	2	0
Brazil	6	46	0
Chile	12	24	1
Jamaica	2	22	0
Mexico	3	7	0

Source: Vuylsteke (1988a), table 1, Annex E, pp. 169-72.

Table 20-5. *Poland: Capital Value of the Largest State Enterprises, 1990*
(billions of US dollars)

Number of enterprises	Net income[a]	Estimated capital value			Ratio to household financial savings[b]		
		P/E=6	P/E=8	P/E=10	P/E=6	P/E=8	P/E=10
Top 100	2.9	17.6	23.5	29.4	1.6	2.1	2.7
Top 200	3.6	21.6	28.8	36.0	2.0	2.6	3.3
Top 300	4.0	23.7	31.6	39.5	2.2	2.9	3.6
Top 400	4.4	26.3	35.1	43.8	2.4	3.2	4.0
Top 484	4.6	27.5	36.7	45.9	2.5	3.3	4.2

a. Data are annualized from January-June 1990.

b. Ratio includes household holdings of cash and domestic and foreign currency deposits in the banking system, which totalled US $11 billion in mid-1990.

Source: Authors' own calculations. Data were provided by the authorities and *Informacja Statystyczna*.

out. Third, the enterprises could be sold mainly to foreigners. None of these alternatives would be remotely acceptable on a political or economic basis.

Interestingly, there is one case in which a country did try to sell a large number of enterprises very cheaply in the context of an enormous credit squeeze—Chile, during 1975-78, just after the coup that toppled Salvador Allende and brought Ernesto Pinochet to power. There, 232 firms were rapidly sold to the public through leveraged buy-outs. The outcome in Chile confirms the worst fears of such a process.[34]

Not only did the Chilean experiment produce weak firms and undue concentration of wealth, but the government was (rightly) attacked for selling the firms at very low prices to the few financial groups that had some access to cash. According to Rolf Luders, a former Chilean finance minister (1979-81) and a strong advocate of privatization in general:

The first round [of privatizations] was carried out in the midst of a deep structural transformation process, during which there was little interest on the part of foreigners to invest in the country, and which was accompanied by considerable political, social, and economic uncertainty... These debt-led privatizations carried out in an economically unstable environment contributed to generate a considerable degree of *financial asset concentration, financial instability, and some important macroeconomic problems.*[35]

Ironically, because the newly privatized firms were undercapitalized and heavily indebted, many of them collapsed during the financial crisis of 1982-83 and had to be re-nationalized.

One novel approach might rescue initial public offerings from the problem of limited purchasing power. The government might transfer purchasing power to the public in direct grants rather than loans. This is the basic idea behind *voucher schemes*. The government issues purchasing power in a kind of voucher (scrip) that can be used solely to purchase shares. The initial distribution of vouchers can be made on an equal basis for the entire population or according to other criteria. Care would have to be taken to ensure that vouchers do not become money substitutes, otherwise the issue of vouchers could lead to a sudden expansion of the money supply that is not synchronized with the sale of shares.[36] As will be mentioned later, the voucher schemes are still likely to suffer from the other weaknesses of initial public offerings: their time-consuming nature and their inability to create an effective ownership structure.

In particular, the use of a voucher scheme in connection with initial public offerings may involve prohibitive administrative costs. If individuals swap vouchers for shares, the pattern of share ownership will involve a dispersion of holdings in small lots. A company worth US$10 million—medium-sized by Polish standards—might be in the position of distributing only $300,000 in dividends per year (with a 15 percent rate of return and a 20 percent dividend pay-out ratio). If a voucher system involved the sale of 500 enterprises to 25 million adult Poles, it could well lead to 100,000 or more shareholders per enterprise. As a result, the administrative costs would leave few resources for profit distribution.

The discussion in Eastern Europe of privatization through initial public offerings has led to the notion that only profitable enterprises would be privatized. Accordingly, the marginal or unhealthy enterprises would be left to the government to restructure or liquidate. This proposition arises naturally from an approach to privatization based on the case-by-case sale of enterprises, because the apparent difficulties of valuing and marketing enterprises may not be sustainable. It would be preferable for all enterprises regardless of their financial position to be corporatized and quickly put into private hands. There are several reasons not to leave the marginal and unhealthy enterprises in the hands of the state. First, these enterprises could remain in state hands for a long period as the government tries to determine whether restructuring or liquidation is appropriate. During this time, the enterprises would be targets for further asset stripping by an unrestrained management. Second, a corporate board of directors will be more competent and less subject to political pressures than the government in guiding the restructuring and, if necessary, liquidation.

An Illustrative Plan for Large-Scale Privatization in Poland

The discussion now turns to how the considerations of the previous sections can be integrated in a single, workable plan. The goal would be to complete the privatization of the 500 largest state enterprises in Poland's industrial sector within a period of four years. While the privatization strategy of the Polish government is still evolving and is likely to change further after the presidential elections, it probably will share some—although certainly not all—of the features that outlined here. Indeed, it should be stressed once again that the development of this proposal has benefitted from extensive discussion with Polish officials in crystallizing the ideas.

To achieve a rapid privatization, a common track would be followed for most of the large enterprises. This approach has two advantages: the minimization of negotiation between the state and the individual enterprises; and the routinization of the process. Most firms would be privatized in tranches, with each "slice" of shares transferred or sold to a different kind of investor. A minority of firms would be sold outright in a standard kind of privatization (either a public offering or a private sale).

At the beginning of the process, each of the 500 largest enterprises would be corporatized, that is, converted into a joint-stock company with the shares initially issued to the state as 100 percent owner. An initial board of directors would be appointed according to the privatization law: two-thirds of the seats would be appointed by the government (most likely by a private investment group that would be hired to advise the government), while one-third of the seats would be elected by the workers. The initial board of directors would serve for one year.

A few enterprises would then proceed with a British-style privatization through initial public offerings, private sales or auctions, although these enterprises are not discussed in this paper. (The privatization law should leave room for individual firms to pursue these routes, especially when private bidders come forward.) The bulk of the enterprises would begin the privatization in tranches. The first tranche would be the transfer, or possibly sale, of shares to an enterprise's workers. Most simply, the government could mandate that the workers receive 10 percent of the enterprise shares for free (the law provides for the sale to workers of up to 20 percent of the enterprise for half price). The allocation of shares among the work force would be determined by the manager with approval by the new corporate board. On this particular issue, it may be wise to require that the worker representatives on the board of directors also approve the share distribution plan among the workers.

In addition to the 10 percent distributed to the workers, around 5 percent of the shares would be reserved for compensation for the managers and the corporate board. Managers could receive stock options or outright share ownership as part of an incentive compensation package. It is expected that the distribution of shares to managers as part of their compensation package could provide an important early spur to increased efficiency within the firm.[37]

The second tranche of shares, around 20 percent of the total, would be used to capitalize a new private pension system. The shares would be distributed to several new pension funds, which would in turn be distributed to enterprises and individuals to back retirement payments. Each pension fund would receive a portfolio of enterprises and would be responsible for the active oversight of the corporations in its portfolio. It could also trade its shares.

During the following few years, enterprises would be "hooked up" with the new pension funds according to the size of the enterprise and the age and wage distributions of the employees. The basic idea would be for the state to scale back its own social security payments that are now made directly from the budget, and to increase the payments being made by the capitalized pension fund.[38] The actual transition from budgetary expenditures to payments by private pension funds could be phased in over a period of 5 to 10 years. If the pension funds receive the income from 20 percent of the shares of the 500 top enterprises, the annual earnings of the pension funds would equal about $900 million, or about 20 percent of the annual pension payments now made from the central budget.

The use of share distribution to capitalize the pension system is not without complexity, and numerous logistical problems will have to be resolved to distribute claims in a fair way and reduce social security payments from the government in line with growing benefits from the private plans.

The third tranche would consist of 10 percent of the shares and would be used to capitalize the existing state-owned commercial banks and the insurance sector. Commercial banks would receive 6 percent of the shares (60 percent of this tranche) and would be expected to develop into active investors along German lines. At the same time, the commercial banks themselves would be converted to joint-stock companies and prepared for privatization.

The capitalization and commercialization of commercial banks would have two main benefits. First, as active investors the commercial banks would begin to play an important role in scrutinizing the management of enterprises. Second, the capitalization would also help the banks to improve their weak balance sheets, which need recapitalization in any case. It is estimated here that with 6 percent of the shares in the 500 largest enterprises, commercial banks would receive a transfer that is the equivalent of about 10 percent of commercial bank gross assets.

Privatization schemes that rely in large part on the free distribution of shares are sometimes said to be disadvantaged in that the government foregoes a large, potential revenue source. While this point may be true when shares are distributed freely to workers or households, the revenue loss may not be incurred when public or quasi-public institutions are capitalized, as in the case of the pension funds and the commercial banks. The capitalization of the pension system will reduce the requirement for budgetary funding of the social security system by an equal magnitude. The capitalization of the commercial banks will likewise reduce a future claim on the budgetary resources of the banks by anticipating the need for a commercial bank re-capitalization.

The fourth tranche will consist of 20 percent of the shares of the enterprises, which will be distributed generally to the adult population of Poland (roughly 25 million). This part of the share distribution *will* cause a loss of wealth for the state sector, since the distribution to households will not be recouped by budgetary savings elsewhere. There are two prevailing models for how to distribute these shares. In one model, the shares of the enterprises would be distributed to several private investment trusts (which are closed-end mutual funds), whose shares in turn would be freely distributed to the adult citizens of Poland. After the initial distribution of the shares, the investment trusts would be free actively to manage their portfolios.

Each individual would receive one share in one of the investment trusts, so that if there were, say, 10 trusts, each would have around 2.5 million subscribers. The investments trusts would pass through dividends and other income to the shareholding public after deducting the fund's expenses and fees. Each trust would be managed by a Polish entity but would contract with a foreign advisory firm to assist in the establishment of the trust, in the active management of assets and in the administration of the dividend distribution.

An alternative model suggests free distribution through vouchers. Individuals would receive vouchers with a fixed face value in the domestic currency. Shares would be tendered at a fixed price after a quick valuation. Households could either buy shares with their vouchers or buy claims on investment trust companies, which in turn would use the vouchers to purchase the tendered shares. The government could encourage the households to deposit their shares with the investment trusts as a sound method of diversification.

This second approach has won widespread support in Poland and is viewed as politically superior to the direct distribution of investment trust certificates, since it offers more choice to households. On the negative side, however, it is vastly more complicated and could in fact greatly slow the privatization. With the voucher plan, unlike the plan to distribute investment trust shares, there must be a valuation of individual companies as well as a time-consuming public offering. In addition, the vouchers could be complex to issue and process.

The free distribution of investment trust shares could be completed within about one year, while the system relying on vouchers would probably take a couple of years longer. In either case, after this phase is completed, the government will retain roughly 35 percent ownership in the partially privatized companies. A second board of directors would have to be formed upon the expiration of the one-year term for the initial board appointed by the government. The second board would be elected by the shareholders for a three-year period. The shareholder groups created by the pension funds, the banks and the investment trusts would presumably dominate this board of directors and, thereby, firmly establish control over management. The board of directors could be elected by cumulative voting (essentially, proportional representation) to make sure that each of the major holders of shares places representatives on the supervisory board.

Following the free distribution of shares, any number of methods might be used to dispose of the remaining government holdings, including public offerings, private placements of shares and further free distributions. Of course, if share sales are the predominant means of disposing of the last tranche, the government will have to undertake a careful valuation of each enterprise and prepare the sale. In addition, the government may wish to encourage enterprises and investor groups to come forward with privatization proposals in a decentralized manner, provided that each deal receives an adequate degree of scrutiny. In certain cases, the government may wish to retain a minority holding and can look to Western European experience for an appropriate pattern of government equity positions in the corporate sector.

The French concept of selling a block of shares to a "stable core" of investors is an attractive technique for disposing of the last tranche. In the case of Poland, the government would entertain bids from domestic, foreign or mixed investor groups. It should be possible to establish a stable core for most of the 500 largest enterprises and complete the privatization of these enterprises within a three-year period. The stable core would eventually become the primary investor group and, because it would be entrepreneurial in nature, would take a dominant role in supervising corporate management. In time, the supervisory role of pension funds, investments trusts and commercial banks, although important, would no longer be the main force monitoring and controlling management behavior.

Central Features of the Illustrative Plan

In concluding this section, what are regarded to be the central features of the plan, and what are regarded as illustrative but not fundamental are stressed. Several key steps are identified here: corporatization that will establish the legal basis of the new economic system; a partial distribution of shares to workers and managers for political and incentive reasons; and the distribution of some shares to financial intermediaries such as banks and mutual funds, which will have some early responsibility for appointing corporate boards. Once this process goes forward for the bulk of the largest few hundred enterprises, it is not vital what fraction of shares the government holds—it could range from 30 percent to 50 percent of the enterprise. In the latter case, however, the government would likely be a mostly silent partner in the daily management of the enterprise.

The proposition that long-term management of the enterprises will be enhanced if the government can sell a significant block of each enterprise to a core buyer is accepted. This process will take time. The risks of waiting, however, will be significantly reduced if a large part of the enterprise is already in private hands and if the preliminary struggle over the form of ownership, corporate versus worker management, for example, is decisively settled in favor of a corporate structure.

Conclusion

The most daunting challenge facing the countries of Eastern Europe today is the transfer of state property to private hands in a manner that is rapid, equitable and fiscally sound. To achieve this goal in the Eastern European context is particularly difficult, because it requires the complete redefinition of property rights and wealthholding in the society and the creation anew of the basic institutions of a market financial system. This paper has reviewed the enormous scope of the privatization task and suggested principles that should govern the privati-

zation. The case of Poland was used to illustrate the political, legal and logistical problems that lie in the way of privatization. A concrete plan for privatization in Poland was presented, aimed at demonstrating how these constraints can be met and how the main economic objectives can be achieved.

Poland, and other countries of Eastern Europe, must devise strategies for privatization that ensure that the transformation of the ownership structure goes forward uninterrupted. The standard, case-by-case approach based on initial public offerings is prone to get bogged down for political, economic and logistical reasons. An alternative approach is needed.

The rapid conversion of state enterprises into corporate form and the distribution of tranches of shares to various groups in the population, including workers, commercial banks, pension funds and mutual funds, are advocated here. This strategy differs substantially from the standard methods of privatization that have been used in the West: the sale of shares in an initial public offering and private placements to investor groups. The free distribution of shares helps to sidestep the difficult, costly and time-consuming process of enterprise valuation, as well as the scarcity of financial capital in private hands in Eastern Europe. More importantly, corporatization combined with the free distribution of shares can occur quickly. Rapid privatization is needed to combat the inevitable social, political and economic problems associated with the lack of corporate governance.

It is vital to establish effective governance quickly. The first, and urgent, task is to introduce a provisional system of corporate governance that can monitor the management and prevent the managers and workers from squandering the capital income and capital assets of the firms before full privatization takes place. The second, and long-term, task is to foster a structure of ownership in which the new private owners will be in a strong position to manage their newly acquired assets.

Notes

1. This paper originally appeared in *Brookings Papers on Economic Activity* 2 (1990): 293-341.

2. For a discussion of the authors' preferred strategy for making the transition to a market economy in Eastern Europe, see Lipton and Sachs (1990). For two other discussions of a comprehensive strategy for transition to a market economy in Eastern Europe, see Blue Ribbon Commission: Project Hungary (1990) and Kornai (1990).

3. There are, of course, exceptions. Trenchant recent analyses may be found in Kornai (1990) and Milanovic (1990). For an excellent overview of the privatization experience throughout the world, see World Bank (1988).

4. Cited in Milanovic (1990, p. 45). For evidence on the rise of institutional investors in the United Kingdom and Japan, see Cosh, Hughes and Singh (1989). They report that in the United Kingdom, for example, financial institutions held 58.9 percent of the value of listed

securities in 1985, up from 44.8 percent in 1976 (table 6, p. 16).

5. Small-scale privatization is moving forward in Poland. Approximately 17,000 retail outlets had been privatized through September 1990. It is still not clear, however, if the government will be able to achieve its target of privatizing roughly two-thirds of the retail establishments during 1990.

6. The available evidence in Poland suggests a surge of private sector activity during 1990, with high rates of return and the rapid establishment of new enterprises. According to the official data, approximately 360,000 new private enterprises had been established during January-November 1990. However, the data are subject to many biases. Many establishments are not registered in order to avoid taxes; other establishments are simply shell organizations created to reduce taxes for other related businesses.

7. The authors' own views evolved during the policy debate in 1990 in favor of a free distribution of shares, and their views have been heavily influenced by several of the contributions mentioned in the text.

8. As is mentioned later, the idea of a "stable core" was central to the French privatization process in the mid-1980s. Notably, Kornai (1990, p. 91) independently stressed the importance of such a stable core in his recent book.

9. These data are out of date and overstate the extent of state ownership in many cases, such as in France and the United Kingdom, which have reduced the share in the 1980s.

10. In Poland, the social democratic faction within Solidarity argues for a more gradual, less free market strategy of reform.

11. According to official statistics, there were 231,000 private establishments in the industrial sector in 1988. These firms tend to be very small, with an average employment of two workers. Polish Authorities estimate that the private industrial sector accounts for only about 5 percent of sectoral output, although this figure is almost surely understated by the high level of activity in the underground (and therefore under-reported) economy.

12. For an extensive discussion of the difficulties and trade-offs involved in privatizing natural monopolies and other firms in noncompetitive environments, see Caves (1990) and Vickers and Yarrow (1988).

13. Sixteen firms have been dropped from the top 500 firms owing to a lack of adequate data on performance during the first half of 1990. The remaining 484 firms are used here as a proxy for the top 500.

14. This section draws heavily upon the research of Moffatt (1990) of the Washington law firm of Hogan and Hartson. The authors thank Joseph Bell for sharing this research material.

15. While the focus is on the phase of reform Communism in Poland after 1980 in contrast to the period of strict central planning before that time, it should be noted that the extent of centralization and decentralization waxed and waned throughout the post-war period. In the early years after the war, workers councils exercised some measure of management rights. These rights were largely lost with the Stalinist crackdown in the late 1940s, when the instruments of central planning were strengthened. There was a brief thaw in 1956 (at the time of Khrushchev's attack on Stalin at the 20th Party Congress), in which workers councils were again invigorated. By 1958, however, they were once again demoted in real influence.

16. See the discussion on Kornai's concept of the soft budget constraint in Kornai (1990), as well as other references therein.

17. For an excellent discussion of the different forms of governance of state-owned enterprises, see Milanovic (1990).

18. As reported by Moffatt (1990, p. 18) regarding the Amending Law on State Enterprises, March 9, 1990.

19. The average real wage in industry increased by 15 percent and 12 percent in 1988 and 1989, respectively. See Lipton and Sachs (1990).

20. The possibility that the workers might appoint a minority portion of the board, as in the company law in many Western European economies, is not being ruled out here. However, Poland's company law, which dates from the 1930s, does not have any such provision for worker representation.

21. For a sophisticated theoretical discussion of this point, see Dreze (1989). Dreze summarizes his findings as follows (p. 114):

In economies operating with uncertainty and incomplete insurance markets, it is natural to find capital hiring labor [rather than labor hiring capital], because efficient labor contracts in capitalist firms are easier to draw and monitor than efficient equity contracts for labor-managed firms.

The point is that it is generally more efficient for the owners of capital to hire labor than for laborers to rent capital.

22. See Blasi (1988, table C-2, pp. 264-66), which reports the proportion of firms owned by internal employee funds (ESOPs, retirement funds, savings funds, stock-purchase plans, etc.) in the case of Fortune 500 companies. There is not a single case in which an ESOP plan contains as much as 15 percent of the shares of a firm and only 7 firms of the Fortune 500 for which an internal stock fund of any kind contains more than 20 percent of the shares.

23. The value of this discount is to be capped, however, at less than the value of one year's average compensation of the workers in the firm.

24. The seminal contribution linking dispersed ownership to ineffective corporate governance is Berle and Means (1932). An enormous debate has arisen concerning ways to solve the governance problem and the extent to which it is a problem. Some economists, such as Demsetz (1983), suggest the problem is largely overcome in practice through a combination of managerial compensation based on stock prices and through an adequate size of share ownership by minority shareholders. Empirical evidence tending to support the Berle and Means hypothesis has recently been provided by Morck, Shliefer and Vishny (1988). In particular, these authors show that an enterprise's market valuation (measured by Tobin's Q) tends to be lower when management holds a very small share of the enterprise capital than when it holds a moderate amount of enterprise capital.

25. The main problem is that takeover bidders usually gain very little from a hostile takeover and therefore often do not undertake the effort even when efficiency considerations would recommend it (see Grossman and Hart 1980). On the other hand, some takeovers may go forward even when they are not justified by efficiency, if the takeover results in a gain in wealth for the bidder, not as a result of a rise in efficiency, but by a transfer of wealth from some stakeholders in the target firm. See Shleifer and Summers (1988).

26. For discussions of the French concept and development of the "stable core" (*noyau stable*), see Friedmann (1989a and b).

27. In the recent debate about the shortsightedness of American and British firms, considerable admiration has been expressed for the German and Japanese patterns of corporate governance. The argument has been summarized as follows:

Much recent criticism of the City of London by British industrialists is rooted in the belief that institutional investors are too willing to sell out to an opportunistic bidder without having due regard to the longer term strategy of the incumbent management. Institutional fund managers, it is said, operate on a different time horizon from industrialists and are prone to behave as speculators rather than owners. Unlike the bankers who have played such an important role in corporate governance in West Germany and Japan, the insurance companies and pension funds which dominate the more equity-oriented markets of the English-speaking economies are remote from the boards of companies in which they invest. The resulting pressure on management for short term performance, it is argued, is inimical to capital investment and research and development. (Plender 1990)

The argument seems to have found a recent practical response as well. French commercial banks, for example, are now moving to emulate the German pattern of bank ownership of industrial capital. (*Economist* 1990.)

28. Sheard (1989) contains an excellent discussion of the role of the commercial banks in corporate governance in Japan. He explains how "the main bank system in Japan substitutes for the 'missing' takeover market in Japan," or "to put it somewhat differently, the main bank serves to internalize the market for corporate control." (p. 407) Sheard stresses that corporate governance by a main bank economizes on scarce information, a fact of enormous practical relevance in Eastern Europe today.

29. The large banks were created by the dissolution in 1989 of the state mono-bank. These banks are therefore still in the state sector and have little actual experience in corporate oversight or loan analysis. However, they will have to play a vital role in reconstruction in any event and therefore their administrative capacity will have to be built up. The banks should receive shares of state enterprises, however, only when the banks themselves have a clear timetable for privatization and have a demonstrated program for enhancing their capacities to engage in corporate oversight. Initially, the shares could be transferred to each bank as a trustee of the government's shares, with the ownership actually shifting to the bank only upon privatization of the bank.

30. Some people have called for an even more active role for financial institutions by calling for the creation of holding companies that would immediately become majority owners of the state enterprises. Advocates of the holding company approach believe that it is crucial to create a dominant investor, with a majority stake, at once and later arrange for the sale of shares that would transfer corporate control. Here the view is that it would be dangerous to entrust the ownership of a large number of state enterprises to a single, untested financial institution. Such an arrangement would, in all likelihood, exacerbate problems of market power and would impede restructuring and liquidation. Moreover, there would be no clear mechanism under which the holding companies would ultimately divest themselves of the enterprises. As long as the holding company maintained its control, there would be a period of limbo during which time it would be difficult to create the financial institutions needed for a market economy.

31. See, for example, "Independent Directors with Bite on the Board" (1990, p. 19), which reviews the article by Gilson and Kraakman (1990).

32. See Franks and Mayer (1990) for evidence that hostile takeovers in the stock market play a larger role in the United Kingdom than in Germany in correcting "managerial failure." In Germany, a change in management is not commonly associated with a change of ownership.

33. If, on the other hand, valuation is done in a mechanical way, without close approximation to true economic value, privatization will inevitably generate large windfall gains and losses that can become focal points for political protest against the entire privatization.

34. For three analyses of the debacle of Chilean privatization in the 1970s, see Luders (1990), Hansson (1990) and Yotopoulos (1989).

35. Luders (1990, p.3).

36. It seems that the most effective way to ensure that the vouchers do not become near-monies is to limit their liquidity by issuing them in registered and non-tradable form.

37. For a discussion of managerial compensation schemes and their effects on firm efficiency, see Murphy (1985).

38. In essence, the income for part of the retirement payments would come out of enterprise profits. These profits are now financing the accumulation of physical and monetary capital by the enterprises. It is likely that as the enterprises are pressed to pay out part of their earnings to the pension funds, the retained earnings of the enterprises would fall, with a consequent fall in domestic investment spending.

References

Berle, Adolf A., and Gardiner C. Means. 1932. *The Modern Corporation and Private Property*. New York: MacMillan.

Bhagat, S., A. Shleifer and R. Vishny. 1990. "The Aftermath of Hostile Takeovers." Discussion Paper 87. London: LSE Financial Markets Group, June.

Blasi, Joseph R. 1988. *Employee Ownership: Revolution or Ripoff?*. Cambridge, Mass.: Ballinger Publishing Company.

Blue Ribbon Commission: Project Hungary. 1990. *Hungary: In Transformation to Freedom and Prosperity*. Indianapolis, Ind.: Hudson Institute, April.

Caves, Richard. 1990. "Lessons from Privatization in Britain: State Enterprise Behavior, Public Choice, and Corporate Governance." *Journal of Economic Behavior and Organization* 13:145-69.

Cosh, A.D., A. Hughes and A. Singh. 1989. "Openness, Innovation and Share Ownership: The Changing Stgructure of Financial Markets." Working Paper 74. Helsinki: World Institute for Development Economics Research, October.

Demsetz, Harold. 1983. "The Structure of Ownership and the Theory of the Firm." *Journal of Law and Economics* 26:375-90.

Dreze, Jacques H. 1989. *Labour Management Contracts and Capital Markets: A General Equilibrium Approach*. Oxford: Basil Blackwell. *Economist*. 1990, August 4.

Franks, J., and C. Mayer. 1990. "Capital Markets and Corporate Control: A Study of France, Germany, and the U.K." *Economic Policy* 10:189-231.

Friedmann, Jacques. 1989a. "Sur l'experience de privatisation: et sur les noyaux stables." *Commentaire* 45:11-18.

_____. 1989b. Lecture presented at the Israeli International Institute in Tel Aviv, September 14.

Gilson, Ronald, and Reinier Kraakman. 1990. "Reinventing the Outside Director: and Agenda for Institutional Investors." Working Paper no. 66. John M. Olin Program in Law and Economics, Stanford Law School, Stanford, California. August.

Grossman, Sanford J., and Oliver D. Hart. 1980. "Takeover Bids, The Freerider Problem, and the Theory of the Corporation." *Bell Journal of Economics* 11:42-64.

Hansson, Ardo H. 1990. "Capital Market Development and Privatization." Unpublished paper. World Institute for Development Economics Research, Helsinki, July.

Hinds, Manuel. 1990. "Issues in the Introduction of Market Forces in Eastern European Socialist Economies." Mimeo. World Bank, Washington, D.C. March.

Informacja Statstyczna [Statistical Information Monthly] (1989, 1990 and various issues). Warsaw: Central Statistical Office.

"Independent Directors with Bite on the Board." 1990. *Financial Times*, September 4, p. 19.

Jensen, Michael C., and Kevin J. Murphy. 1990. "CEO Incentives—It's Not How Much You Pay, But How." *Harvard Business Review* 90:138-53.

Kornai, Janos. 1990. *The Road to a Free Economy, Shifting from a Socialist System: The Example of Hungary*. New York: W.W. Norton and Company.

Lewandowski, J., and J. Szomberg. 1989. "Property Reform as a Basis for Social and Economic Reform." *Communist Economies* 3:257-68.

Lipton, David, and Jeffrey Sachs. 1990. "Creating a Market Economy in Eastern Europe: The Case of Poland." *BPEA* 1:75-147.

Luders, Rolf J. 1990. "Chile's Massive State Owned Enterprise Divestiture Program, 1975-1990: Failures and Successes." World Bank Conference on Privatization and Ownership Changes in East and Central Europe. (Forthcoming.)

Milanovic, Branko. 1989. *Liberalization and Entrepreneurship: Dynamics of Reform in Socialism and Capitalism*. Armonk, N.Y.: M.E. Sharpe, Inc.

——. 1990. "Privatization in Post-Communist Societies." Mimeo. World Bank. Washington, D.C.

Moffatt, Gregory. 1990. "Memorandum: Employee Participation in State-controlled Enterprises in Poland, Hungary, Yugoslavia, Czechoslovakia and the Soviet Union." Unpublished. Hogan and Hartson, Washington, D.C.

Morck, R., A. Shleifer and R.W. Vishny. 1988. "Management Ownership and Market Valuation: An Empirical Analysis." *Journal of Financial Economics* 20:293-315.

Murphy, Kevin J. 1985. "Corporate Performance and Managerial Remuneration: An Empirical Analysis." *Journal of Accounting and Economics* 7:11-42.

National Center for Employee Ownership. 1989. "The Employee Ownership 100." May.

Plender, John. 1990. "Malaise in Need of Long-term Remedy." *Financial Times*, July 20.

Rudolf, Stanislaw. 1988. "The Objective Nature of the Democratization Process in the Workplace." *Comparative Labor Law Journal* 9:399-431.

Sajko, Kresimir. 1987. "Enterprise Organization of Eastern European Socialist Countries—A Creative Approach." *Tulane Law Review* 61:1365-82.

Sheard, Paul. 1989. "The Main Bank System and Corporate Monitoring and Control in Japan." *Journal of Economic Behavior and Organization* 11:399-422.

Shleifer, Andre, and Lawrence Summers. 1988. "Breach of Trust in Hostile Takeovers." In Alan J. Auerbach, ed., *Corporate Takeover: Causes and Consequences*. Chicago: University of Chicago Press.

Tomlinson, Alexander C. 1990. "Proposal for a Hungarian National Investment Trust." Mimeo. Washington, D.C.

Vickers, John, and Vincent Wright. 1989. *The Politics of Privatisation in Western Europe*. London: Cass.

Vickers, John, and George Yarrow. 1988. *Privatization: An Economic Analysis*. Cambridge, Mass.: MIT Press.

Vuylstecke, Charles. 1988a. *Techniques of Privatization of State-Owned Enterprises*. Volume 1, *Methods and Implementation*. World Bank: Washington, D.C.

——. 1988b. *Techniques of Privatization of State-Owned Enterprises*. Volume 2. World Bank: Washington, D.C.

——. 1988c. *Techniques of Privatization of State-Owned Enterprises*. Volume 3. World Bank: Washington, D.C.

Yotopoulos, Pan A. 1989. "The (Rip)Tide of Privatization: Lessons from Chile."*World Development* 17:683-702.

Markets and Institutions in Large-Scale Privatization: An Approach to Economic and Social Transformation in Eastern Europe[1]

Roman Frydman and Andrzej Rapaczynski

This paper provides a systematic approach to the problem of privatization in Central and Eastern European economies. The approach is systematic in the sense of providing a theory of what privatization is supposed to accomplish in Central and Eastern Europe and of supplying a means for evaluating the relative advantages and disadvantages of different privatization strategies. While the case of Poland is the focal point of the discussion, the analysis is intended to be applicable to the region as a whole.

Why Privatize?

The first thing to understand about privatization in Eastern Europe is that, in contrast to other countries and given the environment in these transitional economies, it does not entail a simple transfer of ownership from the state to private individuals. Rather, it is a process by which the very institution of property, in the sense in which lawyers and economists employ the term, is re-introduced into Central and Eastern European societies.

At the core of every socioeconomic order is the problem of the efficient use of socially available resources. Whenever the use of these resources is not restricted, the so-called "problem of the commons" arises. Consider the case of a primitive society in which no one has exclusive rights to land and all members of the community are free to use it for their own purposes. In this society, every time a person invests time and energy to cultivate the land, he or she bears all the costs of producing the crop but can only derive a small part of its benefits; conversely, whenever any person removes something from the commons, he or she derives all the benefits of what is removed but bears only a fraction of the costs of producing it. In a system of this kind, there is a systematic incentive to underproduce and overconsume, and the re-

sources become depleted at a rate that may not be socially desirable.

There are two standard ways of dealing with the problem of the commons: regulation; and the creation of property rights. In the first case, a communal decision is made concerning the use of the common resources, and this decision is then coercively enforced against those who attempt to free-ride on the efforts of others. In the second case, resources are assigned to the exclusive use of individual agents who, because they have to pay all the costs and derive all the benefits from the use they make of the resources, have appropriate incentives to choose those uses that yield the greatest net benefit. In the first case, the social use of resources is made on the basis of political decisions; in the second, it relies on the maximization of individual interests, in conjunction with the market as a mechanism for allocating resources.

While all societies use political decisions to regulate certain aspects of the economy (in particular those in which market mechanisms are vitiated by persistent free-riding and externalities), the socialist systems of Central and Eastern Europe made practically all decisions related to production[2] through the political system, with factory personnel playing the role of state functionaries. The name "command economy" conveys precisely this eschewing of market mechanisms, as well as the fact that all property-related arrangements in general were replaced by an administrative system in which the state preferred to control the behavior of each agent directly, rather than relying on the agent's own pursuit of self-interest. In this sense, the socialist economies of Central and Eastern Europe did not have *any* property system (including state and not just private property) governing their productive activities. It is not surprising, therefore, that in all Central and Eastern European countries it is nearly impossible to answer the simple question of who owns what in the state enterprises: legal determination of ownership was irrelevant under the old system, which instead directly prescribed the conduct of factory officials.

The need to re-introduce the very institution of property into the productive resources of Central and Eastern European countries means that the structural reform of their economies cannot proceed primarily at the macroeconomic level. This realization, given the recent reform efforts in a number of Central and Eastern European countries, is of great importance.

The case of Poland is instructive. The first stage of the economic reform there, known as the "Balcerowicz Plan," consisted of a series of macroeconomic measures, such as credit restrictions, wage restraints and the reduction of subsidies, designed to arrest the inflationary pressures in the economy. The effects of this series of measures was in part predictable: first prices shot upward and then inflation slowed quite dramatically and prices remained relatively stable (although not as stable as had been hoped). Among other expected effects was a fall in production and a rise in unemployment, although to an extent different than expected and perhaps for reasons that had not been foreseen.

The authors of the Balcerowicz Plan also expected that the macroeconomic measures undertaken since January 1990 would result not only in the elimination of the strong inflationary pressures evident at the end of 1989, but also in the creation of the basic conditions for a market economy. The lifting of subsidies, together with other monetary measures, were expected to result in a re-adjustment of prices. The possibility of assessing the costs and revenues of each enterprise more realistically was in turn supposed to provide proper incentives for management and to put state enterprises on a sound footing. Privatization would merely complete the process begun by the macroeconomic reform: when the market could be used to determine the real viability of individual enterprises, they could then be valued and gradually sold off through a variety of well-known techniques.

It is a relatively safe proposition that, without some fairly dramatic steps at the microeconomic level, the hope of achieving a structural adjustment of the Polish economy through the macroeconomic stabilization program could not have been fulfilled. The reasons are related precisely to the absence of an appropriate legal and organizational structure at the enterprise level.

The structure of the Polish enterprises, as with those of the other countries in the region, is still largely a function of the old regime, and the behavior of their managers is determined by the conditions under which they operate. Polish enterprises at this time are not even structured as joint-stock companies. They are governed by state-appointed bureaucrats—the so-called *nomenklatura*—who used to respond to other bureaucrats higher up in the mammoth hierarchy of the planned economy. This hierarchy has by and large been dismantled, and the enterprises are supposed to go it alone. However, in the absence of any new external control over management, the old *nomenklatura* people, instead of maximizing the enterprises' returns, are scrambling to find the best deal for themselves. Some are trying to convert the state enterprises into their own fiefdoms that they can then convert into joint ventures with foreign participants, whereby they will get a hefty pay-off and the foreigners will get the enterprise for a song. Others are attempting a home-grown "privatization" by which, without any capital input or another legitimation, they might end up as owners of the previously state companies. Most managers, however, absent their traditional bureaucratic support, are trying to maintain themselves by forging a new alliance with their workers, to whom the reform has given an inordinate amount of power at the enterprise level. The managers are willing to decapitalize their firms and neglect all measures that might require sacrifices by the work force, while maintaining salaries and employment at the highest possible levels.

In this situation, the freeing of prices and the emergence of markets for the products manufactured by state enterprises are by themselves not sufficient to discipline the managers' behavior. Without the pressure of shareholders who can cashier the management that does not produce high enough rates of return on a firm's investments, the only sanction the product market provides is bankruptcy. However, before reaching that point, a state enterprise can exist for a long time with its traditional inefficiency by using up its sources of credit, cutting back on reinvestment or at best coasting along on the borders of profitability. Further, when a bankruptcy does occur, no mechanism is available for restructuring to put things right.

Thus, reliance on the product market as a disciplinary mechanism, with its threat of bankruptcy, is potentially very dangerous. To be sure, some enterprises should be closed. However, insofar as inefficient management might cause a large number of potentially viable enterprises to go bankrupt, a lot of resources might be wasted and the economy might plummet, without there being any clear way of moving out of the depression.

The only way to remedy the crippling inefficiency of post-socialist state enterprises is to move as fast as possible toward a genuine property regime. An immediate move that, although of limited scope is of considerable practical importance, is to introduce a new legal system of genuine *state* property, even before a transfer of ownership from the state to private hands takes place. This corporatization, or, as it is sometimes called, commercialization, would entail an immediate transformation of all state enterprises into joint-stock companies (with the treasury being the sole shareholder) and the appointment of outside directors. Establishment of a genuine form of state *property*, especially in a society with no significant private sector to shape the behavior of state-appointed directors, cannot result in a far-reaching improvement in the functioning of the enterprises. It can, however, provide some remedy for the worst cases of mismanagement and abuse now common in the Polish economy.[3]

Nothing will remove the need for speedy privatization. It should not be seen as the last stage in the transition from a centrally planned economy to capitalism, a stage during which the final touches are applied to an already functioning system. To the contrary, insofar as privatization consists of a transfer of control into the hands of private shareholders who, in a mutually competitive environment, are trying to maximize the returns on their investments, it is an indispensable condition for efficient control of the performance of management. This control over management is, in turn, the essence of genuine restructuring, that is, of the transition from a command economy to a true market order in which not only the value of particular products, but also of the enterprises producing them, is determined by the relation of supply and demand. Unless this process is completed, the reform efforts in Poland and the other Central and Eastern European countries will probably fail, and the economic situation is likely to deteriorate even further.

The General Principles of Privatization

To have a chance of working, a privatization plan must satisfy four main requirements:

(1) speed. The privatization must be accomplished quickly, as must be evident from what has been said already. If privatization, as is argued here, is the core of the process by which state enterprises are restructured, the economic reform in Central and Eastern Europe cannot proceed without a radical transformation in ownership.

(2) social acceptability. As antiquated and inefficient as Central and Eastern European industry is, it has been built at the cost of enormous sacrifices by the general population over the last 45 years: the industrialization program initiated in the 1950s has been pursued through drastic cuts in consumption. Although governments relaxed the austerity somewhat in later years, the policy of investment in heavy industrial infrastructure has retarded the rise in living standards. If the governments were to sell this indus-

try at prices the public saw as very low, popular opinion might turn against the privatization program as a whole.

The people of Central and Eastern Europe also have a somewhat ambivalent attitude toward the privatization program and the concept of a market economy as a whole. On the one hand, nearly everyone understands that a move in the direction of capitalism is necessary and can be expected to yield, in the long run, significant improvements in living standards. On the other hand, it is also clear that, in the short run, the move toward a market economy means further sacrifices in the form of potentially high rates of unemployment, something the people of Central and Eastern Europe are not familiar with.

Finally, while a certain amount of differentiation in levels of wealth based on risk-taking and superior business acumen is usually socially acceptable, an extremely unequal distribution of wealth that creates a permanent division between the haves and have-nots is inherently destabilizing. It might be especially dangerous in Central and Eastern Europe, where people have become accustomed to a certain amount of equality and where the current political climate is not very stable. Great attention must therefore be paid to choosing a strategy of privatization that does not exacerbate the anxieties of the population, but rather gives it some tangible stakes in the success of the undertaking.

(3) *effective control over the management of privatized enterprises*. The move away from bureaucratic control over the economy cannot mean a simple removal of all control mechanisms with respect to the functioning of the enterprises. This important point does not appear to be widely understood and was apparently responsible for the belief that the removal of price controls and the emergence of markets would by themselves usher in a significantly more efficient system of production at the enterprise level. In fact, decision-making in a complex modern economy, involving as it does extensive information to make even the most trivial decisions and a complicated system for allocating responsibilities, requires a whole panoply of institutions that properly structure the incentives of the actors involved and reduce the complexity of real-world situations to a manageable number of relatively simple rules. In other words, when governments eliminate the control mechanisms of the command economy, they need to replace them with mechanisms that play the same role as the control institutions in a Western market economy, which have evolved over time and which are often taken for granted.

Prime among these institutions is a system that provides incentives for managers of enterprises to maximize the interests of shareholders. In a properly competitive environment, this condition requires that production be structured to serve the interests of consumers. In developed capitalist societies, this task is accomplished, with varying degrees of effectiveness, through a variety of institutions, such as takeover mechanisms (supported by the whole legal, financial and organizational infrastructure of the stock market) or an elaborate banking system that supervises company management (the system in Germany and Japan). Without something to play a similar role in the Central and Eastern European economies, privatization could result in the extreme fragmentation of holdings and no effective system of external supervision of enterprise managers. This situation in turn would undermine the whole meaning of privatization, which, as argued here, involves not just a simple change of ownership but rather a radical restructuring that transforms the incentive system of the economic agents at the enterprise level.

(4) *assured access to foreign capital and expertise.* Nearly everyone understands that the capital-starved and heavily indebted Central and Eastern European economies badly need Western funds to modernize their aging industrial infrastructure, introduce new technologies and so forth. It is equally clear that the region also needs Western know-how and management expertise, without which it will not be able to use properly whatever Western financial aid is made available or to bring its production up to the standards of the developed world. What is less often realized, however, is that Western expertise is most needed in the effort to construct the general infrastructure of a modern market economy, particularly the control institutions that will supervise management at the enterprise level. To be effective, the entry of foreign capital and expertise into Central and Eastern Europe cannot take place through advisory and consulting services. The only way in which Western financial institutions can play a truly creative role in the region is to base their entry on sound business principles, that is, to afford them the opportunity to gain or lose by their activities. This condition in turn means that the privatization program must create the conditions that make entry attractive from a business point of view and that the entry take place in a properly competitive environment.

While serious Western participation in the construction of the infrastructure of market economies in Central and Eastern Europe is needed for a successful shift from the bureaucratic command systems in the region, the entry of foreign capital gives rise to special political problems and raises additional questions of legitimation. The people of Central and Eastern Europe very much want to catch up with the Western world, and they expect to be helped in their efforts to do so. At the same time, they are afraid that foreign capital will come to dominate their economies and jeopardize their economic and political interests.

To succeed, a privatization plan for Central and Eastern Europe must, on the one hand, provide a clear avenue for the entry of foreign capital and expertise, but, on the other hand, must place this entry in a setting that makes it acceptable from the point of view of Central and Eastern Europeans' perceptions of their own interests.

The Problem of Valuation

Privatization requires that a value be established for enterprises to be privatized. The state could convey the title to some private party without assessing the enterprise's value, but such a naked transfer would not accomplish anything, quite apart from the legitimacy problems it might raise. The purpose of privatization is not to transfer a title but to initiate a restructuring of enterprises and a rationalization of the Central and Eastern European economies. For these objectives to be met, someone *must* evaluate the potential of each enterprise to be privatized, that is, assess its relative value as compared with other possible investment opportunities. Only in this way is it possible to decide where best to invest the limited resources available for upgrading the economy.

Given the absence of a developed market economy in Central and Eastern Europe, there are seemingly insuperable obstacles to the use of the traditional forms of enterprise valuation. The traditional methods essentially aim at an "objective," that is, inter-subjectively recognized, assessment of the value of an enterprise. In the case of a publicly traded company, the inter-subjective element is self-evident, since it is equal to the price obtainable on the market at any given time. At the same time, individual valuations may differ from the market price.[4] In the case of a privately held company or a fully state-owned company for which a market price is not available, different individuals may have different subjective assessments of the company's value that cannot be separated from the valuation. In the general context of a market economy, however, it is possible to come up with some approximations of the price that would be arrived at by the market itself, since the agent doing the valuation will in part base the estimate on a number of analogies to the methods commonly used by investors in the market under similar conditions, such as price/earning ratios, the firm's performance over the last few years and the average prices of similar enterprises on the market.

An "objective" valuation does not make much sense under the conditions in Central and Eastern Europe, since without markets it is impossible to establish any reliable benchmarks against which to measure the value of the enterprises. Data from the period when the enterprises functioned within the regime of a command economy tell nearly nothing about a firm's present value. The peculiarly Central and Eastern European institution of inter-firm credit, that is, the mutual indebtedness among companies along the production process, introduces a further element of uncertainty into the already clouded company books: around 40 percent of the book value of some of the companies being prepared for privatization in Poland consists of outstanding liabilities from other enterprises, many of very long standing. Without evaluating the soundness of all the enterprises owing money to the firm, it is impossible to predict what portion of these funds will ever be recovered. Similarly, there is no basis for arriving at a valuation by analogy with other enterprises of the same type because there is no capital market. With no reliable track record, it is impossible to make an informed guess about how a given firm would do in a free market economy. This situation is exacerbated by the fact that Poland's economic condition changes all the time, and it is impossible to predict the state of the whole economy or even its segments a few months ahead. The state still sets the long-term interest rate, about which some assumptions are necessary to calculate the present value of future streams of income, and its future course—even for the next few months—is largely unknown, even though relatively small variations in the interest rate may very radically affect the estimated value of an enterprise.[5]

All these factors combined mean that, given conditions in Central and Eastern Europe, the "objective" elements of valuation are *de minimis* and that the subjective elements, although present in any valuation, will dominate the assessments of companies during the transition to capitalism. First, because there are no reliable benchmarks for an objective assessment, the agents who perform the valuation must make more or less arbitrary guesses about such things as the real value of fixed assets, the appropriate price/earnings ratio or the interest rate for the next few years. These guesses will naturally differ from person to person. Second, when the market does not convey certain types of information through the pricing system, the variations in the information available to individuals increase dramatically. For example, someone in-

volved in shoe manufacturing will have a lot of information about conditions in the shoe industry, which normally the price system would disseminate to the world at large but which remain private in the absence of a market economy. Third, when assets are largely illiquid (because there is no established market), certain assets, quite apart from any informational disparities among agents, will have very different values to different people. A beer producer, for example, might put a very high price on a ton of yeast, but the same yeast will be useless to a shoemaker, who, if he cannot readily resell it to someone who needs it, will not offer any price for it. Fourth, by the very fact that an agent has certain plans with respect to some assets for which he is bidding, he is in possession of information that other people, such as accountants or outside consultants who will not be involved in the exploitation of the assets in question, are lacking. Again, this informational disparity is compounded by the absence of historical knowledge concerning the most predictable uses of even the most standard resources. Finally, every valuation involves some skill or "hunch" or "tacit knowledge" that is not quite arbitrary (some people, using their "hunches," do consistently better than others) but that cannot be explained in objective terms understandable to a third party. For example, a good venture capitalist does not base his assessment of a firm's prospects exclusively on the value of its assets, price/earnings ratios and the like. Rather, the capitalist attaches the greatest importance to the "feel" of management's skills, an assessment that, although intangible and often impossible to explain, may be decisive for the venture's success.

The predominance of subjectivity in valuation poses significant problems for a privatization program, primarily because even to the extent that valuation is not arbitrary, it is impossible to explain or legitimize in objective terms. As a consequence, any help or advice that might be gained from even the most reputable consulting or accounting firms is likely to be worthless. These advisors must explain their conclusions to their principals, a task that is, under the circumstances, impossible. In turn, for a privatization model to have a chance of working, it must avoid making the valuation the responsibility of the state (which, to legitimize its decisions, must use outside consultants and try to arrive at an "objective" valuation). Instead, *the burden of valuation must be placed on those parties that, like an ordinary investor in a market economy, will bear the consequences of their decisions. Only these parties can rely on their subjective estimates without having to explain their reasons.*[6]

Even if the burden of valuation is placed on the party that will bear the consequences of its decisions (deriving extra gains from having arrived at a more precise valuation than other parties and experiencing losses by making errors greater than the others), the remaining high degree of uncertainty may make agents very reluctant to risk their assets on the basis of very imprecise guesswork. If, for example, an investor must decide whether to purchase some shares of Nowa Huta (a somewhat antiquated steel mill in Poland) or a piece of real estate in Switzerland, the uncertainty in assessing the value of Nowa Huta will make the investor choose the safer investment in Switzerland. The exception might be if the price of Nowa Huta were discounted to such an extent as to make it competitive. However, the public might perceive that price to be too low, and serious problems of legitimation could arise.

To deal with this assessment problem, the risk to or the uncertainty of the assessment of the agents must be reduced. A way to accomplish both these objectives is *to reduce the universe of competing opportunities relative to which the agent must evaluate the enterprise in question.* In the example just given, if the agent has no choice but to invest some of his assets in one of the privatized enterprises in Poland, his valuation problem is reduced to an assessment of the value of Nowa Huta relative to other Polish enterprises and no longer to all other possible investment opportunities. Not only is the problem of the size of the discount required by the uncertainty lessened, but the uncertainty itself may be reduced as well. The reason is that large areas of uncertainty are found with all enterprises and may therefore be ignored for purposes of internal comparisons.

Special privatization vouchers accomplish precisely this reduction in the universe of competing investment opportunities. Making the agents bid for the privatized companies using a specially restricted form of currency (vouchers), which cannot be used for any other purpose, rather than having them use money, eliminates all the other options that compound the already serious valuation problems.

The Sale Model

Privatization in Central and Eastern Europe cannot follow the sale models elaborated in recent years in such countries as Great Britain or France because of the imperative of speed in the privatization of most Central and Eastern European industry and the difficulty of valuation. In these highly developed Western European countries, privatization had an entirely different focus than is the case in Poland: in those countries, the task was not restructuring the national economy but merely the sale of a few state-owned enterprises that were functioning in a fundamentally market environment dominated by private property. Prior to their privatization, state enter-

prises in, say, Great Britain were having to operate in competition with other private companies, and their managerial systems (even if often less efficient than those of their private sector analogues) were basically a product of the surrounding capitalist business culture. If some of these state enterprises were in the red, it was relatively easy to provide a measure of subsidies and reform so as to bring them, within a relatively short period, into profitability and to put them up for sale. The sale itself was also rather easy: in a full market economy, which is characterized by most of industry being in private hands, a developed stock market and the use by all enterprises of modern accounting methods, the process does not differ very much from that of a private, closely held corporation "going public" by issuing shares to investors at large. It is enough for the state to hire the services of an investment firm (or a consortium of such firms), which underwrites the issue and sells the shares to the public.

This simple description of privatization in the West suffices to show that it cannot serve as a model for privatization in Central and Eastern Europe, where capital markets do not exist and the aim of the privatization is to introduce the structure of the market economy. The very idea that most enterprises can continue to be owned by the state until they are profitable, in order to be sold off afterwards, cannot be taken seriously: the state has been unable to run these enterprises efficiently for 45 years and is not likely to change now, even if it is no longer Communist. Had the state been able to take care of the enterprises it owned, there would be no need to privatize them.

Even when abstracting from this problem, there is still the valuation problem, which makes an ordinary sale through a public offering (with or without an underwriter) impractical. Even if this problem is also ignored and it is instead assumed that a market economy exists that makes such an undertaking meaningful, valuation is costly and time-consuming. The valuation of over 6,000 state enterprises in Poland (or even of the 500 or so biggest firms) would take decades and undermine the entire privatization exercise.[7]

Even if all these problems were assumed away (by proposing, for example, that all state enterprises be auctioned without any preliminary valuation in the hopes that buyers would be able to make some decisions on the basis of scarce information), there is still one more crucial argument against large-scale privatization through public sales, especially in those countries in which a stabilization program has eliminated the accumulated overhang of the local currency. With Poland as an example, the authors have calculated that, under the very optimistic assumption that people are prepared to spend 20-30 percent of all their savings to buy shares in the privatized enterprises, the amount of money available to purchase the state companies would be between 2.4 percent and 3.6 percent of their book value. While this last number says relatively little about the "true" value of the state enterprises, the discrepancy is staggering enough to make clear that, if purchases by foreigners are left aside for the moment, privatization through sales would amount to a giveaway that would increase the inequalities by several scores. Given that the public does not see the differences in wealth in Poland as a legitimate reward for thrift or industriousness but rather as spoils distributed by the old regime to its loyalists, the giveaway would cause the new authorities tremendous political problems.[8] (If, on the other hand, the government tried to avoid the accusation of giving away the national wealth to the old *nomenklatura* by setting prices too high, it would risk not finding enough buyers, a situation that might have the very harmful effect of lowering the general level of confidence in the Polish economy.)

In Poland at least, sale of a large proportion of Polish industry to foreign investors would pose similar practical and political problems with as serious (if not more so) consequences. In any event, contrary to widespread fears of foreign domination among the Poles, foreign capital is by no means eager to invest heavily in the Polish economy. It might be very hard to find foreign buyers unless the prices offered are very low. That eventuality is very unlikely, since the threat of being accused of giving away the national wealth to foreigners was sufficient to cause the authors of the Polish privatization law to restrict foreign entry and require special permission for any foreign interest to acquire more than 10 percent of a privatized enterprise. This limitation, in conjunction with the proposed preferential sale of up to 20 percent of the shares in an enterprise to its workers, makes investment in Poland even less attractive to foreign investors, who might be seriously hampered in their efforts to restructure the company (as that measure might often require significant lay-offs) and put it on a sound business footing.

For these and similar reasons, it is clear to most people, at least in Poland, that large-scale privatization cannot be accomplished through sales. Nevertheless, the state is still trying to sell at least some state enterprises through one or another form of public offering, with the hope that a significant portion of the shares might be sold to a foreign investor who would become an active participant in the restructuring efforts.

Beyond the technical difficulties, a number of political issues that are involved in valuing enterprises to be sold through a public offering of the British kind have to be considered. Note the following coincidence. According to the Polish privatization law, a considerable portion (up to 20 percent) of the shares of state enterprises will be sold to employees at discount prices. Management is also frequently interested in buying a large enough block of shares to allow it (perhaps in coalition with the workers) to maintain control. Both these groups, which have access to key information and are often in a position to keep it secret, are therefore interested in having the enterprises valued as low as possible so as to strike the best deal for themselves. The Ministry for Ownership Transformations also does not want to set the price too high, since the enterprise might not sell. After months of preparation and the expenditure of hundreds of thousands of dollars, failure to sell would be regarded as proof of the ministry's inefficiency. The end result might be that if a foreign buyer is not found for a significant block of shares, a substantial portion of the ownership of the privatized enterprises will end up in the hands an alliance of workers and the old *nomenklatura*, with the rest being held by small shareholders (if they are found) who would be too insignificant to interfere. All in all, the situation might not be very much different from the present one, in which there is no significant outside control over the enterprises.

Preservation of the *status quo* could be avoided if a foreign investor were found to purchase a significant block of the shares of each privatized enterprise. For this reason, bringing in foreign capital would need to be an integral part of a program of selling selected state enterprises for cash. However, as noted, it is by no means obvious that foreign capital is willing to enter Poland under the conditions being offered. If the foreign investor can buy no more than 10 percent of the enterprise (the portion that can be held without special dispensation under the privatization act), 20 percent of which enterprise is controlled by the employees and a significant portion of the rest by the *nomenklatura* management, the investment will not seem promising. To make the investment more attractive to foreign investors, they must be given an opportunity to buy a large enough block of shares to ensure some influence, at a price that is sufficiently low to outweigh the uncertainty.

While the entry of foreign capital is of crucial importance to the restructuring in Central and Eastern Europe, it is not clear that investment is the most advantageous form. First, this type of foreign capital does not constitute a productive investment since it is goes into the state treasury. Not only may the money not be put to best use in this way, but also, given the very high external debt of most Central and Eastern European states, large inflows of the proceeds from privatization might create intensified pressure to increase the debt repayment, in which case the money would flow right back out of the country. Second, the fundamental rule of trading is not to sell before prices go up. In view of the general political and economic situation in the region, the prices of the privatized enterprises are now likely to be very low. If, however, after several years the general situation improves and the enterprises are restructured, the same companies might be worth several times more. If the condition of the Central and Eastern European economies cannot be improved without selling a very substantial portion of existing assets to foreigners, perhaps the price is worth paying. However, if there are other ways to utilize foreign expertise that do not involve mortgaging the country, the restructuring of the Central and Eastern European economies should bear fruit for the people of the region.

Finally, assume that, despite all the difficulties, it is possible to privatize a portion of state-owned enterprises through traditional forms of sale. Since only the most profitable enterprises are likely to find buyers, the companies selected for British-style privatizations will be the few most attractive plums of the Central and Eastern European economies. What will happen to the rest—and, with them, to the economy as a whole?

Free Distribution Models

Given that the sale model of privatization is not viable, the restructuring of the Central and Eastern European economies must involve more unconventional means. An important element of an unconventional strategy is rapid privatization through a program of free distribution of the shares of the state-owned companies. There are basically *three variables* around which to analyze free distribution plans. The first concerns the *beneficiaries* of the free distribution: to whom is the ownership being given away? The second is the *mode of distribution*: are the shares to be distributed directly or through some intermediaries, or will the beneficiaries receive some form of currency (vouchers) with which they can choose which shares to acquire? (The mode of distribution is decisive with respect to whether the beneficiaries will have some say over which shares they receive.) The third variable is the *role of the beneficiaries in the governance of the privatized companies*: are they to become active or passive owners, and if they are to be passive, who will supervise management?

Labor Ownership

The most deeply flawed free distribution proposals envisage a giveaway or heavily subsidized sale of the shares of state-owned enterprises to their workers. From the point of view of social justice, free or subsidized distribution to workers involves fundamental inequities, since the workers who are employed in the most valuable factories will receive an undeserved windfall, while many other citizens, including those employed in state administration or the private sector (potentially the most dynamic and entrepreneurial segment of the population) will be left with nothing. Quite apart from considerations of equity and the distribution of wealth, this proposal is very wrong from an economic point of view. The principal interests of the workers—employment and remuneration—do not parallel at all the interests of the public (which wants the best products at the lowest possible price) or the long-term requirements of the economy as a whole (which requires long-term investment and growth in productivity). Moreover, if the individual workers were in some ways restricted in their ability to sell their shares, the plan might impede the transfer of control to an outsider whose input could discipline management behavior. Effective supervision would have to come from the workers themselves, and there is very little evidence that such supervision, especially in an economy in which worker-owned firms do not really compete with firms organized along more capitalist lines, can produce the desired results. In other words, as with some of the flawed sale plans, a program of free distribution to workers threatens to leave things much as they are now in countries such as Poland and to impede economic restructuring.[9]

Despite the dangers of worker giveaways, many Central and Eastern European countries face very considerable political pressure to move in this direction. In Poland, this pressure has resulted, despite initial resistance by the government, in a series of provisions in the privatization law that allow workers to buy, at seriously discounted prices, up to 20 percent of the shares of the companies in which they are employed. Any privatization program in Poland will probably have to be reconciled with a significant element of worker participation.[10]

If possible, the potential damage resulting from this giveaway should be contained in some way. One method is to give the workers a choice between their right to acquire shares in their companies via this avenue or to receive the benefits of other forms of free distribution to which they may be entitled (*qua* citizens, for example), rather than allowing them to have both opportunities. Another is to restrict the shares acquired in this way to beneficial ownership, without the right to appoint directors or otherwise actively participate in the governance of the company.

Free Distribution to the General Public

While a giveaway of shares to workers poses both equity and efficiency problems, a program of free distribution to the citizenry at large offers the promise of an equitable and potentially efficient solution to the need for speedy privatization. The main advantages of a free distribution program are twofold: it reduces the problem of valuation; and it eliminates the issues related to the shortage of domestic capital or the reluctance of foreign investors to enter.

A giveaway program cannot eliminate the valuation problem entirely, however. It might be possible to execute a free transfer of ownership to some party without worrying about valuation. At the same time, as stressed, if privatization is to result in a restructuring of the company and not just a transfer of ownership, someone will have to value the enterprises to decide the best way to restructure each company. Similarly, the choice of who should be entitled to exercise the control associated with ownership (and not just to enjoy its benefits) requires some method of discovering the party best able to supervise the restructuring. The best (indeed, probably the only) way to make this determination is to find the party who puts the greatest *value* on the enterprises.

A free distribution program can, nevertheless, reduce the valuation problem because at least some of the most troublesome aspects can be left out of the accounting. Prime among the aspects that can be ignored is the need to express the value of the privatized companies in monetary terms (a task that requires establishing their value relative to all other investment opportunities, such as real estate in Switzerland or paper mills in Sweden). Instead, the allocation problem may be dealt with even if the valuation is done in some form of restricted currency, such as vouchers that can be used only to purchase shares in privatized companies (a limitation that narrows the universe of opportunities to the set of the companies to be privatized).

Even more obviously, free distribution programs eliminate the problem of the shortage of capital: regardless of whether the shares in the privatized companies are distributed directly to the beneficiaries or whether the beneficiaries are given vouchers with which to acquire them (either at a pre-set price or at an auction), there is no danger of the state being unable to "sell."

Free distribution to the public at large also solves most of the legitimacy problems associated with selective giveaways and the sale model. Selective giveaways are, by their very nature, suspect: there can be no satisfactory (sufficiently objective) answer to the question of why one person is more deserving than another.

Similarly, given the valuation problem, inherent in sales in the Central and Eastern European context is the question of whether a given asset is being sold at a price that corresponds to its "real" value (whatever that means). Inevitably accusations of covert selective giveaways arise. If, on the other hand, the privatization program distributes the state-owned assets in some demonstrably equal manner, the giveaway needs no special justification. This point is especially true for Central and Eastern Europe, where it makes eminent sense to say that all of society has paid a very heavy price for the construction of the national industry in the last 45 years.

The main problem with free distribution to the public at large is assuring that the new owners, either directly or through representatives, exercise sufficient control over management of the privatized enterprises. Otherwise no change in the *status quo* can be accomplished, and industry will not be restructured. Some free distribution schemes can be immediately eliminated as unacceptable because they do not meet this criterion. Suppose, for example, that the state wants to distribute the shares of the privatized enterprises directly to the population at large. Clearly, without determining the relative value of each company with respect to every other company to be privatized, any attempt to give different portfolios of shares to different people must raise serious questions about equity, since there is no way to assure that one portfolio is worth as much as another. An implicit principle underlying direct distribution of shares to the population at large is that every person should receive exactly the same portfolio. As such, each person would have to receive the same number of shares (say, one) of each company to be privatized. In a country such as Poland, each company would have to issue at least 35 million shares and would end up with 35 million shareholders. The coordination problems the shareholders would face in their efforts to supervise the management are so staggering that no supervision would be possible, and management would be subject to no external control.

Problems of this kind are endemic to many other free distribution schemes. Suppose that, given the difficulties just described, the state decides not to distribute the shares directly to the population but rather to issue special vouchers that are distributed in equal numbers to all citizens who can then use them to "purchase" (either at a pre-set price or at an auction of some kind) shares in the privatized companies of their choice. Through such an indirect distribution, it is possible to avoid the extreme outcome of companies with 35 million shares. The problem is that the voucher "capital" of any individual purchaser is insufficient to allow him to acquire more than a small fraction of any one enterprise.[11] As a result, the ownership of the privatized companies would be extremely fragmented, and no effective mechanisms for shareholder control would be possible (at least for some time). This problem needs to be solved if free distribution is to be a viable basis for a privatization program.

The Problem of Control

The Core Investor

One way to deal with the problem of control—one that has been proposed by some in connection with the privatization discussion in Poland—is to combine free distribution to the population with the sale of a significant block of shares (around 10 percent or more) to a "core investor" who would assume an active role in the restructuring and subsequent supervision of management.

Some of the difficulties related to the core investor idea were raised in the analysis of the sale model. For a number of reasons, the core investor must be a foreigner: very few Central and Eastern Europeans could afford to buy a significant block of shares in a large company, nor are there many people in the region with sufficient expertise to facilitate and supervise the introduction of modern production and management techniques, and only a foreign investor can facilitate contacts with potential foreign joint-venture partners or entry into foreign markets. One possible problem is that the core investor would be the only significant investor in the company despite having a relatively small block of shares. It might be very hard to dislodge this investor given that corporate raiders are not likely to appear for some time. In turn, unless other shareholders have large enough stakes in the same enterprise to exercise a restraining force, the core investor would basically be subject to no control. If the investor does not provide adequate supervision or exploits the company in favor of other (foreign) entities in which he or she has a higher share of ownership, no one would be in a position to do anything about it. The most troublesome aspect of the core investor idea, however, is that, as noted, for both political and economic reasons it might be very difficult to get foreign investors to enter the Polish market. A privatization plan that relies on finding a core investor for every company to be privatized does not have a realistic chance of moving rapidly enough to restructure the Polish economy.[12]

Financial Intermediaries

The other, more promising, way of resolving the control problem associated with free distribution is to *separate ownership from control* and to assign the latter to special intermediary institutions. These intermediaries are usually envisaged as holding companies or mutual funds, which would be the legal owners of the shares of the privatized enterprises, although they may also hold these shares in some looser form of trust accounts on behalf of individual small investors. If the intermediaries are the legal owners of the shares of the privatized enter-

prises, individuals in turn would hold the shares of the intermediary institutions themselves, so that they would be indirect beneficial owners of the assets held by the intermediaries. The intermediaries may then perform various services on behalf of the small investors, from pooling their resources for purposes of diversification to making all kinds of investment decisions on their behalf to, most importantly, exercising supervisory functions with respect to the management of the enterprises in which they are invested.

A number of privatization proposals involve financial intermediaries of one kind or another. Their respective advantages and disadvantages are analyzed here systematically. Again, there are *several variables* around which a taxonomy of intermediary institutions can be devised. Five are listed below before turning to the discussion of concrete proposals:

(1) *the relation between the intermediaries and the state*, including the role of the state in their formation and later functioning, the conditions of entry that determine the existence of the intermediaries and the nature of their regulation.

(2) *the relation between the intermediaries and the small investors* for whom the intermediaries, perform a variety of services. Of particular importance here is the way in which small investors acquire shares in the intermediaries and the degree of choice they have concerning such issues as entry and exit.

(3) *the relation between the intermediaries and the companies in which they are invested*, and particularly the way in which the intermediaries acquire the shares of the companies in which they invest and their level of involvement in the supervision and control of the management of these companies.

(4) *the relation between the intermediaries and other kinds of financial institutions*, especially banks and investment banks.

(5) *the relation between the intermediaries and foreign and international financial institutions*, in particular the role of these institutions in organizing and managing the intermediaries, as well assisting Central and Eastern European participation.

The intermediaries and the state. Several privatization proposals for Poland envisage the state setting up financial intermediaries. According to some proposals, the state would appoint the directors of the funds (in one of the plans, they would be nominated by the Ministry of Ownership Transformations and confirmed by the Parliament), and the intermediaries would receive the shares of the privatized companies directly from the state according to a set formula (one of the plans, for example, proposes that each of five funds receive 4 percent of the shares of each privatized enterprise). In many of these plans, the government would strictly control the number of intermediaries and would use them as an exclusive medium to distribute the free shares (so that, at least initially, individuals could only own shares in the intermediaries and not directly in the privatized enterprises).

Plans of this kind run very serious risks of making the intermediaries new bureaucratic institutions that would be closely associated with the activities of the state and dependent on the state for their existence and functioning. A foreseeable effect of such an arrangement would be a dramatic reduction in the funds' readiness to make decisions on the basis of ordinary business principles, their reluctance to take risks of any kind and, above all, their security in the assurance that the state, closely identified with the intermediaries in the minds of the public, would have to come to their aid if either they or the companies in which they were heavily invested were in danger of going under. Another obvious risk is that the small number of intermediaries might encourage their collusion and empire-building tendencies.

The only way to make the intermediaries adhere to genuinely business-oriented control functions with respect to the management of the companies under their supervision and of making their interest closer to that of their shareholders rather than the state bureaucracy is to make them private, profit-driven institutions functioning in an environment that forces them to compete for the favor of their shareholders. This approach does not mean that the intermediaries should be unregulated; rather, they must be independent of the state. Among the most important areas to be regulated is how the funds' management is compensated, so as to tie its interests as much as possible to its performance on behalf of the funds' shareholders and the long-term interests of the economy.[13] Similarly, while the state may limit the number of intermediaries, its authorization to operate should not be an administrative, bureaucratic decision; instead, it should auction a certain number of licenses to operate an intermediary to private parties satisfying certain basic conditions.

Clearly, state regulation of the intermediaries is a very broad subject related to the totality of their operation. Some aspects of this problem are discussed in this paper. However, the issue really requires special treatment that touches on nearly the entire field of securities regulation.

The relation to the small investor. The main question regarding the relation between the intermediaries and small investors is whether the latter would be able to choose the intermediaries in which to invest or would automatically receive a certain number of shares in them. A corollary to this question is whether individuals could invest in the shares of the privatized enterprises directly or would have to acquire the shares of the intermediaries.

There is a certain appeal to restricting individual beneficiaries of a free distribution to shares in the intermediaries, rather than devising ways of allowing them to acquire shares in the privatized companies themselves. Similarly, there are some advantages to not giving the beneficiaries, at least initially, the right to choose the intermediaries whose shares they are going to hold. The reasons for these restrictions are always the same: administrative simplicity (which eliminates a lot of the transaction costs involved in other solutions) and the informational barriers facing small investors, which would limit their ability to avail themselves of the benefits from the choice were it available. Thus, for example, if the shares of the privatized enterprises were somehow distributed among the intermediaries (the constraints on this possibility are discussed later), it might be administratively much simpler to give every citizen one share in each intermediary, rather than worry about devising a scheme that allowed individual beneficiaries to choose among the intermediaries or to acquire shares in the privatized enterprises directly. This point is particularly relevant since any such scheme would involve a costly distribution of vouchers to all the individuals involved, who would then choose between using them to purchase shares in the privatized enterprises or to acquire an interest in the intermediaries. It might also be argued that, if given this choice, most individuals would not know how to use it, and finding out might require more effort than the choice itself would be worth, given the small investments involved.

A decision to restrict consumer choice in these matters also has its costs. Consumer choice might be quite uninformed in a situation in which, as is the case in all Central and Eastern European countries, there is no reliable information concerning the relative value of the alternatives among which the consumer is supposed to choose. Nevertheless, consumer choice itself means the disappearance of an important factor that could potentially provide a significant element of external control over the intermediaries' performance. If the intermediaries had to compete for the vouchers to be received from the public at large, or if they had to "sell" their shares in some other way, their success would in part depend at least on the satisfaction of the people they are supposed to serve. If, on the other hand, the shares of the intermediaries are automatically distributed to the beneficiaries, the dependence of the intermediaries on the consumers must diminish and that on the state must increase, if for no other reason than because the decision concerning their creation would have to be made not by the consumers of their services but by the state. (If the consumer has no choice about which intermediaries to "invest" in, their entry must be a state decision.) Some forms of consumer approval could still play a role in the intermediaries' behavior; it would be possible, for example, to tie the compensation of managers to the price of the shares of the intermediaries. However, the fact that at least the initial position of the intermediaries would be independent of consumer choice might allow some funds to entrench themselves, especially if their origin in a state decision were to lead to their having leverage over state assistance in adverse times.

Another, and perhaps more significant, cost of disallowing the beneficiaries of the free distribution to own shares in the privatized companies directly is a long-term concentration of all shareholding in very few hands. While some concentration of holdings is desirable (since it allows for effective control by shareholders), the exclusion of the small investor makes a genuine securities market less likely to arise. If there were 10, 20 or even 100 shareholders in the country, most of whose holdings consisted of large blocks of shares that gave them privileged access to inside information, the volume of trading would certainly be very small; indeed, it would be so small that all trading would likely be private, and most holdings would likely remain illiquid. In the long run, this situation might not only seriously impede the creation of stock markets, but it might also make the intermediaries very difficult to value and leave them forever "closed," i.e., incapable of moving to a system in which they would have to redeem their shareholders' shares on demand.

The "closed" nature of the funds is related to another possible means of consumer control over the management of the intermediaries: the possibility of exit. As long as the fund remains closed, exit is possible only through the sale of the intermediary's shares to a third party. The illiquid nature of the intermediary's assets might make the market price of its shares an unreliable indicator of how it is doing. On the other hand, given conditions in the region, illiquidity of the fund's assets is entirely unavoidable, at least for the time being: it will be a while before the privatized companies in which the intermediaries are invested will have a reliable market price. Still, it is worth considering "opening" the funds (i.e., obliging them to redeem their shares through the sale of a portion of their assets) in the future, since this measure would not only make their valuation more reliable but might also allow for the dissolution of some and a move away from a system in which the intermediaries

are a fixture on the economic landscape of Central and Eastern Europe.[14]

The relation to the privatized companies. There are two main issues under this heading: how active a role the intermediaries play in exercising the control function on behalf of the small investors; and how the intermediaries will acquire shares in the companies to be privatized.

The two questions are related to some extent, since the mode of acquisition may determine the suitability of the intermediaries to exercise the control function. In fact, the most important question concerning the allocation of shares in the privatized enterprises to the intermediaries is how to assure that they take an early interest in examining the potential of the companies to be privatized and compete among themselves to spot the most effective ways of restructuring them. They will do so only if they can determine, at least in part, which companies they will acquire and if their blocks of shares will be sufficiently large to permit them to influence management and prod the restructuring in the most promising direction.

For this reason, unlike in the case of the allocation of free shares to individual beneficiaries, a simple solution involving the allocation of shares to the intermediaries in some random or mechanical fashion has very little to recommend it. Although it could be argued that the initial mode of distribution does not matter since the intermediaries will later trade among themselves to reach the allocation they want, this approach is not appropriate. It is desirable that the intermediaries begin researching the companies to be privatized as soon as possible. The best way to insure their doing so is to force them to make important allocative decisions by a fixed date (as is the case when the allocation takes place through an auction, for example). Second, once an initial allocation is made, some intermediaries immediately find themselves in a better position to evaluate some companies than others because they have access to inside information. At the same time, the informational asymmetries among the potential traders put some parties at a distinct disadvantage. As a result, they may be reluctant to trade.[15]

Third, trading presupposes a number of institutions to facilitate it, such as stock markets with well-established prices for the shares to be traded and specialists who help effectuate certain transactions by underwriting them. In their absence, trading may be very difficult. In Central and Eastern Europe, the funds may not have at their disposal any large amounts of cash with which to trade, especially in conjunction with a privatization plan that relies on free distribution. If most transactions have to take the form of barter arrangements, trading will be very slow, and the needed reallocation of resources may take a very long time (during which the Central and Eastern European economies will languish and the reform movement might collapse under populist political pressures). Finally, back-door transactions among a small number of agents are an open invitation to collusion among the intermediaries.

Underwriting, the allocation mechanism by which shares of privatized companies are initially assigned to the intermediaries, is the most complex and difficult part of any privatization plan involving free distribution. To understand the difficulties, remember that free distribution is necessary because the traditional sales mechanism will not work under Central and Eastern European conditions. In the case of large issues of shares (as opposed to isolated transactions among individuals), this mechanism normally involves an underwriter who assumes the risk of selling the whole issue for a small percentage of the sale price. Whatever the considerable advantages of this solution, it cannot be used in Central and Eastern Europe without some very significant changes. Even if the shares of the privatized companies were sold for money, the uncertainties of valuation and the absence of any track record of past transactions or of specialists who know the local conditions would make the underwriting extremely risky. Even assuming someone foolhardy enough could be found to engage in it, the underwriting fees would be so staggering as to make the exercise impractical from the point of view of the state.

Nevertheless, there have been some interesting proposals to use a modified underwriting mechanism in the context of a free (or near free) distribution of shares.[16] The problem is to find some way to underwrite without forcing the underwriter to risk enormous amounts of money that could be used elsewhere. In other words, the idea is to change the incentives for the underwriter in such a way that, instead of risking a large amount of ordinary currency, he or she would be risking future proceeds from the activity of underwriting itself. The underwriter might, for example, obtain free credit from the state (in the form of vouchers or some other arrangement) and use it to pay for the shares of the issue he or she would underwrite. If the underwriter makes a mistake and is unable to "sell" (again for vouchers) all the shares at the price he or she expected, he or she will be punished by having the profits reduced to zero and perhaps forfeiting some initial deposit.

The issue that should be considered in connection with the underwriting idea is that some other mechanism would be needed to help choose the underwriters themselves. This mechanism could be a multi-criteria selection run by the state or could be an auction. If the first alternative is chosen, the process is likely to end up being quite arbitrary and drawn out. If the second is chosen, it might be preferable to move directly to a different allocation system in which the shares of the privatized companies are themselves distributed through an auction mechanism.[17]

In an *auction*, which is another way to allocate the shares of the privatized companies to the intermediaries, the shares could be "sold" at a special auction during which the intermediaries (as well as private individuals, if permitted) bid for them with the vouchers they receive (depending on the plan) or from their own shareholders.

The main difficulty with a privatization plan involving intermediaries is designing an auction that can accomplish, without the use of real money, the following objectives:

(1) allocation of the shares of the privatized companies in such a way as to reflect the relative valuations by the intermediaries.
(2) acquisition by the agents of adequately large blocks of shares in the privatized companies to permit them to implement their restructuring plans and ensure that every privatized company has at least one (and optimally more than one) large shareholder (so that none are left with no effective outside control).
(3) revelation of some information about the relative valuation of the privatized enterprises by the bidders both to the other bidders during the auction (so that they can adjust their bids to what they learn about the emerging market prices) and to the general public.
(4) clearing of the share-for-vouchers market (at least approximately) so that bidders are not left with worthless paper at the end.

Devising an auction that satisfies the above conditions is a very complex task. However, although the authors are still working on the details of the design, the task does not appear impractical. The main features are described below (a more detailed discussion of the auction design is presented in appendix 2).

The enterprises to be privatized should be divided into several groups, each comprising no more than 150-200 companies. Each of these groups should be auctioned off separately. After the first group is sold, there would be an intervening period during which the new shareholders would elect the boards of directors of the enterprises and the policy-makers and the public would be able to assess the initial consequences of the chosen strategy of privatization. To avoid inter-temporal problems related to bidders' trying to apportion their vouchers among all the enterprises scheduled to be privatized, the vouchers for each privatization phase would be issued separately, and the validity of the vouchers would expire at the end of a given phase. In effect, the vouchers would be a form of self-liquidating credit extended by the state to the public for the duration of each privatization phase.

The preliminary design for the auction of each group of companies privatized at a given phase involves several stages in which the agents are asked to rebid several times. The actual sale would take place according to a rule that facilitates convergence and limits the agents' strategic manipulation. A key feature of the proposed auction is that the enterprises *would not be auctioned off seriatim*; all would be bid for *simultaneously* at every stage.

There would be two basic components of every auction, which would be handled separately. In the first, the agents would be able to bid for, say, three large blocks of shares in each company—one of 20 percent and two of 15 percent. (This system is designed to ensure that each company will have some large shareholders who will exercise effective control.) In the second one, the remainder of the shares would be sold through a different procedure: the agents would apportion their remaining vouchers among the companies of their choice and would receive a number of shares determined by the level at which the prices would clear.

As to *the level of the intermediaries' involvement*, they would fulfill a number of roles, from relatively passive to very active. At one end of the spectrum would be institutions modelled after the American ones, which, as a rule, must diversify very broadly and cannot hold a large stake in any single company. As such, they cannot take an active part in supervising the management of the companies in their portfolios. Intermediaries of this kind serve mostly to pool the assets of their shareholders for the purposes of diversification and access to expert advice. Institutions of this kind would not be suitable for the restructuring of the Central and Eastern European economies.

At the other end of the spectrum are the financial institutions prevalent in Germany and Japan, which have very significant stakes in the companies in which they have invested and play a very active role in supervising management. While the authors believe that the Central and Eastern European economies need precisely these kinds of institutions to supervise the restructuring, there are clear agency problems that must be guarded against when one shareholder controls the whole corporation and can exploit the other owners. While it is beyond the scope of this paper to explore in detail the legal framework and incentive mechanisms that might be the most appropriate for reconciling the requirements of management supervision with the protection of minority shareholders, the importance of

such an exploration needs to be emphasized here. It is, for example, likely that deeper analysis will yield a number of restrictions on the relations of the intermediaries and the companies in which they have invested. Prime along these lines is putting some cap on the percentage of the shares an intermediary may own in any one company (35 percent seems a good candidate in light of the research on American companies) and resolving a host of restrictions on self-dealing and conflicts of interest. The analysis may also suggest mixing the intermediaries with other significant investors (such as the core investor), whose incentives may be structured in a different way, so as minimize the agency problems involving the intermediaries.

The relation to other financial institutions. A corollary of the matter just discussed is the relation of the intermediaries to other financial institutions, especially banks and investment banks. Again, the American model could be followed, in which fiduciary institutions such as mutual funds are forbidden by law from engaging in the provision of other financial services, on the theory that conflicts of interest may lead them to abuse their fiduciary duties to their shareholders. At the other extreme, once again, is the German model, in which banks supervise companies on their own behalf as well as on behalf of their trust account clients, in the process also lending money to the companies under their control (thus further increasing their leverage). Somewhere in the middle is the standard investment house, which may arrange for the financing of companies short of capital, place directors on the boards of companies to guard the lenders' interests and provide expertise in the management of companies in which the investment firm's clients have a stake.

An important part of the regulation of financial intermediaries in Central and Eastern Europe will be determination of the degree of their separation from the other types of financial institutions. It is clear that the closer their relations are, the greater is the potential for conflict of interest and the greater the need for other kinds of regulation (such as restrictions on self-dealing). On the other hand, one of the greatest *lacunae* in the Central and Eastern European economies is a modern banking system and other types of modern financial institutions. Moreover, setting up the infrastructure for an intermediary, which involves establishing local branches, opening up accounts for individual beneficiaries and similar tasks, is not unlike setting up the infrastructure for a standard bank. The absence of restrictions that prohibit intermediaries from providing banking services may greatly facilitate the establishment of a modern banking system and help privatized enterprises obtain financing for their operations. Similarly, the fact that there are no stringent restrictions on combining the fiduciary services of the intermediaries with merchant and investment banking services may allow the intermediaries to become a very flexible source of funds for privatized enterprises: they could make the excess funds of some companies available to others in their portfolios, in this way channelling domestic savings into investments. They could also arrange for financing from outsiders. These services may be particularly important if the intermediaries are linked to Western financial institutions, since they could then serve as a bridge for foreign banking expertise and a window to Western sources of debt financing.[18]

The relation to foreign financial institutions. The importance of the entry of foreign capital and expertise into Central and Eastern Europe is reiterated here. Also emphasized is the reluctance of foreign capital to enter some Central and Eastern European countries such as Poland, and the reciprocal fear in those countries of foreign domination. Thus, serious political problems hinder the entry of foreign investors, at the same time that their entry as advisors is of little use.

The entry of foreign banking and investment banking institutions is very appropriate to the setting up and running of the financial intermediaries under the privatization program. First, foreign expertise may be badly needed to help establish the infrastructure of a modern capitalist economy, with which the region has had practically no experience. This infrastructure is particularly important, since it permits the emergence of market forces and makes possible a chain reaction of growth and development. Second, the foreigners would be entering not primarily as buyers of Central and Eastern European industry (although part of their compensation might, and should, include stock options) but rather as managers of the funds working on behalf of the local owners of the underlying assets. Since their success would directly contribute to raising the value of the equity in local hands, their presence might be more easily accepted than it would be in other contexts. Moreover, if relations between the funds and their shareholders are structured in such a way that the capital being managed by the intermediaries is directly proportional to the number of local citizens who chose that fund over others, the degree of foreign influence over the running of the local economy could be seen as exactly proportional to the welcome of the local population.

While foreigners have a very important role to play in the intermediary institutions, for many reasons it might be appropriate to implement their entry into joint ventures with local partners. This approach would speed up the transfer of expertise to the local population and fur-

ther legitimize the role of foreigners in the privatization. To facilitate the formation of joint ventures, international banking institutions could aid the Polish partners through grants and subsidies, while, should the Polish government require the intermediaries to make some payments (in the form of security deposits or license fees), it could also offer special reductions in those payments in proportion to the degree of Polish participation.

Conclusion

Privatization in Central and Eastern Europe does not entail a mere change in ownership. Rather, it involves a complex social and economic transformation aimed at changing the way every company is run and every business decision is made. Without a rapid transition to private ownership and a dismantling of the rigid Communist structure of industry, these economies will continue to decline.

Moreover, privatization is not just a goal of the market-oriented economic reform. It should also apply to the process whereby the companies are privatized so that competition and market mechanisms can be used from the very beginning to decide who should be in charge of the restructuring. Otherwise, the state will decide what to do with each enterprise, and the economy will remain bogged down in the same bureaucratic quagmire that has paralyzed it for 45 years.

While private institutions should have exclusive responsibility for the restructuring, the state can influence the process by providing the general legal and regulatory framework. Among other things, the law would regulate the incentive structure of the intermediary institutions, prescribe anti-trust rules and tariffs and provide a safety net for the work force in transition.

What distinguishes the approach espoused here from the others is its unique combination of several seemingly incompatible features. It combines widespread ownership and a measure of social justice with concentrated control and economic efficiency. It avoids the initial monetary valuation of enterprises, while immediately allocating the productive resources to the private agents who value them most. It confers ownership on the citizens of Central and Eastern European countries while providing a link to foreign financial institutions capable of assuring access to the world financial markets and expertise in management supervision. Above all, it offers a chance to move very fast toward a novel system of economic governance that could result in effective private control of Central and Eastern European industry.

Appendix 1. Valuation of State Enterprises in the Polish Economy: A Brief Case Study

The valuation of a state enterprise, called X, is discussed here as a case example. The Polish government plans to offer X for sale to the public in the fall of 1990. The government asked a prestigious British accounting firm, called A here, to appraise the firm. The present discussion is based on that firm's preliminary appraisal. While the final appraisal may differ from the one presented here, even this brief discussion of the preliminary appraisal illustrates the fundamental problems inherent in "objective" valuations performed by independent experts on behalf of Central and Eastern European governments. It will be shown that, of necessity, valuations of Central and Eastern European enterprises have to involve predominantly subjective judgments. Thus, to be really legitimate, they should be performed by agents having a genuine stake in the future of the privatized enterprises.

Firm A used three standard methods of valuation: the book value of the enterprise's assets; the price/earnings ratio; and the discounted value of future profits or operating cash flows.

Firm X has assets in the form of buildings (partly under construction), machinery, tools, equipment and motor vehicles, outstanding receivables and inventories. The pro forma balance sheet as of December 31, 1989 (see table 21-1-1) shows that the government valued the fixed assets at US$3.7 million, which represented 52 percent of the appraised net value of the assets. However, in the absence of a real estate market and of secondary markets for machinery and equipment, the government had to value the assets in an apparently arbitrary manner. The accounting firm A reports that the government recently revalued the fixed assets of X by $2.2 million, that is, by 146 percent. This unexplained revaluation accounts for 31 percent of the value of the company's entire net assets. The valuation of the fixed assets is further clouded by the inclusion of the unfinished Center for International Cooperation, a "white elephant" X is building in the provincial Polish town of Kielce with a view to hosting international conferences. In the absence of markets, A reports having understandable difficulty valuing the center. Together, the government revaluation of the fixed assets of X and the value that A has calculated for the center amounted to $3 million, or 81 percent of the appraised value of X's fixed assets and 42 percent of its net asset value.

The balance sheet also shows that inter-firm credit (the result of the notorious practice of inter-company lending) represented 43 percent of X's assets ($7.9 million due from X's debtors) and 87 percent of X's liabilities

Table 21-1-1. *Pro Forma Balance Sheet of Firm X as of December 31, 1989*

(US$ millions)

Fixed assets	3.7
Inventories	1.8
Cash and bank deposits	4.8
Debtors	7.9
	18.2
Bank loan	(0.8)
Creditors and provisions	(9.7)
Welfare fund	(0.6)
	(11.1)
Net assets	7.9

($9.7 million due to X's creditors). The prevalence of this credit and substantial uncertainty associated with its repayment are additional complications in the valuation. As mentioned in the third section, establishing the value of this credit requires evaluating the financial position of all the firm's debtors and creditors. In turn, however, those enterprises are likely to be burdened with their own inter-firm credit arrangements, and so on. In sum, the calculation does not provide any reliable idea of the company's real worth.

According to A, the second method used to value X—using the price/earnings ratio—is more applicable because the main business of X is the export of labor services. As such, the firm's value depends primarily on the quality of its management. However, as is typical for Central and Eastern European economies, X derives a considerable portion of its earnings from exports to Comecon countries. The artificial nature of the historical prices and exchange rates in these countries makes computation of meaningful figures for earnings highly problematic. The computation is further complicated by the prevalence of inter-firm credit.

The absence of securities markets in Poland forced A arbitrarily to fix the price/earnings ratio at 3. The resulting value of X was (at least) $17 million, with a potential error of $8 million. A simple check of the robustness of this calculation shows that had the uncertain price/earnings ratio been set at 4 instead of 3, the potential valuation error would have been $16 million, or 94 percent.

The third method, which is based on discounted future cash flows, requires projecting cash flows and the proper discount rate. Here, A had to make several "key" assumptions. First, it assumed that the future rate of profit of X would be the same as in 1989, the year before the Balcerowicz Plan. Again, typically for the Central and Eastern European economies, it is very unlikely that the pre-reform data were relevant for forecasting the future.

Second, A projected that sales to East Germany in 1990-91 and 1992-94 would be between 30 percent and 120 percent of the 1989 figure, whereas sales to the Soviet Union, Czechoslovakia and Hungary would amount to 30-75 percent of the 1989 sales. Third, it was assumed that the rate of inflation in all countries in which X operated would be the same in future years. Because of the inherently unknowable nature of the environment in which X would be operating in the future, A also had to make a number of other equally arbitrary assumptions to "compute" future earnings. Finally, faced with the impossible task of determining the discount rate, A used a figure of 25 percent supplied by the Polish Finance Ministry.

The peculiar outcome of this procedure is that despite the arbitrariness of all the numbers A used, the value of X that the discounted future cash flows yielded was virtually identical to the one obtained with the price/earnings ratio method. The only way to explain this outcome is that the seemingly arbitrary assumptions were carefully tailored to yield the reported coincidence of results.

Appendix 2. The Polish Government's Large-Scale Privatization Plan: A Preliminary Analysis

On November 21, 1990, the government of Poland announced a comprehensive privatization plan, *Rzeczpospolita*, which it is proposing to implement in the near future. One part of the plan, which deals with the privatization of some 500 largest enterprises in Poland (responsible for about 70 percent of the country's industrial production), utilizes the framework presented in this paper, although it also contains some elements proposed by others. While the plan may undergo a number of modifications as a result of changes in government, it is expected that its main features, as described below, will be implemented.

The Plan

The enterprises presently owned by the state will be divided into several categories. A basic dividing line will separate the 500 largest enterprises from the "small and medium size" ones (some 2,000 industrial companies and 3,500 others). The latter categories will be privatized through sales or liquidation, while the former, with a few exceptions, are to be given away.

Each of the 500 large enterprises will first be converted into a joint-stock company. Following this corporatization, 10 percent of the shares will be given (free of charge) to the workers,[19] while the state will retain another 30 percent and the remaining 60 percent will be transferred to new owners with the help of privatization vouchers.

The 500 enterprises will be disposed of in several phases, with 150-200 to be privatized in the first one. An appropriate number of vouchers will be issued for each phase, with one-half going to the public at large (each citizen receiving one voucher), one-third to the Social Security office (to capitalize the state pension fund) and one-sixth to a number of state banks. Thus, citizens will receive vouchers equivalent to 30 percent of the value of the privatized enterprises, the Social Security office 20 percent and the banks 10 percent.

The state will then invite the creation of a number of intermediary institutions that will offer shares in themselves in exchange for vouchers. (Entry will be free, so that any person or institution, foreign, domestic or mixed, will be able to create an intermediary as long as it satisfies the minimum conditions specified in a special law.) The vouchers the citizens receive will have to be used to "purchase" shares in the intermediaries, with each person having a choice as to which intermediary to invest in. The banks will be free to use the intermediaries or to trade on their own account. The Social Security office will have a choice of depositing all or some of its vouchers in the intermediaries or of creating one or more special pension funds of its own.

Once the vouchers are transferred to the intermediaries, the 150-200 companies privatized in the first phase will be sold at a specially arranged auction, such as the one described in this paper. The state will also deposit the 30 percent of the shares it owns with the intermediaries according to some predetermined formula.[20]

However, the state will not become an ordinary shareholder in the intermediary institutions; instead, it will apportion its shares to the intermediaries and limit its role to the appointment of one director to the board of each intermediary. The intermediaries will be responsible for selling the state's shares in each privatized company to other investors, either by private placement or in the open market. Once a certain percentage of the total state holdings administered by a given intermediary is sold, the state director will resign from the board of the intermediary.

The transfer of ownership and control having been completed, the intermediaries and other shareholders for each company will appoint new directors, and the restructuring will begin. The new owners (with, it is hoped, the intermediaries in the dominant position) will be free to change the management of the privatized companies, to split them up (or perhaps combine them, as long as no anti-trust violations result), to sell a part of their holdings, to approve various joint-venture arrangements between the privatized companies and other entities (foreign or domestic), and so forth. The sale by the intermediaries of the 30 percent of the shares they hold on behalf of the state will, it is hoped, allow "core investors" to become involved in a number of the privatized companies, as well as (together with the transactions involving the 10 percent of the shares held by individual workers) to create a market for a sizable proportion of the shares of the privatized companies. This situation would increase the liquidity of the assets held by all the shareholders and allow for a market valuation of the privatized companies and intermediaries and for the possibility that some of the funds may become "open."

Analysis of the Plan

This plan is clearly a big step in the right direction. The choice of a free distribution model of privatization for a large part of the industrial sector raises the hope that the plan may be executed in a reasonable amount of time without the worst kinds of political problems.[21] Insofar as the plan envisages the sale of a substantial portion of the assets of the 500 largest companies, it postpones that sale until the intermediaries are in charge and the restructuring is underway. As was stressed, the general level of confidence in the Polish economy might be much higher at that point, while the presence of the intermediaries on the boards of directors of the privatized companies might reduce the costs of monitoring for outside investors and thus reduce the investors' *ex ante* risk and raise the prices of the shares. Moreover, the fact that the intermediaries, rather than the state, will be looking for buyers also insures (if the intermediaries' incentives are set correctly) that the timing and price will be better.

The plan's proposal to distribute vouchers to individuals allows for the free entry of the intermediary institutions and removes the state from a significant role in their creation. This process, together with the auction scheme, which makes the intermediaries take an early interest in particular enterprises, puts the intermediaries in a clearly competitive posture with respect to one another and raises the hope they will not degenerate into inert bureaucracies.

In addition to the elements discussed in this paper, the government plan contains a number of other elements that raise very interesting possibilities but also some significant dangers. The most controversial idea is that the state keep 30 percent of the shares of the privatized companies. State shares are undesirable in and of themselves: as argued, this heavy involvement of the state poses the risk that the intermediaries will be politicized, as well as the specter of an eventual bail-out of in-

efficient intermediaries. If budgetary considerations are the sole reason the state is proposing the retention of shares, there is very little to recommend the idea as opposed to a simple taxation scheme.

However, the state's shares are designed to accomplish another objective: to provide for the possibility that a part of each company's assets might be sold to the public or to a "core investor." Both these possibilities have something to recommend them. While it has been argued here that a core investor was unlikely to be found in the initial stages of the privatization, it is conceivable that he or she could be brought into a number of the privatized enterprises within a few years. Moreover, while the core investor, if he or she were to be the only big shareholder, could engage in exploitative behavior with respect to the rest of the shareholders and be very difficult to dislodge, that danger does not apply when the core investor has to share his or her authority over the company with a number of other large players, such as the intermediaries or pension funds. To the contrary, his or her presence on the board of directors might have significant benefits. To begin with, the core investor may have enterprise-specific expertise that the other large shareholders (which are basically financial institutions) may lack. Even more important, the core investor, having a different type of interest from the other large shareholders, may counterbalance their influence when it is not in the best interest of the company and their own shareholders. This possibility could arise because the structure of the institutional investors, such as the proposed intermediaries, always raises the possibility that the incentives of their managers may not be not fully compatible with the interests of their shareholders. These "agency problems" may be limited, but they will probably never be completely eliminated. In fact, the absence of robust stock markets in Central and Eastern Europe will limit the range of devices to be used to evaluate the performance of fund managers and determine their compensation and may make the situation worse in this respect than it is in many other countries. The fact that the representatives of the institutional investors might have to negotiate their strategies for the privatized companies with a player whose incentives significantly differ from theirs may protect the company (and indirectly the shareholders of the intermediaries) from possible over-reaching.

A core investor will not be found for all companies. In these cases, the government's plan foresees that the intermediaries managing the state's shares would sell them, within some reasonable time, to the public. This act might also have the beneficial long-term effect of strengthening the market for the shares of the privatized companies so as to increase their liquidity and allow a more reliable evaluation of the intermediaries' performance.

At the same time, it must be stressed that the existence of a significant state portion in the privatized companies raises serious difficulties. While the government's plan proposes eliminating the state completely from the management and boards of the privatized companies and to reduce its role in the intermediaries to one director on their boards, this solution might not work. It is easy to underestimate the political pressure that can be brought to bear on the state when it is seen as able to resolve a problem that a powerful constituency considers very urgent. For example, if the state is known to have a 30 percent ownership in enterprises that are laying off massive numbers of workers (as might happen in the initial stages of restructuring), the state could face irresistible pressure to exercise a more active role. This eventuality is all the more likely if some other big shareholders, such as state banks and state pension funds, are perceived (not without reason) as belonging to the state and as easy subjects of governmental pressure.

State shares pose a host of technical problems that might be very hard to resolve. First, it is not clear how its shares are to be distributed among the intermediaries (without which the role of the state would be even harder to limit). On the one hand, it would perhaps be easiest to distribute the state's share in proportion to the rest of the assets of each intermediary, so that the state would end up owning 33-1/3 percent of everything each intermediary owned. However, the state's shares in any given company would then be divided among a large number of the intermediaries. This situation would make sale to a core investor that wanted to buy all the state's shares or at least a large part of them very difficult, since the transaction costs of negotiating with many sellers might be very high. On the other hand, for reasons too complex to enter into here, any other arrangement might create serious distortions in the behavior of the intermediaries.

The second technical problem relates to the sale of these assets by the intermediaries. Given the enormous scope of the state's holdings (30 percent of the total), setting an arbitrary date (say, three to five years from the time of the initial auction) as the deadline for selling the state's assets (especially if the remaining 5,500 state companies were also to be put up for sale during the same period) would wreck absolute havoc with the securities market. On the other hand, leaving the decision on timing to the intermediaries could avoid a "fire sale" effect, although some incentives would have to be created for the intermediaries to sell the assets at all. The difficulty of designing an incentive scheme and its potential for creating serious distortions in the behavior of the intermediaries as fiduciaries of their non-state shareholders (the citizens) parallel the already mentioned problems in devising an appropriate distribution scheme for the state's shares.[22]

Overall, while the requirement that the intermediaries divest themselves over time of a certain proportion of the assets under their management may be a good idea, it is not clear that these assets ought to belong to the state until they are sold. Moreover, even if the state were to retain those assets until they were sold, 30 percent is much too large a portion for this purpose. Something on the order of 10-20 percent would be much less dangerous.

The idea of capitalizing the state pension fund by giving it 20 percent of the shares of the large enterprises has even more attractive aspects, although the dangers are also significant. While many budgetary outlays may be better covered through taxation than through privatization, the "pay as you go" pension system is not only very burdensome on the budget, but it also constitutes a much larger burden for each generation that must pay the full cost of the pensions for the retired population, rather than allowing their own savings to grow with the economy before they are drawn on to pay for the old age pensions.

At the same time, the objective of capitalizing the pension fund is not fully in harmony with the purpose of restructuring the Polish economy, which appears to be the main objective of the privatization. The key issue, again, is the very size of the pension sector and its close association with the state. To understand the dangers, it is enough to note that if the Social Security office were to distribute its vouchers evenly among all the intermediaries, it would hold 33-1/3 percent to 40 percent of the shares of each intermediary (depending on what the banks did with their vouchers). It would be by far the biggest single shareholder and the dominant player in this sector of the economy. Alternatively, if the Social Security office did not deposit its vouchers with the intermediaries but were to invest them directly, and if, say, 20 intermediaries were created, the state pension fund would be between 10 and 13 times larger than the average intermediary. This situation, combined with the fact that the pension fund is a state institution, means that the state, even without counting the 30 percent of the shares owned by the treasury, would continue to dominate the economy.

It is not easy to design a satisfactory solution to this problem. The obvious answer is to split the state pension fund up into at least 20 separate funds so that its power would be somewhat dispersed. However, a formal breakup may not be sufficient, for the state would still control each pension fund separately. Under sufficiently strong political pressure it might simply coordinate the actions of all the funds to produce a desired outcome. Perhaps the only way to avoid this possibility is to "privatize" the social security fund, in the sense of giving some non-state parties vested, legally protected property interests in each pension fund. The best candidates for such beneficiaries would be the insured themselves. Thus, for example, individual accounts could be set up for each insured person and the property rights over the account transferred from the state to the beneficiaries.[23]

The next element of the government's plan—the distribution of 10 percent of the shares of the privatized enterprises to the nine state banks—appears to be unnecessary. In their present form the banks are simply state institutions, and there is no reason to believe they would be either independent of the state's political goals or contribute meaningfully to the restructuring. The apparent purpose of their inclusion was a desire to capitalize them and make them stronger. However, they are themselves candidates for a privatization program and thus a part of the problem rather than the solution. As was pointed out, the future of the Polish banking system lies in the further development of the intermediaries rather than in the existing state banking system. However, the banks may have an important role to play in this process, since they are the natural domestic partners of the foreign organizers of the intermediaries. The state banks possess an extensive infrastructure, including local branches, contacts within the world of the state enterprises, and local expertise. As such, they may have quite enough to offer to the new financial institutions. Giving them additional capital in the form of the vouchers (the value of which may be as high as $2.5 billion) appears unnecessary.

More generally speaking, it must be realized that the assets to be distributed are limited. The main goals of the privatization effort must be kept firmly in mind in choosing the beneficiaries. Among the top priorities is to make sure that the corporate governance structure that arises out of the privatization program be efficient and that a sufficient level of popular support be secured for a program that, while it is clearly in the long-run interest of the country, may inflict substantial costs on society in the short run.

With respect to the first objective, care must be taken that the intermediaries receive enough vouchers that their formation is truly attractive and that they can reach sufficient critical mass to bid successfully for the large blocks of shares offered during the first stage of the auction described in the paper and envisaged in the government's plan. Only then will they be able to play their role as prime overseers of the restructuring. Viewed from this perspective, giving 30 percent of the privatized enterprises to the state and 10 percent to the state banks entails a potentially substantial cost in terms of the future restructuring effort.

This argument is reinforced by considerations of legitimacy. The authors' back-of-the-envelope calculations show that the value of the whole giveaway (for the 500 largest companies) under the present government plan, even when measured according to quite optimistic criteria,[24] amounts to about $180 per person. While this amount is not insignificant given Poland's condition (especially considering that several members of each family will receive vouchers), it is still not very large and is likely to be spread over several years. Given this fact, serious consideration should be given to eliminating the giveaway to the banks and reducing the state's share to no more than 20 percent. As an additional measure, workers receiving free shares of their enterprises should not be allowed to receive the vouchers as well. A simple argument that this approach is more than fair is that the average giveaway to a worker, under the government's plan, will be more than eight times greater than the value of the vouchers received by the average citizen[25][Thus, giving the workers a choice between the two forms of giveaway should not lower the program's legitimacy among them (in many cases they get a very good deal[26]), while it might make more assets available to the citizenry at large.

Finally, the government's plan is not clear about the way in which the remaining 5,500 companies will be privatized. This paper discussed in some detail why the prospect of selling a large number of companies quickly is not realistic. Quite apart from this problem, however, it is important to note that, for many of the reasons mentioned above, as well as because some of the smaller companies are the most dynamic and potentially the easiest to turn around quickly, a substantial portion of these enterprises should be included in the giveaway scheme.

Appendix 3. Money and the Question of Voucher Denomination

One issue that often arises in conjunction with proposals to use vouchers as part of a free or subsidized distribution program is whether to combine the use of vouchers with the use of money in the privatization and whether vouchers distributed to the population or the financial intermediaries should have some monetary denomination. This appendix explains why those approaches are inappropriate.

This approach means that the price of the shares to be sold is expressed in regular currency. As a result, some of the valuation problems involved in the ordinary sale of the privatized companies would hamper the privatization program. A further problem is that the vouchers would have to have money denominations, a requirement that raises additional issues.

The amount of the vouchers to be issued is a serious problem. Insofar as the state is concerned, the vouchers are like money: the state must accept them as payment for equity *in lieu* of local currency at face value. The total value of the vouchers issued must therefore have some relation to the total value of the enterprises to be privatized. The task of valuation is then even more daunting: not only must each enterprise be valued separately, but also the value of all of them combined must be estimated at once.

Even though the vouchers would be denominated in a certain amount, their market value (either explicit if trading is allowed or illicit if it is not) is certain to be much less than that amount. Moreover, the discount is likely to be very significant, since not only is the use of vouchers restricted to long-term investment but also the "real" (i.e., market) value of the shares bought for them is very uncertain. The psychological effect might be that people would feel cheated: the government would be telling them they are getting, say, a 1,000 zloty subsidy, while they see the voucher as worth, say, 300. The resulting political liability might exceed the gain from the free distribution.

Given that the (real or hypothetical) market value of the vouchers would be much less than the nominal value, the use of the vouchers in an auction would only confuse the budding price system. Nominally, shares would be bought for, say, 1,000 zloty, while their market value outside the auction would be much less.

In the face these issues, what would be gained by combining the use of money with the vouchers? Two reasons can be put forward. First, the budget would be hurt if the state could not sell at least a part of the enterprises for cash. This argument is a serious one. However, the state has alternative means of raising funds, and even if these means were not otherwise more appropriate, the effect of the sale of enterprises on the privatization would be enough to make them so. In any case, the alternative ways of raising revenue are more appropriate. A consumption tax (such as a value-added tax), for example, would increase the savings rate rather than absorbing the savings available for investment. A corporate tax, while perhaps not practical in the short run (and perhaps, since it involves double taxation, not a good idea in

the long run) offers a steady flow of revenue instead of a one-time injection to cover the budgetary expansion that in later years would have to financed from other sources.

Second, the people who have money would not be able to use it to acquire greater than average shares in the privatized enterprises. This argument would have some force if it could be assumed that the people in Central and Eastern Europe who have savings are the more entrepreneurial element who should not be excluded from acquiring a greater share. This reasoning does not, however, appear sound. To begin with, the distribution of savings in Central and Eastern Europe is more likely to reflect past political connections than a genuine entrepreneurial spirit. Further, the sale of state enterprises would soak up savings that might be needed for other investments (such as the opening of small businesses). In addition, if trade in vouchers without any denomination is allowed, the people who want to invest more than their allotment would be able to buy more vouchers on the open market. Finally, a good privatization proposal would envisage that the shares of the privatized enterprises (or at least those of the intermediaries) would be traded on the stock exchange soon after the initial privatization auction. Those who want to invest their savings in long-term investments would have the opportunity to do so, and the process (more orderly and extended in time) would contribute to the establishment of genuine market prices for the privatized enterprises. (It should also be noted that the price of the vouchers or the shares acquired for them would be higher if the vouchers were the only means of payment at the initial auction. In this case, people at large would have a greater sense of having obtained something valuable, a perception that would raise confidence in the privatization as well as in the economy as a whole.)[27]

Notes

1. The first version of the authors' privatization proposal, suggesting the institutional setting analyzed here, appeared under the title "Privatization in Poland: A New Proposal" in June 1990. A revision of that paper was published in Polish in *Res publica* in September 1990 under the title "Sprywatyzowac Prywatyzacje: Nowa Propozycja Przemian Wlasnosciowych w Polsce" [On Privatizing Privatization: A New Proposal of Ownership Transformation in Poland].

The authors are grateful to Ned Phelps for his comments and interest in the ideas presented here from the very beginning of this project. They also thank Professor Bronislaw Geremek, Minister Jacek Kuron, Drs. Marcin Krol and Aleksander Smolar, and Messrs. Lejb Fogelman, Damian Kalbarczyk and Henryk Wujec for their early encouraging reactions. In addition, they thank the following people for discussions and comments: Professors Bruce Ackerman, William Baumol, Bernard S. Black, John C. Coffee, Marek Dabrowski, Owen Fiss, Harvey J. Goldschmid, Jeffrey Gordon, Irena Grosfeld, Stanislaw Gomulka, Henry Hansman, Cezary Jozefiak, Barbara Katz, Alan Klevorick, Grzegorz

Kolodko, Michael Montias, Joel Owen, Mark J. Roe, Susan Rose-Ackerman, Roberta Romano, Jacek Rostowski, Jeffrey Sachs, Alan Schwartz, Ferdinando Targetti, William Vickrey, Stanislaw Wellisz and Charles Wilson and Messrs. Andrew Berg, Ian Hume, Grzegorz Jedrzejczak, Stefan Kawalec and Jacek Kwasniewski.

Roman Frydman also gratefully acknowledges the grant for this project from the C.V. Starr Center for Applied Economics at New York University.

2. Agricultural production in Poland was the most significant exception.

3. Thanks are owed to Professor Jeffrey Sachs for alerting the authors to the importance of corporatization.

4. One of the reasons for this difference may be that an investor may be prepared to pay a premium for a certain block of shares that would yield control of the company. Another may be that an individual assessment of the company's future differs from that implied in the market price.

5. To show the difficulties and the arbitrariness of the valuation of Central and Eastern European enterprises, appendix 1 presents the case of an enterprise valued by a prestigious British accounting firm for the Polish government in connection with the privatization program there.

6. Katz and Owen (1990) make a similar point.

7. A look at the number of enterprises re-privatized in Britain during the 10 years of the Thatcher administration gives an idea of how time-consuming valuation and sales are.

8. Many of the problems listed here would cease to be serious if so many vouchers were issued that most transactions took place in vouchers anyway. If so, there would seem to be no reason to use money-denominated vouchers at all, especially since they appear to offer no advantages.

9. The interests of the workers are important and do need to be protected by institutional arrangements. The appropriate mechanisms, however, are trade unions and governmental regulation of employment conditions, rather than worker ownership.

10. Appendix 2 discusses the Polish government's recent privatization proposal.

11. Appendix 3 discusses the problems involved in attempts to combine the use of vouchers with ordinary sales and the question of whether privatization vouchers should have monetary denominations.

12. Core investors may still be helpful for many companies. However, it would probably be more appropriate to bring them in at a later stage, when the other important players are already present on the company boards and the price of entry is likely to be higher.

13. The design of the compensation structure and of the control structure of the intermediaries themselves is one of the most complex and important tasks of any privatization proposal that envisages a significant role for the intermediaries.

14. Formation of the stock markets may also be furthered by either forcing the intermediaries, or giving them an incentive, to divest themselves of a part of their holdings through public offerings. Appendix 2 discusses this possibility in the context of the Polish government's privatization proposal.

15. The authors are indebted to Bulent Gutelkin and Gavin Wilson's Memorandum of August 10, 1990, to Messrs. Krzysztof Lis and Stefan Kawalec of the Polish Ministry of Finance for this point.

16. Two advisors to the Polish Ministry of Finance, Professors Stanislaw Gomulka and Stanislaw Wellisz, provided some interesting ideas on this matter.

17. This road has been chosen by the Polish government, as described in appendix 2.

18. The latter may be especially useful, given that the limitations on the entry of foreign capital may restrict the availability of foreign equity financing. In many situations, especially applicable to the Central and Eastern European context, in which share prices may be depressed for some time, debt financing has many advantages over equity.

19. The privatization law that the workers receive up to 20 percent of the shares of the privatized enterprises at half price, not to exceed the value equal to their last year's wages. The present plan abandons the idea of selling the shares at half price and the limitation relative to last year's income because of valuation difficulties.

20. Beyond specifying that the state will not be able to hold shares in the privatized companies directly and will have to use the intermediaries, the government's plan does not specify the formula to be used to distribute the state's holdings. Presumably, vouchers may be used in this connection as well.

21. The first phase of the program is to be completed in 1991, with over half the assets of nearly all large companies being in private hands by the end of 1993.

22. The problems alluded to here arise from the fact that the intermediaries' interest in the state's shares is significantly different from their interest in the shares of the non-state parties. (The difference in the interests of the state and the other parties is a similar situation: the state wants to get the best price for its assets, while the other parties want to maximize their long-term returns.) With respect to the non-state parties, the intermediaries stand to make money from the management fee, while, with respect to the state's shares, they can expect some percentage from their sale. Since the returns themselves and the strategies for their maximization are likely to vary in several respects, the managers of the intermediaries may be tempted to exploit some of their fiduciaries (by, for example, using some of the resources under their management to beef up the prices of others).

23. The mechanism for accomplishing this system requires separate treatment that so far has been absent from the government's proposals.

24. A price/earnings ratio of 5 is assumed here, a figure that is quite high for the Polish economy. There is also some question whether the earnings (based on the first six months of 1990, when profits may have been depressed but when wages were frozen) are reliable.

25. The factor of 8 does not depend on the value of the assets involved; it simply follows from the relative percentages in the giveaway and the proportion of beneficiaries in each class.

26. It should be kept in mind that the average wage at the time when the data used here were collected was about $80 per month.

27. Another important question is whether it is good policy to consume all the capital reserves people in Poland are holding in order to feed the state treasury, instead of utilizing them for other badly needed investments.

References

Katz, Barbara, and Joel Owen. 1990. "A 'Big Mac' Approach to 7Denationalization."*Comparative Economic Studies* XXXII (3):82-92.

22

A Note on the Privatization of Socialized Enterprises in Poland[1]

Manuel Hinds

The government of Poland is designing a strategy for the massive privatization of socialized enterprises. The proposed strategy would transfer ownership of these enterprises to the private sector through both sales and transfers without payment. Preparation of this plan suggests the government has concluded that large-scale privatization is needed. The fact that the proposed plan includes transfers without payment suggests further that the government realizes this approach is the only one to rapid privatization.

This paper assumes that the government recognizes these points. It also assumes that the enterprise reform would include not only privatization but other actions such as the breaking up of monopolies, enforcement of financial contracts and resolution of the issues of compensation of the previous owners of identifiable property.

This paper focuses on mechanisms for privatization once these general issues have been resolved.[2] The next section briefly discusses the privatization scheme the government is now considering, including its long-term objectives. The following two sections present an analysis of the scheme, the first section focusing on the requisites of privatization, the second on the extent to which the proposed program meets those requisites. The final section suggests some modifications that could improve the effectiveness of the proposed program.

The paper does not present a complete analysis of the issues of privatization. Its purpose is to contribute to the ongoing discussion by suggesting ways to carry out a rapid privatization that results in the development of capital markets and improvement in enterprise management.

The Government's Proposed Approach

The Nature of the Privatization Scheme

The government's proposed approach to privatization involves, as the initial step, its reassertion of ownership rights over the capital of the socialized enterprises. Once it does so, it would transfer 20 percent of the shares of each enterprise to five newly created holding companies. Subsequently, these holding companies would transfer their shares without payment to the population. Because the shares would be immediately tradable, they would encourage the emergence of a capital market. Moreover, as a result of the transfer of the shares to the population, the enterprises would become private institutions.

Simultaneously, the government would sell another 10 percent of the shares of each company to the banking system and another 10 percent to the workers of each enterprise. The latter would most likely be sold on preferential terms. The government would retain the remaining 60 percent for subsequent sale, to take place after the prices of the shares have been firmly established in the capital markets.

According to the plan, the shares would have unequal voting rights. Those transferred to the holding companies, banks and workers, although representing only 40 percent of the claims on the capital of the enterprises, would carry majority voting power. Thus, although the government would retain most of the shares, it would effectively be transferring control of the enterprises in part to the private sector (the privatized holdings and the workers) and in part to the banks (which belong to the government).[3]

The proposed approach has several advantages. First, the central government would be able to transfer control over the enterprises to the other sectors relatively quickly. Second, although the government would be surrendering enterprise control rapidly, it would eventually cash in on the benefits of the expected improvement in management because it would at some point be selling its 60 percent of the shares. Third, the plan gives the workers of the enterprises an incentive to accept the demise of labor management.

At the same time, the proposed plan embodies certain features that would jeopardize achievement of the objectives of the privatization. Those objectives are discussed below, while the problematic features of the plan are analyzed in the fourth section.

The Long-term Objectives

Poland's privatization has two main, related purposes: to improve the management of enterprises; and to disperse economic power among a large number of agents. The relationship between the two objectives is complex, however. The dispersion of economic power is desirable because it directly benefits income distribution and political diversity. In addition, up to a point, it reinforces the objective of improving management, given that excessive concentration of economic power leads to inefficiency. On the other hand, excessive dispersion of ownership can also lead to inefficiency. Without a controlling shareholder, management is free to do whatever it wants with the enterprise, and the result can be chaos. Therefore, a delicate balance between these two objectives is needed.

As the experience in Poland painfully demonstrates, efficiency requires that enterprises be managed by someone who will defend the interests of capital, that is, someone who will strive to maintain and increase the enterprises' capital through economic management of its resources and judicious investment. In the absence of an owner, it cannot be expected that somebody else will play that role since they can benefit more by taking away from the owner's income than by defending the owner's interests. This point is recognized in economic theory as the principal-agent problem, and history has proven its validity again and again. Managers not subject to the discipline of owners tend to mismanage the enterprises. They are not natural advocates for capital. They have their own interests, which, if left alone, they will pursue rather than those of capital.

The principal-agent problem does not pertain only to public sector enterprises. It also occurs with private corporations when their ownership is too dispersed. In this case, each shareholder has such a small sum at stake that it is not attractive for him or her to spend time and money trying to control the managers. As a result, the managers' power goes unchecked, to be used to appropriate the rents of capital through huge wages and benefits exactly as happens with workers in labor-managed enterprises. Enterprise efficiency suffers, and the prospects for growth are diminished.

In market economies, the problem of mismanagement is solved by take-overs. Entrepreneurs who believe they can manage an enterprise more efficiently than the current managers can buy enough shares to control the enterprise. They then fire the managers and appoint their own. Take-overs are also used to remove inefficient owners and allow quick reallocation of the capital. In many cases, the managers buy the enterprise and, as owners, impose discipline on the firm. Because of these mechanisms, the unchecked power of managers does not long survive in market economies.[4]

The Requisites of a Privatization Scheme

To be successful, a privatization scheme must meet certain requisites, as discussed below: facilitation of the role of entrepreneurs; speed of privatization; equity; and other oft-cited requisites such paying the government for the shares it transfers.

Facilitation of the Role of Entrepreneurs

It is clear that to achieve the objective of efficiency in an economy with dispersed ownership of capital, it is necessary to allow entrepreneurs to emerge and to bid for control of the enterprises when they see a possibility of improving their management. Thus, a privatization plan should make it relatively easy for potential entrepreneurs to put together the resources to take over control of enterprises to improve their management both at the time of the privatization and later. As will be discussed, the government's proposed plan makes this process very difficult, if not impossible, at least in the initial years.

Speed of Privatization

In economies where the private sector is already predominant, as in the United Kingdom, the speed of privatization is important but not crucial. The reason is that the benefits of privatization, although important, are marginal relative to the functioning of the economy as a whole. In Poland, in contrast, speed is crucial because inefficient enterprise management is causing rigidities that are hampering stabilization and economic growth.

In addition, the socialized enterprises are perceived to be a government responsibility, and their failure to spur economic growth is blamed on the government.

There is also an informal perception, even if denied formally, that the government is financially responsible for the enterprises, which play on that perception by asking for subsidies and privileges. This behavior is evident nowadays. Enterprises have refused to carry out the reforms needed to improve their efficiency. (In a market economy, a liquidity squeeze comparable to that imposed by the government under the stabilization program would have forced them to do so.) Instead, they have been pursuing tactics that permit them to avoid changing in the hopes the government will bail them out if they fail for lack of liquidity. For example, at the time of this writing the food industry was threatening a shortage of supplies if the government did not bail it out.

The government needs to resolve this situation as soon as possible, whence the premium on speedy privatization—the faster it takes place, the better. (Later it will be shown that the proposed government plan will not achieve the necessary speed.)

Equity

Another requisite of privatization is that it be fair. That is, if shares are transferred without payment, they should be given equally to all citizens. If shares are sold, the buyers should pay the market price. The proposed government plan achieves equity through transfers without payment to the population but may face serious equity problems in the sale of 20 percent of the shares to the banks and workers.

Other Oft-cited Requisites

Other features are frequently mentioned as necessary for privatization. Foremost among them is that the state be compensated for the transfer of the assets. Another is that to appreciate the assets, people need to pay for them. Still another is that enterprises should be in mint condition to be privatized. That is, the enterprises should be made more efficient prior to transferring their ownership.

These requisites are derived mostly from the model of privatization developed in the United Kingdom in the last decade. This paper maintains that what worked in the United Kingdom may not do so in Poland because the circumstances there are completely different. In fact, not only are these requisites unnecessary for Poland, but meeting them could be damaging because they conflict with more fundamental requisites, such as speed in improving management practices. The following paragraphs explain the rationale for this assertion.

Shares should be sold. There are two main arguments for selling enterprises rather than transferring their ownership without payment. The first is that, on equity grounds, the government should be compensated for the assets it is transferring. The other is that people will not appreciate the assets if they do not pay for them.

Neither argument is compelling. As to the assertion that the *government should be compensated for assets being taken away from it,* the government is just an intermediary that owns the socialized enterprises on behalf of the citizenry. Compensating the government for the value of the assets makes sense only when they are transferred to a sub-set of the population. In this case, however, the payment would not be compensation to the government, an abstract entity that is only a representative of the citizenry. Rather, those acquiring the assets would be compensating the other citizens by paying the price of the assets to the government. If, as in Poland, the assets are being transferred to all the citizens, who have been the ultimate owners all along, then this compensation is unnecessary.

The second argument—*that people do not appreciate the value of the assets if they do not pay for them*—presupposes that the people benefitting from the rents of the capital have paid for it. Such is not the case. The important point is that associating the benefits of ownership with the burden of management creates a strong incentive for the owners to devote energy to management. This relationship does not exist in the current system.

Furthermore, the statement that people do not appreciate what they have not paid for is only a half-truth. It is only true where the giving away is a ongoing feature of society. It is not true in the case of a once-and-for-all transfer. Receiving shares without payment does not detract from their appeal if the recipients know they will be quite valuable afterwards because no more shares will be given away once the process is finished.[5] A clear example of this point is that most people appreciate what they inherit.

It is likely that some people will not appreciate the shares. However, many others will recognize immediately that getting the shares is a once-in-a-lifetime opportunity. They will want to buy whatever the first group wants to sell. From an economic point of view, it is good that the second group acquire the shares, since they will devote their efforts to making their shares profitable.

Some people may not appreciate the value of the shares at the outset because they do not understand what the shares are. For social reasons, it is desirable that the process be designed in such a way that people have time to come to appreciate the value of the shares.

(The fourth section, on transition, gives some ideas on how to achieve this objective.)

Enterprises should be improved before transferring their ownership. As noted, another commonly mentioned requisite of privatization schemes is that the enterprises be put in mint condition before privatizing them. This requisite embodies two assumptions. One is that the government intends to sell the shares, an assumption that is not always true.[6] The other is that the government may get a higher price after it invests in improving the enterprise than it would otherwise. This assumption is highly debatable.

Nobody would be interested in acquiring, even at zero or a negative price, an enterprise that is functioning under a system that ensures continuous losses and precludes sound management. Thus, nobody would be interested in buying shares in enterprises that are controlled by their labor force or unruly trade unions or that are subject to arbitrary government regulations. The government does need to eliminate these problems prior to privatization. However, once this condition is met, it is very likely the value of the enterprises would decline rather than increase should the government attempt to improve them.

The experience of the 1970s is highly relevant in this respect. The Polish government invested heavily in the modernization of the socialized enterprises, borrowing abroad to finance the process. Because the investments did not generate the cash flow needed to service the related debt, the international financial position of the country deteriorated. Huge losses have accumulated in the banking system (both valuation losses related to the stock of the external debt and collection losses). The government should not repeat this experience.

It can be argued that the stabilization program has corrected the disincentives, ensuring that investments will be carried out efficiently. However, the incentives prevailing in the labor-managed enterprises still do not encourage efficient investment. As is becoming obvious in the current stabilization effort, socialized enterprises do not react to market signals in the same way that capitalist firms do because they do not have an advocate for capital in their ranks. Despite the current liquidity squeeze, socialized enterprises have, as noted, failed to take steps to improve their efficiency. Furthermore, even if the government reasserts its ownership of the enterprises' capital and passes control over to holding companies, the investments are not likely to be efficient unless the private sector carries most of them out. The reason is that the public sector lacks the flexibility and motivation of the private entrepreneur. In addition, if the state

is the major owner in the economy, it will easily bureaucratize the whole process.

The presence of foreign advisors will not change these facts. Poland should not lose sight of the fact that it will face competition from highly efficient Western corporations that are not controlled by foreign advisors but by down-to-earth entrepreneurs. No public sector corporation in the world is a competitive threat in the international markets. No country dominated by public sector enterprises is a major factor in the international markets.

Even in predominantly market-oriented economies, such as the countries in the Organisation for Economic Co-operation and Development (OECD), public sector corporations have shown an inability to operate without huge injections of capital from the state, which, in the eyes of the European Common Market (EEC) in the recent controversy over Renault, are more accurately described as subsidies.[7] Moreover, the Bank's experience in restructuring public sector enterprises all over the world is quite discouraging. There is no reason to believe the experience in Poland will be different.

How Well Does the Government's Plan Meet Its Objectives and the Requisites of Privatization?

This section looks at how well Poland's proposed privatization scheme would meet both the long-term objectives of the effort and the requisites for successful privatization (speed and equity).

The Long-term Objectives

It is doubtful the proposed plan would improve management and decentralize economic power as much as is needed. The main reason is that the initial distribution of voting power in the enterprises would tend to concentrate management power in the five holding companies and a limited number of banks. Assuming that the shares the government keeps have no voting power and that the voting power for all the shares involved in the first 40 percent the government transfers is equal, the holding companies would control 50 percent of the votes and the banks and workers 25 percent each. Moreover, as discussed below, the resulting ownership structure would not be conducive to improving efficiency for several reasons: the potential for bureaucratization of enterprise management; the excessive power the managers of the holding companies would have; the potential for collusion among the holding companies; the creation of conflicts of interest within the banks; the creation of obstacles to the emergence of entrepreneurs who would try to improve management; deterrence of foreign investment from the EEC; and return of investment decision-making to the government.

Potential for bureaucratization of enterprise management. The operation of enterprises is an extraneous activity for banks, while the power of shareholding workers or people buying shares from them would be too disperse to influence their management. Therefore, most likely the five holding companies would end up running the enterprises.

Given the number of enterprises to be privatized, each holding company would find itself having to manage thousands of them.[8] The logistics of this task are such that the holding companies would become gigantic institutions that most assuredly would become bureaucratized. It would soon become difficult to distinguish the holding companies from the former branch ministries. The only difference would be (presumably) that the holding companies would be responsible for enterprises engaged in a range of activities, unlike the situation with the branch ministries.[9]

Excessive power to the managers of the holding companies. The power of the managers of the holding companies would go unchecked because the ownership of these companies would be quite dispersed. Gaining control over an important share of any of the holding companies would require an extremely large amount of money.[10]

As a result, it would be extremely difficult for potential entrepreneurs in the private sector to acquire sufficient voting power in these companies to have a say in their management. The population would most likely react to the situation with apathy, which would ensure that nobody would challenge the power of the holding companies' managers.

In addition, the accumulation of economic power would become the first priority of the managers of the holding companies. Even if their normal objective were to maximize their profits, it is very probable that the concentration of economic power would become the real objective. Moreover, as noted, the objectives of the managers are different from those of the owners. Commanding one-fifth of the industrial power in the country is more attractive than any compensation the dispersed owners could give the managers as a reward for efficiency. The managers' power would be so great that they could appropriate such compensation. In addition, they would enjoy enormous political power. Under such circumstances, to keep and enhance their power the managers would tend to hoard shares rather than trade

them. The same would apply to bank managers. This practice would negate the objective of creating a flexible capital market.

Collusion of the holding companies. There would be a natural incentive for the managers of the holding companies to collude with each other to exercise monopoly power in the different markets of their enterprises. It is very easy to conspire against competition when five people control all the markets.

Creation of conflicts of interests within the banks. There would also be strong incentives for the managers of the holding companies to collude with those of the banks and for banks to use their financial power to maintain and expand their empires. This problem is extremely grave because, on top of all the negative effects of having a small group of people controlling the economy, this situation would create a serious conflict of interest for the banks.

In the proposed scheme, the banks would control some 25 percent of the voting power and would have a substantial amount of money at stake in the enterprises. In this situation they would tend to give preference in their lending and pricing decisions to their own companies and to be lenient regarding the creditworthiness of those enterprises. Such practices are a clear recipe for financial crisis.

The example of the Federal Republic of Germany is frequently cited as proof that linkage between enterprises and banks does not necessarily lead to bad credit decisions. This example ignores the fact that banking supervision there has been strong and has emphasized an arm's length relationship between the banks and enterprises. Furthermore, the banking regulators have discouraged the banks from increasing their current stakes in the enterprises and from participating in new enterprises (the banks acquired their current positions in the enterprises as a result of debt-to-equity swaps in the 1930s).[11]

On the other hand, there are numerous examples of countries where an ownership linkage between banks and enterprises has resulted in financial crises. The list includes Spain, Chile, Yugoslavia, Mexico and even Poland itself (where public sector banks have traditionally financed public sector enterprises to comply with implicit or explicit government wishes).[12]

Even where banks do not lend money to the enterprises they own, they will also not be likely to invest in shares, because shares are more risky than the assets banks normally carry, their value is volatile and both the cash flow and income they produce are unpredictable.

Obstacles to the emergence of new entrepreneurs able to improve the management of privatized firms. Under the proposed plan, it would be even more difficult for potential entrepreneurs to acquire control of individual enterprises than to take over the holding companies. Even if they were able to buy all the shares in the hands of the workers, they would still not be able to exercise control over the enterprises because the banks and holding companies together would have 75 percent of the votes.

Problems for foreign investment from the EEC. The unequal voting rights on the shares pose other problems. For one, they detract from the transparency of the capital markets. For another, the inequality would likely become an obstacle to economic integration with the EEC. According to *The Economist* (1990), "...the EEC will almost certainly restrict, or even outlaw, multi-tier share structure...."[13] The inequality would also hinder investments by EEC investors in Polish enterprises. For these same reasons, Sweden will probably eliminate its system of unequal voting powers. It makes no sense for Poland to adopt a system that other countries are dropping for good reasons.

Giving the power to allocate investment back to the government. Most importantly, the proposed system would run counter to one of the primary objectives of the reform program—that of transferring from the state to the private sector the power to decide the volume and allocation of investment. Whereas transferring the assets from the public to the private sector does not require the use of savings, if the assets were sold, savings would have to flow from the private to the public sector. That is, to pay for the 60 percent of the shares the state would eventually sell, the private sector would have to use savings that it could be investing. It would then be up to the government to allocate the investment of those savings. The purchase of 60 percent of the capital of most enterprises would also use up the better part of private savings for a long time.[14]

Summary. In many respects, the proposed scheme would not meet the government's long-term objectives. It would create substantial rigidity in the system. It would discourage the development of capital markets because it would be practically impossible for entrepreneurs to take over the holding companies and enterprises. The equity markets would therefore not afford mobility for domestic capital. The scheme would also hinder foreign investment from the EEC. It would reduce flexibility in the allocation of banking credit because the banks would tend to give preference to the companies they own. The enormous power of the managers of the holding companies would endanger economic freedom, especially if they collude, as they are likely to do. In this suffocating environment, new entrepeneurs would fail to emerge. Even if they were to emerge, however, they would not have command over the savings necessary for investment. In short, if Poland adopts this privatization scheme, it will simply exchange one variety of monopolistic control over the economy for another, equally damaging, one.

A vivid example of the problems that the scheme could cause is provided by Chile in the late 1970s and early 1980s. In those years, the government sold many industrial enterprises and banks. Since only a few people were willing and able to buy the enterprises, five groups that also owned the banks ended up owning most of them enterprises. These groups used the banks to finance their own enterprises. The result was the largest financial crisis Chile had ever suffered and one of the worst, relative to the size of the country, in any place in the world in the recent past. Chile is not the example to follow.[15]

Speed

Given the problems analyzed above, the proposed privatization scheme would not create the flexibility the economy needs rapidly enough. In fact, it would introduce no flexibility to speak of. Even if the aforementioned problems were ignored and it were assumed that flexibility would emerge eventually, the privatization would proceed too slowly because of the enormous obstacles entrepreneurs would face in taking control of the enterprises.

Equity

As noted, transferring shares without payment to the population meets the equity requirement. However, the sales of shares to the banks and workers pose a serious equity problem. The reason is that there is no way to value the enterprises without a capital market. In fact, the current state of the Polish economy makes the valuation of public sector enterprises even more difficult than is the case in market economies. There the public sector enterprises are operating in an environment in which the price of the factors of production and other basic prices are set by competition in the private sector.[16] The market-based system also allows reasonable projections of the cash flows generated by investments. This situation would not pertain at the start of the privatization in Poland, where the government would still own the majority of the enterprises and factor markets and competition would not yet exist.

Trying to resolve this problem by hiring engineers to value the enterprises entirely misses the point. All the engineers can do is estimate what the value of the assets would be in a foreign market economy, which is what they know. However, it is clear that the same equipment has a different value in, say, Sweden than in Poland. The potential for commercializing products, the wage level, the cost and availability of complementary services, the quality of inputs and all the other factors that determine comparative advantage are different. Particularly important, the risks are different. Nor are these differences negligible: they can mean the difference between becoming rich or going bankrupt.

The value of the shares to be sold at the outset of the privatization would have to be set arbitrarily. Most likely, the market price of the shares would be extremely low. The riskiness of the investment because of the uncertain future of each enterprise would reduce the price, while the proposed scheme would further depress the price of the shares sold to workers and banks. Since the sales would be made to specified buyers, there would be no other bidders, so that it would be a buyers' market.

The government may feel comfortable with undervaluation of the shares sold to enterprise workers. Undervaluation would smooth the process, facilitating the elimination of the controlling powers of the Workers' Councils. However, underpricing the shares sold to the banks is not easily justified.

Desirable Modifications to the Proposed Approach

As stated, the proposed scheme is basically sound. Its problems could be solved easily with some modifications, as proposed in this section. It should be noted, however, that these ideas are preliminary. The intent is to indicate the direction of changes rather than spell them out in detail. These and other ideas should be discussed exhaustively and compared with alternative schemes during the design of the program.

The discussion in this section focuses on seven proposed reforms to the scheme the government is considering. The first two recommendations relate to general rules regarding the development of capital markets, while the rest apply to the privatization. The seven reforms are:

- All shares should be given equal voting power.
- The banks should not be allowed to buy shares.
- The program should discriminate among different kinds of enterprises. A scheme for transferring shares without payment to the population as a whole is an adequate solution for the large and medium-size in-

dustrial enterprises but not for the small ones or for those engaged in services such as transportation, storage and retailing. State farms could also be treated differently.

- The role and number of the holding companies should be revised to ensure that they behave in a way consistent with the desired flexibility in the capital markets.
- The amount of shares to be sold to the population should be drastically reduced so that the amount of savings transferred from the private to the public sector is minimized.
- A mechanism to ensure that entrepreneurs are able rapidly to acquire control over the enterprises during the transition should be designed.
- The measures need to be properly sequenced, especially with respect to the privatization and the restructuring of enterprises and banks.

Equal Voting Rights

As noted, unequal voting rights for different shares undermines transparency, opens the door for pressure groups to enhance their powers, may cause problems for foreign investment and serves no purpose that cannot be obtained through other, less problematic means. These points should not preclude firms from issuing commonly preferred shares, which are subordinated debt.[17] The sale of preferred shares, however, should be something that enterprises decide on in the future, and savers should decide if they want to buy them.

Prohibition on Bank Purchases of Shares

Selling shares to the banks presents serious problems. Most probably, the sales would lead to inequity in the process, a misallocation of resources and financial instability. The government should not only refrain from selling shares to the banks, it should also prohibit them from buying any in the open market. At the very least, it should limit the amount of shares the banks can buy to a very small portion of their equity capital.

Following the international conventions recently adopted on the capitalization of banks (Cooke's Committee), their capital requirements should be estimated on an individual basis, based on the riskiness of their portfolios. That is, banks with higher risk portfolios should be required to maintain a higher ratio of capital to assets. The higher the level is that banks may invest in shares, the higher the capital requirement should be.

One exception to this rule should be that banks can accept shares as collateral and foreclose on them if necessary to collect. However, regulators should ensure that the value of the shares is heavily discounted when accepted as collateral (to cover the risk of the volatility of equity stock) and that the banks sell the shares thus acquired to the public in general within a prescribed period (not to exceed one year).

Need to Discriminate among Different Groups of Enterprises

Currently, big conglomerates control the provision of many services that specialized, smaller enterprises could provide much more efficiently. Examples of areas where this situation is particularly true are transportation, retailing, storage, distribution and all kinds of services that give mobility to products. Typically, the big conglomerates provide these services only for their own purposes. That is, they transport, store and distribute only their own goods. This practice adds to their monopolistic power in their main line of business. Additionally, since nobody else provides these services for other purposes, the development of other businesses that also need the services but cannot get them—either because they do not have the capital or because their demand for the services would not justify investing in them—is constrained.

Although it makes sense for some big enterprises to have their own distribution network, at a time of rapid decentralization of these services the functioning of the economy must be lubricated. These services should be available to anyone and should be provided competitively. Since most of these services can be operated profitably on a small scale, it is probable that new businesses will be created to provide them. However, for the sake of speed, the process should be accelerated by separating those services from the big conglomerates and privatizing them quickly. Furthermore, privatization of these services can be carried out efficiently by dismantling the units providing them and then transferring the individual assets. An example would be trucking, with the trucks being transferred individually. Other examples are retail and storage facilities.

These assets should be transferred through sales. They are small enough to sell easily, and the problem of valuation does not exist or is minimized. Because the assets can be used for multiple purposes, estimation of the profits that they could generate is easier. In the case of trucks, for example, international prices can be used. Unlike in the case of complicated production facilities, trucks will always be needed, and their opportunity cost is clearly their price in the international markets. The prices should be low enough to attract many bidders. In this case, the best course is to auction the trucks of socialized enterprises. A similar procedure can be followed with the other assets involved in the distribution and commercialization of goods.[18]

Sales of these assets should proceed as quickly as possible to facilitate trade. The sales can be financed by the banking system without any inflationary effect as long as the government does not spend the proceeds of the sales. Instead, the proceeds should be used to repay the government's debt with the National Bank of Poland. In turn, the National Bank should sterilize the money. That is, it should not grant credit or in any other way create money with these resources.

The Poland/World Bank/EEC Task Force on Agricultural Sector Reform has produced several suggestions on the privatization of state farms and cooperatives specifically (see Schumacher 1990). The state farms could be treated either as large business complexes and privatized using the same scheme as for large industrial enterprises. Alternatively, the government could establish a system for leasing the land. Under this scheme, enterprises would rent the land from the government but would manage them to maximize their own profits.

Small-scale industrial companies could also be sold at public auction, following the same procedures as those for the service enterprises. The following paragraphs refer mainly to the privatization of medium- and large-scale industrial companies.

Achieving Flexibility: The Role and Number of Holding Companies

Regarding medium- and large-scale industrial enterprises, the government needs to solve two problems: how to privatize efficiently; and how to improve the management of those enterprises that remain in the socialized sector. In both regards, holding companies can play a useful role, although the identity and organization of the holding companies are different in the two cases.

Holding companies as managers of public sector enterprises. Management of the assets that would remain in the socialized sector may be improved by organizing them under one or several holding companies that are responsible for maximizing the return on their capital.[19]

Holding companies may be useful because the mobility of the factors of production requires that decisions on investment and disinvestment be taken by representatives of the owner rather than those who manage the enterprises. The mobility of capital comes precisely from decisions by owners whether to: invest the profits of their enterprises in the same enterprise or in other activities; liquidate or restructure loss-making firms; or sell firms. These decisions can only be taken by an agent *external* to the enterprise whose fate is being decided, that is, by the owner, who should decide how much to invest and in what activities and enterprises.

Thus, there are two levels of management of socialized enterprises, both concerned with obtaining the highest yield from the capital being managed. The kind of manager needed at the enterprise level would be responsible for making the enterprise profitable and for convincing investors (both public and private) to put resources into it. The manager needed at the second level, which could be organized as a holding company, would provide for the mobility of resources across the socialized sector and between it and the private sector. At this level the manager would work within a capital budget constraint, which could be lifted only by the enterprise's being profitable and by convincing the holding company that future operations would be more profitable than the alternatives open to the holding company. The two levels of management should be integrated under one set of rules and perhaps only one institution.

Organizing public sector enterprises into holding companies would not solve the overall economic problem of managing Polish enterprises. Privatization is necessary to create a critical mass of economic agents reacting to market signals in an efficient way. The factor markets will not emerge without large-scale privatization, and in turn the holding companies managing the public sector enterprises would not have to use the prices of the factors of production as given quantities established by the market. There would no point of reference with which to judge their behavior. As a result, they could easily become yet another layer of bureaucracy, as has happened in many other countries, such as Algeria and Egypt.[20]

The long-term role of privatized holding companies. Holding companies present many opportunities for privatization, as well as many dangers. On the positive side, they can bring about all the benefits that institutional investors provide in market economies. However, as was pointed out, they can also become an obstacle to the development of capital markets and the emergence of entrepreneurs. Thus, the potential benefits of having institutional investors should be balanced against the danger of creating institutions that would conspire against the emergence of markets. This balance can be achieved through specialization.

There are at least two requirements of capital markets. First, they should be able to mobilize resources from the population and make them available for investment. This condition requires their offering a varied menu of instruments through which savers can invest in accordance with their attitudes toward risk, liquidity and other preferences. Second, the capital markets should promote judicious investment of those savings. That is, they should encourage the efficient management of enterprises. To

this end, they should promote the continuous emergence of entrepreneurship through transparent competition for the use of savings, as well as competition for the control of enterprises. The system should be very flexible, allowing for voluntary and involuntary take-overs.

Institutional investors can play a very useful role in meeting both requirements of a market. However, to be effective, they should specialize more on the side of mobilizing and allocating financial resources than on becoming enterprise managers. Rather than being instruments to control enterprises, the holding companies should be mechanisms to offer diversified risks to savers. That is, they should become mutual funds, mainly concerned with providing a solid return on the savings of their participants. Their comparative advantage is that they can pool the resources of many people to invest in a bundle of instruments offering different degrees of risk and expected profitability, including a mix that offers lower profitability but also lower risks than is true of investments in the shares of individual enterprises. This approach places their products between bank deposits and equity investments in individual enterprises. Many people would be attracted to them.

To achieve the objective of maximizing the return on the savings of their participants at a given level of risk, the mutual funds should remain independent of the enterprises they invest in. That is, they should be able to invest and disinvest quickly, basing their decisions only on risk and profitability, something they would not be able to do if they were concerned with control issues. Their interest in management should be limited to making sure the companies they invest in are properly managed. They should vote on management issues through their investment strategies. If they do not like the management of a company, they would not invest in it.[21]

Institutional investors are a powerful mechanism for encouraging good management, even though they do not choose the managers directly. Their power is transmitted through the price of the shares, which fall if savers do not buy them. If the mutual funds disinvest in one company or refrain from investing in it, the groups controlling the enterprises get a strong signal that they have to improve their management. Thus, specialization does not preclude institutional investors from playing a useful role in improving the management of enterprises. A regulation prohibiting them from using the voting power of their shares would prevent their perversion into holders of monopolistic power.

Having strong institutional investors that are focused on the profitability of their portfolios would be helpful for other reasons. By investing most of their resources for the long term, they would be a stabilizing force in the market. They would also help make the market transparent. Their relatively large size would allow them to invest time and money to gather information and analyze it in order to invest their resources better.

In summary, the role of the holding companies should be changed from that of controlling units to that of institutional investors. The rules under which they operate should be drafted accordingly. For example, use of their voting powers would be prohibited. If the government opts for this role for the holding companies, they should be called institutional investors or mutual funds instead of holding companies. The remainder of this paper refers to them as institutional investors.

Linking the creation of mutual funds with pension reform. One possibility the government may wish to consider is linking the creation of the mutual funds with reform of the pension system. Wide diversification of investments by these institutions from the outset would make them safe enough to meet their long-term responsibilities. If the government gives away the ownership of these institutions, it might as well transfer to them the pension obligations being covered directly by the budget.

Presently, Polish pensions are based on a pay-as-you-go system. That is, current contributions are used to pay current obligations. No capital has been accumulated to cover the obligations. The problem is that reductions in the growth rate of the population will have a detrimental effect on the viability of the system, as the pension liabilities will increase while the contributions decline, with the government having to cover the difference. The US social security system, for example, is in difficulty because of the decline in the birth rate following the "baby boom." [22]

In Poland, the government could capitalize the pension system with some of the shares to be given away. However, to make the transfer without payment equitable, the resulting pension system should cover the entire population. To make it more efficient, its management should be privatized and made competitive, even if the system is public in nature. To this end, the government would pass laws requiring all workers and their employees to make monthly contributions to a pension fund, but with the freedom to choose which fund to contribute to.

Some of the institutional investors created during the privatization could be established as competing pension funds, while the rest would be set up as straightforward mutual funds. Although a detailed discussion of how to carry out this plan is beyond the scope of this paper, the section on the role of the holding companies in the privatization provides some suggestions.

The number and size of institutional investors. Regardless of their shape as mutual funds or pension funds, the number of institutional investors should be increased considerably from the five suggested in the current proposal. A balance should be struck between making them numerous enough to encourage competitive behavior and making them big enough to have a diversified portfolio. One hundred might be a good number to start with. Of these, 10 could be pension funds and the rest straightforward mutual funds. The sizes of the institutions could differ, with the pension funds being bigger than the others in order to accommodate the pension liabilities. [23]

Even if they number 100, the size of the individual institutions being privatized will be too big if they keep most of their initial holdings. The bulk of the shares should be owned individually, at least at the start of the process. This approach would give more flexibility to the process and would make it easier for entrepreneurs to emerge and take control of individual enterprises. It would also provide flexibility to individuals who prefer to have their shares pooled so that they can organize their holdings as they want. Some may want to establish true holding companies; others may prefer to have mutual funds that specialize in certain types of business; others may prefer to have only friends as fellow shareholders. If the institutional investors keep most of the shares, the individuals will have to accept the government's design, at least in the short and medium terms.

In short, the institutional investors should begin operations holding only a minority of the shares of the privatized enterprises. The bulk of the shares would go to individual investors. However, institutional investors can also be used to transfer shares in enterprises to individuals, in addition to transferring their own shares to them. Toward this end, the government could give the institutional investors two packages of shares, one of which they would keep and the other of which they would transfer. In addition, the institutional investors would transfer their own shares to the population.

Minimizing the Transfer of Private Savings to the Public Sector

The government should retain a portion of the shares for subsequent sale. One reason is that management should be controlled during the transition period. If the privatized holding companies are precluded from using the voting power of their shares, there would be a period when the government would have to manage the enterprises because of a lag between the time the shares are given away and the emergence of groups able to control the enterprises through the acquisition of shares in the free market. During that period, the government should keep enough shares to ensure control.

Beyond the reasons already cited, the government needs to sell part of the assets to raise the resources needed to resolve the problems created by the previous regime. Foremost among these is the need to restructure and recapitalize the banking system. The government will have to take on this responsibility as nobody else will want to: recapitalization of the banks essentially involves the absorption of past losses, and no private investors are going to use their savings to cover the losses of others.[24] The government may use the proceeds of the sale of shares in the enterprises to recapitalize the banking system.

To achieve these objectives while minimizing the savings syphoned off from the private sector, the government should retain only the minimum required to ensure control in a dispersed market. The amount should be no more than 10-20 percent of the shares. Further to minimize the negative effect on private savings, the government should use the proceeds from the sale of those shares to recapitalize the banks.[25]

The precise amount should be based on estimations of the amounts needed to recapitalize the banks. For its part, the government would get revenues from the sale of small industrial and service enterprises, which it would transfer 100 percent through sales.

Facilitating Control by Entrepreneurs over the Enterprises

It is very doubtful that the government's management will be very efficient during the transition. However, its control should at least help avoid the chaotic situation that would develop if nobody were to exert control over the enterprises. Nevertheless, the government should minimize the duration of its control during the transitional period. The process should be designed so that private entrepreneurs take control of the enterprises as soon as possible. There are two complementary ways to accomplish this task. One is to use management contracts during the transition. The other is to design the distribution of the shares in such a way that facilitates take-overs.

Management contracts. To expedite the process, the government may sign management contracts with qualified foreign or local entrepreneurs, paying for the management services but also offering an option to buy a part or all of the portion of shares retained by the Treasury within a specified period (say, after three years) at a predetermined price. This system would give the managers a powerful incentive to manage the enterprise efficiently so as to increase the market value of the shares. In the process, they would benefit all the shareholders.

This system should not preclude take-overs by potential entrepreneurs buying shares in the free market. For this reason, the shares the government keeps and the amounts promised to the contract managers should be only the minimum necessary to ensure control when initial trading in the shares takes place. If the contract managers want to maintain control in the face of a potential take-over, they would have to buy more shares in the market.

Distributing bundles of shares. As was suggested, the government should distribute two kinds of shares without payment to the population. One would be shares in the mutual funds, the other shares in the individual companies. To simplify the process, initially the composition of the bundles of shares from individual companies could be the same as those from the mutual funds. If, as is proposed later, the composition is determined so as to cover a wide range of activities and geographic locations of enterprises, the expected return on these shares would be close to the average that all the privatized enterprises would generate. This approach would be helpful for people who do not have a clear idea what they want to do with their shares, since, if they just kept the bundle of shares, they would obtain the average rate of return and the same return on their shares in the mutual funds. Other people might want to change the composition of their shareholdings, a positive step because it would lead to trading in the shares and ultimately to the establishment of prices for the assets and transfer of control over the enterprises to emerging entrepreneurs.

Protecting people who do not understand the process. Protecting people who do not understand the process is important initially for equity reasons. However, the protection should be provided in a way that does not endanger the success of the privatization. One way is to phase the transfers without payment so that the benefits and losses that people can experience in managing their shares become clear before the second round of transfers takes place. In the long run, these people could exchange all their holdings for shares in the mutual funds, which would carry low-risk, balanced portfolios. They would be able to shift from one mutual fund to another by selling and buying shares.

Sequencing and Transitional Issues

The difficulty of the transition should not be underestimated. The deep structural reforms needed to introduce market forces will cause considerable turmoil during the adjustment period. Many people may suggest gradual implementation of the process so that the economy has time to absorb some of the traumatic shocks before having to cope with others.

This paper espouses the opposite point of view. The market is an all-encompassing system whose benefits can be experienced only when all, or most, of the economy is functioning under its rules. Partial application of market forces is likely to misdirect entrepreneurship away from productive activities into speculative ones. This eventuality would hamper completion of the reform. It is better to address the turmoil quickly than to go through a protracted process that does not afford the benefits of the market. Although a full discussion of the difficulties of the transition is well beyond the scope of this paper, the following paragraphs discuss a few of them.[26]

Accounting. Any privatization scheme requires a change in the accounting system. The systems developed in the Western economies should be adequate, and establishing a new, basic set of books for the enterprises should therefore be a relatively quick task if the government establishes a basic set of accounts to be kept for tax purposes and sets a deadline for the change-over. To accelerate the process, the government should allow companies to hire foreign consultants to help them make the transition.

No reconstruction of the records of past operations is needed. New operations, however, would have to be recorded consistent with the operation of the market and the tax system. For bookkeeping purposes, the initial valuation of the assets could be arbitrary, to be adjusted after, say, two years, when the capital markets are more developed.

Enterprise restructuring. The government should avoid investing in the restructuring and modernization of enterprises, leaving this task for the private sector. If it were to manage the restructuring of the socialized sector, the most likely result would be inefficient investment and outright waste.

As long as the banks remain in the public sector, the socialized sector will enjoy considerable political power over the banking system as a result of the pressures exerted on both the central and local governments. In response, the tendency of the banking system will be to lend to the socialized sector, to the detriment of the private sector. Experience shows that socialized enterprises tend to invest very inefficiently. Most likely, then, the flow of resources toward the socialized enterprises would not only starve the private sector of resources but would also result in substantial waste.

To encourage the growth of the private sector and avoid wasteful investment, the government should prohibit investment of public sector and banking system funds in enterprises in which the government has a majority stake. Any investment in socialized enterprises should be financed out of the enterprises' own resources.

The government should also stay away from coordinating the restructuring, limiting itself to facilitating the process through fast privatization of the socialized sector, cleaning up and privatization of the financial system and creation of the infrastucture needed to foster the mobility of resources. Creating inter-ministerial committees to control or coordinate the restructuring and modernization of enterprises would most likely slow the process and discourage private sector efforts.

The fiscal effects of privatization. The transfer of ownership is a zero sum game: both the increase in the public sector's wealth and in the income derived from it would be counterbalanced by matching declines in the wealth and income accruing to the government. If the government does not reduce its expenditures in line with its reduced wealth and income, or reduces it in amounts smaller than the increased expenditure in the private sector, the effect on the economy would be inflationary. This effect, however, is likely to take place independently of the method used to privatize. The government will lose the income from the enterprises even if it sells them.

Notes

1. This paper talks about a government proposal that preceded the one discussed in chapter 21, "Markets and Institutions in Large-Scale Privatization: An Approach to Economic and Social Transformationin Eastern Europe," by Roman Frydman and Andrzej Rapaczynski in this volume. Although the proposal was never implemented, the points made in Hinds' paper are still relevant, and it was therefore included in the conference papers.

2. For a discussion of the relationship of ownership issues and stabilization and economic recovery, see Hinds (1990).

3. Selling shares to the banks cannot be considered privatization, at least as long as the banks remain part of the public sector.

4. As a result of the imprudent financing of leveraged buy-outs, fashionable in the 1980s, take-overs have acquired a bad name. These particular buy-outs constituted, however, only a very small minority of the changes in ownership that took place in that decade. In a market economy, transactions related to the control of enterprises occur continuously. Nor is control sold just because the enterprise is doing badly. In many cases the owners sell because they think they have a better use for their capital (they want to concentrate their efforts in other areas or they have financial obligations that need rapid cash mobilization).

5. This argument is the mirror image of the recognized non-distortionary effect of lump-sum taxes on the subsequent behavior of the taxed agents.

6. For a more detailed discussion of the relative benefits of selling and giving away shares, see the third section.

7. Getting rid of the fiscal burden imposed by the dependence of public sector corporations on the government's budget is one of the

main reasons behind the current trend to privatize in the OECD countries.

8. Even if management is shared with the banks, each bank and holding company would still be responsible for a very large number of companies.

9. Some mutual funds in large market economies have investments in thousands of enterprises. These funds do not, however, intervene in their management. They are passive investors that hold shares just to get capital rents. In contrast, holding companies that manage enterprises typically handle a much smaller number. In the scheme proposed for Poland, the holding companies would be the control type.

10. Buying 20 percent of the voting stock of one holding company, for example, would be equivalent to buying 2 percent of the total enterprise voting stock in the country.

11. Another frequently cited example is Japan. However, the economic and social organization of Japan is quite unique and can hardly be taken as an example of what would happen in a Western culture such as that of Poland.

12. When reforms are being planned, it is better to rely on the average experience of many countries than on that of exceptional ones. One clear example is the concentration of economic power in Sweden, where a small number of conglomerates control a sizable portion of the country's gross domestic product (GDP). This situation has not resulted in a lack of competition or efficiency. On the contrary, many Swedish enterprises are among the most competitive in the world. However, not many people would use the Swedish example to argue for concentrating wealth in a limited number of families as a way to achieve competitiveness.

13. The term "multi-tier share structures" refers to a structure of shares with unequal voting powers.

14. The price of the shares kept by the government would be lower than those in the hands of the other owners because the former would not have voting power. Nevertheless, buying them would transfer substantial savings from the private to the public sector.

15. To resolve the crisis, Chile dismantled the large conglomerates that controlled the banks and enterprises, sent a large number of companies into bankruptcy and took control of the largest commercial banks, recapitalized them and sold them to new owners. After that experience, the government changed its strategy for privatization completely, the new aim being to spread the ownership. Since then, the enterprises have been quite successful.

16. Competition for the factors of production and other inputs exists even if the publicly owned enterprises are not in the same line of business as the private ones.

17. Subordinated debt means that, in case of a liquidation, the claims of the holders of these liabilities defer to any other liability holders except those represented by common shares. That is, if the enterprise is liquidated, all other liabilities are paid first, then those of the preferred shares are paid and finally those of the common shares.

18. It might make sense for some big enterprises to retain some of their distribution infrastructure, including storage facilities. However, the process should be biased toward complete decentralization to create a clean slate so that all enterprises have access to those services and to stimulate competition. If it is profitable for some enterprises to acquire distribution networks, they should do so in the future, as part of their natural expansion. The government, however, should avoid rebuilding the current monopolistic structure.

19. This point is critical. Efficiency will not improve if maximization of profits is not the sole aim of the managers of public sector assets.

20. For a more detailed discussion of ways to improve the management of public sector enterprises and the need to create a critical mass of private enterprises to help improve the management of the public ones, see Hinds (1990).

21. Specialization is desirable in part to avoid conflicts of interest. It is also needed because the expertise required for managing an efficient institutional investor is different from that needed to run a holding company. The former is financial in nature, while the latter is mainly management of real resources.

22. This problem affects only the pension liabilities of the system. Private pension funds are based on the accumulation of resources.

23. It is desirable that the number of pension funds be kept small because they need to be supervised closely as a result of their provision of a public good. A Superintendency of Pension Funds should be created, responsible for supervising prudent management of the pension resources.

24. See the section on the recapitalization of banks.

25. The timing of this recapitalization most probably will not coincide with the collection of the revenues from the sales. This financial problem is, however, soluble (see the section on the recapitalization of banks).

26. This section does not touch on many important transitional issues, such as the sequencing of bank reforms and enterprise restructuring and needed fiscal and monetary policies. For a discussion of these and other transitional and sequencing issues, see Hinds (1990).

References

The Economist. 1990. "The Wallemberg Empire." June 23, p. 76.

Hinds, Manuel. 1990. "Issues in the Introduction of Market Forces in East European Socialist Economies." World Bank. Washington, D.C.

Schumacher, Augustus. 1990. "Structural Reform of State Farms in Poland: Short, Medium and Longer Term Options."

23

Comments on David Lipton and Jeffrey Sachs, "Privatization in Eastern Europe: The Case of Poland," Roman Frydman and Andrzej Rapaczynski, "Markets and Institutions in Large-Scale Privatization: An Approach to Economic and Social Transformation in Eastern Europe" and Manuel Hinds, "A Note on Privatization of Socialized Enterprises in Poland"

E. Borensztein

There can be little disagreement that privatization is both the most important and the most difficult of the economic reforms the countries of Central and Eastern Europe face. The papers by Manuel Hinds, Roman Frydman and Andrzej Rapaczynski, and David Lipton and Jeffrey Sachs all provide trenchant analyses of the challenges of privatization.

There are some fundamental points on which the three papers agree: privatization must be speedy, for there are large costs in delaying it; it must be comprehensive, as opposed to pursuing a case-by-case approach; and it must be distributive rather than based on the sale of assets. There are, however, important points on which the authors disagree. The two main ones are: the difficult problem of how corporate control should be structured; and the desirable role of the state and other financial institutions in the new market structures. Although the three papers refer specifically to Poland, basically everything said is applicable to other previously centrally planned economies attempting to shift to a market economy.

As to the urgency of undertaking privatization, a point on which the three papers agree, Poland, and in fact most Central and Eastern European countries and the Soviet Union, find themselves in a no-man's land in which, although central planning no longer operates as a system, the lack of private property and a clear profit motive impedes the emergence of a full-fledged market economy system. In this situation, there is no clear authority to monitor the behavior of enterprise managers. Moreover, the perception by managers whose tenure is highly uncertain creates perverse incentives for excessive wage and bonus payments, low levels of investment and a squandering of the assets of the enterprises. It is

not a coincidence that almost all Central and Eastern European countries have instituted taxes on excess wages that penalize increases above certain limits, with the taxes at rates that reach several hundred percentage points of the wage increases. An extreme consequence of this poor incentive system was the emergence of "spontaneous privatizations," as described by Frydman and Rapaczynski and by Lipton and Sachs, which took place especially in Hungary and Poland.

Thus, there is agreement that privatization must proceed at once, even at the risk that the inefficiency of the system of public enterprise management and control blunts progress on all reforms. The question, then, is how to proceed with the privatization?

The second important point of agreement in the three papers is that privatization cannot be accomplished by conventional sale methods for a number of reasons, including: the near impossibility of obtaining a meaningful valuation of the enterprises; equity and political consideration; the lack of domestic savings; a lack of burning interest on the part of foreign investors to invest heavily in purchasing enterprises; and the political unacceptability of heavy foreign investment, even if it were likely. Therefore the idea of a free distribution of equity to the public in general, the "voucher scheme," appears to be necessary in terms of speed and comprehensiveness, and also on the grounds of equity and political acceptability.

The government cannot, however, simply issue the vouchers and sit back. Because of the thin dispersion of ownership, managers effectively would be subject to no supervision because it is not worthwhile for a small stockholder to incur the considerable cost of monitoring management while receiving only a minimal part of the benefits. This issue is the problem of corporate governance. It is the most difficult challenge of any proposal for distributive privatization.

On this point the three papers have important differences. Hinds propounds, as a final objective, a system of enterprise control that is essentially the same as that in the United States and the United Kingdom. In this system, publicly held equity is an important component of capital, and take-overs are the main mechanism of management discipline: if an enterprise is perceived to be poorly managed, some investor group will attempt to acquire it and introduce changes in management and adjustment measures.

By contrast, Lipton and Sachs consider the take-over mechanism as essentially flawed and propose instead a detailed plan of corporate control by several financial intermediaries (mutual funds, pension plans, banks, etc.), to which a "stable core" investor would eventually be added. Although these financial intermediaries would be privately owned, they would be created by the government, which would endow them with certain equity holdings. Their initial directors would be nominated by the government.

Frydman and Rapaczynski propose a different plan. They are not averse to take-overs but believe that the development of stock markets and sophisticated financial securities will not be possible for a long time. Therefore they also propose that mutual funds act as the controlling shareholders of the enterprises. However, in contrast to Lipton and Sachs, Frydman and Rapaczynski propose free entry into the mutual fund market, competition among the mutual funds to obtain vouchers from the public, and auctioning of enterprises to the different mutual funds in such a way as to ensure one or more large shareholders (at least initially).

Starting a complex system of private ownership without any previous experience, institutions or entrepreneurs is Herculean work, and all of the proposed alternatives have some weak points. The corporate structure envisioned by Hinds requires the emergence of both entrepreneurial investors with sufficient capital and well-developed financial markets that will provide the complicated financing that take-overs many times involve. Their emergence might take a very long time, and in the meantime the government would remain in control of the enterprises. Further, there are serious doubts about the efficiency with which they would operate.

Lipton and Sachs's framework would achieve privatization of the majority of industrial enterprise capital in the shortest time. However, the structure of corporate governance appears to be too rigid; it does not leave any margin for spontaneous developments that may be appropriate to the technical and informational resources of the country. Given that corporate governance is an area in which economic theory has not produced conclusive or universal results, it might be prudent to leave more room for spontaneous adjustment of the system.

Frydman and Rapaczynski's proposal has the interesting element of private initiative from the very beginning. By the same token, however, choosing an appropriate mutual fund may require too great an informed decision on the part of the general public, and the establishment of a large enough number of mutual funds may be hampered by the lack of domestic expertise and reluctance of foreign investors. Moreover, the auction process could be excessively complicated, and it is possible that not all enterprises could be sold to qualified investors. The state might end up saddled with inefficient enterprises and face politically costly liquidation decisions.

It seems clear that no strategy is dominant and that any plan will involve unavoidable trade-offs between desirable objectives. One evident area where a trade-off is unavoidable is between speed and comprehensiveness on the one hand and the extent of private initiative on the other: if privatization is to be accomplished at once, in the sense of both ownership and control of enterprises passing to private hands, there must be extensive state involvement and little room for private initiative in designing the corporate governance structure.

At one end of the spectrum is the Hinds proposal, in which the final structure of who is going to own what and how is it going to be run are left completely to private initiative, although the state would continue to operate public enterprises until the markets and entrepreneurs developed. Effectively, privatization would not take place until markets and entrepreneurs had been established. At the other end of the spectrum is the Lipton and Sachs proposal, in which the state decides at the outset everything from shareholdings by each party to seats on the board of directors. Frydman and Rapaczynski's proposal lies somewhere in between this trade-off, given that establishment of intermediaries and auctioning of enterprises would take several years.

Hinds counters that large holding conglomerates as in the Frydman and Rapaczynski and Lipton and Sachs proposals would become powerful empires not subject to the threat of take-overs or proxy fights. That situation would not be consistent with adjusting the size of firms or the scope of their activities, both of which might have become overextended. An alternative worth considering is that of using private holding companies as the privatization agencies, with a predetermined termination date, as proposed in Blanchard, et al. (1991). This alternative is not very different from Hinds' proposal except that the holding companies that control the enterprises would be private and profit-motivated instead of state agencies.

Decisions on breaking up the enterprises, selecting buyers, etc. would all be made with a profit objective. Although this proposal cannot avoid the above-mentioned trade-off in that the state must play a prominent role in establishing and launching the holding companies, the holding companies would be only a temporary device, so that different forms of corporate governance could develop over time.

Regarding the role of the state, the three papers also contain different conceptions. In addition to assigning the state a role in setting up and nominating directors for the different financial intermediaries, Lipton and Sachs reserve a relatively large share for the state in the privatized enterprises (illustratively some 30 percent), although most of it probably would eventually be sold to "stable core" investors. Although in a lesser proportion than that of its holding shares, the state would have seats on the boards of directors.

Frydman and Rapaczynski would prefer to keep the state completely out of the picture if possible with regards to both the establishment of financial intermediaries and participation in enterprise control.

Hinds questions the merits of having a large public stake in enterprise capital, based on a different perspective. As the state sells this stake, it will absorb a large portion of private savings and crowd out private investment. While this scenario is true, some increase in government revenue would be needed in any event unless the privatization strategy alters significantly the level of government spending, and the only issue is to choose between a tax increase or maintaining the rights to income-producing assets.

Another point of disagreement is the role of the banks in the new corporate structure. Lipton and Sachs propound that the banks receive shares in the enterprises (which would also solve their need for capitalization) and that they become active in enterprise control, inspired by the German or Japanese models. (In the United States the Glass-Steagall Act prohibits banks from owning equity, and they cannot participate on corporate boards as lenders).

Hinds argues strongly against a role for banks in the ownership and control of enterprises because of a potential conflict of interest. Frydman and Rapaczynski, while supporting universal banking (allowing banks to own equity), do not predetermine a specific role for banks. To back up the case about problems with conflicts of interest, Hinds cites the Chilean experience after the first wave of privatization. A few powerful conglomerates were generated that owned both banks and their largest customers. After a few years they ended up as massive failures and in financial crisis. The state had to renationalize a number of enterprises and banks to avoid their closing. It is interesting that when Lipton and Sachs note the Chilean experience, they attribute the failure to excessive leverage in the privatized enterprises. On balance, given the necessary fragility and absence of well-developed financial markets (at least initially) in Central and Eastern Europe, the Chilean experience appears more relevant than the German or Japanese ones and suggest caution in establishing close relationships between banks and their clients.

There is one point on which the three papers appear to agree but this commentator does not: the problem of the monopolistic structure of markets, including both horizontal and vertical integration. Lipton and Sachs consider this issue and conclude that, in Poland, a sufficient degree of competition is assured by the existing market structures and foreign competition. This conclusion appears to contradict the views that attribute the large increase in prices after price liberalization in Poland to "monopolistic pricing." In any event, in the more centralized economies of Central and Eastern Europe, such as Czechoslovakia, the problem of monopolistic market structure should certainly be dealt with. Given that breaking up monopolies is certainly easier and less litigious before than after privatization, action on market structure appears to be the necessary starting point of privatization.[1] A related issue is the likely existence of an excessive size and/or vertical integration for some firms, which has resulted, for example, from uncertain access to inputs. This issue is different, because enterprises themselves would benefit (to the extent that they are not compensated by gains in market power) by divesting divisions or activities. Thus this type of break-up would not require government intervention. However, this type of inefficiency increases the risks that corporate structures exist that could support a tendency to empire-building.

The three papers contain elements that are extremely valuable not just for Poland but for any of the previously centrally planned economies attempting a transformation into a market economy. Although it is impossible to design a privatization proposal to fit all the reforming Central and Eastern European economies, some countries (such as Czechoslovakia and Romania) are attempting large-scale privatization in ways not unlike those followed by Poland. Moreover, the analysis in these papers may be even more important for those economies that may follow the case-by-case traditional approach to privatization (as seems to be the case with Hungary).

Notes

1. This point is effectively argued by Tirole (1991), who also puts forward a proposal for joint work by authorities and international institutions to ensure competitive market.

References

Blanchard, Olivier, Rudiger Dornbusch, Paul Krugman, Richard Layard and Lawrence Summers. 1991. *Reform in Eastern Europe*. Cambridge, Mass.: MIT Press.

Tirole, Jean. 1991. "Privatization in Eastern Europe: Incentives and the Economics of Transition." Mimeo. Massachusetts Institute of Technology. Cambridge, Mass.

Part VIII

Summing Up and Overview

24

The Symposium in Review and a Glance at the Future

Stanislaw Gomulka, Johannes F. Linn
and Jan Svejnar

Comments by Stanislaw Gomulka

The intent of this conference was for participants to leave better informed and wiser about the best way for Central and Eastern European socialist countries to proceed with the transition to a market economy based on private ownership. In this context, the papers cover an unusually wide range of topics. This transition may be seen as the latest, and by far the most important, stage in a long history of reforms. In several socialist countries, the original centrally planned economy of the Soviet type first became a modified centrally planned economy of the Hungarian type and then a market-oriented socialist economy of the Polish-1990 type. Within the next five years or so it is to be changed into a fully fledged market economy of the Western type. In discussing these developments, the authors have identified the reasons for abandoning a particular system and embracing specific reforms.

At this time of deep economic crisis in the USSR and Central and Eastern Europe, it is easy to overlook that the traditional centrally planned economies once were capable of respectable, on occasion even impressive, growth. However, the post-1975 slowdown came sooner and was deeper than in the capitalist West.[1] This disparity provided the empirical support for much of the Western understanding of these economies. The social tensions that developed during the slowdown, indeed stagnation, forced the governments in two key countries, the USSR and Poland, to abandon prudent macroeconomic policies. This action very quickly led to an open crisis: it appeared that their economies were disintegrating and the political authority collapsing. The crisis may be seen as the necessary precondition for abandoning the socialist experiment and persuading the population at large to accept the high cost of transition to a market economy, as well as the inequalities and uncertainties to be expected under such a system.

The discussion at the conference suggests that the transition typically involves four phases:

- *Phase 1* centers on macrostabilization, if needed, and on the liberalization of prices, the latter to include (internal) convertibility of the local currency and the dollarization of trade with former Council for Mutual Economic Assistance (CMEA) partners. This phase is preceded by a short preparatory period in which the government takes measures, such as the elimination of the budget deficit and the monetary overhang, to establish the right "initial conditions."

- *Phase 2* is about structural adjustment. It involves the commercialization and privatization of state enterprises and the development of labor and capital markets. It is also a time of big changes in the composition of the output of products and the reorientation of links in international trade. It begins with phase 1 but continues some three to five years longer.

- *Phase 3* is intended to induce the recovery of growth from the deep recession brought about by the supply shocks and contractionary demand policies of phases 1 and 2. The recession produces high unemployment, typically of more than 10 percent of the labor force and hopefully less than 20 percent. The recovery should begin in phase 2 and continue for several years after the end of phase 2. It will be driven by the export sector and private initiatives, fueled by the underutilized resources of labor, land and capital. The new laws on property ownership by foreigners and full remittance of profits abroad will attract foreign investors. In the case of Poland, there should also be an agreement on the reduction of foreign debt and/or debt service payments. The catching-up with Western Europe should begin in this phase.

- *Phase 4* is a period of sustained, balanced growth, accompanied by a macroeconomic policy intended to produce a low-inflation environment.

Much theoretical analysis and policy debate in Central and Eastern Europe have focused on phases 1 and 2. Four models of transition may be distinguished in these phases: (1) the German supershock strategy; (2) the Polish (classical) model; (3) the proposed programs in Hungary and Czechoslovakia; and (4) the presidential (compromise) model for the USSR. The major distinguishing factor among them is the speed with which the domestic prices for tradables are brought to international levels, the subsidies are removed and the domestic markets are opened to international competition. The essence of the transition is the shift in the job of allocating resources from planners to prices. Speed refers to the time taken to put a proper price system in place. Speed, however, also has implications for the depth of the recession.

This latter point leads again to the helpful role of crisis in creating the necessary commitment to deep and rapid reforms despite the high cost. The early literature on reform tended to imply the presence of substantial and immediate benefits from market-oriented changes. However, the current reforms in Central and Eastern Europe entail a major discontinuity in systemic change, with large shifts in demand and large redistributions in the incomes of households and enterprises. In this situation, resources used inefficiently will quickly become unemployed, and their restricted mobility will ensure that they remain unemployed for a prolonged period. The reformers and nations of Central and Eastern Europe must be prepared for a "long march," which they must accept as unavoidable.

While price liberalization may produce large short-term costs, privatization is likely to bring about large and long-term changes in the distribution of wealth and income, with profound social implications. The defensive behavior of state-owned enterprises in Poland this year highlights the need to accelerate the privatization rapidly, and to do so despite the virtual absence of intermediary capital market institutions, such as mutual funds or private pension funds, and the lack of internal financial capital. The issues to be solved include the method(s) of pricing assets, the extent and method of distributing the free shares, the potential use of existing institutions such as banks and the state pension fund, and the role of foreign capital. The two conference papers on these issues contrasted the virtues of state-driven and market-driven marketization. Both call on intermediate capital market institutions, which would need to be created, to play a key role. It is therefore worth noting that neither the Hungarian program nor the Polish plan rely on these institutions. They see a role for them, but only in the later stages of privatization.

Comments by Johannes F. Linn

As someone who is not a specialist on reform in the socialist economies in Central and Eastern Europe, I listened with great interest to the discussion of the previous sessions and found there was a lot to learn. The participants addressed five principal questions. They are reviewed briefly, followed by a summary of the emerging answers.

The first question is whether the socialist economies should undertake reform. There was no disagreement around the table—an affirmative answer was virtually taken for granted. This unanimity is, however, one of the great miracles of the present time, given that a little over a year ago the answer would have been a lot less clear, at least as far as official representatives from the Central and Eastern European countries were concerned.

Second, there is the question of where the reforms ultimately should end up. That is, what is the economic system toward which the Central and Eastern European countries are and should be striving? This gathering did not discuss this question to any great extent, and it is addressed below.

Third, what is the appropriate timing and sequencing of reforms? Much of the debate around the table focused on this question. In the end, it appeared that the debate came out not far from the conclusions drawn by Stanley Fischer and Alan Gelb in their papers. The core of their answer to this question is that the timing and sequencing of reform *packages* that include some progress and action on virtually all fronts throughout the reform need to be considered. The challenge for the policy-maker then becomes one of keeping a large number of balls in the air at the same time and carefully timing the progress in each area so that it has a maximum favorable impact on the overall progress of reform.

The fourth and important question is how the reforms are to be designed and implemented in practical terms. Some of the papers considered issues of detailed design and implementation, but overall the discussion was perhaps too far removed from the practical reality policy-makers in the Central and Eastern European countries face. Much more needs to be done in this area.

Finally, some participants asked how the impact and progress of the reforms can be measured and monitored with available national statistical indicators. It is likely that the reforms will push activity out of the measured into the non-measured sectors of the economy. If so, the costs of adjustment (as reflected in the measured decline in economic activity in the measured state sector) may be overstated relative to the benefits of reform (which would be reflected primarily in the private, parallel and non-measured sector). This situation may affect both the professional assessment of the impact of the reforms and their political sustainability, as people and politicians understandably focus on the official national statistics. Improvements in the economic and social indicators are therefore a high priority, both through refurbishing the conventional national statistical systems, as well as through ad hoc surveys at the firm and household levels to provide a quick snapshot of the impact and progress of the reforms.

To return to the second question with more detailed comments—what is the economic system toward which the socialist economies in transition should ultimately aim—it is an important area where research and policy analysis should provide more guidance to policy-makers. The comments here focus on each of five areas: ownership rights; labor markets; monetary institutions; trade; and the role of government.

As regards *ownership and property rights*, it appears that over the last 12 to 18 months there has been a sea change in Central and Eastern Europe in clarifying that the goal of reform is to establish private property rights as a critical component of a market-based competitive economic system. The role of economists in establishing this goal was perhaps surprisingly small, although Manuel Hinds and Janos Kornai have recently come to the forefront in postulating that without widespread private property rights successful reform of systems is not possible. The lack of clear guidance from economists on this question is surprising in view of the strong evidence, at least for certain sectors in traditional market economies, that indicates that efficient allocation of resources, especially efficient levels of investment, are only possible where private ownership rights are clearly established. This conclusion is true for agriculture, housing and urban land, small-scale industry and services. Perhaps the only area where there may be room for debate is to what extent large-scale industrial firms and banking institutions can remain in some form of social ownership. The conclusions of this debate should be of intense interest to those socialist countries that retain a strong commitment to universal, or near-universal, social ownership of the means of production, such as China, Viet Nam and, until very recently, the USSR. Of course, how to get from a system of predominantly state or social ownership to one of predominantly private ownership is also a major question. Nevertheless, having a clear goal in this regard is a major step forward that most Central and Eastern European countries now appear to have taken.

In the area of *labor market reform*, it seems that a clear understanding of and agreement on where the reforming socialist countries should and want to end up is lacking. There are some distinct models for labor market arrangements in the industrial market economies. The United States is characterized by high labor mobility and low employment combined with low job security and a relatively meager social safety net. Western Europe, in contrast, has traded labor mobility and low unemployment for high job security among those employed and a relatively generous social safety net. It would be useful if the economists could help clarify the trade-offs among these models and perhaps other alternatives and point out to policy-makers the importance of setting clear goals in this area.

With respect to *monetary control*, there was little disagreement around the table that economic reform must begin with the establishment of firm controls over aggregate monetary and credit flows. However, it appears that in some Central and Eastern European countries, in particular Czechoslovakia and the Soviet Union, continuation of central monetary management and currency unity is no longer taken for granted. In Western market economies the benefits of monetary integration and independent monetary control are well understood. The potential risks and costs of a fragmentation in monetary authority in the Central and Eastern European countries should be carefully considered before moving too far in the direction of disbanding current monetary arrangements.

In the area of *trade*, there was general agreement that the socialist economies should establish open trade regimes with a significant export orientation. While this goal was generally accepted, in practice the tendency may be in the opposite direction. Barriers to trade among the Central and Eastern European countries may spring up as the CMEA arrangements break down, and, at least within the Soviet Union, there is a rising incidence of internal trade barriers that could very quickly result in significant disruptions and efficiency losses. External trade liberalization and maintenance of free internal trade should remain clear goals of reform, even as temporary difficulties arise in transition.

Finally, there is the issue of what should ultimately be the *role of the government* in the newly reformed, former socialist, economies. Should the state retain a large share of responsibility for the provision of social and physical infrastructure, as has traditionally been the case in Western Europe? Or should privatization be pursued even in this area, with the state giving up state control over utilities and mining, transport and communications, education and health? Again, what will be the role of government in providing a social safety net during the transition as well as in the longer term? Considering the rapid increase in the incidence of poverty in some Central and Eastern European countries, more attention will have to be paid to this question.

In sum, there are still a lot of questions to be answered and a lot of work to be done. Nonetheless, this conference has helped provide answers to some questions while sharpening the pursuit of answers to others. The effort was worthwhile.

Comments by Jan Svejnar

A number of presentations and discussions at this conference have stressed the importance of macroeconomic stabilization. Another point, made somewhat less forcefully, is that a substantial microeconomic adjustment is crucial if the overall package of policies is to succeed. This observation is very important since a number of successful stabilization programs have become unravelled because of inadequate microeconomic adjustment. As a result, the focus of these concluding comments is on several microeconomic issues that need to be given special attention if the economic transformation in Central and Eastern Europe is to be successful.

Capital Market Imperfections

The capital market in Central and Eastern Europe is severely underdeveloped. There are very few banks, and those that exist are undercapitalized and frequently act in collusion with one another. The banks also have a very limited number of loan officers capable of appraising and evaluating investment projects. On the other side of the market is a large number of potential entrepreneurs who will need access to credit to launch and develop their businesses. The situation is probably worst in Czechoslovakia, with about 200,000 registered small businessmen eager to start operations and 10 commercial banks that have virtually no trained staff.

The bottleneck in the financial sector has obvious economic and social implications. In the Central and Eastern European context, the problem is exacerbated by the paucity of small- and medium-sized firms, the lack of significant personal wealth and the ongoing or imminent lay-offs of redundant labor from the large state enterprises. The limited ability of a large number of small entrepreneurs to launch (labor-intensive) businesses because of a malfunctioning banking sector will have a considerable negative effect on the allocation of resources, growth and social welfare.

Inter-enterprise Credit

In response to the restrictive monetary policy, state or socially-owned firms in virtually all the Central and Eastern European countries have resorted to inter-enterprise credit to counteract the credit crunch. The phenomenon was first detected in Yugoslavia in the mid-1980s, where it contributed to the subsequent onset of hyper-inflation. At present, it is particularly serious in Czechoslovakia, Hungary, Poland and Yugoslavia.

The reliance on inter-enterprise credit represents an attempt by firms to resist and postpone the painful adjustment to ongoing changes. From a political and economic standpoint, however, this initially innocuous activity can become dynamite. It usually starts as a large number of independent responses by individual firms, some of which are increasing their payables and others of which are ignoring the growth of their receivables. Once the mutual indebtedness becomes large, the government is confronted with large-scale insolvency. With unemployment growing and living standards on the decline, this collective insolvency problem is likely to induce even economically conservative governments to abandon restrictive credit policies and bail out the failing firms en masse.

Labor Market Institutions and Distortions

Four interrelated issues stand out with respect to the functioning of the labor markets in Central and Eastern Europe. First, it is argued that labor exercises considerable influence over wage- and employment-setting and, if unchecked, could use its power to undermine the reform. Second, heterodox macroeconomic policies respond to this and related fears by imposing some form of wage control. Third, a salient feature of socialism is that it has greatly diminished worker effort. Hence there is a great need for wage incentives (rather than wage controls) to generate rapid growth in productivity and product quality. Finally, the state or socially owned enterprises are widely perceived to have considerable amounts of redundant labor, and there is a feeling that it is not being reduced rapidly enough.

The labor market is very important: its institutions and functioning could make or break the economic transformation. It is often treated somewhat mechanically at the macro level, but present circumstances in Central and Eastern Europe suggest it needs special attention. In particular, the major problem is that the imposition of wage controls, while aimed at moderating potentially excessive wage demands, usually reduces the incentives for greater effort and work quality.

In considering the design of optimal labor market policies, one aspect that ought to be taken into account is that worker participation in management is a phenomenon with strong appeal in Central and Eastern Europe. The system has worked relatively well in the Federal Republic of Germany (West Germany) and Austria, to mention just the neighboring countries, and the example is visible. Moreover, spontaneous tendencies to establish participatory institutions are a tradition in the region. For instance, although Hitler abolished participatory schemes and trade unions, both re-emerged in most of Central Europe after the war. The Communist regimes eliminated them in the late 1940s and early 1950s, but whenever the central controls were lifted, workers' councils or other forms of participation sprang up.[2] It is plausible to surmise that a tendency is being observed that most likely will not be stopped by democratically elected governments.

The question that naturally arises is whether the phenomenon is negative or positive from the economic standpoint. The economic theory on participatory and unionized firms suggests that in competitive environments these firms do not behave very differently from their profit-maximizing counterparts. Empirical evidence indicates that the economic effects are indeed not negative[3]; the functioning of the West German and Austrian economies has been consistent with this claim. A potential problem that could arise during the economic transition is that insider power could generate perverse behavior by the firms in imperfect markets. However, the West German and Austrian experience with the re-introduction of participatory schemes when these economies had imperfect markets in the late 1940s and early 1950s is quite acceptable. Moreover, recent theories and empirical work suggest that participatory firms generally react to external shocks by adjusting wages and other benefits rather than employment. This pattern is consistent with what has been observed in West Germany, Yugoslavia and Poland, and it suggests that the presence of rents and shocks during the economic transition would be reflected more on the wage than on the employment side of the labor market.

The policy implication of the above findings is that, in general, limiting the scope for rents and soft budgets is essential. Moreover, rather than destroying incentives through wage controls, appropriate policies should set a realistic capital tax (dividend), enforce competitive prices by opening up the economy and strongly encourage the entry of new (private) firms.[4] These policies will go a long way toward getting rid of the short-run problem without introducing significant new distortions.

Finally, the issue of labor redundancy merits a few words. The phenomenon is clearly a serious one that has to be dealt with. The growth of new (private) firms is the most promising way of absorbing laid-off workers and making involuntary separations socially acceptable. At the same time, it is important to heed the evidence from developing countries that the reduction of redundant labor in state-owned enterprises is a painful, often expensive and especially drawn out process.[5] In this context, the finding in the Frydman and Wellisz paper in this volume that Polish enterprises reduced their labor force by 7 percent in 1989 and 10 percent in the first eight months of 1990 attests to a rapid decline in the redundant labor force by international standards.

Notes

1. For a discussion of this issue, see Gomulka (1990).

2. This was the case in the former German Democratic Republic and Poland in 1953, Hungary in 1956, Czechoslovakia in 1968, Hungary and Poland in the 1980s, and Czechoslovakia in 1990.

3. For recent surveys, see, for example, Blinder (1990).

4. It is notable that until recently Yugoslav policy has failed on all these fronts.

5. The Chilean experience is an exception because the lay-offs were carried out forcefully and sometimes with the aid of especially appointed outside directors.

References

Blinder, Alan, ed. 1990. *Paying for Productivity*. Washington, D.C.: Brookings Institution.

Gomulka, Stanislaw. 1990. *Theory of Technological Change and Economic Growth*. London and New York: Routledge, chapter 9.

Participants

Piotr Aleksandrowicz
Rzeczpospolita, Poland

Mark Allen
International Monetary Fund, Warsaw

Leszek Balcerowicz
Polish Ministry of Finance

Wojciech Bienkowski
Warsaw School of Economics

Jan W. Bossak
World Economy Research Institute
 Warsaw School of Economics

Pawel Bozyk
Warsaw School of Economics

Bogumila Brocka-Palacz
World Economy Research Institute
 Warsaw School of Economics

Guillermo Calvo
International Monetary Fund,
 Research Department

Joshua Charap
Ministry for Economic Policy and
 Development of the Czechoslovakia Republic

Simon Commander
World Bank, Economic Development Institute

Lucjan Ciamaga
Warsaw School of Economics

Vittorio Corbo
World Bank, Macroeconomic Adjustment
 and Growth Division (CECMG)

Fabrizio Coricelli
World Bank, Macroeconomic Adjustment
 and Growth Division (CECMG)

Marian Crisan
Rumanian Investment Bank

Marek Dabrowski
Polish Academy of Sciences, Institute of Economics

William Easterly
World Bank, Macroeconomic Adjustment
 and Growth Division

Stanley Fischer
World Bank, Office of the Vice President
Development Economics, and Chief Economist,
 and Massachusetts Institute of Technology,
 Economics Department

Jacob Frenkel
International Monetary Fund, Research Department

Roman Frydman
New York University, Department of Economics

Alan Gelb
World Bank, Socialist Economies Reform Unit

Janusz GoLebiowski
World Economy Research Institute,
 Warsaw School of Economics

Stanislaw Gomulka
London School of Economics

Leszek Hajkowski
World Economy Research Institute
  Warsaw School of Economics

Miroslav Hrncir
Institute of Economics (Prague)

Danuta Hubner
Warsaw School of Economics

Erika Jorgensen
World Bank, Socialist Economies Reform Unit

Janusz Kaczurba
Polish Ministry of Foreign Economic Relations

Stefan Kawalec
Polish Ministry of Finance, Warsaw

Elzbieta Kawecka-Wyrzykowska
World Economy Research Institute
  Warsaw School of Economics

Miroslav Kerous
State Bank of Czechoslovakia

Miguel Kiguel
World Bank, Macroeconomic Adjustment
  and Growth Division

Grzegorz W. Kolodko
Warsaw School of Economics,
  Research Institute of Finance

Jerzy Kozminski
Polish Council of Ministers

Johannes F. Linn
World Bank, Country Economics Department

Nissan Liviatan
Hebrew University of Jerusalem and
  World Bank, Macroeconomic Adjustment
  and Growth Division

Gabor Oblath
Institute for Economic and
  Market Research (Budapest)

Roland Pac
Institute for International Trade (Warsaw)

Ryszard Rapacki
Warsaw School of Economics

Andrzej Rapaczynski
Columbia University, Law School

Petru Rares
Rumanian Agency for the Promotion of Investments
  and Economic Assistance from Abroad

Andrew Rasbash
Delegation of the European Community (Warsaw)

Werner Riecke
Hungarian National Bank and Institute for
  Economic and Market Research (Budapest)

Luis A. Riveros
World Bank, Macroeconomics Adjustment
  and Growth Division

Roberto R. Rocha
World Bank, Macroeconomic Adjustment
  and Growth Division

Dariusz Rosati
Institute for International Trade (Warsaw)

Jacek Rostowski
Polish Ministry of Finance

Eugeniusz Rychlewski
Warsaw School of Economics

Jeffrey Sachs
Harvard University, Department of Economics

I. T. Singh
World Bank, Socialist Economies Reform Unit

Andres Solimano
World Bank, Macroeconomic Adjustment
  and Growth Division

Monika Sowa
World Economy Research Institute
  Warsaw School of Economics

Jack Spilsburry
U.S. Department of State,
  U.S. Embassy (Warsaw)

Jan Svejnar
University of Pittsburgh, Department of Economics

Vito Tanzi
International Monetary Fund,
  Fiscal Affairs Department

Ulrich R.W. Thumm
World Bank, Europe, Middle East and
  North Africa Department

Stanislaw Wellisz
Columbia University, New York, and Polish
  Ministry of Finance

John Williamson
Institute for International Economics
  (Washington, D.C.)

Marian Wojnar
Foreign Trade Research Institute (Warsaw)

Jozef Zieleniec
Charles University (Prague)